THE PRINCE OF WALES TOUR

A DIARY IN INDIA

THE PRINCE OF WALES TOUR:

A DIARY IN INDIA;

WITH SOME ACCOUNT OF

THE VISITS OF HIS ROYAL HIGHNESS

TO THE COURTS OF

GREECE, EGYPT, SPAIN, AND PORTUGAL

WILLIAM HOWARD RUSSELL

GYAN

Published by

Gyan Publishing House
5, Ansari Road
Daryaganj, New Delhi-110002
Phone: 011-47034999, 9811692060
E-mail: books@gyanbooks.com

Distribution Network
gyanbooks.com
India, USA, Canada, UK, Australia

ISBN: 978-93-7014-290-9 (PB)

First Published, 1877

2nd Impression 2025

Printed at: Gyan Press, Delhi.

THE PRINCE OF WALES TOUR, A DIARY IN INDIA
Author: WILLIAM HOWARD RUSSELL

H. R. H. THE PRINCE OF WALES.

Photographed from Life by Lock and Whitfield.
July 17, 1876.

THE PRINCE OF WALES' TOUR

A DIARY IN INDIA;

WITH SOME ACCOUNT OF

THE VISITS OF HIS ROYAL HIGHNESS

TO THE COURTS OF

GREECE, EGYPT, SPAIN, AND PORTUGAL.

BY

WILLIAM HOWARD RUSSELL.

WITH ILLUSTRATIONS BY SYDNEY P. HALL, M.A.,
ARTIST IN THE SUITE OF H.R.H. THE PRINCE OF WALES.

SECOND EDITION.

LONDON:
SAMPSON LOW, MARSTON, SEARLE & RIVINGTON,
CROWN BUILDINGS, 188, FLEET STREET.
1877.

DEDICATED

BY PERMISSION

TO

HIS ROYAL HIGHNESS

ALBERT EDWARD,

PRINCE OF WALES.

TO THE READER.

A FEW words to the reader to explain some matters connected with this book. It is a Journal or Diary kept from day to day, in which the Prince of Wales is the central figure round which all the things, persons and events mentioned in it revolve, so that if his name and title occur repeatedly in the same page, it is necessary, from the nature of the work, that they should do so. The impressions recorded by the writer are his own; and if, as is rarely the case, opinions are expressed on questions of policy or of government, they must not be ascribed to anyone but to him who states them. Wherever the word "we" occurs, the reader is prayed to take it as meaning "the Royal party," not as the pronoun in an editorial sense, or as indicative of any intent to involve the identity of the Prince with that of the gentlemen who accompanied him.

WILLIAM HOWARD RUSSELL.

Middle Temple, 1877.

INTRODUCTION.

The Prince of Wales told a distinguished audience which had been invited by the Governor to meet him at a State Banquet soon after his arrival in Bombay, that "it had long been the dream of his life to visit India." The idea of a tour in the Eastern possessions of the Crown appears to have been first suggested by Lord Canning, whilst he was still in India, to the Prince Consort as part of the education of the Heir Apparent; and it was no doubt included in the great scheme of instruction devised for the Prince by one who thoroughly appreciated the value of the eye, when it is quick and observant, in aiding the other faculties in the acquisition of knowledge, and the power it has of impressing the mind—

> "Segnius irritant animos demissa per aurem,
> Quam quæ sunt oculis subjecta fidelibus et quæ
> Ipse sibi tradit spectator."

It is probable that the Prince Consort, with his acute intelligence, would have perceived the advantages of sending the Prince of Wales to learn something of the Empire over which he was one day to reign without any such suggestion, and that he would have recommended the Queen to include her Indian dominions in the programme of travel laid down for him. Lord Canning—the first Viceroy, as Lord Northbrook was the last—ruled India more absolutely, perhaps, than his successors, because he was charged with the conduct of affairs during the greatest strain to which the Imperial Power had been subjected; but he was deeply convinced, even in the hour of triumph, of the necessity of creating some substitute for the prestige of the great authority which had been overthrown for ever. The East India "Company" to the princes and peoples of India was not an empty abstraction. In the recesses of the national brain, mixed up with images of mythological personages and of their heavenly attributes, there was a dim conception of it, as of a great physical force, of which there were manifestations in the paraphernalia of executive power, the dignity of the magistrature, and in armies terrible with banners. To the princes and peoples the Governor-General was, after all, only the servant of the "Company," for they saw that the haughtiest and most powerful of them all was so swayed by its decrees that, if the "Company" pleased, he could be swept clean off the scene of his apparent domination. When the Queen's Proclamation, which may be styled the Magna Charta of India, was read to the Chiefs assembled at Allahabad on the 1st November, 1858, there were few of them—and they were not many there—who could understand what was the power which had destroyed the East India Company, and what authority replaced it. The Oudh Talukdars, who remained in arms, would not give faith to promises made to them in the name of "the Queen." Even the soldiers of the British regiments of the East India Company's army refused to recognise the right of the Crown and of Parliament to transfer their allegiance and services without their consent; and a very great danger arising from their discontent, which Lord Clyde and Sir W. Mansfield regarded with profound apprehension, was only averted by management and concession. The Governor-General saw how desirable it was, at a time when the basis on which our authority rested had been shaken to the very foundation, that India should have an outward and visible sign of the personal existence of the Power which had control of her destinies; and he appreciated the great benefits which would accrue from personal intercourse with her princes and people to one who would occupy a position in which he must exercise immense influence over the direction of affairs—not the less because exercised indirectly and without responsibility. But the Prince of Wales was only seventeen years of age. Circumstances, such as the lamented deaths of Lord Elgin and General Bruce, caused the intended visit to be deferred, after it had been accepted as an incident in a general scheme of travel; and the activity of the Prince's disposition found opportunities for development, meantime, in tours in foreign countries, and in constant participation in functions of State importance, or of a national character, at home. The journey of the Duke of Edinburgh, which had been seized upon by the Princes of India as an occasion for lavish offers of splendid hospitality, and for profuse munificence, had given already some indication of the manner in which his elder brother, Heir to the Throne, would be fêted and welcomed whenever he could go amongst them.

But the deplorable assassination of the Earl of Mayo, coupled with the memory of other sinister events, suggested the necessity of caution, and increased the dread of responsibility of those who were charged with the action of government in such a matter. The Prince of Wales could not travel incognito in India. His movements would be known to all the world beforehand. There, no doubt, were men who would esteem themselves happy in venturing their lives on the chance of destroying one so dear to Feringhee rulers. Religious passion "and study of revenge, immortal hate," might arm many a desperate hand; and certain exhibitions of the fanaticism of the Wahabee, or of the strong prejudices of the Hindoo, showed that the apprehensions of those who considered that no precautions should be neglected were worthy of the gravest consideration.

In the winter of 1874, the project of a tour to India in the autumn of the following year became the subject of anxious deliberation, and communications passed between the authorities with a view to an understanding as to the manner of the visit. There were obstacles to be overcome, or at least there were objections to be removed in high places, for such an expedition had never been undertaken by any personage in the Prince of Wales's position in any period of our history. Royal visitors India has had and to spare. They came upon her—nameless Chiefs at the head of their invading hordes—long ere Alexander, well knowing that there were more worlds to conquer beyond its waters, was obliged to abandon the object of his heart's desire on the banks of the Beas. Timour and Baber, Mahmoud of Ghuznee, and Nadir Shah—these were terrible visitors indeed. Each represented the temporary overthrow of ancient dynasties, invasion, and widespread destruction, or conquest, occupation, and the permanent establishment of foreign rule. More recently there have been visitors of royal races of a more amiable type. Prince Adalbert of Prussia rode by the side of our victorious Generals in one of the most famous of Indian battle-fields, when the supremacy of Great Britain was challenged by the Khalsa. The King of the Belgians, ere he was called to the throne, included part of India in his course of travel. The Duke of Edinburgh, in the course of his interesting but rapid excursion, had some experience of the honours which would await the Heir to the Throne. But the position of the Prince of Wales, not only in its relation to the State at home and to the Indian Government, but in its bearings on the politics of Hindostan, was totally different from that of any previous visitor. Never, with the exception of the Prince Regent, had an Heir Apparent been so much before the public eye, and never had any Prince of the Blood in direct succession to the throne been entrusted in the lifetime of the reigning Sovereign with so large a part of the functions of Sovereignty. The Prince was, owing to circumstances of which no one questioned the force, in such a position that it seemed scarcely possible that his absence from the country for half a year and more would not be attended with serious inconveniences. Those who followed the course of his life, as it was evolved from the exercise of one public act after another, best understood how incessant had been his labours in endeavouring to meet the demands of the country for Royal sanction and personal encouragement of the works of which they are considered the fitting complement. The Prince of Wales, however, felt that it was his "mission" to go to India, and he resolved to fulfil it. But for the strong insistance of the Prince, the dream of his life might not have been realised; and whatever advantages may be derived from the tour must be attributed to the power of volition before which obstacles vanished, and to the force of conviction which defeated objections and overcame dissuasion. In the beginning of January, 1875, it was known that the project was seriously entertained, and soon afterwards it was spread abroad that the visit would be made in the ensuing autumn. Long before the intention was communicated to the world at large, programmes were sketched out and plans were prepared, the Indian authorities were consulted, and the

Residents at great Native Courts had warning that the Prince might appear among them.

On the 16th of March the Marquess of Salisbury made an official announcement to the Council of India of the intended visit of the Prince of Wales, and the Council then passed a resolution that the expenses of the journey should be charged on the revenue of India; but at a meeting of the Council on the 27th of April, they passed a further resolution that it was only the expenditure which was actually incurred in India which should be charged on the revenues of that country. The 'Times' of Saturday, March 20th, contained a short paragraph to the effect that the report of the Prince of Wales' intention to visit India towards the close of the year was true. This statement must have appeared to those in authority to have been a little too absolute, for on Monday, 22nd, there appeared another paragraph, inserted in the space usually allotted to official announcements, as follows:—"We have authority to state that the report of the intention of his Royal Highness the Prince of Wales to visit India is well founded, and that his Royal Highness will leave England for that purpose—should no unforeseen obstacle arise—in the month of November. Sir Bartle Frere will accompany the Prince of Wales at the express wish of his Royal Highness." A flood of articles was at once poured out by the press. There was a general expression of opinion that it was right for the Prince to visit Hindostan. India had lately gained a new and rather painful interest for the people of England. The country, they were told, had just been rescued from the jaws of famine. About that time the deposition of the Gaekwar of Baroda and the inquiry into his complicity in the attempt to poison Colonel Phayre, caused people who would have been puzzled a short time before to decide whether the Gaekwar was a person or a thing, a man or a State, to read about India. The general relations of the great feudatories—the Chiefs of States with Treaty rights—and of the Crown were critically examined, and many homilies were delivered on the duties of Sovereign States to their dependencies, and on the blessings of civilisation to uncivilised nations. A sensation of surprise was experienced by many people at the discovery that there were Native States in India which had some sort of autonomy—a despotism tempered by Residents—and something like alarm evinced when the papers reproduced from an Indian journal a most formidable-looking muster-roll of the "armies" of the Native Chiefs, with their many thousands of horse, foot, and cannon.

The common "Aryanismus" of the races was, however, much urged on the notice of the world as a reason for mutual relations. It was pointed out that the Hindoo and his master were after all made of the same clay, that "Blacks were not so black—nor Whites so very white." It may be quite true that at some period, which conjecture cannot aspire to reach, Central Asia, the *sæva mater* of nations, poured forth the hordes which peopled Europe and Hindostan alike, though it is as difficult to persuade the Englishman of to-day that the Hindoo is his brother as it was to impress on the average Englishman of the early part and middle of the last century that the Negro was a brother, or that he was a man at all.

"An immense respect (wrote the 'Times' on 23rd March) is due from the conquerors of India to the venerable kingdoms, institutions, and traditions of which they have become the political heirs, and an adequate manifestation of this feeling has always been one of the great wants of our Indian administration. Changes of dynasty are the lot of all nations, but the English dominion must in some respects have represented this revolution in a peculiarly unpalatable form to a people with whom the hereditary principle is not a secondary but a primary nature. The rule of strangers, who to their eyes carry no hereditary dignity, could not fail to be especially distasteful." These are sentiments which many Indians feel; but the policy of the Prince's visit was eventually justified by the impression produced by his presence. There were not wanting some who predicted greater benefits than could reasonably have been expected from it; nor were others who asserted that the difficulties of the Government of India would be increased, by the paling of their splendours, left voiceless. Hitherto they would appear to have been false prophets.

The final step was taken. There were reasons which would always justify uneasiness at the protracted absence of the Heir to the Throne from the United Kingdom; but there were also reasons which rendered it highly desirable he should visit that portion of the Empire, in right of which the Crown is Imperial. If there was a feeling that there would be a void in society and in all the great functions over which Royalty usually presides while he was away, it was felt, too, that his Royal Highness had earned his right to such repose, and that he was entitled to a little respite from ceremonial observances. The effects of the protracted, and all but mortal, illness which brought the nation, as it were, to the doors of Sandringham, rendered it expedient that the Prince should not be exposed to another winter in England if it could be avoided. The anticipations of repose were scarcely justified, for there was but little cessation of work in India; but the strength and energy which the Prince displayed proved that his medical advisers had judged rightly of the beneficial effects of escape from an English winter.

It was now necessary to provide the Prince with a following suitable to one who would be regarded by princes and people as an Imperial Ambassador of a rank and dignity towering far above the highest of their ancient dynasties. But those who imagined that the presence of the greatest statesman or noble would lend additional dignity or importance to the Heir Apparent's avatar, could not have understood how very ignorant and indifferent most of the Chiefs and the masses of the people are to what pass in Great Britain as matters of deepest gravity. The more intelligent natives are acquainted with the names and views of those who deal with Indian topics in Parliament; but the Resident, the Collector, and the Magistrate represent to them the whole force—they certainly do not always represent the splendour—of the State. The Duke of Sutherland's name, known so widely in Great Britain, had reached the ears of comparatively few in India. On the other hand, the name of Sir Bartle Frere, which only became familiar to all people at home after his successful mission to Zanzibar, was a household word with millions of people in Bombay and in the north-west of India. In the early part of 1875 the latter was informed that the Prince of Wales wished to have the benefits of his experience during the Expedition; and about the same time, or somewhat earlier, the Duke of Sutherland received an invitation to form one of the suite to which his rank gave such weight. Lord Suffield, the head of the Prince's Household, was naturally selected to accompany his Royal master; Colonel Ellis, Equerry to the Prince, who had served in India, was also nominated, and was charged with most delicate and difficult functions in administering, in conjunction with Sir Bartle Frere, the affairs of finance and presents. Major-General Probyn, whose confidence in the success of the visit, which he strenuously advised, was strong from the beginning, was engaged in making arrangements for horses, transport, and sporting at an early period of the year. Mr. Francis Knollys, the Prince's Private Secretary, completed the list of selections from members of the Royal Household. A valued servant of the Queen, Lord Alfred Paget, Clerk Marshal, who had known the Prince from his earliest childhood, undeterred by any consideration respecting the possible influences of an Indian climate on a frame which, despite robust health, had lost the resisting forces of youth, was desirous to accompany one to whom he was so much attached, and his desires were gratified. The Rev. Canon Duckworth was selected as Chaplain to the Prince, and Dr. Fayrer was entrusted with the onerous and responsible duty of watching over the Prince's health. The Earl of Aylesford, Lord Carington, and Colonel Owen Williams, personal friends, were invited to join the party. Lieutenant Lord Charles Beresford, who had accompanied the Duke of Edinburgh in his Indian tour, lent his unflagging gaiety, his practical knowledge and professional experience, to the Royal suite, which received another agreeable accession in the person of Lieutenant FitzGeorge, of the Rifle Brigade. Mr. S. P. Hall, whose sympathetic and skilful pencil had gained him high reputation, received a commission to sketch the incidents of the tour. Mr. Albert Grey, Private Secretary to Sir Bartle Frere; and the writer of this record, temporarily attached as Hon. Private Secretary to the Prince, completed the list of those who formed the suite of his Royal Highness.

There was but one cloud resting on the horizon to which all eyes were turned. Those concerned in the government of the State, and responsible to the country for the trust on which so much depended, could not but perceive the objections to the absence of the Princess of Wales from her children; and it was equally obvious that it would be most unwise to expose them to the climate of

India at the time of life when it is most dangerous. It may well be conceived how painful it was to know that a separation, which would cause so much grief to her Royal Highness the Princess of Wales, was drawing near at hand.

When the map of India was laid on the table, immediately there came to the surface the difficulty of getting many places within the limits of the time which the Prince could devote to his visit. In a general way, the limits of his Royal Highness's tour in India were marked by the thermometer. Dr. Fayrer was very decided in putting the beginning of November as the earliest date at which the Prince should arrive, and in fixing on the early weeks of March as the latest period at which he ought to attempt to come home through the Red Sea. There were certain broad lines to be followed; but a line ends in points, and at the outset there was some hesitation in determining whether it would be better to begin at Calcutta or at Bombay. The claims of Cashmere and of Ceylon seemed to clash. The passes into Cashmere are not open till the hot weather has begun in the plains, and it was of the first necessity that the Prince should not be exposed to long journeys at unhealthy seasons, and to rapid transitions from cold to heat. Several attempts were made to divert the Prince from his purpose of visiting Ceylon, but he was inexorable as well as penetrating; and it is said that once, at one little "Indian Council" at Marlborough House, there was a map produced in which Ceylon did not appear, when the routes were being laid down and discussed, but that a Royal demand, "Where is Ceylon?" rendered the stratagem, if such it were, of no avail. The trip to Cashmere assumed an uncertain aspect; that to the Deccan was, for several reasons, doubtful; but to Ceylon the Prince adhered with invincible firmness, undeterred by "sanitary considerations" and medical reports, which, sooth to say, were damaged in their authority by the very opposite opinions of the *cognoscenti*. As early as the third week in May, the routes of the Prince were laid down from the 17th of October, on which day he was to set out on his voyage, to the date of his arrival in Calcutta, before Christmas Day. Already the Residents at the Native Courts were enabled to convey most satisfactory intelligence respecting the manner in which the Princes had received the announcement that the Prince would visit India; and the demands made for his Royal Highness's presence a few days here and a week there, urged with the most perfect conviction, could not have been satisfied in a twelvemonth. Already requests were made from India that there should be no further delay in buying horses for the Prince and his suite; and it was suggested that an officer of the rank of Major-General, with a proper Staff, should be placed at the head of the carriage and transport department. At the period of which I speak, the Government had given no intimation of their intentions as to money; and if the Prince was to start in October, there was not much time to order carriages and gifts of honour; but until the money had been voted, it would have been impossible to have laid down any precise scheme of expenditure. The preliminary arrangements were, however, advanced as far as was practicable. It was decided that the presents should be placed in the charge of a special Staff from the India Office; that gold and silver medals should be struck for presentation to the Chiefs; and it was further understood that the Queen would issue a warrant to authorise the Prince of Wales to hold a special Chapter of the Order of the Star of India at Calcutta.

The interest which was taken in the visit increased as

the country had time to reflect upon the subject. Articles in the press, and communications between the authorities in India and at home, increased in number and importance. Whatever might be the wishes of the Government, it was plain that the Prince could not be other than paramount when in India; and it was therefore matter of consideration that his exalted position should not cause that of the Viceroy and Governor-General to be unduly depreciated. It may now be asserted that the apprehensions which were entertained on that ground had no solidity. Even if the brightness of the Viceregal luminary had been subjected to temporary eclipse, it is evident that there could have been no permanent diminution of it after the Prince's transit, and that as long as the transit was occurring, no official measures could have prevented some little dimming of the splendour of the official sun.

On the 15th of April Mr. Hankey put a question to the Government. He asked "whether it was intended, in the event of the Prince of Wales visiting India, to propose to Parliament to make such provision as would enable his Royal Highness to discharge such duties as might be considered befitting his position as the representative of Her Majesty with becoming dignity?" Mr. Disraeli's reply evinced a certain dislike to any early announcement of the intentions of the Government; he would not even admit that the Prince was going to India at all, and described the question as "hypothetical." He apprehended, he said, that, in the event of the Prince visiting India, he would not visit it as the representative of the Queen. The Viceroy would continue to fulfil the duties of that office. But he might say generally, that if the Government had to make any public communication on the subject the House of Commons would be the first body in the country to which that communication would be made.

Doubtless, on grounds which commended themselves to official prudence, Mr. Disraeli refused to acknowledge that there would be any demand made on the Exchequer, even as late as the 3rd of June. Replying on that day to Mr. Leith, who asked "whether the expenses of the Prince of Wales would be charged to the Imperial or to the Indian Exchequer?" the Prime Minister protested against honourable members "assuming that there was to be a grant of public money proposed, and on that assumption asking questions" which should be reserved till such a proposal was made. On the 5th of July, however, Mr. Disraeli gave notice that he would the week following make a statement on the House going into Committee of Supply respecting the visit of the Prince to India, and that he would submit an estimate of expenditure. On the 8th of July the Premier made the promised statement to a full House, and succeeded in attracting the sympathies of his audience in no ordinary degree to the objects of the Prince's intended journey; but in the phraseology of the Minister there might be detected a sense of the responsibility which rested on those who had any share in sanctioning the enterprise. He alluded to the previous travels of the Prince in various parts of the Queen's dominions, and drawing a distinction between what was best suited to those who were, and to those who were not, Royal personages, observed that though he could not say that travel was the best education, he would venture to assert that travel was the best education for Princes. But the visit of the Prince of Wales to India would be, he said, unlike his previous travels. The rules and regulations which sufficed for the Prince in Canada and in the Colonies would not be adapted for India. One remarkable feature of Oriental manners was the exchange of presents between visitors and their hosts. The Viceroy, thought that ceremonial presents need not be given or received, but it was necessary to place the Prince in a position in which he could exercise the spontaneous feelings of generosity and splendour which belonged to his character. It was also necessary to gratify the feelings of the Native Princes. The ordinary rule was that the presents made by Native Chiefs were sold, and the amount carried to the credit of Government, which made presents of corresponding value to the donors; but it was evident that, on the occasion of the visit of the Prince of Wales, such a course would be undignified and distasteful. The Prince would be the guest of the Viceroy from the moment he landed on Indian soil. That was the strongly-expressed opinion and wish of the Viceroy, who highly approved of the visit, and believed it would be attended with great benefit to India and to this country. The expense of that part of the reception would not be considerable, for it would be confined to the rites of hospitality, and the sum of 30,000*l.* had been mentioned casually as the amount which might be charged against the Indian Budget on that head. The estimate of the Admiralty for the expenses of the voyage to and from India, and of the movements of the fleet in connection with it, came to 52,000*l.* With respect to other charges, Mr. Disraeli pointed out that the Prince did not go to India as "the representative of the Queen," but as "the Heir Apparent of the Crown." Without interfering in any way with the legal and constitutional character of the Viceroy, the Prince would nevertheless be placed in a position which would impress the mind of India with a sense of his real dignity and importance. To meet the personal expenses of his visit, it was proposed to move a vote for a sum of 60,000*l.* in the next Committee of Supply.

This announcement of the intentions of Government was almost disappointing to the country. Letters, in which the impolicy of a stinted allowance was demonstrated, and strong reasons were adduced for the assertion that the sum of 60,000*l.* would not suffice for the legitimate and becoming expenditure of the Prince, appeared in the public papers. The distinction between the appearance of the Prince in India as the representative of the Queen and as the Heir to the Throne might have been understood by the House of Commons, or by logical minds in Europe, but it was one which, as events proved, the natives of India could not appreciate. When the resolution was brought forward in Committee of Supply, on the 15th of July, Mr. Fawcett considered it necessary to raise a discussion which was much to be regretted. He moved, as an amendment, "that it was inexpedient that any part of the expenses of the general entertainment of the Prince of Wales should be charged on the revenues of India." Mr. Fawcett's objections to the vote were founded partly on sentimental, partly on abstract politico-economical reasonings. He pointed out instances in which India had been charged with expenses for entertainments of an Imperial character with which India had nothing to do—such as the Ball to the Sultan, the visit of the Duke of Edinburgh, the carriage of Royal presents to England, the fee of 400*l.* paid to the Dean and Chapter of Westminster for the erection of the monument to Sir Herbert Edwardes—and introduced other matters which might have been appropriate in a general discussion on the distribution of taxation and expenditure, but which had no bearing on the Prince's tour. The honesty of purpose of Mr. Fawcett and the value to India of his laborious advocacy cannot be doubted, and there may be need of both, especially in a body which is dealing with the resources of a country in which the principle that taxation and representation go together has no existence. The debate which ensued was interesting and animated, but the great weight of authority was against Mr. Fawcett, and he was not supported by the leaders of the various sections of the Opposition. The Liberal party, or the Whig section of it, certainly seemed rather disposed to attack the Government on the ground that their proposal was illiberal and parsimonious, and there was some talk of an amendment in quite a different sense from that of Mr. Fawcett. Lord Hartington was known to have expressed most generous views as to the Royal allowance, and there is no doubt that had a quarter of a million been asked it would have been granted—a much larger sum, indeed, was named out of doors for the probable expenditure, and there were people who went about deploring the fate of the Chancellor of the Exchequer, who would certainly be called upon for 500,000*l.* or 750,000*l.* for the Indian expenditure. In a house of 446 members Mr. Fawcett found only 32 to agree with him in the view that India should not contribute to the expenses of the tour. It may be very fairly asserted, however, after the experience of the great interest which the Prince's presence created, that if the people of India had enjoyed the franchise they would have disapproved of the conduct of any representative who objected to a contribution to his Royal Highness's expenses from the Indian exchequer. It is not easy to comprehend the exact nature of the reasons which led Mr. Disraeli to insist on the necessity of the Prince of Wales being the "guest" of the "Viceroy" in the face of the fact that he was moving the House of Commons to make adequate provision for the extra expenditure which would be necessitated by the visit, and that he was expressly intimating that the cost of the Prince's entertainment in India would be borne by the Indian Budget. He, however, pressed the point with energy, and drew a vivid picture of the extraordinary pomp and circumstance which would necessarily surround the Prince if he were to go as the representative of the Queen. "He would have to exchange the presents of Europe for presents of Ormus and of Ind. He would have to hold Durbars, to travel with Princes in his train. He would not only be present at feasts—he would preside at festivals." Now all these things the Prince did in his non-representative capacity. The Prince exchanged the presents of Europe for the presents of Ind, and perhaps for some which might have come *viâ* "Ormus;" he held Durbars, he was attended by Princes, he presided at festivals, and yet he did it all for less than the sum which Parliament granted, under a sort of protest from Lord Hartington, strengthened by many expressions of opinion in and out of the House, on account of its inadequacy. The 'Times' next day wrote, what every one said and felt to be the truth—"The Prince must exercise extraordinary powers of management if Mr. Disraeli has not to ask for a supplementary estimate next year." Not only was the sum not exceeded, but there was a small surplus; not only was it not necessary to propose a supplementary grant, but it was the pleasing duty of the Minister, after a careful audit of the accounts had been made, to report that there still remained some money, which it was proposed to leave at the Prince's disposal with the unanimous consent of the House. It is only just to state that at all the Courts where the Royal visitor was welcomed there was no lack of souvenirs and no stint of princely largesse, and, avoiding any odious comparisons, that the presents made in India, if necessarily wanting in the infinite variety of form and diversity of nature which were exhibited in the gifts of the Native Chiefs, were of great substantial value and of beautiful workmanship.

As to the tour itself, those who read the following

pages will see the force of the metaphor of Bacon, that "Princes are like to heavenly bodies, which cause good or evil times, and which have much veneration, but no rest." According to all testimony, there has been no evil but much good caused by the visit among the princes and people of Hindostan, and it would be unjust to attach to it any consequences which may result from acts supposed to be justified by the enthusiasm with which the Prince was received, or to be called for by State and policy convenience. The famine which is now ravaging so much of the land which the Royal traveller saw wreathed with smiles and decked in gala attire, would have occurred whether he had gone or not; but the suffering people have now the consolation of knowing that they have secured the active sympathy of a powerful friend; and the Native Chiefs, and those whom they rule, under the protection and supreme sway of the Paramount Power, have the assurance that the attention of their fellow-subjects at home has been directed to their condition with a keener interest, and with a determination that they shall be ruled in righteousness and justice.

FROM LONDON TO BRINDISI.

L'ENVOI.

THIS narrative of the Prince of Wales' tour, as far as my personal knowledge of it is concerned, must begin at Brindisi, as it was there that the two divisions of the Royal suite were united. The Queen was at Balmoral Castle at the time of the Prince's departure from London, which took place on Monday, October 11th, some days earlier than the date which had been determined upon in the early programmes. On Sunday, October 10, the Prince and Princess attended Divine Service in the Chapel Royal. They received the Duke of Edinburgh and the Duke of Connaught at luncheon. In the evening there was a farewell dinner at Marlborough House, to which the members of the Royal Family then in London, and a few personal friends, were invited. In the forenoon, Dean Stanley preached an eloquent sermon in Westminster Abbey (the text taken from was Esther i., viii. 6), in which he expatiated on the journey "of the first Heir to the English Throne who has ever visited those distant regions, which the greatest of his ancestors, Alfred the Great, one thousand years ago, so ardently longed to explore." He concluded with an earnest prayer that the visit might leave behind it, on one side, "the remembrance, if so be, of graceful acts, kind words, English nobleness, Christian principle; and on the other, awaken in all concerned the sense of graver duties, wider sympathies, loftier purposes. Thus, and thus only, shall the journey on which the Church and nation now pronounce its parting benediction be worthy of a Christian Empire, and worthy of an English Prince." The circumstances under which the Prince of Wales was about to visit India, and those under which Alfred the Great desired to open commercial relations with it (there is scarcely any ground for stating that he ever contemplated a visit or longed to go to India) differed very considerably; but a study of the old travellers' stories leads one to think that, given the means of locomotion and time, it was not so very difficult to reach "Cathay and Ind" in remote times as it might be supposed to be from later narratives.

The chronicles of the day relate how deep an interest was taken by the public in the arrangements for this enterprising journey. On Monday all the morning and evening papers published leading articles, in which the warmest aspirations, not quite free from uneasiness, on account of "considerations which should quicken caution, though they need scarcely cause anxiety," were expressed for the Prince's happiness and safe return. "The life of the Prince of Wales," observed the leading journal, "is a very precious one; how precious, indeed, in the judgment of the country, the national anxiety in the autumn of 1871 indisputably showed; and his welfare is dear to us all." The great crowd which assembled on the evening of October 11th to bid him "God speed," at Charing Cross Station an hour before the departure of the special train, afforded ample testimony to the truth of these words.

There was, of course, a Royal Guard of Honour on the platform; but there was also a gathering of friends, for whom the station was all too small. When the Prince and Princess made their appearance, and walked slowly down the platform towards the train, between the line of soldiery and the great concourse of people, there was a demonstration, in which it would be hard to say whether a feeling of sadness at the Prince's departure and at his wife's emotion, or the desire to assure the Royal couple of enduring and affectionate loyalty, predominated. Cheers and waving of handkerchiefs—moistened eyes, quivering lips—and many an audible "God bless you!" At 8 o'clock P.M. the train glided out of the station. The memorable journey had fairly begun. At 9.20 P.M. the train stopped at Ashford, where the Duke of Edinburgh and the Duke of Connaught bade the Prince of Wales adieu. At 9.53 P.M. the train reached Dover, where 6000 or 7000 people had assembled along the approaches to the Admiralty Pier. All the naval, military, and civil authorities were in waiting to receive the Royal travellers. There was a Guard of Honour of the 104th Regiment, a detachment of the 78th Highlanders lined the pier platforms. The weather had been very rough for some days and nights previously, but wind and sea had obsequiously gone down, and there was every promise that no severe test would be applied to the qualities of the *Castalia*, which had been engaged for the passage. As the train stopped opposite the steamer, her bulwarks were lighted up by red and blue lights, which cast a strong glare on the anxious faces of the great crowd, and as the Prince and Princess stepped on board the steamer there was an outburst of cheering, renewed again and again with genuine enthusiasm. The Trinity House tender and other vessels in harbour lighted up sides and rigging. The Mayor and Corporation of Dover repaired on board to present an address, which was "taken as read," and for which the Prince said he was "much obliged." Then, at 10.10 P.M., three rockets gave the signal for departure. As the *Castalia* moved from the pier there was a clamour of valedictory voices, which followed her far out into the night. In two hours she arrived at Calais. Here was the saddest moment of the many which had been casting their solemn influence over the day. The Princess of Wales was not going on shore, but had resolved to stay on board, and return to England in the early morning. The train was to start at 1.50 A.M., so that there was short space left. The grief of that hour can now be regarded as a sorrow that has past, through the light of the happy meeting this year. At 2 A.M., October 12th, the train left the Calais station, and arrived at the terminus of the Northern Railway in Paris at 7.20 A.M. It so happened that the President, Marshal MacMahon, and a few gentlemen were there at the time, waiting for a train to take them to a shooting party. The Prince was welcomed by the Marshal and his suite with great cordiality and respect. He was received by Lord Lyons, who was in attendance with the members of the British Embassy. Entering his lordship's carriage, the Prince drove to the Hôtel Bristol, where he received numerous visitors; but it was officially understood that his Royal Highness wished to be incognito in Paris. He dined at the British Embassy that evening. Next day, October 13th, the Prince visited Marshal MacMahon, and lunched with him at the Elysée. He subsequently received a return visit from the Marshal. At 8.40 P.M. his Royal Highness and suite left by the ordinary train for Turin, which they reached at 7 P.M. next evening, 14th October. Resting at Turin for the night, the Prince continued his journey at 9.40 A.M. next morning, reached Bologna at 5 P.M., October 15th, and after a halt of an hour and a quarter, went on in the ordinary train, which was provided with Royal saloon carriages, to Ancona, where he got out for a few minutes to receive the expression of the good-wishes of a small gathering of English people who had been waiting on the platform to bid him "God speed!" Although the Prince was incognito, he could not escape official recognition, and he had been the unwilling object of every kind of attention throughout his journey;

and so it was that as the special train flew along through the night to Brindisi, the travellers, whenever they woke up and looked out, were aware of the presentment of prefects and sub-prefects in black coats and white cravats, of officers, guards of honour, crowds of people, and blazing lights on the station platforms.

In order to facilitate the overland journey through France and Italy of so large a party with great quantities of baggage and many personal attendants, Lord Alfred Paget, Lord Carington, Sir Bartle Frere, Colonel Owen Williams, Major-General Probyn, the Rev. Canon Duckworth, Mr. Albert Grey, the writer of this record, and a detachment of the Royal servants, preceded his Royal Highness, and left London, some on Saturday evening, October 9th, and others on the day following, for Paris, where they remained till Tuesday, October 13th, when they started for Brindisi, which they reached on the 16th of October. The 14th of October was passed in Bologna, but the day's repose, such as it was—for there was very much seeing of sights to be done—had its small grief to follow. It was necessary to arrive a clear twelve hours before the Prince; and at 1.30 A.M., October 15th, the whole of the first division, instead of being fast asleep, were under arms in the breakfast-room of the hotel, waiting till Groot, the excellent courier "in charge," had vanquished the difficulties connected with sleepy waiters, porters, bills, and the transport department, and gave the word that we had only to descend to the carriages which were waiting to take us to the train. There was an excellent saloon-carriage and a sufficient number of *coupés* ready, and at 3 A.M. we glided out of the Bologna station into a storm of rain and wind which lasted for several hours, and made some among us turn an uneasy eye on the grey, leaden-looking Adriatic with its fringe of surf, which came in view in the course of the day. Ancona and Foggia furnished a few minutes' halt, food, and news of the Royal progress. We reached Brindisi after a run of twenty hours from Bologna, and at 11 P.M. the train drew up alongside the platform close to the jetty, where there was a body of blue-jackets and Marines from the *Serapis*, to take charge of the baggage and to keep the Italian porters in order. There were also some friends waiting to greet the travellers. The rain had ceased and the wind had abated. The stars shone through the cloud-rifts, and, looking seawards, there was a great glory on the waters, for a few yards out from the pier lay the *Serapis* with her long line of ports lighted up, her white sides and golden scroll-work gleaming brightly in the glare of the gas-lamps on shore, and of the lanterns displayed at the companions and over the sides to show the way. Her boats were alongside the pier; and leaving Groot and his auxiliaries to contend with the piles of luggage which were shot out on the platform, we embarked, and in a few seconds more were standing in the blaze of lamps in the saloon, where sheen of snowy damask, and glitter of silver and glass on the long table, gave note of welcome supper. Captain Glyn received the members of the suite, and the officers did their best, late as it was, to induct them in their cabins, and make them at home; and we found Mr. Hall already installed on board, as he had preferred taking a passage from Portsmouth to the overland journey.

CONTENTS.

CHAPTER I.

DEPARTURE FROM BRINDISI.

CHAPTER II.

FROM THE PIRÆUS TO GRAND CAIRO.

CHAPTER III.

SUEZ TO ADEN, AND ADEN TO BOMBAY.

CHAPTER IV.

BOMBAY.

CHAPTER IX.

CALCUTTA.

CHAPTER X.

CHAPTER XI.

IMPERIAL DELHI.

CHAPTER XII.

THE KUMAOUN—TERAI—NEPAL.

CHAPTER XIII.

CHAPTER XIV.

CHAPTER XV.

LIST OF ILLUSTRATIONS.

Full-Page Engravings.

Full-Page Engravings.

(*Continued.*)

Smaller Engravings.

Smaller Engravings.

(*Continued.*)

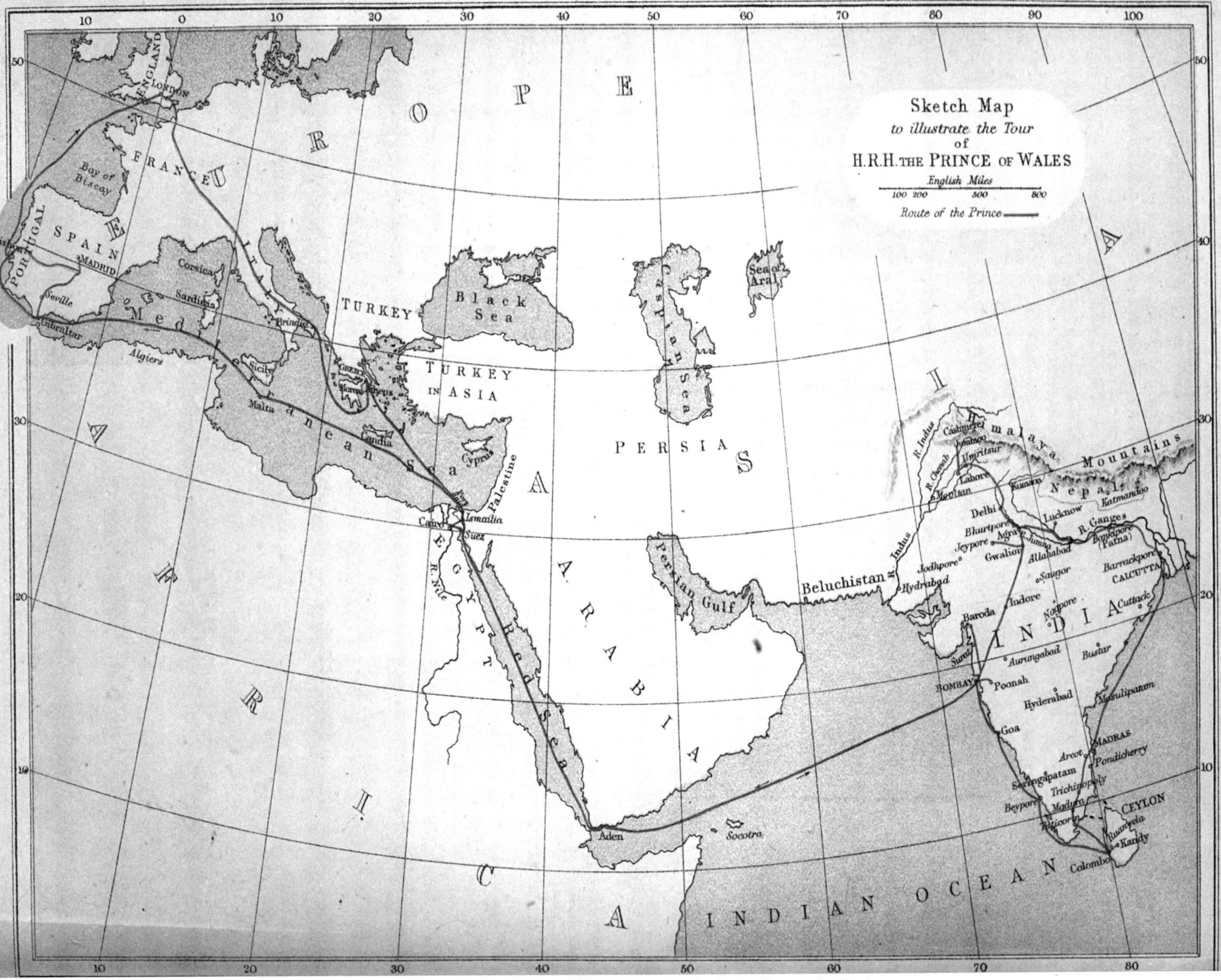
Sketch Map
to illustrate the Tour
of
H.R.H. THE PRINCE OF WALES
English Miles
100 200 500 800
Route of the Prince
EUROPE
ASIA
AFRICA
ENGLAND
LONDON
FRANCE
Bay of Biscay
PORTUGAL
SPAIN
MADRID
Lisbon
Seville
Gibraltar
Algiers
Corsica
Sardinia
Sicily
Malta
Brindisi
ITALY
TURKEY
Black Sea
TURKEY IN ASIA
Candia
Cyprus
Mediterranean Sea
Palestine
Cairo
Ismailia
Suez
R. Nile
EGYPT
Red Sea
Caspian Sea
Sea of Aral
PERSIA
ARABIA
Persian Gulf
Aden
Socotra
Beluchistan
R. Indus
R. Chenab
Cashmere
Jummoo
Umritsur
Lahore
Mooltan
Himalaya Mountains
Kumaon
Nepal
Katmandoo
Delhi
Lucknow
R. Ganges
Bankipore (Patna)
Bhurtpore
Agra
Jumna
Jeypore
Gwalior
Allahabad
Jodhpore
Hydrabad
Saugor
Barrackpore
CALCUTTA
Indore
Nagpore
Cuttack
Baroda
INDIA
Surat
Aurungabad
Bustar
BOMBAY
Poonah
Hyderabad
Masulipatam
Goa
MADRAS
Arcot
Pondicherry
Seringapatam
Trichinopoly
Beypore
Madura
CEYLON
Ruanwela
Kandy
Colombo
INDIAN OCEAN

BOWS OF THE 'SERAPIS.'

THE PRINCE OF WALES' TOUR.

CHAPTER I.

DEPARTURE FROM BRINDISI.

Preparations on board the *Serapis*—Brindisi—Reception of the Prince—Departure—Life on board—"Cleaning-up"—Muscular Christians—First Sunday on board—Cape Malea—Reminiscences—The hermit—Last "look round"—The Piræus—Modern Greek—The Palace at Athens—Tattoï—Constitutional troubles—Departure from Athens—Farewell at sea.

OCTOBER 16TH.—It was very early indeed when the preparations for the reception of the Prince commenced on board the *Serapis* this morning. The Royal special train was expected to arrive at 8.30 A.M. Several hours before that time, strenuous efforts to clear away the mass of personal baggage outside the cabins on the main-deck disturbed the sleepers, who, after the fatigues of the journey of the previous day, would gladly have remained at rest a little longer; but the inexorable first lieutenant and officers of the watch directing their forces of sailors, marines, and Chinamen to make a passage between the piles of portmanteaus from the gangway to the foot of the saloon-companion, speedily dissipated any dreams of indulgence in such bodily infirmity. As to the minor inconveniences of "clearing away" boxes and "lumber" outside cabins on these occasions, they best can paint them who have felt them most. There were stowaway corners and crypts under the staircase, and shelves fixed across the main-deck, concealed by green curtains, for portmanteaus; but this did not suffice for all, especially as the shelves were appropriated by a few who had many boxes. The mode of access to the saloon and to the State apartments was rather a weak part of the constitution of the ship, but it was perhaps unavoidable. The companion-ladder was on the port side of the main-deck, and visitors were obliged to pass by the sleeping-cabins to the staircase which led to the saloon on the upper-deck.

There was little time before the arrival of the Royal train to make ourselves familiar with the ship which was to be our home for so many days and nights, but her great length of deck, the beautiful order and exquisite cleanliness of everything visible aloft and below, produced a favourable impression at the first glance. The cabins varied in size and in fittings; some had two ports, others one, but all were well-appointed. They were beautifully fresh and neat, not overdone with ornament or gilding, but there was room for such decoration as the occupants might deem most appropriate. In each cabin there was a large and comfortable-looking sofa which was converted into a bedstead at night, but the fate of these was speedily sealed, as shall be related hereafter. A writing-table with drawers, a chest of drawers and dressing-table, a washing-stand, a bath, shelves and nettings for books, clothes, boots, and looking-glasses—what more was needed? There was ample light when the outer ports were not closed. It must be confessed that the stories of her behaviour in the run from Portsmouth outward, and the reputation she had acquired as a "tremendous roller," caused some misgivings among the weaker vessels; and many secret and confidential inquiries were addressed by them as soon as they got on board to the officers and passengers respecting the conduct of the *Serapis* in the voyage from Malta to Brindisi, the results of which were very satisfactory and comforting. The suite received invitations from Captain Glyn and the officers to the ward-room as honorary members of the mess.

There is an Old-world look about Brindisi. When the line of mail steamers to the East galvanised the port into a fitful activity for a few hours once a week, there were great expectations raised of a glorious future, and it was predicted that the town would become the centre of a considerable commerce. Land was largely bought on speculation, the harbour was dredged out and improved, a new breakwater was completed, houses were built on a large scale, and all seemed going on well, when Venice was "discovered," and the old Queen of the Adriatic enticed the roving affections of commerce from her disconsolate rival. One advantage was gained by the temporary importance of the place which the inhabitants perhaps did not appreciate. The incredible filth and nastiness of the streets were somewhat abated, and the manners of the inhabitants improved. Many travellers still prefer the long, tedious, and trying journey from Turin to Brindisi to the sea route from Venice, and there is nothing to be said against their fancy if they disregard the dust in summer and the cold in winter, the evil baiting-places on the way, and the monotony of the rail with its borderings of olive plantations and tideless sea, where the excesses of the storm are denoted by lines of stagnating sea-weed. Now Brindisi was very gay. Landwards floated in the strong southerly breeze over the houses the flags of many Powers, for there are many Consular personages in the town. The Civic Band was playing near the railway station, the custom-house guards in full uniform were drawn up on the quay to which the *Serapis* was moored, and there was close to her a crowd of fully a hundred persons apparently listening to a lecture on marine architecture from an ancient mariner who had surely never beheld such a gallant craft before. Seaward, near the interesting old fort in the middle of the harbour lay the Italian ironclads, *Castel-Fidardo* and the *Reina Maria Pia*, which had come round from Spezzia in a gale of wind, H.M.S. *Hercules*, H.M.S. *Pallas*, the Royal yacht *Osborne*, and a few steamers and sailing-vessels—British, Greek, and Italian—all dressed in their best, to do honour to the Prince of Wales, with bunting streaming out flat as sheets of coloured glass in the stiff souther, which sent the surf flying over the breakwater, and brought up with it from time to time drenching showers. The members of the suite appeared in uniform for the first time; the ships' officers were what is nautically called "in full fig;" and as the drum summoned the crew to quarters, it was a pleasure to look down from the quarter-deck on the clean, smart men-of-warsmen ranged below in their spick-and-span new white raiment ready to man yards at a word. It was nearly 9.30 A.M. when the Royal train was signalled, in less than half an hour afterwards the Prince of Wales descended from his carriage at the Railway Station. The Prefetto and sotto-Prefetto, and the authorities of the district, on the platform, received

EMBARKATION ON BOARD THE 'SERAPIS' AT BRINDISI.

his Royal Highness, who acknowledged their salutations, shook hands with Count Maffei and one or two of his personal acquaintances, and walked to the steps where his barge was awaiting him. With the Prince came the Duke of Sutherland, the Earl of Aylesford, Lord Suffield, Lord C. Beresford, Lieut.-Colonel Ellis, Mr. F. Knollys, Major Stanley Clarke, Sir A. Paget, and the members of the British Legation who could be spared from Rome, the Italian Minister of Marine, Vice-Admiral di San Bon, and his naval aide-de-camp, &c. The Civic Band played "God save the Queen" and the Italian National Air; the Royal Standard (of the Prince of Wales) was run up in the barge the moment he was on board; the British and Italian men-of-war manned yards, and running up the Royal Standard, fired a Royal salute. The fine effect of the sudden outburst was greatly increased by the drifting smoke, which was whirled away rapidly by the breeze to leeward, instead of hanging round the ships and obscuring hull and rigging. In a couple of minutes more the Prince of Wales was ascending the ladder to the port gangway of the *Serapis*, where he was received by Captain Glyn and the officers of the ship. On every occasion of his Royal Highness's arrival or departure in public the same ceremony was observed on board. The Royal Marines and the detachment of R.M.A. were drawn up on the main-deck to the right of the larboard gangway, the Band of the Royal Marines on their left, the officers standing in a line from the gangway to the entrance to the main-deck cabins. The instant the Prince put his foot on board or quitted the ship, his Standard was run up or hauled down, yards were manned; the Band played "God save the Queen," officers and guard of honour saluted with the usual honours. The guard of honour mounted on the main-deck to receive personages entitled to salutes could not "present" arms, as the bayonets would have come in contact with the deck overhead, but Major Snow got over the difficulty by inventing a new exercise and *maniement des armes*, which answered quite as well as the old.

The arrangements on board were found to be very satisfactory. The Italian Minister of Marine was loud in his approbation of the great size and airiness of the ship, and of the perfect order on board. Breakfast was served soon after the Prince's arrival, and then, after a short promenade on deck and final message, came "the word that must be spoken." At 11.15 A.M. the British and Italian Ministers took leave, with many expressions of their respectful interest in the expedition, and good wishes for the safety and happy return of the Prince. The first thud of the screw caused the great frame of the ship to quiver from stem to stern, and the *Serapis* moved slowly seaward in the wake of the *Osborne*, which was followed by the *Hercules* and *Pallas*. The moment of her departure was telegraphed to Athens, where the Prince was expected on Monday. Again the iron throats of the cannon uttered a deal of sulphurous breath and the crews of the men-of-war shouted. The Prince went forward to the bridge, where there is a kind of room or wooden box with windows at three sides, a table for charts, chairs, telescopes, and glasses. The steering-wheels are underneath, and there is a good look-out fore and aft over the decks from the platform, which is nigh sixty feet above the sea. In ten minutes we saw the *Osborne* make a graceful curtsey to an incoming wave, the first of the numerous family outside the reef which, leaping on each other's backs in their anxiety to welcome it, were awaiting the little squadron; but when it came to her turn, the lofty *Serapis* scarcely deigned to notice their salutations, and only gave a slight nod of her head as if to show she was not regardless of all the laws of maritime propriety. But notwithstanding that dignified nonchalance the company which sat down to dinner did not include all those who came on board the ship, and there was in several cabins hidden but audible suffering. This was the first time of wearing the *Serapis* dress—a blue jacket with silk facings and household buttons, black trousers and black necktie—which was pronounced to be a successful substitute for the mess dress and the civilian black coat of evening life. The Prince went round the decks before dinner and inspected "the Farm,"—the various animals he was bringing out as presents to the King of Greece, and his horses from the Sandringham stables, but he did not appear at table. However, he came out of his room after dinner, and in the evening sat in the charming little "fumoir" on the quarter-deck, to which access is gained from the saloon below by a winding staircase. It is windowed with plate glass, panelled in white and gold, and provided with sofas. There are doors at each angle, a small book-case, barometer, clock, &c.; on the panels are fine photographs of the two young princes in sailors' costume, and a frame of exquisite photographs of the Princess of Wales and the Royal children. The Band stationed on the upper-deck played from dinner-time till past 9 o'clock, and proved to be very steady on its legs in the sea-way, and of excellent quality. The speed of the vessel was regulated methodically by Admiralty Orders, as if the winds and seas were factors of small consequence. An average rate of 264 knots in the 24 hours, or 11 knots an hour, was the basis on which the calculations of the programme depended, and about 48 revolutions per minute of the *Serapis* screw corresponded with the required mileage. There was a fair but strong wind, which eased the screw and enabled the ship to set a good spread of canvas, but there was too much wind and sea towards nightfall, as she was off the coast of Cephalonia, and sail was reduced. The lights are extinguished in the cabins at 11 P.M., but those in the saloon are left burning till the Prince retires for the night. There are, however, great lanterns along the main-deck, which cast their rays upon the darkness where the marine on duty passes up and down outside the entrance to the cabins, and reveal "Bobêche," the Prince's French poodle, scampering about in search of "Flossy," another canine favourite, or of some other less substantial playmate. He seems under the impression that there must be a dog or two hidden on board, and has already made search all up and down the decks, investigating the secrets of his water prison-house with so much success that he was quite lost for about an hour, and baffled all attempts to discover him, so that it was feared he had gone overboard. However, Bobêche had not the least idea of doing anything so foolish.

October 17th.—The wind and sea abated during the night, and the *Serapis* slid very quietly through the placid waters; but soon after dawn a gentle breeze sprung up nearly right astern, and all square canvas was set—*Osborne* in her station, but no sign of *Hercules* or *Pallas*. The first sound which pierces the dull hubbub of the throbbing engines and of the cleaving of the waters outside is the bugle-call, which sets all the servants in motion—or ought to do so—on the main-deck. Then comes the tumult of "cleaning-up" outside the cabins and on the decks, but we are spared the horrible marine infliction of "holystoning." The planking is covered with oil-cloth, which is swabbed and washed. The cleaning-up is done by certain loose-limbed sinewy Chinamen—quiet, orderly fellows, with a full allowance of tail, who do not appear to recognise "Tom

Fat" as a man and a brother, though his tail is of irreproachable length. Perhaps his Christianity has cut him off from his brethren. Presently electric bells begin to tinkle, and various figures, draped after the antique, appear outside the cabins, and hold converse on the main-deck whilst they await their turns for the bath, exchanging ideas about the weather, past, present, and to come, and the sensations which the sea has caused or which it yet menaces. The athletically disposed take to various strengthening exercises. Dr. Fayrer, armed with two mugdahs or Indian clubs, whirls them round his head with an air of entire resignation and devotion, diligently improving his already very respectable biceps, and Canon Duckworth gives demonstration that he is no bad representative of the school of muscular Christians. Sir Bartle Frere is one of the very early risers, and begins his work before breakfast hour; but no matter how busy he may be, he never minds any interruption, and is always ready to give information, of which he has such ample stores in most matters, with the greatest cheerfulness.

A fair muster at breakfast, Lord Alfred Paget turning up at 8 A.M. with sailorly briskness, and most of the others being an hour later. At 11 A.M. the Church pendant was hoisted, and the Rev. Canon Duckworth read Divine service in the saloon before the Prince, suite, and domestics. Land was seen on the port bow at 1.45 P.M.; and soon after the little squadron passed Navarino Bay. An Italian brig saluted the Royal Standard, dipping her flag three times, and Captain Glyn gave orders that the *Serapis* should dip also, which was much better than taking no notice of the civility, although it was not strictly in accordance with the etiquette to do so under the circumstances. The steamer *Graphic* of Hull, actuated, no doubt, by excessive loyalty and curiosity, but troublesome for all that, as if the sea were not wide enough for all, would get in our way. There have been recent painful incidents which render these demonstrations undesirable. As the time at which the Prince was expected at Athens was settled "to the minute," it was necessary to reduce the speed of the ship to eight knots, in order that we should not arrive too soon. At 4 P.M. Mount Taygetus was visible. The approach of the Prince was telegraphed to the telegraph station near Matapan by the code signals. It would not be at all a novel remark to offer that it would have been a great advantage to the democracy of Athens if they could have learnt exactly when the Spartan galleys might have been expected off Ægina. The sea belied its traditions this our first Sunday on board, for it became almost dead calm as soon as we were off Cerigo, and a bright moonlight rested on the crestless swell which still agitated the sea. There was a glorious sunset—beautiful exceedingly—a great fire on the western horizon, which cast a purple glow over the sea, and flung a broad hemisphere of saffron, gold, and green into the sky. All the company turned up on deck, and watched the radiance in silence.

All the late absentees appeared at dinner to-day, and in accordance with the custom which was established on the first day of the Prince's appearance on board, and which was never departed from during his voyage, a certain number of the ship's officers were invited to the Royal table, invitations being given to all the officers in turn. The dressing bugle sounded at 7 P.M., and at 7.30 P.M. the company assembled in the large saloon astern, in the fore part of which the table was laid. The Prince came out of his room a few moments earlier, and went round to say a few words and shake hands with the officers; the signal for dinner was given by the Band playing "The Roast Beef of Old England," His Royal Highness led the way and took his place at the forward end of the table. Lord Suffield sat at the other end aft, and the suite and guests settled down pretty much as they pleased, till use established a settled order in the intermediate seats. Towards the close of dinner, the Prince rising said, "Her Majesty the Queen," and the company rose also and remained standing whilst the Band played the usual bars of the National Anthem. Then after dessert the Prince left the saloon and went up to the divan on the quarter-deck, where coffee was served, and sat for an hour or two listening to the Band or engaged in conversation.

After dinner the Band varied the musical entertainment in the programme by singing a chorus from *Stabat Mater* very finely. We were near Cape Malea at the moment, and I thought of the time twenty-one years ago when the Rifle Brigade—the advance guard of the British expedition to the Crimea—on board the *Golden Fleece*, woke up the echoes of the same headlands with the strains of their jubilant song—

> "Soldiers! merrily march away!
> Soldier's glory lives in story,
> His laurels are green when his hair is grey,
> And it's oh! for the life of a soldier!"

How many of the joyous Riflemen are alive now? There are Norcott, Elrington, Colville, Newdegate, Egerton, and some two or three more perhaps. Sir Bartle Frere told me that thirteen years before the time of which I speak he passed this very Cape Malea in a Greek brig, on his way to Alexandria to make essay of the newly-found "overland route," of the which—as far as water was concerned—he had, ere he arrived at Bombay, a very long and varied experience in the Red Sea and the Persian

Gulf. It is said that the hermit who lived in a cave in the face of the cliff in those days, and who was held in reverence by superstitious mariners, is still abiding there. It is probably a hereditary office—"l'Hermite est mort! Vive l'Hermite!"

Before turning in, those with nautical tastes generally go forward to the bridge and have a little weather talk. The Prince rarely if ever retired for the night without taking this "look round," and having a few minutes' conversation with the officers on duty.

October 18th.—"We shall be in the Piræus in a couple of hours, they tell me!" First news this morning. The speed of the ship was reduced, as the Prince's arrival had been fixed for 9.30 A.M. Already Cape Colonna could be discerned, and the ruins of the Temple of Minerva, crowning "the marble steep," were shining in all the glory of their untarnished marble in the morning sun. On our port side lay the rugged shores of ancient Calaurea, where stood the Temple of Neptune, in which Demosthenes, almost within sight of the beloved city which his eloquence could not save from the proud foot of the conqueror, died by his own hand. The island now called Poros, from a small peninsula near it, is the site of a naval arsenal. Ahead, on the port bow, was Ægina, with the bulk of Mount St. Elias towering aloft, just flecked by a few snowy cloudlets. Presently the coast of the Gulf seemed to come out to meet us. Salamis lay on our port bow. Looking straight over the stem the spectators beheld, glistening in the sun, the mountain ranges which inclose the little plain of Attica. The pure, clear air renders the outlines of the landscape wonderfully distinct, but it is difficult, nevertheless, to believe that the figure of Minerva—which, with gilt helm, spear, and shield, surmounted the Parthenon—was visible at Sunium, a distance of forty miles and more, unless, perhaps, when the sun was reflected from the polished surface. Beneath the high chain which sweeps round from the range of Parnes, fencing out rude Bœotia, there stretches the broken hill-land to the west, north, and east of the city. "There is the Acropolis!" "You can see the Parthenon quite plainly now!" To the left of the Temple we could discern Mount Anchesmus, and beyond the sheer downfall of Pentelicus, clad in white marble, and, nearer, Lycabettus; and on the starboard bow towered Hymettus. The fair panorama unfolded itself rapidly. The white houses of the city cowering at the base of the Acropolis, the domes of Greek churches, and the piles of recent public edifices became more definite; and the confused, cloud-like appearance on the verge of the sea which the Piræus first presented to the sight, was resolvable into a mass of houses, in front of which was a pulk of ships' masts close together, with bright coruscations of colours playing over them as the innumerable flags fluttered in the breeze.

"Adsunt Athenæ, unde Humanitas, Doctrina, Religio, Fruges, Jura, Leges, ortæ atque in omnes terras distributæ putantur, de quorum possessione, propter pulchritudinem, etiam inter Deos certamen fuisse proditum est."

How different is the present reputation of the "Ancient of Days"! Neither humanity, religion, learning, nor laws emanate from her bosom, and the old world only gives back with niggard hands some of the blessings which she owes to her benefactress, and distils out of the great reservoir of her wealth a few drops to refresh the arid plains in which were nursed all that can decorate life and bless mankind with knowledge. They who were charged with the care of the *Serapis* just now, however, had not much time to think of anything else except the difficulty of guiding such a vast ship through the narrow entrance to the anchorage of the Piræus, which is far more suited to an ancient trireme than to a modern troop-ship. In the days of sailing-vessels it could not have been easy to have entered, unless with fair winds, and it is related that when Captain Clarke took in the *Braakel* in 1812, not without doing her a good deal of damage, the people flocked down in thousands to gaze on such an unwonted apparition.

Steam enables sailors to tackle such difficulties as are presented by the narrowness of the Piræus with confidence, though not without care, and now the water seemed blocked up with the mass of shipping; but, as we glided out of the Pass, we could see there was a kind of avenue between the British men-of-war and those of other nations, and the ships, yachts, and small craft which crowded the ancient port, left for the vessels to keep in. It was a very pretty sight; every ship dressed in colours, the crews of the men-of-war in white in the yards; marines drawn up with presented arms; officers in groups on the quarter-decks; boats with men and women waving hats and handkerchiefs flying in and out amid the lanes of vessels. The Prince, who was dressed in full uniform to receive the King, surveyed the scene which looked so bright in the bright sunshine. His *compagnons de voyage*, Murray in hand, were ogling the landscape through their glasses, or recalling ancient memories. The guns thundered, bells rung on shore, cheers rose from the waters and floated away from the throats of the sailors manning the yards and rigging of the craft which lay so close and packed in the little harbour, that there was not much room for the *Serapis* to scrape through to her anchorage. The Royal Greek yacht *Amphitrite*, with the Standards of Great Britain and of the Hellenic Kingdom flying from main and fore, and the Russian sloop lay close at hand on the port bow, and the American corvette, *Juanita*, on the starboard quarter. The pilot thought the ship was in the right place off the pillars. "Let go the starboard anchor!" Over went S.B. The usual rumble and grating, like a charge of fifty steam rollers over a rough pavement, followed for an instant—and for an instant only—the chain cable had snapped at the fourth shackle, and the starboard anchor, having severed its connection with the ship, was lying at the bottom on its own account. "Let go the port anchor!" A quick, hot command this time. Over went B.B. Again the rattle of the chain through the hawsehole was heard for an instant—and for an instant only—the cable had parted—the port anchor was rejoicing in its liberty alongside its fellow. Except the sailors, no one knew what had occurred; but as the *Serapis* fetched leeway under the influence of the stiff breeze, Captain Glyn, who had been till this moment looking somewhat uneasy about the berthing of his ship, passed aft with a fine calm on his brow, to look out astern and murmured gently "We've lost both anchors!" on the quarter-deck. The steam had been blown off from our boilers, and there seemed imminent risk of a catastrophe. Either the *Serapis* would crush up the whole flotilla of wooden vessels like so many egg-shells, and run aground, or she would be impaled on the spur of one of our own ironclads. Every one ran to the side, looked over, and then glanced astern, where the shining iron stems of the *Hercules* and *Swiftsure*, as they rose and fell gently in the swell, flashed a kind of signal to beware of contact. Their bows would have gone through the thin iron of the *Serapis* "as a knife cuts butter." Gathering way rapidly, the *Serapis* came down on the astonished Greeks on board the yacht; but the King of the Hellenes, who is a thorough sailor, saw what was the matter at once, and sent the crew forward to fend off the coming mountain. In a second more there was a loud crash and snap as the *Serapis* avenged the damage done by the yacht's bowsprit to one of her boats by the abrupt removal of that spar, and then continued her career astern. There was speedily a scene of much activity all round us. Off came the Russian's boat with the end of a warp, and landed it cleverly on board the *Osborne*, which had her steam up, and was manœuvring to help her erratic consort. There was not the smallest confusion, but there was a good deal of excitement on board. In a very short time the warp was made fast on board the *Serapis*, her way was checked just in time to avoid the danger of fouling, and, forging ahead again, she was brought up to her old ground, and then let go both sheet anchors, which held her fast at last. As soon as she was anchored (10.30 A.M.), King George came off under a Royal salute from all the shipping, yards manned, &c., and was received at the side by the Prince, who conducted him to the saloon, where the members of the suite were presented to His Majesty. Sir J. Drummond, Admiral Boutakoff, and many Russian, American, Austrian, and Turkish officers hastened on board to pay their respects to the Prince. These were followed by officers in uniform—naval, military, consular, and diplomatic—so that the decks of the *Serapis* presented a very animated appearance, in keeping with the scene outside, where the waters were crowded with boats and sailing craft, filled with people turned out in their best. At noon the members of the suite were told off to the boats alongside, to lead the way to the landing-place of the Piræus, about a quarter of a mile away. On the platform there was a deputation, and probably an address, but the first comers had to drive off to the terminus before the Royal party landed, and did not witness the reception. They passed to the carriages from the steps through the guard of honour and troops lining the sides to keep off the crowds of curious who pressed upon them—a medley of races in great variety of costume, among whom there were not many women. These mostly looked out of the windows of the rather poor houses, much given to entertainment of sailors, and suggesting the idea of a Greek Wapping, which line the way here. There was abundance of green wreaths, bunches of flowers and banners along the streets to the Railway Station, which was prettily decorated—scarlet cloth laid down on the platform—banners, &c.—a gathering of well-dressed ladies, the various ministers and ex-ministers, the diplomatic body, the clergy of the Greek Church and others, the civil magistrates, the Town Council (τὸ δημοτικὸν Συμβούλιον 'Αθηνῶν), the Nomarchs of Attica and Bœotia, the Demarchs of the Piræus and of Athens, the Ὑπουργοὶ, &c.—to receive the Royal party, whose arrival was announced by another salute of cannon and by loud cheering.

The Royal train was in readiness, the engine puffing impatiently to get off, and after some delay, connected with baggage, the King and the Prince, greeted by the peculiar sort of cry which is the Greek substitute for a cheer, left the station. There was some curiosity manifested by the people in the suburb of the Piræus, for they mounted on the walls to look at the train; but the peasants, men and women, at work in the olive-groves and in the fields, only paused for a while, some doffing their hats, and then resumed their labours. There were Royal carriages, an escort of cavalry, guard of honour, band, &c., in attendance at the Observatory Station in the outskirts of Athens, where the King and the Prince alighted, and a greater gathering to welcome them than there was at Piræus.

There a state procession was formed; all who took part in it were in full uniform. The carriages, escorted by the *Chevaux Légers*, set out at a slow pace, in order to give the people an opportunity of seeing the guest of their King. It was a hot and dusty drive from the station to the palace, but the great crowds which lined the streets (ὁδὸς Αἰόλου, ὁδὸς Ἑρμοῦ, &c.), and filled the windows and balconies along the route to bid the Prince welcome, had endured the fierce rays of the sun and dust of the roads some hours before he appeared. In the present day there are few distinctive marks about the dress of the better-off classes in European cities, and the ladies and gentlemen who looked with so much interest on the Royal visitor and his suite were pretty much like the inhabitants of any other large town. There was a good deal of an *esprit moqueur* about the crowd, and people in good coats and hats pointed at the novel uniforms with more freedom than is usual in Western cities. There were sprinklings of Greek costumes to be seen here and there among the poorer sort, and a large proportion of those "indescribables," with unwashed faces, and felt hats of strange shapes, furnished by all the nationalities of the world, who may be seen in Levantine towns. And as of the people so of the dwellings. The new streets are formed in right lines of very lofty buildings of the Haussmann type. There are no "old houses." The Acropolis looks down proudly on what is, take it all in all, the newest city out of the United States. In the rear of the principal streets, which are nearly as wide as those of Munich or of modern Paris, are lanes of humble cottages, of modern construction and of no particular type, "the huts where poor men lie." But with this newness of look there was one thing ever before our eyes during the long drive to the Palace which prevented our forgetting where we were—the characters and the names on the walls and the shop-fronts which exercised—well, let us say—the ingenuity or memory of the suite, and afforded them a distraction. There were many flags flying in the streets. The majority were Greek, next Russian, next Italian, then English and French; but the Crescent on the Red field of the Turk was rare indeed. The Athenians did not cheer, but they talked loudly, and a buzzing sound preceded the cortege; the ladies waved handkerchiefs from the windows; the police, who are dressed like infantry soldiers, had not much difficulty in keeping line, save in front of the numerous cafés, which were thronged with people, and emitted clouds of tobacco-smoke. Certainly ten men out of eleven smoke cigarettes.

The aspect of the Basilikon is imposing. The Palace is well placed on an elevated site at the base of Mount Lycabettus, commanding a fine view towards Hymettus and the mountains on one side, and facing the modern Place, in which are the principal hotels. The portico, the colonnade, and much of the exterior are built of the pure white marble of Pentelicus, which towers behind it in the distance; and much of the interior is decorated with or constructed of the same beautiful material. The vast hall is adorned with columns of marble; the courts, by which the Palace is divided, contain two of the loftiest and finest State saloons in Europe, which are only used for great banquets or royal festivities. Great corridors run along the length and breadth of the Palace, which is a quadrangle of 300 feet by 280. On the first floor, which is at a great height from the basement, are suites of rooms of large dimensions—too large to be easily warmed in the severe cold of the Attic winter, of which one is reminded by the German stoves in the corners of each bed-room and sitting-room. The King's apartments are charmingly comfortable; the Queen's suite bears the evidence of an exquisite taste, and of tendencies which in an English house would be called "ritualistic." There is a Greek Chapel in the Palace for her Majesty and for those of her attendants and others who belong to the Orthodox Church; and there is a separate Chapel for the King. In the public apartments and on the terraces there are some pictures, treated in the heroic manner, of the great frescoes of Cornelius. These are painted, I believe, by Danes or Germans, for modern Greece has not yet found her Apelles. From the front windows there is a wide-spreading view towards the city and the country in the direction of the Piræus, and a glimpse of part of the Acropolis.

Before the entrance there was a guard of honour, with band and colours, a company of infantry, clad in uniform with some resemblance to that of the French line, except that the men did not indulge in *garance* pantaloons. On the steps the officers of the household of the King and Queen, and a crowd of functionaries, were assembled, many of them in the picturesque dress of the Court—which was adopted by King Otho to please the national taste—gold-embroidered jacket and vest, sash, stiff white fustanelle, a cap like a fez with an elongated bag, decorated with a long gold tassel, and embroidered gaiters. There was a small gathering of people in the open space between the shrubbery and railings which fence off the Place from the front of the Palace, for in Athens, as in most cities which boast of a Royal residence, there is no restriction on the use by the public of the walks about the palace. The King of the Hellenes led his guest into the great hall, and thence to the Royal apartments. Presently those who accompanied the Prince were summoned to the saloon where the Queen was standing with her children—the Duke of Sparta, Prince George, the Princess Alexandra, and Prince Nicholas—and the ladies-in-waiting, and were presented to her Majesty by his Royal Highness. Her Majesty's manner is exceedingly gracious, and for each she had a kind word, and for those whom she had known before a little speech, which proved she had a Royal memory. Nor did she forget to express her great regret that circumstances had prevented the Princess of Wales coming so far with the Prince on his way to India. Then came a general dispersion to the rooms, mostly of great size and well found, where the servants were already unpacking portmanteaus for a change from uniform to plain clothes. There was a little difficulty in establishing communications between the Greek gentlemen-in-waiting and our own people; even Canon Duckworth, whose Greek was of the freshest and best, was at fault when he came to "hot water" and the like. The Highlanders in the Royal train were especially disappointed in the expectations which had been raised in their breasts by the appearance of kilted Albanians, that Gaelic would serve as a medium of converse; but there was an excellent Corfiote who had picked up English in the old days of the British protectorate, and there were German-speaking men, remanets of the Othonic period in attendance, and so, after a time, all things went pleasantly and well.

The King and the Prince of Wales went out for a drive in mufti, and Mr. Malet, of the British Legation, came to the Palace to conduct those who wished to see the Acropolis, the Theatre of Bacchus, and as many of the sights as could be taken in before dinner. There is no city in the world, except Cairo—where spick-and-span new Italian and French villas smirk under the shadow of the Pyramids—which presents such contrasts between ancient and modern civilisation as Athens. From the

Acropolis you see the smoke of tall factory chimneys, rapidly increasing in number near the port, streaking the bright blue sky of Attica, and the railway from the Piræus traversing the plain where once flowed, and now trickle, the Cephissus and Ilissus. Separated from the base of the citadel by the space whereon lie the Areopagus, the Agora, the Theseum, the Pnyx, the Dionysiac Theatre, to the W. and S.W. rise the streets of the new city, its Greek churches, and lofty white houses glistening in the sun, and the imposing public buildings — the National Academy, the University, the Polytechnic School, and the Museum — which indicate that there is a "living Greece," and that learning, science, and the arts are remembered in the land of their birth. These, however, appear very justly to shun the fanes of the older city, although the Temple of the Winds, and one or two monuments which stood outside the boundaries of Athens, on the north side of the Acropolis, are included within the limits of the fast growing quarter which has the brand of Munich and Paris upon it. Since the Prince was last here the Venetian Tower has been removed from the Acropolis, and its place knows it no more. However great the force of the æsthetical reasons for the demolition may have been, I am not sure that the general effect of the grand mass of ruins, as seen from the lower ground, has not been injured by the removal.

At dinner the young Princes came to their places at table, and when dessert was over took leave, going round to each guest, shaking hands, and bidding him good-night in the most charming, frank, and pleasant way. The boys resemble their mother — blue, serious eyes, serene brows, and wonderfully fair skins. The Queen expressed much interest in the expedition, and seemed to think that the Princess of Wales could have had no difficulty in visiting India; at all events, "she thought the Princess might have come as far as Athens." After dinner the King and Queen and the Prince of Wales drove out to see the lighting up of the rock and the temple of Jupiter Olympius, which was wound up by a very effective exhibition of fireworks, with clever combinations of colour, including an escutcheon of the Royal Arms. But surely in the strict application of *τὸ πρέπον* the Acropolis ought not to be desecrated by fireworks? Or if that be begging the question—is it not a "desecration" to make the Acropolis the scene of a pyrotechnic display? Whilst we were going over the Erechtheum and Parthenon we came on gangs of workmen fixing the stands for rockets, Roman candles, and similar *feux d'artifice* along the façades. It must be admitted that the display pleased thousands of spectators, and that it was very beautiful. The great crowd which assembled to see the Prince and the fireworks behaved with much consideration, although it could not be expected they would prove utterly indifferent to the desire to have a close view of the Royal personages.

The King was delighted with his presents from England, which were delivered from the *Serapis* in the afternoon. There was a steam-launch, an Alderney bull and cow, a ram and sheep, and a few fine specimens of the British pig, which came, I think, from Sandringham.

Tuesday, October 19th.—It was somewhat amusing to make out in the morning paper, the 'Stoa,' the account of the Prince's landing yesterday, which appeared under the date of October 7th, and to try to identify the persons in attendance upon the Prince. Here they are:

1. Ὁ Δοὺξ τῆς Σούθερλανδ, ἱππότης τῆς Περικνημῖδος.

2. Ὁ Λόρδος Σούφιελδ, λόρδος ἐν ὑπηρεσίᾳ καὶ ἀρχηγὸς της Αὐλῆς τοῦ Πρίγκηπος.

3. Ὁ Κόμης Ἀϋλεσφόρδ.

4. Ὁ λοχαγὸς τῆς ἐφίππου Β. φρουρᾶς καὶ ὑπασπιστὴς τοῦ Πρίγκηπος λόρδος Κάριγκταν.

5. Ὁ κύριος *W.* H. Ῥοῦσσελ ἐπίτιμος ἰδιαίτερος γραμματεὺς τοῦ Πρίγκηπος.

Ἡ Α. Μ. ἡ Βασίλισσα ὑπεδέξατο τὸν Πρίγκηπα ἐν τῇ αἰθούσῃ τοῦ Θρόνου ἔχουσα παρ' αὐτῇ τὴν μεγάλην Κυρίαν καὶ τὰς τρεῖς δεσποινίδας ἐπιτίμους κυρίας.

Τὸ ἑσπέρας, τῇ 7 μ. μ. ἐδόθη γεῦμα εἰς ὃ ἐκλήθησαν ὁ πρέσβυς τῆς Ἀγγλίας καὶ ἡ κυρία του, καὶ οἱ δύω γραμματεῖς τῆς Πρεσβεία, οἱ ἀνωτέρω πέντε καὶ οἱ ἑξῆς 8 :

1. Ὁ ἐντιμότατος *Sir Bartle Frere*, ἀνώτερος ταξίαρχος τοῦ τάγματος τοῦ Ἀστέρος τῶν Ἰνδιῶν καὶ ταξίαρχος τοῦ τάγματος τοῦ Λουτροῦ.

2. Ὁ ὑποστράτηγος *Probyn* ἑταῖρος (*compagnon*) τοῦ Λουτροῦ, ἀνώτερος ἀξιωματικὸς ἐν τῇ ὑπηρεσίᾳ τοῦ Πρίγκηπος.

3. Ὁ ἀντισυνταγματάρχης Ἀρθοῦρος *Ellis* τῶν ἐπιλέκτων τῆς φρουρᾶς, ἀνώτερος ἀξιωματικὸς κ.τ.λ., ὡς ἀνωτέρω.

4. Ὁ κ. *Francis Knollys* ἰδιαίτερος γραμματεὺς τοῦ Πρίγκηπος.

5. Ὁ Γενικὸς χειρουργὸς *Fayrer M. D.* ἑταῖρος τοῦ παρασήμου τοῦ τάγματος τοῦ Ἀστέρος τῶν Ἰνδιῶν, ἰατρὸς τοῦ Πρίγκηπος.

6. Ὁ ὑποπλοίαρχος Λύρδος Κάρολος *Beresford*, ὑπασπιστὴς τοῦ Πρίγκηπος.

7. Ὁ αἰδεσιμώτατος *Canon Duckworth*, ἱερεὺς τῆς Α. Μ. τῆς Βασιλίσσης τῆς Ἀγγλίας καὶ τοῦ Πρίγκηπος.

8. Ὁ ἀντιναύαρχος *Drummond*.

Ἐκτὸς τῶν ἀνωτέρω σημειωθέντων δώδεκα, τὴν ἀκολουθίαν τοῦ πρίγκηπος ἀποτελοῦσι καὶ οἱ ἑξῆς ὀκτώ:

1. Ὁ ὑποστράτηγος Λόρδος Ἀλφρέδος Πάγετ, *I*[er] *Ecuyer, Sous-Maréchal* τῆς Α. Μ. τῆς Βασιλίσσης.

2. Ὁ πλοίαρχος *Honnath H. Carr Glynn*, ἑταῖρος τοῦ τάγματος τοῦ Λουτροῦ, ὑπασπιστὴς τῆς Βασιλίσσης, Κυβερνήτης τοῦ δικρότου Σέραπις.

3. Ὁ συνταγματάρχης *Owen Williams*, διοικητὴς τοῦ συντάγματος τῆς Ἐφίππου Φρουρᾶς.

4. Ὁ ὑπολοχαγὸς *Augustus Fitz-George*, ἔκτακτος ὑπασπιστὴς τοῦ Πρίγκηπος.

5. Ὁ Ταγματάρχης Στάνλεϋ *de A. C. Clarke* (Δ' σύνταγμα τῶν Οὐσσάρων.)

6. Ὁ κυβερνήτης τοῦ πυργωτοῦ *Osborne* κ. *Durrand*.

7. Ὁ κ. Ἀλβέρτος Γρέϋ ἰδιαίτερος γραμματεὺς τοῦ σὶρ *Bartle Frere*.

8. Ὁ καλλιτέχνης Σύδνεϋ *Hall*.

We were warned last night to be up early, as the

day was to be devoted to an excursion to the Royal farm and country house at Tattoï, about two hours and three-quarters' quick drive from Athens. The house is situated on the slope of the mountain-side near the site of the ancient Dekelea, which closed the most eastern pass over Parnes into Bœotia. Not very long ago the robbers who rendered travel so precarious, and residence so disagreeably exciting in Greece, very much affected this vicinity. When I write of these gentry's habitat in the past tense I do so out of respect for recent information, but I am bound to say that the road from outside the village of Marousi up to the farm of Tattoï was patrolled by soldiers, and that there were cavalry pickets stationed at regular intervals all the way in addition to the permanent posts of infantry who were observed around the small block-houses which command the hill-tops. It was not very far from Tattoï that Lord Muncaster's party were seized, and the tragedy for which Greece paid so dearly commenced. Four years have elapsed since the occurrence of the dreadful affair called "the Greek massacre;" and the indignation excited in civilised Europe, and the serious consequences to the Greek Government which ensued, may be said to have been the death of brigandage. Mr. Erskine was quite right when he said in his despatch that if it was quite understood that the nation would have to make good any loss inflicted on foreigners, owing to the neglect and mismanagement of the Government, the latter "would soon discover the means of putting a stop to a state of things which is mainly due to the supposed exigencies of party warfare, and which is a disgrace to any community calling itself civilised." M. Zaïmés was then Prime Minister. General Soutzo was Minister of War. The former declared that the brigands were acting in concert with the Chiefs of the Opposition. There were men who had declared, months before the tragedy, that something would happen which would bring about a crisis. They were quite right. The massacre caused a ministerial crisis. It did more—it delivered Greece from a national curse.

There must have been, judging from the few anecdotes we heard from our Greek friends, many reminiscences of adventures on the road, which patriotism probably stifled; but it would seem as if the brigandage which disgraced the neighbourhood of the capital, and which was too often used as a political instrument, has been really extirpated, or at least very nearly suppressed.

The country near the city is tolerably fertile. There are large tracts of uncultivated land before we reach the Cephissus; but in the olden days the wastes which are now covered with hibiscus, thyme, prickly shrubs and weeds, doubtless bore corn, olives, and fruit. These grow abundantly in the valleys, where the villages nestle in orange-groves and vineyards, because there is running water, though it is nowhere abundant.

The peasants along the road were fine hardy fellows, not differing in appearance or even in dress very much from the better sort of contadini in Southern Italy. As the carriages, escorted by the Chevaux Légers, who retain the uniform which King Otho adapted from Bavaria, whirled by in clouds of dust, the wayfarers touched their hats or stood with head uncovered, and then continued their course, not stopping to look back, or seeming to take much further interest in the cortege, but quite respectful whilst in the presence. There were relays of horses, guarded by the pickets on the road, but there were not, as there would be in most countries, groups of people near at hand to watch the arrival and departure. The women seemed to do more than divide the labour of the fields with the men. There is a good bridge over the Cephissus, which ran—if the word can be applied to its feeble and shrunken thread, which almost merits the derisive epithet of "*ποδονίφθη*," or foot-bath—in a deep ravine, with great boulders along its course; but the bed had the characteristics of that of a torrent. From the bridge there was a steep ascent, and the road climbed a steep hill-side, covered with pine-trees and oak, the former of which gave out a

TATTOÏ.—COUNTRY RESIDENCE OF THE KING OF GREECE.

strong resinous odour. For about an hour's drive the road wound through this wood, through the glades of which were caught bright glimpses of the sea away toward Salamis on one side, and on the other the hill-fronts gradually rising towards Marathon. Then there came the marks of enclosure—fences and walls and cleared spaces, where the greensward had taken the place of oak and firs. Finally we entered a wild kind of park and passed along an avenue to the King's Villa, which is like a large Swiss chalet, with extensive outhouses and offices. There are magnificent trees in front of it, and breakfast was spread on a table in the open air beneath their shade. There was a wine of very curious taste, named Resino, which the King commended for sanitary properties, but the faces made by those who tasted it for the first time indicated that, like the late Lord Derby, they would prefer enduring any normal maladies for which it might be a specific to taking the medicine. The Farm, in which the King takes great pleasure, was visited afterwards; nor was a vineyard close to the chalet, in which abounded grapes of wondrous size and great sweetness, left unnoticed. In the park—if that it may be called so where Nature has so much of her own sweet way—there is a Gazebo or Belvedere, recently erected, from which there is a beautiful view; and here, by the King's orders, are deposited the various antiquities which from time to time are dug up by the labourers in making drains and ponds. There is already a very respectable collection of cinerary urns, fragments of statuary, pottery, portions of marble columns and capitals, and it is intended to make further researches. Many of these were found near the site of Dekelea. After a saunter through the very charming grounds and a scamper on horseback, for which the horses of the King and of the Chevaux Légers were impressed, the party set out on the return to Athens, where there was to be a grand State Banquet at the Palace in the Prince's honour. My companion, Admiral Sachtouris, aide-de-camp to the King, who had been in the British navy and is an excellent specimen of a Greek naval officer, told some interesting stories of his native island of Hydra, which still furnishes the best sailors to the Greek navy, royal and mercantile. The island not very long ago nearly depopulated itself in an immense migration. Not less than 4000 Hydriots went off to the United States, where many acquired competence and where some made fortunes, as a proof of which they sent home large sums for beneficent purposes; but with that extraordinary attachment to abstract "Greece," which many of the Greeks, however, show rather in their death than in their life, they came back in old age to their native island to die. One Hydriot returned a short time ago "an Admiral in the United States navy" (so said Admiral Sachtouris) "and sought in vain for a trace of his kindred;" and so went away once more to America. Notwithstanding that extraordinary drain, Hydra is flourishing, and still keeps up its supply of able and excellent sailors.

It was dark before Athens, over the site of which there was a bright halo from the illuminations in the streets, came in view. Anticipating the Prince's return, discharges of rockets were going on from the Acropolis and from the ships in the Piræus which lighted up plain and sea.

The streets were filled with masses of people, through which the carriages went at full speed. Balconies crowded, windows ablaze, Chinese and Italian lanterns and transparencies, testified to the desire of the Greeks to do honour to the guest of their King. The Banquet gave occasion for the King to assemble all that was eminent in public life, literature, and science in Athens. In the saloon before dinner there was a striking scene. Most of the older men of the company appeared in their palikar dresses, than which nothing could more become their fine faces and figures. Conspicuous among the crowd, which glittered with lace, orders, and decorations, moved M. Boulgaris, a most patriarchal-looking old man, dressed in a furred robe and soutane, with a skull-cap on his massive head, a bright, keen, eager eye set under a broad brow, and a face like that of Titian's "Doge." There were men, too, whose names are familiar to students of Greek politics as those of leaders of Ministries which last, on an average, some half-dozen months—M. Tricoupi, now in power, a young man with a very intelligent, earnest, and expressive face, M. Zaïmés, M. Comoundouros, M. Deligéorgis, M. Delyannis, &c.—each representing the nucleus of possible combinations of party-men uniting to obtain power and oust the men in office, rather than distinctive political principles.

Covers for 120 were laid in the Great Hall, which would do credit to the palace of an Emperor, and is finer than many banqueting-halls where monarchs of the first rank give their feasts of honour. It was built, if I mistake not, in King Otho's time, and displays a prodigious wealth of the purest marble. The immense height and grand dimensions of the place render it possible to keep the air tolerably cool when many hundred of wax lights are burning. The cooking was French, the attendance Greek, and the military Band played often enough to take off the stress of conversation. There were no speeches, and only two toasts. When dessert was over, the Prince took the Queen's arm, and led her forth, followed by the King and the company, to the other great room, where ices, &c., were served; and a conversazione ensued, which lasted an hour or more. Many presentations were made to the Prince, who must by this time be tolerably well acquainted with nearly every one of the busy, keen, restless politicians who fret and fume their lives away in Athens. They put one in mind of a grand intelligence—a mind full of ardour for action—cased in a puny frame. The tenement of Greek clay is all too small for that fiery Attic soul. The men of Athens may be still "δεισιδαιμονεστέροι," but they have exchanged the direction of their thoughts nowadays. They prefer pictures to statues.

Proud of steam-engine, ironclads, recent empire, immense wealth, and prodigious luxury, the descendants of the rude islanders,—who were in a state of primeval savageness, fighting for their lives with wild beasts and each other, armed only with flint weapons, and living in caves, at the time when the dwellers in Athens were carrying philosophy and the arts to a pitch of excellence which has left its mark above our highest efforts—can only set themselves on a satisfactory elevation in comparison with modern Greeks by assuming that the latter are not descendants of the ancient races of Hellas. The Greeks of this latter period are indeed apt to swagger as if each of them could point to his descent from Alcibiades. They provoke an ill-bred, and perhaps unjustifiable, disposition to draw a line somewhere, and to cut them off from the grand inheritance they claim—not only the inheritance of the past, but the succession to a stupendous future.

The affairs of Turkey were naturally the subject of much conversation, but the statesmen who were presented to the Prince did not talk politics. The insurrection in the Herzegovina interests every one at Athens, and most of all the King, who, young as he is, possesses the political capacity to a high degree, and foresees the risks to the peace of Greece and of the world which will arise from the prolongation of the contest. At present there is no outward sign of dangerous excitement, but the "Great Idea" is not dead—it is only sleeping. There is a fixed idea that Turkey must break up, and that her bankruptcy just announced points to a speedy dissolution, which some say looks suicidal. Every Greek feels—most say—that of right, Crete, Epirus, Thessaly, and half of Macedonia should be theirs, and that they have a clear reversionary right to Constantinople.

There was some trifle to relieve the solid pudding of discourse; and one gentleman said that when he saw the *Scrapis* adrift "he thought she was going to destroy the whole Greek navy at one blow." An American officer added that the Prince of Wales had been "most liberal! His Royal Highness has made the King a present of a bull, cows, sheep, pigs, and—*two anchors.*"

October 20th.—I desired the excellent piper Maclachlan, who is in attendance on the Duke of Sutherland, and was lent to me—not in his musical capacity—to call me early, as I expected a visitor—not to be later than seven. He not being as familiar with Greek as with Gaelic, could not set the living machinery connected with cold and hot water supply for bath and shaving in order. Any way, he was late by an hour; and so it was that the visitor I expected came in and found me in bed. The visit, however, was not in vain; and for an hour I listened to most interesting information on the present condition of Greece—the difficulties which beset her; the admirable qualities of the people; the causes which have operated to retard her progress, or rather to prevent its more rapid march; and the outlook, full of hope—if a few "ifs" be happily gratified. To find the source of many mischiefs, it was only necessary to place one's hand on the rock which well-meant people intended as the basis of a splendid national edifice, but which they put over the mouth of a well—the Greek Constitution. My informant did not say so, nor would he admit anything of the kind; but, following his conversation closely, it could be easily seen that all, or nearly all, the dangers with which good government in Greece was threatened arose from that ridiculous Constitution given at the time of the Independence.

It is unnecessary now to inquire whether the National Assembly of Greece was or was not responsible for the Revolution of 1862, which drove King Otho from the throne after a reign of twenty-nine years; but it is very necessary to inquire whether the present condition of the kingdom is such as satisfies the just expectations of the Three Powers, which formerly gave, and now guarantee, the independence of Greece. When the National Assembly, in March 1863, declared a young Prince of the Royal Family of Denmark King of the Hellenes, under the title of Giorgios I., it accepted towards the Monarch, then a lad of eighteen years of age, responsibilities which have hitherto been repudiated or ignored. Not only has he been exposed to misrepresentation and unjust suspicions on the part of some of his subjects, but he has been deprived by the selfish struggles of faction of the support in his office on which a Constitutional monarch has a right to rely. He has been thwarted and opposed in his efforts to establish good government by continuous intrigue, and by scarcely concealed disloyalty and ill-will. Full of generous sentiments, animated by the highest motives, and "consumed by the love of his people," he has been consistently, if not purposely, baffled in his endeavours to develop the resources of the country, and to divert the thoughts of the people from vain aspirations after Eastern Empire to solid industry and practical improvement of the resources of their country. There is in the Royal Palace at Athens a picture of Prometheus bound to the rock, with the vulture tearing at his side, whilst in the distance appears the form of the victim's deliverer. The young King may be pardoned if he sees in the work a subtle allusion to his own fate; though he may not be able to detect the means of his deliverance. He is bound in chains to a Constitution which he alone of all men is forced to recognise. The most bitter partisan cannot say he has been unmindful of his oath, or neglectful of his duties. For twelve years he has only been absent from his kingdom ten months, and he has applied himself to the serious hard work of kingcraft with an assiduity and success which have won the admiration of his ever-changing Ministers. No one knows Greece better, or more thoroughly understands her position in relation to the rest of the world. Master of the language, he has made it his business to inquire into the working of every public department; and no lawyer in his kingdom—and there are many lawyers in Greece—is better acquainted with the Constitution with which she is afflicted. But all these high qualifications, attributes, and aims on the part of the Chief of the State are rendered almost impotent for good by the mischievous activity of political parties which that Constitution has, if not created, at least encouraged. The normal condition of the Government is "crisis," and as there are no political internal questions to divide the members of the Assembly into great parties, the King has to deal with men who only represent their own interests and the cupidity of their followers. There remain, then, not measures but men—not policies but passions—not wholesome political strife, but personal intrigue and self-seeking. The doctrinaires, and the party which advocated "The Great Idea," have received a severe blow by the fate of the Cretan Insurrection, and are at present quiescent, or have, at least, desisted from an open propaganda; but they still exist. "I do not say," observed a foreign statesman, who knows Greece well, "that M. Comoundouros, M. Deligéorgis, M. Zaïmés, M. Delyannis, or M. Boulgaris have no individual views: on the contrary, the latter, at all events, has very decided intentions, and would be a man of action if the means were at his disposal; but that any differences of opinion on public questions which may exist between the leaders of parties are not considered for a moment if a movement or combination be needed to turn out the adversary of the hour, who is an adversary because he is in place, and that the facility with which such combinations are effected is, owing to the working of the Constitution, destructive of any hope of a stable Government, and of permanent improvement and progress." There are neither Tories nor Whigs, Conservatives, Liberals, nor Radicals in Greece; and, with one exception, the men who come in and the men who go out, work in the same lines in and out of power. The present Assembly consists of 188 members, and according to the Constitution there must be an absolute majority of all the members to enable a Minister to carry a measure. The Premier of the day cannot continue in office if he cannot command the votes of ninety-five followers; and when the Tricoupi Cabinet, which came into power to preside over the creation of the Assembly which has just finished the verification of the returns of its members, found that it could only muster thirty votes, and that M. Comoundouros, M. Zaïmés, and M. Deligéorgis would not support it, there was no choice left to M. Tricoupi but to resign. When a Minister is forced to take such a step in England, he advises the Queen to send for the leader of the party which has sat at the other side of the House during his term of office, and the King of Greece has hitherto generally acted on a similar principle, and has called in the statesman who commanded the largest number of adherents. That gentleman usually accepted office with alacrity, and informed the King he had such promises of support as enabled him to look forward with confidence to the formation of an enduring Ministry. So it was some years ago when M. Comoundouros came into power, and M. Zaïmés and M. Deligéorgis assured the King they would give him their aid; but in a few hours these gentlemen united their forces once more, and turned M. Comoundouros out. At the present moment, the men whose names head the list of candidates for place can muster, as near as can be judged, the following number of votes:—

Comoundouros	60
Zaïmés	40
Deligéorgis	35
Tricoupi	20
Delyannis	15
Boulgaris	13
	183

If M. Comoundouros, elected President, seeks to form a Cabinet, he must come to the King, for the King will not send for him. When he appears his Majesty will have a right to demand some guarantees that he can command a majority, and that he will not expose him to another "crisis" in a few days; but as the other leaders have already broken their promises, it is not probable that the King will be satisfied with anything short of a written promise that those who induce M. Comoundouros to come forward will sign a declaration of their readiness to support him when he is placed in office. The directness of his honest Danish nature, fortified by his youthful education at sea, is evidenced in every act of his public life, and it disconcerts the subtlety of Greek politicians much more than any finesse. Not that the King is by any means deficient in tact or statecraft, but that he conceives it is safer to follow a straight course than a crooked one. Hitherto he has steered his course through a sea of troubles with extraordinary skill and judgment, but it is to be feared that there are great trials in store for him.

The *Chanson de départ* sounded early in the Palace. A general packing-up—one stage more in the journey eastward to be made; the short visit to Athens terminates to-day. The King, attended by his constant companion, a splendid Danish boar-hound, who has a little wee black doggie to wait on him in turn, came round the corridors, and paid visits to the suite.

There was a reception by the King and Queen after breakfast, and subsequently those who had not received the honour on a former occasion, were decorated by the King with the Order of the Redeemer, and made Grand Crosses, &c. The departure of the Prince from the Palace was made, as he came, in state, and he was accompanied by the King and Queen, and by several members of their Court, to the Station, and thence to the Piræus, where arrangements had been made for their reception and for an excursion to sea. There was a Guard of Honour, an escort of the Chevaux Légers, and a considerable crowd outside the portico and in the square before the entrance. The officials and the servitors of the Palace, in very picturesque uniforms and costumes, rich with embroidery, but wearing that head-dress already described, which, for all its long tassel, puts one in mind of the Turkish fez, were drawn up in order in the corridor and hall. The Prince and suite were *en grande tenue*, and as they drove through the streets to the train, it seemed as if the crowd were more warm in their greeting, and a little more demonstrative in their marks of respect. There was certainly more waving of handkerchiefs and cheers. The Athenians were evidently acting on one part of the Homeric advice—to speed the parting guest.

There was a strong breeze blowing seawards, and the scene looked as bright and beautiful as it did on the morning of our arrival. Under a thundering salute from the *Hercules* and *Swiftsure*, the Greek gunboats and the Russian *stationnaire*, *Psezouapé*, the King, the Queen, and the Prince, went off to the *Serapis*, which had her steam up ready to start. By the aid of divers, after much hard work, she had managed to recover both her anchors by noon to-day. Admiral Boutakoff, Admiral Drummond, &c., were invited to breakfast, to which so many were bidden that even the great length and breadth of the *Serapis* could scarcely furnish room for them. After luncheon, the King and the Prince went on board the *Hercules*, and soon after their return the *Serapis* stood out to sea; but not quite without another trouble, for, as they were weighing anchor, it was found that her cable had fouled the cable or the anchor of the *Hercules*—and she was obliged to leave it—No. 3 lost *pro tem.*—in the Piræus. Then, just when she had got under way, and her head was pointed to the narrow channel between the marks, the *Assyrien*, a French steamer, steamed right in her course, and threatened to make a collision or taking the ground inevitable. These are things of a sort which try the marine temper. As the two vessels scraped past each other, Captain Glyn probably was thoroughly glad to be out of the Piræus, where he seemed at one time likely to make a longer stay than would have been altogether agreeable, and felt that the Frenchman was, at all events, not polite. The *Amphitrite* and the *Osborne* followed astern. The weather was all that could be desired, and their Majesties were apparently delighted by the excursion to sea. There was an exchange of souvenirs, photographs, &c. The Band played nearly all day. Tea was served on deck, and then came a state dinner, in levee dress. Night fell—deep blue, not black — her mantle studded with stars. Then up rose the moon; not yellow, but brightest silver. It is only further west that "the sun looks like the moon, and the moon looks like a cheese." The Greek fishers must have gazed in wonder on the *Serapis*, a phantom argosy of white and gold, all her ports gleaming high above the wave; her attendant yachts hung with lanterns, which scarcely vibrated, so placid was the sea. The island of Hydra was reported in sight, seven miles on the starboard beam, the island of St. George on our port-quarter. It was now 10 P.M. The *Serapis* and her consorts lay-to. The steam-launch was in readiness; the crew manned the sides; as the King and Queen appeared on the main-deck and took leave of the Prince, ere they stepped down the companion, the Marines presented arms, and the Band played the Greek national anthem. At the instant the bulwarks of the *Serapis*, in the ports of which lights were placed from stem to stern, were lined by the crew burning blue fires; and at the yard-arms, up to the royals, appeared, bright as if in the sunshine, sailors with blazing portfires. And then what a sight it must now have been for those out at sea, and to the dwellers in the islands, when the *Serapis* and *Osborne* burst into active eruption, with maroons, shells, and fountains of many-coloured flame, and, vieing with each other, sent flights of hundreds of rockets into the sky, where they seemed to wage a mimic war and to sow the heavens with new but evanescent constellations! The effect, even to those on board, was very beautiful; the *Serapis* admired the *Osborne*, as she no doubt was admired by the *Osborne* and the Greek yacht. There was but one inconvenience from the beautiful display, and that was caused by the dropping of the burning composition into the launch ere it could be shoved off, and some little damage, or fear of it, to the dresses of the occupants. The Prince went off to the *Amphitrite* and took leave of their Majesties under their own flag; and when he came on board again, the *Serapis* and *Osborne*, with parting cheers and bouquets of rockets, steered their course for Port Said, and the King and Queen returned to their famous but agitated little capital.

KING AND QUEEN OF GREECE LEAVING THE 'SERAPIS.'

STUDYING RELIEF MAP.

CHAPTER II.

FROM THE PIRÆUS TO GRAND CAIRO.

Theatre Royal, *Serapis*—Sports and Pastimes—The Saloon—Port Said—The Suez Canal—Ismailia—The Palace of Gezireh—The Khedive—Investiture of Prince Tewfik—The Pyramids—"Why go to India?"—Departure from Cairo—Farewell to Suez.

OCTOBER 21ST.—At dawn Crete was in sight on our starboard bow. Surely there never was more stately ship nor gentler fortune in these waters! Not a breath of wind. The crew beat to quarters, and were exercised at putting out an imaginary fire, and in closing the water-tight compartments, to which recent occurrences at sea had given unusual interest. The sectional drawing of the *Serapis* which is nailed up on the main-deck forward is awful to contemplate. It represents a mighty maze of pipes, valves, stop-cocks, and machinery, which sets one thinking; and Mr. Hulton, the first lieutenant, who is always working down below, said it was a week's hard practical study to master the secrets of our floating prison-house. At noon the thermometer marked 70°. The awning fenced off the sun's rays, but they glanced fiercely from the bright blue sea, which spread out sailless, birdless, and apparently fishless, to desolate-looking Santorin. In the afternoon there was a gentle breeze right astern, the sea crisply lapping the sides of the ship, which was so steady that the Prince and his friends could play deck tennis, an adaptation of lawn tennis, which did very well indeed, only that the balls were apt to fly overboard. Whereupon it was enacted that he who knocked a ball overboard should pay one sovereign fine; howbeit at the end of the voyage there were less balls out of the many provided than sovereigns, but that was a matter of detail. Pistol practice at marks hung to the yard-arms varied the tennis-playing.

In the evening, the Prince and the company repaired to the after-part of the quarter-deck, on the starboard-side, where a very pretty little theatre had been set up. Chairs were placed on deck from the wheelhouse forward to the companion. Behind these were ranged the picturesque masses of the crew and the marines, some in the rigging and mizen-chains, others on the bulwarks—a very attentive and enthusiastic audience. There was a drop-scene, well executed by one of the men, representing the *Serapis* leaving Portsmouth. When the curtain was raised it revealed an elevated stage of moderate capacity, provided with a piano and the inevitable troop of Ethiopian Serenaders, furnished by the bandsmen, sailors, and marines. The stage manager was Mr. Smith Dorrien, one of the lieutenants, and the theatrical company was furnished by the ship's crew; the Magnus Apollo was an A.B. sailor named Spry,—a fine, manly-looking tar, with a big beard, and a burly voice, and with a turn for versification, for which the rules of rhyming needed to be stretched a little.

A CHRISTY MINSTREL PERFORMANCE ON BOARD THE 'SERAPIS.'

He was evidently a favourite with the crew, for before he had said a word he was cheered, and his song on "Optional Cocoa" was received with wild enthusiasm. Now "Optional Cocoa" seemed a recondite subject, but it was one well known to his audience. They roared at every satiric touch of Mr. Spry, as he recounted his experience of life as one of the seamen on board a ship of the Channel squadron, in which, by the Admiral's orders, it was "optional" for the crew to take a cup of cocoa in lieu of some more stimulating beverage. The entertainment was diversified by clog-dances, hornpipes, sentimental ditties, and "regular fore-bitters," by various legs and voices, and it was brought to a close at 11 o'clock by "God save the Queen," sung by the company with a chorus from the audience, and the ship's company, Prince and all, standing with heads uncovered. All the men enjoyed it very much, and the encouragement given by the Prince's presence was very grateful to those concerned in providing so much harmless pleasure for their fellows.

The following was the programme :

H.M.S. 'SERAPIS.'

CHRISTY'S MINSTRELS.

21st OCTOBER, 1875.

OVERTURE	Encore	BAND.
OPENING CHORUS	"We niggers are free"	COMPANY.
SOLO	"Pretty little dark eyes"	SEIDON.
SOLO	Napolitaine	SNELL.
COMIC	"Hat and Feather"	BRANDON.
COMIC	"Kingdom's Coming"	HOLMES.

PART II.

SOLO	"Nellie's Answer"	COSTER.
COMIC SKETCH ..	"Statue Blanchia"	HOLMES & BRANDON.
DANCE	Break Down	DUFF & HILL.
COMIC	"King Coffee Dust"	SPRY.
PLANTATION	Walk Round	COMPANY.

October 22nd.—Dr. Fayrer, full of hygienic wisdom and sanitary precautions, gave counsel yesterday that the generous energy of the French chef should be restrained; that the number of hot dishes at breakfast should be reduced to two; that attendance at lunch should be, like cocōa in the Channel squadron, "optional;" and that three courses at least should be struck off the dinner *menu;* and next (this) morning the new rules came into effect. All day the *Serapis* screwed steadily along with her head pointed Egyptwards, the *Osborne* following at her prescribed distance. There were many means of passing the time pleasantly on board in such fine weather. There was a large relief chart of India against the side of the Prince's sitting-room to study. There were many books—novels in French and English, voyages and travels, works relating to India, biographies, history, and literature, heavy and light—in the drawing-room bookcases; and there was another smaller collection in the quarter-deck saloon. There were chess and backgammon boards in the saloon—seldom used, however, as the attractions of tennis were greater, and there were pistol practice and the general amusements of the deck, such as quoits and ball. There were letters to be written at the many well-furnished writing-tables; a little music to listen to when Prince Louis of Battenberg or some other less gifted amateur could spare half-an-hour; inspections of the horses and animals; visits to the bridge, to the ward-room; and there was last, not least, the never-failing solace of a siesta in one's cabin when the pen began to falter and the words on the paper danced before the wearied eyes.

October 23rd.—The speed of the vessel was once more reduced to eight knots, as it was when we were running for the Piræus, lest the vessels should arrive too soon at Port Said; but at dawn, this morning, the look-out man reported that the harbour-light was in sight. The engines slowed, until the little squadron only just crept through the discoloured sea, for we were still too early. The land-fall of Port Said is not easy, for the strip of beach on which the town stands is not six feet above the water-level; but the Light House is very lofty, and there are also a few date-trees to mark the site, and close to them there were now visible a clump of masts and rigging, and a tall flagstaff which seemed to rise from the sea. At 7.30 A.M. those on the deck of the *Serapis* could distinguish the colour of the flags flying from the Consulates on shore, and from the shipping inside the breakwater, conspicuous among which were H.M.SS. *Invincible* and *Pallas*, which had arrived from Brindisi. The men-of-war and the Egyptian yacht *Mahsa* saluted as soon as they made out the Royal Standard. At 8.30 A.M. the *Serapis* and *Osborne* entered the Canal, and proceeded slowly ahead between the two breakwaters to their moorings off the Custom House; the *Invincible*, *Pallas*, and Egyptian frigates manning yards and cheering; the bands on deck playing "God save the Queen;" and a guard of honour of Egyptian infantry drawn up on shore, with band and colours, presenting arms and saluting with martial flourishes of trumpets.

Port Said has ample stores of bunting; and there was a great display of it; but the people were not very demonstrative, and although there was a considerable crowd of the dwellers in that accident—which cannot be called lucky for them, at all events—on shore, there was not any cheering. There was some curiosity shown by the population near the shore, but the coal-heavers and the dredgers went on with their work as usual, and people were to be seen up the long sandy streets, lined by wooden huts, who could not be tempted to the water's edge to look at the Royal personages and their suites in all the splendour of full-dress uniform. The bulk of the people are French by birth or naturalisation. Certainly they are French by feeling, and they still cherish the recollection of the hostility England displayed to the enterprise, to the success of which she now so largely contributes. It is the most curious spot on the face of the globe. On the strip of land between Lake Menzaleh and the sea there is pitched, tent-like on the loose sand, which rises over the shoes where asphalte or planking has not been deposited, a city of wooden houses, laid in perfect parallelograms, and furnished with shops and magazines, where every article of European luxury can be had. Outside, on the same belt of sand, in a condition akin to savagery, there is a settlement of Arabs. The commerce of one quarter of the world passes by the city, but few traders land, and none remain there. The population, which probably exceeds 15,000, lives, however, on the crumbs of that commerce; and the most singular fact connected with this singular place is that the whole of the townspeople, and of the natives around it, depend for fresh water on the work of a steam-engine sixty miles away, which drives it from the Sweet-water Canal at Ismailia to feed the reservoirs at Port Said. Perhaps there is no place in the world which contains members of so many different nationalities. In addition to the Arabs and fellaheen, every European country has representatives—Tunisians, Algerines, Syrians, Moors, Hindostanees, Persians, Chinamen—who mingle with people from all the isles of the sea, and yet, I was told, that serious crimes are not frequent. The place has created itself and its police; but Port Said, as all the world knows, owes its existence to M. de Lesseps' determining that the end of the Canal—or the beginning, if you like it better—should be at this precise point. It was but a point on the sea-beach extending from Damietta to the coast of Palestine, and it was selected to be the site of the Port, because the sea-soundings off that point gave greater depth of water than at other points in the curve.

As soon as the *Serapis* was abreast of the quay of the Custom House, where the guard of honour was stationed, Major-General Stanton, Consul-General, came on board to pay his respects, and to take orders respecting the arrangements for the journey on to Cairo. There was a great "turning of keys and grating of locks" as baggage was sorted out to be transferred to the *Osborne*, and a mighty hurrying to and fro on the main-deck to get all things in readiness. A State pinnace put off from the Egyptian yacht, with the Princes Tewfik, Hussein, and Hassan, in very rich uniforms. They were accompanied by Nubar Pasha, Mustapha Pasha, and other officers of the Khedive's Court.

The Prince had on his Indian helmet and plume, blue undress frock coat, with Field-Marshal's insignia, and white trousers—the suite according to order. The helmet is a very presentable headdress. The military men wear a veritable *pickel-haube*, with a spike on the top like the end of a classical spear; gilt for regulars, silver for yeomanry and militia, metal scale chin-straps to match. The civilians rejoice in a brass or gilt knob instead of a spike (less dangerous in thunderstorms); but after their arrival in India it was found that the metal chin scales were not legitimate, and that there was nothing like leather for them, and the scales were accordingly lightened. The Prince received the Egyptian Princes with much warmth, and engaged in conversation with them until they rose to return to their yacht, which was to follow the *Osborne*.

In future it will be scarcely necessary to say that "the Prince was accompanied by the members of his *suite*." It may be taken for granted that Æneas was always followed by his faithful friends—"*Fortis Gyas, fortisque*

Cloanthus"—and that, as far as outward adornment in the matter of uniform was concerned, their appearance was regulated by that of his Royal Highness.

After the departure of the Egyptians, the light baggage having been transferred to the *Osborne*, the Prince, attended by Major-General Stanton, shifted his flag from the *Serapis* to the *Osborne*, which went up the Canal, with the Royal flag flying at the main and the Egyptian at the fore, at ten knots an hour, under a salute from the *Invincible* which made the wooden habitations of Port Said shake to their not very stable foundations.

The last time a Royal Standard floating over these waters indicated the presence of the head of a great Power, was when the Empress Eugénie, leading one of the most glorious naval processions ever witnessed in the world, opened the Suez Canal, along which we were now speeding towards Ismailia. It was certainly a tribute to the genius and insistance of Baron de Lesseps that the Heir to the English Throne should be seeking India by a route the idea of which was so much in disfavour in England for so many years, and the execution of which was both secretly opposed and openly discountenanced by the most powerful of English Ministers as politically dangerous and as practically impossible. It was that opposition which created the Canal — in the first place, by stimulating French feeling on the subject of English jealousy, and tickling the mouths of French money-bags by appeals to national vanity; and in the second place, by forcing Baron de Lesseps to call in the aid of mechanical genius to provide the means which were denied to him by the Egyptian Government when they removed the labourers, in consequence of the representations of our Government that the *corvée* was, in fact, "slavery," and that the scenes of misery which accompanied the making of the Mahmoodieh

Canal must not be repeated so late in the nineteenth century.

The Prince took great interest in the scene which was presented on either side of the two narrow mud walls marking the course of the Canal through Lake Menzaleh—the broad expanse where the water and the sand of the Desert mingle, undistinguishable one from the other, save that boats, busily engaged in fishing, marked the outlines of flotation, and that vast flocks of flamingoes and pelicans, standing breast-deep, showed where the land was rising to the surface of the *lacus piscosus.* By special order the *Osborne* was allowed to proceed at a speed forbidden to ordinary vessels; and as the wave impelled by her bow broke on the banks, mullet and other fish, disturbed by the unusual rush of water, bounded repeatedly high in the air. When the *Osborne*, followed by the *Mahsa*, rushed past the *elevateurs* and dredging stations on the banks, and the small reed-huts and houses of the *employés*, the men of many nations paused for a while at their labour, and now and then raised a cheer, or raised their caps respectfully as the notion burst upon them that a great Prince was passing. No more difficult pilotage can well devolve upon a man than that of the Canal, narrow as it is, for every inch of water must be measured accurately, and the slightest turn of the wheel will send a ship pretty hard and fast for the time; but the French pilot knew his work thoroughly. Indeed, Captain Glyn, and other naval officers who had experience of the management of the Canal in all its details, gave unqualified praise to the excellent method and precision of the service. The nicest management, of course, was needed in the case of vessels encountered in the way, of which there were not a few—the *Scotland* of London, the *Montgomeryshire*, and others. The Peninsular and Oriental steamer *Pekin*, with the passengers of the broken-down *Deccan*, was passed about half-way to Ismailia. From men up masts, rigging, and yards, and from her crowded deck, came repeated cheers for the Prince of Wales; but as he stood on deck, with a great crowd of persons in the same kind of dress, all of them with lorgnettes to their eyes trying to make out their friends on board the *Pekin*, it is probable there were doubts as to his identity, until he raised his cap in acknowledgment of the cheering. Amongst the passengers by the *Pekin* were the special correspondents of the London and other papers on their way to India. The Royal visit to Cairo just enabled them to reach Bombay a few days in advance of the Prince.

The great stretch of Lake Timsah, on which Ismailia is built, attracted special notice, when it was explained to the travellers that where navies can now ride triumphantly there was but a few years before a desert, and salt-pits, and barren rock; but the Prince was familiar with the scene, as he had visited it with M. de Lesseps before the Canal was opened. At Ismailia, which the *Osborne* reached at 5 P.M., every preparation had been made—infantry and cavalry guards, and a force of military-looking, well-dressed, and active Egyptian police—to show the Prince all fitting honour. Carriages, comprising all the resources of Ismailia in the way of vehicles, with auxiliaries from Cairo, conveyed the Royal party to the station; but the luggage was not quite so mobile, and there was a delay of some half-hour before everything was transported from the steamer to the baggage-vans. The American saloon and state carriages, so familiar to many recipients of the Khedival hospitality, were in readiness, provided with a train of valets and ample store of refreshments. The Egyptian Princes Tewfik, Hassan, and Hussein, Nubar Pasha, Mustapha Pasha, and the officials of the Court, busied themselves with the necessary preparations for departure, which chiefly consisted in the carriage of the baggage from the shore to the station, but that was at last effected. And as the sun was setting on the horizon, which melted into the grey Desert in the distance, the train glided, amid loud cheers from a crowd of several hundreds of persons, among whom were many French ladies and gentlemen, out of the pretty station of Ismailia on its way to Cairo. The Moslem Pharaoh has not neglected the interests of his country like the Turk. In the memory of young men the Desert and the land between the Bitter Lakes and Cairo were roadless—no vehicle travelled where there is now regular railway traffic—the camel and the ass afforded the only means of conveyance.

It was then past six o'clock, but the line was clear, the carriages in good order, and the train, carefully driven under the orders of Betts Bey, ran continuously through to Cairo at the rate of forty miles an hour, and at nine o'clock drew up at the platform of the Shoubra Road Station. The Khedive, in gala uniform of blue and gold, and with all his orders on, surrounded by his ministers and by the foreign Consular body, stood waiting for the Prince, beside him towered the Grand Duke Alexis of Russia, in naval uniform, attended by his officers. There was a full battalion of infantry drawn up from end to end of the platform, the passages were lined with soldiery, and another regiment was on duty outside the station. The Prince was in full uniform. The station was as light as day, from gaslight and torches, and the *coup d'œil*, as the Khedive advanced to meet his guest—and the whole mass of men in uniform, lace and jewels moved along the platform—was striking. There was a most warm greeting. The carriages of the Khedive, turned out faultlessly, were waiting. There was a host of runners and masalchees to precede them, and the Prince and his host drove off amid cheers, music, and clattering of sabres through the well-watered streets of the new quarter of Cairo, and turning to the west, passed the Nile by the Iron Bridge to the Gezireh Palace which had been assigned for the Royal residence.

The Khedive, having installed the Prince in his sumptuous quarters, took leave, and was driven to Abdeen, at the other side of the river, which seems to be his favourite abode. The Gezireh Palace was, I think, built for the reception of the Empress Eugénie; and it is certainly in some respects worthy of its purpose. The rooms are exceedingly handsome and well furnished—large armoires; mirrors against the walls, of course; and lustres, or many-dropped chandeliers, from the ceilings. The floors covered with French carpets; the bedsteads of brass, with musquito curtains. French ormolu clocks; Austrian furniture, which should be marked "fragile," covered with damask; rich curtains, badly hung, and sometimes hooked back on common iron staples driven into the walls; marble-topped washhandstands and chests of drawers; tables with exquisite cut-glass service, *fleur d'orange* water, sugar for *eau sucré*, scent flasks, and last, not least, small bottles of ammonia to assuage the pangs of insect bites, if haply such there were. There are some very fine objects from the Great Exhibition of 1867 in the rooms. Late as it was, the table was laid, and dinner was served with creditable alacrity. Then came coffee, pipes, and bed. I believe we lodge in the very rooms where but a short while ago Zuleika, Hanoum, Fatima, and others, lorded and ladyed it supreme. All the ladies of the household have gone off to some other viceregal retreat; but I am not quite sure of the point, and do not care to ask. Anyway, the palace would delight St. Kevin. It is perhaps a little too near the river for the safety of the walls, but the situation affords agreeable prospects. The suite, servants and all, were lodged without any difficulty within the walls. Musquitoes were "out of season," but some of the Royal party declared other things were "in," and one sufferer cried aloud and spared not.

October 24th.—Early in the morning the black-coated servitors, each with red fez on his head, badge of public or State employ, began their scurrying work along the corridors—not noiselessly. They are the housemaids of the Palace. They are of all races, and are supposed to speak French or Italian.

The prospect from the Palace windows is exceedingly interesting. There is the money-making muddy river beneath you, and along yonder bank a selvage of Nile boats, with naked masts and long lateen yards triced to the top; a broad belt of houses, such as can only be seen in Cairo, above the roofs of which—seen through a golden haze, which is but the fine dust raised by the slippers and feet of the multitude, and lighted by the rays of the sun—rise the minarets of mosques in the incongruous company of factory chimneys. Further still, towards the east and south, the rock, on which stands the Citadel, and the slender minarets and dome of the Great Mosque come out high and clear, and the barren shelves of many-coloured rock of the Great Mokattan ridge trending towards the Nile. The Nile is now almost bank-full; it is rushing past my windows at such a rate that the country-boats, with their vast sails bellying out with the strong breath of the north wind, can but just stem its stream. The Palace of Gezireh abuts on the left bank of the river, which swirls and gurgles against the buttresses of the garden wall, and circles in deep, eddying pools in the angles of the embankments, to the great joy of the catfish and other Siluroids, which rise heavily at pieces of bread and floating offal. At the other side of the river lies Boulak, which is called the Port of Cairo, but which is part of the city all the same. The ruins of houses in the stream, the overhanging banks, the ends of walls, and the masses of masonry rising out of the current, show how destructive the river is in some of its moods. When the Nile is at its highest it does much harm, and it is mischievous even when it does most good. There is no solid basis for masonry to be found till the rock, some forty feet below the great alluvial bed, has been reached, and few can afford the expense of laying such deep foundations. The weakness of the Grand Barrage, a magnificent work which few visitors to Cairo ever visit, is mainly due to the want of an adequate ποῦ στῶ, and the difficulty of finding that essential has much increased the cost of bridging the river, and of building near it.

The air is delicious, as it generally is at this period of the year, and until the sun gained power after noon there could not be a more perfect day. Breakfast was laid out with a great pomp of plate, exquisite fruit and flowers on fine *épergnes*, the beautiful china service made expressly for the Khedive, in one of the saloons on the drawing-floor, looking out on the Nile. The servants in the Viceroy's fine livery, which is not sparing of gold lace, were Frenchmen, and they were directed by higher officials, also French, in black Stambouli coats and fez caps. From the breakfast-room, which contains two good pictures and a couple of busts, one of the Khedive, and a noble piece of marble work as a chimney-piece at one end, there is but a step to the saloon leading to the Great Hall of Audience, the windows of which open on the balcony overlooking the main entrance and the garden. This saloon is furnished with splendour; richly-gilt divans and easy chairs, marble-topped tables, &c., are placed round the sides. A group of chiboukjees, in the unvarying fez and black suit of frock, vest, and trousers, stood apart at one of the doors; and at a signal these, demure and noiseless, appeared with coffee in exquisite little wafer china cups, placed in golden holders, set with diamonds, rubies, and emeralds. Then they brought in long pipes, ready lighted, and there were few who refused the luxury of a fragrant whiff of tobacco, which seems necessary to the full enjoyment of the East. The fresh air and the perfume of the flowers tempted some to the balcony. Beneath it were pacing the sentries of the Khedive's Foot Guards, tall, broad-, if flat-backed, Egyptians, clad in white—gaiters, breeches, tunic, gloves, all white—save the red fez, the swarthy face, and the black belts. The French postillions, in jack-boots and buckskins, laced blue and scarlet jackets, red vests, shining oilskin hats, with Viceregal cockades and powdered "bobs," were lounging by the steps—the very reproduction of the men, if not the men themselves, whom one saw riding the pecherons of the Imperial Court when Fleury and St. Meurice ruled the equipages. There was not a sound except the grating of the sentries' shoes on the gravel, and the screams of the peacocks from the aviary. Just outside the carriage-sweep begins the sward of the garden, in which there are a menagerie, artificial lakes and ponds, rocks, cascades, and clumps of trees and flowers. The garden is bounded on the right by the river, and on the left by a wall, beyond which lies the level spread of irrigated and cultivated land up to the foot of the Desert, guarded by the Pyramids of Gizeh. At 11.30 A.M. the Prince and his suite and servants assembled in the Saloon of Audience for Divine service. The Rev. Canon Duckworth read the prayers and lessons for the day to the little congregation. As the words of Christian thanksgiving and prayer came from the clergyman's lips, "O! Praise the Lord, all ye heathen; Praise Him, all ye nations!" we heard the grating tramp of the Mahometan sentinels and the Arabic commands of the officer relieving guard below. When service was over, the Prince went out in one of the Viceroy's open carriages to the other side of the Nile, to visit the Viceroy at the Palace of Abdeen, and to see the Princes of his family at Kasr-el-Nil. He was in uniform, for it was a ceremonial visit. In his absence there was full leisure for those who were not detained in the Palace to go to Cairo, and carriages were in readiness for any who wanted them. It was only necessary to send some of the Longjumeau postillions for one, and it was at the door in a few moments. There was a very ample lunch at two o'clock, which caused Dr. Fayrer some anxiety; but with the certainty of a State banquet at the Palace of Abdeen at seven o'clock, forbearance was a duty which forced itself on the understanding of the most reckless. A State banquet at the Viceroy's is a very serious matter; "no expense is spared," and we may be certain those who have to make the charges are not over ready to cry, "Hold! enough!"

When the Prince returned from his afternoon visits it was almost time to dress for dinner at the Viceroy's. There was an escort of cavalry for the cortege of the Prince from one palace to the other, and the road was illuminated all the way by lamps and pans of fire. The road from the Palace of Gezireh to the Iron Bridge runs parallel to the stream, from which it is only separated by a narrow belt of low land, which is partially inundated. On the other side are the Viceroy's Horticultural Gardens and Conservatories. The road is an elevated causeway—a dyke with a broad top, in fact—and is bordered by trees, which although they have not been very long planted, afford a pleasant shade. The great bridge is a very noble work indeed; and as one sees the dense streams of camels, donkeys, carts, and pedestrians which throng it, moving to and from the city, the wonder suggests itself how they did, or managed to live without it. The suburb between the Iron Bridge and the Hezbekieh is undergoing a surprising change. It was once covered with miserable sheds, narrow lanes of tumbledown Egyptian houses and waste patches, filled with heaps of refuse, and here and there cultivated plots a few yards square. The houses have been pulled down, the lanes no longer exist. Fine streets, well lighted with handsome lamps, and bordered by trees, run in converging lines towards the Opera House. Charming villas and detached houses, in the French and Italian style, have been finished, or are in course of erection, along the course of the projected thoroughfares. Verily this Egypt is still a land of wonders! The new rooms of the Abdeen Palace are not merely viceregal but imperial in number, size, and decoration, and the Banqueting-room is worthy of any Court in Europe. To outward appearance the Khedive's Court is at least royal. On his service, carriages, &c., there is the likeness of a kingly crown; his State is regal; the Consular persons accredited to him are Ministers in all but name; and salaries, and the *charges de la Cour*, are on a scale worthy of a considerable Power. But all that is maintained for a purpose—not from any personal love of splendour and luxury, for no one is better pleased with a simple, quiet life than Ismael Pasha. He is very happy when he can get out of gold-laced coats, put his jewelled scimetar and sash away; slip on his black Stamboulee coat, easy shoes, and sit down with a friend in a quiet corner for a little conversation, which on his side is always original and fresh, and is sustained by the aid of cigarettes, of which his Highness keeps a store for himself and his friends in his breast coat-pocket. To Europeans he speaks French, to his secretaries and to those who wait on him he generally addresses Turkish, and to the Egyptians he talks in Arabic. His powers of calculation are extraordinary, his conception rapid, his memory acute, and his love of work inexhaustible. He has a fair fund of anecdote, and appreciates a joke most thoroughly, for all his Turkish gravity. As an instance of his sagacity and foresight, it is related that when he returned to Cairo, after his visit to England and France, he expressed the strongest opinion that a "war with Prussia was intended, or at least was inevitable, and that the Emperor, who then seemed at the summit of his splendour and power, was on the verge of a precipice." To the Prince of Wales he seems to have a very strong regard and liking, and he does all he can to contribute to his Royal Highness's enjoyment. The Viceroy stood with his sons and officers of State, and received the Prince at the entrance of the Palace. He was in State uniform, with riband and orders, but the effect of the fine lace-embroidery in which Turkish uniforms excel is greatly diminished by the ugly simplicity of the fez. A guard of honour was drawn up in the court. The staircase was lined with Albanians and the various *valetaille* of an Oriental Court. When the Khedive, leading the Prince to the Hall of Audience, had taken his place, the new comers were presented to him. There can be no more agreeable manner than that of the Viceroy; he was particularly affable to the English as well as to those with whom he was acquainted—the Duke of Sutherland, Lord Alfred Paget, Lord Carington and others. With very few exceptions, every one in Government employment speaks French, and the old French leaven which once turned all things Egyptian into French is still working and still powerful. That influence, indeed, is well justified when such a man as M. Mariette represents it. The Viceroy's physician, M. Bourgières, is one of the most agreeable and lively of companions, and has the reputation of great skill in his profession. To their compatriots are due mainly the beautification of Cairo, the Opera House, the creation of scientific institutes, and the promotion of learned societies in the capital and in Alexandria, which have done so much for Egyptian history, and for the cultivation of literature and philosophy. There were some European ladies, the wives of Consular personages or of Europeans in Egyptian employ, present at the dinner; but the civilisation of the Khedive's Native Court does not go so far as yet as the threshold of the door of the Temple sacred to Woman's Rights. The "Shrieking Sisterhood" of the Moslem demand not to be driven out of, but to be let stay in the harem and in seclusion. Mahometan women think they exercise more influence over mankind by having their children and husbands all to themselves, when they see them in familiar intercourse, than they would possess if they were to enjoy the sad liberty of being flattered by every one.

Later in the evening the Viceroy and Nubar Pasha had a long conversation with Sir B. Frere and General Stanton. The repudiation by Turkey of the conditions upon which she contracted such heavy loans naturally causes a lively emotion at Cairo. It is evident that underlying all the reticence which a personage in his condition is obliged to maintain, the Viceroy thinks the funeral knell of the Sick Man is likely soon to sound if the Powers do not take heed to his case. And what next? *Jam proximus ardet.* Nubar Pasha gave the most emphatic assurances that the finances of Egypt were in a sound state, and that she was quite able to pay her way; but he foresees that the acts of the Sultan's Government will very much depreciate Egyptian credit, and favour combinations against it. The articles in the English press attacking Egyptian budgets, and the general distrust of Government statements evinced in London, were spoken of; and the Khedive broached the idea of applying through General Stanton to the British Government for the services of an experienced officer of the Treasury to investigate the public accounts and examine the financial system, and he expressed the utmost confidence in the result. Sir B. Frere approved of the notion. Mr. C. Pennell and Mr. Acton, two gentlemen formerly in the Treasury, are now engaged by the Khedive as heads of financial departments. The tendency in Egypt is certainly to accept England as her guide in finance, at all events.* But there were still graver matters to discuss. The insurrection in the Herzegovina gives rise to the deepest anxiety. The expenses of the war are enormous, and if it be long protracted, Turkey will be crushed into the lowest depths of insolvency. The dread which is felt of European intervention, and of a joint partition of the Dead Man's effects, is not disguised. "And in that case will England take charge of Egypt?" The Khedive, indeed, did not ask the question or suggest it; but it was asked, and the subject was discussed; and when some one said, "England will probably await the march of events," a Minister exclaimed, "Without any policy? Without any attempt to direct it? Cela vous portera plus loin que vous ne croyez." It was very interesting to observe the small group talking in a corner so gravely, whilst the crowd of officers and courtiers, clouted with orders and blazing with gold lace, moved about the brilliant saloon chatting and laughing, amidst a great clatter of plate and glass, and the servants passed in perpetual procession with refreshments. The Prince returned to Gezireh in the same state as he came, and there was a line of lights, which made the road from Abdeen to the Palace as clear as day.

---

* It may be taken for granted that the origin of Mr. Cave's mission dated from this conversation.

October 25th.—At 11 A.M. the Prince inspected the arrangements which had been made for the investiture of Prince Tewfik, the Viceroy's eldest son, with the Order of the Star of India. In one of the very handsome apartments of the Palace chairs of state were arranged, and the insignia of the Order to be conferred were placed upon a marble table. The 3rd Battalion of the Egyptian Guards formed up outside the Palace, and lined the way from the gate to the steps of the Entrance Hall. The Viceroy's orderly officers remained outside. Shortly before half-past twelve, the trumpets announced the arrival of the Viceregal cortege, which came up in great state, with an escort of smart-looking cavalry, the Viceroy, his sons, and ministers, in full uniform, blazing with jewels and gold lace. Two of the Prince's aides-de-camp received his Highness at the steps, and led him to the Prince, who stood at the foot of the grand staircase, with the Duke of Sutherland on his left, and Sir Bartle Frere on his right, the other members of the suite lining the hall at each side from the entrance to the staircase. The Prince wore a Field-Marshal's uniform, the Duke of Sutherland the Riband of the Garter, and Sir Bartle Frere the insignia of the Star of India; the suite were in full dress. The Prince, having shaken hands with the Viceroy, led him upstairs, and thence through the two state-rooms to the Saloon, where the investiture was to take place. Dr. Fayrer, who was assisted by General Probyn and Colonel Ellis, read the warrant, under the sign-manual of the Secretary of State, by order of the Queen, for the investiture. The Prince of Wales, standing, addressed Prince Tewfik, with great dignity, in the following words:—

"Sir,—I consider it a high privilege, a high duty, and it is a great gratification to myself personally, to be able, in the presence of your Highness, to carry out the commands of Her Majesty the Queen, who has charged me with the duty of investing you with the ensigns of the Order of the Star of India. It is not the most ancient of our English Orders, but it is one highly valued by us for the distinction it confers on those to whom it is granted for their services in India. The Queen has determined to confer this especial mark of consideration, Sir, for your self and family, because of the goodwill Her Majesty bears towards His Highness the Khedive, himself a member of the Order, who has always shown himself a true friend to the English nation, and has done so much to promote the safety and convenience of our communication between England and India, in facilitating the transit of our troops and commerce. I trust that in fulfilling this charge with which the Queen has intrusted me I may be adding another link to strengthen the bonds of friendship which already exist between England and Egypt."

The Viceroy, who seemed to feel the honour conferred upon his house, and spoke with emotion, turned towards the Prince, and said :—

"Monseigneur! Je suis profondément touché du témoignage et de l'honneur que Sa Majesté la Reine a conféré à toute ma famille en daignant nommer mon fils Grand Commandeur de l'Ordre illustre de l'Etoile des Indes. Par une délicatesse qui rend sa faveur royale encore plus précieuse à mes yeux, Elle a daigné charger Votre Altesse Royale de conférer elle-même les insignes de l'Ordre à mon fils, afin de témoigner à tout mon pays que Votre Altesse Royale partage les sentiments que sa Gracieuse Majesté veut nous porter. Recevez, Monseigneur, mes plus vifs remercîments. Recevez-les encore pour vous être souvenu que, sur la route de votre Empire des Indes, il se trouve un pays qui s'est toujours vu encourager, par le Gouvernement de Sa Majesté et la nation anglaise, dans la voie du progrès et de la liberté commerciale. L'honneur conféré à mon fils, la présence de Votre Altesse Royale, seront, croyez-moi, Monseigneur, pour moi, ma famille et pour mon pays, le plus grand encouragement pour persévérer dans cette voie."

The Prince of Wales then taking the Riband of the Order from the cushion, on which it was held by General Probyn, passed it over Prince Tewfik's neck, and fastened the Collar over his shoulders. The Prince expressed his great sense of such a signal mark of Her Majesty's favour in a few graceful words, and the Viceroy took leave, and went off, as he had come, in state, with his sons and ministers. Then came a change of dress not at all dis-

CAIRO.—START FOR THE BAZAAR. (ROUT OF THE DONKEY-BOYS.)

agreeable, and mufti was the order of the day for lunch at Major-General Stanton's. There was a tremendous clamour of donkey-boys outside the house; for to enjoy Cairo a donkey-ride is, for the traveller, no matter how distinguished or illustrious he be—that is, if he likes it—a *sine quâ non.* The Vicéroy relates even now, with a comic mixture of merriment and horror, how the Empress Eugénie compelled him once upon a time to mount one of these useful animals, and to exhibit himself to the utter amazement of his subjects, in the full light of day, tearing full speed down the main street of the bazaar.

It is now full Bairam time; but the Prince, nevertheless, managed to do a good deal in the way of shopping and purchases, and returned at half-past four o'clock to the Consular headquarters, where six of the Viceroy's *chars-à-bancs* and carriages were in waiting to take him and party to the Pyramids. The *chars-à-bancs* were drawn by six pecherons, ridden by postillions in the old Imperial fashion, jack-boots, gold-laced coats, leather breeches, glazed hats, and cockades. The road, in spite of all the previous watering, was very dusty, for the party was a little late; and ere the carriages emerged from the shady avenue of trees, which now extends more than half-way to the Pyramids, the sun was setting in a dull haze behind the desert outline beyond Gezireh. There was a crowd of at least a thousand people, men and women, in Frank clothing—Paris bonnets, gay coats and umbrellas, and all the accessories of civilised attire—clustered round the Chalet in which the Prince was to dine; and there was an immense gathering of the Arabs with their well-known Sheiks, whose mission it is to seize on the unwary traveller and carry him up to the topmost row of the masonry which is piled above old Cheops. These poor Pyramids! How commonplace they are becoming!

Dinner over, there was a dance by a party of Ghawázee, or Egyptian dancing girls (for whom see Lane's 'Modern Egyptians')—"girls" by courtesy—stumpy gipsy women, voluminously clothed from the waist downwards; bare arms loaded with bracelets; thick, coarse, black hair, heavy with gold coins; posturing, quivering, and sliding to and fro on their pretty feet, to the clatter of the metal castanets and bangles, and to the monotonous but not unmusical sound of the native orchestra which accompanied them. The heat in the Chalet was rather trying, and the company were probably not loth to leave the dance and go outside, where there was a strange weird exhibition, which, notwithstanding revulsion of æsthetical feeling, will probably be repeated on all similar occasions till the Pyramids become nothing more than stands for fixed pieces like those at the Crystal Palace or the Alexandra Park. But it must be admitted that Cheops prepared a very grand and extensive site for these displays. First, the Great Pyramid was illuminated by rows of blue lights along the layers of the masonry; next, flights of rockets were let off from the sides and summit, and from the base, many of which flew high above it, and let fall a rain of stars; then came red and blue lights, then pans of saltpetre at the angles of the Pyramid were ignited and threw up a peculiar bluish flame on the faces of the Arabs who superintended the *feux d'artifice*, causing the most extraordinary contrasts; but it soon died away, and was succeeded by red and yellow and green flames. The glare was blinding. When the lights flashed on the sea of upturned faces and of white-turbaned heads, the effect was sufficiently striking to justify such a use of the Pyramids—at least so it seemed to most people. The Prince stood amongst the crowd, who seemed very much interested in observing in what way he took the fireworks, which, however, were no novelty to him. One little maiden, after a long consultation with the members of her family, stole timidly up to the Prince to request that he would allow her to shake him by the hand, to which he laughingly assented. She said she was "Kate Batchelor from the United States;" and she returned in the highest state of satisfaction to the bosom of her family. Darkness stole, or rather dropped all of a sudden, over the Pyramid, and the Royal party were whirled back again to Cairo, not without some risk of *contretemps* on the road, because it was difficult to avoid the vehicles—

ILLUMINATION OF THE GREAT PYRAMID.

ships of the desert and others—which thronged it; but the Prince got back in time to drive to the Palace, change his dress, and see part of the piece 'Les Trente Millions de Gladiator' admirably played at the Opera House by the French Company. The Khedive was waiting to receive him, and there was a very full house; but I believe most people were rather glad when the curtain dropped, and it was time to retire and drive back to Gezireh to bed.

October 26th.—Much interest is taken in the Prince's voyage in Cairo. It seems to many people a strange and wonderful thing that he, who has so much at home to love and care for, should go out to a distant land in search of doubtful pleasures; but there are some who quite appreciate his motives, and the Viceroy especially is struck with the enterprise. Cherif Pasha, who is a devoted sportsman, would gladly resign office to have a chance of killing the tigers and other wild beasts, of which he has heard, and sadly resigns himself to quail and snipe. Nubar Pasha ponders over the *haute politique* of the situation; others deal with the considerations which render India interesting to Egyptians, for there is a great fear that, in case of the Sick Man's immediate dissolution, Egypt would be treated as a part of his estate, and that England would claim it as her share by reversionary interest. The Egyptians would not, perhaps, cry their eyes out if the Turk were to die; but they fear very much that in a faction fight over his grave their own little property might be appropriated. They would like nothing better than a kind of International Commission to regulate the finances of the Empire, and to act as physicians to cure the patient of the most fatal of the diseases by which he is menaced. Talking of the East, one of our Egyptian friends on the platform said, "I doubt, after all, whether you will do much better at Calcutta than at Cairo. They have no opera there; we have one of the best in the world. They have no ballet; except Vienna, we have got the best. The climate is abominable; ours, at least at this time of the year, delightful. The cooking is, I am told, but middling; ours is first-rate, at least I hope you found it so. Their wine is bad; we intercept the best champagne and claret on its way. They have no tobacco worth smoking. Why go there?" When he was told there were other things to live for beside these, he said, "I daresay there are; but I don't know any people who like them better. As to seeing *ryots*, we can show you *fellahs;* and there is no form of Government which you have in India which you cannot study to better advantage up the Nile."

After breakfast there was much bustle in the corridors of the Gezireh Palace, for there was need to send on the baggage in advance to the station, which is half an hour's drive, away at the other side of the river. Then there was a gathering in the great ante-room of the officers and others, to whom the Prince desired to give souvenirs; these were introduced, one after the other, to his presence, and were sent away with a pleasant speech, a shake of the hand, and a cadeau.

"Great are the charges of him who keeps another's wealth." When the Prince of Wales leaves the Court of one in Royal or distinguished place who has lodged him and his following, those who have to distribute the souvenirs of his visit have much of which to think. Photographs and portraits for those in high position; snuff-boxes, rings, pins, watches and chains, arms—lorgnettes, and then haply the solid rouleaux, which represent the "gratifications" called baksheesh by the Oriental vulgar—these must be taken out of the Treasury, and marked off, and ticketed, and appropriated. The Prince gives his presents in *genre* with his own Royal hands—the specie is distributed by humbler agencies.

The outward world knows little, and probably does not care to know, how great are the troubles and cares which weigh on the inner life of those around the great. Everything appears to the public eye to go so smoothly and well that no anxiety is manifested to learn how it is all done. There is the *Serapis*, splendid in white paint and gold, obedient as a well-trained steed to the rider's hand. What need to dive into the engine-room and see how the machinery is regulated? When the Prince of Wales comes or goes, everything for his coming or going seems as if it happened in the order of nature; but could one only see the anxious faces, and the calculations, and the consultations, and the pre-arrangements, he would be able to judge how far those who are hidden behind the folds of the Purple have to do with the arrangements for its complete effect.

The Khedive, the Princes his sons, and his ministers, visited the Prince at one o'clock, and took leave of him, although they were to meet him at the station to see him off with all honour. We were sitting enjoying the early chibook (spell it any way you please) after lunch, when the Khedive was announced, and every one hurried off. His Highness and his suite were in plain clothes. The Prince received him at the top of the staircase, and after a few moments' conversation they retired into the Prince's ante-chamber. Presently there came a summons for one of the suite, and he obeying it, returned with a broad green and red riband and Badge, and men knew that he had received from the hands of the Khedive the decoration of the Medjidié. To do the Prince honour, these decorations were conferred with no sparing hand. There were some who had already received the honour, and these were advanced in dignity; but those who had it not were decorated each in degree.

At 2.10 P.M. the Prince was at the Railway Station with the Viceroy and all his house, and there, with many kind speeches and friendly expressions, he took leave of his Highness. When the Prince was leaving, the sons of the Viceroy proposed to accompany him, but his

Royal Highness would not hear of it; "it was a long journey," he said, "and he felt quite sensible of their kindness." It would appear that there was a real friendship between the Viceroy and the Prince, and they parted with cordial manifestations of good-will. General Stanton, Nubar Pasha, Mustapha Pasha, and others accompanied the Prince, and once more the great American saloon carriages were under way rattling towards Suez. The journey was hot and dusty.

At Zagazig the special train halted for ten minutes, and the staff of vice-regal servants passed up and down the carriages with ices, fruits, champagne, soda-water, and such like luxuries, and informed us at the same time that there was a complete dinner, with a staff of servants, cooks, &c., ready in the train, and that it could be laid upon the table in half an hour. From Zagazig the train sped on through the land of Goshen, and an hour ere reaching Suez the sun set, round as a shield, falling abruptly as a red-hot shot beyond the verge of the desert, and leaving us in darkness. The train was due at 7 P.M., and it wanted but a few minutes of that time when it ran through the Suez station, where great crowds had collected from the ships in the harbour, and from the teeming bazaar, who cheered and yelled as the special dashed past towards the pier. Then, looking seawards, the welcome lights of the *Serapis* and the *Osborne* shone their welcome over the water. The Egyptian men-of-war, with masts, yards, and sides brightly illuminated, formed striking objects in the roadstead. Rows of soldiers with blazing torches lighted up the landing-place, where the Pacha of Suez, the officers of the port, and a guard of Egyptian infantry were waiting to conduct his Royal Highness on board the tender which was to take him off to the ship. It was some time before the baggage, which had filled six fourgons at Cairo, could be transferred on board the *Serapis*; and as the Prince was going off, Mr. Gibbs, Superintendent of Telegraphs, handed in a telegram with the news in London up to 2 o'clock that day, and the name of the winner of the Cambridgeshire, which had been run a few hours before. On visiting the saloon it was felt that the Red Sea was not far off, and the punkahs over the dinner table were set in motion for the first time. It was found that the sweep of the punkah was rather too low, and when the Prince stood up to give the health of the Queen, in accordance with custom, he was obliged to stand on one side till the living machinery on deck could be induced to stop their monotonous labours. When everything was ready, Nubar Pasha, Mustapha Pasha, General Stanton, and the other officers and officials took leave, and were conveyed on shore; and presently, amidst a general illumination, discharges of rockets, and cheers, the screw of the *Serapis* sent her ahead, and the Prince of Wales was steaming down the Sea of Jubal for India.

"THE PUNKAH."

ADEN.—SOMALI BOY CHASED BY A POLICEMAN.

CHAPTER III.

SUEZ TO ADEN, AND ADEN TO BOMBAY.

Sinai—The Red Sea—A visit Below—Bed and Board—Aden—Landing of the Prince—Arab Sultans—The Aden Address—Turks in Arabia—The first Levee—Sultan of Lahej's Petition—The "Hanging-tanks"—Exiles in Aden—Subsidized Chiefs—Something wrong Below—Programme for Southern India modified—Guy Fawkes at Sea—A Sunday's Routine—Approaching Bombay—Anticipations.

OCTOBER 27TH.—The dawn found the *Serapis* with the constant *Osborne* in company at regulation distance, running at the rate of twelve knots an hour, afterwards increased to thirteen, out of the narrow Straits of Jubal into the wider expanse of the Red Sea. We have shipped multitudes of Egyptian flies; the most daring, active, and aggressive of their pestilent race, and they make the early morning hideous. There was a fond but erroneous belief entertained by some of the suite that they had seen Sinai soon after sunrise, but the identity of the sacred mountain does not seem to be well established, and the peak which is generally thought to be Sinai is hidden from view by the outer ridges of the chain. At 1 P.M. the Peninsular and Oriental Company's steamer *Peshawur*, bound for Suez, came close up, with yards manned handsomely, all her passengers on deck waving hats and handkerchiefs, and crew cheering lustily. The *Serapis* stopped; a boat was lowered and manned; the *Peshawur* lay to, and for a moment it was thought that a mail for England would be sent on board her; but the letters were not quite ready; and so, after a short exchange of courtesies, the ships—to the great relief of Captain Glyn, who was apprehensive of the effects of any avoidable delay—proceeded on their respective courses, the band of the *Serapis* playing "Home! Sweet Home!" the *Peshawur* saluting the Prince's standard with lowered ensign, and the passengers and crew again huzzaing lustily. The Prince stood on the bridge, and acknowledged the compliment and these marks of respect by touching his cap and by repeated bows till the steamers went ahead full speed. The quarter-deck substitute for lawn tennis was tried with great success in the afternoon, but, in spite of the awning, it was warm work, for the sun was tyrannous and strong—82° in the shade. The library was a great comfort for those who had leisure to read, and the charts, laid out on the table, and relief maps were diligently studied. By the time we reach India most of us will probably know something more of the Empire and of its history than we did before. The excellent band of the Royal Marines under Mr. Kreyer practises for an hour at 11 A.M., plays at lunch from 2 till 3 P.M., and at dinner (7.30 till 8.30 P.M.), and often for an hour or two later, so that there is no want of delightful music; but it must be confessed that, with all these means of enjoyment, the high temperature and the general monotony of life at sea tend to promote slumber at unusual times.

October 28th.—A profound calm during the night; but

a gentle breeze sprung up after daylight. At 4.10 A.M. we passed Dædalus Shoal and its disconsolate Light-house, rising on a kind of gridiron frame above the sad sea wave. There were signs of life in the upper story, and a flag was flung out from the staff. It was erected by the Egyptian Government, which has done the lighting of its coasts in an admirable manner. All ports open. It is not easy to sleep in the early morning—the sun rises on my side of the ship, which, as the world is ordered, is quite inevitable, for I am on the port side, and we are steering East; but it is unpleasant, like many other inevitable things. Out of the port I see far away the land of which we know so little—not much more than we do of Central Africa, although Arabia is inhabited by one of the most ancient, interesting and indomitable races in the world, and is the birth-place of the founder of a faith which alone of all creeds shows no sign of receding before Christianity. They are still fierce and proud—it may be said they are the only Eastern nation which does not *fear* the power of Europe, or hold Europeans in some sort of respect. Woe to any white man who lifts his hand to an Arab, or shoves him to make place in the streets of Jeddah! "See, extending from the Euphrates southwards, the vast country, washed by four seas, touching Europe (if we admit Syria to belong naturally to the Peninsula), Africa, and Asia—left altogether to barbarism because there is no gain to be had out of it! No one cares for the Arabs save the Turks, and their solicitude is to subdue the people. They are passed by and neglected by all the world. Where are the Christian missions in Arabia? Where are the schools? Look at the map, and see a space nearly as large as Europe, with the mark of our ignorance upon it, 'Desert from Mecca to Oman.' I don't believe it!" At this stage I am interrupted by my early marine with a cup of coffee, and soon the ship awakes, electric bells ring, "Tom Fat" is summoned by my neighbour, servants are roused out from the depths of what the subalterns call Pandemonium, baths are ordered, quaint figures flit about in light attire, paying a round of visits from hammock to berth. "Well! How did you sleep, old fellow?" "I never was so hot in all my life." There never were more pleasant or more agreeable companions. There is still, in spite of the heat, a gymnastic performance about tubbing time, in which Dr. Fayrer and Canon Duckworth lead the exercises—simple evolutions with mugdahs, or Indian clubs, of which sets of different weights and sizes were sent on board by the dockyard people. Sometimes the Prince takes what is called "a cruise" between decks before breakfast, and visits the cabins to see how every one is going on. At noon we were inside the tropics (lat. 23° 39′ N., long. 35° 46′ E.). The thermometer in the cabins marked 81°, but owing to a following wind from the north, the want of ventilation made the heat seem greater. There were sixteen Arabs shipped at Suez to aid the seventy European firemen as coal clippers, but they did not stand the heat below (146°) as well as the latter. Hearing that the stokehole was considered to be very hot, his Royal Highness paid it a visit. The Duke of Sutherland was of course one of the party. The black and grimy stokers, who were interrupted for a moment in their labour to make way for strangers, were evidently delighted and gratified when they saw the Prince, in the full glare of the fires, in their midst. Having inspected the shaft-gallery, and had a good look all round down below, the Prince ascended to the main-deck in a state of very considerable perspiration. Some honeybirds and a kestrel were shot, and the gig was lowered and sent off to pick up the latter, which went astern at a great pace—or rather, was left behind very rapidly till the ship stopped. By the time the bird was found, the gig was some miles away from the *Serapis*. The *Osborne* gave the boat a tow; but it was an hour before we were going ahead again. In the evening there was an amateur concert and reading in the little theatre on the quarter-deck, and several of the blue-jackets acquitted themselves very well. Captain Glyn acts as Lord Chamberlain's reader of plays and dramatic censor, but the melodious captain of the forecastle, on the spur of an encore, slipped in an impromptu which caused immense delight to the pit and gallery. It was not, however, at all objectionable. It was merely meant to be a little satirical, and chiefly dealt with the expedition of the gig's crew after the hawk, for which the sea name appears to be "nanny-wiper."

October 29th.—At 10 A.M., the thermometer marked 83°, wet bulb, 79°; temperature of sea, 86°; specific gravity, 1·0030; wind S.W. Dr. Fayrer was summoned to attend several cases of "heat exhaustion." Ice and brandy-and-water are specifics for most of these. The domestics on the lower deck, where the bull's-eyes cannot be kept open, were considerably affected. As the day wore on the heat increased, and gradually stole over one like sleep. Starboard at least 1° hotter than port side. The paint in the cabins has become clammy. This state of things developed a display of energy and latent power in the suite after noon which was quite astonishing. The beds and bedsteads in the cabins were unanimously voted to be a mistake. They were "stuffy," and, moreover, having been filled in a hurry with feathers which had not been properly dried, they were not sweet smelling; and they were cleared out *vi et armis* by their occupants. The leader in the work of destruction was "the author of their being," so to speak, for he it was who ordered them, or approved of them, when the vessel was being fitted up. In fact, they were not fit for the Red Sea; and although they resisted strenuously, and held on with brass claws and iron nails to the frames, the cushions and mattresses were torn out, and pitched out on the deck by sheer strength. The frames were made comfortable by means of wooden stretchers, but the cabins were so hot at night that a demand was made for hammocks. Several of Seydel's excellent light nettings were on board, and were slung outside the cabins on the main-deck. Lord Suffield, Lord Carington, Lord C. Beresford, Colonel Ellis, Mr. FitzGeorge, and I, found "these pendent nests" very comfortable. Lat. 19° 42′ N., long. 39° 3′ E., distance run 270 miles. The Prince, notwithstanding the temperature, played at "lawn" tennis in the afternoon. Great numbers of sand-martins kept up in the wake of the ship; and many of the little fellows came on board and rested on the rigging. The kestrels follow them undauntedly to-day, and one more of them fell a victim to the Prince's gun. Fishing-lines were put over the sides, but not even a flying-fish could take a bait going fourteen knots an hour through the water. In the evening there was a solitary rubber of whist—the only game which has been played since the departure from Brindisi—and it did not last very long. The heat was too great, although the players were in the very lightest clothing.

The correspondence between the Resident at Hyderabad and Sir Salar Jung, a copy of which had been sent on from England, was read and discussed among the old Indians, and I think there was only one opinion expressed respecting the taste and tone of despatches, which intimated that the Resident believed the reasons assigned for the Nizam's inability to go to Bombay were fictitious, and that the Dewan had some secret purpose to serve in asserting that the journey would, according to the phy-

LAWN TENNIS ON THE 'SERAPIS.'

sicians, be dangerous to the life of the boy, who is delicate and nervous, and who has never yet been separated from his mother. It is well sometimes that we have no foreign critics, no external public (in Europe or Asia) to bear upon our conduct in India. I say sometimes, because I believe that generally our rule will bear criticism.

The propriety of sending on the *Osborne* ahead to Aden to announce the Prince's arrival was considered, but the idea was abandoned, as "something" might happen, and it would be awkward if the *Serapis*, which is "forced" a good deal, were to strike work in mid Red Sea.

October 30th.—The wind rose, and as it was right ahead, our speed was knocked down a knot an hour. Through the port caught glimpses of *Osborne*, pitching so as to bury her bows, whilst we in *Serapis* scarcely moved to the sea. At 9 A.M. the thermometer stood at 84° in my cabin. Some of the suite feel the effect of the great heat. A Turkish bath is an excellent institution, but if a man plays tennis till he is at boiling-point, and then dashes into cold water, he may suffer for it. Lord C. Beresford had a touch of fever, which by no means interfered with his animal spirits when he was awake, though it caused "Tom Fat" considerable anxiety. Lord Carington, also, is not as well as we would wish. The servants complain of the short supplies of "ice" in their den. What a luxurious age it is! Think of the Portuguese caravels, laden to the water's edge with armoured men; or of the Greeks returning from India up the Persian Gulf! "But who can hold a fire in his hand for thinking of the frosty Caucasus?" Wind sails were fitted to the ports, and a variety of light costumes was exhibited. At noon, observations gave lat. 16° 7′ N., long. 41° 15′ E., 250 miles since 12 o'clock yesterday. The island Gib-el-Teir, an extinct volcano, was seen right ahead, like a cloud on the water, about an hour afterwards. Deck tennis was still in vogue after lunch, and was eagerly worked at till it became too dark to play. At 2.30 P.M. the centrifugal pump got out of order—slowed for an hour during repairs. Passed Gib-el-Teir at sunset. The rude fantastic outlines of what was called by some one on board "an awful monument of the angry passions of the youthful world" riveted many a glass; every one anxious to detect some sign of life on those awful crags where life has never been —not a blade of grass, nor shrub—nothing but cinders—scoriæ—still coloured by the tremendous furnace hues. The sea, which had been rising gradually with the increasing force of wind, now attracted the attention of some of the weaker vessels, who retired within their cabins, and did not appear at dinner. The *Scrapis*, head to wind, was still wonderfully steady; but the lights of the *Osborne*, as seen from the stern windows, indicated that those on her deck were obliged to submit to considerable deviations from the perpendicular. Towards midnight a cry of distress came up from the deeps, for, unwisely courting ventilation, some of the suite left their starboard ports open, and suddenly along the side of the ship there came a long, curling, crisping wave, which just overlapped the sills, soused bedding and clothes, deposited an inch or two of water in the cabins and ran aft, rejoicing at the mischief it caused. Sir Bartle Frere, Canon Duckworth, Mr. Knollys, Mr. Grey, and myself were among the victims of the "water baby," and some of us had to look out for dry quarters on tables or sofas above. The deck saloon was turned into a sleeping-room for the nonce. After such a warning there could be no doubt as to the necessity of "putting up the shutters," and ports on both sides were lowered and secured for the night. Towards 11 o'clock P.M. the force of the wind—a strong south-easter—became so great that it might fairly be called half a gale. The Prince, who goes on the bridge every night before he turns in, went up as usual, in light waterproof, and remained till past midnight enjoying the freshness of the wind, and watching the sea-horses tossing their white manes as they rolled past the ship in headlong charges into the darkness of the night.

October 31st, Sunday.—The gale abated towards morning, but left a high confused sea behind it. I do not believe Captain Glyn turned in all night. All ports shut. Wind S.S.E.; thermometer 82°; water 86°. Mocha on port beam at 10 A.M. At 11.15 A.M. the Rev. Canon Duckworth performed Divine service in the saloon. Prince and suite in blue frock-coats and white trousers. Service private—that is, the ship's officers and crew were not present, but had service on the main-deck. Perim—a gigantic blistered clinker, the vitrified dross of the submarine furnaces once so busy in this part of the earth—with the British Standard flying on an elevated peak, and a group of very unpretentious dwellings on its arid ridge, came in sight. There was a guard of honour—the little garrison of the island—drawn up on a ledge above the sea, and his Royal Highness had his first view of her Majesty's native troops; for the detachment belonged to the 2nd Bombay Native Infantry (Grenadiers). He had fully acquainted himself with the reason of their being there, and certainly was not indifferent to their singular residence. As the *Serapis* came nearly opposite the flagstaff, down came the ensign, the twittering of a *feu de joie*, repeated three times, ran along the little line of infantry, and the feeble rattle and cheers, or what sounded like them, were borne down to our ears on the breeze. It is to be hoped that the general dwellers of Perim, who sat perched on the rocks like cormorants, could make out the Prince, who touched his cap repeatedly in acknowledgment of their tokens of respect. The *Serapis* ran out of Bab-el-Mandeb (the "Gate of Wailing or Affliction"?) at 3.50 P.M., and signalled to the *Osborne* to proceed at all speed to Aden, which was 95 miles distant, to announce the Prince's coming.

November 1st.—"Rouse up! Aden is in sight!" But so it had been since 1.30 A.M. As the morning sun pierced the light covering of fleecy clouds which benevolently sheltered us from the full fierceness of his welcome to the East, the barren savagery of the awful forms into which the volcanic eruptions hardened when their fires went out was concealed in the play of light and shade and shifting colour, for the lava and scoriæ, of which Aden is made, have infinite variety of all hues save green, and present every sort of outline except the round. The ships in the harbour, dressed out with flags could be made out through the glass at 6 A.M., and many hundred feet high above them could be seen a solitary ensign fluttering from a staff erected on a towering lava shaft of Ras Morbat. At 6.30 A.M. the batteries saluted the distant flag of the Prince. Then, as the *Serapis* screwed gently landwards, the white bungalows and houses, like patches of snow, giving a delusive impression of coolness, against the Vandyke browns and red and sennas of the volcanic background of craters and lava walls, varying from 700 to 1700 feet in height, by degrees began to define themselves. Presently we could make out that the sides of the rugged cliffs were covered with human beings, that there were many flags in front of the low white-roofed houses, and that there was a red line behind the platform which was indicated as the landing-place. For once Aden looked gay and bright indeed, and had decked herself in holiday attire. The Prince went up on the bridge to gaze upon the first fortified possession of the Queen and

"Empress of Hindostan,"* and looked on the scene with evident interest. Just at that moment, as if to call to mind what are the foundations on which that Empire to which he is heir mainly rests, the mail steamer from Bombay (the Peninsular and Oriental ship *Lombardy*) appeared from behind the projecting Ras (headland), to the north-east. A large Arab dhow, laden with people who had no great interest in the event of the day, if one might judge from their keeping on their outward course, was obstinately bowling along to the west; another dhow stood in towards the harbour under all sail close hauled; but there were no other moving objects except a few gulls on the water. At anchor in the roads lay H.M.S. *Osborne*, H.M.S. *Vulture*, an Egyptian sloop of war, a French mail steamer, three British steamers, and two or three sailing ships, flying every flag they could find. At 6.45 A.M. the *Serapis* ran down towards her moorings in West Bay. Then from a lava peak 800 feet high there spurted forth a bolt of snowy smoke; the thunder rolled over the tremendous crags, and the report of the cannon woke all the grim steeps into life, and seemed to invite the rivalry of their ancient fires. Gun succeeded gun, battery followed battery, opening suddenly again and again from unexpected bluffs and mounds far away. The *Vulture* and Egyptian frigate joined in chorus as the *Serapis* with the Prince's standard flying, let go her anchors and brought up off the landing-place, about one mile from shore. The effect of the salute was very fine. Before the anchors were well down, the Somali

---

* This was written on November 18. The passage was published in the 'Times' the same month in accidental anticipation of the formal assumption of the title by the Queen under the provision of an Act of Parliament. It was believed by the writer at the time that by the Proclamation of Allahabad the title was legally assumed by her Majesty.

boys, familiar to all visitors to Aden, came alongside, paddling their frail canoes, which resemble the longitudinal section of a large cigar, and hold at most two of these naked, curly-headed young vagabonds, who are more at home in the water than on land. They at once began to call for money to be thrown overboard that they might show their skill in diving—very different from their congeners at Greenwich in the whitebait season—and their appeals were answered by a shower of pence. They expected more precious coins from such a noble ship, no doubt, and the first Somali who came up from a deep dive after a penny made a horrible grimace as soon as he rose to the surface and saw the piece of money, the colour of his own skin, which he had rescued from the depths. The Prince watched their gambols for some time, and shot a couple of gulls, which they dashed at like water-dogs, and fastened to a string, that they might be hauled up the side. Certainly, next to otters or seals, there are no such swift, keen-sighted divers, and the way in which they get into their miserable leaky canoes, which must be baled out incessantly, is very adroit. Civilisation is making way among them, for, though they still dye their hair red, and twist it into corkscrew curls defying imitation, they have adopted simpler styles of ornamentation in head-dresses, and wear drawers or loin-cloths. Soon after 8 A.M. the Prince came on deck, wearing Indian helmet, plumes, blue frock undress, Field-Marshal's insignia, and white trousers, the suite being ordered to appear in parade dress, or civil uniform, helmets, and white trousers. Presently, the Resident, Brigadier-General Schneider and Staff, Colonel Penn, R.A., &c., came off in full uniform, to pay their respects, and to take the Prince's pleasure as to the time of landing, and the arrangements for his reception. There was a brief space of time to prepare despatches and letters for home, and to send on telegrams to India.

The Resident then returned to shore. A little after 9 A.M. the Prince embarked in the State barge, to which his flag was transferred from the main; the shore batteries and the ships saluted again; the *Serapis* manned yards; the Marines, under Major Snow, were drawn up on the main-deck, the band playing "God save the Queen." The *Lombardy* manned foreyards in very creditable style, and her crew and passengers cheered bravely. About 9.30 A.M. the Prince landed at the triumphal arch or covered way prepared for his reception. The platform was laid with scarlet carpeting, and was covered with an awning, or shamianah. At the water-step stood in front the Resident and the officers of the Staff and of the garrison of Aden. On the left stood the Foreign Consuls, the officials and Residents—European, Asiatic, and African—of every kind of dress, complexion, and aspect.

On the right side were drawn up the Arab Chiefs, the Sultan of Lahej, his brothers, and some six or seven other Chiefs or "Sultans" from the mainland, in most picturesque costumes, who first attracted the Prince's attention. They received his Royal Highness with a kind of proud deference. One Sultan could not come on account of fever, but most of those whom we subsidise to give and protect the carriage of supplies to the garrison attended. It is a pity some opera costumier could not have seen them. He might enlist a legion of supernumeraries before he could find such a picturesque creature as one of the Sultan's brothers. Figure and face might have belonged to some clothed statue but for the eye, which burnt and flashed like glass reflecting the rays of the desert sun. Impossible to convey an idea of his splendid repose, or to describe his dress, which terminated (alas!) in a pair of socks and French bottines.

The Prince, acknowledging the loud cheers which greeted his landing, walked down the platform to the esplanade at the end, where a guard of honour of one hundred men of the 2nd Battalion, 25th King's Own Borderers Regiment, with their colours, was drawn up in front of a handsomely-decorated Stand, which contained all the ladies of the garrison and Station, some in European and some in Asiatic costumes. On the front of the Stand waved the Prince of Wales's plumes, composed of one hundred ostrich feathers, and, emblazoned in gold and blue, an inscription bade the Royal traveller "Welcome." As he emerged from the shelter of the awning into the bright sunshine, and his eye rested on the extraordinary gathering of natives on the crags and rocks, where they were nestling like sea-fowl of curious plumage and colour, he might well have been struck with admiration at the unpremeditated picturesqueness of the scene. There were weird and wonderful types of humanity from the opposite coast of Africa, wearing hair, resembling small snakes, stiffened like quills, or falling down like red fungi on each side of their faces, the men often far over six feet in height, with dazzling white teeth, scanty clothing, and legs which might be taken for mop-handles; fierce-eyed Arabs, demure Hindoos, sleek Parsees from Bombay, and varied specimens of the teeming populations which come from the Persian Gulf and the Coast of Africa to Zanzibar, and from the shores of the country marked as Arabia Deserta in our maps. Such dresses, as well as such absence of apparel, although he has now travelled in many lands, and has seen many strange sights, had never yet met the gaze of the Prince.

When the Prince returned to the shamianah, Mr.

Cowasjee Durshaw was presented by the Resident. This gentleman has, by honourable industry, raised himself to a high position in Aden. He is a Parsee, and he wore the distinctive head-dress of his people, which was adopted from the Hindoos, flowing robes of pure white muslin, trousers of the same, and shoes turned up at the toes. He proceeded to read an address from a handsomely illuminated volume.* At first his voice was somewhat

---

* As this was the first address which the Prince received to the east of Europe, it is worth while to print the text, which was very handsomely emblazoned and bound in an illuminated cover. The Parsees telegraphed both address and answer the same night to Bombay for the information of their community.

"To his Royal Highness Albert Edward, Prince of Wales, Duke of Saxe Coburg and Gotha, Duke of Cornwall, &c.

"May it please your Royal Highness,—

"We, the undersigned inhabitants of Aden, representing the mercantile community, humbly beg leave to approach and welcome your Royal Highness on arrival at the first British possession belonging to her Majesty's vast dominions in India.

"We feel gratified for the opportunity thus afforded us of expressing through your Royal Highness our loyalty and devotion for Her Most Gracious Majesty the Queen and Empress of India.

"We fully appreciate the motive which induces your Royal Highness to visit India, and confidently believe that it will tend still further to cement the cordial understanding that now happily subsists between her Majesty's British and Indian subjects. We desire to acknowledge with gratitude the blessings we enjoy under the mild and just sway of her Majesty's Government, as exemplified in the yearly increasing prosperity of this important military settlement. When Aden was captured in 1839, being the first of the territorial conquests that have been made during the glorious reign of Queen Victoria, it was only a small fishing village; but under the fostering care of British rule it has expanded, as your Royal Highness will this day see, and it has become a large and prosperous town, containing a population of nearly 30,000 souls, composed of many creeds and races, and with an import and export trade showing transactions valued at upwards of two millions sterling. We recognise in your Royal Highness's visit to India a desire to become acquainted with the manners, customs, and institutions of its people, which cannot fail to be productive to the teeming populations over which your Royal Highness is destined hereafter to reign. To commemorate your Royal Highness's visit to Aden, we have set aside the sum of Rs. 20,000, to found a charitable dispensary, which, with your Royal Highness's permission, we propose to style the Prince of Wales's Charitable Dispensary. We beg, in conclusion, to express to your Royal Highness our earnest hope that your Royal mother, our most gracious Sovereign, may long be spared to reign over us, and also that her Royal Highness the Princess of Wales and the Royal children may

tremulous, but as he read on he acquired confidence, making a low bow whenever he had occasion to allude to the Queen, the Prince, or Princess, and pronouncing his English very plainly, he came at last to the end. His co-religionists, a knot of eminently respectable, intelligent-looking men, dressed for the most part with greater richness than their spokesman, listened to the address and to the Prince's reply with the profoundest attention.

The Arabs were somewhat bored, it struck me, with both the Parsees and with their address, and looked disappointed when the Prince walked towards the carriages prepared for him and his suite. The Peninsula is not rich in such vehicles, but the Resident and the chief merchants had collected enough of Victorias and four-wheelers for all the suite, not without calling in the resources of Bombay. The guard presented arms, the people cheered loudly, and the cortege, escorted by Major Stevens' Aden Troop—very picturesque cavaliers from India, in red turbans, dark tunics, and jack-boots, mounted on fiery little horses, and armed with tremendous sabres—preceded by a body of Shootee Sowars—Native troopers riding fast dromedaries—set out along an excellent road, to visit "the lines," which extend some six miles from end to end. The sides of the road were lined by H.M.'s 25th Regiment, the 2nd Bombay N.I. Grenadiers, the Royal Artillery, and by detachments of Native Sappers, Gun Lascars. The European troops wore Indian helmets, the Native troops turbans with distinctive

---

enjoy, with your Royal Highness, long lives of peace and happiness, surrounded by all the blessings this world can give.

"We beg to subscribe ourselves your Royal Highness's most obedient, humble servants,

"COWASJEE DURSHAW, and others."

badges. Along the greater part of the route crowds of "Natives," kept in order by vigilant, yellow-turbaned policemen, assembled at the best places. Of the 30,000 souls in Aden, there were few who did not come to look at the Prince, though there were some who stood afar, as if fearful of coming too close. A crowd of bheesties watered the dusty road in vain. When the clouds opened for a moment, the sun let fall rays like red-hot iron bars, and umbrellas and dust-coats were in requisition.

The Prince passed under many triumphal arches (six or seven at least), each with appropriate inscriptions and devices, visited the new works, saw the tanks, and halted for half an hour at the Mess-house of the 25th (K.O.B.), where there was a collation, which was very welcome. Thence he continued his inspection of the "lines," passing through the tunnels, and getting out of his carriage at the Victoria Bastion to take a look from the top of the rampart over the low spit which connects Aden with the mainland. In the distance there could be made out a few trees and a small white walled hamlet—the outpost of the Aden Horse. The Turkish outposts were at Thiais. They extend thence across Fow, at the distance of 120 miles from our outposts. A new Pasha had come to command at Sana, and he had just given the Hashad Arabs a complete defeat. The proximity of the Turks and the movements of the Egyptians along the opposite coast cause uneasiness at Aden. If it were the object of our Government to precipitate the collapse of the Ottoman Empire, they would be pleased to hear that the Sultan is keeping up an army of 30,000 or 40,000 troops against the Arab tribes, at an incalculable cost. There surely seems to be no solid reason for the smallest jealousy of Egyptian influence over the tribes which the Khedive is taking in hand on the African side, for it must be our interest to see a settled administration along the coast, and to deal with civilised, instead of savage government.

The climate seems favourable to the production of a somewhat light and acid humour. The inscriptions over some of the designs of the cantonments indicated the existence of a certain caustic fun, which may be the result of a residence on this somewhat over-sunny peninsula. Over the portal of one building was inscribed "*Morituri te salutant!*" On inquiry it turned out that the place was the garrison slaughter-house. On another building was depicted a blazing yellow sun of a sinister aspect, winking one eye at an arid waste of stones, dotted with scanty herbage and half-starved camels, with the legend "Welcome to Araby the Blest!" Some classical artist had limned a dark young lady, in native garb, advancing to meet an unmistakable Britannia, with the words, "*Mater pulchrâ filiâ pulchrior!*" A materialist had designed a pile of champagne bottles, with the motto, "Thirsty Aden drinks to thee!" In front of the modest library was the inscription, "Hail! Author of our joy!" There were endless "Welcomes," and "Hails," and "Good wishes," and a "Cead mille failthe." "Freedom for all under the British Flag!" "Great Britain and India united for ever!" "Hail, electrifier of loyal hearts!" "Hail, Royal scion of a noble Queen!" "Happy and glorious is the reign of Victoria!" "Aden owes her prosperity to Britain;". "Our Arab tents are rude for thee." There were few if any Arabic or Ordoo inscriptions, and only one or two in French or other European language.

Above the portal of the Main Guard, which is situated in the throat of a narrow ravine at the Pass—a rift in the rugged crater wall, so wild and dark that one might pardon those who thought the Inferno lay inside—were written the words "Halt! who goes there?" As we passed the grinning mouths of the guns which seemed to ask the question, there was no reply; but the inscription, "Pass, friend! And all's well," greeted the Royal visitor at the exit. On another archway there was emblazoned a "Hearty Welcome," which, when the Prince returned through the gate on his way back, was replaced by "Farewell, Albert Edward! our hearts go with thee!"

At 12.30 P.M. the Prince reached the Residency, a large bungalow, situated on an elevated peak of one of the higher ridges of Aden, and looking down on a quiet bay hundreds of feet below. It is a plain, unpretentious, and not very extensive quadrangle, of which, though it was decked out with much taste inside, any great Indian civilian would not think much as an official residence. The gardens were laid out by Colonel Playfair when he was Resident, with the assistance of Dr. George Birdwood, who sent the frankincense trees, which form such interesting objects, from Bombay.* The sight of shrubs and flowers so green and bright, in a setting of rugged scoriæ is very refreshing. There is a very interesting flora at Aden, for all its barrenness, and Mr. Mudd, the Prince's botanist, made valuable additions to his collection here.

Mrs. and Miss Schneider were presented to the Prince. After lunch his Royal Highness held his first levee in the Indian dominions of the Queen—for Aden may be considered as an outlying dependency of the Presidency of Bombay—in the outer room in the Residency, which was in some degree cooled by the current of air through mat hangings outside the porch, and by verandahs jealously excluding the sun. Captain Hunter, Lieutenant Kennedy,

* The descriptions and figures of three new species of the genus Boswellia, which were discovered by Dr. Birdwood, appeared in the 'Transactions of the Linnean Society' in 1869.

Lieutenant Sealy, and the officers of the Aden staff—Military, Marine, Judicial, Medical, &c.—were duly presented by the Resident. Mr. Jones, the Garrison Chaplain, Father Francis, the Roman Catholic Chaplain, in cowl and cord and sandal shoon, were not forgotten. The Foreign Consular officers presented the Prince with an address; Herr Ganslandt, Consul for Germany, offered a few words of congratulation, apparently on his own account. There was also an Egyptian officer, who said he came in the Khedive's name to offer a welcome to the Prince. The principal merchants of Aden were introduced. Next came the reception of the Arab Chiefs—very real men to look at—with a sort of proud suspicion and disdain in their glances at all save the Prince—and all picturesque and sufficiently graceful; the most interesting, spite of the attractions of his wild-eyed brother, was the Sultan of Lahej, who was introduced by the Resident to the Prince of Wales "as a faithful ally of the Queen." This Chief, Fadhil bin Ali al Abdala, Sultan, who succeeded Fadhil bin Mohun last year, is of olive complexion, mild aspect, with soft lustrous eyes, black moustache and small curling beard. He was richly dressed, and fully armed with scimetar and pistols; but to the horror of the old Indians of the party, he was in stockings and boots instead of bare feet. General Schneider held the left hand of the Sultan in his right, and between the Sultan and the Prince stood the native interpreter. In a few graceful words, the Prince expressed his acknowledgments, on behalf of the Queen, of the services rendered by the Sultan to the garrison of Aden; and as a souvenir of his visit he pinned one of the medals struck for the Indian visit, and to which there was attached a blue riband, on the Sultan's left breast, and then put a massive gold ring, with the initials A.E., on the Sultan's finger. The ceremonial was

DECORATING AN ADEN CHIEF.

explained by General Schneider, through the interpreter, to him of Lahej, who never looked at either medal or ring while in the Prince's presence.

For all his pride and pleasure the poor Chief was nursing a small wound. He had been refused "the completion of his joy." Here is the translation of a letter which will explain his grief:—

From SULTAN FUDHL BIN ALI, of Lahej, to GENERAL SCHNEIDER, C.B.

A. C.

I inform you that your letter dated the 10th October has reached me, and its contents are understood. It has delighted me exceedingly, as it contained the news of the approach of H.R.H. the Prince of Wales, the future King. I also became very glad for your invitation to come to Aden on that day. I hope that you will complete my joy by allowing me to enter Aden with at least one hundred men, and after the meeting I will leave the town at once, because I am only coming to see one who is a most powerful and majestic friend. Although the meeting will take place only for a moment, it will be enough. If you will not permit me to come with one hundred followers, I will still come to pay my homage to the great Prince, but it will be with grief, and it is not proper to wear sorrow while all my friends are rejoicing; so please keep sorrow away from me, by giving permission. May you remain for ever.

18 *Ramzan*, 1292.

The Resident, however, did not think it expedient to grant this humble petition. It is to be hoped, nevertheless, that the Sultan went back with a light heart. General Schneider appears to understand the Chiefs and to be liked by them, and he would not have rejected the demand without good reasons for it.

Aden may be regarded as our Indian Gibraltar. There is an evidence of the cost of Empire in the cemetery where rest so many of our people—very numerous indeed for the size of the place. They do not fall in battle, but they fail on the homeward voyage—too often deferred till all hope is over—from India. Whilst the Prince was at the Residency, Captain Glyn visited the grave of his brother

Richard, who was buried at Aden on his way to England at the close of the Mutiny, and old comrades of the Rifle Brigade and friends will be glad to learn that the place where he rests is carefully kept, and that all about it is in order. There is no ancient record of travel in which this cinder-heap is not mentioned as a place of importance. It has now been 37 years in the possession of Great Britain, and yet it is only within the last 17 years that the restoration of the fifty and odd reservoirs, some of which were probably constructed more than 1260 years ago, was undertaken; so that for nearly a quarter of a century we allowed a rapid ruin to fall upon these wonderful works which uncivilised and barbarous nations, as we call them, perfected. When Captain Haines visited Aden, four years before we attacked and took it, several of the reservoirs—"the hanging-tanks up the hill-sides"—were in perfect order. The "fine remains of ancient splendour" which Salt saw in 1809, have now all vanished. If we were to leave Aden to-morrow, the works which would record our presence would be few indeed—a mess-house or two, a small quay, a light-house, some batteries and stone walls, and imperfect restorations of the doings of others. And yet the very names of the makers of the great tanks which we are clearing out are unknown, and the impression left on the minds of the general Briton quartered in the place by the operation is, very probably, that *we* are executing great conceptions never thought of in the dark ages. Playfair's 'History of Yemen' gives a most interesting account of the efforts made 500 years ago to convey water into Aden. When the first system of reservoirs was restored and constructed in 1857, a single fall of rain, we are told, gave a larger store of water than all the wells would have yielded in a year. Proud of steam-power, however, we preferred condensers to any attempt to take the goods the gods provide us, and for a long time were glad to pay 6*s*. or 7*s*. for 100 gallons of very vapid oxide of hydrogen.

The population of Aden is housed, for the most part, in wigwams. The place is a penal settlement for India, and people whom it would be inconvenient to keep in Bombay and its dependencies are deported to this garrison, over the entrance to which the inscription above the Gates of the Hell which Dante saw might well be placed, although it could not add to their misery. Jaswunt Rao Jasood, one of those alleged to have been engaged in the attempt to poison Colonel Phayre, was deported here by order of the Government of India, and was in Aden at the time of the Prince's visit—probably not at large—and there were possibly others connected with the same business; but the writ of Habeas Corpus does not run in these parts of the Queen's dominions. As far as I know, there was no judicial sentence of any kind against Jaswunt Rao Jasood. The two Maharajas and Sir Madhava Rao, indeed, dissented so completely from their European colleagues as to say that they did not believe the Gaekwar had instigated any attempt against Colonel Phayre's life, and, *pro tanto*, they acquitted those who were on trial, or whose guilt was being inquired into; but all the same, the Indian Government deposed the Gaekwar, and sent Jaswunt Rao and others into exile. When the Prince was at Baroda, a petition was delivered at the Residency from the family of Jaswunt, praying that they might be allowed to communicate with him at Aden, but the Prince could not interfere in the matter.

There is a regulation which is founded on the assumption that Aden commands the Red Sea, and that Great Britain is the mistress of that sea, which, if enforced, ought to enable the British authorities to exercise enormous influence. Every vessel carrying more than thirty passengers, natives of Asia or Africa, from any port east of the Cape of Good Hope to any port in the Red Sea, or from any port in the Red Sea to any port on the East Coast of Africa, must touch at Aden, and not depart without a clean bill of health. But why thirty? Or how can the number be ascertained? These questions are not easily to be answered. The sea-imports of Aden in 1874–5 were no less than 2,050,837*l.*; the exports were 1,278,365*l.*; total of exports and imports, 3,329,202*l.* Where the difference, amounting to 772,472*l.*, between the incomings and outgoings went, it is difficult to conjecture. But it is a very unpleasant fact for Manchester, that American piece-goods are sold here at a higher price than English manufactures, and are sent from Aden to Mocha and Hodeida in very large quantities. There are eyes from Germany, France, Austria, Italy, Holland, Sweden, &c., upon us at Aden, for there are Consular officers to represent these Powers; but Turkey and the United States seem to leave us to our own devices. The garrison of Aden consists of a Battalion of Queen's troops, a Battalion of Native troops, two Batteries of Royal Artillery, one Company of Indian Artillery, one Company of Indian Sappers and Miners, and the Aden Troop belonging to a regiment of Bombay Cavalry. The political and military functions are in the hands of the Resident, who is also charged with the administration of justice, in which he is assisted by subordinate officers and the Cantonment magistrate. He is the Sovereign's representative, to whom the Arab tribes look, if not for protection, at any rate for the payment of annual subventions; and it is a curious, if inevitable, feature in the dealings of the British Government with their very odd allies here, as well as on the North-west frontier of India, that it pays them tribute instead of receiving tribute from them. We may put any gloss we please on the fact, but the naked truth which the payees perceive under it is, that they receive our money to be quiet. The Abdalees and the Fadthalees were our bitter enemies for several years after the British occupation; but they were beaten into treaty-obligations; and to the Chief of the first tribe (Lahej) we pay 6942 German crowns a year; to the Chief of the second—Sultan of the Fadthalees, 2160; and to the Chiefs of seven other tribes, little gratuities varying from 80*l.* to the modest sum of 8*l.* per annum. We are supposed to be the protectors of these tribes against the encroachments of the Turks, and the eye of the Resident is supposed to look across the narrow sea, also keep a keen glance on the opposite coast, and watch the uncanny doings of the Egyptians.

There are now ninety-four guns in position, and heavy guns are much needed on two of the points. Ten 9-in. guns are to be mounted immediately; but they have been lying exposed to the weather for the last five years. There ought to be at least three more batteries between the Camp and Steamer Point, which are six miles apart. In consequence of a recommendation of Lord Sandhurst in 1864, the Native Artillery are to be removed, and replaced by fifty Lascars, who are of no use as garrison gunners, and do not know enough drill to enable them to fire a salute. There is one point from which an enemy's steamer could reach the coal depôts. This should be secured.

Having taken leave of Mrs. Schneider and her daughter, the Prince walked down the steep path from the Residency to the beach, where the steam-launch and boats of the *Serapis* were waiting in a secluded little bay. There was no crowd to witness his departure; no one except a few Arab fishermen, who did not heed what was going on. The many who were loitering about the platform and triumphal arch were no doubt taken by surprise when the guns fired a salute, and the manned yards of the *Serapis* and *Vulture*, and the cheers of the crews, announced that the Prince was going on board without returning from the Residency to the landing-stage. The Resident and the principal officers of the Staff, the commanding officers of her Majesty's 25th (2nd Battalion), K.O.B. (Colonel Wallace), and 2nd Bombay Grenadiers (Lieut.-Colonel Stanley Edwardes), Colonel Penn, R.A., Major Stevens, Aden Troop, Commander Brooke, R.N., &c., were invited to the Prince's table on board the *Serapis;* and a dinner was also given by the ward-room officers to the officers of the garrison. The town, the lines, and the batteries were lighted up and illuminated at nightfall. At 9 P.M. Brigadier-General Schneider and officers took leave of the Prince, and returned to Aden. At 10.30 P.M. the *Serapis*, with the *Osborne* in company, quietly got under way, and steamed out into the placid ocean for Bombay.

November 2nd.—Our log-book is a record of dry accomplished facts, for "incidents" are distasteful to our excellent and practically-minded Captain; all non-essential matter is carefully eschewed; even the capture of a "booby" or a "noddy" would not have been entered. The wind was generally light and favourable—that is ahead, so as to make the boilers draw. The distance allowed per 24 hours was 246 knots, and at 48 revolutions the *Serapis* did that run very readily "when nothing went wrong." At noon our position was determined to be lat. 12° 59′ N., long. 47° 22′ E., there being only 1′ difference between the ship's place according to dead reckoning and that given by observation. Distance from Aden, 134 miles; from Colaba Light House, 1510 miles. The thermometer rose to 81°, the temperature of sea-water was 78°. Nor birds, nor ship, nor fish proper, were visible, but the sea abounded in incredible quantities of jelly-fish of all sizes, from the bigness of a florin to that of the top of one's hat, which, exhibiting many pretty colours, were floating at various depths—some nearly on the surface of the water, and some far down as the eye could reach. At 2.10 P.M. there was a sensation. The ship suddenly stopped. Every one was instant in inquiry, "What is it? Why are we stopping?" The cause was soon explained. A condensing pipe was out of order. It was set to rights in a quarter of an hour, and the vessel proceeded on her way; but in little more than an hour the screw again ceased to work. Then great Mr. Oliver, Inspector of Machinery afloat—a hard-headed Oliver Cromwell sort of Scot, master of his work — took off his coat, and dived down the ladder into the interior of the murky turmoil of boilers, pistons, and furnaces, to direct the operations for the repair of the machinery. The Prince and the Duke of Sutherland also descended into the engine-room, to see for themselves what was wrong. This time it was the soft metal stuffing of one of the pipes which had melted, and the water was going into the stoke-holes. In an hour and a half the needful repairs were effected, and the *Serapis* resumed her course. Some censure was bestowed on the jelly-fish, which were said to have got into places where they had no right to be. At 6.21 P.M. there was a sunset of such miraculous beauty that every one came up on deck to see it. The sea was of an intense purple, almost black; the sky on the horizon, for ten or twelve degrees, was of a flaming saffron, softening and spreading upwards in a fan-shaped radiance of amber and yellow which melted into the tenderest and most delicious green. Long after the sun had set the glory of that wonder of harmonious colour haunted the western sea.

November 3rd.—It was a dead calm all day. The sea was more animated. Flying fish skimmed away over the smooth roll of the ocean, the repose of which was broken now and then by the plunge of a large fish in pursuit of the much-persecuted creatures which, between the bonitos and the gulls, have no peace either in sea or air. The waters are reported to be much favoured of sharks here; and towards noon certainly we were gratified by the sight of a school of whales, which kept, however, a good way from the ship. It was well they did, for rifles were immediately got in readiness to cause them inconvenience if they came within shot. The wondrous drift of jelly-fish continued. Scarce a square yard of water without its indolent citizen. There below him were others in layers far as the eye could reach—hour after hour for hundreds of miles. We lowered buckets over the side, but the ship went through the water at too great a speed to permit us to catch any. What a wealth of life! What a subject for research! At noon we were in lat. 14° 2′ N., long. 51° 37′ E., 1250 miles from Colaba Light House, Bombay; the ship running 12 knots. There was a solitary ridge, like a cloud, resting on the water, visible on the port beam, which was pronounced to be Ras Fartak, a wall-like steep some 6 miles long and 1900 feet high, which is quite inaccessible from the sea. It was said to be some 80 miles distant as we steered, and to be in a savage part of vast unknown Arabia, where the people of the Coast are given, it is believed, to sore ill-treat traveller or luckless mariner. There is some trade, especially in dead sharks'-skins and fins, nevertheless, in the small maritime towns along this coast farther north. This day there was a council of deliberation held in the saloon to consider the bearings of the news received at Aden as to the existence of cholera in Southern India, and to decide upon the route to be taken in consequence; and after full discussion it was resolved that the visit to Trincomalee should be given up.

As an illustration of the influence on events which trivial matters may exercise, I may mention how it came to pass that the Prince's tour in Southern India was so modified and altered. Before leaving England, one of the suite received a letter, intended for publication in a newspaper, from Mr. J. B. Norton, enclosing a communication from an officer of Engineers, which pointed out the grave dangers which would attend a visit to the districts at the time of year indicated in one of the programmes to it. As it was considered inexpedient to create alarm in the public mind, the letter was put aside. One day it met the eye of the gentleman for whom it was intended, who communicated the contents to Dr. Fayrer; and he considered it of sufficient consequence to be made known to Sir Bartle Frere. A telegram was despatched from Egypt to the authorities at Bombay, to make inquiry into the truth of the statements as to the danger of visiting the districts in question. When the Prince arrived at Aden, the answer to these inquiries came back by telegraph, to the effect that although the risk of fever appeared to be exaggerated, there could be no doubt that the neighbourhood was at that moment unhealthy, as cholera appeared to be spreading among the villages surrounding the hills where the Prince's sporting camp would have been pitched. It became necessary to modify the programme, and to suspend any decision respecting that part of it until further information could be procured after our arrival at Bombay.

At 3.40 P.M. there was a stoppage of the engine once more. This time it was the cover of the bilge-pump of the main engine which had become disorganised. The bilges had been pumped out, and a good deal of work had been done in the engine-room to-day, so that when the accident occurred it was not considered of any consequence, as it was known that everything was in good order. In half an hour or so the vessel went on at increased speed to make up for lost time. At 6.20 P.M. the *Osborne* signalled that she could not keep up at the rate of 12½ knots, and our speed was reduced 1 knot an hour accordingly.

November 4th.—The ship's company exercised at small arms, and were inspected by the Prince. At noon we were in lat. 15° 14′ N., long. 56° 23′ E.; 964 miles from Colaba Point; sea like glass. There was a concert in the theatre on deck after dinner; but the comfort of the audience was interfered with, and their enjoyment of the entertainment diminished, by showers of smuts and clinkers from the funnel, which were driven aft by the head-wind. Some amateurs who appeared for the first time were stricken dumb from stage fright; their voices died in their throats. The bandsmen sang some part songs and glees very excellently well. Alister, the Duke of Sutherland's piper, in all his bravery, made a promenade round and round, with his pipes playing gaily; but he rather fretted on the narrow stage, for your piper is nothing if he cannot strut up and down with martial swagger, swelling like a pouter pigeon. The leading comedian tried a little tragic part—a reformed pickpocket *à la* "It's Never Too Late To Mend"—and the gods roared with laughter at his pathos, to his great discomfiture.

November 5th.—The continuous steaming for five weeks is rather too much for the engines, and repairs and a thorough overhaul are much needed, and will be executed at Bombay. At noon we were 654 miles W. of Colaba

Light House (lat. 16° 18′ N., long. 60° 55′). There was a disturbance among the Arabs shipped at Suez as stokers respecting the choice of sleeping-places, the top of the sheep-pens being much coveted for that purpose. After dinner the Prince went on deck, where the crew had prepared a very elaborate Guy Fawkes, with a long wig and bands, villainous countenance, lantern, &c., complete, which was brought aft to the sound of fog-horns, tin-kettles, and all kinds of abominable noise. To this the Arabs, who perceived there was a tomasha going on, thought they would add an entertainment of their own. They accordingly crowded up on the upper-deck, with false beards, coloured faces, &c., and were quite enjoying themselves in their own fashion, when it was perceived that they were very rudely interrupting the legitimate drama, whereupon they were sent back whence they came, and even further, and had good reasons afterwards to repent their intrusion. When the Arabs had been removed, one of the crew read an indictment against Guy Fawkes, and pronounced sentence upon him, which ended with the committal of his body to the deep. A floating stage was ready at the side, Guy Fawkes was placed upon it, and when the port fire was lighted the stage was let go and dropped into the sea. To the great disappointment of the contrivers and the spectators, the stage capsized, and Guy Fawkes was whirled astern on his side; but it was fondly believed that the fire would not be extinguished, and that the rockets, maroons, and other explosives with which he was charged would go off after a time. Eyes were strained to catch the first fizz in the distance; but, to the grief of every one but the captain, who "didn't see the fun" of having these fireworks blazing under his counter, Guy Fawkes never righted himself, and was lost in the darkness. It would be curious to learn what became of him. The thing would float about for weeks, and might cause many a false alarm and strange surprise at sea.

November 6th.—A wind from north-east fresh enough to mark "3" in the log, and to make one look out through the open port now and then to see if a wave was likely to come inboard, heralded by a crest of foam; but, though it often threatened, the breeze was not strong enough to summon the dreaded men who come round the cabins to secure the dead-eyes. The sea was still full of jelly-fish, apparently drifting about in a helpless way, but bent doubtless on important business. For all their flabby purposelessness, these creatures can vex steam-engines and men, for they are sucked into the pipes, and are solid enough to clog them. It was resolved to send the *Osborne* in advance to Bombay with letters, and at noon she ran up very close, and in reply to the Prince's hail, Commander Durrant said he hoped to get in by 10 o'clock on Sunday night. A boat was sent off to her with despatches at noon, and in a few minutes the *Osborne* was steaming away fourteen knots an hour, and showing the road to Colaba Light House, leaving her consort to do as well as she could without her. The observations at noon gave lat. 17° 23′ N., long. 65° 35′ E.; distance run, 264 miles; and distance to Colaba Light House, 420 miles. The thermometer stuck to its point, 80°—81°, with tenacity, night and day, but we are becoming used to it. The Prince's horses stand the temperature very well, and seem none the worse for it when they are taken out for their morning's walk up and down the deck. Commander Bedford has been introducing some sanitary improvements among the Arab stokers, the importance of which have been forcibly impressed on them, and it is to be hoped that their manners will also partake of the benefits of these disciplinary reforms. The excellent author of the 'Sailors' Pocket-Book' would be an admirable ædile on shore.

November 7th.—An easterly breeze, blowing just strong enough to give a good draught to the furnaces. Divine service on deck to-day. The Rev. Canon Duckworth read the lessons and preached a short sermon. He was assisted by the Rev. Mr. York, chaplain to the *Serapis*, who composed a simple hymn for the voyage, which was sung with fine effect by the trained men, officers, and crew. As many of the crew as could be accommodated on the main-deck, the Royal Marines, and the officers, &c., were present, and joined in the hymns and responses. All wore snowy caps, jackets, and trousers, and the bronzed and bearded faces afforded the only relief to the mass of white which filled the quarter-deck under the awning. Rarely has a more clean-looking, picturesque, or attentive congregation been anywhere assembled. The Prince, attended by the military members of the suite (blue frock-coats and white trousers, swords and spurs), inspected the Marines and Artillery detachment (R.M.A.) on the main-deck, and was much pleased with their appearance. His Royal Highness also went round main-deck cabins, some of which have been by this time worked up to a high degree of beauty, especially that of my neighbour, Lord Charles Beresford, for the adornment of which Tom Fat has indented on the resources of the ship in the way of brass-headed nails to an unconscionable extent. The thermometer hovered about 80°, and now and then ran up to 82°. At noon the result of the observations, which were laid as usual by Staff-Commander Goldsmith on the saloon table as soon as they were worked out, gave our position as 165 miles from Colaba Light House, which means that we shall see "India" early to-morrow morning, and make the landfall somewhere about Bombay—our inheritance from Catherine of Braganza, in virtue of her Portuguese dowry. It is wonderful, when the comparative ignorance and helplessness of those ancient mariners are taken into account, to think how boldly they sailed those seas, and ventured on "the great void," so full (void as it was) of the terrors which must have beset them of the unknown. The knowledge of what had been done before them was lost. They were not encouraged by an acquaintance with the records of Egyptian exploration, or of later Greek enterprise. M. Mariette asserts that it is beyond gainsaying that the Egyptians not only traded from the Red Sea with India, but that they sailed down the coast of Africa, doubled the Cape of Good Hope, and, turning northwards, reached the Straits of Gibraltar, and so arrived at last at Alexandria, or the port which was at the spot where that ancient city now stands. As Archbishop Whately said when he was shown the slate on which St. Kevin crossed from Wales to Ireland, and was asked "if he doubted the fact?" "I cannot say that I do, but I think if he did it St. Kevin was a *very lucky fellow*." With all our modern science and measured mileage of the sea, there was some little anxiety among our officers in the small hours about sighting Colaba Light House. "You see, Sir," said an astute navigator, on whom the exploits of the ancients were being thrust, "they did not know their dangers, and they were bold accordingly; they made no allowances for deviation of compass or set of tides and currents, for they were ignorant of them; and so they were as jolly as sand-boys. They had no Lloyds and no Boards of Inquiry; no courts-martial; and if they went down, there were no newspapers to make a howl over them." Practical commentaries these on the advantages of the dark ages! But regarding the arrival at Bombay in the light of a certainty, it must be said that there was one perpetual prophecy as to the Prince's progress which was never falsified. Programmes, indeed, were subjected to change, but when the telegraph announced that the Royal fleet, or train, or cavalcade, would arrive at such a place on such a day, the fulfilment of it was pretty certain. Thus there were many advantages gained, and much ease and contentment given to those who were to receive and to see the illustrious visitor. So it was, too, that words which were not to be spoken or heard for many days were read and answers prepared beforehand, so that when the Prince arrived at any point where he was to be greeted with a thoughtful and elaborate address of welcome, he was not obliged to deliver a hasty and inconsiderate acknowledgment. Before the *Serapis* left Aden it was known what the Corporation of Bombay would say to the Prince, and similar foreknowledge was obtained, where an impromptu reply would, in many instances, have been hazardous.

The work of getting ready for landing has been going on since Friday, and the holds of the *Serapis* are yielding up mountains of cases. The Prince's presents alone form portentous piles between decks; and as to gun cases, boxes of ammunition, portmanteaux, boxes of wood and of metal, and all the farrago of a grand shikar party, the eye that did not see the stratified masses round which valets and mariners and Chinamen hovered, and on which they climbed for hours, can never hope to behold the like unless the Prince goes to India again.

It may readily be imagined that the near approach to India causes reflection, and fills men's minds with various emotion. Sir Bartle Frere is about to revisit the scene of the labours and services of his life, and to see in the city, which is yearning to receive him, the substantial proofs of his beneficent administration. Major-General Probyn is returning to the country in which he won his spurs; but he is charged with a load of care which he would gladly change for the conduct of a charge at the head of his troopers; because trustful as he is in the divinity that will hedge the Prince, he knows what dangers there are ever lurking in that cruel thing called "a crowd," and he has had much to do with this expedition. Dr. Fayrer is also about to place his foot on the shore of a land where he has worked hard for many years of his useful career, and wielded sword and lancet with equal assiduity and honour, but on his strong shoulders there rests a moral burthen and responsibility which he of all men least depreciates. Lord Charles Beresford is familiar with the wild sports of the East, and is joyous at the thought of fresh encounters with pugnacious "pig" and ferocious tigers, but still more elate at the thought of the pleasure it will afford the Prince to "get his first spear," and to have a warm corner in the jungle. Lieutenant-Colonel Arthur Ellis has served in India, and he looks just now as though he were oppressed by awful visions of masses of Maharajas and Nawabs, and rows of Rajas waiting on shore, holding out their hands filled with diamonds, pearls, rubies, emeralds, &c., of fabulous value, surrounded by piles of Kinkob, shawls, brocade, and all the wealth of Ind, ready to precipitate themselves on the Prince, to each of whom must be given some adequate return. When the list of these Potentates was received the other day, and the account of the presents they intended to make was read, there was a moment's deep despondency, and a declaration of bankruptcy by anticipation was imminent. The other members of the suite, with the exception of Lieutenant Fitz-George, had all the pleasures of novelty to which to look forward—new scenes, new life, new sport, new pursuits. For the Duke of Sutherland, who had been diligently "reading up India" during the voyage, there was a store of investigation of natural resources, studies of agricultural improvements, irrigation, mining, the state of princes and people; for Lord Alfred Paget there was the acquaintance to be made with manners and customs of Native Courts, and the gratifying exercise of an active intelligence in observing the habits of Anglo-Indian life, and in seizing the distinctive points which make the Anglo-Indian something not quite the same as an Englishman or Englishwoman in India. For Lord Suffield there was the pleasant combination of the duties of a high officer of state about the person of the Prince, and of the pleasures of a keen sportsman—good with rifle and gun, and firm in the saddle—in a new field; and to similar obligations, and to the anticipation of similar enjoyment in the chase Lord Aylesford and Lord Carington had superadded a task imposed by their personal attachment, which happily had no need for its exercise. Mr. Knollys had the certain solace of having plenty of work to do, and so in degree each of the voyagers had something to think of—some a great deal. But the centre of all—the Prince—what of him? The country he had left was still straining its gaze in the track of the ship that bore him, still listening with all its ears for the reports of his progress, there was no empire or kingdom in Europe which did not take note of his journey. There were hundreds of millions of human beings waiting to feast their eyes upon him—the whole state of Hindostan from the Viceroy to the humblest Sepoy were in expectancy of his coming. Well. There was the Prince of Wales writing at one of the tables in the saloon, with a pleasant smile on his face—now and then stopping to caress "Flossy," or to address a word to those near him—perfectly calm and composed, the traces of the once natural sadness caused by his parting nearly all effaced—for at every port telegrams come and go—"all is well" at Sandringham and at home—and he is looking forward with resolute dignity to the ordeal which he is told he must undergo, and to the opening of the drama in which he is not merely the principal but the only figure.

THE PRINCE SHOOTING BIRDS ON BOARD.

THE BHEESTIE, BOMBAY.

CHAPTER IV.

BOMBAY.

First Sight of India—Bombay Harbour—The Viceroy and the Governor of Bombay—The Landing—The Prince and the Chiefs—The Bombay Address and Reply of the Prince—The Procession—Bombay Streets—The burra khana—First Morning in India—First Reception—" Private Visits"—Maharajas of Kolhapoor and Mysore—Máhárána of Oodeypoor—Rao of Cutch—The Gaekwar of Baroda—Sir Madhava Rao—Sir Salar Jung—Rajpoots and others—Rewa Kanta Chiefs—The Hubshee—Birthday Rejoicings—Unpleasant News—The Thakoors—The Levee—Return Visits—Byculla Club Ball—Bombay Jugglers—Box-wallahs—Caves of Elephanta—The Banquet.

NOVEMBER 8TH.—The Colaba Light House was not sighted as early as was anticipated, but the reflection of the light on the water could be made out about 1.30 A.M. The ship, being then only some 25 miles distant from land, was eased, and at 4 A.M. the engines were almost stopped, just going fast enough to keep the *Serapis* in her place till it was time to make the run into the harbour of Bombay. The morning was very bright and beautiful. A glorious sunrise promised one of those fine days which are somewhat too common in this part of the world, and the thermometer marked 80° with a persistency which led the observer to think that the instrument must have received a permanent injury. Soon after 6 A.M. the highlands over Salsette, and the Ghauts to the south and east of the city, were plainly visible from the ports; the peaks of Elephanta and the Mahratta Queen could be made out some time before the masts of the men-of-war in the bay could be seen. The Prince came up and stood on the bridge, while Captain Searle, the Master-Attendant, who had boarded the *Serapis* outside, explained the principal points of interest in the fair landscape. At 8 A.M. the ships of the East India Squadron, under his Excellency Rear-Admiral R. J. Macdonald (Commander-in-Chief), viz., *Undaunted* (flag), *Briton*, *Daphne*, *Philomel*, and *Nimble*, as well as the harbour ironclad turret-ships *Abyssinia* and *Magdala*, and the ships of the Flying or Detached Squadron, under Rear-Admiral Rowley Lambert, *Narcissus* (flag), *Raleigh*, *Topaze*, *Doris*, and *Newcastle*, dressed, and fired a salute with magnificent effect, though the *Serapis* was rather too far at the time. They lay in echelon in two lines, the Indian Squadron on the port, and the Detached Squadron on the starboard, side of the grand sea-alley through which the *Serapis* was to pass. Behind the Light House, which rises out of the sea like one of the huge painted candles to be seen in foreign churches, there lay spread out, when the smoke rolled away, the fair panorama of the Bay, fenced in by the blue Ghauts, with the fleet in front, and enclosing in its arms the great expanse of buildings, steeples, and houses, which gives some impression of the importance of the city of Bombay; but the scene was once more shut out by the rolling cloud of smoke from the broadsides and forts, which drifted slowly away before the land breeze northward. It was just 9 o'clock when the *Serapis*, the Prince's stately yacht, entered between the lines of the men-of-war, the marines drawn up and presenting arms, officers in full uniform with uncovered heads, and the crews on the yards cheering, ship after ship. The fleet then fired another salute, the bands on board each ship playing "God save the Queen" and "God bless the Prince of Wales." The spectacle is not one to be described. There might be naval displays with more lively backgrounds, greater life and animation in flying yachts and countless boats and steamers, crowded with people and gay with flags, elsewhere, but where out of India could be seen such a stretch of coast fringed with tropical vegetation and lighted by such a sun?

All the arrangements for the reception of the Prince had been so thoroughly worked out before the arrival and landing that there was scarcely anything that could happen which had not been provided for. The order of the procession, the visits of the Viceroy and of the Governor, the forms to be observed, had been arranged. When the *Serapis* came to her moorings, many boats came off with the members of the Staff of the Viceroy and of the Governor, which are, I believe, called in India, Deputations, to pay their respects to the illustrious guest.

There had been some little trouble between the authorities by sea and land. A Commander-in-Chief on the East Indian Station and an Excellency afloat in harbour was something new at Bombay, and the Governor and Council had assigned Rear-Admiral Macdonald a place in the order of dignitaries on the opening day, which he would not accept, feeling that he represented in his person and office the honour of the service. To show how far below the Prince of Wales the greatest was, the Commander-in-Chief declared he could not salute Viceroy or Governor once the Royal Standard was flying in harbour; but all these clouds were happily dispersed in the end, and the Admiral's rights and office were recognised, and Viceroy and Governor had their salutes in due course.

Six hours elapsed between the arrival of the *Serapis* in harbour and the reception of the Viceroy on board, but there was plenty to be done and to be seen meantime—constant arrivals of persons of greater or less importance, visitors, persons on business, Sir Bartle Frere being especially in request. The officers to whom the Prince and the Royal party were so deeply indebted for their comfort and well-being came on board and were introduced to his Royal Highness. They were Major-General Sam Browne, V.C., Major Ben. Williams, Major Bradford, and Major Sartorius, V.C. The first-named officer was charged with all the transport arrangements, trains, carriages, baggage, and the like. The second was entrusted with the care of the stud-horses, syces, &c. The third had, perhaps, the most difficult and arduous post, for he had to look after the safety of the Prince's person, and to act as the head of the police. The fourth had the control of the tents and *valetaille* and service of the Royal camps. Among these four officers there were two Victoria Crosses and only six arms, for "Sam" Browne had lost one of his in an action near the Rohilcund Terai near the end of the Mutiny, and Major Bradford had to suffer the loss of one by amputation, in consequence of injuries received from a wounded tiger. There are few men whose four hands could do as much work as these gallant soldiers managed with only two. Major Henderson, who has been specially attached to the Prince because of his great attainments as a linguist and of his acquaintance with Oriental etiquette and knowledge of Native Courts, was also admitted to an audience. There was need to land and despatch the baggage in advance, excellently managed by the experienced servants entrusted with it. The ship between decks presented quite as bustling and lively an appearance as the harbour outside, where native boats of novel shape and rig, laden to the water's edge, and steam-launches and men-of-wars'-men furrowed the water between the lines of shipping. The *Serapis*, gazed at eagerly by tens of thousands, whom we could see on shore, and by the multitudes on board the vessels moored in the stately bay, was the centre of all eyes. The two Rear-Admirals, Macdonald and R. Lambert, and senior officers of the fleet were received at 10 A.M., soon after the vessel anchored. There was lunch to which several of the visitors were invited at the usual hour. It was now nearly 3 o'clock, and those in attendance on the Prince were told off to their places, for Lord Northbrook, Viceroy and Governor-General, was about to make his appearance on board. Shortly before that hour a salute from a battery on shore, immediately taken up by the ships of both the squadrons and by the floating batteries, announced that his Excellency had embarked at the Dockyard; and presently a barge with the Viceroy's standard was seen approaching, and, punctual to the moment, the Governor-General stepped on board, and was received with all the honours due to his official rank. Lord Northbrook was attended by Mr. Aitchison, Secretary of the Foreign Department, by several members of his personal staff, the Military Secretary, Colonel Earle, his private secretary, Captain Baring, &c. He was conducted by Lord Suffield between lines of the Prince's aides-de-camp and suite along the corridor of the main-deck, which was covered with scarlet cloth, to the companion leading to the saloon, at the top of which stood his Royal Highness.

There had been some sort of notion abroad that the meeting of the Prince and the Viceroy would be attended with difficulties affecting their relative position and precedence—not in rank, because of that there could be no question—but in state ceremonial before the world; but it was at once evident that such anticipations were unfounded, and that the Prince of Wales and Lord Northbrook perfectly understood what was due to themselves and to each other; nor was there, I believe, as far as they were concerned, the smallest interruption to the perfect *entente* established at the very commencement of their intercourse, although an inadvertent interference of one of the Viceregal Staff at one time caused temporary annoyance.

The Prince, having presented the members of his suite to the Viceroy, who in turn presented his Staff to his Royal Highness, retired to a sofa with him, and engaged in conversation for some time. Presently it was perceived from the commotion at the landing-place in the Dockyard that the Governor was about to embark. At 3.25 P.M. the saluting battery commenced again, and Sir Philip Wodehouse was seen coming off to the ship. He was attended by the Commander-in-Chief of the Presidency, Lieutenant-General Sir Charles Staveley, the members of Council, among whom were two Parsee gentlemen, Mr. Wodehouse, his private secretary, and his aide-de-camp. He was received by the Prince with much kindness. The usual presentations were made. In half an hour his Excellency took leave, and returned to the Dockyard to join those who were waiting for the landing of the Prince.

When it was time for his Royal Highness to set his foot on the shores of India, on which we had been gazing all day, there was some curiosity to observe in what order the Prince and Viceroy would take their seats, but according to marine views, whether by accident or not, Lord Northbrook unquestionably gave precedence to his guest, for he stepped on board the launch first, and remained standing until the Prince had descended the

THE FIRST STEP ON INDIAN SOIL.—LANDING AT BOMBAY.

companion and had taken his place beside him in the stern of the boat. Once more the cannon spoke, the crews aloft cheered, bands played, marines and guards of honour on deck presented arms, officers saluted as the Royal Standard passed each man-of-war, and from all the shipping uprose a mighty shout. The Prince's barge was preceded by boats bearing the members of the suite, who had to land before him. Looking back from one of these, a noble pageant, lighted up by a declining sun, met the eye—the hulls of the fleet, bright streamers and banners, long rows of flags from yard to yard and mast to mast, white boats, a flotilla of steam-launches, gigs, pinnaces, and a crowd of onlookers hastening fast as oar could send them in wake of the Royal barge to the Dockyard.

The flotilla sped on shorewards. A vast triumphal arch, spanning the water-way between two piers, but gay with banners, branches and leaves, and with decorations of palm and cocoa-nut, appeared in front of us. It could not be imagined that this dockyard stair in its normal state was one of the most commonplace and ugly of landings. But it had now not only been decked out with all the resources of art, which in this land are various and fantastic, but there was assembled beneath its great span perhaps the most strange and picturesque assemblage ever seen of late days in any part of the world. On each side of the way, under the vaulted roof, were long lines of benches rising in tiers, draped with scarlet cloth. This material was also laid down on the avenue to the gate, a hundred yards away, where the carriages were waiting. In the front rows sat or stood, in eager expectance, Chiefs, Sirdars, and native gentlemen of the Presidency, multitudes of Parsees, rows of Hindoos, Mahrattas, and Mahomedans dressed in their best—which was oftenest their simplest—a crowd glittering with gems and presenting, as they swayed to and fro to catch sight of the Prince, the appearance of bright enamel, or of a bed of gay flowers agitated by a gentle breeze—the officers of the Government, the Corporation with its address, the Municipal body of Bombay, and the naval and military officers who could be spared, representatives of the faculties, corporate bodies, dignitaries, and all the ladies who could be found within the radius of some hundreds of miles, and who had hastened to greet the Prince with their best smiles and bonnets. An abundance of sweet-smelling flowers, many of rarity, was displayed in pots along the avenue, and others commingled with shrubs of new forms were arranged in masses near the entrance —banners hung from the roof,—words of "Welcome," in various characters were inscribed in gold over the entrance. I shall say nothing of the appearance of the Chiefs just now, inasmuch as there will be plenty to write of them hereafter.

The mode in which the Prince was to make his first appearance before the Queen's subjects in India had been the subject of some consideration and discussion. Oriental ideas of dignity and grandeur, which insensibly acquire influence over the minds of Europeans after a residence in the country, suggested that splendidly caparisoned elephants would form the most fitting mode of carriage for the Prince, the Viceroy, the high officials and their suites in his Royal Highness' procession through the city to the Government House at Parell. The animals were all ready, but it was resolved not to adopt the Indian custom. As alternatives, there were carriages, or a cavalcade. The latter would have been the most effective manner of entry. It would, as we now know, have given the people more satisfaction, and would have enabled them to identify the Prince with greater ease; but such an ordeal as a ride of six or seven miles or more through rivers of illuminations would have been more than human nature could have undergone, even if equine patience would have endured it. So it was decided that the entry should be made in carriages. A reference to the Appendix will show what were the official regulations, and it must be said, considering the difficulties which are found in enforcing arrangements of the kind, that they were well observed.

When the Prince came on shore, the anxiety of the Chiefs to see him was almost painful. For once they were much agitated, and the proudest departed from the cover of their habitual reserve, and from the maintenance of that staid deportment which the Oriental Turveydrop considers the best proof of high State and regal dignity. The Prince was at first shut out from their view, or was only revealed at times in the centre of a waving mass of cocked hats, plumed helmets, uniforms, European dresses, in which he was scarcely distinguishable; but when they could identify him, the frankness of his smile, and the candid look with which he surveyed them, produced on the instant a favourable impression; and when he paused to return their salutations, with hand uplifted to his helmet, a closer inspection more than confirmed the idea which their quick perception of character enabled them to form of his courtliness.

Some who saw the Prince as he landed thought they observed that he had a graver cast of countenance than was habitual with him a few years ago, and said they did not know whether to attribute it to the sun, which was unusually hot for the time of year, or to the emotion caused by the novelty and grandeur of the scene, accustomed as he was to such sights. Others wrote that he "seemed serious and even sad of aspect" as he walked up the landing-stage from the Royal barge, and that he "returned the salutations which greeted him with a preoccupied air that betrayed emotions working within." But at all events his answer to the address of the Corporation was delivered with the utmost clearness of elocution, and in a manner which gained the hearts of those who saw him, if, indeed, they at all required any gaining.

When the strains of "God save the Queen" died away in the hum of many voices, the Corporation, the members of which had been eagerly awaiting for the moment, advanced, headed by Dosabhoy Framjee, the Parsee chairman, in the pure white robes in which his race rejoice, and in the headdress worn by his people which the Prince had already noticed at Aden. He said:—

"MAY IT PLEASE YOUR ROYAL HIGHNESS,—

"We, the Chairman and Members of the Municipal Corporation of Bombay, esteem it a high privilege to be allowed in the name of the Corporation and of all the inhabitants of this City to greet your Royal Highness at your landing on the shore of India, with an address of loyal welcome. We rejoice that your Royal Highness should have selected Bombay as the starting-point of your Indian travels; for this city is in itself perhaps the most striking example India can present of the beneficial results that may be produced by the impact of Western civilization on Oriental character and institutions, and of the success that may attend earnest and judicious efforts to reconcile all the various races of this country to British rule.

"Bombay may lay claim to the distinction of being a Royal city, for this island first became an appanage of the Crown of England through forming part of the dowry of Charles II.'s Portuguese bride, and during the two centuries that have since elapsed, Bombay has had every reason to be grateful for this fortunate change in her destiny. From a barren rock, whose only wealth consisted in cocoa-nuts and dried fish, whose scanty population of 10,000 souls paid a total revenue to the State of not more than 6000*l*. a year, whose trade was of less value than that of Tanna and Bassein, and whose climate was so deadly to Europeans that two monsoons were said to be the life of a man, she has blossomed into a fair and wholesome city, with a population that makes her rank next to London among the cities of the British Empire, with a municipal revenue amounting to 300,000*l*. a year, and with a foreign commerce worth fully forty-five millions, and yielding in customs' duties to the Imperial Treasury three millions a year. All this material prosperity she owes to the strong and wise Government which has secured her in the enjoyment of peace and order, of equality before the law, of religious liberty, and of freedom of trade, and has thus given confidence to men of all races and creeds—Europeans, Indo-Portuguese, Hindus, Mahomedans, Parsees, and Jews—to pursue their various callings under the shadow of the British flag.

"We gladly, therefore, seize the occasion of your Royal Highness's presence amongst us to record our sense of the blessings of British rule, and to assure your Royal Highness of our devotion to the throne which has become the enduring symbol of concord, liberty, prosperity, and progress to all the multitude of nations that own the benign sway of Queen Victoria. We beg that your Royal Highness will convey to her most Gracious Majesty the expression of our loyal sentiments and of our gratification that her Majesty has sent the heir to the Crown amongst us to become personally acquainted with the people of India. We regret that your Royal Highness's Consort, the Princess of Wales, so much and so deservedly beloved by the English people, has not been able to accompany your Royal Highness on this journey, to learn for herself in what honour her name is held in India. We pray that the God of all nations may watch over your Royal Highness, and bring your happy design of visiting India, of which we to-day witness the auspicious commencement, to as happy a conclusion, so that it may be blest with good fruit hereafter in the strengthening of the ties of mutual interest, esteem and good-will which already bind the Imperial State of Great Britain to its greatest dependency.

Given under the Common Seal of the Municipal
Corporation of Bombay.

Chairman.
Secretary and Clerk.

The Prince's reply was happily conceived. He said:—

"It is a great pleasure to me to begin my travels in India at a place so long associated with the Royal Family of England, and to find that during so many generations of British rule this great port has steadily prospered. Your natural advantages would have insured a large amount of commerce under any strong Government, but in your various and industrious population I gladly recognise the traces of a rule which gives shelter to all who obey the laws, which recognises no invidious distinctions of race, which affords to all perfect liberty in matters of religious opinion and belief, and freedom in the permit of trade and of all lawful callings. I note with satisfaction the assurance I derive from your address, that under British rule men of varied creeds and nations live in harmony among themselves, and develop to the utmost those energies which they inherit from widely separate families of mankind, whilst all join in loyal attachment to the British Crown, and take their share, as in my native country, in the management of their own local affairs. I shall gladly communicate to Her

Majesty what you so loyally and kindly say regarding the pleasure which the people of India derive from her Majesty's gracious permission to me to visit this part of her Majesty's Empire. I assure you that the Princess of Wales has never ceased to share my regret that she was unable to accompany me. She has from her very earliest years taken the most lively interest in this great country, and the cordiality of your greeting this day will make her yet more regret the impossibility of her sharing in person the pleasure your welcome afforded me."

Then the Prince, with Lord Northbrook by his side, advanced slowly along the carpeted avenue, at the end of which a band of Parsee girls in white were awaiting him with garlands and baskets of flowers. He stopped from time to time to speak to the Princes who were presented to him by the Viceroy, the first being Sir Salar Jung, who is only a Prime Minister, but who represented the State of Hyderabad. He shook hands with most of them, and was especially gracious to the younger Chiefs, sympathising perhaps with the cares which must fall on such young shoulders in time to come. Each Chief had his Mentor, his "Political," by his side, and had a setting of Sirdars around and behind him. A bystander wrote :—"Even the Mahratta Sirdars, who have not much besides their dignity to stand upon, were charmed, apparently, with the gracious presence and winning smile of the future Emperor of India; and when he spoke to each of them in turn and seemed to take a real interest in them, even Oodeypoor smoothed his troubled brow, and forgot his grievance against the Government which had set the Gaekwar above him. We doubt if a native noble left the pavilion without feeling gratified at the notice taken of him; and it only shows what a mighty power lies hid in that little word 'tact,' when a kind smile and a courteous phrase can efface in a moment the remembrance of innumerable imagined slights inflicted by a generation of stiff-necked and narrow-minded officials."

Those of his suite who had to enter the carriages in advance had actually left the shed before the Prince landed. There is one inconvenience attendant on the position of those who are taking part in a procession. It is that they see very little of it—they are seen (and they are unable to ascertain whether that produces a gratifying effect on the beholders or not); but on such an occasion they may be sure that they are regarded with the utmost indifference, if, indeed, they are not looked upon with absolute contempt and dislike as mere obstructions and impediments to the full enjoyment of the one great object which all have come to behold. I am enabled to write nothing of what happened in the Dockyard on the landing except from hearsay. But of what I saw from the landing-place to Government House I am able to record my own impressions. Any spectator along the line of way could give a much more interesting narrative and describe more fully the effect of the procession itself. By one of these it was compared to a Doge's wedding as represented in the old pictures, save that it was on land instead of water, and that the *Bucentaur* passed between masses of human beings instead of gliding down canals lined by gondolas. That may be far-fetched. Of one matter, however, connected with this procession I cannot speak in terms of praise. There was no music: there was, indeed, the band of the 3rd Hussars, but it was silent. The band of the 7th Fusiliers was at the landing. On such an occasion as this nothing would have been more inspiriting than the performance of martial music by mounted bands placed at intervals in the line of the procession, nor would it have been amiss had there been a greater display of cavalry and even of foot regiments, for the pace was not so fast as to have taxed the powers of marching, and the effect of the spectacle would have been enormously enhanced by such an addition.

The Prince emerged from the Dockyard—a salute was fired by the artillery, and the procession, the head (in the sense of the beginning) of which had already awakened the curiosity of dense multitudes a mile in advance, moved forward, and those who were by nine carriage-lengths ahead of the vehicle of State, in which the Prince and Viceroy were seated, heard a roar piercing through the wild tumult of voices for a moment, as a gun at sea breaks through the noise of wind and wave. At every station in India had been heard a Royal salute where guns were to be found to fire it, and it may be safely said "that never was there so wide-spread and noisy announcement of any event made known to so many people at the same time as the arrival of the Prince of Wales in India."

The impression produced by the aspect of the streets can scarcely be conveyed in any form of words; certainly if one were to try to set the sights down on paper, he might well be puzzled. He would have to give an account of every yard of the many miles through which the Prince passed, each presenting extraordinary types of dress and effects of colour. There was something almost supernatural in those long vistas winding down banks of variegated light, crowded with gigantic creatures tossing their arms aloft, and indulging in extravagant gesture, which the eye —baffled by rivers of fire, blinded with the glare of lamps, blazing magnesium wire, and pots of burning matter—sought in vain to penetrate. For the most part the streets indulge in gentle curves, and as the carriages proceeded slowly, new effects continually opened up, and fresh surprises came upon one, from point to point, till it was a relief to close the eyes out of sheer satiety, and to refuse to be surprised any more. After several miles of these melodramatic effects, no wonder there was an inclination to look for one welcome little patch of darkness to receive us in its grateful recesses ere the night was over. Certainly it was a spectacle worth going far to see—the like of it will never probably be seen again. This is generally said of any spectacle of any unusual magnificence, or of extraordinary grandeur; but taking it all in all, I believe that very few who witnessed the sight would care to miss it, or to go through it all once more. To the spectators, no doubt, the passage of the cortege of the Prince, who was the central point on which all eyes turned, presented an absorbing attraction. But it was a pleasure which lasted but for a moment, for the carriage was soon out of sight; and then silence gave way to the noisy interchange of ideas as to what had been seen, for there was no certainty among the mass of natives respecting the Prince's place in the procession. To those who were passing between these animated banks of human beings, there came at last an ennui, and a sense of sameness, although, as I have said, every single yard of the way was marked by many distinctive types. Who could take them all in? Windows filled with Parsee women—matrons, girls, and children—the bright hues of whose dresses, and the brilliancy of whose jewels, emulated the coloured fires burning along the pavement—scarcely attracted one's notice before it was challenged by the next house filled with a crowd of devout Mahommedans, or by a Hindoo temple opposite, with its Brahmins and its votaries on steps and roof; flanked appropriately by a Jew Bazaar, or by an Armenian store, or by the incongruity of a European warehouse; or was solicited by the grotesque monitors on a Jain Temple. For if the changes in the chess-board are so numerous as to furnish matter for profoundest calculations, the extraordinary varieties of race and population in Bombay present endless subjects for study, to which only one thing was now wanting—adequate time. Night had long fallen; at last the whisper came from the front and ran down the line—"We are nearly at home," and Parell received the Prince with all due honour, the most illustrious of the many guests who have been sheltered under the roof of the old Jesuit convent.

Up to the gates of the Park, illuminations and crowded thoroughfares, guards of honour, and salutes once more, and an official instalment in the mansion which was ablaze with lights and prepared for the occasion with the utmost regard to effect—clusters of turbaned scarlet-coated servitors in the hall and on the steps, the Governor's Body Guard lining the corridor and staircases, and now the day was to be wound up by a banquet in the Great Hall.

The accommodation afforded by Parell is not very extensive, although the dining-room is exceedingly fine and large, and the State apartments sufficiently imposing; but any way, it was necessary that the greater number of those in attendance on the Prince should be accommodated in tents; and on each side of a broad avenue, formed by noble trees, there was a fair camp prepared for their reception, with crowds of servants waiting to be engaged "on approbation"—Portuguese boys, in blue jackets and white trousers, and Bombay natives, contending for choice. Outside the main street of the camp were tents for the servants; for a Battery of Artillery, and for a detachment of the 2nd Queen's Royals, and the quarters of the vast miscellaneous gathering of people which is inevitable at any centre of power and authority in India. The tents were ready—beds, tables, chairs, washing apparatus, lamps, tubs, but alas! there was one drawback. The soil was not very dry, and the tents were pitched on wooden platforms, which did not afford very equable support, and as one walked, the planks went up and down, giving a general impression of an earthquake about the premises. Then, too, there were horrible suspicions of snakes, for Parell is built close to a swamp, and the lower part of the lawn may be said to melt into it.

The description of a dinner-party, even of the grandest, cannot be made interesting. The impression produced by the change of colour and of costume of the domestics at a burra khana does not last very long, or, if it does not subside rapidly, it is overcome by irritation at an appearance of alacrity and prompt obedience which is falsified by results; but the novelty of the scene at Sir Philip Wodehouse's table, where the glare of Indian liveries and the picturesque effects of Oriental attire were seen for the first time, must have been felt by the strangers. Besides the Governor's servants in their fine turbans and robes, there was in attendance a small battalion of those engaged for the Prince in new liveries of the native fashion—a flat white headdress, with a broad band of gold lace running diagonally from the scarlet top to the side, scarlet surcoats buttoned to the throat, richly embroidered with gold lace and the Prince's plumes in silver on the breast, laced on the sleeves, edged with gold lace, and confined by rich cummerbunds, but—"desinet in piscem"—the glittering personages so fine above wore thin white trousers, and went barefooted. Those specially attached to the Prince's service were fine-looking fellows, and so completely devoted to their work, that they would have seen all the company die of hunger sooner than give them a morsel. One there was whose place and duty it was to stand behind the Royal chair with a long fan to chase away the flies. Two other were engaged on State occasions to cool the air by the slow lateral movements of the great hand-punkahs. So far as I remember, there was only one Indian noble of high rank at the feast, and that was Sir Salar Jung.

The health of the Queen was drunk with extraordinary enthusiasm, but the few words which prefaced the health of the Prince of Wales were followed by what in such company might be described as a storm of applause. There was a State reception in the grand drawing-room upstairs after the banquet, and the Prince remained till near midnight, conversing with the various guests with unflagging energy, but the departure of the Viceroy for Malabar Point was the signal for the breaking-up of the company. Not one of the least of the strange sights to-night was that afforded outside by the carriages, and the lights of the running footmen in attendance on them, which reminded one of what might have been seen in the neighbourhood of Covent Garden, or of the Grand Opera in Paris on the night of a fancy ball. The heat did not abate, and it contributed not a little to the exhaustion of the labours of the day, and to the effects of the passage through the fiery furnace of the streets. There were very few even of the youngest who did not rejoice when it was time to walk down the steps of the Government House, and make their way along the avenue of trees to their tents where the watchful "boys" were sitting ghostlike in their white robes, waiting to see their masters to bed. There was an appearance in the sky over the city as of a great fire. Camp fires blazed around. "Is it not all like the description in the 'Inferno,'" observed a friend to me, "where the poet says—

'Sovra tutto 'l sabbion d' un cader lento,
Piovèn di fuoco dilatate falde,
Come di neve in alpe sanza vento.
Quali Alessandro in quelle parti calde
D' India vede sovra lo suo stuolo
Fiamme cadere infino a terra salde'?"

There was the stir of an army not yet reposing. Challenges of sentries, neighing and clatter of horses, and from afar came the dull beat of drums and the monotonous chants of the camp-followers outside Parell, for these are very night birds. "Boy! Close the tent! Bund-Kharo! Good-night!"

November 9th.—Very early risers must men be who want to work in India, if not elsewhere. Once more in a tent, with black faces all around one! People and trees and surroundings all different—mango-trees and mango-birds, the gold mohur-tree, cocoa-nut and toddy-trees (*Borassus flabelliformis*), the wheeling kites overhead—higher still, the soaring vultures—the cry of the great woodpecker, and the chattering of the familiar minar—a new land, but a glance revealed that you were in India, and you felt it too. There is the Head-quarters' barber, in a great red Mahratta turban, waiting outside—a handsome smooth-faced fellow who makes his English go a long way, and who is a master in his art, though his fingers are deadly cold, and he is for his trade overfond of garlic. Him, be sure, you will never lose sight of as long as you are in India. There is the bheestie with his water-skin ready to fill your tub. There is the syce with your horse outside, if you are minded for a morning ride. There is the sweeper hovering in the distance, the khelassies or tent-pitchers awaiting orders, the khitmutgar with a cup of coffee, and the Bombay "boy"—in my case one Jivan—a slight, quiet, demure-looking man of forty or so—who has already taken possession of my property—boxes, bags, clothes, money and all—to the intense astonishment of Maclachlan, who would have resisted his assumptions by force, but that I told him it was the custom of the country. These and others. Each tent is a centre of existence to seven or eight of the people called "Natives," to whom you are for the time being lord and master. The impudent and irrepressible crows, which are already marking you for their own, are taking accurate note of your proceedings, and studying your character from the branches of the mango-tree overhead, and have been trying your patience by making a prodigious cawing and croaking on the top of your tent. Looking up the grand avenue toward Parell, you see the sentries pacing before the portico, the Royal Standard floating overhead, and the Sowars mounted and ready for duty outside. There are busy groups of people before every tent on each side of the main street, and word comes round that in a couple of hours breakfast will be served, and that, two hours later, every one is to be in uniform, in readiness, to assist at the reception of the Princes and Chiefs in Government House.

There was but little time to look around one, although the shade of the noble trees in the garden at the back of Government House, and the display of new plants and flowers, and the lake with its terraced margin were very tempting, and made one envy General Probyn his quarters in the detached bungalow inside. The Prince of Wales's birthday is to be duly honoured all over Hindostan India at noon; and the first object which greeted his eyes this morning was a portrait of the Princess, which had been entrusted to Sir Bartle Frere for this happy occasion. Probably he never had a more trying day, for accustomed as he has been to the performance of nearly all the duties of Royalty and to administer its functions, his Royal Highness had now to make himself acquainted, at very short notice, with formalities of a novel character, to which the greatest importance was attached, and, before the eyes of a most sensitive and watchful Court of Princes and Chiefs who had been accustomed to such routine all their lives, he had to go through ceremonies which, if not ridiculous, struck a stranger as frivolous or unmeaning. The heat even at 8 A.M. was quite sufficient to warn us that we were in India, and yet the Prince was obliged to wear a uniform of European cloth, laden with lace and buttoned up to the throat, and to stand and sit for hours, going through the same kind of labour with each of the Rajas whom he received, who after a time must have appeared very much like the same people who had just left the room and were coming back again—figures lighted up with jewels, followed by crowds in white robes and gay headdresses. A little before 10 A.M. the members of the suite who were not on out-door duty were directed to repair to the inner audience chamber on the drawing-room floor of Government House. At the entrance stood two gorgeous people in scarlet and gold surcoats and turbans, with massive gilt implements in their hands. Servants, similarly dressed, with gilt batons of curious form held like swords, were ranged along the sides of the room. Twenty-four chairs were placed on the left of the silver Throne which had been prepared for the Prince at the end of the room on a cloth of scarlet and gold. Behind this seat stood four servitors—two with peacocks' feathers and horse-tails, and two with the broad fans, familiar to every one who has seen a picture of an Oriental reception, which were moved by the bearers to and fro on the long stems on which they were resting. On the right of the Prince's Throne twenty-four chairs were ranged, with a second rank behind. On the wall behind the Throne was a portrait of the Queen. In front, and extending about three-fourths of the length of the room or hall, was "the Carpet," which plays such a large part in Durbars. The programmes do not use that word on the present occasion, and style the ceremonies of to-day "private visits." It was mentioned in the early correspondence on the subject, that the Prince could not hold "Durbars;" but it would have been very difficult to have detected much distinction between these and the private visits, except in the fact that the Chiefs were introduced separately and had separate audiences. Thus certain grave questions connected with precedence were evaded. But *the* "carpet" was there—the kudometer, if the word may be coined, by which Viceroys and others measure the degree of consideration and honour which is assigned to the durbarees, or those entitled to be received in Durbars. In the centre of the purple or crimson cloth, which was provided with gold-lace borders, there was an emblazonment of the Royal Arms and motto in full. It is with reference to the outer edge of this carpet, and to the exact number of steps taken by Prince or Viceroy from the Throne along it that the rank of the visitor is determined.

As yet the Prince of Wales has only been seen by the multitude, and has only exchanged a few words with the Chiefs. He has been surrounded by Europeans and has been at a "burra khana." Now he is to receive those Chiefs who have come from all parts of the vast Presidency, larger and more populous than many kingdoms. They have already had a kind of rehearsal, for the Viceroy has held a Durbar at which, *mutatis mutandis*, every form has been observed which will be followed to-day.

Be good enough to read this official document, and you will see what is laid down. It is "No. I., Programme for the reception of His Highness the Raja of Kolhapoor by His Royal Highness the Prince of Wales, No. I., Foreign Department," dated Bombay, 6th Nov. 1875, and addressed to "Political Officers concerned," and others. It runs thus :

"At 10 A.M. on Tuesday, the 9th November, 1875, his Royal Highness the Prince of Wales will receive a private visit from his Highness the Raja of Kolhapoor.

"The Raja will be accompanied by nine of his principal Sirdars and by the officer on duty with the Raja, and will be escorted from his residence by a party of cavalry.

"Major R. W. Sartorius and one of the Prince's aides-de-camp will proceed on horseback 500 yards from Government House, Parell, to receive and conduct the Raja to the Prince's residence.

"Major P. D. Henderson and an aide-de-camp will receive the Raja as he alights from his carriage, and will conduct him to his Royal Highness's presence.

"The Prince will receive his Highness at the edge of the carpet, shake hands with him, and conduct him to a seat on his right hand.

"On the right of the Raja will sit the officer on duty with the Raja, and the Sirdars in attendance on his Highness according to their rank.

"The other British officers present will sit on the Prince's left, in the order of their rank.

"After a few minutes' conversation the attendant Sirdars will be introduced by Major Sartorius, and will present the usual nuzzurs, which will be touched and remitted.

"Uttur and pân will then be given to the Raja by the Prince. Major Henderson will present uttur and pân to the principal attendant Sirdars, and Major Sartorius to the others.

"On the departure of the Raja, the Prince will conduct his Highness to the edge of the carpet; Major Henderson and an aide-de-camp will accompany his Highness to his carriage; Major Sartorius and an aide-de-camp to a distance of 500 yards from Government House; and a party of cavalry as far as his Highness's residence.

"A salute of 19 guns will be fired on the arrival and departure of the Raja.

"A guard of honour will be drawn up in front of Government House, and will present arms as the Raja passes.

"Full Uniform to be worn,

"P. D. HENDERSON.

"*Political Officer on the Staff of*

"*His Royal Highness the Prince of Wales.*"

The Prince came into the Throne-room shortly before the time fixed for the first reception. He looked at the gorgeous Chair of State with its golden arms, one representing a lion the other a bull, as if he thought it was somewhat too fine. The Duke of Sutherland in blue and silver, wearing the Riband of the Garter; Major-General Lord Alfred Paget in uniform of Major-General; Sir Bartle Frere in official uniform, with the Riband of the Star of India; Lord Suffield in State uniform as Head of the Prince's Household; Major-General Probyn (uniform,

Equerry); Colonel O. Williams (uniform, Royal Horse Guards), Lieut.-Colonel Ellis (uniform, Equerry), Lord Carington (uniform, Royal Horse Guards), the Earl Aylesford (Yeomanry), Lord C. Beresford (uniform, Lieut. R.N.), Dr. Fayrer (uniform, Surgeon-Major), Mr. Knollys (Household), and others; some on the Prince's left hand in order; others on duty outside; and others, again, engaged in the trying task of galloping up and down in the hot sun in attendance on Rajas, were all in their places.

A little before 10 A.M. the guns of the R.A. battery in the Park outside began to fire a salute, and before we could count the nineteen coups to which his Highness is entitled, the Raja of Kolhapoor drove up to the front of Parell House with a great flourish in a grand carriage drawn by four horses, with servants in beautiful liveries of blue and silver, and a magnificent fan-bearer behind, wielding a blazing machine to keep the sun away. He was received as per programme, led up the steps into the Hall, so up the grand staircase lined with the Governor's servitors—then into the corridors, and so conducted to the entrance of the Throne-room. There he stood for a moment. But inexorable fate in the shape of Major Henderson led him forward towards the Prince, who had risen and advanced with great dignity down the carpet to meet him. At the edge he stretched forth his hand and took that of the Raja, whom he drew towards him kindly. After the Raja trooped the Sirdars, each holding his sword by the sheath, which has neither straps, buckle nor slings, and is thrust into the cummer-band when it is borne in action. A few phrases of courtesy were exchanged between the Shahzadah and the descendant of Sivajee (who can tell how many degrees removed?), adopted by the amiable Prince of Kolhapoor who died six years ago. Chatrapati Maharaj Raja Sivajee IV. is a

Mahratta, twelve years of age, and belongs to the Bhonsla family. He was attired in purple velvet and white muslin, and was encrusted with gems. His turban was a wealth of pearls and rubies; his neck like an array of the show-cases of some great jeweller. The Raja is as yet a mere child, despite his years, and seems as if he would be the better for a little course of cricketing or of some other bodily exercise. The State, which is ruled in his name, contains upwards of 3000 square miles, and more than 800,000 people, and has a gross revenue of 3,047,243 rupees.

It was interesting to watch the face of the Raja as he raised his eyes to meet those of the Prince. It wore an expression of pleased surprise as his Royal Highness, coming to the regulation spot on the edge of the carpet, with a pleasant smile took the hand of the little Chief and led him opposite the silver chair, where he left him with a bow, and sat down. The Political Agent then conducted the Chief to the chair on the right of the Prince, leaving another for the officer who acted as interpreter. The Raja's quick, soft eye rolled down the line of the suite opposite, and then remained fixed on the Prince; and his Sirdars—who sat in a row, contrasting very much indeed, in their Oriental bravery of shawls, jewels, and tissue of gold, with the plain uniforms of the Prince's suite opposite—watched every gesture of both. A few compliments were exchanged, but the remarks at such a reception are of an official character. Then it came to the turn of the Sirdars. Each rose in turn and advanced to the foot of the Throne or chair of State, salaaming low, and presented to the Prince a kerchief containing gold mohurs. This the Prince touched with his right hand and remitted, and the Sirdar walked backwards as instructed, not always with ease, to his seat. When these presentations were ended, the Prince and all present rose, and his Royal Highness taking from those in attendance a gold and jewelled scent bottle, shook a few drops of perfume (uttur) on the Rajah's pocket-handkerchief, and then from another rich casket took the betel-nut (pân), wrapped in fresh green leaf covered with gold foil, which he placed in the Raja's hand; Major Henderson, as per programme, doing the same for the Sirdars. The interview was at an end, and the Prince led his Highness to the sacred verge, and thence he was conducted to the entrance, where he vanished with his face still turned to the Throne. The Maharaja went off as he came, in great state.

Scarcely had the echo of the salute for him of Kolhapoor died away when the guns once more opened, this time firing twenty-one rounds, to announce the coming of the Maharaja of Mysore. He is the adopted son of the Maharaja who died in 1867, and the restoration of his House is one of the most remarkable political acts of any recent Indian Government. His Highness, an intelligent-looking lad of thirteen years of age, is the subject of a great experiment, and represents the results of the subversion, by English hands, of the Mahomedan power founded by Hyder Ali, and the restitution of a Native State to the rule of a Hindoo House, which, strictly speaking, had no direct right in virtue of descent to enjoy it. It was for some time doubtful whether the adoption of Chamrajendra Wadia by the Maharajah in 1865 would be recognised; but six months after his death, the lad, then not quite seven years old, was installed on the throne, and was placed in the charge of most careful and laborious officers, whilst the affairs of the ill-governed State were retained in the hands of the British Government, but will be handed over to him when he is eighteen years old, if he "shall then be found qualified for the discharge of the duties of his exalted position, and subject to such conditions as may be determined at the time." The State contains 27,000 square miles, and a population of more than 5,000,000 souls. The revenue is put down at 10,820,000 rupees, and it pays an annual subsidy to the British Government of 2,450,000 rupees. The jewels which literally hung on him must be of enormous value. One stone of the many of his necklace is said to be worth nine lacs of rupees. Some of the suite smiled as the Band outside played the duet of the brave Gendarmes, "We'll run him in," by way of prelude to his entrance to the audience chamber. He wore a coat of black velvet. His neck, wrists, arms, and ankles, were encircled with strings of pearls, diamonds, and rubies. His turban was graced with an aigrette of brilliants of large size, and a large tuft of strings of big pearls and emeralds hung down on his shoulder from the top. His Sirdars were equal in splendour to such a Chief. The same forms were observed as before, but the visit lasted a little longer. The Prince expressed his pleasure at hearing the little Maharaja speak fluent English, and on being informed that he loved the chase, was a good shot, and could play cricket, and sent him away in evident contentment.

He who came after Mysore was regarded with some curiosity. Who could be indifferent to the presence of one who claims celestial descent, and has his claim allowed—whose blood is of such heavenly blue that marriage with a daughter of the house is only to be obtained at the cost of a province, and who is, according to Tod, the living representative of the only dynasty which, with the exception of Jaisalmir, "outlived eight centuries of foreign domination in the same land where conquest placed them, and who now holds the territory which his ancestors held when the Conqueror from Ghizneh first crossed the 'blue waters' of the Indus to invade India"? Sir Thomas Roe, indeed, asserts that the House of Oodeypoor is descended from Porus! The Máhárána is a young man of the highest race in India, and, if all tales be true, of considerable force of character. He boasts of the oldest pedigree in the world, and "looks a gentleman all over." He speaks English, is tall, good-looking, and very fair—of a fairer hue than the average Europeans of the South—and is of very dignified manners and carriage, with an air as if he were conscious of his origin, and meant to keep up the traditions of the House. But what can he do at the best? What career is open to him? He rules, but does not govern; and unless some change be introduced in the system, the instruction given to the Native Princes in English and other learning, and the cultivation of their minds, with all the concomitant knowledge of history, and the birth of new ideas—patriotism, ambition, and the like—will prove not only mischievous but disastrous. He was dressed all in white—turban, robe, and pantaloons; but on his headdress there was an aigrette of magnificent diamonds, and he exhibited on his neck and on his arms some great pearls and rubies, and his gold sash was ornamented with a buckle set with the finest brilliants. His sword-hilt and sheath were richly studded with precious stones. The Sirdars in his train were attired in green satin and brocade and white turbans, and were more resplendent than their Chief.

The Máhárána has but nineteen guns; his State contains 11,614 square miles, and a population of 1,168,000 people. The revenue is about 4,000,000 rupees, of which 20,000*l.* goes as tribute to the British Government. The Prince, who is not yet of age, was adopted by the late Máhárána, and is the son of the elder of his two uncles, both of whom were excluded from the succession. The Prince and the Máhárána seemed, to use a common phrase, to get on

A DURBAR AT BOMBAY. INTERVIEW WITH THE GAEKWAR OF BARODA.

very well together, and there was evidently a good deal of sympathy in the interview.

The Rao (Pragmul) of Cutch, who rose from his sick bed to pay homage to the Prince, came next—a tall, dignified, portly man, walking with great difficulty; so ill, indeed, that he only returned to his State to die, to the great grief of his subjects and of all who knew him. There are only seventeen guns allotted to him. The Prince did not go further than the middle of the carpet to meet the Chief; but the Rao and his Sirdars made a very impressive appearance for all that. Next to the Prince himself, the Rao seemed desirous of seeing Sir Bartle Frere, and the same remark applies to all the Bombay Chiefs, amongst whom the ex-Governor had left most pleasant memories. The "good" that men do oft lives with them. It was touching to think of the painful journey this infirm old man had made to pay homage to the Prince and see him for a few moments. He retired with evident satisfaction. The State is small—6500 square miles, exclusive of the Ran, which contains 9000 square miles. The population is under half a million, and the revenue is but 1,500,000 rupees. It was harshly dealt with by our rulers in times past; but they did some good too, and now they are doing justice. It was now ten minutes past eleven o'clock, and more than an hour had gone by in the performance of these ceremonies, when twenty-one guns announced that some one of Royal dignity was near at hand.

All eyes were dazzled when Maharaja Syajee Rao, the little boy whom the Government of India installed as the Gaekwar of Baroda, stood at the threshold of the door—a crystallised rainbow. He is a small, delicately-framed lad for his twelve years and more, with a bright pleasant face. He was weighted, head, neck, chest, arms, fingers, ankles, with such a sight and wonder of vast diamonds, emeralds, rubies, and pearls, as would be worth the loot of many a rich town. It is useless to give the estimate I heard of their value, and the little gentleman has more at home. We all know his history, and how he owes his position and his future inheritance, whatever it may be, to the attempt made to poison Colonel Phayre, and to the selection by Jumnabaae, widow of the predecessor of the ex-Gaekwar, now somewhere in custody, of a little scion of the House of Pilajee, who founded the family, and whose descendant (Pertab Rao) little dreamt of the revival of the branch in the person of his son. He was met at the edge of the carpet, and strode with much solemnity to his seat side by side with the Prince. Sir Madhava Rao, Sir R. Meade, and a noble train of Chiefs came with him. The first is one of the most noteworthy men in India; the second is distinguished as a soldier and as a diplomatist, and is deemed by the Government worthy of the highest trust and of the most responsible posts.

The State of Baroda contains 4399 square miles, and a population of more than 2,000,000. The Gaekwar coins his own money; has an army of 5 batteries (20 guns and 400 gunners) and 3126 infantry, 2 squadrons of horse, and an irregular force of 5000 cavalry and 7400 footmen, costing the State 40 lakhs of rupees, or 400,000*l.* annually —*a quoi bon?* But Baroda has treaties; it is bound to have a "contingent," and we control the manufacture of salt, and the right of opening ports. What the revenues are seems rather indefinite, but every one believes Sir Madhava Rao will place them on a sound footing. Baroda is now the subject of an interesting experiment. The ability of a Native administrator to construct a fabric out of the ruins of systems which covered every kind of disorder and corruption will be fairly tested. Baroda rules itself. Only in certain matters which do not interfere with the full development of its resources or with its good government does the Paramount Power pretend to exercise control, or does the Resident become justified in making representations to the Durbar. The term "Paramount Power" is objected to by certain Indian newspapers. It is, however, perfectly applicable and absolutely correct. In no place has the term been more fully justified than in Baroda. The present Regent is one of the men who rise to the surface in Hindostan by sheer strength of talent, industry, and intelligence superior to all the forces arrayed against them. A Mahratta Brahmin, forty-seven years of age, he may be said to have been born in the purple of Premiership, for he is a son of one Prime Minister of Travancore and nephew of Vincat Rao, who filled a similar office. He was educated in the High School of the Madras University, where he was at one time Acting-Professor of Mathematics and Natural Philosophy; he subsequently filled several posts in the Civil Service, and was then appointed tutor and companion to the Prince of Travancore. He finally was made Dewan or Prime Minister of that State in 1858, in which capacity he acted for fourteen years with such eminent ability, and with such benefit to the British Native rule, that he was made Knight of the Star of India, and was offered a seat in the Legislative Council, which he declined. In 1873 he was invited by Holkar to become his Dewan, and administered the affairs of Indore with success. When the Viceroy deposed Mulhar Rao, and it became essential to place Baroda in the hands of a Native statesman, the British authorities applied to Sir Madhava Rao, who accepted the grave responsibility. What, with the advice and assistance of Sir R. Meade, he has done already promises well for the future. He has reconstructed the Revenue system, the Police, the Courts of Justice, and has reformed the whole administration of the State. He has acted on the principle of paying all Government officers very high salaries, so as to secure able men, and to diminish the temptations to peculation and corruption which operate so powerfully in countries beyond the bounds of Hindostan; and it is stated, on very good authority, that justice is administered, and order and law established and maintained, with firmness and certainty. The village watchman still exercises his calling, but he is well paid and is made directly responsible for his village; so, onwards and upwards, in all branches of the Administration, Sir Madhava Rao has so organised the offices that there is no ground of complaint of inadequate or irregular payment, while the Revenue shows a large and rapid increase. He has not begun by sweeping away all old institutions and customs, tearing up tradition by the roots, and leaving a bleeding and irritating surface to receive the application of new ideas, but he has worked on the old basis and repaired the ancient structure. Here we have a man of the intellectual type of that Purnia of Mysore described by an illustrious Englishman, who said, when speaking of Talleyrand, "He is like Purnia, only not so clever;" but Sir Madhava Rao is, in point of character and directness, greatly the superior of Wellesley's typical Brahmin Minister. The visit of the Gaekwar lasted a minute or two longer than usual, for the Prince asked several questions, and conversed with Sir Madhava Rao and Sir R. Meade. The forms prescribed in the programme were duly observed, and the Gaekwar, whose cortege and escort were very splendid, departed.

Next we had one of the most interesting events of the day. It was the reception of his Excellency Sir Salar Jung, G.C.S.I., Vikar-ul-Umra, Nawab Khurshid Jah, Nawab Ikbal-ud-daula, and the other members of the deputation representing His Highness the Nizam of Hyderabád. The Nizam's Minister was dressed with studied simplicity in a long robe of dark green cloth, over which he wore the riband, G.C.S.I., a plain gold waist-belt, and a very small white turban, which set off his well-developed brow and fine but melancholy face to great advantage. The Prince received Sir Salar Jung, who led the deputation, in the middle of the carpet. He shook hands with him, and the members of the deputation. Few words passed, but the Minister seemed diffident. His reserve may be accounted for by the apprehension that he would be regarded as a *persona non grata* on account of the inability of the young Nizam to appear, but there was nothing in his reception by the Prince after dinner last night, or in the manner of his Royal Highness to-day, which gave any outward sign of displeasure. Sir Salar Jung did not speak until he was spoken to. After a brief conversation, he presented on his own behalf a nuzzur of 101 gold mohurs, which was touched and remitted. The eight Ameers who had been previously presented were introduced by Major Sartorius, and offered the usual nuzzurs, which were touched and remitted. A salute of twenty-one guns was given to the deputation as representative of the Nizam, who is entitled to that number, and not to Sir Salar Jung, who is personally only an Excellency. The Minister retired with his Sirdars, who were much more splendid than their leader, and who did not wear a very contented aspect for reasons unknown to us.

After him came Keshree Singjee, the Maharaja of Edur, a fifteen-gun Prince, a handsome, soft-faced, voluptuous-looking youth, who was more at his ease than any of his fellows. His father was a K.C.S.I., and Member of the Legislative Council of Bombay, and the Prince is a minor, and is receiving his education from a tutor appointed by the Director of Public Instruction. His State, which has a population of only 220,000, is scarcely defined as to its boundaries, but is accurately measured as to revenues, of which the net amount is 25,000*l.* a year. The Prince advanced only three paces to meet him, and led him for so many when he was leaving, but the Chief went away in excellent humour and full of smiles, followed by his six chief Sirdars in very fine dresses. He congratulated the Prince on his birthday, and hoped for the honour of a visit from him at Edur.

Next came Sir Charles Napier's old friend, Meer Ali Morad, of Khyrpoor, in quaint Sindian headdress, with a dyed beard, who talked to the Prince of his shooting days with the most perfect frankness, and expressed his regret that he could not show him some sport in the way a M.F.H. would lament a hard frost to a winter visitor; but he was not entitled to even one step in advance, and was received by the Prince standing fast before the throne. However, he received his uttur and pân from the Royal hands. Though he is only sixty-one, he seems very old, and he retains his cheerfulness under rather trying circumstances. It is of not much benefit to revert to the very doubtful circumstances under which he was made Rais after Sind was annexed, but for him it is enough that he was deprived of the title and of most of his land in 1850, because he claimed more than he was entitled to, and that he was left only what his father bequeathed him. He is very poor and very proud, and has very little power or influence, but he is considered by sporting men "not a bad sort of fellow," and he made a very favourable impression. His Beloochee Sirdars were of the fiercest and finest-looking we have yet seen. When he left it was a little after noon, and if the Prince was not tired of the standing up and sitting down in that heated room, some of his suite certainly were. However, there was no respite save for a minute or two, when the Prince walked into the outer hall and looked out from the verandah on the Park outside, which was filled with the people in attendance on the visitors. There was still much to be done.

After these great personages had been received and dismissed, their Highnesses the Nawab of Joonagurh, the Jam of Nowanuggur, the Thakoor Sahib of Bhownuggur, the Raj-Sahib of Dhrangdra, the Raja of Rajpeepla, the Dewan of Palanpoor, and the Nawab of Radhanpoor, were received in private audience, a very interesting group of picturesque personages, mostly in bare feet and fine turbans—of whom there are probably few persons in or out of India who have heard anything, even the names, unless the officials immediately charged with the administration of the India House and Foreign Office.

The Nawab of Joonaguhr comes of a race of soldiers, the first of which known to Indian history seized on the district of Torith, from the capital of which the Chief takes his title seven generations back. He pays out of his revenue of 600,000 rupees a sum of 28,394 rupees to the British and a sum of 36,413 rupees to the Baroda Government. The Jam of Nowanuggur enjoys revenues of 600,000 rupees, of which 50,312 rs. go to the British Government, 64,183 rs. to the Baroda Government, and 4893 rs. to the Nawab of Joonagurh. He is the head of the Jahrejah Rajpoots, and his ancestors, coming from Kutch, established their rule in 1542 by force of arms; and one of them made an attempt to shake off the authority of the British Government in 1811, but was quite unsuccessful. The Thakoor Sahib boasts a pedigree of nearly nine centuries, and now rules a prosperous little State with a revenue of 800,000 rupees, of which he pays 130,000 rs. annually as tribute to the British

Government. Dhrangdra is a small State, but its Chief, a Raj Sahib, is head of the Jhulla Rajpoots. He has 160,000 rupees a year, of which he gives 40,000 rs. as tribute. The Rajpeepla Chief seemed to be under the influence of considerable excitement, as though he were angered by something, and exhibited some temper when one of the officials placed his hand on his shoulder to direct him to his place—a most vivacious, bright-eyed, sprightly man who was evidently anxious that his little son should be noticed, and was immensely pleased when Sir Bartle Frere spoke to him, and said a few words to the boy on leaving. He comes of a Rajpoot race, which maintained its independence till the time of Akbar, and he still rules over an area of 4500 square miles, and enjoys a revenue of 375,000 rupees, of which he pays 20,000 rupees annually towards the maintenance of the Guzerat Bheel Corps. He possesses the power of trying any but British subjects for criminal offences. The Dewan of Palanpoor belongs to an Afghan family, which came to Bahár in the time of Humayoon, and became masters of large territory, but they were deprived of much of their possessions, and all that remains to them now is an area of 4384 square miles, peopled by 178,000 people, and a revenue of 300,000 rupees, of which he pays 45,512 to the Gaekwar. Radhanpoor is a little district of 833 miles square, with a population of 46,000 souls, and a revenue of 250,000 rupees. It pays no tribute, but it has in lack of protection to submit to black mail from its neighbours. The Chief is descended from a Persian adventurer of Ispahan, who carried his way with his sword, and left sons to develop his fortunes. One of these became possessor of large part of Guzerat, but his descendants suffered the loss of much of it at the hands of the house of Baroda. He has power to try for criminal offences.

At 12.50 P.M. their Highnesses the Raja of Baria, the Raja of Loonawara, the Nawab of Balasinoor, the Raja of Chota Oodeypoor, the Raja of Soonth, the Sir Desai of Sawant-Wari, the Raja of Dharampoor, and the Nawab of Jinjera successively paid private visits to the Prince. The ceremonies were the same as at the preceding visits, except that on the arrival and the departure of the Raja of Baria and of the Raja of Dharampoor a salute of nine guns was fired, whereas the others had eleven guns each. These Chiefs generally belonged to the Rewa Kanta States. The first of them is a young man, who is owner rather than ruler of a small territory of 1600 square miles, with a revenue of 75,000 rupees, of which 12,000 rupees are paid to our Government. The second has a still smaller estate and revenue; and he must be poor indeed, for out of less than 4200*l.* per annum he pays 1600*l.* to the British and 230*l.* to the Raja of Balasinoor, who rules over 400 square miles, and enjoys its revenue of 40,000 rupees, from which 11,079 rupees go to the British Government. These small Chiefs and the Ruler of Chota Oodeypoor (who has an estate 3000 miles square, and a revenue of 100,000 rupees, of which 8770 rupees go to the Gaekwar) belong to races and families closely connected. But the Raja of Soonth, who has only a little estate of 900 square miles, and a revenue of 22,000 rupees, claims descent from the ancient Rajas of Malwa. He is reduced to an income of 2200*l.* a year, of which he pays 600*l.* to the British Government. The Sir Desai of Sawant-Wari is in a protected condition. In 1730 his ancestor was an ally of the British, who were glad to make a treaty with him for the plunder of the famous Angria, and to give him all the conquered territory except Gheria and Kenneree. His successors were piratically inclined; and our dealings with the race were not conducted with clean hands. The present man is an opium-eater, and his State (900 square miles and 153,000 people, with a revenue of 200,000 rupees) is managed for him. Of the Dharampoor Raja little is known, even to Captain Malleson, except that he administers the affairs of 15,000 people, whom he can try for capital offences, and that he has a revenue of 90,000 rupees, of which 6500 are paid in tribute. The Hubshee Chief, Nawab of Junjeera, or Jinjeera, Ibrahim Mahomed Khan, did not attract as much attention as the singular history of the State he rules, the race he represents, and the character of the man merited. The Nawabship is of very curious origin. Nearly 400 years ago certain Abyssinians, who in those days had relations with the Indian States on the coast, obtained permission to land 300 boxes (the number is suspicious) of reputed merchandise on the island. Each box contained a soldier, and the living imports seized on Rajpoori and Jinjeera. The Abyssinian admirals, who administered the affairs of these parts subsequently, under the Ahmednuggur Kings, were elected, and were styled Wazeers, and an African Colony grew up and waxed so strong, that the Seedee Futteh Khan, their Chief, not only defeated the Peishwa's army, in 1659, with great slaughter, but maintained his independence. Sivajee in person took Rajpoori in 1661; but was effectively held in check by the Fort of Jinjeera. Though he conquered every other part of Konkan, Sivajee never could obtain possession of the island. Finally, the Seedee Chiefs acknowledged the sovereignty of the Peishwa; but the extraordinary vitality of these Abyssinian admirals, and the long-sustained independence of their State, are among the curiosities of history. Jinjeera now contains only

324 square miles, 83,000 people, and it yields a revenue of 330,000 rupees a year. The first time he ever left his island was when Sir Bartle Frere was Governor. He started with the intention of visiting Bombay; but his heart failed him when he came in sight of the harbour, and saw the great mass of shipping. In fact, the Hubshee Nawab was profoundly suspicious of his neighbour, and obstinately —shall I say wisely?—refused to have anything to say to us. He would not make any treaty, enter into any arrangement, nor acknowledge any obligation; he would pay no tribute, and permit no foreigner to live in his State. Naturally, therefore, when there was a leisure moment, the British Government interfered on the general ground of "misconduct and oppression;" and although they were indifferent to their existence for more than half a century, the Bombay authorities, in 1867, deprived the Nawab of his criminal jurisdiction. He came to Bombay to pay his respects to the Duke of Edinburgh in 1870, and sought the recovery of his powers, but in vain. He had, perforce, to agree to do as he was bid, and now all goes well.

The first sensation experienced when the last of the durbarees had departed was naturally enough one of thankfulness. Who does not feel a sense of relief when a levee is at an end? And this was a levee held under difficult circumstances. There was yet much for the Prince to do ere his birthday could become yesterday. The Viceroy was received, and had a long conversation with the Prince before the latter left Parell House on a very interesting occasion. He went to pay a visit to the *Serapis*, where the crew were enjoying a dinner provided by the Prince, the men of the *Osborne*, I believe, being similarly treated. There was a fine work of the confectioners' art ready in the saloon, which the Prince cut, and his health was drunk with much feeling. Telegrams were exchanged between Sandringham and Bombay. The passage of the Prince between the shore and the ships was, of course, made with pomp, salutes, and yards manned, flags, music, cheering; and when he landed, the city, which had been in great excitement since yesterday, was beginning to light up, for this was the happy occasion for which the native world had been longing—the general illumination of the fleet and of the town—a spectacle that never can be forgotten. It was a surprise even to those who had passed through the streets the night before.

The ships were so brightly illuminated that the great bay seemed as if it were filled with rows of fiery pyramids. The sea that lapped the sweep of the bay and all its curvings from Malabar Point to Elephanta was fringed with flame, and broke on shores of fire. The Prince, attended by the Viceroy, the Governor, the officers of State, of the Army and Navy, and the Chiefs, drove through the principal streets from Mazagone to Parell, passing by every public building and object of interest on the way. None who have not seen an Indian illumination can imagine the beautiful effect of the soft light of the buttee, or the oil-lamp, a small saucer of baked clay, with a piece of cotton-wick. The lamps were fed incessantly by men and women with cans of oil. The inscriptions were monotonous, and rarely deviated from the stereotyped "Welcomes;" though now and then one came upon an exceptional expression, such as "Tell Mamma we're happy,"—"Welcome thee, our future Emperor,"—"Welcome our future father and King," and the like.

A State banquet was given by the Governor in honour of the Prince's birthday.

"It has long been my earnest wish," said the Prince in returning thanks for his health, which was proposed by the Governor—"the dream of my life—to visit India; and, now that my desire has been gratified, I can only say, Sir Philip Wodehouse, how much pleased I am to have spent my thirty-fourth birthday under your roof in Bombay. I shall remember with satisfaction the hospitable reception I have had from the Governor and all here as long as I

THE BUTTEE-WALLAH.

live, and I believe that I may regard what I have experienced in Bombay as a guarantee of the future of my progress through this great Empire, which forms so important a part of the dominions of the Queen." These few words were prophetic and true to a degree which few dared to anticipate. A reception, attended by many of the Native Chiefs, in addition to the elite of the European community, followed, and the festivity was not brought to a close till late at night.

November 10th.—The Governor-General sets out to-day on a tour, and when he takes leave of the Prince will see him no more till he receives his Royal Highness as his guest in Government House, Calcutta. The "act of respect" has been performed, and having welcomed the Prince to India, Lord Northbrook departs with his Staff and Body Guard, and exhibits his state to the Chiefs of Rajpootana, and to places seldom if ever visited by his predecessors. Whilst the Prince is engaged in a sedulous execution of the programme prepared for Bombay, official intelligence of the spread of cholera renders it very doubtful if the shooting excursion in Southern India will be practicable. Colonel Michael, who was charged with the arrangements, and who is quartered in camp, hopes that the reports will turn out to be exaggerated. After breakfast the last series of visits began. When the Prince had taken his place before the Chair of State once more, and all things had been rightly ordered, the minor Chiefs, who had been fast assembling, were marshalled in the outer rooms to be presented. First came Chiefs of Kattywar, of the second class, whose distinctive title is "Thakoor Sahib," and who exercise legal jurisdiction in the Kattywar Courts for capital offences, unless the accused are British subjects. There were a certain number of retainers allowed to each, but these were not presented to the Prince; and the Chiefs are not entitled to return visits from him. Each Thakoor was led by one of the Staff to the threshold of the Audience Chamber, where he was received by Major Henderson or Major Sartorius, who, taking him by one hand, walked slowly up, and announced the Thakoor's name. The "conducting" of the Chiefs was a curious ceremony. The Political Officer took the hand of the conductee in his own, and thus led him to the presence as if he were in some sort of custody; and the appearance was intensified by the attitude at times of another officer at the other side of the honoured person. The Thakoor made obeisance, the Prince bowed, and then the Chief was pointed out his chair on the right of the Prince; his followers took their seats in the chairs behind him. The Chiefs retired in due order, followed by their retainers and salaaming to the Prince.

This formula was followed closely, and it was repeated, *mutatis mutandis*, in the case of Chiefs of equal rank. It will be seen that to Rajas and Nawabs of lower degree there was not accorded the favour of a personal reception outside the Government House by a member of the Royal suite. The higher honour—which means that when one officer of the suite had had quite enough of trotting as hard as he could 500 yards up and down in the sun, he was relieved by another, and that when one equerry or aide-de-camp had done his share of the receptions of Chiefs, another took his place—is greatly prized.

The first who came, the Thakoor Sahib of Morvee, is owner of 125 villages, with a population of 91,000 souls, and a revenue of 65,000*l.* a year, and pays a tribute of 4000*l.* Next, though his revenue is only 12,500*l.*, out of which he pays 1200*l.* to Government, came the Thakoor Sahib of Wankaneer. The Thakoor of Palitana, a Rajpoot, aged thirty-one, whose State contains a population of 52,000, and whose city is in high repute among Rajpoot pilgrims, was next. Another Rajpoot — the Thakoor Sahib of Derole—a poor man, with a State of sixty-one villages, a population of 18,500, and a gross revenue of 15,000*l.* a year—followed. After him came the Thakoor of Limree, a minor, pupil of the Rajcoomar College, whose revenue is estimated at 21,000*l.* a year.

Then came the Thakoor Sahib of Wadhwan, Raja of Rajeer, also a minor, and pupil at the Rajcoomar College, who draws 35,000*l.* a year from his villages, pays 3250*l.* to the British Government, and 6230*l.* to the Nawab of Junagarh, who seems to be the greatest of these Chiefs. Next, at 12.20 P.M., six Sirdars of Sattara, the Deccan, and Konkan, who do not possess the power of life and death, but who belong to families of the most extraordinary antiquity, were received. The first was the Swamee of Chafool, but he was by no means the first in point of birth; for the Punt Prithinidee of Aond, who was presented after him, boasts of a title higher than the Peishwa's own, and still holds part of the lands his fathers held from Sivajee. Punt Sucheo of Bhore, who has a jagheer of 500 square miles, came next; then the Chief of Phultun (400 square miles), the Chief of Vinchoor, C.S.I., and the Raja of Jowah. When these were dismissed, which was done in ten minutes, there was still a third body of Chiefs to be presented to the Prince. These were the Raja of Moodhole; the senior and junior Chiefs of Sanglee, and of Meeruj; the Chiefs of Koorundwar and of Ramdroog. The Raja of Jowah and the junior Chief of Sanglee would have made a sensation anywhere. In raiment and face and figure these men were various—some were laden with jewels, some were plainly clad, but as each sat sword in hand he looked a gentleman—better sitting, awkward as it is, than walking in the horrid restraint of patent leather shoes or *bottines*. Their behaviour was admirable—no staring or pushing, no curious gestures or expressions of surprise, but perfect self-possession and repose.

Hitherto opportunities of appreciating the force of the sun not in the shade have not been many, but the drive this afternoon amply atoned for want of experience of that sort. The Prince, accompanied by Sir Philip Wodehouse, left Parell, with all the usual honours of guard, band, colours, and salute, at a quarter past 3 P.M., escorted by a body of the 3rd Hussars. Although this is the cold season, the sun was intensely hot, and the smallest protection—such as a shady piece of road—was eagerly welcomed. There were many thousands along the route, but the many tens of thousands of people had disappeared. Some time after 4 P.M., the Prince alighted at the Secretariat, an enormous pile of buildings, not unsightly or incommodious, where the chief clerks of the Government, who rejoice in the title of "Secretary," carry on their business. Here he was received by the Chief Justice and Commander-in-Chief, the Members of the Council, the Roman Catholic Bishop, the Commander-in-Chief of Her Majesty's naval forces in India (I take the order from the official programme), and was attended to the Presence Room. Having taken his place on an elevated dais in a large room, honoured by that style and dignity, the door was thrown open, and the levee commenced. It may be an excellent institution in Europe, but in Bombay, in a temperature approaching that of the dog-days, it is certainly one of the least agreeable ceremonies that can be, whether for Europeans or natives. The former were naturally desirous of paying their respects to the Prince, although the utmost notice he could bestow upon them was a bow as their names were announced. As to the native gentlemen, some of them appeared so utterly astonished and unhinged as to lose all power of locomotion; so that it was necessary to seduce them gently away from the Royal presence, or occasionally, indeed, to direct their uncertain steps with more vigour than politeness. It may be imagined what the effort of standing in a smothering atmosphere for more than one mortal hour, and making at least two thousand bows in the time, must have been. However, at last, the levee was brought to an end. The doors were peremptorily closed at 5 o'clock, and many were left outside, too late to have the honour for which they so much longed. A much more pleasing ceremonial followed, although it was not without its share of toil—the Children's Fête, held upon an open space near the harbour,—which afforded a very pretty spectacle. Boys and girls of all castes, classes, and creeds, dressed in the most brilliant colours, were collected under their various teachers, to the number of 7000, with banners flying, and insignia denoting the schools to which they belonged, driving one again for comparison to the oft-used image of wide-spread banks of flowers in full bloom; and these were in full bloom, if not with ruddy cheeks, at least with that peculiar light and glow which indicate youth and health in this part of the world, and with an intensity of eye which, except in Spain and Italy, is not seen out of India; and as the Prince, almost with difficulty, made his way up to the elevated stand where he was to hear the song in his honour, and to present himself to the little multitude, the cries, the cheers, and hurrahs, which arose, indicated their possession of excellent lungs. Finally, he was almost smothered in garlands and wreaths of flowers. The Parsees were remarkable for the richness of their dresses, and for the startling effects of colour which they exhibited. The evening was fixed for the return visits, which began after the inspection of the children.

When the Prince returned the visits of the Chiefs at their own residences the restraint and silence, which had been so remarkable, vanished. There were, to be sure, formalities duly prescribed in printed circulars, but the Prince spoke unreservedly to the Chiefs, and the effect of his ease and kindness was magical.

The first visit was to the Maharaja of Kolhapoor, four of whose principal officers escorted the Prince at

6 o'clock from the Esplanade, near the Secretariat. The Chief's residence, hired for the occasion, was some distance from the Fort. The crowds of natives in the streets, augmenting in density as the procession reached the place where guards of honour, artillery, triumphal arches, illuminated gardens, and a bungalow of great size, as light as day, indicated that the Prince was expected, were interested to the utmost, especially the Hindoos, who took it as a compliment to themselves that the Shahzadah was about to honour one whose lineage they so much respect. In the court before the door the Native forces of the State were represented by some very picturesque cavalry and footmen. The Sirdars of Kolhapoor, surrounding their Raja, were arranged outside the house. The hall was full of retainers, and the staircases were lined by warriors and servitors armed to the teeth. As to the tumult of music and cannon, the drumming and flourishing of trumpets and instruments of auricular torture, which arose when the Prince, descending from his carriage, was received by the Raja, it must have been heard to have been appreciated. The State apartment was very richly decorated, and was not wanting in chandeliers, coloured prints, and mirrors. The Prince and the Raja, hand in hand, advanced between the lines of seats arranged at each side of the room, and sat down in chairs at the end. The Sirdars sat on the left, the English on the right. The Prince expressed the pleasure he had in meeting with a Chief with whom it was possible to converse. He was aware that the late Raja had died at Florence, on his way to England. He much regretted the occurrence; but he trusted that it would not prevent the Raja from visiting him some day, and he would be always glad to hear of the progress made in his education. Then came a presentation of all the Native officers to the Prince by the Political Officer on duty,

each of whom presented his nuzzur, which was "touched and remitted." While this interview was proceeding, the presents were being laid out in an adjoining room. Then the Maharaja gave the Prince uttur and pân, and conducted him to his carriage, which was met outside by a deputation of the Sirdars of Oodeypoor. Then another drive through crowded suburbs and under illuminated arches to the residence of the young Chief, who had an enormous establishment of armed retainers and troops, horse and foot, drawn up in his court-yard, in addition to the British guard of honour, band, and colours, and to the artillery. "God save the Queen;" Royal salute; the same exchange of ceremonial speeches and presents. The Prince pleased and flattered the Máhárána greatly, it would seem, by the simple remark that he had heard of the great antiquity of his house, and had read in history of the gallant deeds of his ancestors. He regretted that his limited stay in India would prevent his visiting the capital of such a distinguished and ancient race, which he had heard was one of the most interesting and beautiful in India. As the Máhárána was going back to his capital in order to meet the Viceroy, who was setting out on a tour to Rajpootana and the Central Provinces, the Prince expressed a hope that he would not remain unnecessarily in Bombay on his account. The next visit was to the Gaekwar. Four of the chief Sirdars of Baroda came to the gate of the residence of the Máhárána of Oodeypoor to escort the Prince to the residence hired for his Highness near Malabar Hill. The Gaekwar met the Prince at the step, and conducted him upstairs to a seat in a long room lighted most brilliantly, and when the Durbar was set, the sight was very fine, for the Court of Baroda is still magnificent. It is hard to find small-talk for a little boy like the Gaekwar, but the Prince charmed him by speaking of illuminations and horsemanship. The Gaekwar is very fond of riding, and his Royal Highness encouraged him to persist in it. As he was in the carriage which came immediately behind the Prince's, he could see the illuminations to perfection, and he expressed his pleasure with childish freedom; but he did not seem quite so cheerful when the Prince alluded to his studies, said he would watch over his career with interest, and hoped he would pay especial attention to English, which he would find so useful. He enjoined him not to neglect his writing. The Prince, before leaving, had an interview with Jumnabaae, who may be called the "Queen-Mother," and then drove off, followed by the Baroda Sirdars, back to Parell.

And then it was just as much as one could do to get to his tent, and rub off the smut and black of illumination and flaring torches in a welcome bath—once a shower of unctuous rain was let fall from a triumphal arch on the State carriage and its occupants, owing to a jar given to the frail edifice by the wheel—dress, and run to the House to get to one's place before the Prince and the Governor led the way to the Banqueting Hall. When dinner was over, there was a movement for the grand Ball given by the Byculla Club, of which all European Bombay had been talking, thinking, and dreaming for weeks; but it was not given to every one to have strength for these festivities, which, after all, were like those exotics which are chiefly valuable because they flourish under adverse circumstances. There were always absentees, or some who treated such occasions as men do the cold water plunge of the Russian bath—popped in and hopped out again. Perhaps the Duke of Sutherland and Sir Bartle Frere were among the latter, and certainly Canon Duckworth was of the former, but the Prince was never known to disappoint expectations, or to throw a chill over such gatherings by retiring early—"Royauté oblige" with him; and the Byculla Ball was, by all accounts, worthy of his presence, and was a great credit to those who had the management, and who were seen to grow old prematurely under the weight of care, till all wrinkles were smoothed by its brilliant success. The jackals and minars, which had been welcoming dawn round my tent, were banished by the cheerful voices of my neighbours as they returned, one of whom was good enough to come in and give me his first and freshest impressions of the ball, and to assure me I had "missed one of the jolliest things a fellow could see—good rooms, good supper, good wines, good music, good partners, and capital floor."

November 11th.—After breakfast hour a train of ragged fellows, some leading apes and others carrying bags, was seen coming up the main street of the camp. These were followed by seven or eight ugly, shapeless, elderly women, in bright drapery, with what are here considered to be musical instruments in their hands. They squatted apart—conjurors, ape-leaders, singing women—under the shade of the trees in front of the tents. Presently the Prince sauntered down from Government House and took a seat in front of the tent of Lord Charles Beresford, and the charmers and conjurors prepared for their exhibition; but the natives had no idea of the rank of the person before them. The camp-followers and soldiers from the tents near at hand gathered round, till one of the suite, remembering what had occurred on a similar occasion in India, cleared them away. The juggler and the snake-charmer first showed off all the orthodox tricks of their confraternity. They were two only—a withered vivacious juggler and a ragged snake-charming confederate—chatty old fellows, whose skin hung on their bones as if it were cracked brown paper. They did clever "passes," swallowed and spat out fire, exhibited an inexhaustible water-vessel, and walked on wooden pattens, held on by the feet making a vacuum with the sole. The juggler suddenly produced two cobras out of one of the baskets, which had been turned over, inside out, in our presence. A thrill went through the spectators as the reptiles, hissing fiercely, raised their flaming eyes and hooded crests and reared on end as if to strike the garrulous charmer. It was not the drumming or the playing of his friend on the dry gourd which drew the reptiles out of cover. The snakes danced to the music of a gourd drum, but it was with rage and fear, not with pleasure. Dr. Fayrer opened the jaws of the larger with a stick while the man held it, and showed the Prince where the fangs were *not*. Meantime a mango-seed, which we had seen placed in the earth, was growing rapidly, and the old fellow in an interval of snake-charming exposed a bright green tree, some 18 inches high in the ground, where he had apparently only put in a seed, covered with a dirty cloth. Then another of the famous legendary feats of the Indian juggler was executed. A shallow basket, about 18 inches high and 3 feet long, with a cover, was placed before the Prince. It was plain "there was no deceit." It was a basket, and nothing more or less, and it was put on the bare earth before our eyes. A lad of twelve or so, slight of figure and pleasant of face, with not an article of dress on him save his loin-cloth and turban, came out from the group of natives near at hand. Him the jugglers, chattering the while, bound up hand and foot, *à la* "Brothers Anyone," with strong twine. Then the old fellow slipped a sack of strong netting over the lad, and squeezed him down on his haunches so that he could tie the cords securely over the captive's head; he then lifted him from the ground to show how securely the sack was fastened. He put the boy into the basket with great force, as it seemed, and appeared to have difficulty in fitting the lid on the top. When that was done, the older juggler began to talk to the basket. Presently the lid was agitated, the cord and net were jerked out on the ground. The juggler ran at the basket, jumped on the top, stamped on it in a fury, crushed in the lid, took a stick and drove it through the wicker-work. He lifted up the lid. The basket was empty! Then came a voice as of the lad who had been inside it, and lo! up in the branches of one of the trees near us was just such a youth! It was certainly a very clever trick, and done with the most simple adjuncts. The mango-tree, when it was next uncovered, appeared hung with tiny fruit. The ape-men showed off their favourites, which had been trained apparently to turn the British soldier into derision, and went through the manual and platoon exercise in a shockingly reckless manner, winding up with a general quarrel. Finally the singing-women began a ditty; but a few staves were quite sufficient to prove that the taste for native music must be acquired.

The accounts from the hunting-grounds left no doubt that cholera has broken out epidemically in the district which lies between the coast and "Michael's Valley." Reports from the *shikarries*, enough to make one feel exceedingly bitter against the cholera and its untimely visit, represent that bison and ibex are swarming all around the site of the intended camp. But Dr. Fayrer was quite resolute; nothing would induce him to consent to the Prince's passing through the cholera-infected region, where there was also fear of catching fever. With heavy hearts it was decided that the landing at Beypore must be, if not abandoned, at least excluded for the present from the programme. It was no comfort to learn that we were to have the opportunity of seeing the Baroda Highlanders. This eccentric-looking corps was the creation of a former Gaekwar, who succeeded in procuring all the materials for Highlanders except the men. He could not help Indians having brown skins; and no matter how a real Highlander's legs may be burnt by the sun, they cannot assume the Oriental bronze. The "Highlanders," about 300 strong, came marching up gaily to the strains of their own bagpipes, which were just as musical as though they were tuned by Alister MacAlister himself, and drew up in line outside the entrance to Parell. They wore what seemed to me the clothing of a Highland regiment. Probably their coats might have been new when purchased, but certainly they were not made for them. In coats, kilts, bonnets, and feathers, stockings and shoes, they were as like Highlanders as could be—quite as tall, or taller, if not so broad as the average of Scotch battalions; but there was one startling innovation in the costume. Whether to imitate the colour of Briton's flesh or from motives of decency I cannot say, but anyhow, the Baroda Highlanders wore pink calico breeches, which came down below the knees, over which their stockings were drawn above the calf of the leg.

The return visits of the Prince to the Maharaja of Edur, and to Chiefs of equal and minor degree whom he had received, but whom he could not see at their own residences, were made at 3 P.M. at the Secretariat, in a room set apart for that purpose, each Chief being assigned an apartment which was provided with chairs of State and double rows of seats. On the Prince leaving the first Chief, he was met at the door of the reception-room by the next, to whom he then paid a short visit.

It did not strike me that it was either a satisfactory or becoming arrangement, and I was not surprised to hear that it had caused annoyance to the Chiefs when the Viceroy called on them in the same way, but the honour of receiving the Prince was some compensation. To the eye all went well, and there was a pleasant if "warm" interchange of civilities; in fact, the heat in the rooms was just on the verge of being unbearable. The good people of Bombay had been for some time preparing a dinner in honour of the Prince's visit, to the sailors of the fleet, to which his Royal Highness proceeded when these return visits were over, and it was a good idea well carried out and thoroughly appreciated. And to hear these two thousand sailors cheer when they saw the Prince of Wales enter and advance to the centre of the canvas hall, all draped with flags, was great comfort in itself—a sort of marine assurance that there was, without Chauvinism, no want of the old stuff which some think thinned and worn-out by chafing innovation! No wonder the Prince wanted to see them as they saw him, and so he called for a chair to stand upon, and mounting the plank with a glass in his hand exclaimed, "My lads!"—such a combination of roar and laugh as broke out at this!—"My lads! I am glad to meet you all! I drink your good health and a happy voyage home!" Well, it would be very difficult to say what these two thousand men would not have tried to do at the Prince's bidding when he spoke these words. I am glad their only task was to keep quiet and get on board, and that they did in most orderly fashion—albeit they put the wreaths of flowers on their necks, and ornamented their caps with the little flags which graced the table. There never were better behaved fellows, not only at the vast feast spread in immense tents wherein tables had no time to groan under beef, pudding and beer, and had to bear a good deal of dancing all during the festivities, but in the streets. Moreover, on this day there was a fête of great grandeur, if of excessive ritual; the Prince laid the foundation stone of Elphinstone Docks with Masonic honours—not honours merely, but ceremonies of the most orthodox complication and elaborateness. The only mistake lay, perhaps, in inviting the Chiefs to come and see, and placing them where they could not see anything. It was a surprise to the ignorant to see Parsee, Mahomedan and Hindoo members of the craft, but they were there in considerable numbers. There was an address and reply—there was a procession of Masons in all their glory, and then the stone was laid amid great rejoicing. When that was done, the Prince had to take off his Masonic robes and go through yet another duty ere dinner time. I shall not attempt any description of what occurred on these occasions, although each had distinctive features—exchanges of courtesies, presentations, and presents, garlands and uttur and pân, pleasant speeches, magnificent dresses, and immense and costly preparations.

The return visit to the deputation under Sir Salar Jung and other high officers from the Nizam of Hyderabad was paid at 6.15 P.M. The Nizam's deputation attended the Prince to the entrance of the villa which had been engaged at large cost for the use of the representatives of the minor—at present almost an invalid under his mother's care. The reception was one of great state and formality; but the conversation was of a friendly and gracious character. The Prince's demeanour, under the circumstances, was a matter of great moment to these Sirdars; but there was not the least appearance of reserve on his part. The Maharaja of Mysore was visited afterwards, and the programme fixed the Royal arrival at 6.30 P.M. The Sirdars of the Rao of Kutch awaited the Prince, who paid a visit to their Chief on leaving the Maharaja. Another dinner and a reception at Parell brought the day to a close.

November 12th.—There is news of something more than

the average sickness in the fleet, and the death of a boy on board the *Serapis* from cholera is reported. Before breakfast the *box-wallahs* came down in force upon the camp, generally selecting, by a sort of natural or trade intuition, tents the proprietors of which were likely to be good customers. Ganesh, Lord Charles Beresford's kitmagar and factotum, however, afforded him efficient protection, and gave some very useful information respecting the value of the articles for sale, which, without that assistance, if taken at anything like what they were offered for, would certainly have been dear. Some of the customers entered into the traffic in a novel spirit, offering to toss "double or quits;" and after a time the astute Bombay box-wallahs entered into the idea, and eagerly accepted it. Lord Carington, who had at first very fair success in tossing, "won" a ring. The man had asked fifty rupees for it; Lord Carington offered to toss whether he would give twenty or forty, or something of the sort. He won, and was very much pleased, not so much at the value of the ring as at "doing the box-wallah;" but, on inquiry, he ascertained that the ring might have been purchased, at the very outside, for two rupees in the bazaar. Presents offered by the Chiefs, and accepted by the Prince, are already pouring in to Parell in great quantities. Groups of Native Police are constantly on duty, watching porters carrying cases and boxes, who are followed by the jealous officers of the Chiefs, into the rooms where they are consigned to Mr. Isaacson, of the India Office, who has charge of them. The Political Agents had informed the Government of Bombay what presents would be made and what would be the value of them; in some instances apparently directing, or at least advising, what the presents should be. Thus, one Political Agent writes that he will advise his Chiefs when they go to Bombay to buy 5000 rupees' worth of Surat manufactures. Another Agent is told by the Government that his Chief is not expected to make any present at all. In other instances the Agent states that the Chief does not intend to offer presents. In others, the Agent expresses "little doubt that the Chief would present a specimen of work costing" so much. The Duke of Sutherland went off at an early hour, to inspect the various institutions of Bombay, under the guidance of Surgeon-Major Hewlett, and no better could be.

The Prince was entertained in the evening at a banquet in the caves of Elephanta, to which invitations were necessarily limited. This was not the first time that these caves, of which Heber, Dr. Wilson, Forbes, and many others of a long list of travellers, British and foreign, have given descriptions, have been made the scene of a Christian festivity; but the natives, it is said, do not regard such apparent desecrations of their holy places with anything like the feeling with which we should see a number of Brahmins indulging in the excesses of the Holee festival, or Mahometans celebrating the Mohurrum inside Westminster Abbey. The Brahmins are, according to one local paper, men of resource, for they told the Hindoos in Bombay that the Prince of Wales and the Europeans went to Elephanta to worship the Deity there, and to do *juttra* to Shiva. Two steamers conveyed the Prince and the favoured guests of the Governor from the Bay across to the island, where they were landed at the pier, not without difficulty, for the water is shallow. The sun had set, and the disembarkation was effected by torchlight carried by men wading up to their middle, sufficiently picturesque in themselves, and there were fires on the beach, and an illumination—how often must that word be written?—to guide the vessels. There is a steep winding ascent to Garipuri—"the City of Caves"—for three quarters of a mile, which was lighted up by lamps suspended from a continuous framework of bamboos. One thousand and one steps, men said, to the top. It seemed more like ten thousand, and as we mounted "the boldest held his breath for a time," now and then, and the coolest was very hot, nor did any despise the halting-places on the way, or disdain to look out on the Bay where the men-of-war lay, tricked out with dotted lines of light like strings of stars, preparing for the great effect which was to glorify the return of the Prince. When the visitor enters the excavations, passing through the double row of pillars, which look as though they were supporting the mountain, or the squared mass of it, here chiselled into a grand portico, he sees the work of men who must have been, as Mr. Maclean remarks, imbued with a religion in which there was an element of sublime mystery and awful grandeur now completely lost in practices which are grotesque and contemptible. But these creations, solid as the rock, are perishing—these idols of stone are crumbling away, although they are not, it is believed, a thousand years old. Their stony eyes seemed to be glaring on the great array of tables covered with cloths and plates and dishes. The faces of extraordinary power and beauty, the gigantic forms cut with decision and boldness which challenge admiration and wonder, may seem to us to violate the rules of proportion and to indicate vicious taste, but it should be remembered that they are but the efforts of the sculptors to convey their impressions of beings of divine not of human type—Mahadeva, the three-faced god—the goddess with a single breast, Paravati, the wife of Shiva—the sculptures around the shrine of Linga—all indicate struggles to express in stone the attributes of extraordinary beauty, power, strength, fecundity.

I confess that Elephanta did not appear to me a happy choice for a dining place *per se*, although sufficiently curious and novel. In broad daylight, when the view over the Bay could be enjoyed from the shelter of the cool caves, I can fancy that the island would not be a bad resort for a picnic party, provided always they cleared away the debris of their feast; but when the excavations are lighted up and the feast spread, the glare and heat of torches and the smell of oil, combined with the close reeking air, produce an odorous temperature by no means enjoyable by any but an Eskimo, who would find the combination very agreeable. The cooking or warming of the dishes must be effected inside, in chambers dedicated by the laborious contrivers to religious or superstitious use; and the vast halls were filled with the inappropriate incense of chandeliers, lamps, and candles, suspended from the roof ranged round the pillars, and placed on pyramidal stands on the floor. The Prince and the Governor and the *dii majores* sat at an elevated table, at right angles to which were ranged the tables of the general company, and when the feast was over, and the toasts of the Queen and of the Prince had been given by Sir P. Wodehouse and received with acclamation, the party made an inspection of the chambers of the Temple, admiring especially the massive columns with their beautiful carved capitals—works quite apart—and then escaped to the outer air, and descended the steps under the trellis archway of lamps, now hotter than ever, towards the pier. But before they reached the beach the island suddenly became volcanic; the double mountain begun to glow with fires; on the summit above the caves spirted up tongues of coloured flames, and then followed eruptions of rockets—we were in for more fireworks! It was rather a *sauve qui peut* from the sticks in some places; and when the Prince's launch pushed off from the shore it seemed as though Elephanta were resolving itself into red, blue, and green fires. And yet this was but a preparation—a kind of pyrotechnic prelude to what followed, when the procession of boats, escorted by the steamers, approached the two squadrons of the fleet, and passed down an alley of ships discharging volleys, in which the *Osborne* and *Serapis* were conspicuous as ever in their rivalry of fireworks.

> " Fire answers fire !—and thro' their paly flames,
> Each battle sees the other's umbered face."

I can say no more except that it was, all in all, perhaps, the most impressive of all the many displays of the kind made for the Prince's honour, and for the delectation of those who came to pay it to him. The moon, sailing in state in the bright starlight above, instead of diminishing the beauty and brightness of the scene, cast over the bay a sheen which increased greatly the pleasure which the eye conveyed to the beholder, the illuminated hulls and rigging of the ships, the coloured fires, the rocket flights were reflected in the silver mirror, and it was difficult to say where the sky ended and the sea began—the boats seemed to float on some new innocuous Phlegethon. But all that's bright must fade, and people must sleep ! and so the Prince landed and drove off to Parell, and that day was ended.

SWAMP SHOOTING.

CHAPTER V.

Visit to Baroda—Battle of Kirkee—Poonah Address—Gunnesh Khind—Rumours of War—Sivajee—The First Review—Going Somewhere—Ball at Parell—Departure for Baroda—The Reception—State Elephants—Residency at Baroda—Baroda Highlanders—The Gaekwar's Court—Scenes in the Arena—Sensible Rhinoceros—Zoologicsl Collection—Shikar Party—Cheetahs—Deer-Stalking—Native Officers—Palace of the Gaekwar—The Queen and the Gaekwar—Quail Shooting—Visit to the City—Return to Bombay—Uncertain where to go—Visitors to Hyderabad—A Hindoo Wedding—Departure from Bombay.

NOVEMBER 13TH.—At 5.30 A.M. all the servants in camp were turned out to send off luggage to the train, which started for Kirkee at 7 A.M.—that is, it was to have started, but it really did not go off for an hour and a half later. The news from the hunting-grounds in the south is still worse; Colonel Michael is in despair. He says that cholera is always to be found in India; that if its presence is to deter the Prince from going to his Valley it ought to prevent his going anywhere. But anyhow, the roads which had been made up the hill-sides for the Prince's accommodation to that happy Valley have been destroyed in a tremendous rainstorm. There has been no rain here, so everything seems to be against the expedition.

A special train to convey the Prince and suite to Poonah, 119 miles, was at the station close to Parell at 11 A.M. There was a guard of honour of Volunteers —Europeans, of course—whom the Prince inspected, and to whom he expressed his satisfaction at their appearance, and his approbation of the movement which has now extended over India; every Station of considerable size has its own corps. This was the first occasion on which the Prince travelled by rail in India, and he had now the first opportunity of becoming acquainted with the wonders of "*bundabust*," which are supposed to be so remarkable there in all Government departments. To each carriage was affixed a label with the names of those of the suite who were to occupy it; and in the same way the vehicles in which they were to be seated on their arrival were told off, generally with great exactness, all through the tour.

Sir Bartle Frere has recorded that an officer, who was quartered at one of the first stations we stopped at outside Bombay, Tannah, when it was an outpost, in 1808, was Brigadier in command of Peshawur, more than 1000 miles north of it, in 1858; but it may be doubted whether that vast stride was made quite over terra firma. There are some who think it would have been better to have dug down in what we had, for solid foundations for our power, than to have been so eager for new territory. But anyway, the Russian can point to no longer leap in the last fifty years than that wonderful skip from Tannah to Peshawur.

The ascent of the Bhore Ghaut and the scenery of the line have been so often described, that it would be as superfluous to say a word about it, as it would be to give an account of the road from Aberdeen to Ballater; but at all events, it may be said that it was a very interesting journey, and the Prince and his followers enjoyed it all the more because, as the train mounted the gradients to the summit level, the heat sensibly diminished.

Kirkee, the scene of the battle which determined the fate of the Mahratta Empire, was reached in due time. It is just fifty-eight years and one week ago since by this roadside there was fought that action of momentous consequences to British rule; for the results were the fall of the power of the Peishwa and the establishment of that of the Company in the Deccan. But very few cared now to know about Bajee Rao, the last of the Peishwas, for we were all eager to get to Poonah and to rest. It is, however, not to be left unnoted that the success of the British in that battle, which was a crowning victory, was due, in great part, to the extraordinary attachment of a native regiment—not to the ruler of their own country—but to Ford, their European leader. The regiment belonged to the Peishwa's infantry, but fought against him at the command of an European Commandant. There is a good deal to be thought of in that fact, and it would be well if our Government could always get men of the same stamp as Major Ford to lead native regiments. There was not much to be seen from the train at Kirkee—a plain sufficiently dry-looking; rows of bungalows, and lines of trees by the roadside; a British battery firing a salute; a crowd of soldiers' wives, and children, European and Eurasian, outside the railings, and officials and the guard on the platform, which was decorated with flowers and flags. In a few minutes more the thud of another salute was heard ahead, and the train stopped. Many officers, civil and military, and a great gathering of the "Station," greeted the Prince as he stepped out on the platform, with much enthusiasm. Sir Charles Staveley and his staff, and Lord Mark Kerr and his staff, and every one who could get there, were waiting to receive the Royal visitor, who drove in State through the Cantonments and the outlying suburbs, which are so creditable to the powers that be.

The procession suddenly pulled up in the sun, between the lines of soldiers, which formed a bright border to the variegated flower-bed-looking crowd of natives behind. It is always difficult for those who are in some sort engaged in the smaller business of ceremonials to become cognisant of more than their own part in it. They are like the actors behind the scenes, waiting till their turns come, save and except that they take more interest in that which is going on in front. "An address, of course!" And so it was, for the elders of Poonah, headed by a venerable-looking man with a noble beard, were on a platform, beyond which was a fair arch of triumph; by the roadside, and behind and on each side of them, were many European ladies and natives, who gave the Prince most loyal welcome. These we saw when our turn came to pass the stand. It was the Honourable Khan Bahadoor Poodumjee Pestonjee who read the address, which was enshrined in a fine casket of silver, whereupon was an image of Gunputty, God of Wisdom, with a lotus in one of his four hands, and his faithful mouse in attendance. The Prince made a gracious reply, and was much cheered. And then on and on through miles of road and street lined with soldiers, British and Native, and crowded with people, mostly Mahrattas.

It was 5 o'clock P.M. ere the Prince reached Poonah, and then there was a long drive to the Government House of Ganesh (or Gunnesh) Khind, of which we had heard before — the *bête noire* which Mr. Fawcett turned out occasionally in the House as "a typical instance of the extravagance and insubordination of the Governors of Bombay." Sir Bartle Frere, who was with the Prince, underwent a little raillery on the subject, but, standing in the magnificent marbled halls of the Palace, he might say "Circumspice!" He had, however, a good deal more to say, and more germane to the matter, which is somewhat complicated. In an able minute, Sir Bartle Frere seems to candid minds to have established the points, that he built a very fine dwelling for future Governors, that he acted within his legal powers, that he was not insubordinate, and that he had not, when he retired from the Government of Bombay, expended all the money at his disposal. The Palace and buildings cost 175,000*l.* But India is a very dear place for some sorts of work—papering a small room here cost 30*l.*; making a door, 38*l.*; the marble cement for the State Drawing Room, 360*l.*; and so on. Anyway, there is the Palace—if not quite a thing of beauty and a joy for ever, at least a very imposing structure, with noble tower and fair frontage—state-apartments of the grandest—conservatories, gardens fresh and blooming—placed on a commanding site, with a view over the undulating plains and strange tumulous scenery of the Deccan. The Prince was received here in state worthy of him, and his standard flew out from the tower as he set foot within the threshold of the Palace. The generals and officers, military and civil, attended, and were duly presented.

After a stroll through the charming grounds of Gunnesh Khind, the party in waiting on the Prince broke up, and sought out their lodgings. Some were quartered in the Palace, others were provided with accommodation in houses in adjacent compounds. The dispersion at Gunnesh Khind was inevitable, because that stately residence, with all its grandeur, does not possess the merits of extensive accommodation; but there were carriages provided to take the guests to and fro. The Duke of Sutherland and Lord Alfred Paget were told off to Bungalow No. 1. The Rev. Canon Duckworth, Mr. Hall, and myself were informed that we were to lodge at Bungalow No. 2. "Where are they?" "Oh! any one would tell us." The Duke, Lord Alfred, and myself were put in one carriage, which was driven by a coachman in the Governor's livery, aided by another domestic in fine garments, and we set off full of confidence. At first there was the Park, then there was a pretty guard-house and a fine Clock-Tower, and a noble porter's lodge and gate to admire; after which came a nice drive in the country. On we went. Poonah was in sight. Still the coachman drove on. But where was Bungalow No. 1 or Bungalow No. 2? Suspicion began to cloud our thoughts and interrupt our speech. "Ask him where he is going?" But alas! the coachman and his fellow were Mahrattas, and understood only their own tongue, so that indifferent Ordoo was quite thrown away on them. There were a few Europeans loitering on the road to take chance of seeing the Prince; but not one of them had ever heard of Bungalow No. 1 or of Bungalow No. 2. An artillery non-commissioned officer, who had been quartered for months close at hand, could not even direct us to the Clock-Tower, to which we desired to return. He had never seen it. By ingenious pantomime, not unaccompanied by vigorous demonstration, the coachman was at last induced to abandon his apparent object of taking us to Central India, and to turn back towards Gunnesh Khind. This time Sir P. Wodehouse moved his staff to explicit ordering, and eventually the party were installed in their bungalows.

There was a State dinner, and a dance, which was, I think, suggested by the Prince as an enlivening process.

Among the guests was Count Seckendorff—a clever linguist, and a man of observation and resource, with a fine taste in art, and of merit as an artist—who is visiting Lord Napier of Magdala, whose acquaintance he made when he was attached by his Government to the Head-quarters of the Abyssinian Expedition. His father was well known in the diplomatic service in London, where he represented Prussian interests for some years. He has a good deal of the hardheadedness of his race; but he is kind-hearted, and willing to serve a friend, as I had occasion to know when he was on the Crown Prince's Staff at the time we were together in France and at Versailles.

November 14th.—Mr. Kanné, who superintends the arrangements for the Royal travels, having accompanied the Prince so far, starts early to-morrow morning with letters to deliver to the Princess of Wales and the Queen. Alarming telegrams that Russia had set three army corps on a war-footing, ready to move at a moment's notice, came later. It appeared quite possible that the expedition would be abandoned, for in case of war it would not be expedient for the Prince of Wales to be away from Great Britain. Canon Duckworth preached at the Station Church, which was very much crowded, as it was expected that the Prince would have attended. However, having been at Divine service in Government House in the forenoon, he only visited General Staveley's quarters, where he had tea.

November 15th.—Early in the morning Mr. Kanné came knocking at the door of the bungalow wherein Canon Duckworth, Mr. Hall, and myself were lodged, to get the letters which were lying on the table; but so sound asleep were we, that he had to leave without obtaining admission. It was not comfortable to find that the servants showed so little vigilance. I woke up later, found the letters, and despatched one of the many natives—who were lying outside in the verandah, rolled up in their calico garments like lumps of dough—to the Railway Station, which was some miles away, and the man made such good use of his slender legs that he caught Mr. Kanné just in time.

At 6 A.M. the Prince started to visit the famous Temple of Parbuttee, rather to the discomfiture of some of the suite, who scarcely believed that so early a start, designed overnight, would be carried out in the morning. One of them even ventured on what is called "backing his opinion," that the chief of the expedition would not be punctual, for a small amount, which was lost, and duly paid to the winner. Two of the suite who were late, found that the old saying of "the more haste the less speed," was true in India as well as at home, and came down with, or parted from, their horses as they rode, *ventre à terre*, to overtake the party. The ascent to the Temple, which is effected by a long flight of stone steps, exceeding steep, and in some places rugged, was made upon elephants, and the Prince now had his first experience of a mode of carriage with which he became familiar enough ere he left the country. Chota-hazree (small breakfast) was served at the base of the ascent to the lofty hill on which towers the fortress-like Temple. There was a gathering of devotees, fakirs, beggars, to welcome the visitors; but here, as elsewhere, due precautions were taken to prevent intrusiveness or mobbing. The Prince inspected the interior of the great pile, was shown the shrine of Shiva, looked at the idols, and had a conversation with one of the priests, a very astute Brahmin, who, having learned all that he could of English dialectics, and possibly the rudiments of Christianity, had reverted with increase of subtlety—but not with much credence, it would seem, from what he said respecting the details of his religious exercises—to the practices of his faith. He was an exceedingly good, if not an interesting, specimen of the cultivated Brahmin *à l'anglais*, a master of logic, of a philosophical humour, coupled with a mocking spirit, which perhaps would have developed into an exhibition of some stronger feeling had he dared to indulge in it. He was made happy in the way he most valued, by a gift to the Temple from the Royal hand. From a window-like slit in the wall of the Temple, the last of the Peishwas beheld the rout of his forces on the plains of Kirkee below, and could possibly perceive that the deadliest blow was struck by the troops on whom he most trusted for the success of his treacherous attack. It was more than a defeat—it was the overthrow of an Empire and the destruction of a dominant race. Recent visitors have attempted to gather a moral from the history of that defeat, and have inferred that our Power is perfectly secure, because 2800 well-drilled men, of whom 800 were Europeans, once routed 18,000 scratch cavalry and 8000 infantry, provided with fourteen pieces of Native artillery. Such hasty assumptions form a very unsound basis for the convictions of men who may influence State policy. Whilst the Prince was at Parbuttee, the Duke of Sutherland and Lord A. Paget, under the guidance of Colonel Fife, visited the great artificial lake which serves as the head-water of a vast scheme of irrigation connected with the Moota, and the renowned stronghold called Singguhr, i.e., the Lion Fortress, eleven miles from Poonah, which was captured so wonderfully by Sivajee. It is built on the summit of a block of basalt so steep and high that the only means of reaching the fortress is by a laborious climb on one's legs, or by using the legs of the porters who carry you up in a palanquin in about an hour. Sivajee, the Mahratta hero, was not gifted with very heroic attributes, according to our conception—" Bloody, resolute, and cruel,"—he was, however, full of energy, resource, and subtlety, undaunted and indefatigable. From the Temple you can see the ruins of Torna, the first fort he captured, as well as Raj-guhr, the first which he founded, in the Deccan, and a vast extent of rolling country scarred with watercourses, and streaked by mountain ridges, which are broken here and there into detached truncated blocks, frequently crowned by ruined fortalices.

On the Prince's return from the Temple to Gunnesh Khind there was a discussion respecting future plans and programmes. Opinions differed every hour as accounts came in, each with a new version of the state of the South: at 7 A.M. it was reported that the hills were free from disease; all were happy at the prospect of the visit to the shooting-camp, and remained so till 8 A.M., when a telegram reported "cholera still rife." This was followed by one at 8.30 A.M., that there was sickness at Coimbatore; which was succeeded by another at 9 A.M. to announce that cholera was spreading generally over Madras and Southern India. This last despatch, being official and positive, seemed final. Alteratives and plans to consume the time between the Prince's departure and the date fixed for his arrival in Ceylon were suggested, for the Bombay programme promised to be speedily exhausted. Besides, it could not but be felt that whilst the Governor and his officers were engaged in the agreeable task of entertaining the Prince, the work of Government was almost at a standstill. Many places, such as Ahmedabad and Baroda, were named; and finally it was resolved to ask Ceylon when she would be ready, and meantime to visit, if possible, the city of the Gaekwar.

A review of the Poonah Division was ordered at 6 P.M., but it was rather later when the Prince came on the ground, a flat plain, which is used as a course for the races, so dear to the hearts of the civilians and soldiers, not to speak of the mem-Sahibs, of the Presidency. There was a very considerable concourse of Natives, among whom the Mahratta turban largely predominated, and all the Europeans who could manage to be there congregated near the flagstaff, where they seemed but a little dark patch on the broad white selvage of the indigenous multitude.

There was not a very large force to show, nor were the Native regiments good specimens.* As the eye gets accustomed to the local colour, the faces of Europeans strike one as being almost unwholesomely pale, and the helmet projecting over the brow, and casting a shadow on the upper part, gives an appearance of attenuation, and causes the features to look shrunk and small. Lord Mark Ker, although he admitted that recruits were too numerous, and explained that the Native battalions were not at their full strength, did his best with the materials that he had. The Prince and some of his suite mounted; others were on foot or in carriages. Riding strange horses, mostly "Walers," given to the high spirits and capers of their tribe, and going at a great pace, several of the horsemen were unfortunate. One was thrown heavily; another, not attached to the Royal party, was carried by his steed among the spectators; so that, on the whole, there was some little excitement apart from the military spectacle. Before the march past was over it became too dark to make out much more than the fact that there were troops moving in quarter-distance column in front of the Grand Stand. It was "black as pitch" when Captain Hogg, of the Poonah Horse, exhibited his plan of dismounting cavalry, which has been thought highly of by some authorities, but of which there was no opportunity of forming an

* See Field State.—Appendix.

opinion under the circumstances. The merit claimed for it consists principally in the way in which, as it was explained, the horses of the dismounted troopers are held, so as to enable a larger proportion of the troopers than is possible under the ordinary system, to act as infantry, and to resume the functions of cavalry very quickly.

The Prince returned to Gunnesh Khind by the city and Cantonments, which were illuminated with great brilliancy. Need I add that there were fire-works, triumphal arches, inscriptions—that the streets were thronged—that buttees and fires, blue, red and green, revelled aloft and alow—that there was abundance of music of the native kind—and that every one was glad to get to Gunnesh Khind, and to pack up his recollections of Poonah—very pleasant on the whole—with his portmanteau, which was to be packed off to the Kirkee Station before dinner? There was a farewell dinner at Gunnesh Khind, and at midnight the Prince and his company drove to the special train at Kirkee, where the servants had arranged luxurious beds in the carriages, and in half an hour more they were rattling away from the former capital of the Peishwas on their return to Bombay, sleeping as securely as if they were at home.

November 16th.—There were few who were awake at sunrise and saw the wild scenery of the Ghauts gradually developed in the early morning, but those who were by chance so fortunate had reason to be grateful. The train arrived at the station outside Parell at 7.30 A.M., and the Prince at once drove to Government House. Here the situation was reviewed once more. When the necessity of "going somewhere" was forced on the consideration of the Prince's counsellors at Poonah, and, earlier in the day, many places were mentioned and discussed before Baroda became the favourite. There were several reasons for caution and investigation before the Prince could be advised

"SHAHZADAH PASSES!" NATIVE BAND AT POONAH.

to go to the capital of a State which had lately been the scene of the remarkable and exceptional political trial which had agitated not merely India, but had extended its influence to public opinion in Great Britain. The deposed Ruler was known to have many adherents, despite his crimes and misgovernment. Sirdars who declared the tyrant's rule intolerable, have since been heard to express sorrow for his fate and for his misfortunes. The old Court followers of Mulhar Rao have been disarmed and scattered abroad, but who could guard against the presence of one or of twenty desperate men in a city of 90,000 or 100,000 people? The Baroda Government, however, was confident. The former Resident, Sir R. Meade, whose knowledge of the present condition of the place carried immense weight with it, was in favour of the visit, and was satisfied that there would be no risk in going there, and the Governor of Bombay was relieved of a responsibility which he might have been unwilling to incur had the excursion of his Royal Highness been dependent on him alone. In all matters of the kind the Prince of Wales submitted with the utmost readiness to the advice and opinions of the Indian authorities. Finally the Governor-General, when it was suggested that the Prince of Wales should honour the young Gaekwar by going to see him in his capital, gave his concurrence and approval. So, after many pros and cons, it was settled that the Prince might safely visit Baroda. There were promises of excellent sport, and there was also the opportunity of seeing a Native Court still flourishing close to one of the capitals of British India. The result was that the Prince of Wales saw a place rarely touched by the foot of the stranger, and had a reception which, if it were wanting in the glare, enthusiasm, cheers, and infinite variety of forms, ceremonies, and entertainments which welcomed him at Bombay, was entirely Oriental—

the source of much enjoyment to himself, and of great service, it is believed, to the State.

New colours were presented by the Prince to the Marine Battalion, as the 21st B. N. I. are called, at 4 P.M., on the open space near the Secretariat, and the ceremony attracted an enormous mass of people, among whom, conspicuous for their carriages and costumes, were the Chiefs still lingering in Bombay, and the ever-present and picturesque Parsee ladies and children. The prayer which, according to "Regulations," the Chaplain is wont to deliver on the presentation of colours to a Christian regiment, was necessarily omitted, but every other portion of the detailed and elaborate, if not imposing, formality, was duly observed. The old colours, inscribed with many names, mostly unknown to Europeans, and not so ancient as the corps, which was raised nearly a century ago, were accepted by the Prince, and carried home to England to grace the walls of Sandringham.*

After another burra khana at Parell, there was a grand ball, the last for the good people of Bombay, and the Nawabs and Rajas who came had an opportunity of seeing how European ladies and gentlemen dance to amuse themselves instead of looking at others do it for them. However, there are some Europeans who prefer seeing a ballet to engaging in the pleasures of square or round. The Chiefs scarcely rallied round the supper tables, although some of them are known as "quiet drinkers," *chez eux*. When we see dancing Rajas and waltzing Nawabs in India, we may be sure our work is almost accomplished; but, to judge from the modest way they avoided beautifully dressed ladies to-night, it would seem as if the day were yet far to seek.

* See Field State.—Appendix.

November 17th.—"Farewell the tented field!" Farewell the crows and minars, which seemed to think it their bounden duty to insist on early hours being observed by those under their protection, and who cawed and chattered ere the sun rose, regardless of the fact that they went to bed when he set the night before, whereas their victim had not long lain down! To-day we pack up and clear out from under canvas. Those who are going to Baroda to-morrow are only to take what is necessary—some are to shoot—others are to look on. The heavy baggage is to go on board ship. In the afternoon the Prince left Parell, which had been in such constant fête since his arrival, and which was now fast emptying out the offerings from the Chiefs, and sending them to the boats.

The presents, upwards of 400 in number, from the Bombay Rajas and Chiefs, included specimens of every variety of Indian workmanship—tissues, brocade, cloths, arms of all kinds, jewellery, gold, silver, and metal. On the whole the offerings were good without being too fine. The Raja of Kolhapoor, in addition to an ancient jewelled sword and dagger, estimated to be worth 6000 rupees, has assigned a sum of no less than 20,000*l.* for the admirable purpose of founding a hospital, to be called after the Prince of Wales. The presents of the Nizam, rich in swords, fire-arms, carpets, gold cloth, and the like. were especially interesting. The Gaekwar of Baroda offered a tea-service of silver, of native workmanship and design, made at Madras under European superintendence: shields of layers of silk, closely pressed together, which resist a sword-cut or the thrust of a lance from the strongest arm; a pearl necklace from the Maharanee, a very beautiful ornament which had graced the necks of ladies of the Gaekwar's family, the pearls of excellent colour and size, with an emerald and diamond pendant, for the acceptance of the Princess of Wales. A diamond brooch with pearl pendants was also presented to her Royal Highness by the Maharanee. The Rao of Cutch sent an exquisite collection of the famous work of his State, which has a deserved reputation in India. Upwards of thirty pieces of silver and gold, flower-vases, tea-services, varieties of articles for the table, formed a very sufficient illustration of the excellence of the workmanship, and of the taste of the workmen.

The Prince had many to remember at Parell; and there was a little levee in the Hall when he was about to take his place in his carriage. There was not, however, any great gathering of people along the roadsides, as they probably were not aware of the hour of his departure. The sun was furious, and the Prince after a dusty drive once more saw, doubtless with pleasure, the sea, and the ships awaiting the moment of his embarkation for the utterance of their noisy welcome. The bay shone like a mirror—not a breath of wind. Dr. Fayrer, who has seen a good deal of other parts of India, expressed his opinion of Bombay in the "cold weather" in energetic terms, and most of those on board could sympathise with him. In the evening Sir Philip Wodehouse, his staff and suite, and others, came off to dinner, and there was a very pleasant evening, enlivened by the music of the band and India table-talk, till the guests departed for shore. The ships were again illuminated and in active eruption.

November 18th.—A night of great heat and sleeplessness, or, at best, of broken dreams, in which you could not decide whether you were under a tent, or in a railway carriage, or on an elephant, or at sea. "What noise of falling rockets in mine ears!" Indian "bundabusts" begin early, and the tumult of packing began to rage outside the cabins soon after dawn. The Native servants who came on board with their masters from Parell, and had slept on the hammock chests, not looking much the better for their "snug lying," glided ghost-like about in their new quarters. The main-deck was the scene of immense activity from 6.30 A.M. till noon, when the steamer for the shore luggage came alongside. The magazines of small arms were opened up; rifles and smooth-bores, cartridges, pistols, shooting-clothes got ready, and there was a ripping up of tin cases, and a rending of timber, not conducive to rest or to literary pursuits. When the luggage was off, there was a little calm, but no repose. Every one bathed in perspiration; the air on board is what may be called "muggy." Most of us were driven out of our berths, and sitting in our very light clothing on the main-deck, outside our cabins, looked like icebergs on a sunny day. At 10 A.M. the thermometer 86° in the shade between decks. At 1 P.M. the Prince went with the Duke of Sutherland on board the *Undaunted*, to lunch with Admiral Macdonald. Dinner was half an hour earlier than usual; and the Prince and suite were dressed in patrol jackets to start for the journey to Baroda. Captain Glyn was confined to his cabin by a slight attack of fever; Lord C. Beresford was compelled to remain on board in consequence of his fall at Poonah; the Prince went round and said a few words to them before he entered his steam-launch. About 8.30 P.M. the Royal party landed at the Apollo Bunder. There were some hundreds of Indians, Europeans, and Parsees, at the landing-place, and a few hundreds more were collected along the route to the railway. Outside and inside the Station there was a large assemblage, wherein the Parsees were conspicuous. They have always been very much to the front. It is to be regretted that they are not more important as an element of strength, for they feel fully the advantage of living under British protection. They are very rich, very commercial, very acute, and sufficiently civilised; they are attached to a rule which protects them and enables them to make money. No one, however, supposes the Parsees could fight for us, or that, if left to themselves, they could do so successfully on their own behalf.

The railway to Baroda traverses the island on which Bombay is built, and is carried by a series of bridges and embankments over the estuaries and rivers which mingle their waters in the low-lying district close to the sea, across Salsette, and so northwards by the small Portuguese settlement of Damaun, the existence of which was a novelty to many of us.

November 19th.—All the party were fast asleep in their snug beds in the train when good General Sam Browne, like a blustering East wind, came round knocking at the windows of the carriages. "Get up! get up! We shall be at Baroda in twenty minutes!" A great scrambling to get at clothing and uniforms ensued, and scarcely were we attired ere General Browne's words were verified. At 7.20 A.M. the train arrived. The Gaekwar, with Sir Madhava Rao at his side, and groups of resplendent Sirdars behind him, Mr. Melvill, the Agent of the Governor-General, and the officers of the British Government, civil and military, in full uniform, stood on the platform at Baroda, which was beautifully decorated with green wreaths and festoons, and decked in flags and flowers, to welcome the Prince. Outside there were triumphal arches, and a vast sea of dark faces under the red Mahratta turban —and turbans of every hue, green, white, and blue—was visible; and a mighty gathering, which might be counted by tens of thousands, spread out along the roadside far as the eye could reach, all looking the same way, all eyes fixed on one and one object only—the son of the Empress, the Shahzadah of Hindostan. A regiment of Baroda Infantry in yellow coats and quaintly-shaped shakoes was drawn up before the Station. Two squadrons of Lancers belonging to the State were formed in their rear, and presented a very pretty show in their powder-blue uniforms and turbans—the bands on the flanks. The Prince exchanged greetings with the Gaekwar and Sir Madhava and the British officials. Such a clang of drums and brass and braying of clarions arose when he was seen! As the Guard of Honour (of her Majesty's 83rd Regiment, under Captain Windham) presented arms, the Gaekwar's infantry, to the roll of kettledrums and trumpet flourishes, did the same. The Prince took the little Maharaja by the hand, sat down and spoke with him for a short time. He then passed outside to the steps leading from the entrance of the station, before which towered an elephant of extraordinary size; on his back was a howdah of surpassing splendour, which shone like burnished gold in the morning sun, and which was either made of gold or of silver gilt. It was covered with a golden canopy. This exquisitely finished carriage, reported to have cost four lakhs of rupees, was placed on cloth of gold and velvet cushions, fastened over the embroidered covering that almost concealed the outline of the great elephant, which stood swaying his painted proboscis to and fro as if he kept time to the music of the bands outside. His head was coloured of a bright saffron, and on this ground were traced quaint scrolls. His proboscis was especially ornamented in different coloured patterns, and his ears were stained of a pale yellowish-green. His tusks had been sawn off to the length of three feet, and false tusks of greater diameter, also shortened, were wedged over them by bands of gold. His painted legs were encased in thick round coils of gold. The mahout was attired in a costume befitting such a gorgeous charge. Attendants stood by with State umbrellas, fans of peacocks' feathers, yaks' tails, and streamers of scarlet and cloth of gold, which they waved before the Prince, others held the silver ladder for him to ascend to the howdah. After a short pause to survey the scene, the Prince and the Gaekwar descended the steps. The beast in golden raiment, in a succession of convulsive heaves and jerks, dropped down upon what elephants rest upon. The ladder was placed against the howdah, and the Prince, carefully helped, stepped up, the Gaekwar followed and sat by his side. Sir Madhava Rao, in small white turban and purple velvet robe, took his place. At the word to rise, the mountainous creature swayed to and fro, and the Prince held on strenuously to the rail in front while the animal was establishing itself on its fore-legs. The attendants, with State umbrella, fans, and yaks' tails, clung by the sides. Then, as the elephant made its first stride, the clamour of voices and of sound deepened and grew and spread onwards, and the artillery began a salute which announced that the Prince and the procession had set out. The next elephant, stained a French grey, or slate colour, and red, his proboscis richly arabesqued, was even larger, but he was not so quiet. His howdah was of burnished silver, on a cloth and cushions scarcely less splendid than those on the Royal elephant. Massive rings of silver encircled his tusks and legs; his mahout and attendants were dressed to match. The Duke of Sutherland and Mr. Melvill got on the second elephant. The third elephant, which was rather of a difficult disposition, and by flourishes of its tail and aberrations of its proboscis, caused thrills of anxiety to its riders, bore Sir R. Meade, Sir B. Frere, and myself. Other elephants, each painted and stained in different fashion from his fellows, and each with his peculiar howdah and trappings, stood in line behind. To the right a row of these animals, to whom the adjective "sagacious" belongs of right, knelt down in line, as if dressed by a drill sergeant, and remained making salaams till the Prince had passed. Then they arose and followed in the procession. Beyond the line of elephants clearing the way in front of the Prince was an advance guard and escort of the 3rd Hussars, under Captain Gibson, which only arrived three hours before from Bombay, and turned out smart and fresh as possible after a tedious journey of more than eighteen hours. In the rear were three guns of E 9 Battery R.A., under Captain Georges; Major Wakefield's detachment of the 83rd Regiment furnished the infantry escort. A detachment of the Gaekwar's Artillery, a cavalry band, a troop of the Baroda Horse—irregular cavalry—a great crowd of Parsees, Sirdars, and small Chiefs, Mahrattas, Guzeratees, on horseback and on foot, followed.

The interest taken by the population in the Prince's movements is gratified by the full accounts in the Native papers, which are generally accurate. It is very curious to watch the groups collected round the happy possessor of a programme whenever there is a procession, and to see them checking off the various personages in the carriages, who are not infrequently out of their places, so that the impressions conveyed by their observations are not seldom erroneous. To them, however, Tyrian and Trojan are much alike; but the offices held by various members of the suite are subjected to strange translations in the different languages of the people. Even here in Baroda, they had their programmes, and scanned the occupants of the howdahs very keenly, though their great anxiety, now happily set at rest without any manner of uncertainty, was to see the Prince. Sir Bartle Frere, Sir R. Meade, and Mr. Melvill were the only Europeans of whom they had ever heard before, and the finest sort of uniforms and most valued decorations and orders, surmounted by the spiked helmet, could not have struck a crowd accustomed to the bright robes and jewels of Native Chiefs.

The procession set out in single file to the famous Residency, some three miles distant, with a pomp and circumstance which only the East can show, for surely of all the vehicles on which human pride and state were ever borne, the caparisoned elephant is the grandest and most striking, and those of the Gaekwar's excel in stature and (always excepting No. 3) in dignity of deportment. The cavalry which lined the way, the native carriages, the crowds from the Station to the Cantonments beyond which lay the Residency, and the novelty of the procession, invested the Prince's entry to Baroda with unusual interest. The whole of the way, every inch of it, was bordered by a light trellis-work of bamboos and palm strips, hung with lamps and festooned with bright green leaves and flowers, and there were at intervals grander arches and clusters of banners. It was astonishing to see how much had been done in the time. Due praise should be given to Mr. Hill, Engineer to the Government, for the skill with which he designed devices and illuminations which made the road gay by day and resplendent at night. The people seemed very comfortable, no sign of the wretchedness we are so fond of attributing to Native rule; and the city, so far as we could judge, was clean and bright to a degree. At the Cantonments the two Native regiments, the 9th Bombay Native Infantry and the 22nd Bombay Native Infantry, and the rest of the 83rd Queen's were drawn up in front of their lines with bands and colours, and saluted.

There was very short notice of the visit. The Indian city is large; the English station very small. The resources were few. Mr. Melvill only arrived a day or two before the Prince came, and Indian hospitality was driven to its wits' ends, but not to the end of its resources. The Residency is a wretched, tumbledown, old place, with very small accommodation. The Prince had a small suite on the ground-floor. Sir Bartle Frere had a room next that of the Duke of Sutherland, on the first floor; Major-General Probyn occupied the historical (recent history) apartment in which Brigadier Phayre's poisoned chalice was prepared, and his window looked out on the spot where the pommelo juice fell and the poison was scraped up; Lord Aylesford had the room adjacent. Major-General Browne, Colonel Ellis, Dr. Fayrer, Mr. Grey, Mr. Hall, &c., lived in tents, not of the best, at the back of the Residency, pitched so as to form three sides of a square. These tents and furniture were sent up from Bombay. "Doubling up" generally was the order of the day and of the night.

The procession arrived at the Residency in an hour. There was then a Durbar, at which the Sirdars were presented, and the suite were presented to the Gaekwar. When the leave-taking came, the Prince led the Gaekwar to the entrance. The elephants, with gold and silver howdahs, and the whole of the brilliant sowaree, were waiting there, with the guard of honour and the Gaekwar's own escort. He mounted to his seat, and with the clang of music and measured throb of cannon, which gave him his Royal salute, returned to his palace at Baroda, some three miles distant. Then Mrs. and Miss Melvill were presented to the Prince, and the officers on duty and attached to the Staff were invited to table, and there was subsequently a reception or levee for European officers. Before the hour fixed upon for the return visit to the Gaekwar, the Prince shot a few specimens for the naturalist, in a small tope close to the house, which was full of parrakeets, woodpeckers, orioles, and other birds which were seen by him at liberty for the first time.

It was 3.30 P.M. when the Prince set out to pay his return visit to the Maharaja. Native policemen lined the streets, and Sowars kept guard at the crossings. At various stages there were guards of honour of the Gaekwar's troops—the Horse in leather helmets with scarlet tufts, red-embroidered tunics, breeches, and boots—a uniform devised probably by some of the old foreign officers formerly at his Court; one of the infantry regiments in the Highland uniform already described, which seems so curious, and which, nevertheless, suits the brown faces wonderfully well, and would be quite correct were it not for the ridiculous pink calico tights beneath the kilts. Trumpet flourishes, roll of drums, presented arms, standards lowered, spoke of ancient discipline. There were many vestiges of barbaric and costly state which must have often vexed the souls of honest economical British Residents, and have caused the unsympathetic and practical British Government to cut off slice after slice of territory to satisfy creditors and to insure payment of debts. The city is curious. There are drains covered with wood along each side, and some idea of a path for foot-passengers, but there is no pavement. The houses generally consist of two stories; the ground-floor, raised above the level of the pathway, open to the front, is used as a shop or a store; the first-floor has a verandah and a balcony of carved wood, which is painted in some bright colour—red, yellow or sea-green—so that the effect is very brilliant. The Hindoo temples are small and unobtrusive. The shop fronts and verandahs were filled with Mahrattas in their large red turbans and white robes, or Guzeratees from the up-country in smaller headdresses. A parti-coloured crowd, two or three deep, sat or stood—keen-eyed, curious, and quiet—along the mile and a half of winding streets through which the cortege passed. There were respectful salaams, and now and then some Parsees cheered; but the attitude of the multitude was one which it would be difficult to characterise if it were judged by European standards. Few women were visible, but abundance of children of both sexes, in the lightest costumes, were held up by the men to see the show. The Prince passed under the Clock-Tower gateway, which was the *place d'armes* during the troubles that followed the deposition of Mulhar Rao. It is placed at the intersection of the two main streets, and is still occupied as a military post. Soon afterwards the procession came out on the road to the old Palace, and defiled through a triumphal arch (of which there were many on the route), near which the children of the Gaekwar's schools were drawn up. The Palace is one of the ordinary residences of Native Princes, built under European inspiration, and presents a poor front; but there was a great display of mirrors and lustres inside, and the attendants were in fine costumes.

On the arrival of the Prince, he found the little Gaekwar with all his jewels on, Sir Madhava Rao in studied plainness of attire, with a background of Sirdars and shrewd-looking Parsees, waiting to receive him on the steps at the portico. The Maharaja is, as one of the suite said, "a boy such as one may see all over the place"—with soft mild eyes, and sad subdued look. There were three boys of the stock of the Gaekwars picked out for adoption in the succession to Mulhar Rao by Sir R. Meade, and after three interviews the widow of Khandee Rao selected him. One wonders if he is as happy in his diamonds and emeralds as he was when he was running about his native village. The

Maharaja led the Prince upstairs to a room, hung with large chandeliers, with coloured prints on the walls. They sat side by side for a time, during which the Prince talked pleasantly through Sir Madhava Rao's interpretation. The Sirdars, Ministers, and officials under the Native Administration were presented, and offered nuzzurs, which were duly touched and remitted. A wreath was placed round the Prince's neck by the Maharaja—uttur and pân went round—and the Prince was led by his host to the door of the Maharanee's apartment. Jumnabaae is an exceedingly engaging and graceful lady, not yet thirty years of age, with a pleasant face, bright eyes, and agreeable smile. Her hands and feet are particularly small and well-shaped. The former were not overdone with rings, but her Highness would probably not be able to take a long walk by reason of toe-rings, one of which, on her left foot, seemed to exercise some control over her motions. She was unveiled, but from time to time she drew, as if instinctively, her tissue shawl over her head. She held her little daughter, "who," said the Maharanee, "would have been Gaekwar had she been a boy," by her knee, and the child's governess, an English lady, sat a little behind her. The Maharanee was delighted with Bombay; honoured beyond expression by the Prince's visit; hoped that he would like Baroda; and was much interested in the success of his shooting-party, as to which she had given orders. The Prince presented his suite, and started for the Agga, or the arena for wild-beast combats, where he arrived shortly before 5 P.M.

The Agga is an enclosure of 180 yards long by 60 yards broad, with walls 20 feet high. These walls are pierced by low archways, into which the men engaged may retreat in case of being attacked by the animals. At the western extremity there is a Grand Stand three stories high. On entering the gateway two elephants were seen, one tied to the wall opposite the Grand Stand, and another chained to the wall on the right of it. As soon as the Prince had taken his place in the front, with the Gaekwar by his side, two wrestlers, quite naked except at the waist, advanced, and after profound salaams, grappled. The pulwans of Baroda are not so famous as those of Lucknow, but these fellows were masses of brown muscle—a little abdominous, perhaps—but still of enormous power. Other athletes came into the field, so that there were at first four, and afterwards six, groups of flesh—animated Laocoons—striving, writhing, and rolling about in the dust, in such knotted coils of arms and legs as baffled discrimination. They were matched so well that only once did the applause of the spectators announce a victory and a defeat—the great feat of strength by which one of the wrestlers, uprooting his antagonist from the ground, prizes him over his knee, and throws him over so that both shoulders touch the ground. The wrestlers advanced to the stand, salaamed to the Prince and Gaekwar, and retired. One of the elephants was then let go, and we saw that its tusks had been sawn off short, and that it was a beast of infinite *bonhomie* of countenance. But it had a temper of its own. After some insults from the people in a safety arch, which seemed to exercise it amazingly, and which it resented by trying to tear down the wall, it was provoked beyond endurance by others who came out with spears and red cloths. It suddenly trumpeted, and made a charge, which sent the recreants flying into their recesses again. Then it stood, pondering on the situation, in the centre of the arena. While it looked at the Prince of Wales and other distinguished visitors, as if it were conjecturing what they thought of it all, the elephant at the other end of the enclosure was let go free. When the elephants perceived each other, they advanced kindly as if to inquire after each other's health. But the persecuting band who followed them would not have it so. By shouts, lance-pricks, and other aggravating acts, they inspired the beasts with the belief that they ought to be enemies. They accordingly put down their heads and fought; but these sagacious creatures were, I think, only making believe. They merely put on the gloves and had a few rounds. Certainly there was hard hitting and tremendous head-collisions; tusks rattled and clattered, proboscis met proboscis in intricate convolutions, the vast hulls shook under the strain of combat; whether they really meant mischief or not it was impossible to determine, for at the critical moment when they had tied their trunks up in a knot, men with squibs at the end of spears let them off under the combatants' bellies. I am sorry to say the heroes bolted. After a pause, however, the combat was renewed. The elephant which seemed to have had the worst of it in the last bout, by some dexterous manœuvre now managed to turn his enemy's flank, and butted him on the quarter and stern with such force that—amid the cheers of the crowd—he turned and fled, smitten heavily, and "rammed" by his pursuer till he was brought up by the wall, when the men with rockets and squibs came in once more, and the combatants were separated. The manner of securing the elephant when the fight is at an end is clever. While his attention is directed to men in front, who menace and tantalise him with spears and flags, others, armed with large iron clamps, watching their opportunity behind, clip first one and then the other of his hind legs in the implements, over which they lasso strong ropes, so that the beast is unable to run, and is thus led off to his quarters. The prettiest little *entr'acte* followed this combat. Just as a third elephant was led out and provoked to a proper state of indignation and temper, a lithe compact sowar, mounted on a croppy little horse, with a jerky action and a jaunty step, came into the arena. The cavalier perked up to the beast, which stood balancing itself, now on one leg, then on another, and flopping its proboscis about angrily. There is a strong antipathy between horse and elephant, but the horseman cantered his steed close up to the brute in a very confidential manner. The elephant appeared to take no notice of the sowar, who had not even a whip, and guided his horse by hand and the stirrup-irons. Suddenly the elephant uttered a short, sharp trumpet-note, and made a furious rush at his tormentor. It seemed as if man and horse must die. The end of the proboscis was all but on the rider's shoulder; a murmur ran round the arena—a cry of horror—which was changed into a burst of applause—as the sowar, with a plunge of the sharp edge of his stirrup-iron, shot away, wheeled round, and, before the elephant could get himself together again, was capering provokingly at his flank. Again and again the scene was repeated, till the elephant was not able to run, but the sowar was never so near capture afterwards. Every one admired his perfect coolness and horsemanship; and when the elephant was fairly tired out, his victor rode away among renewed plaudits. Not always is it so: sometimes the rider and horse are overthrown; and we were told of horses trampled to death, and of riders only escaping by getting between the elephants' tusks. Khandee Rao, the Gaekwar who preceded Mulhar Rao, was very fond of these sports, and, like the Roman Emperor, whom he resembled, it is said, in other ways, he would often descend into the arena and contend with his pulwans. I daresay they were perfect courtiers, and knew better than to "grass the Gaekwar."

The bar across the end gateway was now lowered, and half-a-dozen men came in, tugging at a rhinoceros. He had heavy chains on his legs, and was "roped" before and behind—a captive Behemoth. However, this was all "make-believe," too, for when the ropes were slipped off, the unwieldy thing toddled about grunting like a pig, and looked as if he wished to follow his keepers. Presently another rhinoceros was introduced to his fellow. Two merchants could not be more amiable on first introduction on 'Change. They came nose to nose, as if to exchange civilities, but the attendants began to excite ill-feelings by poking and patting them alternately, and by horrid yells, and one rhinoceros—lowering his head till his chin, or lower jaw, rested on the sand—made a thrust with his snout at his friend. The blow was hard, as the noise it made testified, but it was delivered on an adamantine front. It was at once returned—the crowd were delighted. There were quick encounters, blow for blow, till it occurred suddenly to the first rhinoceros that it was nonsense to get heated and worried all for nothing, so he turned round and made off as hard as he could lumber towards the gateway. But the bar was down; his backers and friends reproached him for his want of spirit; he was again goaded up to his antagonist, who was standing as though he too were wondering what it all meant, when he received a treacherous dig in the side, which made him quiver from stem to stern. Then he turned, and the brutes, with levelled rams, had a keen bout, in which they were deluged with cold water to keep up their courage by the attendants, till the former runaway performed his retrograde movement again, to the amusement of the audience, nor could he be induced by threats, abuse, flattering fondlings, and abundance of cold water to renew the fight. It was evidently a relief to the less cowardly when his antagonist ran off, and he did not show any inclination for pursuit. *Exeunt* two degraded rhinoceroses, for neither could be described as "game" or heroic!

Two buffaloes, which next stepped into the ring, were animals of very different mettle. They rushed to the encounter. The arena rang with the clatter of their horns. It was real fighting; with strained hind-quarters, heaving sides and lashing tails, they strove, head to head, with passionate fury. But equals in rage, they were not matched in strength; the smaller gave way, and was pushed back, slowly at first, and then at a run, till he fairly turned his flank. In an instant he was hurled on his back, for the conquering buffalo dashed at the exposed side, and, putting down his head below the belly of his enemy, butted him right over. There was no lack of courage on the part of the other, for, worsted as he was, he got up and renewed the conflict, but, after one desperate rally, in which the result was not doubtful and the damage to the defeated buffalo not slight, he was—not ingloriously—driven off the ground. An exhibition of fighting rams followed; but the champion, covered with garlands and brocade, was considered too good for anything on the ground, and the contest was left to rams which had their spurs to win. There was nothing of the timidity of the sheep in their engagements. The fury of their charges, the tremendous cracks with which their heads met together, were worthy, we were told, of great praise, and I certainly would sooner see them than a couple of prize-fighters at home, or than the pugilists with iron knuckledusters who exhibit sometimes at Baroda. Libra would not incline towards one Aries rather than to the other, and the rams were led away. When these contests were over, some of the zoological curiosities, in which Orientals as well as other people delight, were introduced. I believe the Prince might have had the whole collection had he expressed any desire on the subject. A nylghau driven in harness—not very tractable; a pair of black bucks, harnessed and drawing a small carriage; parrots in cages, &c., were paraded in front of the Grand Stand for the Prince's inspection; and last, but not least, a Royal Bengal tiger was led out, lank, fiery-eyed, and savage, uttering growls, but scarcely capable of mischief, for hind-legs and fore-legs and body were bound with ropes, held by ten men at arms' length on both sides. Nevertheless, he was not by any means pleasant to look upon, and did strike out viciously with his right fore-leg, and very nearly laid hold of one of his guides.

The Prince now rose, thanked the Gaekwar and Sir Madhava Rao, and returned to the Residency. Night after night one lives in a constant state of illumination. The consumption of oil at Bombay, Poonah, and Baroda must have been wonderful. Chinese lanterns and myriads of "buttees" made the lines of the Cantonments and the Stations almost bright as day, and the routes from the Residency to the City, and to all the camps, blazed with lights suspended from trellis-work of bamboos. After an interval devoted to business and a change of dress, the Prince and suite drove over to the lines of the 9th Native Infantry, where he was received with due honour by Colonel Thompson and his officers, and dined with the regiment, which seemed very sensible of the honour. It was the first occasion on which a Native corps had ever entertained an Heir-apparent, and every effort was made to render it agreeable.

November 20th.—The cold was felt rather keenly last night by the outsiders. In the original programme the Prince was to have gone from Calicut for Coimbatore early this morning. Alas; how "the best-laid schemes of mice and men gang aft a-gley!" We were starting for the deer preserve of the Gaekwar for a day's sport. Noises outside at 4 A.M.; lights in the tents at 5 A.M.; shooting-clothes in request, and much tribulation among native servants unfamiliar with the language of detail. At 5.30 A.M. the members of the suite who were to go with the Prince assembled at the Residency, which was already lively enough, for servants were busy preparing the "little breakfast," which in England would do duty for a big one. The rays of the sun just slid over the tops of the trees which surround the building and touched the tips of the lances of the escort, and the bayonets of the sentries —the sentries of the 83rd Europeans being outside the line of the Native Infantry. Breakfast was hurried over, the Gaekwar's carriages were at the door, trumpets flourished, the guard presented arms, and at 6.15 A.M. the Prince and suite whirled away in a cloud of dust to the old railway station. Mr. Melvill, Sir R. Meade, Colonel Thompson, Major Bradford, Lieut.-Colonel Barton, Captain Jackson, and other officers and officials accompanied him. The special train—two saloon carriages and a van—rattled off to a place some eight miles distant, where the Prince was to begin his shikar. The line runs through a country of exceeding richness—level as a billiard-table, but so wooded and crop-laden that it was quite impossible to get a glimpse of the horizon except where the tent-like heights of Pounagurh, which people fondly believe to be a Hill-station, rose above the trees. So it is that Baroda city, with its 90,000 inhabitants, lying close at hand, is invisible. It is not half a mile from the line, and yet there is no trace of smoke or dust in the clear sky above the human turmoil. There were not many of what are called "Natives" about, for they were at work in the fields, which, rich in growth of hemp of extraordinary height, maize, cotton and dhal, stole away under cover of the trees, to the sea, forty-five miles to the West, and spread far East to the confines of British India. Social gatherings of monkeys were much agitated by the train. Wayfaring peasants halted to take the look, which seems obligatory all over the world, at the locomotive and carriages. In half an hour the special halted at a station, where the Kasee Shab-ood-deen, representing the Baroda Durbar, was present with a great gathering of elephants, shikarees, sowars, camels and oxen, to receive the Prince. There was an escort of the Haik Pagah, or the Gaekwar's Body Guard, in charge of a very gaily dressed young officer, who would have made a sensation at a costume ball in his green satin robe, and scarlet and gold clothing. There were sowars and lancers capering over the plain; and altogether the scene was bright and animated as eye could see. Some half-dozen of Probyn's old Horse were there—splendid-looking Punjaubees, whose eyes flashed with pleasure as they recognised their former leader. To these were given the rifles and ammunition. Five or six cheetahs—I am not sure which—surrounded by their attendants, were standing upright on cars drawn by oxen, their eyes hooded, lashing their lank sides with their tails, hissing and purring by turns like monster tabbies. There were also ugly, fierce-looking dogs of the Persian type—half greyhound, half deerhound—in leashes, and eight falconers with splendid peregrines and inferior short-winged falcons on their wrists. The Prince inspected the cheetahs with interest; one was taken from his cart for closer investigation, at which it hissed savagely till it was stroked into good humour by its keepers.

The Prince then mounted an ox-cart with the Duke of

Sutherland, and the rest of the suite followed on similar vehicles. This mode of conveyance was intended to permit the sportsmen to approach the black buck, which are accustomed to see long trains of hackeries or bullock waggons traversing the fields. The carts were, however, too highly ornamented, it is said, and the cortege was much too large. The elephants and sowars halted in the rear. The party then drove on to a vast plain called the Preserve. After a short time, herds of black buck were seen grazing amid the cotton-grass. They were much wilder than usual, and kept edging away from the carts, which were driven in a tortuous line, and worked like a fleet seeking to bring an enemy to action. The deer moved off towards thicker cover. Black buck are supposed not to mind carts, but they certainly were very vigilant on this occasion. Perhaps it was the novel costume, helmets, and London shooting-clothes, or the unusual length of the procession, which set them on the alert. At last a cheetah was slipped from the cart at a herd some fifty yards distant, and singled out a buck, which bounded with amazing springs across the plain. The cheetah, being distanced, gave up the chase after a dash of about 500 yards, which is said to be about the longest run they ever make, as the animal generally gives up after the failure of his first rush. The hunters now divided and beat in different directions, and many herds of deer were again seen, but they, too, were very wild. At last, after much manœuvring, a cheetah was brought sufficiently close, and was unhooded. It sprang from the cart at a herd and pulled down a buck, which was engaged in fighting with another, catching it fast by the throat. When the cheetah seizes buck or doe the agony is short, for the shikaree runs up, and, after the customary ejaculation, "May it be lawful!" puts an end, with keen blade, to the victim's struggles, and "grollocks" it, *more Scotico.* The blood of the poor deer was given to the cheetahs, as a broken-up fox is the reward of the hounds. The sportsmen mounted the carts again, and in half an hour got near another herd. This time two cheetahs were slipped, and each pulled down its victim.

Those who slip staghounds after haunched or broken-

THE PRINCE OF WALES IN SHOOTING COSTUME.

legged deer in the Highlands cannot logically charge those who follow this sport with cruelty, but it is not one which commends itself to Europeans. The cheetahs were sent back; and the Prince tried stalking, but it was with difficulty the hunters could get within a long shot. The usual course is to drive till deer are seen, and then get out and walk alongside the cart, which is directed towards the herd. Even after the party broke up into detachments, the herds were wild and shy, and his Royal Highness had only one chance, and that a very poor one, before 10 o'clock A.M. The heat then became oppressive, but the Prince stood the sun wonderfully well, and marched through the deep stuff as if he were used to it, while Peter Robertson trudged after him, thinking, perhaps, that a little of the sunshine might well be spared for the valley of the Dee. Dr. Fayrer insisted on the virtues of umbrellas and shade, and at 11 A.M. the sportsmen mounted their horses, and rode to the Palace, or shooting-seat, of Muckunpoora, a large block of building in the centre of a wide-spread plain. On his way the Prince came to a pool where there was a herd of buffaloes, guarded by a couple of little girls, and, dismounting from his horse, went towards them to get a shot at a paddy bird. The sight of a white man was too much for the guardians of the herd, and they fled across the marsh with piteous cries, not at all reassured by the shouts of a sowar who was despatched to comfort them. The shelter of the Palace, where breakfast was laid out in a room with thirty-six enormous lustres and as many side-lights, was very welcome.

The sportsmen, perforce, rested till 3 P.M., when the sun became somewhat less powerful, and then set out to try for black buck. At 5.30 P.M. the Prince returned with a fine buck, which he had killed at 200 yards, and Colonel Ellis with a doe. The day ended pleasantly, if the sport was a little disappointing—a great authority having promised the Prince at least twenty shots. At 6 P.M. the Prince drove back to Baroda. Sowars and police patrols were posted at intervals along the road, and a cavalry escort guarded the carriages. The Prince arrived at the Residency, where he was received with the usual honours, at 7 P.M., changed his shooting-dress for uniform, and dined with the Colonel and officers of the 22nd Native Infantry in the Cantonment at 8 P.M. The mess-room was very prettily decorated with garlands, wreaths of flowers, banners, and trophies of arms. At one end of the table were some fine skins of tigers shot by Colonel Nuttall, and the Prince of Wales' plume on the wall behind his Royal Highness was creditable to the skill of the contriver. Colonel Nuttall proposed the health of the Queen, and then that of the Prince of Wales, who, after an expression of the pleasure he felt at meeting the officers, and an acknowledgment of their very gratifying reception, gave the health of the regiment. Colonel Nuttall, in returning thanks, said the memory of that night would live in the annals of the regiment for generation after generation. The grounds around the mess-house were brilliantly lighted, and the Cantonment and the road to the Residency illuminated.

November 21st.—Jackals last night; parrots, minars, and crows, aided by a vigorous sun, early in the morning, could not banish slumber altogether; but, tired as we were after an early turn-out and a long day, it was not easy to sleep. The "Hookumdarr?" of the Sepoy, and the "Who comes there?" of the British soldier, pierced the single canvas of the tents very persistently, and to aid these lively influences, there was a perpetual tomtom-ing and a tomasha-ing outside Baroda. The coldness of the weather, in comparison with that at Bombay, set all the servants coughing terribly. And so I saw the sun rise above the trees. Odd creatures of natives, undoing the turbans they had bound their heads in, were crawling about the camp in the increasing warmth, like half-drowned flies trying to come to life; others, crouched on their hams, were cooking their rice; others, petition in hand, waiting outside the line of police, for it is difficult to persuade them that the Prince cannot redress all their wrongs.

The Rev. Mr. Polehampton, stationed here as Garrison Chaplain, one of the athletic family so well known for their prowess as oarsmen, came over from Cantonments to the Residency, and the Prince and suite attended Divine service in the large reception-room.

The Native officers of the 9th B. N. I. and of the 22nd B. N. I. were presented to the Prince by their Colonels in the afternoon. Each came forward as his name was called, presented his sword with the hilt towards his Royal Highness, who touched it, and the officer then passed on, making a military salute, with his hand to his turban. They were a fine-looking body of men, but it struck me that they were far too advanced in years for the active discharge of regimental duties.

At 7 P.M. the Gaekwar's carriages were at the Residency. Half an hour later the Prince, with Sir R. Meade, Mr. Melvill, Sir Bartle Frere, and the members of the suite, drove to the Palace of the Mohtee Bagh. Perhaps his Royal Highness saw nothing in India more curious than he witnessed on the way. Outside the Cantonments there was a bridge, spanned by triumphal arches most brilliantly illuminated. Men holding blazing torches stood along the parapets. But placed at the corners, and perched on stages and towers along the battlements, were the most grotesque and terrible things I ever beheld out of a dream. They looked like plaster statues. From beneath glistening tiaras or bonnets, wigs of snaky hair flowed over opaque white faces, which were set on tinselled bodies decked with wings of scarlet, picked out with gold and silver tinsel, which projected from the shoulders. Dresses resembling Elizabethan sacques, of brocade and tinsel, concealed all shape or form. In the inanimate hands were held stiffly bouquets, fans, swords or lances; but we started with horror when we saw the eyes—veritable coals of fire, set in those white stony faces of the wildest aspect—turn as we passed them. Some thought the spectacle ludicrous—to me it was horrible. It seems that on such occasions young people of the lowest castes dress themselves up thus at the expense of the Native Court, and keep their finery as perquisites by right. Every road was marked out by lamps. The very trees of the groves adjacent were hung with lamps. There were lamps before all the houses. Lamps were strewed broadcast over the fields. There were ornamental towers and triumphal arches blazing with lamps. Chinese lanterns innumerable swayed wherever they could be hung. Behind these lights stood a silent, solemn, brown-faced crowd; and the effect of these lights on enormous masses of white-clothed figures produced combinations to drive an artist to despair. When one thinks that for all that distance, through a city where the authority of the Empress's Government has been so very sternly and, as many think, unjustly asserted, the Prince passed almost within reach of an arm outstretched from the roadway, and that not a word of offence or gesture indicative of disrespect on the part of those myriads could be heard or seen, it must be admitted that the people of Baroda are, at all events, well-mannered.

Once more we saw the Baroda Highlanders, the Baroda Horse, the gold and silver guns,* and the beautiful carriages of the Maharanee Jumnabaae, drawn by magnificent oxen, with gilt and silvered horns, covered with trappings of gold and silver tissue. The Gaekwar's band played "God save the Queen;" his artillery fired a salute, his troops presented arms. The Gaekwar, Sir Madhava Rao, Shab-ood-deen, and the Ministers received the Prince on alighting at

* See Notes.

the steps. Unreservedly, trustingly, the Prince, followed by his handful of friends, passed into the Palace among the masses of swarthy retainers of the Court, all armed to the teeth, with the hand of the Gaekwar in his own. As a *divertissement* before dinner, the company were invited to inspect the Crown jewels, laid out on three tables in an adjoining room. They were well worthy the admiration of those who had such an opportunity of seeing concentrated riches. Let me tell a story. The late Gaekwar was fond of jewels. There came a merchant with certain precious stones, valued by him at 90,000*l*. The Gaekwar wanted money. So, said he, "I will buy the jewels; and if you give me 30,000*l*. down, I will give you an order for 120,000*l*. on the Treasury." The jeweller agreed; he gave the Gaekwar the money, and he handed him over the jewels, for which he got a receipt and an order on the public purse for 120,000*l*. When the Gaekwar was removed, the jewels could not be found, and the jeweller is now pressing the Baroda Government for the payment of his little bill. I fear he is not likely to get it.

When dinner was announced, the Prince led Mrs. Melvill downstairs to a long narrow pavilion in the garden. The dinner was in the European fashion—Baroda fashion in the old days was said to be apt to disagree with one—and it was not very long, which was a mercy. Towards the end Sir Maḍhava Rao appeared, leading in the Gaekwar. The Prince rose and made room for him by his side, Sir Madhava Rao standing at the back of his chair. After a short conversation, Sir Madhava, in the name of the Maharaja and Maharanee, proposed, in English, the health of the Queen, which was drunk with all honours, and next gave that of the Prince of Wales. The Prince, in returning thanks, expressed the pleasure he felt at being in

Baroda, and his gratification at the cordiality of his reception. He thanked the Maharaja and the Maharanee for their kindness, and could assure them he would never forget his visit. The Maharaja was yet very young, but he had a great career before him. He predicted that the Maharaja, inspired by the able counsels of Sir Madhava Rao, would devote himself to promoting the welfare of his people, and would exert himself to develop the resources of the country he was called on to govern, so as to insure the continuance of friendly relations between the two Governments. He gave the health of the Maharaja and the Maharanee. Sir Madhava, in reply, said the Maharaja and the Maharanee requested him to return their most grateful thanks for the manner in which their health had been proposed and responded to. They certainly regarded that as the happiest moment of their lives. Long had they been gazing on photographs of English Royalty. It was now their felicity to see that Prince who was heir to a sceptre whose beneficent power and influence were felt in every quarter of the globe; which dispelled darkness, diffused light, paralysed the tyrant's hand, shivered the manacles of the slave, extended the bounds of freedom, accelerated the happiness and elevated the dignity of the human race. They were grateful that the Prince had come from his distant northern home, traversing seas and oceans, as the gracious messenger of a gracious Queen. He had come to inspect an empire founded by the heroism and sustained by the statesmanship of England; to witness the spectacle of indigenous principalities relying more securely on British justice than could mighty nations on their embattled hosts. He would be greeted everywhere with enthusiastic loyalty and fervent devotion on account of his illustrious mother, and on account of his exalted position; of the motives which prompted the visit, and of his own right Royal affability and graciousness. His visit to Baroda could never be forgotten, never could fade in their memory. The occasion would be commemorated by history, and would ever be associated with renovated strength and renewed stability of the State. He had only to add a fervent prayer that their Royal guest would complete his progress to his satisfaction, and that he might have reason to regard with peculiar favour the weighty interests of the Princes and peoples of India; that he might carry back to his Empress mother, and to the British nation in general, most gratifying messages of loyalty to and attachment on the part of divers nations, professing different creeds, differing even in colour and costume, but united in gratitude for the benefits of British rule and influence.

After dinner, the Prince, Gaekwar, ladies, and company returned to the Palace, where a clever performer played on a simple apparatus of cups of different sizes filled partially with water, to an accompaniment of zithers. Two girls afterwards sung characteristic music, and there was dancing of no great merit, although the performers, it was said, were highly esteemed. Coffee was served, and there was a display of beautiful fireworks. At 10.30 P.M. the Prince paid a visit to the Maharanee, and expressed his pleasure at the visit, and his gratification at the sporting arrangements. The Maharanee was evidently greatly pleased at the Prince's expressions, and was very gracious to the suite. She came out with the Gaekwar, and bade them good-bye at the steps of the Palace.

The Prince drove to the Station at 11.25 P.M., where a special train was waiting to convey the party to the shooting-ground south of Mehmoodabad. Mr. Shepherd, Collector of Kaira, a famous shot, was charged with the arrangements. Those who were not to go with his Royal Highness, or who were excused by him, returned to the camp, and made the most of their time next day.

November 22nd.—The Duke of Sutherland and Mr. Grey went by special train to Ahmedabad with Colonel Barton, and greatly enjoyed their trip to that ancient city, and to its monuments and temples. The nights are cool, if the Bombay standard be accepted; but the heat in the tents was of an aggressive character, and drove the thermometer up to 88° at 11 A.M. In reality, shooting in the open is not so trying, although it may be more dangerous, than writing or working in the shade, even at a considerable reduction of temperature. Just as the sun rose, the Prince and his party got out of the train prepared for immediate action. There were elephants, camels, ponies, tongas or country carts, waiting for the sportsmen, a capital set of beaters, and a fine stretch of country under such crops as quails affect—jute, bagrie, &c. It was not long before the fusillade began; quail rose and dropped rapidly; but it was not always easy to find the birds in the thick green crops. There were three kinds—the grey, the rain, and the button quail. One of the party killed a peacock, and now and then there were partridges and hares. The Prince made a large contribution in the shape of a sarus (crane), which was found near some swampy ground, to the collection which Mr. Bartlett is preparing. About 10 A.M. the bag was found to consist of 111 quail and sundries. The Prince and party then rode to an old Temple, beautifully situated over the river, where they found breakfast. The special train was reached at noon, and at 1.30 P.M. the Prince arrived at the Residency. Then there was a *relâche* of two hours for lunch, and change of clothes for the pig-sticking expedition to Dubka, some eighteen miles south of Baroda. The party drove in open carriages to the ground, where they dined, and slept in two travellers' bungalows. The road was carefully guarded and patrolled, and the quarters were protected against intrusion for the night.

November 23rd.—The pig-stickers were up early, and rode off to try their 'prentice hands at the most popular of Indian wild sports; but the crops were very thick, and somehow or other the pigs did not show as it was expected they would. Some good boars broke, and went away; but at last the Prince had a chance of "getting his spear," as it is called, and killed a pig.

The Duke of Sutherland, Sir Bartle Frere, and I took a drive through Baroda. The streets were filled with bullock-carts and foot-passengers; consequently the yelling of the official in scarlet behind our carriage was incessant and deafening. We visited the potters' quarters, where the manufacturers were working their primitive wheels, turning out earthenware chatties at 1 pie each. One told us he could make 120 in the day, all told, which would give him more than 3*s.*, but out of that he would have to pay for fire for baking, and for clay. Nothing could be more quiet, civil, and courteous than the demeanour of the crowd. We drove by an ancient crenellated brick wall, with round towers and casemates, from which protruded the muzzles of iron cannon—a work older than the Mahrattas. So on to a magnificent tank, 500 yards square, where elephants were bathing, people washing and drawing water, the surface covered with rich green scum, broken by the gambols of fish and water-serpents. It is 12 feet deep, and has not been drained nor cleared for many years. The priest of the Hindoo Temple near at hand came out and invited us to enter. The inner idol was not shown, but in the outer shrine we could see the image of a cow or ox covered with gold tissue. There were many Brahmins inside. Though some had frowns on their brows, they were civil. One elderly priest told us there was a sermon and service, by reason of a foundation from Khandee Rao, open to all, every Monday; and he pointed out a lad of eighteen as the best of the preachers. Our guide showed at the end that he was as well up in asking a fee as if he were a true British verger. Driving back, we skirted the Palace of Bhow Scindia, the luckless Minister whom the deposed Gaekwar is said to have done to death. The irons and manacles forged by Mulhar Rao's orders for his brother's favourite and Premier now lie in the Residency. When we are told that Bhow Scindia had nothing to drink but salt water and pepper, in equal proportions, that he wore these chains and lived for fifteen days on such diet, it must be admitted, by those who believe the story, that he had, at all events, a very fine constitution. We passed next through the quarter of well-to-do citizens, and observed strong police stations and guards, as well as mounted men on guard at various places. It struck me that the Shroffs of the *beau quartier* regarded the strangers with less friendly eyes than the poorer classes, who were, however, negative in their demeanour. Some of the fat, sleek people sitting before their money-bags were absolutely scowling. Perhaps they had bad news of Turkish or Egyptian securities.

The hunting-party returned in the afternoon, and the Prince received deputations and addresses from Ahmedabad and Surat. It is to be regretted that Surat, which possesses interesting remains of the early representatives of British enterprise, was left unnoticed, and that the mosques, tombs, temples of the famous old city, the seat of Mahomedan dynasties and Hindoo houses for so many years, could not be visited; but Ahmedabad had not yet recovered from the effects of the dreadful inundation, and it would have been difficult to have made the necessary arrangements for Surat at short notice. The departure for Bombay was not so fine as the entry, but it was nevertheless made an affair of State, and the Gaekwar and all his people attended the Prince to the Baroda Station. Illuminations, bands, escorts, of course; but the platform at the Station was in darkness, and Sir Madhava Rao was in some apprehension lest advantage might be taken to do mischief to the Prince or to the young Gaekwar in the confusion. Owing to changes in the arrangements, there was some delay in getting up the carriages and starting the train.

November 24th.—The special train arrived at the Church Gate Station, Bombay, at 8.40 A.M. Sir Philip Wodehouse and his Staff, the Admiral, Captain Glyn, Lord A. Paget, Lord C. Beresford (quite recovered), Mr. Fitz-George, &c., were awaiting the Prince's arrival, and procession was formed to the Dockyard, where steam-launches were in readiness to convey the party to the *Serapis*. It was not considered expedient to return to Parell, or remain on shore, on account of the prevalence of sickness. There were renewed consultations respecting the arrangements for the tour after leaving Bombay. It was settled that after visiting Goa the *Serapis* shall call at Beypore, and that if the reports are unfavourable, she will go on to Ceylon, where the Governor is making every preparation for the Royal visitor.

The Prince dined with Admiral Macdonald, who is invited to take a passage to Calcutta, and whose flag-ship, the *Undaunted*, will proceed to Colombo. It was only by the exercise of Mahratta-like cunning, or of sturdy self-will, that any one could escape the pains and penalties of programme, or evade the grasp of official notifications. The Prince "Rex est et super grammaticam," but he was nevertheless very careful of prescribed covenants with the public, and it was only by hard work that he contrived to obtain relaxation. The Duke of Sutherland and others visited the institutions and sights of Bombay, and saw their friends at their ease without the "magna comitans caterva," but it was not possible for the Prince to imitate the good Haroun al Raschid. The Towers of Silence—of which no more at present—the Holy Tank and Temple of Walkeshwar, the Crawford Markets, the European Hospitals, were all duly visited before the Prince left Bombay, but each demanded its exertion and its "special" bundabust. The flourishing sect of Khojas, who acknowledge as their Chief the descendant of the Old Man of the Mountains, the veritable head of the Assassins, were gratified by seeing the Prince pay a visit to Agha Khan and his sons, the Persian Princes—for particulars of whom and of their history, please read the interesting papers in 'Macmillan's Magazine' from the charming pen of Sir Bartle Frere.

Whilst the Prince and his party were enjoying themselves at Baroda, Lord A. Paget, Major Sartorius, and Mr. FitzGeorge, &c., were engaged, in charge of Mr. Larcom, in search of tiger at Rajpoori. The *Osborne* arrived there on the 19th. Lord A. Paget, Mr. Larcom, &c., leaving the ship early on the 20th, made a good bag of wild fowl; Major Sartorius, Lieutenants Fitz-George and Gough, &c., had fair sport among the woodcocks. On the 21st, Lord Alfred Paget and others, leaving at 7.30 A.M., landed about two miles up the river. Under the orders of Mr. Larcom, the party toiled over hillside and through jungle until nightfall, without result. They landed again on the 22nd. Came on distinct recent traces of a tiger; so it was evident that they had been sitting down not many yards away from the beast during lunch. Perhaps he did not like the white umbrellas of some of the party. The sun was hot, and umbrellas were no doubt useful; who does not remember the story of the Royal Bengal, who was driven off in his charge on a picnic party by the sudden unfurling of a sunshade? The Jinjeera tiger might have been animated by similar antipathies. At all events, he was not killed. This short trip was a great relief to the ship's company. The crew made up water parties in a decided fashion; sixty "salts" hauling away at the ship's net astonished the villagers every evening. By the light of a big bonfire on the beach, alternately working cheerily up to his neck in water, and running foot-races, "Jack" managed to enjoy himself completely. To compensate for the scarcity of game, the party managed to bring back plenty of fish.

November 25th.—The steam-like clouds floating over Elephanta and the shore-line, and clinging to the surface of the water this morning, gave an indication of the heat which was not belied even when the sea breeze was freshest. Every one felt the influence of the climate. The very shipping, whilom so gay, had a depressed air, which corresponded too well with the sanitary condition of some of the crews; the pendants and ensigns drooped in the morning haze; a Vandervelde calm. The *Doris*, we know, is not at all healthy. The *Philomel* was away to the Malay Peninsula, despatched the night of the Byculla Club Ball, in consequence of the receipt of a telegram announcing the murder of Mr. Birch at Perak. Although we leave Bombay this evening, the route is still unrtaicen. A telegram received from the highest quarter gave expression to the anxiety caused by the reports of cholera, and the shooting excursion in Southern India may be considered as definitively abandoned. Dr. Fayrer and Dr. Hartwell, whose name has been so long associated with sanitary reform, and who has done such good work in the city of Bombay, think there are symptoms of an impending outbreak of cholera all over the Madras Presidency. The programme for the tour, so carefully drawn up in London and in Calcutta, has been cut to ribands. Every day brings its despatch, every despatch has dashed so many hopes and plans. Not needlessly nor in vain were warnings given that the set calendars in which the Prince's steps were measured and his hours told off should not be relied on. There was not in all these linked sweetnesses one small space left for a day's break down—for an accident, for even a headache or indisposition. The fleet has been an object of great attraction to the Rajas and natives of all classes, and even the high-caste Brahmin was not superior to the curiosity of seeing the *Serapis.* Commanders and First Lieutenants feel on such occasions very much as a man does who sees a loutish fellow tread with muddy feet on the tail of a lady's robe, so that the patience of Commander Bedford was sorely exercised by hosts of strangers. But now the Rajas, to the great relief of the saluting battery, have nearly all gone away, pretty well cleared out, poor men! and there was only one nine-gun-wallah to notice the loss of this morning. The *Serapis* was, however, thronged by visitors on business, and many friends came to take leave in the "cool" of the morning (thermometer 88°), notably of Sir Bartle Frere, whose name is ever grateful in Bombay, notwithstanding the small carpings of economists who object to spending the money of the people in the improvement of the city and county in which they live. There was also that liveliness of motion—going and coming—between deck, which denotes an impending arrival or departure, and many cases full of presents were being shipped and sent down the hold.

There was some anxiety respecting a detachment of the party (Lord Suffield and Mr. Knollys) which should have been on board early this morning; but they returned at breakfast-time from a visit to Sir Salar Jung at Hyderabad, which had proved very interesting and agreeable. They had not seen the Nizam, who was too ill to receive even his tutor, Captain Clerk.

The Prince landed at noon to take leave of the Governor. It was a state ceremony, and the men-of-war and the vessels in harbour dressed and saluted, the crews manned yards, and cheered; but there was naturally some diminution in the manifestations of loyal curiosity which marked the first appearance of the Prince. The landing was at the Peninsular and Oriental Steam Company's Dockyard at Mazagone, where there were very few persons to receive the Prince, because he had arrived before the time at which it was understood he would land. There were the band, colours, and guard of honour of 100 men of the 20th Native Infantry, the escort of the 3rd Hussars, and a half battery to salute. Mr. Souter was, of course, on the spot—where has he not been, and where is he not, wherever the Prince has been or is expected?—and he sent off for the vehicles; but he heard, perhaps with some dismay, that his Royal Highness wished, instead of driving direct to Parell, the way to which had been duly lined and patrolled by police, to visit the house of Sir Munguldass Nuthoobhoy, where there was a wedding festivity, which he intended to honour by his presence. Off flew a mounted Chief of the Bombay sbirri to make such dispositions as were possible to clear the new route of all impediments. The mansion lay in an out-of the-way part of the town;

suburban; but it was worth while to go there, for it is not given to every one to see the interior of a Native mansion at such a time; and the visitors saw not only the interior of the house, but the ladies of the family, and the young men who were enjoying the festivity, and the bridegroom himself, who was a marvel of brocade and gold and silver lace and tinsel, with a tiara on his head, so that he might well have been taken for the bride. And in such attire was he to proceed on a champing charger, escorted by his friends, to bring his wife to her new home. Poor lad! He seemed oppressed by fatigue, and no doubt would have given a good deal to have had the equestrian exhibition struck out of the programme. The house contained some good rooms, furnished in the mode which commends itself to the Oriental taste; and there were mirrors, musical clocks, mechanical contrivances, chandeliers, and engravings, notably of British and European personages, in abundance. The ladies were in flutters of delight at the visit, and Sir Munguldass Nuthoobhoy gave full expression to his feelings at the honour conferred on him. There was a great crowd of Bombay merchants. Several were pointed out as being worth so many lakhs of rupees, some as being worth millions of money; and of these the chief were presented to the Prince—then uttur and pân, and good-bye. The quantity of flowers in and outside was astonishing, and the scent overpowering; nor did any who entered escape the be-wreathment and garlanding, which form part of all ceremonies, the Prince being especially festooned with the choicest. There was an impression in the minds of some of the visitors that they had been at a Parsee's wedding, for the full-dress turban of the Bombay banker or bunneah has been adopted by the Parsees, and many think that it is their exclusive right to wear it. Away to Parell—streets lined, but not any great crowds of people. The Horse Artillery troop fired a salute; a guard of honour, furnished by the 26th Native Infantry, with band and colours, was in front of the House; but a glance down the avenue showed that all the canvas was down, and that life in the tented field was over for the present. The visit to Parell was very grateful, surely, to the Governor and to the Prince; but most of all, perhaps, to the Chief of Police (to whose activity, zeal, and administrative skill so much of the success of the Bombay festivities has been due—not a serious accident, not a riot, nor a fire); for the Prince, whose eye is quick to detect merit of the sort, thought it would be a proper recognition of Mr. Souter's services to bestow on him the honour of knighthood; and there were few happier men in the land that afternoon than the gentleman who felt the touch of the sword held by the Prince as the accolade was bestowed, and heard the words, "Rise, Sir Francis Henry Souter!" There was one small drop of bitter in the cup. The new knight had a hereditary right to be proud of "Frank," and he was styled "Francis;" but he was rendered content by the assurance that he could call himself "Sir Frank," as he preferred it. After tiffin and sitting for photographs, the Prince left Parell to go on board the *Serapis*. At the Dockyard there was a guard of honour of the 2nd Queen's, band and colours, under Captain Holt. The decorations had been furbished up, and, instead of "Welcome," over the entrance, there was "God speed." The interior seemed comparatively empty, for most of the Rajas were absent. There were present, however, the Raja of Radhanpore, the Raja of Dranghdra, the Nawab of Jinjeera, and the Raja of Palitana, each with followers gorgeously dressed, and there were several of the white-gowned and turbaned Sirdars of the Deccan. Sir Michael Westropp,

Sir Charles Sargent, Mr. Justice Kemball, Mr. Justice Melvill, Mr. Justice Green, Mr. Justice Bayley, the Hon. Mr. Scoble, the Hon. Mr. Rogers, the Hon. Mr. Gibbs, Major-General Kennedy, the Hon. Mr. Ravenscroft, Mr. Lee-Warner, Captain Morland, Captain Robinson, Mr. Barrow, Mr. Spencer, Mr. Orr, Sir Jamsetjee Jeejeebhoy, his sons and brother, the Hon. Vishwanath N. Mundlik, the Hon. Beecherdass Ambaidass, Mr. Nowrojee Manockjee Wadia, Mr. Manockjee Curtsetjee, Mr. Homejee Cursetjee Dady, Mr. Cursetjee Furdoonjee Paruck, Mr. Limjee Nowrojee Banajee, Mr. Pheroshah M. Mehta, and many others, and a great company of ladies, bouquets, kerchiefs, new dresses and fresh smiles, bright, fair and faithful to the last.

The Prince walked slowly down the scarlet cloth, stopping frequently to shake hands with and speak to gentlemen and ladies who had been presented to him; and, as he looked round, he noticed Sir Jamsetjee Jeejeebhoy, walked over and shook him by the hand. He touched his helmet in answer to salutes from gentlemen who were not within reaching distance. A crowd of officers and other gentlemen followed him to the Royal barge. The Prince stood engaged in conversation with Sir Philip Wodehouse, and several other gentlemen, for a few minutes. Then he stepped back, shook hands with almost everybody present, being anxious that none of those who had been introduced to him should be missed. The barge shoved off amid deafening cheers, not only from those in the yard, but from thousands who lined the piers and thronged the Apollo Bunder. Five minutes after, a salute from the ships of war announced that the Prince had arrived on board the *Serapis*. The Governor and his suite and others were received, and paid their parting respects on board the *Serapis* in the evening;

some, as Major-General Browne, Major Bradford, Major Sartorius, Major Ben. Williams, to rejoin the Prince, others to their posts, all with recollections of a few graceful sentiments more treasured than the substantial souvenirs which were so freely bestowed. The list of those latter would be long; but the name of Captain Robinson should not be omitted, nor the thanks the Prince conveyed to him and the Department over which he presided. At 5 P.M. the *Serapis* slowly moved ahead, with the faithful *Osborne* in her usual station, the *Raleigh* (freighted with all the special correspondents of the London papers and others, including Count Goblet d'Alviella, of the 'Independence Belge,' and M. de Coutoley, of the 'Temps,') in a line parallel to her, and the *Undaunted*, flag of Rear-Admiral Macdonald, astern.

At 6 P.M. the rays of the Colaba Light House, which had first welcomed the Prince to the East, were casting their gleam over the waters in our wake, and almost as uncertain in his wanderings along the coast as Vasco da Gama himself, the illustrious guest of the Viceroy of India was setting out to see what the Fates would send him on his cruise down the western coast of Hindostan.

"HAULING THE SEINE."

CHAPTER VI.

Visit to Goa—A Portuguese Settlement—New Goa—Old Goa—Mancheels—The Cathedral—The Bom Jesus—A Fishing Excursion—Coast Scenery—Beypore—Cholera prevalent in the Shooting District—The "Moplahs"—A Remembrance of Tippoo—Otter Hunt—Quilon—The Tambarettes.

NOVEMBER 26TH.—The *Serapis* continued her course south at a distance of some fifteen miles from land. The sea-line marked by a well-defined wall of cocoa-nuts; inland, elevated plateaux, leaving intermediate ranges cut up by valleys and sweeping plains. But what activity and life amongst people, to us as unknown as they were to the Portuguese when first their daring caravels ploughed these waters! Close to land were running, as if engaged in a regatta, fleets of fishing-boats, with outriggers and lateen sails, and here and there larger native merchantmen. All day long they passed to and fro, up and down, now and then coming quite close, the crews rousing themselves up to stare at the unwonted bulk and grandeur of the great steamer, such as was never before beheld in those seas. At long intervals, wherever the coast offered a sheltering bay for commerce, there were traces of the works of former conquerors, and of races no longer in power. We passed Malwan in the course of the afternoon, and soon afterwards Fort Melundy, a remarkable work, about 400 yards long, with sixteen bastions, built of dark-coloured stone. At 1.30 P.M. the *Osborne* was signalled, and Colonel Ellis was sent on board with despatches to announce the arrival of the Prince, and to make arrangements for his reception at Goa. The Governor had been already informed that a visit might be expected from his Royal Highness, and preparations were made to do him every honour. In the course of the afternoon, the sea being perfectly calm, a remarkable appearance in advance of our course caused some uneasiness on board, till the cause of it was understood. It was an elevated line of water in the shape of a Λ, the sharp end being at the distance of several miles, and the sides gradually extending outwards, so that it looked exactly like the sea marking a reef, right on the centre of which we were running full speed. The *Raleigh*, which was on our port quarter, was signalled to, altered her course, and came up on the starboard and astern; but after a close inspection through the glass it turned out to be nothing more than a long double ripple in the placid sea, the effect of the *Osborne's* course, although she was so far ahead as to be hull down at the time. At 5 P.M. we sighted Cape Aguada, which is north of the entrance to the river on which Goa and Panjim lie. It is a bluff, brown mound, with some buildings on the pointed summit, and with a fort, or rather a wall with a few guns mounted on it, at the base. At 7 P.M. the *Serapis* and *Raleigh* anchored about two miles out from shore, the *Osborne* being stationed inside. The night passed quietly, but they had some difficulty in preventing the Portuguese authorities coming off to welcome the Prince, and they were very anxious to fire another salute.

November 27th.—The morning sun lighted up the glistening sides of the *Serapis*, the warlike bulk of the *Raleigh*, and the graceful lines of the *Osborne*, and of her small sister, the *May Frere*, as they sat on the quiet roll of a waveless sea, which lapped the verge of the wide spread of green cocoanut-palms fringing the shore. The number of pendants, and the array of steam-launches, barges and gigs passing to and fro between the vessels, gave a fitting appearance of state to the little squadron flying the Prince's standard and the British ensign in Portuguese waters. Landwards were a few fishing or coasting boats, with broad lateen sails and high sterns. Then a low broken range of hills, above the outline of which rose higher and more regular summits. Here and there the detached tumular formations so frequent in this part of India were visible, and on one of these, close to the beach, was perched the Light House, which looks like a fortified work. To the south crop up a few small islands. The settlement of Goa-Panjim is situated on the south bank of the river, some three miles from the headland. The town could not be seen from the anchorage, but one large house embowered in trees, and several smaller residences on the rising ground, could be made out through the glass.

At 8 A.M. the Prince of Wales, in undress uniform, and his suite, Captain Glyn, Captain Tryon, Commander Durrant, &c., were conveyed in two steam-launches to the *May Frere*. The *Raleigh* woke up the echoes with her big guns, and, before the salute was over, the cloud of smoke, curling in creamy folds and mounting upwards, hid all but the men on the top-gallant yards from view.

At 8.45 A.M., as the despatch-boat ran past the ancient water battery at the north side of the creek on which Panjim is situated, the Portuguese fired a very creditable salute of twenty-one guns and hoisted the British standard. There were very few craft on the river, and no Portuguese or European vessels; but as we were entering the creek, a steamer, which had been chartered to carry the Raja of Kolhapoor on his way home from Bombay, passed out to the north with many Native passengers. The boats engaged in fishing were rudely made of thick, coarse planks of dark wood, with high projecting sterns; the rowers were all but naked. They are a squalid people to look at, very dark, like most of the natives of the coast, and do not seem to belong to the race of Hindoos to be seen inland. A coarse cloth, rarely clean, serves as turban, and nothing else have they in the shape of clothes but a very scanty loin-cloth. Their oars are like maltsters' shovels, very nearly similar to those used in Bombay waters, which are poles with flat circles of wood nailed to the end.

The river beyond the bar resembles the Thames below Gravesend, always assuming the cocoanut-palms on the banks as an invariable characteristic. As we came nearer, the resemblance was strengthened by the aspect of New Goa itself, which is exceedingly like old Gravesend. The Government House looms like the old Falcon Tavern, and there are little bits by the river-side which remind one exactly of the more ancient buildings above and below Rosherville. A range of wild ghauts is visible to the east.

When the *May Frere* came up to a line of detached bungalows on the creek, the people ran towards the landing-place, where there was a multitude of persons, some in black hats and evening dress, others in less elaborate costumes, and others in the simple attire affected by the aborigines. The Portuguese turn very brown in these parts, and their native hue deepens greatly in India, where as we travel south the people generally acquire darker tints. The Europeans looked like Hindoos *en costume*, and the entire absence of any sort of womankind added to the bizarre effect of the crowd on those whose eyes had been accustomed to see brilliant Parsee ladies everywhere in Bombay. As soon as the *May Frere* was moored about 100 yards from the Governor's House, a double-banked galley, pulled by eighteen men, who were dressed in a uniform which recalled the costume of the time of Elizabeth, put off. The scarlet caps, in front of which were fixed large silver plaques, worked finely, and said to be 200 years old, may be seen depicted in an old painting (at Venice, I think), representing a naval engagement between the Turks and the Venetians, in which there is a boat in the foreground, rowed by men wearing caps and badges of very much the same form. The galley came alongside, two equerries received the Governor (Viceroy no longer) at the gangway. The Prince stood at the top of the ladder of the quarter-deck, and his Excellency Tavares de Almeida, General of Division of the Royal Artillery of Portugal, and Governor of Goa, &c., ascended, and was graciously welcomed. His Excellency, who was highly *décoré* for services in China, Mozambique, &c., was followed by Senor J. H. da Cunha Rivara, Secretary; Major Albuquerque, Military Secretary; Lieut.-Colonel Pertana, Governor of Damaun (another Portuguese possession near Bombay); Captain J. T. F. Arez, R.N., Captain Fonseca, A.D.C., Captain de Lacerda, A.D.C., Senor B. J. de Lorena, &c. After a few moments' conversation, the Prince, Governor, and suites were rowed to the landing-place of New Goa, where order certainly did not prevail. Though there was no shouting, noise, or violent shoving—still there was a strong desire to close in round the Prince, and the two stalwart Punjaubees who carried the Prince's rifles, which were taken on the chance of a shot, as game was said to be abundant, exercised a very salutary influence in restraining the eagerness of the crowd.

A very small place it is, indeed; but an immense mass of people around the landing-place—of such mongrel aspect that it was very hard to say where Hindoo ended and European began—gave cause for wonder as to where they abode or where they came from, for outside the town all is cocoa-nut. The forces of the Government were drawn up — a European battalion, a Sepoy battalion, and a battery. The Sepoys, with European officers, were very much the same stamp of men as our own low-caste regiments, looking more like Madrassees than Bengalees. They were dressed in blue and yellow. The Portuguese officers smart, but rather sickly. The European battalion, on their right, extended up across the Plaza to the Government House. When the crowd, making a most extraordinary chattering and jabbering, closed in, there was decided agitation of the two mounted officers, whose horses had probably never before been exposed to such an ordeal, and the "present arms" was almost too much for them. The Government House, which is not more than a century old, contains a very interesting gallery of portraits, removed from old Goa: likenesses of all the Viceroys who reigned in the names of the Kings of Portugal from the foundation of their great dominion in India till Viceroys ceased to be, and gave way to simple Governors-General. They may be as apocryphal as the likenesses of the Scotch Kings at Holyrood, but they have an air of genuineness about them; and they stand in ruffs, collars, trunk hose, Vandyck cloaks—right gallant-looking gentlemen. Whether the climate was very deadly, or they made their fortunes very rapidly, it is certain they followed in quick succession, and two came in one year, which, considering the difficulty of the voyages between India and Portugal, is remarkable. The Prince went round the rooms with great interest, and after a time, taking his stand before a seat of honour in a chamber which was decorated with portraits of the Kings of Portugal and of some of his own Royal relatives of the House of Coburg, received the Archbishop of Goa and his clergy, and a number of Portuguese officials, who were presented to him by the Governor. The heat, if not overpowering, was distressing, and the buildings were crowded by the whole population of Goa apparently, who certainly had the Republican attribute of doing exactly as they pleased.

Then his Royal Highness and the Governor embarked in the steam-launch of the *Osborne*, and went three miles up the river to visit what remains of Goa proper, or "old Goa," abandoned more than 230 years ago on account of its unhealthiness. The river washes the remains of a great city—an arsenal in ruins; palaces in ruins; quay walls in ruins; churches in ruins—all in ruins! Long would it take to repeat the stories of our friends concerning the places we passed. As one of them said, "We were once great. We ruled vast provinces in this land. Now you are the masters. Look and see what is left to us!" We looked, and saw the site of the Inquisition, the Bishop's Prison, a grand Cathedral, great churches, chapels, convents, religious houses on knolls surrounded by jungle and trees, scattered all over the country. We saw the crumbling masonry which once marked the lines of streets and enclosures of palaces, dockyards filled with weeds, and obsolete cranes.

Goa! Somehow or other the "Inquisition" comes to one's mind when the place is named. But it has, or ought to have, memories of a nobler sort. The history of the Portuguese in India would point the moral and adorn the tale of a philosophical historian who should write of the decline and fall of empires. The Portuguese can fight, no doubt, as stoutly as they did in days of yore, and if they are not quite so potent in an eminently practical and rather severe theology as they once were, they have not been left ignobly behind in the race of modern civilisation. Da Gama! Albuquerque! These are names to conjure with. It is a place an Englishman ought to visit. It is a place which an English Prince, especially, may visit with great profit. If we are proud of our deeds and of our history in India, and if we are elated by the greatness of the doings of our race, we may be led by the aspect of ruins such as those which the Prince of Wales has been gazing upon to turn our thoughts to the investigation of the causes which sap the foundations of mighty States, and lay the work of statesmen and soldiers in the dust.

At the landing-place some dozen wretched-looking natives were gathered. The distances are great, and if the stranger does not wish to be carried in litters resembling the Simla panjams, here called "mancheels," which are canopied seats slung from bamboos, which are borne on men's heads, he must walk. The Prince and the Governor got into one of these litters, not without some laughter, and were conducted to the Cathedral, which is half a mile from the landing. The road passes under a large arched gateway. In a niche over the arch, beneath one of St. Catherine, stands a painted statue of Vasco da (not de) Gama, and we were told that it was of necessity that each Governor of Goa should go under this archway—" Aliter

Gubernator non potest fieri." There was one of the smooth, well-bred, amiable ecclesiastics, who are ever to be found *in situ*, to show the Prince round and explain everything. The Cathedral inside is of vast and noble proportions, very plain and massive outside. It contains shrines and chapels, and much gilding, many middling paintings, fine old silver work. There were only seven worshippers—all women, all natives—all before one shrine;

THE MANCHEEL.

at least, *they* were real, for the visit was a surprise. What had become of the worshippers for whom these churches had been erected? Or were they the work of Faith and Hope? From the Cathedral the Prince went to the Bom Jesus. On the steps a musical performance welcomed the Prince, which he never heard or saw the like of before. One tall, lanky native gentleman, whose principal raiment was a big drum slung from his neck, belaboured that instrument with one hand, and with the other held to his mouth a fearful tube of brass, from which he compelled the most dreadful sounds. A boy beside him, without the benefit of drum, clanged two cymbals, and a couple of youths joined in, one on a kettle-drum, the other on a drum simple. Above this din rose the ding dong of the small, and the sonorous roll of the great, bells of the church, and the barking of noisy curs. There were no beggars, and that for the reason that there were no people to be begged of. The Bom Jesus is chiefly noted for the shrine of St. Francis Xavier, a man whom the churches of the world may unite in accepting as a true Apostle. It is certainly one of the most beautiful and one of the richest objects of the kind which can be seen anywhere. But it is placed in a very small, dark chapel, and can scarcely be conveniently examined. The treasuries, full of gold and silver cups for the sacred elements, were opened, and their contents and many curiosities were exhibited; then the Prince, having thanked the clergymen who had been his guides, got into a mancheel and was carried down to the landing-place. There was by this time one beggar—a fakir—and he got nothing. The Governor took the Prince a little run up the river in the steam-launch, but they did not go so far as was intended. The Portuguese gentlemen said, however, that they did this to please the Prince, and that to please themselves they would never dream of going abroad in a heat of 85° in the shade. The party returned by water to Panjim—indeed, it would seem as if there were no good roads inland—and then left the boats for the despatch vessel, the heat being too great to render it agreeable to land.

At 12 o'clock the *May Frere* left, with the Prince and Governor, for the *Serapis*, where lunch was served at 1.30 P.M. The Prince took the Governor and suite over the ship, with which they were delighted. At 3 P.M. his Excellency took leave of his Royal Highness, who bade him goodbye at the top of the main-deck ladder. The *Raleigh* hoisted the Portuguese standard at the main, manned yards, and fired a salute of twenty-one guns.

Smooth as the sea was, the surf ran heavily on the spit at the entrance to the river; one of the boats of the *Raleigh*, in charge of Lieutenant Kingscote, was swamped in the course of the day. But the chance of an upset was rather appetising. There was not much danger—no sharks, it was said—and at 4 P.M. a boat pulled off to fish on the beach. The Prince decided on going later, when he had finished his letters. I am not quite sure that his Royal Highness's determination caused unalloyed satisfaction, for the risk in the surf would be increased by darkness. The Prince turned out in fishing-clothes, which would have done very well "for the hill." The boat was towed out by a launch; but before the Prince reached the shore a breaker struck the stern, and thoroughly drenched him and the Duke of Sutherland. It was just enough to laugh at—the sea-water was warm and the beach was near. The fires lighted on the beach showed where the first party were drawing the nets. The fishing was pleasant, if not profitable. The natives are to be credited with a strong love of sport, for, as fuel was not abundant, they came down with parts of their houses and contributed to the fires on the beach. The sailors, hauling at the seine, delighted at seeing the Prince and his friends working in the water, waded and swam cheerily in the surf; but big fish were not in the way, and after three draws of the net there remained on the beach only thirty skate (maiden ray) and some dozens of a fish like a sardine, only somewhat larger, which were certainly inferior to the poor Mediterranean article, and tasted, when cooked next morning, according to a high authority, "like flannel stuffed with pins." Still there was the sense of doing something, and there was plenty of laughter. At midnight the Prince and party returned, "wet to the skin," and woke the sleepers to tell them what had happened. Every one was very glad to see all safe on board again. As soon as the Prince returned, a boat was sent off to the *May Frere*, which proceeded to Bombay with the mail bags to catch the outgoing steamer of November 29th.

November 28th.—The *Serapis* lay at anchor all night, guarded by the *Raleigh*. As the sun, heralded by a glorious golden haze, rose behind the line of the purple ghauts and flung its rays into the blue, yet rejoicing in its myriad stars, the crew warmed into life in the hard and very practical manner of men who go down to the sea in ships, and whose business is upon the waters. Pumps were rigged and hose laid out to wash the decks, and douse the unhappy natives who are unwary enough to sleep "all over the place." Sufferers who have been awakened, as they slept on the deck of a Peninsular and Oriental steamer in the Red Sea, will quite understand the operation. At 5.30 A.M. the *Serapis* weighed anchor, and ran along the shore for Beypore at a speed of 10½ knots an hour, accompanied by her guardian and the Royal yacht. Sea smooth; the irresistible thermometer at 80°. Coast ten miles off—brown bluffs and rocky promontories fending off the waves, a rugged line of blue hills in the distance—and in the intermediate space rolling land, timbered or cleared. There are no pirates to vex commerce now; yet it is not so very long ago that the British Government, represented by the Honourable East India Company, made treaties with the Angria family—a race of pirate chiefs haunting this very coast. A Hindoo pirate seems to be an anomalous personage, but he is not much stranger than an Abyssinian admiral, and these were once, as we have seen, very considerable powers on the West Coast of

India. Marmagoa and St. George's Islands were seen in due course. At 8.15 A.M. we passed Cape Ramas, "a high bluff headland, forming in two level points when seen from north or south." There were several white objects on the shore, which were explained to us to be Portuguese churches, but which had the look of Nestorian places of worship, such as were common further south. About 9.30 A.M. the squadron was again off British territory; Polem, the Portuguese frontier town which lies east of Loliem Point, being twelve miles south of Ramas. The heat increased, and was 87° between decks at dinner time. Lord Carington, who was a little hit by the sun because he will, in his unselfish way, persist in taking the last and the worst place wherever it can be found, is himself again; but, *per contra*, Lord C. Beresford is obliged, after his night's fishing, "to lie up." At noon we were in lat. 14° 29′ N., long. 74° 3′ E., 60 miles from Goa. Divine service on the quarter-deck at 11 o'clock. The Rev. Canon Duckworth and Mr. York, the chaplain of the *Serapis*, officiated. There is an excellent harmonium on board, on which one of the band plays. The reading-desk, covered with a handsome flag, is on the port side. The Prince's chair is placed beside the harmonium, opposite the desk; there is a double row of chairs from the Prince's left, and from the reading-desk and pulpit to the deck saloon. The suite sit here, Captain Glyn facing the Prince and next to the clergyman. At right angles to these, extending aft, are chairs and benches for the officers of the ship; behind the Prince, on the starboard side, are the bandsmen of the choir, the Marines and sailors; the domestics of the Prince and of his suite are on the starboard side of the deck, in a line with the Staff and suite.

November 29th.—Passed Sacrifice Island at 8 A.M.; Cabo an hour earlier. Rocky ridges covered with sea eagles close at hand. Beypore was in sight in an hour more; and about 9.30 A.M. the squadron anchored a couple of miles from the bar, just within view of the Beypore Railway Station. At 10.15 A.M. an effete little steamer, called the *Margaret Northcote*, crawled up alongside from shore, and anchored a cable's length off; and presently a boat came off with Mr. Robinson, Mr. Macgregor, Mr. Logan, and Dr. Houston, in full uniform—and very hot it was indeed—and put them on board the *Serapis*. The reports of the medical officers and of the authorities were conclusive—cholera existed along the routes which the Prince would have had to take. It is easy to say that there was cholera in the places visited by the Prince subsequently; but how fearful a censure would have fallen on the officer responsible for the health and safety of his Royal Highness if he had recommended a visit which turned out disastrously! The gentlemen did not give any advice, but they approved Dr. Fayrer's recommendation, although they knew what chagrin it would cause. The shooting-camps had been formed with infinite labour and expense. Bangalore had arrayed everything that luxury could suggest or wealth procure for the occasion. The Mysore Government had spent many thousands of pounds on preparations for the Prince's reception. Ootacamund was on the tip-toe of expectation, and the good people of the Station had laid out money in the most lavish manner; the Raja of Travancore had been living in the hope that he would have the honour, for which he had made magnificent outlay, of being the host of the Prince. For hundreds of miles the whole population was stirred with the same expectancy. All this was true, but it was true too that there was the cholera among them. Dr. Houston was of opinion that there was no reason to prevent any one visiting the shooting district. There was cholera certainly, but then there is always cholera more or less about these parts. At Alipee there had been twenty-one cases in a month; at Cottiam fourteen cases in a month; there were cases at Mysore and at Bangalore; in fact, cholera was to be found all over the country. One place alone was free—Trivandrum. "Let the Prince go to Trivandrum, then. The Raja of Travancore is there." Alas! "There is nothing to shoot at Trivandrum." And to make matters more aggravating, it was announced that the Annamally and "Michael's Valley" were swarming with bison and deer. Deer may be killed elsewhere, but the last chance of bison is lost when this part of Southern India is abandoned.

The Prince bore the disappointment with much philosophy; and as there was no need of hurrying to reach Ceylon, proposed to run up the river to-day, and accordingly set out in the launch, which towed a dingy, for a little excursion.

The bar is dangerous in bad weather, and though it was quite calm, a "good lump" of a swell was on. There must be abundance of fish here. Shoals of a pretty grey mullet-looking sort leapt out of the water continually; one came into the boat, another would have done so but that an arm was in the way. A shoal of very large but exceedingly knowing porpoises led the launch astray in a bootless chase. They rose, spouting and puffing in the sunshine—their black sides shining as if they were clad in macintoshes—dived deep in the blue wave, and full of their tricks went off below in quite a wrong direction for the sportsman, who pursued only to see them, at the next "show," twice as far. On the left bank of the river, close to the water's edge, stand the few houses which constitute the town of Beypore. A lofty flagstaff, dressed with many colours, a reception platform, and an avenue lined with green branches and wreaths, marked the Railway Terminus, where it was hoped the Prince would have been received. The river is not more than 250 or 200 yards wide above the town; palm-trees clothe its sides as far as the eye can reach. Occasionally one makes out in the gloom beneath the branches the low roof of the native mansion thatched with leaves, but there is no appearance of towns or villages. The launch steamed against the stream and the ebbing tide, and attracted some—but not any great—attention from the fishermen and boatmen, and we began to look out for game, for Mr. Logan said crocodiles were plenty. At one place some of the party went ashore and found a family of boat-builders at their occupation. Mr. Logan explaining that we wanted cocoa-nuts, off went two of their number, who scrambled up trees like monkeys and came down with a dozen. These they trimmed with their axes, cut off a piece at the top and held up the natural goblet full of vegetable milk to thirsty lips.

Mr. Robinson was anxious, however, that the Prince should not land. The "Moplahs" are not to be trusted. These people are descended from Arabs who, at their first coming, married the Indian women, but they now marry among their own people exclusively. Active merchants, keen traders, industrious agriculturists, they are fanatical and furious in matters pertaining to their faith, and under the influence of a very bigoted priesthood. A Moplah is ready to sacrifice his life at any moment in order to take that of a heretic. Armed with bill-hooks, the Moplahs have more than once received volleys of musketry and bayonet charges from European troops without flinching, and they have so completely cowed the native troops that no one would think of sending Sepoys to put down a Moplah movement. They fight till they fall to a man. It is a pity we cannot make use of such admirable material for soldiers, but they will not serve us.

With some interest we asked, when we saw natives on the bank, "Are they Moplahs?" Once only was the answer "Yes," and that was when Muggur Sing ("Crocodile Lion"), one of the Punjaubee horsemen in attendance on the Prince, routed a woman in a yellow garment, who, in apparent trepidation, hurried out of her house with a child on her hip into the jungle, and was followed by two or three lads. Just half a mile above the line of native vessels moored off the Railway Station, Mr. Logan, looking into a small creek, said, "There are otters!" And there, sure enough, mingled with bitterns and paddy birds fishing in the shallows, were ten or twelve of them. They were alarmed by the puffing and screw-beat of the steam-launch, and began to edge towards the cocoanut-trees. The Prince, accompanied by Mr. FitzGeorge and Peter Robertson, got into the dingy, and was rowed gently up the creek, but by the time he was within shot not an otter could be seen. The dingy went on up a narrow channel, between an island and the main, to the deserted works of the Porto Nuovo Iron Company, which made excellent Bessemer steel and iron, but was unable to procure fuel cheap enough to give a profit. The Prince, in spite of the sun, the declining rays of which struck on his back with full force, was still intent on sport, and kept on in advance. Gaily dressed native Christian ladies, floating down the stream to have a look at the Prince, little dreamt that the Sahib in the small boat who was "pottering about" the river was the Shahzadah.

On an eminence crested with trees could be seen the ruins of one of Tippoo's forts. "Do the people remember Tippoo?" "Oh dear, yes! He gave them good reason to remember him and his doings, and they talk of him still." It is the immortality of those who vex their kind—"on parlera de sa gloire." Suddenly a shot was heard, the dingy pulled vigorously towards a circle in the water. An otter had been hit. It rose and made for the bank, was struck by a second shot, and sank. "The divers shall get it to-morrow morning," said Mr. Logan (a very difficult matter, one would think, but he assured us that there were pearl divers at Beypore who could stay five minutes under water—on the which depends a bet), and so the chase continued. Then another shot was heard, and Peter Robertson, in mortal fear of snakes and alligators, was sent ashore to beat the jungle. "Crocodile Lion' was sent to the other bank. Eventually an otter, wounded so severely that it could scarcely crawl up the bank, was driven out; but the creature was so tenacious of life, and so crafty that it was not possible to find him in the thick brushwood and rocks. It was now 6 P.M., and it was getting dark; Captain Gilham, our pilot, became anxious; the Prince, disappointed at the loss of three otters, came into the launch, where the cocoa-nuts full of milk were very welcome. As the launch and dingy in tow passed Beypore, blue lights were burnt and music was heard—a "fantasia" was going on to console the people for losing the Prince's visit. The bar was passed at reduced speed, as there was a long and heavy swell on. As the launch ran by the ever-watchful *Osborne*, a blue light was burnt. It was answered by a rocket and two blue lights from the *Serapis*. In five minutes more his Royal Highness was on the companion-ladder of the great ship, the sides of which gave the idea of a street with triple row of gaslights. The Prince's absence had created a little uneasiness on board, and the steam-launch had been got out. Mr. Logan and Captain Gilham went on board their steamer, and at 7 P.M. the *Serapis* and *Osborne*, escorted by the *Raleigh*, weighed and steered for Colombo.

November 30th.—At 7 A.M. wind light, sea smooth;

speed, 10 to 10½ knots; thermometer, 80°; land scarcely visible on port side. At 8 A.M. faint blue mountain outlines in the distance, which gradually became better defined. At 10 A.M. the coast was closely approached again—that is, within eight or nine miles—the unfailing band of cocoanut-palms running along the beach, and the mountain ranges of Cochin and Travancore in the distance. Found that the bath-pipes were doing the duty of the bilgewater-pipes, which rendered bathing not quite so agreeable as it might otherwise have been.

At noon the squadron was off Quilon. Our latitude was 8° 51′ N., long. 76° 29′ E., distance run since yesterday 153 miles,—difference between reckonings showed a current of 20 miles against the ship. The Fort of Tangacheri, with flagstaff—a British ensign hoisted on the staff—and the houses could be easily made out. Then came in sight the first of the remarkable churches, built on the very verge of the beach, at intervals of two or three miles apart, as far as Comorin, which attest the existence—alas! many centuries ago—of considerable Christian communities and successful missionary labours. Their uniform elevation, snow-white frontages, and apparently complete preservation, render them singularly conspicuous and interesting objects from the sea. The track of whales became obvious. They spouted! "To arms!" was the call on the main-deck; several rifle shots were fired, but none of the whales seemed to mind. At 3 o'clock P.M. Trivandrum, and an Observatory belonging to the Raja, were in sight. The Raja of Travancore is, in spite of his Observatory and his attainments and science, a very strict Hindoo. He rules a fair domain. It is said to be one of the few States which have always been under Hindoo rule and governed by Hindoo laws, but these latter, which dated from 1490, were modified in 1811. The succession is in the female line—that is, the Raja is succeeded by the son of his daughter, not by his son; and the tales in connection with this singular custom are curious. The history of the Tambarettes, or Hereditary Queens of Travancore, may be one of the most interesting in the pages of romance; but we know little or nothing of it. Who was the young Englishman, for instance, with whom the Queen fell in love, and whom, though he declined to marry her, she sent away, in 1685, loaded with presents? How did he get to Trivandrum, and how did he leave? and where did he go to? and why did he refuse her hand? Anjengo, higher up on the coast, was, says Mr. Eastwick, the birthplace of Sterne's Eliza, and of Orme, the historian of British India. Nobody whom any one cares about seems to be born in India now, neither heroine nor historian. The coast line maintains almost a uniform character to Cape Comorin,—a belt of yellow sand, on which break the great snow-white rollers; native boats, looking like basking alligators, drawn up on the beach; Nestorian churches flecking with white patches the cocoanut-tree fringe; a flat stretch of green to the great wall of mountains, broken at the summit into peaks, conical or rounded, and jagged outlines and saw-edges at elevations varying from 3000 feet to 6000 feet. Several waterfalls seamed the lofty ridges of the towering background. At 5 P.M. Cape Comorin was well in sight—"the end of India." The Cape is flat and sharp; the cocoanut-palm pursues it out to the verge of the ocean. Behind rise the Ghauts, their summits covered with mist. The villagers could be seen pointing out the flotilla, and gazing westwards in the track of the setting sun.

At 7 P.M. it began to blow, and at 8.30 P.M. a swish of a sea came in through the windows on the port side, and flooded the cabins of General Probyn and Colonel

Ellis. The night was squally; nevertheless, there were festivities on board, for the promotion of Lord C. Beresford to be Commander was duly celebrated at a dinner presided over by his Royal Highness, to which Captain Glyn and all the officers of the *Serapis* were invited, and after which the Ethiopian serenaders performed on deck.

"IT'S NAE THE TIGERS THAT FEAR ME, IT'S JUST THE SAIRPENTS AND THE LIKE O' THEY!"

LANDING AT COLOMBO.

CHAPTER VII.

COLOMBO, KANDY, CEYLON, TO TUTICORIN.

Colombo in Sight—Taprobané—Birthday of the Princess—The Landing at Ceylon—Departure for Kandy—Railroad Scenery—Kandy—Blood-suckers—The Pera-hara—The Botanical Gardens of Ceylon—"Lightly tread!"—The Sacred Tooth—The double Imposture—Buddhist Priests—Along the Road—A curious "Bag"—Leech-gaiters—The Stockade—Don Tuskerando—"Dead, sure enough!"—Agri-Horticultural Exhibition—The Colombo Ball—Tamil Coffee Pickers—The Evil One in Ceylon.

DECEMBER 1ST.—Colombo lights were in sight before daybreak. The *Serapis* seemed inclined to justify certain traditions relative to her extraordinary powers of rolling last night; but if any one on board felt inclined to consider himself unfortunate, he had only to look, if he could, out of his port in the early morning at the *Osborne*, and see what remarkable ups and downs she was undergoing. Nevertheless, our stately vessel rolled at times quite enough to divert the thoughts of most of us from comparison with anything outside the cabins in our ship. The "bearings" at last became heated in their controversy with the waves, and the speed was necessarily reduced, so that the *Serapis* was late, and was not able to come to anchor in Colombo Roads within three hours of the time appointed by telegraph, which is quite enough to demonstrate the force of the breeze. As the morning dawned—a gradual spread of lighter grey over the dull pall, charged with rain and thunder, which rested on the land—the look-out was not cheerful. There was no patch of blue in the sky. Taprobané was sulky, and refused to put on smiles for her visitor. There was nothing bright or lively to meet the eye, except the white surf which broke on the low coast-line, and washed the base of the interminable array of cocoanut-trees which guarded it. The mountain ranges were hidden in vapours and rain-banks, against which the seagulls seemed of snowy whiteness. The Cingalese outriggers, many miles from land, provided with long wooden arms, projecting at right angles to the side to sustain the log of wood which balances the craft against the pressure of the sail in the heaviest seas, and prevents the long, narrow hull capsizing, with crews out on the log, buried now and then to the waists in the curling waves, threaded their way through the muddy-looking waters, other catamarans, canoes, ballams, and doneys were engaged in fishing nearer shore, and the number of these to the north was so great as to suggest the idea of large flocks of ducks. These boats, no matter what their size, are made with pegs of wood instead of iron, and the planks are sewn together, carvel fashion, by fine cocoanut-fibre rope or cord. The gunwales are sometimes surmounted by a course of wickerwork or compost, to keep out the lap of the water. The Greeks in Homer's day used bulwarks of osiers to exclude the waves. Similar contrivances may be seen in the Nile boats, and even on board the less advanced condition of Thames billyboys. Very likely the Cingalese boats remain as they were in the earliest days, and that the story of the Loadstone Mountain, which drew the iron bolts out of ships, and caused them to fall to pieces, had its origin in the error of some wandering navigator in these seas. As the *Serapis* swept by, the crews—wiry, lithe-figured men, all but naked, their black skins shining in the spray—stared for a while, open-mouthed, and then resumed their labours at oar, or rope, or net.

The approach to the coast of the great island, the fame of which has exercised such an influence over men's minds for many centuries—Taprobané—the mother-land of fables—the country which to the Greeks, the Romans, the Egyptians and the Arabs, offered the same mysterious attractions that the East long did to the people of Western Europe—was regarded with much interest. Every eye was fixed on the fast-developing outlines of the landscape, which grew more distinct as the morning advanced, and the wealth of greenness which renders Ceylon "an Emerald Isle" indeed, displayed itself from the beach up to the swelling hills, the summits of which were lost in curling clouds. The Prince went up on the bridge. The "spicy breezes," of which poets and prose writers speak, did not come out to sea to warn us of the nearness of the land, where so many flowers are said to impregnate the air with their odours—

> "Spargon dall' odorifero terreno
> Tanta suavità, che in mar sentire
> La fa ogni vento che da terra spire."

In fact, the odour which the traveller encounters near the pearl fisheries is anything but that of spices, aromatic plants, and sweet flowers; and if he goes "in the height of the season," and has the wind off the heaps of oyster-shells, he will feel sorry he has a nose to smell withal.

First as ever to welcome the Prince to new lands, the waving white ensigns and the tall masts of the men-of-war were made out, all dressed in colours. Then by degrees the modest elevations of Christian steeples, the Semaphore, the Dutch fortifications, attributed to Cohorn himself, the white-walled, red-tiled bungalows along the beach, and the houses, set in the never-failing frame of green cocoanut-palms. There was amid this green a fluttering of many colours, as if a dejected rainbow had been caught and was striving to get free, which was, the glass told us, the play of innumerable flags and streamers. The pilot came on board. The fleets, with the flags of two Admirals (Macdonald and Lambert) flying, saluted, but the *Serapis* was rather too far out. The rule is that the Royal Standard shall be saluted "as soon as it is seen;" but if the salute be intended to gratify as well as to honour, there ought to be some discretion in the matter. In the present instance all that could be seen was a cloud of smoke, which hid Colombo for a while, and then we heard a distant rumble. In three-quarters of an hour more the *Serapis* had found her way to her anchorage. On such occasions the admirals and senior officers are the first to come on board to pay their respects. It was somewhat too rough in the open roadstead for spectators in fine clothes to come out in the shore-boats. The Governor's aides-de-camp put out from a little bay sheltered by a reef (probably the "Διὸς ἄχρον") on which the surf broke with fury, sending showers of spray high in the air, and causing some uneasiness as to our comfort in going on shore; but the pilot told us that the jetty and platform where the Prince would land were protected from the swell. The officers came to take orders, and await the Royal pleasure as to the disembarkation. Whilst they were explaining the programme of addresses, receptions, and the like, there was plenty to interest those who had never been in Ceylon before. The native boats, with stores of novel merchandise and strange fruit, and—what were of more novelty and strangeness—Cingalese bumboatmen, fruiterers, jewellers, officials, telegraph clerks, and post-office employés, in the native costume, which is to European eyes so extraordinary—their lower man swathed in "women's petticoats," their hair worn in massive rolls at the back of the head, secured by large tortoiseshell combs, "μαλλοῖς γυναικείοις εἰς ἅπαν ἀναδεδεμένος," as Ptolemy wrote—exposing them to a certain amount of what is called "chaff," which they bore with dignified composure, either because they were ignorant or accustomed. At one o'clock the *Serapis* made signal to the fleet; soon afterwards, a Royal salute from ships and forts and a *feu de joie* on shore celebrated the anniversary of the Princess of Wales' birthday.* The Governor was waiting to be summoned on board. After a time he was signalled for, and, attended by the higher officers of the Government, came off in his galley, towed by a steam-barge. They were not sorry to reach the deck of the *Serapis*: it seemed as if they could not get on board without a drenching, and they hopped out on the ladder with great alacrity. Mr. Gregory has long had the honour of the Prince's acquaintance, and was cordially received. Major-General Street, C.B., the officer commanding the forces, Mr. Birch, the Colonial Secretary, and the Staff, were presented, and then the Governor and the authorities returned to shore, where they were anxiously expected by a great crowd of ladies and gentlemen from all parts of the island, some of whom, we were told, had

* The members of the suite sent a telegram to Sandringham congratulating her Royal Highness on the happy recurrence of the day, to which they received a gracious reply at Colombo the same evening.

been in their places since 6 o'clock that morning. It was nearly 4 P.M. before the Prince left the *Serapis*. He was in the uniform, adapted to Indian latitudes, of Field-Marshal—white trousers, and plumed helmet. His steam-launch was preceded by one with a portion of his suite, whose appearance created a great commotion at the landing-place. The *Undaunted*, *Narcissus*, *Immortalité*, and *Newcastle* fired a salute just as the launch's bows, rising on the crest of a sea, appeared round the Point. Tremendous cheering, mingled with wild cries, made the recipients of the undeserved honour feel all the pangs of men engaged in unwitting imposture speedily to be detected. It was a very pretty sight which met their eyes shorewards—a broad water avenue formed by lines of native boats draped with bright-coloured streamers and banners, garlanded with flowers and wreaths of cocoanut-leaves, and crowded with spectators and bands of native musicians. The Landing-Place at the end of this marine avenue was enclosed by a gay pavilion, which was reached by a flight of steps, covered with scarlet cloth, leading under a very striking archway, which was decorated very tastefully with flags and wreaths; but what satisfied the eye, and at the same time caused something like regret at such wastefulness, was the display, as mere ornament, of masses of fruit—jack, limes, oranges, shaddocks, plantains, pine-apples, figs, custard-apples, mangoes, &c., &c. Everywhere flags, fruit, cocoa-nuts, flowers and palm-leaves, triumphal arches. Then, in long perspective, more flags and arches, tiers of spectators on seats and terraces, windows and roofs crowded with figures and faces. On the Landing-Platform stood all the State of Ceylon—the members of the Legislative Council and of the Municipal Corporation ranged at each side of the dais; a kind of throne, placed on an estrade, was ready for the Prince; a table near at hand sustained two caskets. There was a guard of honour of the 57th Regiment (the old "Die Hards"), with band and colours. Conspicuous among the crowd of ladies, some in what may be styled British, and some in Anglo-Cingalese dresses, and of officers, civil, naval, and military, were two remarkable objects—one was a group of officials, in full Cingalese costume—combs, hair-rolls, and petticoats complete; with very small, curved, dagger-like swords, broad baldricks, medallions, and large gold plaques, as large as cheese-plates, on their breasts: the other was a white-haired, George Washington-looking sort of gentleman, in a black velvet Court suit, full lace ruffles, and black silk stockings—which attracted immediate attention. "Who are those natives?" "They are the Mudaliyars—Native swells. That nice-looking old fellow is a Government House man, and he has got all those medals for good service." "Who is that gentleman?" The answer—in a tone of surprise, "What! Don't you know Mr. Layard?"—announced that the gentleman was of high repute in Colombo. When the Prince appeared, a few moments after the landing of the first boat-load, there arose a shout which seemed to imply that the former greeting was not a mistake at all, but a mere exercise to clear the popular throat. The women, I believe, joined in it; but then no one can be quite sure about them here. It was a very hearty outburst. It was repeated oftentimes, and for some moments waves of exulting sound filled the air in successive volumes, to acknowledge each bow of the Prince. Then came the presentation of addresses and the answers.

This ceremony ended, the Prince and Governor led the way up the avenue, lined by the 57th and the Cingalese police, to the large Government building (a custom-house, I believe), at the end of the rows of reserved seats. The spectators on each side were quite delighted; they forgot all their long waiting. The Prince was, as a lady said afterwards, "so close to each and all, they could nearly touch him, and he smiled so pleasantly as he walked along, we saw nobody else!" Outside the seats "the people," wild with joy; a wide-eyed, large-mouthed people, not much weighted with clothing, but in high animal spirits. They ran, shoved, leaped up to get a view even of the waving plume and white helmet. Passing through the halls, which were mostly filled with Europeans, the Prince emerged into the open air to meet, if possible, a greater ovation. A triumphal drive through the town and around by the Sea-Wall, to enable the Prince to see and be seen, gave renewed occasion to admire the enthusiasm of the population, and wonder at the profligate, or, at all events, exuberant, expenditure of vegetable wealth in sacrificial piles of fruit, arches, wreaths, festoons, garlands, and at the quaintness of fancy in decoration, inscription, device, and grotesque representation of the elephant—the creature which typifies the island. It was in some measure like a promenade in the covered ways of a great horticultural exhibition in full fête. Thus the Prince, with the Governor by his side, drove for many miles all round by Colpetty—surrounded by cocoanut-trees, and again cocoanut-trees—the suburban villas surrounded by cinnamon-groves, and almost buried in the richness of real tropical vegetation—and so by Galle-face (the Dutch Galle-baak), round to the place whence he set out. But everything must come to an end, and as evening set in the carriages returned to the Landing, and the boats took the Prince and his following off to the *Serapis*, which Captain Glyn would gladly have seen in smoother water; nor were there any who would have differed with him. There was a State Banquet, at which the Prince entertained the Governor, the senior naval and military officers and authorities, and as many of the officials as the ship could accommodate. Colombo was illuminated beautifully, and the fleet lighted up. The planters kept revel on shore. Never perhaps were there more joyous times in the island than when his Excellency Governor Gregory received the Prince of Wales. There may have been greater displays of wealth and splendour in the old days before them, but then there was always uncertainty of possession and of life; there were wars and rumours of war, the coming of the spoiler, and the cry of the distressed.

December 2nd.—"There's a good deal of sea on, sir; and it's likely they will get a ducking going on shore this morning!" This was the first news which arrived in my cabin with the seven o'clock cup of coffee this morning. There was a natural politeness about my marine which prevented his saying "*you* will get a ducking;" but I knew quite well what he meant. The sound of the lapping waves outside justified the prediction. Already the note of preparation had been sounded between decks, and the servants were busy in getting ready for the journey for Kandy. The baggage was despatched at 10 A.M., and the Prince went on shore at 10.20 A.M. under the usual salute. There is a screen in the steam-launch to keep off the spray from those in the stern-sheets, but all the party did not reach the shore in dry clothes, and the state of the sea during our stay rendered boat work anything but agreeable. Terra firma at last—Governor Gregory, Mr. Birch, Sir R. Morgan, Mr. Layard, full uniform, guards of honour, salutes, crowds of men in petticoats, with combs in front of their *chignons*, "cheering like Britons"—the same multitudes as yesterday—arches, inscriptions, festoons, and cocoanut-tree rejoicings—not much the worse for the day's wear.

From the Landing-Place to the Railway Station one

clamorous crowd, which thinned away from the rear, and rolled in towards the front, around the cortege. The Cingalese type is not strikingly handsome; the yellow tinge in the colour of the skin is less pleasing—at least to my eyes—than the red or dark-brown hue of the native of Upper India; and the hair, if abundant, is very coarse. The teeth do not rival those of the African, and the eyes are not particularly bright. The men are well made, but small. As to the women, except some wretched old hags of the lower order, we did not see a dozen; but as the carriages passed through the suburbs to the Railway Station, we could make out eyes peering through the chinks in the doors and in the stockades of the houses. Amongst the carriages of the special train was one of native manufacture—very creditable to Cingalese builders—light, commodious, well-fitted, and prettily decorated. Well, after some little delay, which caused the usual disquietude to railway directors, managers, and engineers, the Royal train, followed by loud cheers from the gentlemen on the platform, and by the multitude outside, moved off on a run to Kandy, which was from end to end a prolonged scene of excitement and welcoming, in which the eye turned from crowds of people and arches and garlands to some of the softest, and yet grandest, scenery in the world. The day was fine, with just enough of drifting cloud to cast ever-varying fleeting shadows over the grand sweep of hill-side, and there was that sharpness of outline and clearness of detail of the distant mountain ranges which indicate the approach of rain. The railway follows the course of the Great Road, which justifies the skill and intelligence of the makers half a century ago. Outside Colombo the Railway crosses the river, which seems scarcely below the level of the surrounding country, now intensely green with growing rice. I am not about to describe a journey which is made by thousands of persons every year, who think as little of its beauties as if they were going by the Underground Railway from Charing Cross to the Mansion House; but, under favourable circumstances, I should think it well worth while to go from London to Colombo to enjoy such scenery as we beheld to-day. Underneath thick groves of cocoanut-trees, arecas, and jaggery (*Caryota urens*), and an extraordinary profusion of trees—some like the Coral or the Murutu (*Erythrina Indica*), bearing rich pink or crimson flowers; others presenting glowing masses of scarlet buds and shoots; others, like the ironwood-tree, with white flowers and blossoms of purple or lilac—one caught sight of the hamlets in which dwell the cultivators of the sea-like expanse of rice. In the offshoots of the river, and in the pools alongside the rail, groups of natives were tubbing—an operation which is popularly supposed to be confined to England, whereas there are few nations in the world who use water so little for purposes of ablution as the people of the three islands, always excepting the classes with which, within the last half century, the tub is a morning institution.

Along the road are two-wheeled waggons, pretty little humped-back cattle, pack bullocks, Moorish brinjarees, and pedestrians armed with the inevitable leaf of the talipot, which serves as an umbrella against the sun or rain, as the case may be. Occasionally glimpses of Buddhist Temples, perched upon hill-tops, or half-hidden among the ironwood trees, laden with white flowers, which put one in mind of Chinese pagodas. Now and then a group of Buddhist priests, in yellow robes, stand making surly obeisance by the roadside. It would be flattery to ourselves to say that their looks indicated perfect good-will towards the travellers. The tonsure does not by any means suit these gentlemen, whose ears are of enormous size, and whose foreheads, villainous low, tumble backwards into bulging, bullet-shaped skulls. As far as Veyangoda the scenery is pleasant, but rather monotonous. At the distance of a few miles from that station, which is twenty-five miles from Colombo, the ascent becomes rapid, until we reach Ambapussa. Here the spurs of the higher hills begin to strike down into the plains, covered with forest so dense that a ray of sunshine piercing it seems, in the darkness, like a polished steel bar. In the hollows between these spurs are green patches of rice set round by borders of underwood and tropical vegetation. The Prince and the Duke of Sutherland enjoyed the scenery from the engine; and at "Sensation Rock" the whole party enjoyed that supreme delight—a safe danger—contact—all but actual—with destruction, which is exceedingly charming to all who have nerves fit for the peculiar pleasure. It is an exceedingly bold—almost overhanging—mass of gneiss or granite, with that unsteady appearance which gives one the expectation that it will be down on his head as he looks at it; a profound valley runs below. At Pulgahawalla, and indeed at all the Stations, the names of which need not be enumerated, were crowds, inscriptions, arches, to welcome the Prince. The houses were ornamented with green cocoanut-fronds, the split leaves and stems nailed on bamboo-frames, formed in the most graceful devices. At Kadugannawa we reached the summit of the Railway. The line passes by the rock which was bored through for the main trunk road made by Sir Edward Barnes. When that was accomplished the hopes of the Kandyans perished, for they saw in that work the fulfilment of the prophecy that their kingdom should depart when a bullock could be driven through the hill, and a horseman ride through the rock. The hill was tunnelled, and soon afterwards the Kandy mail was driven through the archway. Since the final capture of Kandy in 1815 there have been several uprisings and rebellions: one, the most formidable, in 1817; the last in 1848, which Lord Torrington stamped out with a vigour which nearly brought on him the fate incurred by Governor Eyre in later years. We do not like rebellion at home, but we are very apt to punish those who nip it in the bud abroad; they ought perhaps to wait and see if it is about to become serious. In that case they are not unlikely to incur the odium and punishment of imbecility. The train halted at the summit, and the Prince inspected the column on which are enumerated the services of Captain Dawson of the Royal Engineers, who "planned and executed the road and other works of public utility, during the government of Sir Edward Barnes, K.C.B." It is now forty-five years since Captain Dawson died at Colombo, and it may well be said of him that the good he did lives after him. From Kadugannawa the train sped on to Peradeniya. The Station, which is but a few miles outside Kandy, was decorated with originality. In addition to the ordinary floral embellishments, birds, monkeys, minars, white crows chattered, jumped, or flew as far as the length of their tethers would let them along the platform; immense crowds of Kandyans—many of them wore flowers in their hair, and had nosegays in their hands—welcomed the Prince. It was after four o'clock before the train reached the neighbourhood of the city. All we had heard of the beauty of the situation of Kandy, and of the character of the scenery was fully sustained.

In a deep ravine at one side of the plateau, or, more properly speaking, of the broad valley surrounded by hills, overlooking a still deeper depression, on which the town is situated, the Mahawelli Ganga River thunders in its rocky bed. The small lake by the side of which part of the city is built lends a charming repose and freshness to the scene, which is mirrored in its waters. Wherever the eye is turned rise mountain tops, some bare masses of rock, others clothed with vegetation. There is no idea of a "town" or of a "city" to be realised in what one sees: it is all suburb —verandahed pavilions and bungalows stretching in lines bearing the names of streets; here and there the native houses packed more closely may be termed lanes; but the whole place is as "diffused" as Balham, or Clapham, or any other rural quarter of the great Metropolis. Kandy was once a stronghold of kings, but it was not till the end of the sixteenth century that it became the capital. When that dignity was conferred on the city, it was forbidden to the common people to have windows, or white walls, or tiles to their houses, as these were luxuries for royal use alone. Public buildings, properly so called, there are none, but in lieu of these was one of the most picturesque crowds ever seen. I doubt if ever anything so unmasculine, uncomely, and unbecoming was ever devised as the dress of the great Chiefs. There are various orders of Chiefs. The higher they are the more ridiculously elaborate is their attire. The dress of the upper ten thousand is an enormous stiffened white muslin petticoat, with gigot sleeves, nether garments puffed out as if they were strongly fortified by crinoline, the work of cunning seamstresses, made with exceeding art. On their heads elevated pincushions, like tinselled crowns, singularly unsuited to the climate or to dignity of appearance. The few women visible wore white muslin jackets and comboys, and displayed a considerable wealth of bangles, necklaces, and rings. The becombed heads of the men, which are the rule at Colombo, did not appear to be quite universal.

The number of Chiefs and of Buddhist priests at the Station showed what importance was attached to the Prince's visit by the people, and proved that the Governor had cultivated their good opinion with success. The popularity he enjoyed was among the causes which collected so many people together, for had he been less favoured, some of the Chiefs, at all events, would have stayed away. There was, of course, an address from the Municipal Council of Kandy delivered at the Railway Station, and deputations from all the country for many miles around ; so much to observe that the memory and the eye were fairly overweighted. Endless would be the task of describing miles of decorated roadside, inscription, triumphal arches, festoons and garlands, or the curious devices from the Station till we reached the Governor's house. It was with a sense of relief we found refuge in the "Pavilion," the bedrooms of which open out upon the charming garden. There was, alas! one drawback to a walk in the shady groves, where the air was heavy, with the odour of unaccustomed flowers. A sharp prick above the ankle directed my attention downwards, and I saw a small black body, not much thicker than a pin, which gave decided signs of life, contracting and expanding itself vigorously from one point, just above the shoe. I caught hold of the little black thread in my hand, and pulled it away; where it had been, a spot of blood appeared; in a second the leech fastened upon my finger. The place was swarming with the wretches! I had inadvertently walked on the greensward, populous with these blood-suckers. I instantly fled, and resolved to wear shoes no more in these latitudes.

The Governor entertained the Prince and the notabilities of Ceylon at a State dinner. Lamps and lanterns were waving and swinging in the perfumed breezes. Rows of cocoanut-oil-lamps climbing up the hill-sides to join with the stars ; streamers floating from elevated masts ; clang of music, beating of native drums, blowing of horns, sound of gongs and mighty cheering, which rolled away like thunder along the hill-sides.

Immediately on the conclusion of the banquet, the company were summoned outside. The Pera-hara, now celebrated in honour of the Prince, was out of its ordinary place and time. Instead of being made through the city at a new moon, in the month of June or July, the procession was confined to the route from the Temple to the garden of the Pavilion. Knox describes the ceremony two hundred years ago, when it must have been of a grand and imposing character. In those days the Kings of Kandy were great indeed, and little dreamt of the time when white men, from countries of which they kept many inhabitants in base captivity, would march upon their capital, seize upon the treasures of their temples, plunder their tombs, and scatter their ashes to the winds. It is probable the Kandyans have traditions concerning these things, although we have forgotten them. In Knox's day the Chief Priest rode through the streets of the city upon an elephant, covered in white, with all the triumph that king and kingdom could afford. He was preceded by fifty elephants of the Temple, dressed in rich stuffs and covered with jingling bells, which followed drummers, trumpeters, dancing men, of the wildest and most fantastic figures, and fifers, dressed like giants, the imitation of giant stature being effected by elevated head-dresses. "After the gods and their attendants," says Knox, "thousands of ladies and gentlemen, of the best sort, arrayed in the bravest manner their ability can afford, go hand in hand, three in a row. The streets are made clean. Pennons and flags flutter from poles stuck along the street, which are adorned with boughs and branches of cocoa-nuts, and rows of lighted lamps border the pathways both night and day." But the women of whom Knox speaks do not make their

KANDY.—THE DEVIL DANCERS.

appearance now. Elephants, with priests representing the deities, makers of heaven and earth, and inferior heavenly potentates came next. The Cingalese deny that the images of the gods in their temples, which represent the influence of the Hindoo conquerors on the religion of Buddha, are more than symbols, and say that they are not actually worshipped. Last of all come the soldiers with the commanders, but in Knox's time the King had ceased to ride in the ceremony. Sir Emerson Tennent says the Buddhist priesthood suffered a great loss of prestige "since the loss of the Royal presence, in which it was their privilege to bask. Even their ritual pomp and ceremonials no longer command the same homage from the populace; and the great annual procession of the Pera-hara, with its torchlights, its solemn music, and caparisoned elephants, is spiritless and unimpressive if contrasted with occasions in their memory when it was hallowed by the divine presence of a king." The writer never imagined that in the time so little distant from his own, the heir of the Monarch, to whom has descended greater honours than were ever enjoyed by all the kings of Taprobané, should give once more to these fêtes the prestige of a Royal presence. What the Prince of Wales saw was different from the great ceremonial. There was only a procession of elephants, dancers, and priests belonging to the temples; but it was exceedingly grotesque, novel, and interesting, and it would tax the best pen and pencil to give an adequate idea of such combinations of forms, sounds, and figures. The "devil dancers," in masks and painted faces, were sufficiently hideous. Their contortions, performed to the tune of clanging brass, cymbals, loud horns, and, for aught I know, sackbut, lute, and dulcimer, presented no feature of agility or grace which might not be easily rivalled by an ordinary dancing troop nearer home.

The elephants, plodding along in single file, carried magnificent howdahs occupied by the priests, and were covered with cloth of gold and silver, and with plates of metal, which shone in the light of the torches. The better bred of these animals, and most of them indeed were exceedingly polite, salaamed, and uttered a little flourish of trumpets through their probosces, as they came opposite to the place where the Prince was standing; some knelt down and made obeisance before him; but the propriety of the procession was somewhat disturbed by the cupidity of one which, finding that the Prince had a small store of sugar-cane and bananas, resolved to make the best of his time, and could not be induced to go on without difficulty. This Pera-hara was but a rehearsal of the ceremony fixed for the following day.

December 3rd.—There came in the night-time a refreshing shower, so that all the glorious mass of vegetation in the garden and grounds outside the Governor's house was literally ablaze with brilliant flowers, and the air was heavy with the perfume of yellow champac and of the white roses of the ironwood-tree. As to the colouring and size of the rhododendrons, Indian magnolias, Gordonias, &c., they must be seen to be believed, and then, as Knox says, "not without rubbing of the eye." All the birds were set a-singing, and the woods, if not most melancholy, were at least most musical in force of sound. Indeed, one of the party complained that "a violent woodpecker" close to his window kept him awake all the morning. It is a strange country, for there are in it fishes which walk, climb, and sing; but it would be wrong, perhaps, to say always that the birds sing: the noise they make is certainly too loud to be melodious. After breakfast there was a visit to the Royal Botanical Gardens, which should properly, I think, be called the

Arboretum, situated at Peradeniya, a distance of three miles or so from the Pavilion. Here the Prince was received by Mr. Thwaites, the learned author of the 'Enumeratio Plantarum,' &c., Fellow of the Royal Society, who did the honours of the place with charming vivacity and scrupulous care, allowing no object of the many extraordinary and beautiful specimens of tropical vegetation to escape unnoticed.

I have never seen in any part of the world such an extraordinary exuberance and variety of growth. In addition to every tree and plant properly belonging to Ceylon, there are numbers of exotics, which have been imported, and which grow freely in the open air. Mr. Mudd, the botanist attached to the Prince's establishment, went about in a subdued ecstasy, knife and book in hand, attended by a native gardener speaking English, who seemed an excellent botanist. We entered through a magnificent avenue of the india-rubber-tree (*Ficus elastica*), and drove along sweeping avenues by the borders of the river, through a park-like expanse, which was one marvellous exhibition of the glories of the vegetable kingdom. Orchids in every variety; palms of stupendous size, thickness, and height; talipots, palmyras, date-palms, gigantic clumps of reeds, the coco demar, the traveller's tree, almost shut out the light in places, or were scattered over the green meadow in detached blocks, or concentrated into central masses, over which whirled thick clouds of flying foxes. Perhaps the most interesting and astonishing objects, where all was so new, were the jungle-rope creepers, and elephant-creepers of the *Bauhinia* class, which seem to seize the trees in giant folds, as if intent on their destruction, an object in which, it is said, indeed, these tremendous vegetable reptiles too often succeed. In the gardens nearly all the products which are valuable for commerce have been introduced—cloves, nutmegs, vanilla, tea, chocolate, arrowroot, tapioca, ginger, mangoes, lichens, and every fruit known to the East. It is, in fact, a very noble institution, and a great glory to the island, to those who planned it, and to its present amiable, excellent, and learned director. The flying foxes come here at certain times of the year in enormous multitudes, migrating from spot to spot as they devastate each district. Some we saw hanging, as you see them in the Zoological Gardens, with their heads covered snugly up in the membrane of the wing, and the body hanging by one hind leg from the branch, like strange fruit. Mr. Thwaites said that these foxes caused immense damage, and that the gardens required perpetual cleaning. On the Prince expressing a desire to procure a specimen, a gun was sent for, which probably exposed the Prince to more danger than many things in his travels which were regarded with greater suspicion. Up went the gun, and down came a flying fox. The *Pteropus Edwardsii* was about four feet from one wing tip to the other, and was covered with thick red hair, the skin on the face black and naked, and teeth exceedingly sharp. It is said they are not bad eating, something like hare; but it would be excessive hunger indeed which could induce me to test the fact. When the Prince fired, the creatures showed they possessed the instinct of self-preservation by retiring to greater distances and higher altitudes, but several more were bagged, not without a considerable expenditure of powder and shot on the part of the extraordinary fowling-piece.

At Mr. Thwaites' house, a pleasant Swiss-like chalet, the Prince was shown specimens of tea, of cardamums and other spices, cinchona, live scorpions, and the curious nests of the white ant, of which there were great numbers in the garden. We were warned that if we made excursions into the jungly ground near the river, there were venomous spiders, ferocious ants, ticks, centipedes, to be avoided. Nor were we made more inclined for a walk on being informed that the *Tic polonga* (*Daboia elegans*), a deadly snake, the terror of the natives, was to be met with. The European servants walked about cautiously. As one of them said, "It's not tigers and lions that I am afraid of! It's the serpents!" Before leaving, the Prince planted a small shoot of a Peepul—the Bo-tree, or *Ficus religiosa*—to commemorate his visit.

Any desire for independent excursions had been extinguished by the information that *Tic polonga* might be encountered in the long grass; but that the leech most certainly would come to us, whether we went or not, we were very soon certain, as various outcries testified. "Will you take this off my neck, if you please?" "Hang it! there's one on the calf of my leg!" They came wriggling and jumping along the grass. They must smell one's blood. If you stood on the gravel-walk for a few moments you could see them making their way from all parts of the surrounding country towards you as a common centre of interest. Most horrible of all their properties, they can stand erect on their tails and look out for what is coming.

In the evening there was a banquet at the Pavilion, and then the ceremony of bestowing the insignia of the K.M.G. on the Governor, and of the C.M.G. on the Colonial Secretary, and on Mr. Douglas, in the Audience Hall of the Kings of Kandy, used at present as a district Court House. It is a long low room, the richly chiselled wooden roof upheld by a double line of elaborately carved columns of teak with bracketed capitals: the exterior rooms and corridors are narrow and dark. On the walls and columns are carved flights of geese—or, to speak with accuracy—"the Sacred Goose" of Buddha *passant* is multiplied many times. In this Hall the Kings held Court at night in a dimly lighted recess, to which ministers and courtiers went crawling on their stomachs. It was now thronged by Kandyan Chiefs, Mudaliyars, European colonists, officials, and the jewelled wives of the Kandyan nobility, in snow-white dresses, drawn up on the righthand side below the dais, on which the Prince's chair of State of crimson velvet and the less splendid seat for Mr. Gregory were placed. The Chiefs were presented by the Governor. Round the neck of Dewé Nilimé, one of the most eminent, the Prince placed a blue riband with the Indian gold medal. They were introduced in columns of five, according to their rank, and presently they came back in procession to offer the Prince a handsome silver casket. Whilst the presentations were going on, the thunder roared and the lightning flashed, and the rain fell with tropical violence outside. Mr. Gregory appeared at the head of a small procession—consisting of the members of his suite, Colonial Secretary, Auditor-General—and advanced to the dais, at the base of which he bowed to the Prince. All the company stood up. His Royal Highness announced that he had her Majesty's commands to confer on her trusty councillor, the Right Hon. W. H. Gregory, the dignity of Knight Commander of the most Illustrious Order of St. Michael and St. George, and added that he had great pleasure on personal grounds in doing so. Then the patents, &c., rather tedious documents, in which there were something like injunctions against larceny, were read. The Governor knelt; the Prince gave the accolade with the words, "Rise, Sir William Gregory." The Knight rose and expressed his feelings in a neat speech, amid tremendous cheers, which woke up every echo in the old Hall, and challenged the muttering thunder. Mr. Douglas and Mr. Birch were next invested with the C.M.G., amidst expressions of general satisfaction. The Prince left the dais, and the wives of the Kandyan Chiefs who were as dignified and stately as so many Mistresses of the Robes, were introduced to him. Out of the Audience Hall he passed through narrow passages and serried ranks of Buddhist priests, mounting the steps to the Temple, to see the Sacred Tooth of Gotama Buddha.

The Holy Object abides in a Wihara, or sacred chamber, in a tower adjoining the Malagawa Temple. The European style of the architecture of the tower causes it to stand out distinctly from the neighbouring buildings, and is ascribed to Portuguese captives, employed in its construction by the Kandyan King, Wimala Ilkanna, 270 years ago. The "Dalada," as it is called, is a piece of bone or, as some say, ivory, with a suture up the side, nearly two inches long and one inch round, of irregular cylindrical shape, tapering towards the end, which is rounded. If the article ever was in Buddha's mouth, and if he had a complete set to match, he must have possessed a wonderful jaw, and a remarkable stomach, for it is easy to see that the tooth is not a human molar or incisor. It is, however, at least as real as was the Palladium, or as are many relics nearer home. It has been suggested that it was modelled after the canine teeth which are seen in some images of Vishnu and Kali, but it by no means resembles a true canine. The story of the tooth has been told many times. When Gotama Buddha's body was burned at Kusinara, 2419 years ago, his left canine tooth was carried to Duntapura, the capital of Kalinga, where it reposed for 500 years, till the King sent it to Ceylon. There the Dalada, called Dahta Dhatu, lay till the early part of the twelfth century, when a Tamil Prince of Madura, who invaded the island, carried it off to India, where the Sacred Tooth remained till the King of Kandy, as the gratifying result of a personal crusade and expedition for the purpose, obtained possession of it. But the Dalada's peaceful days were over. Less happy than its former owner, now absorbed in eternal rest, the tooth was the object of constant inquisition, and it was carried about for safety from one hiding-place to another during the constant wars which distracted the island. Sir Emerson Tennent has given a full account, translated from the Portuguese of Diego de Couto, of the capture of the Dalada by Don Constantine of Braganza at Jaffna in 1560. Diego calls it the tooth of an ape, which it certainly is not, and gives the details of its destruction by the archbishop at Goa, in presence of the Viceroy and his officers, and of the prelates, inquisitors, vicars-general, and pious Jesuits, in April 1561. It was these good people who counselled the needy pidalgos, captains, and other temporal persons, to reject the 400,000 cruzadoes offered by the envoys of the King of Pegu for its possession. The archbishop, having received the relic from the treasurer, "placed it in a mortar, and with his own hand reducing it to powder before them all, cast the pieces into a brazier, which stood ready for the purpose; after which the ashes and the charcoal together were cast into the river in the sight of all those crowding to the verandahs and windows which looked upon the water." Many, we are told, protested against the measure, on the ground that there was nothing to prevent the Buddhists from making another tooth, and that the money would have repaired the pressing necessities of the State. They were quite right. The Buddhists were not to be beaten. The Dalada which they exhibit to-day is, they say, "the real and only one;"—that which Don Constantine took at Jaffna was a sham made *ad hoc*. When the King of Pegu, three years after the tooth had been reduced to powder, sent to the King of Kandy to ask his daughter in marriage, the crafty chamberlain of the latter, who pretended to be a Christian, but who was a Buddhist at heart, told the ambassadors that he had hidden the real tooth, and took them to see a facsimile, which he had constructed out of stag's horn, in his house. He was prevailed upon, for a consideration, to yield this tooth up to the King of Pegu, who was in a great delight with his treasure for some time, till he was told that the lady he had married as the daughter of a king was as great a sham as the tooth which had been sent to him. But even then he preferred keeping both the impostures to admitting that he had been deceived, and he informed the King of Kandy, who maintained that he was the possessor of the only genuine relic, that he was quite content with what he had. The King of Kandy doubtless caused the present article to be made at the time. The Wihara, or small shrine, in which the Dalada is kept, is approached from the Temple by a narrow door and staircase; the apartment itself, which is hung with curtains embroidered with curious devices, was redolent of sickening perfume, which combined with the heat of the lamps held by the priests to make the atmosphere almost stifling. The Carandua, a bell-shaped golden casket enclosing the tooth, stands on a silver table. The case glitters with emeralds, diamonds, pearls of great price, and bears a large stone on the cusp at its summit, which is, we were told, of enormous value It is hung round with chains, of which the links are diamonds, emeralds, rubies, and pearls, apparently of very great worth—is elaborately chased and worked in an intricate pattern of which a photograph alone can give an idea. At one side of the table, surrounded by as many as could crowd in after him, the Prince took his place. One priest produced a bundle of keys, which was taken, not without trouble and delay, out of some secret receptacle, and then proceeded to unshrine the relic. Even when the keys were brought, it would seem as if those who were the guardians of the shrine were not very familiar with its intricacies. It was not at the first or the second trial that they found the right key; but at last a sliding spring was touched, and the outer case opening, revealed inside another of gold, also jewelled. This in its turn was opened. Again came in view a new casket like unto its fellow, and so on the operation was repeated, I think, for five times, until at last,

> "Fold after fold to the fainting air,
> The soul of its beauty and love lay bare"—

Buddha's tooth, just as I have tried to describe it, reposing on a golden lotus leaf! No hand might touch this holy of holies. There was an expression of awe on the faces of the priests, which could not have been feigned; the eldest, a venerable man in spectacles, who quivered with emotion, taking up the gold lotus leaf in one hand, was supplied by another of the priests with a small piece of cambric, or of some white textile stuff. Placing this carefully between his fingers, and not allowing his hand to come in contact even with the golden lotus, he took up the tooth and held it for the Prince's gaze. There was, of course, not much to see in the tooth, and, without faith, nothing to admire; and so the Prince, having duly looked at it, departed, and was followed with pleasure by all whose duty it was not to remain inside. But it was very curious to think that so many millions of people, some of them, no doubt, wise and good, spread all over the East, constituting the population of great empires, not destitute of culture, should hold such an object in veneration. The shrines in which it is encased have been made by various Kings of Kandy, and some go so far as to say that the most recent, the exterior, dates from the year 1464, and that the inside case was made two hundred years before that date.

Had it not rained as it did, in downright sheets of water, there would, no doubt, have been a very pretty sight, and characteristic, from the Octagon, where the Prince now stationed himself in full sight of the people. They faced the rain, for all their scanty raiment, with patience for hours; and when the few fireworks which could burst out into life threw a glare on the multitude, the partially undraped figures glistened in the wet like statues of polished bronze. The Pera-hara, devil-dancers and all, passed beneath the Octagon; but the downpour washed all the animation out of them, put out the lights, soddened the drums, choked the musical instruments, and spoilt everything but the good temper and patience of the crowd. Before retreating to the Pavilion, a deputation of Buddhist priests, bearing a very valuable set of the holy books for the Prince's acceptance was introduced. They also exhibited, as they asserted, the "most ancient Buddhist MSS. in the world," and one of the younger priests proceeded to chant in minors, ending in a prolonged high note, from one of the books, in a manner not unmusical, reminding us somewhat of the intonation of the Russian ritual. The reverential air and deep attention of the Buddhists who sat round the reader were very striking; one especially, who, with moistened eyes, raised his hand gently, from time to time, to emphasise a passage, looked at the Prince as if he expected a miraculous conversion. The *séance* ended, the Royal party made the best of their way to the Pavilion. Thousands of people were unable to find shelter, and slept wherever they could. Every house was full, and the verandahs and doorsteps were crowded. The railway carriages and stations were filled by people.

December 4th.—At 7.30 A.M. the Prince, accompanied by Sir W. Gregory, Mr. Birch, and some of his suite, escorted by the Governor's Body Guard, drove to the Railway Station, where Major-General Street, C.B., and his Staff, and a guard of honour, band and colours of H.M.'s 57th, under Captain Collins, were on duty. Colonel Williams, Colonel Ellis, Canon Duckworth, and Mr. Knollys remained at the Pavilion. The special train, preceded by a pilot-engine, ran smoothly through one of the most lovely countries in the world, all fresh and shining from the morning's torrents, which had, however, flooded the fields in many places, and caused land-slips on the hill-sides, over the new line to Gampola. There the Duke of Sutherland, Lord A. Paget, Captain Glyn, and Commander Durrant bade farewell to the Prince for the time, and went to the Governor's Lodge at Newera Ellia (the Royal City of Light), "the Elysium of Ceylon," over the Rambodda Pass, where there is a sanitary station, at an elevation of 6000 ft. above the sea-level. They enjoyed some sport; but the rain which fell on us was equally just to them. At Gampola, as at every station, there were crowds of planters and Cingalese, and the usual decorations. At Nawala-pittya, where our railway journey came to an end, a fine pandal was erected, although the Prince was only to stay there till the carriages were ready. Horses are rare in Ceylon, and transport is carried on in bullock hackeries; but the Governor had collected a sufficient number of vehicles and horses to carry the party on to Ruanwella, a secluded spot, forty-one miles from Colombo. It was reported that two herds of elephants were in the forest, and the local sportsmen were employed in watching them. The planters and ladies of the district gave the Royal traveller a most hearty welcome; nor were the Cingalese, among whom were Chiefs, Mudaliyars, priests, and peasants, less enthusiastic. Soon after we left the Station of Nawalapitiya, the clouds, which had never ceased to hang on the mountain-tops, gradually crept down, and the rain descended once more, at first gently, and then in torrents. It was very disappointing; for such glimpses as we had of the scenery were enchanting—banyans, ironwood-trees (*Mesua ferrea*), euphorbias, satinwood-trees, oaks, acacias, rhododendrons, magnolias, asoca, champac, wonderful creepers—some thick as a mast, and others like whipcord—convolvuli, orchids, &c., sheeting hillside and valley with an infinity of flowers and colour, challenged our admiration, and caused a sentimental sorrow at the aspect of the horrible utilitarian coffee-clearings, where the prostrate trunks of trees lay black and hideous on the dull red soil. Constant exclamations of delight—"Look there! How lovely! Do just turn your head to see that waterfall!" There was an excellent road, which appeared little frequented, and no Europeans were met from the time we left the railway. Heavier and heavier fell the rain, and good as the road was, it was so hard on the horses, that before we reached the Rest House at Kalugala, where the Prince was to breakfast, it was necessary to get out of the carriages and walk. We overtook some of the servants who had been sent on the day before, and found the Prince's gun-cases, &c., lying on the path. The coolies had refused to go further, and when coercion was resorted to, had simply and masterfully retired into the woods, and left the Europeans to their devices. The Governor was almost in despair; but, aided by Mr. Layard and his staff, made dispositions which enabled the servants to proceed.

There was a long halt at Kitulgala, where the rest-house occupied by the Prince commanded exquisite views of the river and secluded valley. The journey was resumed after breakfast, the rain coming down more violently than ever. Ruanwella, 46 miles from Kandy, was reached at 4.30 P.M., long before the baggage arrived. Every one was wet, more or less. The coolies came dropping in slowly towards nightfall with various articles, which were anxiously expected, and as the stragglers came in sight, the excitement of owners waiting for guns, dressing-bags, and changes of raiment was intense. Of course, things which were not wanted came in first. The Prince, the Governor, and one or two members of the suite were lodged in an old Dutch house, the only one in the place. The others were quartered in huts close at hand. The temporary residences erected on such occasions as these are graceful to look at, and not uncomfortable to live in. The house, if so it may be called, in which we slept was formed of bamboos driven into the ground, with a sloping roof, made of lighter slips of the same material, on which palm-leaves were fastened. The edifice consists of a central hall, with four rooms of about 10 feet by 6, constructed of calico and bamboo frames, provided with windows and little doorways opening into the central hall, all finished as though we were going to remain there for a month at least: there is a verandah, about five feet broad, between the outer wall of the house, to which the overhanging roof descends. Ten bamboo pillars sustained the verandah in front, on which hung, by way of ornament, cocoa-nuts, and their flowers, festoons and garlands. At dinner, which was served in an open hall made of bamboos thatched with leaves, there was much talk of elephants and sporting. It was reported that some planters had camped close to the forest where elephants were concealed, and it was feared they might start the herd. This, considering who was going to shoot, was *de mauvais goût*, and that they could hunt when they pleased; but it is probable they erred from ignorance. Mr. Varian and

Mr. Fisher, two young gentlemen of the Forest Department experienced in elephant hunting, Mr. Campbell, Mr. Hudson, and others, attached to the police under Major Tranchell, joined to assist the expedition. The party retired early to rest, and, as a precautionary measure, Dr. Fayrer served out quinine all round.

December 5th.—The rest of the baggage arrived safe, but not sound, during the night. Still the rain continued. The weather was what one might call muggy; and though the palm-leaf roofs had kept out the rain completely, the interiors of the huts were damp and steaming. Wonderful birds—parrakeets, kingcrows, pigeons, barbets, &c.—fluttered from branch to branch of the trees around our temporary encampment. It was yet very early in the morning when Mr. Birch sounded the turn-out to a breakfast of tea and coffee, toast and fruit. The Prince, accompanied by Lord Suffield, Lord Charles Beresford, and one or two others, went out down by the river to procure some specimens for Mr. Bartlett to stuff. The bag consisted of various kingfishers, woodpeckers (*Brachypterni*), a snake or two, snipe, and a Kabrogaya lizard (*Hydrosaurus salvator*), 5 feet 7 inches in length, killed by Lord Carington, which was found to be filled with small crabs. Apropos of snakes, Dr. Fayrer and Mr. Campbell, an active officer of the police force of the island, had an animated discussion. The latter gentleman is a firm believer in the efficacy of ammonia as a specific for snake-poison, and declared that he had cured many cases by the use of it. This Dr. Fayrer declared to be impossible; and when Mr. Campbell asserted that he had cured men who were bitten by snakes, Dr. Fayrer replied that the snakes were not poisonous, and that if they had been so, ammonia could not have saved the patients. I did not like to suggest to Mr. Campbell that he should allow himself to be bitten by an undoubtedly poisonous snake, for so firm did he seem in his belief, that I believe he would have tried it, and I was confident enough in the soundness of Dr. Fayrer's knowledge to think that Mr. Campbell would have fallen a victim to his zeal. In the afternoon there was another shooting excursion in the jungle close at hand. It was said that there were deer and other *feræ naturæ* in it in abundance. The beaters went in to drive for them, and as Lord Suffield was standing on the edge of a swampy patch, amidst tall grass, in a very thick part of the wood, he was put on the alert by the rush of some animal close to him, which afforded a glimpse of a glistening brown hide. He fired, and down went the beast. It was a fine buffalo; but there is some suspicion that it was not altogether in a state of nature. Two pengolins, or scaly anteaters, were captured by the natives for Mr. Layard, who is a great naturalist. In the evening a thunderstorm burst over the camp, and the rain once more came down in torrents. A flash of lightning came so near Macdonald, the Prince's chief jäger, that he fell to the ground, and Dr. Fayrer experienced a numbing sensation from a bolt which seemed to fall close to our dwelling.

As I did not feel very well, and had a good deal to do, I sent my servant over to the mess-hut for my dinner. The poor wretch returned with the exclamation, "Look, Sahib! Plenty leech about!" I looked, and saw he had actual "anklets" of leeches. They hung by scores on his legs, and gave him the appearance of having jet ornaments on his nether extremities.

December 6th.—Rat, tat, tat, beat the rain all night on the leafy roof of our dwelling. When the dawn woke up the noisy birds in the trees around the encampment, the air was so "thick" that the light could scarcely pierce the fleece of white vapour which rose from the reeking earth, but "as the sun ascended the weather mended." The day, however, never became what is called "sunny," but it was steaming hot, and every one of the party lived and moved and had his being in a portable warm-bath of his own, which may be "nothing when one is used to it," but which is very trying before that feat is accomplished. The limp, worn-out natives had an air as if they had been swimming for their lives all night and had just scrambled upon the bank, and were not to the front with their usual alacrity. It was six o'clock. Out of my calico window I could see the police-sentries pacing up and down in the mud before the Prince's bungalow; and in the open shed outside the sportsmen were beginning breakfast, attired in their shooting-dresses. Looking out of my calico door, I saw Mr. Birch looking out of his upon our common table, whereon were laid bananas, oranges, bread and coffee; and after the customary morning salutations, and a hasty meal, Mr. Birch whipped up his young friends, and told them off to their different carriages. The Governor went back to Hanwele, to make arrangements for the return to Colombo. His Royal Highness soon afterwards appeared in a broad-brimmed solar topee, sober-hued jacket and knickerbockers, and "leech gaiters." These necessary additions to one's toilet are stocking-shaped bags of linen, which are pulled over the feet and fastened at the knee before the shoes are put on. They are supposed to baffle the efforts of the denizens of Ceylon forests to suck the traveller's blood. The jungle in which the elephants were abiding was about seven and a half miles south from Ruanwella, and horses had been sent on to await the Prince on the roadside, to take him on by a path cut through the forest to the Kraal. Lord Aylesford, Dr. Fayrer, Mr. S. Hall, Mr. Varian, Lord C. Beresford, and Mr. Fisher went ahead in a mail-coach, which had been relieved from its ordinary duty. The Prince, attended by Lord Suffield and General Probyn, followed in a carriage, escorted by lancers of the Governor's Body Guard; and a third carriage, in which were Mr. Birch, Mr. FitzGeorge, Mr. Thackwell, aide-de-camp, and myself, closed the rear of the little cortege. We drove through a wooded country, in which the view was shut by walls of dense forest, to the main road; and at 8 A.M. we saw a considerable crowd in advance on high ground, on which there is a village called, I believe, Algeda. "Where is the Prince?" exclaimed Mr. Birch. "He has gone on," was the reply. "Where?" "We don't know!" Here was a situation! The Prince's carriage had passed the place where it ought to have stopped. What was to be done? The horses in waiting had not been observed by any of the Prince's party, and those who saw his carriage supposed the coachman was going to pull up further on. There was a pulling up, but not of horses, on account of this incident afterwards. The delay might not seem to be of much consequence, but as the beaters in the jungle had begun to drive the elephants at 7 A.M., or, according to Mr. Atherton's account, nearly an hour sooner, there was just the chance that the whole of the preparations made with so much labour and at so great a cost would come to naught if the Prince were not at his post. Lieutenant Thackwell, one of the Governor's aides-de-camp, ever active and ready, at once mounted a horse; but the animal had a will of his own, and he and his rider were a long time arguing it out before they could agree on a common course of action. Mr. Campbell started off on horseback and Mr. Varian on foot; but the Prince was not overtaken till his carriage had reached the ferry-boat at Avisawella, some good three miles further. The feelings of Mr. Birch meanwhile, as, communing with himself, he walked up and down in a field off the road, were set forth in touching pantomime. Waiting by a roadside is weary work; and Mr. FitzGeorge and myself, after a short conversation with Major Tranchell, who was guarding the entrance to the wood with his police, resolved to walk to the rendezvous. The path, deep-trodden by many feet, led by the side of a clear stream through primeval forest and jungle; and after a walk of half a mile or so, we came on bamboo huts and the embers of fires where the watch had been keeping in the elephants. Then we passed sheds in which biscuits, tobacco, bread, eggs, and fruit were on sale. In fact, within the silent jungle which was spread out before us there were parties variously estimated to number 1200 or 1500 men, who had been engaged for more than a fortnight constructing the Kraal, and keeping an eye on the elephants.

We passed two barriers guarded by police, and arrived at a platform—a sort of Grand Stand—in the forest, on which we found Lord Aylesford, Dr. Fayrer, and others, awaiting the arrival of the Prince. From this we looked down on an immensely high and strong stockade, formed of trunks of trees strongly strutted and stayed, extending across a shallow wooded valley, at the bottom of which there was a tiny rivulet. At the other side of the valley were trees, creepers, and bamboos, so thick that the stockade could hardly be seen twenty or thirty yards off. Beyond the impenetrable forest gloom. Outside the stockade, running across the valley up the hillside, there was a stake net of wood-work, into which the beaters were to drive the elephants after they had been forced past the high rock on which the Prince was to be placed; spears and pointed stakes were piled up to be thrust between the openings should any elephant try to break through. Lining the stockade were some hundreds of men, keeping very quiet.

At 9 A.M. the Prince arrived on horseback, dismounted, and passed through the stockade to the stand. He was attended by Lord C. Beresford and Robertson. Mr. Hall was placed in a tree within sight of the Prince. The yells of the beaters had been audible for some time before his arrival. Mr. Fisher and Mr. Varian went inside the stockade to direct the operations, and then we all waited for an hour patiently. Eleven o'clock, twelve o'clock, one o'clock, came and went. Still no shot. At half-past one o'clock there was a tremendous commotion. The word was passed that the herd was coming down towards the stockade. In effect they did. We heard the beaters' cries coming nearer and nearer—just as in a deer drive in the Highlands. The platform was deserted. Every one rushed to the Kraal, armed with spears or long bamboos to thrust through the interstices and drive back the elephants. Every eye was strained to pierce the forest depths, where bamboos and trees cracked like pistol shots beneath the trampling of elephant hoofs. Thrice the Prince caught a glimpse of a ridge like the top of a loaf of brown bread moving swiftly through the jungle; but it was only for a moment. Suddenly the cries of the beaters ceased, the crashing and snapping noises receded. "The herd has gone back again." "The tusker has charged and broken through." It was the same thing over and over again. All attempts to force the herd towards the stockade failed. In the jungle were two herds. One of only three, led by an old tusker—charged with the death of four European sportsmen and of many cattle—the other of seven—lady elephants. When the beaters came up, the latter put themselves under the old tusker, who proved to be a leader whose courage and coolness were only equalled by his sagacity and strategical skill. He not only refused to be driven, but, charging at the head of his column, he broke through the beaters again and again, driving them up trees for shelter, and utterly spoiling sport. A suspicion arose that the Chief was playing false. He was to have whatever elephants could be "kraaled." If the Prince fired, there was small chance of driving them to the enclosure; it was supposed, therefore, that he had given orders to dodge the elephants past the Prince's stand, if possible. Perhaps he was wronged. He was told that if the Prince did not get a shot, the Kraal would be destroyed that night; and he was seriously spoken to, as if he could control the elephants and the beaters. I do not know if he could. Certain it is, however, that about 2 P.M., after the Prince had been five hours in his stand, and Lord Suffield and others had volunteered to try to dispose of the tusker, a report came that the old hero and the three ladies he was guarding so devotedly had separated from the herd of seven elephants with which they had fraternised, and had escaped clean away into the forest. In vain the beaters yelled like demons; they were charged by Don Tuskerando, obliged to run uphill and to get into trees, and to begin the drive again. At last it was resolved to apply the ordeal which elephants so much dread. Dried timber was piled up in the jungle to windward of the female herd, and set on fire. Mr. Fisher and Mr. Varian marshalled the beaters, and permission was given to some of them who were armed to fire into the rear of the elephants. Presently branches crashed, and trees shook violently, a couple of shots were heard—an elephant rushed, like some great rock, down the hillside within twenty yards of the Prince, who fired, and hit the beast in the head, but it went on and was lost in the forest. In a few minutes Mr. Fisher ran up, "steaming," and said, "Sir! If you will come with me I think I can get you a shot. I have wounded an elephant; I know where he is, and you can kill him." The Prince descended from his post and set out with him creeping through the dense jungle as well as he could. Mr. Fisher and Mr. Varian were on each side and a little in advance of his Royal Highness, Peter Robertson, Lord Suffield, Lord C. Beresford, and Mr. Hall followed in the rear. The heat was great; it was impossible to see two yards ahead. Shooting hats were lost, clothes torn. Suddenly the elephant which had been wounded was discovered through the jungle. The Prince fired—the elephant dropped at once, and lay as if dead. Mr. Hall stopped to take a sketch; but after a while the elephant began first to move, then to kick, and finally to get on his legs; whereupon Mr. Hall, doubting whether he could challenge the *revenant* to an encounter with a lead-pencil, prudently sought safety in flight. Meantime the Prince and his companions were advancing in the jungle towards the place where the principal herd was supposed to be. There was a crashing noise in the forest ahead. The beaters got up into trees. A halt was called. Mr. Fisher and Mr. Varian became uneasy and alarmed, and inexperienced gentlemen thought unnecessarily so. But they knew the situation. Elephants were close at hand, though they could not be seen. At any moment an elephant might rush out; evasion and escape were hopeless, for in such a jungle no man could do more than very slowly creep, whilst the elephant could go through the brush as a ship cleaves the water. All at once, Mr. Fisher perceived an elephant not ten yards off in the very act of charging. The Prince caught sight of it also, fired, and it disappeared in the jungle. The huntsmen continued in pursuit cautiously, but the creepers and thick undergrowth made stout resistance, so that their progress was slow, and not unexhausting. In a few minutes more another elephant was seen, where the bush was

CEYLON.—THE DEAD ELEPHANT.

not so dense, by the side of the rivulet. The Prince took deliberate aim and fired. The great beast toppled, and fell over on its side in the stream, where it dammed up the waters! There ensued a scene of great excitement. The Prince descended the bank, but they called to him to take care. They approached and watched for a moment. The creature did not move; it was "dead, sure enough!" Then the Prince, assisted by the hunters, got into the water and climbed upon the inert mountain of flesh. Down came the natives from tree, stockade, and hillside. Europeans and Cingalese dashed into the stream, and cheered again and again, and the whole party whooped and woke up the glade with their cries, as the Prince was seen standing on the prostrate body—which was not that of the redoubtable tusker. The Prince, according to custom, cut off the tail. As soon as his back was turned, the Cingalese took pieces from the ears as trophies of the day. The Prince was streaming with perspiration, his clothes wet, and torn to shreds. It was getting dark, and quite time to get out of the jungle. The party mounted their horses and returned to the road. Carriages were waiting to take them to Hanwele, where Governor Gregory and others, having gone down the river by boat from Avisawella, were waiting to receive the Prince; but ere he arrived, he met with a little, which might have been a great, accident. At the corner of a small bridge, where there was a deep ditch, the carriage went right over, flinging the occupants on each other. Lord Aylesford was on the box beside the driver. General Probyn, Lord C. Beresford, and Mr. FitzGeorge were inside with the Prince. The vehicle was broken, but the Prince emerged unhurt. His Royal Highness acts on the principle of the late Duke of Wellington, "not to be afraid of a danger when it is over," and the first thing he did was to inquire after "his elephant's tail." It was long after dark when the Prince reached his quarters, and he must have been excessively tired; but he gave a full account to the Governor of his adventures in the jungle, and of his upset. At the latter he laughed heartily; but there might have been very serious results had the coach turned over a few feet further on.

At Hanwele, which is eleven miles from the ferry at Avisawella, there are the remains of an old Dutch Fort. The Prince slept in the Bungalow, or Rest-house, and his followers were quartered in various detached buildings. The Fort is situated on the Kalany Gaṅga, which, swollen by the rains, now presents a noble appearance.

December 7th.—Soon after 7 A.M. the Prince, though there had been a late sitting to talk over the details of the day's sport, to wait for tidings of the wounded elephants, and to read letters and home news in the mail which had just arrived, left Hanwele, and drove nineteen miles to Colombo.

Whilst his Royal Highness and party were travelling by road, I was descending the river Kalany Ganga, from Hanwele to Grand Pass. The boat in which I was a passenger was something like the large vessels formerly used by Europeans on the Ganges, and could have accommodated a dozen persons. In the stern there was a luxurious apartment, intended to shelter one from the sun, covered over with thatch, provided with sofa, table, chairs, &c. Further aft was a kitchen, where the meals were cooked. The crew consisted of four men, who sometimes allowed the boat to glide down the current of its own accord, the steersman astern directing it with an oar-like rudder, sometimes pulled vigorously, and sent it along at a speed of six or seven miles an hour. The river was at the full; broader than the Thames at Greenwich, but flowing through very different scenery. I have never beheld anything, even in our recent journey, so wonderful as the mass of vegetation and the continuous wall of forest on the banks. It could not be supposed that there were any human habitations in such jungle, but at every turn, and there were many, we came upon the natives fishing, and navigating their frail barks, and through the openings in the glades here and there, caught sight of hamlets, which but for the cocoanut-palms that hedged them in, justifying the Cingalese notion that the tree will not live out of reach of the human voice, would be scarcely distinguishable from the foliage around.

A civil native gentleman seeing me, when I landed at Grand Pass, in difficulties for a conveyance to the Governor's house, very kindly harnessed his horse to a gig and drove me to Colombo, where I arrived in time for the Prince's levee, which was attended not only by the Europeans and Cingalese authorities, officials, planters, and gentry, but by deputations from all parts of the island, some with presents and addresses, and by a large number of yellow-robed priests. The presentations were numerous, and the levee was not long over before it was necessary to change and prepare for a visit to the Exhibition at the Agri-Horticultural Enclosure, where a very instructive collection of the products, fabrics, and manufactures of the island, as well as specimens of its natural wealth in minerals and precious stones, &c.; and of jewellery, and the like, were laid out in a very large enclosure. But the tent was crowded, and the weather was too hot to enable the visitors to enjoy the sight. Natheless, it afforded fair occasion to many ladies and gentlemen to see the Prince closely. There was included in the exhibition, in a booth specially erected for the ceremony—but whether designed for the Agricultural or the Horticultural part I cannot assert —the representation of a Cingalese wedding. For those who are curious in such subjects, and who care to learn what the ceremonies are, there are plenty of books extant, and it would be, perhaps, misleading to describe what the Prince saw, as it might have been a "mock marriage," or a Gretna Green business à la Colombo. Nor shall I say more about the exhibition of the detachment of Veddahs than

THE VEDDAHS LAUGH.

remark that they destroyed two phases of faith which had obtained among the visitors. They were such indifferent marksmen with the bow and arrow that they would have been nowhere at a good Archery Club Meeting, and when they were amused they laughed like other people. As to the first, it must be admitted that they had to shoot before the Prince in the midst of an immense concourse; and as to the second, they may have been very much tickled at the idea of being sketched, for when Mr. Hall produced his pencil and book, and began to take notes of them, there could be no doubt of their hilarity, and the harder he looked at them and sketched, and the more they looked at the artist, the greater was their merriment. Sir Emerson Tennent gives the fullest and best account of these curious people, and it is a disheartening reflection that with materials so void of prejudices and dogma, it is impossible to make Christians out of them. Voilà!—"something which gives to reflection!" From the Agri-Horticultural the Prince drove to see elephant arches and trophies, returning to the State Banquet in the Queen's House, to which Sir W. H. Gregory had invited all the people of note and foreign Consuls, to the number of seventy, to have the honour of meeting him; the like of which has never, one may safely say, been seen in any time of Cingalese Kings, or of Indian, Portuguese, Dutch, or English. Nor with that and with its pleasures was the cup quite filled, for a ball of exceeding brilliancy and admirable in every way, at the Colombo Club, followed at 10 P.M. I am not quite sure of the building, though I can aver that it was spacious, airy, abounding in fine rooms handsomely decorated, with excellent music, good floor, and indefatigable dancers. Human nature, not princely, gives way under such stress of enjoyment. Certain of the guests, quite tired out, retiring to the Queen's House, rather early, thought they would like to procure a glass of water or lemonade. They called and rang, stamped and shouted—no one came. Voices were heard all the while clacking in Cingalese close at hand, whereupon, claymore in hand, the Duke burst in upon them. And lo! they vanished "like ghosts at cockcrow" into the woods, or who knows where—but, any way, the Governor the following morning prayed, in much amused trepidation, that next time we might do our spiriting gently, "for" says he, "these fellows think nothing of going off into the jungle, and I don't know where to get others, so that we may be left without servants in an instant." The situation was too grave for the hint to be neglected.

December 8th.—There was general lassitude this morning. The effects of the shooting-excursion in the forest and of the climate are disagreeably evident. Lord Suffield suffers from sore throat; Lord Aylesford has slight fever; Mr. Grey is far from being well, and has to remain in his room. The house was hemmed in with box-wallahs. They were regularly in possession, sat outside all the bedroom doors, and encamped in the passages and garden. Some who had been forbidden admission hovered outside the sentries, and tempted purchasers from afar. Inconceivable rubbish was displayed with much ostentation, and, for anything good, the prices were ridiculous. "Cat's-eyes" were offered for 600*l.*, which were probably worth a third of the sum to those who have an affection for such stones. Nevertheless, there were heavy purchases made on simple principles. "What's the price of this ring?" "That very fine ring, my lord? Sold one like it one thousand rupees, not same good as that." "I'll give you five hundred for it. Come! will you take it?" "My lord, say just eight hundred! I should like to oblige you." "Be off with you." "Will my Lord give seven hundred rupees, and ruin me?" "No, not a penny more than five hundred." "Just say, my Lord, six hundred and fifty, to let me have one rupee profit." "No," &c. The ring, be sure, is sold for the five hundred, and is seldom worth what is paid for it; but there are exceptions to the rule, and some very pretty and valuable articles of jewelry were purchased at fair prices. There were visits promised to Messrs. Leechman's cocoa manufactory, and to Messrs. Walls' coffee factory in the forenoon. The Prince called, on his way to them, to see an enormous tortoise, said to have belonged to the last Dutch Governor, and to be more than a hundred years old. The tortoise, who was "at home," appeared not to be at all sensible of the honour, and to have more than his share of Dutch phlegm. Thence his Royal Highness went, in a very hot sun, to the cocoa manufactory and to the coffee factory, which deserved a visit much better than most show places. In the coffee-picking rooms there were some hundreds of Tamil women and girls, who come over from the mainland with their families. They displayed a surprising quantity of silver bangles, necklaces, bracelets, gold ear-rings, and rings. The workers in any English factory would surely have envied them. Their behaviour was perfect; they neither stared nor giggled. The curious and characteristic jewellery and ornaments attracted the attention of some of the visitors; and the English superintendent was asked to buy what struck them. Indeed, there were independent efforts made at barter by intending purchasers, who held out hands full of money, and pointed out what they affected; but the owners did not appear inclined to sell. When the superintendent came on the scene, it was different. I fear he ordered. No doubt the women received full value, and more, for their ornaments; but they showed no disposition to part with them, and one, as she removed her armlets, was quite forlorn, and hid her tearful eyes with her hand when they were removed. Certainly the ordinary Tamil silversmith in the bazaar can make the articles; but there might have been some feeling among these poor people—some "heirloomry" sentiment about the ornaments.

Messrs. Fisher and Varian appeared at lunch, and reported that the two wounded elephants had escaped to the mountains. At 4.30 P.M. the Prince received deputations, native literates and learned Buddhists, who presented addresses and presents.

The laying of the foundation-stone of the new Breakwater by the Prince this afternoon was an interesting ceremony. There was a considerable assemblage, guard of honour, band and colours of the 57th Regiment, in the enclosure around the stone, which was lowered to its place with the usual formalities, but the eye was most taken with the splendid crew of the *Serapis*. Their bronzed faces, broad chests, and fine stature, afforded a great contrast to those of the "washed-out-looking" and slightly-made men of the infantry regiment, the men of which lined the way to the reserved seats. Colombo is an open roadstead much vexed by ocean, and landing and embarking always are difficult. The undertaking is a great one, and worthy of all success; and the breakers which thundered close at hand spoke very eloquently of the necessity for such a work, which will illustrate the administration of Sir W. H. Gregory.

The Prince, followed by the people to the water's edge, left Colombo for the *Serapis* in the evening. A farewell dinner was given on board to the Governor and authorities. The town and the country round about were illuminated —the fleet and shipping, bright as lanterns, blue and red lights, rockets, maroons, and bombs could make them. With the expression of his perfect contentment to all concerned for his reception at Ceylon, and many acknowledgments of the pleasure he had derived from his visit, the Prince bade his excellent host, Sir W. H. Gregory, and his staff and the chief persons, good-bye.

Friar Jordanus and others have told us many wonderful things about this ancient kingdom. But the quantity of truth—a rare article in the writings of ancient travellers

—which he wrote, all things considered, is remarkable. We did not, indeed, come across the "island wherein there is a lake with a tree in the midst of it, which hath the property of turning everything into gold which is washed with the water, and of curing every wound that is rubbed with the leaf of the tree." There is still quite enough of marvel and novelty in Ceylon to attract travellers, even although they may not be so fortunate as Knox and Jordanus. I am glad to add that none of us in our rambles chanced, as far as I know, to meet with what they both speak of. "What shall I say then?" exclaims Jordanus. "Even the Devil speaketh many a time and oft to man in the night season, as I have heard him." Mr. Mitford presumes to insinuate that it was the cry of a night-hawk which the Friar mistook for the voice of the Evil One; but Knox, in his narrative of adventures, declares that at night he frequently heard Beelzebub calling out in Ceylon. He says, "This for certain I can affirm, that oftentimes the Devil doth cry with audible voice in the night. It is very shrill, almost like the barking of a dog, and this I have often heard myself; but I never heard that he did anybody any harm." (The puir De'il!) "Only this observation the inhabitants of the island (Ceylon) have made of this voice, and I have made it also, that either just before, or very suddenly after this voice, always the King cuts off people. To believe that this is the voice of the Devil three reasons urge, and 'tis so accounted by all the people:—'1st. Because there is no creature known to the inhabitants that cries like it; and (2) because it will on a sudden depart from one place to make a noise in another quicker than any fowl could fly; and (3) because the very dogs will tremble and shake when they hear it. This voice is heard only in Kandy, and never in the lowlands.'" Then he goes on to tell how the Cingalese,

U 2

"when they hear this voice, will curse the Devil, calling him a 'beef-eating slave,' and telling him" (which seems needless) "to be damned. Whereupon the voice always ceaseth for awhile, and seems to depart, being heard at a greater distance."

The Prince had to overcome opposition to his project of including Ceylon in the tour. There were difficulties in relation to other places in the programme connected with the visit, which encouraged those who did not think the island very interesting to persist in objections which it needed persistence to meet and overcome. The Prince has to be congratulated on the result. He greatly pleased the inhabitants, native and European, and he certainly, notwithstanding the weather and some impediments to the execution of the original plan, passed a very agreeable time there. The memories of Ceylon will always be green as the island itself.

A "CRAWL" IN THE JUNGLE, CEYLON.

CARVING A GOD AT MADURA.

CHAPTER VIII.

TUTICORIN—MADRAS.

Tuticorin—Tamil land—Tinnevelly Christians—Madura—The cholera again—Trimul Naik—The Ranee of Shivagunga—Seringham—Trichinopoly—Madras—The Duke of Buckingham's Reception—The Golden Umbrella—The Rajas—Prince of Arcot—Races—Illumination of the Surf—Native Entertainment—Departure.

DECEMBER 9TH.—In the middle watches of the night the *Serapis*, to the great satisfaction of her officers, left her moorings in the roadstead of Colombo, and proceeded to sea. As the first turn of the screw shook the vessel, and as she reeled over in the sea-way, there were probably a few, who turned uneasily in their hammocks, aware of the fact that we were under weigh, and would see Ceylon no more. When the morning advanced, there could be no doubt that we were at sea, and very much so, too. Although sailors might not consider the wind strong, it was powerful enough to raise a lopping sea, which rendered it impossible to enjoy any amusement on deck, and which also, as we afterwards learnt, caused much alarm to the special correspondents, for whose use Sir William Gregory had provided a coasting steamer—the best he could procure—of no great power or size. An uninteresting sea; no vessels or boats in sight. On the right a faint cloud-like land, which melted away gradually in the Gulf of Manaar. Observations at noon gave lat. 8° 1′ N., long. 78° 56′ E. Eighty-six miles since 4 A.M. Tuticorin Light sixty-four miles distant. About 4 P.M. the coast could be made out, and after a time we saw the inevitable palm-trees, which waved their arms to welcome us. But riding outside, some distance from the shore, a brig at anchor afforded unpleasant proof of the roughness of the sea. Staff-Commander Goldsmith, however, did not think much of it, though he was not so well pleased with the soundings, which showed that the *Serapis* would have to give the land a wide berth. Presently the Light House and a coast which put one greatly in mind of the scenery about Shoeburyness, *plus* cocoanut-trees, came in view. At 5.25 P.M. the *Serapis* brought up five miles south of Tuticorin. There was no appearance of any authority with or without a cocked hat. The "locals" were evidently taken by surprise—caught in a *siesta*, or ignorant of the Prince's coming. Commander Durrant came off from the *Osborne*, and had by no means an easy task to board. He and his crew had a ducking, and as he stepped on the ladder he was caught by a wave up to his knees. When he had occasion to go back, he very wisely, if very actively, lowered himself down by a ladder of ropes hanging astern into his gig. At 7 P.M. a boat came off from shore with the Master-Attendant. It was ordered that the luggage and baggage should be ready at daybreak, lighters to be alongside at 5 A.M. to convey them on shore.

December 10th.—At 5 A.M. every one was up and stirring; but not a boat was to be seen. The sea was "rough and lumpy," and it rained during the night. As I was in my cabin I heard a heavy thump on the deck, and was told by Dr. Fayrer that a man had fallen out of the mizen rigging, and was very badly hurt. It was one of the few accidents which occurred on board, and, I am glad to say, the man quite recovered. At 6 A.M. three large boats were seen beating around the point under reefed mainsails. Before they arrived alongside, the *Margaret Northcote*, which is certainly not intended for anything but the smoothest inland navigation, struggled to get near the *Serapis*, and made terribly bad weather of it as she encountered the roll of the sea. She is a very crank little craft, and will go pearl-fishing for herself some day, if she be sent out in bad weather. We gazed with compassion at the group of gentlemen in uniform—Mr. Robinson, Colonel Hearn, Mr. Shaw Stewart, Dr. Stewart, and others—on board, when she came near enough to enable us to see her deck, which inclined sideways occasionally, as if to tilt them into the sea. Compassion for them deepened into commiseration for ourselves, when we were informed that the body of the suite would be transferred on board that very same vessel. To our great regret Lord Suffield and Mr. Grey had to remain on board the *Serapis* in charge of Dr. Watson, as Dr. Fayrer did not consider it judicious for Lord Suffield to expose himself to the land journey, and Mr. Grey was too weak to attempt it. It was a *mauvais quart d'heure* for those on board the *Margaret Northcote.* It seemed as if she never would get her anchor. General Probyn, for once assuming control of a department not his own, stimulated the gentlemen of colour who were engaged at the windlass by fervid orations in, or in what ought to have been, their native language, which they seemed not to understand. At last we reached *terra firma*. The preparations were pretty; but there was really very little time to look about one. A temporary pavilion or pandal had been erected, in which the inevitable address was delivered, and the Zemindars were presented; and when the exchange of courtesies had ended, the Prince walked to the Station, where he waited till the exhausted and exhausting *Margaret Northcote* had delivered her luckless freight. It is scarcely possible to exaggerate the quiet charms of the scenery along the new railway, or the great delight of the people at the combined attractions of the first train and of the Prince. The whole population thronged to the roadside. The tall, erect figures, square shoulders, broad chests, narrow flanks, and straight limbs of the men, struck one almost as much as the graceful carriage and elegant forms of the women. It would be difficult to find a finer race in any part of the world. Their attitudes of wonder and joy were singularly graceful and attractive. Some expressed their feelings by placing their hands, clasped as if in prayer, before their breasts; others held their fingers to their lips, as if to suppress their cries; but as the train passed, one and all clapped hands, as if they were of a London audience applauding at a theatre. A more natural, easy, and well-to-do looking people could not be found in Christendom. Plains green with sugar, rice, and cotton, spread to the foot of the wooded hills of gneiss-rock, which, generally conical were sometimes worn into fantastic outline of castle-like crag and beetling precipice. It is certainly a land, if not flowing with milk and honey, inhabited by a population of sweet and kindly disposition, whose virtues are admitted by the missionaries, and whose exceeding tractability has gained for them "the praise of masters not always given to indulge in over-laudation of any native virtues."

This part of India, which the missionaries call Tamil Land, is larger than Bavaria, Saxony, Wurtemberg, and the German Dukedoms together, and contains a population of about sixteen millions of people. The Nilgherries, rising to the height of 8000 feet; the Pulnee, with peaks 7000 feet high, and their eastern offshoots, diversify the surface; and the watersheds throw off supplies for the great rivers, which become, however, for part of the year, little more than beds of sand. Coffee is planted on the lower ranges; rice, in great quantities, is cultivated in the plains, and sugar cultivation is extending. Indigo and different kinds of grain thrive in parts of the district, if so it may be called, and cotton is not only sufficiently abundant for the wants of the native manufacturers, but gives margin for export. The manufacture of iron, the ore of which is found in large quantities, though not of very great excellence, is still carried on. Here we have the salt tax and monopoly in full force, the French at Pondicherry receiving 40,000*l.* a year for prohibiting the manufacture within their settlements; the revenue of the Tamil district from this objectionable source amounting to about two millions of rupees per annum. One of the German missionaries of the Evangelical Lutheran Society has expressed a regret, in which I certainly share, that the sobriety of the people has been undermined, if not by the English Government, certainly by its legislation, for it has introduced the system of selling the right to make palm-tree toddy to the highest bidder, and drunkenness — once the great disgrace amongst Hindoos, and even a capital offence, and punished with severity under the Mahomedans—is steadily increasing.

At Maniachy, eighteen miles from Tuticorin, a deputation of about 6000 native Christians, including a large body of clergy and catechists, and 1000 boys and girls receiving education in Church of England schools awaited the arrival of his Royal Highness. The Rev. Dr. Caldwell, the able and learned missionary of the Society for the Propagation of the Gospel, and the Rev. Dr. Sergeant, a veteran representative of the Church Missionary Society, surrounded by a considerable staff of English clergy, stood on the platform side by side, typifying the perfect unanimity with which our two great Church Societies are labouring for the evangelisation of India. When his Royal Highness alighted from his carriage, the missionaries were presented to him by Mr. Robinson and Canon Duckworth. Dr. Caldwell read an address of welcome from the Church of Tinnevelly, expressing the devoted loyalty of its members and their deep sense of the special blessings they enjoyed as the Christian subjects of a Christian Sovereign. The progress of the Church of England Mission in this region was sketched, and it was shown how the good seed conveyed from Tanjore by Schwartz, about the end of the last century, and that which was sown broadcast from 1820 onwards by Rhenins, both German missionaries in the employ of English societies, had been nurtured by missionaries since 1840, until the native Christian community in Tinnevelly is the most numerous in India. Christian congregations have been formed in about 600 towns, villages, and hamlets, composed exclusively of converts. The total number of native Christians in the district was stated to be 60,000, who are under the charge of 54 native clergy and 590 catechists and teachers of various grades; and the number of communicants is 10,378. The schools are attended by about 13,000 boys and girls. It is worthy of note that the Christians in Tinnevelly contributed last year 32,483 rupees for the support of their own Church, equivalent in the sacrifice it represents to eight or ten times the amount in England. At the conclusion of the address a handsomely-bound Bible and Prayer-book, in the Tamil language, and offerings of embroidery and exquisitely fine lace, the handiwork of girls attending the Tinnevelly schools, were presented to his Royal Highness.

NATIVE CHRISTIANS AT TINNEVELLY.

The Prince having replied to the address in gracious and encouraging words, the children sang a "Tamil lyric," composed in the Prince's honour, of which the following is a translation, in chorus to a quaint native air:—

"Through the grace of the blessed Lord of Heaven, O son of our Victorious Queen, mayest thou ever enjoy all prosperity!

"It is our peculiar happiness to be subject to a Sceptre under which the leopard and the deer continually drink at the same stream.

"Crossing seas and crossing mountains, thou hast visited this southernmost region, and granted to those who live under the shadow of thy Royal umbrella a sight of thy benign countenance.

"May thy realm, on which sun and moon never set, become from generation to generation more and more illustrious!

"May the lion-flag of the British nation wave gloriously far and wide, and wherever it waves may the Cross-Banner of our Lord Jesus fly with it harmoniously!

"God preserve thee and regard thee with an eye of grace, and grant thee long life and victory, and bless thee for evermore!

"Obeisance to thee! Obeisance to thee, O wise King that art to be! Safely may'st thou reach again the capital of thy realm, O thou whom all men justly praise!"

After receiving this vocal homage, his Royal Highness handed to representatives from each of the schools mango and other seedlings, to be planted in the school-compounds in memory of his visit, and, doubtless, in many a hamlet of Tinnevelly the "Prince's tree" will keep alive for generations the traditions of the hour when the Christians of Southern India, long wont to pray, like ourselves, for "Albert Edward, Prince of Wales, the Princess of Wales, and the rest of the Royal Family," stood face to face with their future Sovereign.

At 12.20 P.M. the train stopped at Kovilpatty, thirty-six miles from Tuticorin. There was a small camp and a handsome mess tent fitted up luxuriously near the Station. The tents belonged to the minor Zemindar of Ettiapuram, who was there with his kinsfolk and tenants, and the usual mighty multitude, to greet the Prince. Once more we had occasion to wonder at the swarming masses, and to admire the fine forms, pleasant manners and looks, and picturesque appearance of the people. There was a halt of half-an-hour for luncheon, and before the Prince resumed his journey he accepted from the Zemindar some articles of trifling value as mementoes of his visit. A little before 5 P.M. the train reached its destination at Madura. The *nil admirari* is a secret of happiness that is now well-nigh lost in India, but there was a lightness and grace in the decorations of the Station and of the streets, and something arcadian in the aspect of the city, which, sated as the eye is with sights, attracted attention. The engine which had drawn the Royal train, hitherto anonymous, was christened the *Alexandra* by the Prince, and the line of the S.I.P.R. to Madura declared to be open. The procession of the Prince from the Station to his residence was like many others, but it succeeded in the object of giving pleasure to thousands of spectators. Flags and festoons were profuse; in the main street there was a white triumphal arch of taboot work in perforated paper, covered with talc plates and silvered plaques, behind which was a screen of red. The arch was surmounted by three domes, with four minarets, two on each flank. There were also eight pandals in the town, in addition to those put up by the Railway Company. The cleansing, scouring, whitewashing, painting, and deodorising, which were the usual precursors of the Prince's visits, were vigorously carried out.

Madura deserves the credit, which its inhabitants at least award to it, of being the most charming town in Southern India. The streets, if unpaved, are broad, ornamented with palm-trees, well swept, and clean. We may believe or not, as we please, that it was once the capital of a kingdom, which sent its ambassadors to Augustus at Rome; but all must admit that the public buildings and temples attest the great prosperity and riches of its more recent native rulers. The people say it is called Madura from a Sanscrit root signifying "sweetness," and the repose of its tanks and groves, and the placid air of its inhabitants, bespeak long freedom from the effects of war and tumult. It is the centre of missionary enterprise, particularly for the American Societies, and the latest accounts of evangelising progress state that there are 139 congregations in the district, with an aggregate of 7000 Christians. In the whole of Tamil Land there are said to be now about 120,000 Protestant Christians. But there is some reason to fear that the Abbé Dubois was right in his melancholy deduction from the labours of his life amongst the Hindoos. There is no permanent increase; in fact, the Christian churches seem to have been more numerous and flourishing in the time of Friar Jordanus than they are at present.

When the English succeeded the Dutch, who had driven out the Portuguese in Southern India the ecclesiastical authorities and missionaries for some time got on exceedingly well with the Churches which recognised the Patriarch of Antioch; but after a while there was a split among those they call the Thomas Christians, one portion adhering to the Anglicans, and another retaining their allegiance to Antioch, and calling their bishops from Syria. The Roman Catholic Church has still flourishing establishments over the land; and as there are varieties of missionaries belonging to sections of the Protestant Church, each working on the account of their own body—Americans, Germans, Danes, and Englishmen—the natives may point to the discrepancies amongst these professors of Christianity as some reason for adhering to their own belief. But the missionaries have, notwithstanding, made greater progress in this region, probably, than in any part of the heathen world. Progress has not always been uniform; and if we compare the condition of the ancient Christian Churches with that of the present establishments, we may find reason to believe that there have been very decided lapses, and not only no progress, but retrograde movements at times. But that there is no reason to despair of eventual success in this part of India is the belief of Sir Bartle Frere and of very high authorities.

In less than an hour the Prince arrived at his charming quarters, situated in front of the Teppa Kollum (or "Floating Tank"), but with the disadvantage of having the public road running between the door-steps and the Tank. The latter is walled round and cased with black granite steps. In the midst of the tranquil lake there is a shrine, or temple, embowered in trees, on an artificial island. There was an inevitable dispersion of the suite. "Where ignorance is bliss, 'tis folly to be wise," and we were well content with the quarters assigned to us; but the distance prevented some of the suite seeing the illuminations and fireworks—or at least any more of the latter than the highest bursting charges. The ladies of the Station were admitted to witness them from the roof of the house, and were presented to the Prince, and there was, I believe, a musical entertainment subsequently. Before dinner the principal personages were received; among them the Native Chiefs, of whom the most conspicuous in more ways than one was the Raja of Pudukotta, commonly called the Tondiman Raja.

His Excellency Raja Ramachundra Tondiman Bahadoor of Putukottai, or Pudducottah, is a small, stout man of forty-six. He speaks English and a little French, as well as Telugu, Tamil, Hindustani, and Mahratta; is a Sudra by caste of the tribe of the Kallar (called "Colleries" by Orme). His State, with the administration of which he has little or nothing to do, covers 1380 square miles, and has a population of 320,000. There are 3000 tanks, some of great size. One peculiarity of the State is that it has no treaty with the British Government, is exempt from tribute, and has independent Courts of

Justice. But, for all that, the poor man has no power, for he is under British suzerainty, and he is controlled even to his expenditure of pocket money by the Political, who can "remonstrate,"—that is, scold and threaten him—*de omnibus*. His subjects can be tried in British territory for offences therein committed; but his little State is a kind of Alsatia for refugees from the surrounding British districts; and his "army" of 21 horse and 126 foot is sometimes suspected of considerable eccentricity in its military capacity. As a punishment for running in debt, the Raja has been deprived of some of his titles, and has lost his guns! But he seems to be a perverse kind of potentate, an incorrigible, for he was as splendid with jewels as any we had seen, and offered presents of great price to the Prince. It is said his jewels are not always in his possession, and that his revenue of 325,000 rupees has many claims on it. This is not a pleasant condition for the representative of a house which is described "as the oldest and truest allies of the British in Southern India, who most materially aided them in their contest for supremacy with the French, especially in the stirring events around Trichinopoly, and in the wars against Hyder Ali and Tippoo." It is said by some learned people that the Tondiman Rajas of the period were mere robber Chiefs, and that we ought to be rather ashamed of ourselves for the alliance. The Raja showed the Prince a most interesting book, consisting of letters, despatches, and correspondence between Clive and others and his ancestors relating to these times.

December 11*th*.—"A horrid whisper ran o'er us as we lay" in our beds in the bungalow where I was quartered, this morning. My servant, with a face perceptibly less dark than usual, informed me that the cholera was amongst us. There was a force of 500 native policemen collected from all parts of the country to keep order and to watch over the Royal quarters, and of these, two, he said, had been attacked in the night, and were now dead men. Apropos of police, it was stated that the administration of this district of 2,500,000 souls is carried on by just seven Europeans.

Trimal Naik, whose name is susceptible of many variations, must have been a great king. He reigned at Madura from 1621 to 1657, and he built palaces, temples (of these no less than ninety-six) and tanks on a magnificent scale. His Choultrie ("Mandapan"), or lodging-place for the idol, which was taken from the Temple near at hand, and deposited for ten days each year in this great edifice, measures 333 feet by 105 feet. It is of iron-grey granite of exceeding hardness. It was built in twenty-two years, and was finished at a cost of a million sterling, just about the time of the outbreak of our civil war between Charles I. and his Parliament. In front of the Choultrie there is a gate-tower, which Trimal Naik did not live to finish. The door-posts are single blocks of granite 60 feet high, covered with the most beautifully sculptured foliage—not one square inch without a trace of that patient labour. The interior presents a display of four rows of sculptured columns 25 feet high. It is scarcely too much to say that there is enough of detail on each of these to need half-an-hour's study. The figures are elaborated with extraordinary richness and abundant fancy. The façade is covered with monsters with lions' heads and bodies, trampling on elephants, and with figures on horseback engaged in killing men and tigers—the horses' feet resting on shields which are borne by soldiers. "As works," says Fergusson, "exhibiting difficulties overcome by patient labour, they are unrivalled, as far as I know, by anything found elsewhere. As works of art they are the most barbarous, it may be said the most vulgar, to be found in India, and do more to shake one's faith in the civilisation of the people who produced them than anything they did in any other department of art."

In the great pillared hall there are statues of the Raja and of his six wives. There is one whose side exhibits a deep gash. The story goes that when the Raja had finished his palace he took his wife, who was a Princess of the house of Tanjore, to witness the great work he had accomplished, expecting her to be struck with amazement; but whether they had had any little conjugal quarrel that morning or not, it is quite certain that the Princess was not moved to the expression of any feeling of wonder or surprise. To whom the Raja —"Has your father, of whose greatness you so often tell me, any building in his dominions at all like this?" "Like this!" she replied; "why the sheds in which he keeps his cattle are finer!" Whereupon the Raja, instead of knocking her down and kicking her, like a good pattern husband, threw his dagger at her—it struck her in the hip and there remained. The excellent missionary who tells the story remarks, "The Prince may have been a little violent, but his haughty wife deserved correction, for neither in her father's palace, which is still standing, nor in the whole town of Tanjore, is there a hall to compare with his."

At the entrance to the Palace, part of which, called Westminster Hall among the European colonists, is about to be converted into public offices, the Prince was received by the Trustees of the Temple and by a large body of Zemindars. There was a guard of honour, and band and colours of the 19th Madras Native Infantry outside. It need not be said that the roads and streets through which he passed on his way from the Collector's house were crowded, and that the numbers at the Palace were prodigious, but even these did not prepare us for the aspect of the ancient Hall of Audience which presented a compact mass of turbaned heads. Although there was a throne-like silver chair placed for him on an elevated dais, the Prince stood while the address was being read in very excellent English by S. Subramania Tyen, Bachelor of Law and B.A., Vakil of the High Court of Madras, Municipal Commissioner, and one of the Trustees of the Great Temple. Having delivered his reply, which elicited great applause, his Royal Highness proceeded to examine the handsome presents which were offered to him by the people and the citizens of Madura, and was then conducted round the Palace In one of the apartments the Prince had an interview with the widowed representative of the Chiefs of Shivagunga, one of whom inflicted a severe defeat upon our forces in times past; a most charming old lady, who had entreated the favour so persistently that it could not be denied to her. She had, it appeared, been engaged in a long litigation with the Indian Government, which had been finally decided in her favour on an appeal to the Committee of Privy Council, and this decision the Ranee insisted on accepting as the act of the Queen. "It was the Empress who had done her justice, and she wanted to thank her son;" and so she brought all the treasures of her house, and her own son and heir, "to express what she felt, and to offer everything she had to the Shahzadah." I have seldom seen anything more touching, on or off the stage, than her gesture and action when, thanking the Prince, she took her son's hand, and placed it between her own, as if in supplication, that the Prince might take it. Thence the Prince went to see the edifice, of which Trimal Naik's palace is but a portico— the shrine of Linga Sunadara ("the beautiful Linga"), said to be founded by Raja Kala Shekaya Pandaya between the fifth and sixth centuries. The towers are certainly much more recent, and were probably built by the last of the Pandayan Kings between A.D. 1450 and A.D. 1500.

At the entrance to the Temple of Minakshee, the "fish-eyed" Goddess, Parvati (who was the wife of Shiva), the Prince was received by the chief priests, and by a crowd of inferior ecclesiastics, if so they may be called, who presented an address. As he, preceded by the guardians and a band of dancing girls of the Temple, passed underneath the Gopura, showers of what looked like gold-dust were let fall by unseen hands from the roof. He was covered with a State shawl. The nautch girls scattered flowers before him, fillets of gold and silver tinsel were placed on his brow and arms, richly-scented garlands were brought in baskets and were passed over his shoulders. The suite were decorated in like manner—Canon Duckworth not escaping, and reminding one of the expression of Bishop Heber on a similar occasion, that "he resembled a sacrifice rather than a priest."

The Temple is a rectangle, with sides 730 feet and 830 feet long, and covers twenty acres of ground. A hall of 985 sculptured columns surrounded by arcades; grand gateways, porticos, shrines; mysterious passages; monster idols, one, "the Belly God," with many worshippers; fearful faces which glared from stony eyes; gliding priests; oppressive odours; the recess, specially illuminated, in which dwelt the deity Minakshee, of which—favour almost without precedent—the Prince and followers were vouchsafed a glimpse—it was all very strange and curious, but somehow impressed one with a feeling of deep melancholy.

The shrine, which cost 70,000*l.*, is surrounded by pillars, on which are carved the gods and goddesses of the Hindoo mythology. It is covered with a stone canopy, from the corners of which are chains of three links carved out of the solid block hanging from the stone, of which they formed part. The dome over the shrine, which has cost 7500*l*. already, and will need a further outlay of 2500*l*., is of copper gilt.

The Tank of the Golden Lotus—the sacred bench presented by Shiva himself for the use of the Collegiate Synod, which would be invaluable to the Civil Service Commissioners—the Golden Dome, &c., were all inspected. Great quantities of the manufactures of stuffs, for which Madura is still famous, were laid out in one of the chapels. Having examined the Temple minutely, at 10 A.M. the Prince was driven to the Railway, where breakfast was laid under a very fine pandal specially built for the occasion. The Tondiman Raja offered elephant's tusks, arms, and various other presents. The inhabitants of Madura presented models of the great Temple and of articles used in the worship of their gods; a gold casket of very fine workmanship; specimens of the manufacture of the place in brass and in various coloured stuffs and kerchiefs. The Ranee of Shivagunga, the interesting lady who was so exceedingly gratified at her interview with the Prince, presented boomerangs of steel inlaid with silver and with gold mountings, showing that the use of the boomerang is not confined to Australia; stone images, ivory carvings, betel-nut-crackers; an ingenious puzzle-padlock in a case, with a dagger inside it; and a sword so finely tempered that it could be worn as a belt, which had a history of its own. It belonged to the Poligar Catabomna Naik, who completely defeated the British forces before his fort at Pangalan Kurichi, in Tinnevelly, in 1801. The revenge we took was equally complete. It certainly does not say much for the magnanimity of our conduct to a brave foe. The fort was carried by assault, and razed to the ground. The town shared the same fate. The sites of both were ploughed up and sown with salt, and the Chief, who was taken fighting in the fort, was hanged.

When the Prince stepped into the railway carriage to continue his journey, the natives renewed their curious clapping of the hands and shrill joyous cries. At Dindigal, a town of 13,000 inhabitants, the name of which often occurs in the history of Tippoo's wars, the Prince alighted from his carriage and walked on the platform to admire the decorations. The fine old Fort, dismantled and in ruins, could be discerned on the commanding site outside the town which rendered it so important. Trichinopoly, 82 miles from Madura, and 198 miles from Madras, the chief and military station of Southern India, was reached at 2.30 P.M. The address, pandals, flowers, triumphal arches, guards of honour, officials in uniform, streets decorated with extraordinary richness and taste, were ready for the Prince. There were two companies of H.M. 89th, one battery of artillery, and three regiments of Native infantry on duty in addition to the Police. Here there were official presentations; and when these were over, the Prince drove to the house of Mr. Webster, where a pandal, decorated in the Native fashion, which cost nearly 1000*l.*, had been erected for lunch and dinner. After lunch the Prince, accompanied by Mr. Robinson and the authorities of Trichinopoly, &c., drove through the principal streets, and crossed the Cavery by a fine bridge to visit the famous Temple of Seringham, which is built on an island formed by two arms of that river. There he was received by the priests, guardians, and attendants, and conducted into the interior. The natives outside sat on housetops, walls, in trees, on the ground, as close as they could pack, and, as is generally the case in the vicinity of the religious establishments, were rather morose of aspect.

The Great Temple is a vast, bewildering mass of gate-towers, enclosures, courts, terraces, and halls, which the eye cannot take in from any one point, and which it is necessary to examine in detail, and therefore to see at a disadvantage. One of the halls which the Prince examined—450 feet long by 130 feet broad—contains no less than one thousand columns of granite! They are, however, except in one place where the roof is a little elevated, not more than 10 feet or 12 feet high, and are necessarily so closely packed that there is little space between, and no vista. But then observe that each consists of one block, carved most elaborately with images of deities, and the like, from top to bottom! The effect can only be compared to something described in one of his dreams by De Quincey. The gateways, pierced in the immense piles of architecture called Gopuras, which surmount them to a great height, lead into a labyrinth of courts, the whole surrounded by a wall 2900 feet long by 2500 feet broad. Some of the gateways have jambs of granite slabs 40 feet high, the slabs which form the roof of the gateway to the north are 24 feet long. These Dravidian architects had certainly immense skill in details, but small knowledge of general effect, and there is no common purpose aimed at in their designs. The view of the numerous gateways, of which there are more than a dozen, from the terraced roofs, and the imbroglio of walls and curious roofs and outlines, were, nevertheless, very striking. It was intended, Mr. Fergusson says, to have run up the pyramidal tower over the main entrance to the height of 300 feet. The same admirable authority tells us that the whole of the Temple dates within the eighteenth century, and that the building was stopped by the French, who seized upon it and turned it into a fortress during the struggle with us.

Trichinopoly was the central point of the struggle

between the French and English for the sovereignty of Southern India; but long before that, its position made it an object of immense importance to all the great Chiefs who were contending for supremacy. In the old times of Mahomedan rule the Governor of Arcot was wont to send round to the tributary States a slipper, supposed to belong to the Great Mogul, which the vassal was to meet at the border of his territory, in order that it might be escorted in state to his capital; but Ranga Kismi, Raja of Trichinopoly, disliking such an admission of inferiority, and, at the same time, fearing to resist compliance with the custom, resorted to excuses and delays, and inveigled the carriers of the sacred slipper stage after stage from the borders of his dominions to his palace-gate. When there, the King desired them to throw the slipper on the floor, which they did; whereupon the King, thrusting his foot into it, exclaimed, "Does your master think I have only one leg? Go back and bring me the other slipper." They did come back, but not until after the King's death; and they returned as conquerors.

There are few miles of this district which have not souvenirs of the stirring times when MM. Bussy, Lally de Tollendal, and Clive fought it out for the mastery of the country. On our way we were shown where the latter saved himself from capture by presence of mind—where he caused a large force to surrender by a ruse—and so on. On his return to Trichinopoly, the Prince visited the old Palace of the Nawabs of the Carnatic, very interesting and curious, now about to be turned into public offices. An address from the inhabitants was read by a Native barrister, and the principal Zemindars and people were presented, or, as Mr. Robinson says, "were pointed out" to the Prince. The deputation from Tanjore was introduced with an address and a finely worked silver and gold casket. The members of the deputation, and several of the Tanjore magnates, were presented by Mr. Thomas, Collector. From this—strange scene for the reception of addresses by a Prince of Wales—the cortege was escorted to the gate of the Main Guard of the ancient Fortress, so many times vivid with musketry and crowned with anxious faces. There was a kind of Grand Stand for the Prince, ladies and gentlemen, and Chiefs, that they might enjoy the fireworks and the grand sight—the lighting of the Rock. However, the sun had not yet set, and the effect of the illuminations was for some time kept in abeyance by that very potent rivalry. The scene was very animated—prodigious multitudes, a large tank with boats below, Clive's house at the opposite side, and above all, the vast pyramid—the Rock of Trichinopoly—crested with the Temple of Ganesa, whose festivals were attended by thousands of pilgrims. Not very long ago a panic occurred at one of these meetings, and before it could be allayed, upwards of 500 persons were precipitated down the sheer precipice over the granite steps, or trampled to death.

When the sun went down the illuminations began to tell their story, and very fine it was. The circular boats on the tank, miniature Popoffkas, discharged rockets and water serpents—the sides of the tank blazed with coloured fires and the lines of the houses were marked by ribands of flame. These lighted up a multitude of faces and colours such as one can see nowhere else. Then, just as the vast rock commenced to glow with the most original pyrotechnic device we have yet seen, out sailed the moon. The winding stairs and ascent, as well as the Temple, were illuminated at the outset; but from the summit there were presently pouring lava-like floods, now blue, now orange, now green, from some overwelling fountain, casing the sides of the great mass, far higher and larger than that of Edinburgh, in sheets of iridescent flame. The Prince expressed to Mr. Patlabhirain Pillay his great admiration of the effect. At 8 P.M. dinner of 50 covers was served in the pandal, to which the Brigadier-General, Commanding Officers, and military and civil authorities were invited; and there was a reception of the ladies of the Station at 9 P.M., which ended in a pleasant little dance, not prolonged after midnight. Then a dispersal to quarters, and exercitations of temper in finding them and arousing the sleeping and tired domestics. Dr. Fayrer and I owe much to the kindness and hospitality of Major and Mrs. Henderson, who caused us to forget how far we were from home. *Homo homini lupus*—they say. In India every one is friend and host to the stranger. On the way home we observed that the roads were closely patrolled, and were challenged several times by zealous guards.

It is with surprise one hears of the precautions taken for his security wherever the Prince rests, for there is no outward sign of them. As you approach the spot where the Royal Standard indicates Headquarters, you see sentries on duty, perhaps a few native policemen at the corners of the avenues, or in front or rear of the house; but they do their work so unostentatiously, that it is only by a close examination of the outposts one can form an idea of the magnitude of the force employed. There are at this moment 762 native policemen engaged in guarding the Prince's headquarters.

December 12th.—There was a heavenly repose in the early part of the day. Divine service in the drawing-room at headquarters at 11 A.M. Then came irruptions of workers in gold and silver, in brass and ebony, and in all the things for which Trichinopoly is famous. There was no more peace, but there was much bargaining for bangles and jewellery. Packing up began at 1 P.M., and at 4 P.M. the Prince was starting, under the usual military honours, from the house of the Collector for the Railway Station, where he was received as on the day of his arrival. There were loud cheers raised as the train moved away, and the ladies were particularly enthusiastic, for that little dance had quite gained their hearts. At Caroor, on the junction of the Amavâlly and the Cavery, the Prince addressed a few words to the Native officials,

BARGAINING FOR BANGLES.

who had prepared the platform very prettily. The line runs along the valley of the Cavery to the Erode junction (S. I. R. and M. R. Railway), where the Collector and district officers of Coimbatore, band, colours, and guard of honour of H.M. 43rd Regiment were in attendance. Dinner was served at 8.15 P.M. Mr. Wedderburn and Colonel Wilkieson were invited to the Royal table. The journey was resumed soon after 10 P.M.

December 13th.—Rattle and rumble all night long, with

the exception of two stoppages from heated axles and two distressful changes of carriages. It comes quite naturally by this time to one to sleep in a railway carriage. At 7 A.M. the train, then nearly an hour behind time, pulled up at Perambore, where very welcome tea and coffee were served on the platform. Instead of 6.30 A.M., it was 8.10 A.M. before the train stopped at Roypooram, outside Madras, not quite at the right place, overshooting the position on the platform of the Duke of Buckingham, who, with his staff, the civil and military officers, the municipal body and dignitaries of the Presidency, the Rajas of Cochin, Travancore, Arcot, Vizianagram, and others, had been long waiting.

When the usual salutations had been exchanged, and the presentations customary on such occasions had been made, the state procession set out from Roypooram Station to Government House, passing through the streets of the native town, and the wide avenue-like thoroughfares which divide the immense compounds of the European quarter of Madras.

The golden umbrella held over the Prince's head was an excellent thought, and relieved many doubting minds. It is not always easy even for those familiar with European usages to make out the principal person in a public procession. The Duke of Buckingham, whose attention to details caused the whole Madras visit to be so successful, seized on the Oriental idea of having an umbrella as a special means of identifying the Prince, and thereby gratified thousands of people. "I am not sure if I have seen him after all," exclaimed a Chief at Bombay, "and I have travelled 600 miles merely to get a look at the Shahzadah!" Another Chief said to the Minister of a Native State, "Think what a way I have come to see the Prince! —think what distances we have journeyed, and yet we are only permitted to gaze on his face for a moment!" "Very true," replied the Minister, "but just think what a way the Prince has come to see you!" The Wallahjah bridge presented an exceedingly interesting appearance. No less than 126 different schools and colleges, with a total of 12,500 students and boys and girls, including the teachers, were ranged on both sides of the elevated stands, each school with its distinctive banners, the pupils also wearing badges and dressed all in their best, some singing, some non-singing, some mixed-singing. On the right, first three Church Schools, the Harris School for the higher classes of Mahomedans; the Roman Catholic Schools; Doveton College, for the higher classes of Eurasians; Convent Schools; Free Church Schools; Scottish Orphanage; the London Mission Schools; the Bishop's Schools; the Church Mission Schools for Hindoo girls and Hindoo boys, among which must not be forgotten the Rev. T. Satthianaden's establishments. On the left, University Graduates; Presidency Colleges; Engineering College; Medical College; School of Arts; Government Normal School; the Government Madrissa School for Mahomedans alone; various Church and Asylum Schools; the Director of Music with his trained choir; Christ Church boys; Military Female Orphan Asylum; Army girls' and boys'; the Eurasian girls of the highest classes of the Doveton Schools; Wesleyan Schools; the three schools of the Raja of Vizianagram; Female Normal Schools; Church and Lutheran Missions; Church of Scotland; Wesleyan; Hindoo Proprietary, and two other schools under pure native management, and the school of Dr. Savarimuttu. As the golden umbrella came in sight of the *Raleigh*, which had just anchored outside, she saluted with fine effect. Government House was reached at 9 A.M. The ladies of the Duke of Buckingham's family, and the members of his staff and suite, were presented to the Prince, who introduced his officers and suite to the Governor. Breakfast was served in the fine saloon on the first-floor. The Prince, having put on full uniform, orders, &c., proceeded to the Audience Chamber to receive the private visits of the Chiefs, which were conducted in the same way as those paid at Bombay, so that no detailed account of them is necessary. Madras had few great Rajas to summon, but those she had were of an interesting type.

The name and title of the Maharaja of Travancore are Sri Padmanabha Dasa Vanjee Bala Rama Varma Kulashekara Kiritapati Munnee Sultan Maharaj, Raja Rama, Raja Bahadoor and Lhamsher Jung, K.G.C.S.I. His Highness is of the Kshatryia caste, forty-four years of age (looks nearly sixty); in addition to Mahratta, Tamil, Hindustani, and Telugu, writes and speaks English with fluency; is a good Sanscrit scholar, and much given to literary discussion with pundits; is fond of music, in which he excels; is an admirable man of business, very punctual and exact; fond of science, and profoundly attached to his own faith. He has a stammer in his speech at times, but his manners are easy and agreeable, and his appearance is dignified, as becomes one who claims an ancestry that dates from 600 A.D. The State covers an area of 6653 square miles, and contains a population of 2,310,000 souls. The annual subsidy to the British Government, fixed by Treaty, is 81,000*l.* per annum. It is a model Native State, and Sheshia Sastry, the present Dewan, a schoolfellow of Sir Madhava Rao, is a man of great intelligence and ability. The Prince gratified the Raja, who came in great state, by his special attention, and by the expression of regret at his inability to visit his State and become his guest at Trivandrum. The Sirdars of each of the Chiefs were presented, and offered nuzzurs in the usual manner.

His Highness the Raja of Cochin is a tall stout man of forty. He is of the Kshatryia caste, and is descended from a Viceroy of the Chola Kings, who ruled in the ninth century. He does not speak English, but he is a thorough Sanscrit scholar, and is well acquainted with Native literature. The State, which contains a population of 600,000, and covers an area of 1360 square miles, is in subsidiary alliance with the British Government, and pays a tribute of 20,000*l.* a year.

The Prince of Arcot was also received. There was a time when the Nawab of the Carnatic was a personage of no small power. The present inheritor of that title, Azim Jah Bahadoor, and his father, Ameer Ood-Dowlah Bahadoor, gained the respect and esteem of all with whom they were brought in contact. The family are now living in Madras, fallen from their high estate, as far as temporal position and power are concerned, but certainly secure in the ownership of that which they have left, and in the regard of those around them, native and European. To show that they were once of some consideration, a small pamphlet of official and other papers relative to their genealogy, &c., has been published, which included such matters as notes from former Governors, asking them to come to breakfast, or acknowledging a supply of dishes from their table. Ameer Ood-Dowlah, in a poem addressed to the Queen, and sent through the hands of Sir Charles Trevelyan in June, 1860, said of himself: "Though I bear that name which means 'Baron of wealth,' yet am I a suppliant for your favour." Alluding to the Proclamation of 1858, he congratulated her Majesty on having assumed the administration of the Indian Empire, and ended with the words: "Through the favour of the Most Holy Jesus Christ, may this assumption of rule prove auspicious to you! May your dominions last till the resurrection"!

More conspicuous than any of these Chiefs by his fine presence and face is the Raja of Vizianagram, who is, however, not as yet entitled to pay a separate visit to the Prince, and is still less entitled to receive one, but who will probably, on account of his character, connections, influence, and charities, be raised in the native peerage, if we may use the phrase, by a discerning Government. He speaks English as well as if he had been born and bred in the land, although he has never left India, and for all his culture and enlightenment he is too good a Hindoo to make it probable that he will come to England unless the Brahmins are unusually liberal. He came frequently to see Sir Bartle Frere. As I was quartered in the same house, I had frequent occasions of speaking to him, and could not but be interested in his conversation, which let in a flood of light on the way in which natives look at things which to us present aspects utterly dissimilar. The subscriptions and useful works to which he makes such great contributions are regarded by him as duties for which he expects no return or consideration hereafter. His religion teaches him, he says, to do these things, and there is no merit in doing his duty, but the neglect of it would be a great offence. However, if a man does not feel it to be his duty to give he cannot be blamed for want of charity. The Raja indulges in a luxury which was once common enough among the great in Christian Europe, he keeps an astrologer; and so one morning, as he was speaking of the Prince's arrival at Calcutta, he exclaimed with a sigh, "I shall not be there to see his Royal Highness land!" "Why, may I ask? There is plenty of time for you to go round by land and meet him. The Duke of Sutherland intends doing so." "Well," replied the Raja very seriously, "I have consulted the stars, and there will be no favourable day for beginning my journey till the 21st, and then I should be too late, but I will arrive in Calcutta in time for some of the festivities." (The intention of the Duke of Sutherland to go round by land was formed some time ago. He wants to see as much of the country as possible, and very naturally objects to the loss of time, as far as such as an object is concerned, which occurs in a voyage by sea.)

A proof of the desire of the Chiefs to stand well with their English friends, and to impress them with a proper idea of their dignity, is afforded by the issue of little memoirs relating to various Rajas who come to pay their homage and respect to the Prince. The Maharaja of Vizianagram, K.C.S.I., claims descent from the Ranas of Oodeypoor, the most illustrious Rajpoot family in India, whose ancestors conquered Oudh at a very remote period, and one of whose more recent progenitors, at the modest date of 519 A.D., conquered more than two-thirds of the present Madras Presidency, and established a dynasty which reigned over the land for 921 years. A Chief of Vizianagram built the present fort in 1712, and had great power under Arungzebe. In 1756, when M. Bussy moved into the Circars, the Raja joined him with 10,000 men. Bussy and his allies attacked a Poligar, who put to death the women and children, and fought till he was killed in the fort. His followers avenged his death by murdering the Raja. Next day an old man appeared, leading a boy by the hand. "This is the Poligar's son," said he to M. Bussy, "whose life I preserved without his father's consent;" whereupon Bussy made the boy, son of the murdered man, the Chief. The Raja got tired of the French, drove them out of his towns, and made overtures to the English at Madras. Lord Clive sent Colonel Ford, in September, 1758, with a considerable force, to aid the Chief on a general buccaneering expedition, in which it was stipulated that plunder should be equally divided, and that conquered countries should be delivered to the Raja, who was to collect the revenues, and to pay 50,000 rupees a month towards the expenses of the troops. The English obtained four of the Circars as the result of their trouble. The following year the Chief died without issue, and one of his wives performed suttee. His aunt was entrusted with the selection of an heir, and chose the second son of her husband's cousin. At this rate a genealogy is very easily manufactured. A good deal of trouble ensued, and for some time these Chiefs were under a cloud; but latterly, thanks to the personal character of the present Maharaja, the influence and position of the house have been increased.

A Levee held by the Prince in the Grand Banqueting Hall at one o'clock was attended by every European and Native who could obtain access or carriage to it. The throng was very great, and the doors were closed before all the gentlemen whose names had been received could find their way to the presence.

A State Banquet of fifty covers to which the chief personages of the City and Presidency of Madras were invited, was given by the Duke of Buckingham in honour of the Prince of Wales in Government House. The Prince retired after a brief reception in the Drawing Rooms, and drove out to Guindy Park, the country seat of the Governor, eight miles from Madras, to spend to-morrow —the anniversary of his father's death—in seclusion. A few only of his Royal Highness' suite accompanied him. The park is beautifully wooded, and full of game. There was no intrusion on the Prince's privacy, and the rest and quiet must have been very grateful.

December 14th.—There were no public functions to-day, but several of the institutions of Madras were visited by those who were not at Guindy, mainly under the guidance of Dr. Balfour. The native choultries, poor-houses and places of refuge for aged and destitute persons, were exceedingly well worth seeing. There were "caste wards," and pariah or no-caste wards—refuges for friendless boys and girls—an hospital for lepers (who were terrible to behold), some endowed by the Government, and some kept up entirely by individual Chiefs. Thus I saw one choultrie belonging to the Raja of Ventnagacherry; another was maintained by subscription; the charities of the Raja of Vizianagram are also conspicuous. The Museum seems much appreciated by the Natives, and it was very pleasing to observe groups—whole families—going round the rooms, and to hear them expatiating in great varieties of speech on what they saw—for the voices of the people in conversation generally are low and sweet. But what a Babel of languages!—Uryu, Tamil, Telugu, Canarese, Maliar, Talu. The Agri-Horticultural Gardens are delightful, and abound in forest and vegetable wonders, not to speak of an attempt at a menagerie.

December 15th.—There were races at Guindy Park, and the Madras world was on the road before 6 A.M. I got up at 5 A.M., and had the satisfaction of seeing my friends start for the scene, under St. Thomas' Mount, where tradition has it St. Thomas Aquinas suffered martyrdom, and of hearing from them all about the races when they came back. These are now as obsolete as last year's Derby; but the sporting world of Madras will long remember the struggle in the Sandringham steeplechase, when Artaxerxes snatched the prize given by the Maharaja of Jeypoor from all the cracks, and when the jockeys ran under the approving eye of the Prince of Wales. The natives take very kindly to horse-racing, and Rajas gave the five or six cups which were run for. The scenes on the course were said to have been very amusing. Many of the native spectators perched in trees; there were strange contrasts between the civilisation of European jockey-caps, jackets, breeches, boots, and spurs, and the turn-out of native aspirants, or at least of one who rode a very losing race in a huge red turban, white petticoats, and parti-coloured robes; between the bustle of very small but fierce jockeys, who strode through the crowd of long-legged natives, and waved them aside as if they were so many rushes; and the calm of great Chiefs, such as the Raja of Cochin, the Prince of Arcot, the Raja of Jodhpoor, who were there, attended by numerous familiars in all their bravery. The heat was strongly felt before the sports terminated. An hour before noon the Prince returned to Madras.

At 3 P.M. the Chancellor, Vice-Chancellor, and Fellows of the University, among the latter of whom were several native gentlemen, capped and robed, proceeded to Government House to present an address from the Senate to the Prince. They were received at the entrance and conducted to the Audience Chamber. The Commander-in-Chief, the Bishop of Madras, and other *ex officio* members of the Senate were present. The address, printed in gold on vellum, was read by Mr. Innes. It gave a sketch of the progress and labours of the University since its foundation in 1857. There was rather a despairing admission that in the present circumstances of the country the Senate could not foresee the period when learning would be pursued for its own sake, but they were satisfied that the other motives which induced students to attend would assist in advancing the objects of the University. The Prince in his reply alluded to the graduates who were filling some of the higher posts in the public service, and congratulated the Senate on its attention to the scientific study of the ancient languages and literature of India, on its encouragement of

MADRAS RACES.

pure science, and on the impetus it had given to general education. After the Senate retired, a deputation of the Freemasons of the Presidency, the district Grand Master, officers and members, presented an address, in which they expressed their satisfaction at welcoming so distinguished a member of the body at Madras, and gave assurance that the craft was flourishing. In reply, the Prince said he would convey to the brethren in England the gratifying information that Freemasonry, and with it the practice of the charity and brotherly feeling which bound the fraternity throughout the world, was encouraged in Madras. The Mysore Commission, including Mr. Gopauliah, Head Sheristadar, and Mr. Ananda Rao, son of Sir Madhava Rao, were introduced, and presented an address expressing their regret that the Prince could not visit Mysore. The Prince, in reply, assured them that he felt very much his inability to see their country, or to go to Bangalore. A picturesque deputation from Coorg, headed by the Assistant-Superintendent, and consisting of Mr. Gunputty, Subadar of Mercava, and two gentlemen in their national costume, presented an address and offerings of Coorg knives and dresses, which were received, and the Prince entered into a short conversation with the members. A deputation from Coimbatore, headed by Mr. Wedderburn, the Collector, Colonel Wilkieson, R.E., Venkatachillum Pillay, &c., also presented an address, and a handsome volume of views of the places the Prince would have seen had he been able to visit their district as he had intended. The Prince, in reply, said that though he had been disappointed, he was glad to think that no risk of health or life had been incurred on his account by the inhabitants of the country.

The afternoon was occupied in making return visits. The Prince, who wore the uniform of the 10th Hussars, drove to Egmore, the residence of the Raja of Cochin, escorted by cavalry and attended by members of his suite, at 4.30 P.M. The formalities on such occasions do not vary. The personage to be honoured by the Prince sends a deputation of his chief officers to escort him to the house, at the entrance to which the Raja or Nawab stands to receive his visitor. There is a guard of honour, the Queen's

A NUZZUR AT MADRAS.

colours and band, furnished by a regiment, in this instance the 13th M. N. I., and an artillery detachment to fire a salute. Then a Durbar and presentations, after which the interchange of presents; the be-garlanding and farewell. Three of the Princes of the Carnatic and Hyder Jung escorted the Prince from Egmore to the residence of the

Prince of Arcot in a street in the native town where there was a guard of honour, band and colours of the 37th M. N. I., a display of the retainers of the house, and a band of native musicians. Among the presents made by the Prince of Arcot was a sword which had once belonged to the Nawab Wallahjah. The third and last Chief who received a return visit from his Royal Highness at Madras was the Raja of Travancore, whose offerings were curious and valuable.

The question of return visits is regulated on principles better understood by European officials than by Asiatic nobles; but the Prince endeavoured to meet the wishes of native dignitaries as far as possible, and strained a point to save them chagrin. The Princess of Tanjore is a lady belonging to the family of the Sivajee (who is spoken of as a mere adventurer; he was a member of a very ancient family), and it created irritation that her salute of guns was forgotten in the absorption caused by the Prince's arrival; but *en revanche*, her master of the ceremonies omitted to make a formal request for permission to visit the Prince. It is understood that her Highness is anxious to secure the title of Raja for her husband, and nothing that can be said, or written, or done, can prevent the people of India, high and low, supposing that the Prince possesses unlimited power. When the Princess was permitted to visit his Royal Highness, she departed from the usages of Mahratta widows, whose custom it has been to receive and pay visits without the restrictions which she considered necessary. She sat with the ladies of the Duke of Buckingham's family in a room, part of which was screened off; into this compartment the Prince was introduced. He could put out his hand to be shaken, but he could not see, or it was supposed he could not see, the Princess's face. She grasped his hand very warmly, and expressed her pleasure at the arrival of the Prince in Madras. Major Henderson, who acted as interpreter, knowing the Princess could speak a little English, requested her to speak in that language, whereupon, with a little laugh, she said, "I am glad to see my Royal Brother." Her Highness asked after "The Queen, my Royal Sister," in right regal fashion.

At 4.30 P.M. the Prince laid the memorial foundation-stone of the new Harbour works, which will inaugurate a great, and let us hope successful, struggle with Nature, and form a very visible and permanent memorial of a visit to which must be ascribed the commencement of so many useful works. The Governor and the ladies of his family, the Members of Council, the Military and Civil authorities assisted at the ceremony, which was exceedingly well-managed. There were bands, colours, guard of honour, troops to line the approaches, and escorts of the Body Guard and 16th Lancers. Beyond the benches on which the company were seated and the upturned sea of faces, the great army of waters was seen hurling the crested heads of its columns on the beach, and the roar of its artillery was heard amid the smoke of the spray—pregnant comments on the utility of the work to be accomplished, if significant, too, of the power of the forces to be overcome and of the audacity of the enterprise. The engineers explained the plans to the Prince, and the stone was lowered in its place with all proper observance. Altogether it was an impressive scene; and the only persons who could have found fault with it, had they known the purport of the function, were the catamaran and massoulah boatmen, who could be seen from the platform riding on the billows, and justifying the mistake of the ancient traveller, who declared that he beheld devils playing at single-stick on the coast. Thence, as it was getting dark, the cortege drove homewards; but on the way, the Prince intimated a wish to see the famous old Fort St. George, which has played such a part in our short eventful history in India. It rained in torrents, and the visit was rather a surprise to the authorities, so that there was more to do than say "Open sesame!" at the doors. Any one acquainted with its story could not find a spot in the wide domains of the Empress more full of topics for reflection; but millions of Englishmen seem to think that the Empire is like Topsy, in 'Uncle Tom's Cabin,' and "'speckt it growed." *Our* romance of Indian history lies concentrated in the days when "furious Frank" and fiery Scot and Saxon fought and intrigued for the possession of the pagoda tree. The keys of Pondicherry and of Carnatic fortresses, cannon and arms belonging to Tippoo, famous chiefs and ancient poligars, each with its tale, are stored in the Arsenal, which seems well kept. Apropos of Pondicherry, let me not forget M. Tillard, the Governor of the French Colonies in India, Commissary-General of Marine, who has come to salute the Prince, attended by officers of his suite, and has been a guest at the entertainments given in his honour by the Governor. M. Tillard, like our friends at Goa, has his memories and regrets, no doubt; but he rules a prosperous and well-ordered settlement, and probably he is personally much happier than if he had larger charges. But a Frenchman of to-day may be pardoned if he feels indignant at the stupidity of his ancestors, when he remembers that the fruits of the victory of de la Bourdonnais, the keys of Fort St. George, and the possession of Madras, were given back to England by the treaty of Aix-la-Chapelle. The Church is full of interesting memorials; the monument to Lady Hobart, recently placed there, which bears an inscription, the words of which will find echoes in the hearts of thousands here who revere her memory, attracted the Prince's attention.

There was another State Banquet at Government House, which was followed by a reception and by a very successful concert, at which the Chiefs of Travancore, Vizianagram, the Prince of Arcot, and other native gentlemen were present. The Governor has a very good band; and M. Stradiot, the master, composed an "Ode of Welcome" to the Prince, which was sung very finely by the Madras Philharmonic Society. The band of the 89th Regiment played some favourite pieces.

December 16th.—In addition to the sentries of Government House in front, and the usual gathering of scarlet-coated and turbaned servants, there were two lads, with high headdresses of tinsel, and robes of bright red and gold, with bows and arrows in their hands. Their faces were decorated with unusual caste markings, and with painted moustaches. Their dresses resembled those in which the Incas are depicted in Kingston's book, and there was a vague Mexican impression produced by the character of the headgear and robes. Mr. Minchin told me these boys belonged to a very ancient race called Uryas, celebrated as warriors in former days. It is the custom of the young people, when their tasks are done in the evening, to play for the amusement of the villagers some part of the great Epic "Ramayanam," by Valuniki, which gives the history of the war between Rama and Ravana, the Demon King. Rama, exiled by his father, is followed to his asylum in the woods by Sita, his wife, and Lechman, his brother. Ravana, King of Lanka (Ceylon), a land of demons, seizes Sita, and carries her off, but Rama and Lechman rescue her, and destroy the demons and their king. Sita was represented by a figure of the size of life, carved with great elegance from a single wooden block, painted of a colour, between the hue of a Cashmere woman and that of a European. It was accepted by the Prince, and sent home to England. This figure was placed between Rama and his brother; on their right was the Demon King in a horrible mask. A reciter and musician stood behind the group. The performance began by a wailing song, to the music of which Rama and Lechman, moving round in small circles, kept time with their feet, while the Demon King nodded his wooden head in very quaint fashion. The voices of the boys were sweet, and their movements graceful. Whatever attractions the play might have for a scholar or for a native audience, it certainly hung fire after a quarter of an hour or so; and when the performers were told they might cut the play short, a look of surprise, perhaps of chagrin, stole over their faces. Next there was a display of jugglery. The performances were directed by Ramchandra Rao, Commissary of Police, one of the most clever and intelligent officials in the service of the State, and at the same time one of the most thorough-going Brahmins in India. There are many men of the kind in India, the number is increasing. He gave us an exposition of Hindoo doctrine one morning, remarkable for clearness and refinement, in which he grappled, if not boldly, at least most ingeniously and delicately, with the abstrusest questions. The Indian juggler has no elaborate apparatus. At the utmost he has a withered scarecrow to assist in his deceptions, but generally he is alone. He is all but naked; and his whole stock-in-trade consists of a stick and a few baskets. He can hide nothing, for he has no place to put anything in. The first juggler, Madhar Sahib, put down a small basket. He chattered at it, and lo! there was an egg on the carpet. Then he put the basket over the egg, chattered at it, turned it over, and out walked a pretty pigeon. Next Madhar placed another egg under the basket. After incantations, out strutted the first pigeon and another exactly like it. Other things did Madhar Sahib, but none so striking, though peas under a thimble have before now exercised the finest intellects, and baffled the greatest ingenuity. Poolee, who came next, converted himself into a magazine of horrors; took live scorpions out of his mouth; spat out stones as large as plums and swallowed them; evolved from internal depths large and small nails and string, till there was a pile of his products before the Prince. Kamatchee, a strong-limbed, comely young woman, began by taking up a handful of earth, which she piled in a heap. Into this she stuck two long needles. She then took her right big toe in her left hand, twisted her leg over her head, and repeated the feat with her left leg and her right hand. Next she stood with her heels to the heap, and bending backwards till she could put her hands on the ground, brought down her face close to the needles, which in the twinkling of an eye were caught up by her eyelids! Syed Khadir and Momee Sawmy—simple, but, as it proved, hard-headed peasants—next made their appearance. Their stock-in-trade consisted of cocoa-nuts. Syed took one, threw it up in the air, and, as it fell, met it with the top of his naked skull, whereupon the cocoa-nut flew in pieces, scattering the milk over the place. Momee did the same. Several nuts were thus brought to ruin on their skulls. To my comfort, a small relative of these gentlemen picked up the fragments and put them in a bag for home use. Valoyoodhum, Syed Cassim, and Imam Sahib exhibited their powers as snake charmers. A girl twisted a rock snake round her neck, and the little Eve unblushingly demanded baksheesh from the Prince. Seven cobras, of the largest size, were set dancing within a few inches of the legs of the company. The snakes were deprived of their fangs; but of their malice and desire to kill there could be no doubt; they struck again and again at their charmers. Imam Sahib—a more ragged and miserable old creature I never beheld, so that growing mangoes does not appear to be a good trade—showed that trick better than I have seen it. Vencatamoodoo and Mauree did what they pleased with flat metal dishes, and the former was a marvel of dexterity, and quite surpassed the grand operator of my youth, Ramo Samee, in terrible ease and rapidity, with knives and balls. Ghoodoo performed the basket trick. The girl was forced into a shallow basket, Ghoodoo proceeded to inveigh against her as if he were counsel in a divorce case; finally, he thrust a sword through the basket, and pretended to gloat over the blood on the blade. But when the eyes of the audience were turned on a child, whom Ghoodoo seized and pretended to behead, a sharp-eyed lady saw the girl gliding like a shadow out of the basket.

December 17th.—The curries of Madras have a reputation all over India, and in Madras the Club has the crowning honour and glory of being considered the best place for curries. The Committee caused an intimation to be made to the Prince that if he would be so good as to accept an invitation to lunch, they would put forth all their strength to sustain their high renown, and to-day was fixed for the tiffin. There were many curries and Indian dishes, and those qualified to judge said that all they tasted were worthy of the occasion. M. Bonnemain, the *chef* on board the *Serapis*, was instructed by native cooks in the mysteries; but the French intelligence, fine and keen as it is, does not penetrate the depths of curry-lore, and the dishes, even after a considerable experience in the arts and sciences of several gentlemen of colour engaged expressly to dress curries, never came up to the Indian standard.

There was a Children's Fête in the People's Park in the afternoon, where the Prince had an opportunity of seeing in all their finery the many thousands of young people who welcomed him on the bridge. An address was presented, and a band of children sang "God save the Queen." Altogether it was a pretty sight, and as the cortege drove slowly down the ranks, the clapping of hands, cries of joy and cheers of the little folk in all the *abandon* of childish happiness, evinced the pleasure they felt at the visit. One could not but feel respect and something like compassion for the good men who pass their lives in educating these children in the hope, not often realised, that some at least will be permanently retained in the fold. From the People's Park the Prince drove to the Island, where he was received by the Commander-in-Chief, Sir P. Haines, and his staff. He mounted, and, attended by the military members of his suite, rode to the line of troops drawn up one side of the parallelogram, the other sides of which were lined by a great concourse of people, most of whom had been squatting there for hours. The troops at the General Parade were one squadron of the 16th Lancers, the Governor's Body Guard, the A and C Batteries, 20th Brigade, R.A., H.M.'s 89th Regiment, the Madras Volunteers, 10th M. N. I., 13th M. N. I., and 37th M. N. I. An incident which illustrates the difficulties of dealing with those who do not understand our ways, occurred. The Raja of Vizianagram came on the ground as the Royal cavalcade was moving off, and mounted a very handsome and showily caparisoned Arab, which was awaiting him. He was attired in a scarlet gold-laced tunic, wore a turban with diamond aigrette, a jewelled sword, gold-lace sash, patent leather Napoleon boots, and heavy plated spurs, and looked a very gallant gentleman. Nothing doubting, he dashed off full speed and joined the Staff as the Prince turned to ride along the front of the line, but he had not been very long in company before an intimation was conveyed to him, that not being a military officer on duty, or not being specially invited, or something of the kind, he had better retire, and he rode back accordingly, and took up his post near the Governor's carriages with an expression of mortification and anger on his face which was only too manifest. The Raja evidently thought he was quite in the right in riding in the Prince's retinue, and it never entered into his head that he could be out of place. The march past made the physical inferiority of the Sepoys and the advanced age of the native officers of the Madras army more conspicuous than they had been when we observed the native regiments lining the streets. There was another observation—that one of the R. A. Batteries had Armstrong guns—the other the new muzzle-loader, but in time the former will be placed in store, and there will be, it is to be hoped, uniformity in the field artillery in India. When the parade was dismissed, the Prince returned to Government House, and thence drove to the residence of the Commander-in-Chief, whom he honoured with his company at dinner.

About 10 P.M. the Prince, attended by Sir C. Staveley, &c., drove to the Pier, where the Duke of Buckingham and a great concourse had been awaiting his arrival for the great "effect" of the Madras week. Seats were placed for the Prince, the Governor, his family and suite, &c., out of the reach of the spray. Men will never see any spectacle more strange—nay, awful—than the "illumination of the surf." Neither pen nor pencil can give any idea of it. It was exciting, grand, weird and beautiful. As if to render homage to the occasion, the wind rose in the course of the day, the surf was high—enormous curling breakers ran between the base-pillars of the pier. The moonlight revealed now and then dark objects rising and falling on the billows, between the outer darkness of the horizon, against which the hulls and rigging of the *Serapis*, *Osborne*, and *Raleigh*, lighted up with lanterns, stood out in relief, and the breakers on the beach. These were massoulah boats and catamarans lying off in the rollers till the time came for setting fire to the lights, which were to burn in, and to illuminate the water. The buildings, transparencies, and triumphal arches, above which rose steeples, domes, and columns, brilliantly illuminated, formed the background along the beach. Southwards, where the rollers swept up to the roadway, rows of natives, facing seawards, with blazing torches and blue lights lighted up an ocean of white turbans. First there were fireworks. The *Osborne* and *Serapis*, emitting volumes of coloured flames, vied with each other in all kinds of pyrotechny. It seemed as if volcanoes were bursting up from the deep. In a grand discharge from the *Raleigh* there were 190 coloured rockets. Presently appeared from afar seawards many flames, dipping and rolling amid the waves, drifting landwards like fire-ships. These multiplied. Occasionally lights flashed right through the rollers from the other side. Suddenly the lines of black massoulah boats and catamarans from the beach dashed into the surf like a squadron of cavalry. With the wildest yells they charged the serried ranks of the foam-crested breakers. Amid a sea now black as ink, now like glistening jet, now creaming in surf, the catamaran men contended with waves, which seemed to be mounds of flame. Sometimes they were swept off, and disappeared beneath the billows, or were seen swimming in the mad turmoil. There was an agonising suspense till they regained their craft, or, striking out with strong arms, were borne in on the surf, and landed safe on the beach. The massoulah boats, swept from stem to stern by the breakers, forced their way out over the rollers to the smoother sea,

MADRAS.—ILLUMINATION OF THE SURF.

only to return, at full speed, and engage with wild emulation in still more animated contests. The hardy fellows, watching their opportunity, by tremendous efforts kept their boats on top of the wave, and, covered with foam, were borne past the pier with wonderful velocity to the beach, yet always emerged safely from the surf.

When that extraordinary scene was over, it was long past 11 P.M., and there was yet another function, and a heavy one to boot—a visit to the Native Entertainment, the scene of which was the immense Railway Station at Roypooram, which had been converted since the Prince's arrival into a vast theatre, nearly 800 feet long and 250 feet wide, decorated with great splendour and richness. An elevated platform covered with scarlet cloth and tiers of benches was reserved for the guests and Chiefs, and in the centre were gilt chairs for the Prince, the Governor and the ladies of his family, the authorities, and the Europeans. The hour fixed in the programme was 10 P.M., and it was midnight when the Prince entered. Many thousands of people, Europeans and Asiatics—the latter, of course, many hundreds to one of the former—filled the place. On the entry of the Prince, which was announced by music and cannon, all the multitude stood up,

> "Their rising all at once was as the sound
> Of thunder heard remote."

When the Prince and the brilliant company were seated, a deputation of native gentlemen advanced to the platform, and, mounting to the dais, presented an address, which was read by the Chairman, in which they expressed the gratification of the native community at the great honour conferred on them by the Prince's presence at their entertainment, and requested his acceptance of the exquisite gold casket, on the top of which was a finely-worked tiger, which was placed on a velvet cushion on a small table in front of his chair. Whilst the address was being read and the Prince was replying, there was time to look about one. A square platform stood in the body of the hall, nearly at the level of the Royal seat; in the centre there was a gilt pole with coloured cordons, like ropes of artificial flowers, from the top. From this platform there was a gangway to a stage, whereon were seated the dancing girls and musicians—the former dressed in the richest and heaviest robes of kinkob, and stuffs of the brightest colours descending from the throat to the ankles, and leaving exposed only the arms, which could scarcely be called bare, as from shoulder to finger-tip these ladies wore armlets, bracelets, and rings—and, moreover, had in their noses and their ears sparkling diamonds—and, set with yellow flowers, in their thick, coarse, black hair, more diamonds, and on their toes rings of precious stones. Just beneath the droop of their crimson or scarlet satin trousers were revealed the sparkling anklets and bangles, which kept time to their movements and to the click of the castanets, with a sharp metallic tingle as they danced. Each lady wore a scarf or shawl, in which she muffled herself up as she sat on the ground till her turn came to dance, when it was called into action and made to play an important part, being held over the head with extended arms, or thrown wide aside, or closely gathered round the figure, in unison with the sentiment to be conveyed by the dance. These were brought under the ordeal of most powerful lime-lights, which threw an intense white glare on the vast sea of turbans and faces, the uniforms and pale features of the Europeans, and caused the jewels of the Rajas and Nawabs on the platform to dazzle one's eyes, and the enormous chandeliers suspended from the ceiling to pale their ineffectual fires. The Kolattam, which opened the entertainment, was simply

THE NAUTCH AT ROYPOORAM.

such a dance as one has seen at stage representations of May-pole dances and merrymaking. The nautch girls advanced, each took one of the cords, and then they danced in and out and round the pole and each other till they had wound themselves into a nosegay-looking knot, and then they unwound themselves—this too often, perhaps, for the perfect enjoyment of those who had done so much in the daytime and who were now sitting into the small hours. The great feature of the entertainment was the performance of the famous *danseuse* Gnyana, for whose services 700*l.*—probably 70*l.*—or perhaps the former sum for all the dancers and musicians—was paid. The little woman, rather pretty and confident, executed a very long "piece" with her feet to the music of the native implements and to the accompaniment of an intermittent chorus, aided by conch shells and solos, and at times illustrated by her own voice; and as the dance appeared to give exquisite pleasure to every ninety people out of the hundred who looked at it, there would be presumption and insular arrogance and prejudice—probably ignorance of the true principles of art-combinations of music, song and dancing—if one were to say that the performance seemed monotonous and exceedingly destitute of variety. When the player on the vina had fairly embarked on the solo, which was to be the musical gem of the evening or morning, it became evident that the enjoyment of the entertainment by the principal person had been sufficient, and he rose to go to the supper-room for a few moments, whence he emerged to drive back to Government House, leaving the native drama, in four acts, to be seen by those who were determined to see, and the songs by celebrated artistes, and the concerted pieces on the vina, dol, and zither saranthé, to be heard by those who pleased to stay.

December 18th.—A meet of the Madras pack at Guindy tested the sporting energies of the weaker sort to fracture; but the Prince, who did not get to bed till nearly 2 A.M., was up and away at 6 A.M. *Quæ regio in terris?*—Here is Squires, whom men and dogs have obeyed at the Pytchley, and who is known to the followers of the West Norfolk—who has led the Austro-Hungarian chivalry after the Esterhazy foxhounds, and has wound his horn by the side of Russian covers—installed as huntsman of the Madras pack, recognised by the Prince, and by more than one member of the field—*κύδει γαίων*! Several of "the following" had "incidents," but the ground was soft; there were adventures by flood and field, broken curb-chains, broken stirrup-leathers, and "staggers"—the latter confined to horses. There was, however, a fine run—said to be nine miles—and a kill at the end. The Prince enjoyed the morning's sport exceedingly. The party returned "hungry as fox" (or jackal) "hunters" to Madras. After lunch, the party inspected the native presents, which were laid out in a tent in the compound; and it is only to be regretted that there could not have been a similar exposition of the gifts made in return by the Prince.

Among many interesting offerings to the Prince at Madras must be specially mentioned an account of the Danish Protestant Mission, Tranquebar, by the Rev. C. E. Kennet, with an autograph letter of George I. (December 22, 1719—January 3, 1720) from St. James's, addressed to "Bartholomæo Ziegenbalg and Johann Ernest Groundler, Missionaries, Tranquebar," offered by the Rev. I. Schwarz, of the Lutheran Mission, Tranquebar, for the acceptance of his Royal Highness. The Princess of Wales would, no doubt, be glad to learn that in this distant land her own countrymen could tell her husband that Denmark was the first Protestant country which (in the reign of Frederick IV., in 1705) sent out a mission for the evangelisation of India. The Ziegenbalg, who is named above, visited England on his return from India in 1714, and the Prince and Princess of Wales of the day received him most courteously, and promised him every help.

There was much to be done in a very short time, for this was our parting day. The windows and the verandahs of the houses and offices were filled—the roofs were covered thickly by people. The patient Asiatics congregated at various points along the route; but certainly there was not one-half the number of those who attended on the day of the entry. A well-bred Native gentleman explained the fact. "There are," he said, "so many thousands sorry for the Prince's leaving that they cannot bear to see it, and so stay away." There was no cheering, except from Europeans; no clapping of hands, but an attitude of profound respect—"a silence which had in it something of reverence, such as that which prevails in a place of worship." At the platform at the end of the pier tramway, the Native officers were presented to his Royal Highness. To those specially mentioned the Prince said a few gracious words. No one who glanced at the faces of these gentlemen—many of them gray-haired soldiers—could doubt that the Asiatic delights in a tangible, visible representation of royalty, and that "veneration" is one of the most pronounced characteristics of his nature. Their bearing was charged, so to speak, with submissiveness. At the landing-stairs many hundreds of Europeans, ladies and gentlemen, assembled, but the Chiefs remained at the place whence the car started. There was a guard of honour, &c., of the 89th Regiment opposite the stairs. The massoulah boats were rising and falling more vivaciously than was pleasant at the foot of the steps. A flotilla of catamarans, each with a flagstaff and flag, lay beyond them.

The Prince remained a few moments on the landing-stage, while the suite cast uneasy looks on the waves which ran between the uprights of the pier. He bade the members of the Governor's family and the ladies and gentlemen with whom he was acquainted farewell, going round and shaking hands with his personal friends. At last came the moment to leave, and as the Prince stepped down the ladder to the massoulah boat, the whole company stood up. A great clamour of "sounds, like breakers in a dream" arose, blessing the Prince and his journey. Watching the rise and fall, he stepped on board the massoulah boat at the first attempt. The Royal Standard was hoisted in the bow, and as the boatmen uttered the first notes of the chant with which they kept time to the beat of their paddles, the crowd cheered, and waved hats and handkerchiefs. There were four large massoulah boats for the Prince and his suite, and they formed line, heading towards the *Serapis*, which, with yards manned, was waiting for her illustrious passenger. A double line of catamaran-men escorted the Royal barge. These mermen have been often described; but no one who has not seen them can form the smallest idea of their skill and daring in a seaway. Familiarity has bred in them contempt for the dangers of the sea. They sit bolt upright on their heels, so that the thigh and the leg are one above the other, like the limbs of a parallel ruler. Thus seated, they are as firm in their places on the narrow plank of wood on which they float above and through the water, as if they were nailed to the catamaran, and work the uncouth pieces of board which they use as paddles with the greatest freedom and security. It was feared there would be some trouble in boarding. Captain Glyn ordered a spring to be put on the cable, so as to bring the ship across the run of the sea and make a fair lee, and the "chair," which was in readiness to hoist up the Prince, was not required. The moment his Royal Highness left the boat the standard at her bow was lowered, and in another instant the guns of the *Raleigh* were duly honouring the Royal flag which floated from the main of the *Serapis*.

May it be said that the Prince was sorry to leave Madras? It certainly would be true; and although there has been no lack of courtesy and kindness to be spoken of in all this Eastern land, it would be only just to say that the welcome of the Duke of Buckingham and the reception given by Madras must remain for ever among the most pleasant memories of the Prince's tour. In Government House there was a combination of the charms of English family life with the state of an Oriental satrap; but the former so far predominated, thanks to the presence of the gracious ladies, who did the honours of the Duke of Buckingham's house with such kindness, that one felt, in spite of strange surroundings, as though he were "at home." Surely it would be advisable, as a means of breaking down the barriers of caste and custom, to appoint to high places in India those who have around them the gentler agencies which in every civilised country exercise such an influence on society? There are sacrifices, no doubt—there are too many instances of them—but it is a great work to be accomplished. The Prince expressed his sense of the Governor's efforts to render his visit to Madras agreeable and profitable in the warmest terms.

At 5.30 P.M. the *Serapis* got her anchor and proceeded northwards for the Hooghly, the *Raleigh* and *Osborne* being astern, starboard and port respectively. The sun was fast sinking behind Fort St. George, but its rays still struck the coloured fronts and roofs of houses facing westwards, and the domes and steeples of the city; touched the salient points of the long façade broken by colonnades and porticoes presented by the sea front, and cast a magic light on the landscape in the background, which melted away amid masses of wood into faint mountain outlines. Venice never looked more beautiful than Madras did, as the long line of buildings, which rise above the surf, the fluttering flags, and the vast crowd on shore appeared to retire from the *Serapis*. The ever-changing hues of the flying spray threw a many-coloured veil over the barrier of human heads, with faces still turned seawards. If the beach of Brighton, from Hove to the West Cliff, under like conditions of sea, sun, and sky, were covered by white turbans and dark skins, there would be some resemblance to the sight that Madras presented; for there are no minarets, mosques, or Hindoo temples, to detract from the European look of the place; and whether it be that the general impression of the situation and architecture of the pier recalls the Steyne and London-by-the-Sea, there is certainly a suggestion about Madras of a Brighton, without east winds, or fogs, or wintry vapours.

DEAD GAME.

THE PRINCE AND THE BEGUM OF BHOPAL.

CHAPTER IX.

CALCUTTA.

From Madras to Calcutta—The "James and Mary" Shoals—The Hooghly—Landing at Calcutta—Government House—Private Visits—Ceremonies—Christmas Day—Chandernagore—Reception of Chiefs at Chandal—Return Visits—Tent-pegging—The Star of India—The Procession of the Order—The Ceremony—The "Awful" Benefit Night—The Zenana.

DECEMBER 19TH (*Sunday*).—The weather at sea was all that could be desired. The thermometer marked only 78°. The wind light and fine, the squadron running through a smooth sea at the rate of eleven knots an hour. Divine service was performed at 11 A.M. on the quarter-deck, by the Rev. Canon Duckworth and the Rev. Mr. York, chaplain. The Prince, Admiral Macdonald, members of the suite, and the ships' officers and company present. At noon our position was lat. 15° 6′ N., long. 89° 16′ E., distance made good from Madras, 166 miles; distance to Light-ship Sand Heads, 492 miles, so that we shall be in before our time, as the *Serapis* will be at the Sand Heads at noon on Tuesday, and will then be only 105 miles from Calcutta, where she could arrive on the 22nd, if all went well. In the afternoon the wind became a little more positive, and blew right ahead, which increased the draught in the furnaces, and we had plenty of steam. This great Bay of Bengal, so terrible in monsoons and so vexed by cyclones, was tranquil as a Highland tarn—not a sail was visible, nor were there fishes or birds to be seen. The *Raleigh* is always a fine object to look at—symmetry (in spite of her stern, which "hangs" in the water), strength, power and speed, seem to be happily combined in her. She fills the mind with a satisfying idea of a man-of-war. We lose her at the entrance to the river, and proceed with the ever-faithful *Osborne*. That pretty fine-weather yacht has proved a great success. Intended only for Channel service and Royal journeys in short sea-passages, she has turned out to be an ocean-going steamer, capable of holding her own in the stiffest breezes and most disagreeable seas, though to say she does not roll and is not wet under such circumstances "were base flattery."

December 20th.—At 2 A.M. the spring of the cylinder gave way, and one hour and a quarter were spent in repairing damages. The stopping of the screw woke the sleepers in hammock and berth instantly. Even Lord C. Beresford, whose marine assurance in such matters is not easily disturbed, was heard to utter a dreamy order to Tom Fat to "see what the row was about." Continued all well. A dead calm. At noon, observations gave lat. 17° 44′, long. 84° 47′; distance run 213 miles. Distance from the Light-vessel in the Eastern Channel of the Sand Heads, 279 miles. The current (N. 43′ E.) set the ship seven miles out of her course. There was consequently a considerable discrepancy between the dead reckoning and the observed position. The ship was trimmed, 350 tons of water pumped in, and chain cables, &c., transferred, to deepen her astern.

To-morrow will be the last day, and will also give us the lowest, of the neap tides, and there are the "James and Mary" shoals, full of terrors for Captain Glyn and all stout mariners, who know that it is really a case of "touch and go" for a ship which runs into their dangerous embrace. After dinner Mr. Smith Dorrien's company gave a musical and dramatic entertainment, which was more than usually lively and successful; and at the close, invitations were given by the ward-room officers, which were accepted by the Prince and some of his suite.

December 21st.—Not a ripple on the water. Lat. 20° 28′, long. 87° 38′. Distance made good at noon, 245 miles. The Light-vessel in the Eastern Channel off the Sand Heads, 33 miles distant. A N.E. current set us 16 miles out of our course. At 2 P.M. the Light-ship was sighted, and at 3 P.M. the *Serapis* was alongside it. Two trim-looking pilot brigs, belonging to the excellent service of the Hooghly Pilotage, were bearing down upon us; and when the *Serapis* anchored, Mr. Daly and Mr. Baker, two officers of the department, came on board. They informed Captain Glyn that he could not cross the bar to go up to Saugor till to-morrow (Wednesday). This was not pleasant intelligence. Of all places in the world where one would like to anchor the Sand Heads is, to put the subject in the most favourable point of view, perhaps that which he would select the last. As the *Raleigh* drew too much water to go up the river at low tides, it was considered better to send her back; and she was accordingly ordered to go round to Bombay. Captain Tryon came on board to pay his respects to the Prince, and take leave. His Royal Highness presented Captain Tryon with fine portraits of the Princess of Wales and of himself, and with other souvenirs. The two ships parted company under the friendly fire of tremendous cheers from the crews. After a little council on the bridge, the Prince expressed a desire to proceed onwards towards Saugor Island. Captain Glyn gave the necessary orders. The *Serapis* weighed, and crept up with sedulous lead-going, till she found it was very dark above and "soft and near" below, and we anchored for the night. A small steamer was despatched ahead to take letters to post on shore.

December 22nd.—Weighed at 6.5 A.M. Passing Saugor Light House, at 9 A.M. Anchored off "Mud Point" at 11 A.M. A very dreary prospect. Practised rifle shooting at buoys and floating marks "because there was nothing else to do." From the time the Sand Heads Light was sighted we have passed nearly two days in these muddy waters—and at one time there was only six inches of water between our keel and the mud. Sir R. Temple, two of his officers, and General S. Browne, came on board from the *Rhotas* just as it was becoming dark, and after an interview with his Royal Highness, returned to their floating mansion. Lieutenant-Colonel Parnell, Captain Durrant, Mr. Prinsep, Lieutenant Clifford, and Lieutenant Gough, were invited to dinner from the *Osborne*.

December 23rd.—The *Serapis* was ready to start at daybreak, but she did not weigh anchor till past 7 A.M., and had some little difficulty in turning in the narrow channel. Messrs. Day and Falle of the Harbour department came on board, and we proceeded with the flood-tide up the great river which, but for the cocoanut-palms, mangoes, and bamboos on the flat shores, would remind one of the Elbe, or the lower reaches of the Rhine—nay, of our own Thames at its widest—till we had mounted into narrower waters, where the deeper channels enabled the vessel to approach the banks. There were crowds wherever there were villages, and discharges of arms and fireworks indicated the desire of the natives and of the local authorities to render themselves agreeable and to do honour to the Prince. After breakfast, his Royal Highness put on his uniform and went on the bridge, where he remained observing with keen interest the rapidly increasing tokens of our approach to the great city—the larger and more frequent villages, the detached bungalows, factory chimneys, fishing and trading boats, merchantmen anchored in the stream, and passing steamers filled with people. There was no necessity for observations, but the steering needed close attention. The channels shift and change in a wonderful manner—"Here to-day, gone to-morrow." At noon there was a general parade of all officers. In an hour the masts of the vessels anchored below Garden Reach came in sight, and the ships of war dressed in flags. At 1 o'clock, the *Immortalité*, *Doris*, and *Newcastle* saluted. The sailors manning the yards of the men-of-war were dressed in blue; signal was made for them to change to white. By the time the Prince was alongside the vessels, the crews were all in apple-pie order. They saluted, cheer after cheer. As the Prince was passing the gardens of the residences of the King of Oudh, the retainers of his ex-Majesty lined the bank, and stood in crowds on the tops of the houses within, in the enclosure, and in the verandahs, but they did not make any sign of welcome. The *Serapis* passed by the great banks of shipping, which lay below Fort William three or four deep, the decks and rigging crowded with people, who cheered vociferously. The guns of Fort William thundered, the batteries on shore re-echoed the sound. From the deck could be seen the countless multitudes on the Maidan, and the lines of the troops drawn up from Fort William to the Government House, and the galaxy of Chiefs and ladies, and the splendour of the official and military uniforms on shore.

When the *Serapis* anchored, Colonel Dillon came off to take the Prince's pleasure as to when Lord Napier of

Magdala should pay his respects. The Duke of Sutherland, the aides-de-camp of the Governor-General, Bubbur Jung—the son of Sir Jung Bahadoor, attached to the Prince as aide-de-camp, in a uniform like that of an English officer with the exception of the head-dress, which was a kind of morion, or skull cap, with a plume of bird-of-paradise feathers, and an aigrette of brilliants and emeralds—and many others boarded the *Serapis*, and a grand array of eminent persons, military and civil, of the Indian hierarchy, all in full uniform, congregated on her decks, which presented a very animated and brilliant appearance. They were received by the Prince very graciously, and many old friends met now after years of separation. The news that Lord Hastings had died of fever contracted on a shooting expedition on the Western Coast was heard with infinite regret and surprise.

When all had been properly ordered for his reception on board, the Governor-General and Viceroy put off from shore to welcome his Royal guest, and once more the fleet, the forts, and the artillery thundered. Lord Northbrook came in full state, with all his suite and staff, and was ceremoniously conducted by the officers and equerries of the Prince to the saloon. The meeting between the Viceroy and the Prince was of a very cordial character, and after a pleasant conversation apart, and the usual presentations, the Viceroy and his officers returned to shore in state, and took their places in the very grand Reception Hall which had been erected on the muddy margin of Prinsep's Ghaut. They were followed at 4.30 P.M., the appointed time, by the Prince, whose arrival was awaited with indescribable anxiety by the magnificent multitude, although they knew that he would not land before the hour set down in the programme. They were luxuriously seated in tiers of seats ranged by the sides of two pavilions draped in scarlet, the roofs of which were upborne by white and gold pillars, wreathed with garlands, roses, and green chaplets. In the space between the pavilions or canopies, there were many couches, fauteuils, and arm-chairs for the great natives invited to assist at the reception. Flags, banners, and flowers decorated the walls, and were suspended from the sides and covering of the pavilions, and beyond there was one very lofty and massive arch of triumph, with the word "Welcome!" A scarlet carpet of great richness was laid in the platform, and the landing-stage and platform were covered with red cloth, and handsomely ornamented. The whole of the *personnel* of the vast administration of the seat of empire was there. As to the crowds of Rajas, Chiefs, and authorities of all kinds, it is only necessary to say they were even larger than those at Bombay.

I shall not attempt any description of the entrance of the Prince into Calcutta, or of the procession from the landing-place to Government House, for such pageants are singularly alike. It gradually grows on one amid all the congregations of men in power, the actual rulers of the land, that the native leaders have a weight and dignity which are but little understood at home. They are growing upon us even though they only come at first like the magnificent supernumeraries of a theatrical spectacle, who appear to lend a glitter and give a picturesque effect to the homelier but more potent characters of the piece. When these ceremonies are over they disappear from our gaze, but we know that they are active behind the scenes. They remain whilst the great actors are changing their parts, and they are still engaged when the stars have at last retired altogether from the boards. The Prince's welcome was not comparable in noise and in the excitement and variety and picturesqueness of the multitude to that of Bombay, but it was, perhaps, more dignified, by reason of its metropolitan attributes. The same result has occurred here as elsewhere. The "people" turned out in myriads to see the Shahzadah. Immense satisfaction is felt at this flesh and blood presentment of Royalty—a peculiar want of human nature has been gratified by the Prince's *avatar*. The arrangements for the landing and procession, if rather simple, were very good indeed, but I fear it would not interest my readers to learn more than that fact, although it cost many weeks' anxious thought and preparation to make them so perfect, and the officers who left the Prince at Bombay have been engaged ever since in getting all things in order—looking after *suspects*, carriages, horses, tents, servants—and doing everything that could be done, to insure the success of the Royal visit to the chief seat of the Government. The Prince was much gratified at all that had been effected, and seemed surprised at the grand appearance of Government House and at the splendour of the Viceregal state. The principal members of the suite were provided with quarters in the house, but on the open lawn in front of it a camp was pitched for the others, who could scarcely be termed less fortunate, inasmuch as they were lodged most comfortably.

The banquet given by Lord Northbrook in honour of the Prince was in all respects worthy of the occasion, and such as could not be accommodated with seats at table in consequence of the great number of official persons who could not be omitted, were overwhelmed with invitations to dinner by hospitable residents. The lights in the houses, the hum of voices, the stir in the streets, showed how deeply the great city was moved by the event which had been so long looked forward to.

Calcutta, December 24th.—The reception of the great Chiefs by the Prince at Government House to-day, although accounted "private," was a very stately ceremonial, conducted with much official pomp and care. The grandiose creation of Lord Wellesley, designed by Mr. Wyatt, one such as no Governor-General would dream of constructing now (it cost 150,000*l.*), lends itself well to such an occasion. It occupies a fine site, and has an imposing elevation and approaches. It is grand, but not solid. The noble portico is gained by a flight of upwards of thirty steps from the carriage drive; thence the vestibule gives on a magnificent hall, divided into centre and aisles by two rows each of twelve massive columns. The walls of the rooms and the pillars are covered with layers of the peculiar Indian cement, called chunam, which, when well polished, is whiter than the finest marble, the ceilings are beautifully decorated. The floors are of marble.

In the carriage sweep in front of the flight of steps at the portico were placed a guard of honour, the band and colours, of the 109th Regiment. On the broad landing at the top of the steps the Viceroy's Band was stationed in front of the portico; mace-bearers, or chobdars, in scarlet and gold liveries, guarded the entrances. Between each pair of columns in the Hall stood, sword in hand, a gigantic trooper of the Viceroy's Body Guard, in scarlet and gold tunic, cummerbund of the same, quaint zebra-striped turban, buckskin breeches, and jack-boots. Advancing between the columns up the centre of the hall, the visitor sees the Throne in an inner room, running at right angles to the hall, placed exactly opposite the entrance. Macebearers and janitors, in the handsome liveries of the Governor-General, bearing chotas and silver maces, were stationed at the entrances of the rooms and inside the Throne-room. Very good portraits (full-length) of George III. and Queen Caroline adorn the wall at each side of the Throne. On the wall, over a sofa in a kind of ante-chamber, whence a door leads to the rooms of the Prince's suite, is a full-length portrait of "Major-General the Hon. Arthur Wellesley, 1803"—an unmistakable likeness as to the face, but not equally accurate, it is to be hoped, as to the legs, which are very feeble. At the end, facing Wellington, is an abominable painting of the Queen in her robes, by Sir George Hayter. The Throne-room at one end has a row of columns forming a recess. The Prince's suite, in full uniform, stood in line in the Throne-room, on the right of the entrance. It has been observed that the Prince does not sit on any of the numerous thrones prepared for him, or avoids doing so as much as he can.

At 10.30 A.M. the approach of the Maharaja of Puttiala was announced by the regulation salute. Puttiala was not one of the finest of the Chiefs by any means, and yet he was, as a friend of mine said, "like a flash of lightning through Storr and Mortimer's." He is son of a man who did England good service by keeping the road between Delhi and the Punjaub clear, and helping us in a most substantial fashion, when it was of vital importance. He is rather a fine-looking man, about thirty years of age, with a melancholy, anxious face. As he was led tenderly along the outer hall by Major Henderson, his eye rested on the empty throne with a puzzled expression; but he looked pleased when he saw the Prince, who had been hitherto hidden by the columns, waiting to receive him in the inner room. The Maharaja made a very low yet dignified salaam. The Prince took his hand, and led him to the sofa at the feet of the picture of Wellington, where he sat with the Maharaja on his left, the Political Officer (Tupper) next, to interpret. The conversation, which lasted eight or ten minutes, seemed to interest the Maharaja greatly; and he was delighted when the Prince referred to the services of Puttiala in 1857. The Maharaja was evidently in very good humour when he was led back to the end of the carpet.*

Scarcely had the clatter of Puttiala's horse-hoofs died away ere the guns announced the Maharaja Holkar of Indore, G.C.S.I. His Highness is a very tall man, with developments such as were attributed to Aldermen before

AFTER THE AUDIENCE.

they took to volunteering and athletic exercises. Conducted by Major Henderson and the Political Agent (Maitland), he came into the Throne-room, rolling from side to side, and just touching his forehead slightly to the suite in a very regal manner. Holkar is very proud and punctilious, and there have been difficulties about his precedence, so great, that the arrangements for a meeting

* Before the Prince reached England he received, with great regret, the news of the untimely death of the Maharaja in the prime of life.

with other Chiefs were attended with trouble. A certain interest is attached to Holkar, because, if report be true, he has five millions sterling stored up for a rainy, or let us say, as we are in India, for a dry day. His two sons and his clever Dewan, Ragonath Rao (nephew of Sir Madhava Rao), and a train of Sirdars took their seats with the suite. It is said the Maharaja is desirous of some part of Kandeish; but he is clever enough to be aware that the Prince cannot interfere. He received the gold medal and riband which is given by the Prince to the great Chiefs, introduced his sons and Sirdars, and left with a cheerful countenance. The Maharaja of Jodhpoor—a most picturesque-looking Chief, followed by a splendid Sirdaree—came next. A very bright, keen eye, and black, bristling whiskers, moustache, and beard, brushed upwards, gave him, at first sight, a fierce look, of which the sad, proud aspect of his small, well-cut features, changed the character on closer scrutiny. But proud he is beyond the pride of the proudest. It is related of him that at a Durbar, when chairs were placed for himself, the Maharaja of Oodeypoor, and another Chief, he exclaimed, "Let Oodeypoor take which seat he pleases; I shall sit above him!" What wealth of gems glittered all over his neck and breast I cannot describe. The many-folded petticoats, like an Albanian fustanelle, worn by the Maharaja, descended nearly to his heels, and reminded one of the robes of the dancing dervishes. The petticoats were looped up by a roll of cloth of gold, forming a thick circular girdle, which hung from the waist and gathered his dress in behind below the knees. His bright yellow turban was bound round his brow by a band of cloth of gold, and displayed an aigrette of diamonds and rubies of great beauty. His Sirdars were attired in a similar way, and seemed to be very pleasant, agreeable gentlemen.

The Maharaja of Jeypoor drove up in a handsome carriage, drawn by four white horses, covered with trappings of cloth of gold, at 11 A.M. He has the reputation of being one of the most enlightened of Indian Potentates. He wears spectacles, which somehow or other never seem to suit Oriental costume very satisfactorily. His Sirdars were very splendid and peculiar in attire.

The cortege of the Maharaja of Cashmere caused the impression produced by previous coruscations to fade away. The state-coach, in which the Maharaja, the Political Officer (Captain Jenkins), and his Dewan sat, arrived at 11.20 A.M. It was preceded by two Life Guardsmen, armed with enormous sabres, in brass helmets and red horse-hair plumes, steel cuirasses—helmets and cuirasses which, unless I am deceived, once belonged to France, and defended the heads and bodies of Imperial Cuirassiers—blue coats, yellow buckskin breeches, and long boots. Four more came behind his carriage, in addition to his escort. His Sirdars followed in five carriages. He is a handsome, well-made man, upright, and more quick in gait and manner than Asiatic Chiefs generally are. He and his Chiefs affect the Sikh headdress—one of the most becoming of turbans, with a pretty, rakish set on the head, and smart, defiant brush, or tuft of bird-of-paradise feathers, in front. As to his aigrette or plaque of diamonds, one can only say that there seemed to be a flash in the air as he turned his head in talking with the Prince. The Maharaja of Gwalior followed. He walked towards the Prince in a kind of eager, courteous, deprecating way, which no actor could imitate. The attachment of Scindia to the British raj nearly cost him his throne in 1858; and he certainly did not increase his prestige among his own people by the discovery and surrender of a supposititious Nana Sahib—heir, in their eyes, of the Peishwa. Scindia delights in soldiering, and a very good judge told me he knew few officers in our service who could put a Division of the three arms through a good field-day so well. His is one of the cases which present formidable difficulties in India. Here is a ruler of martial tendencies, who has no possible career open to him, and whose devotion to drilling and manœuvring must be more or less cause of anxiety to the Paramount Power. He is rough in speech, but that his sentiments are noble may be inferred from his answer when the Bombay Government desired to buy the site for the Palace at Gunnesh Khind. "A man," said he, "does not sell his patrimony; but he can give it to his friend."

At 12 (noon) a salute of nineteen guns was fired, and a closed brougham drove up to the steps, to which the guard (now of the 40th Regiment, relieving the 109th Regiment) presented arms. The door was opened, and a shawl, supported on a pair of thin legs, appeared. On the top of the shawl there was the semblance of a head, but visible face there was none, for over the head was drawn a silk hood, and from it depended a screen of some sort of stuff, which completely hid features which report says are not at all deserving of such strict concealment, though her Highness is nearly forty, which is old for India. This was the Sultana Jehan, Begum of Bhopal, G.C.S.I., a descendant of one of those families which were pushed into place and power by British influence after the Pindarees were stamped down. With her came a daughter, draped and dressed in the same way, and quite as old, to judge from appearance, though the lady is only eighteen. They walked very slowly one after the other up the steps, taking their time about it, as if they were performing some remarkable feat. The Sirdars, among whom were two highly-jewelled lads, said to be her Highness's nephews, and one old gentleman, Jam Allahdeen Khan, a very fine type of a Native Minister, were dressed magnificently. The Begum was very much at her ease, and chatted very pleasantly with the Prince, whilst her daughter engaged in conversation with Sir Bartle Frere.

The last Chief was the Maharaja of Rewah, whose carriage and four, with two postillions in green and gold, top-boots, and breeches, did credit to the Political Officer (Bannerman) in charge of his Highness. The Maharaja is a dignified personage, very well spoken of by all who know him. His family claims very high rank in point of antiquity and ancestry.

The receptions finished, a Levee was held in the Throne-room. The Prince, in full uniform, stood before the throne for more than two hours, bowing to the stream passing before him—the Duke of Sutherland, Lord A. Paget, and Sir B. Frere on his right; and Sir R. Temple on his left, whispering information, which caused the names to be a little jumbled up and some bows to be missed. Notwithstanding the notices, people would bring cards printed in all kinds of texts, instead of having their names boldly and legibly written. It was pitiable to see the state of bewilderment in which Native or European from the mass, barred at the door, passed, with the sun—for it would get through—in his eyes, between lines of uniformed gentlemen, one saying, "Not so fast; wait till your name is called!" another exclaiming, "Turn your head and salaam, Sir!" and looked for the Prince in order to make his bow—wondering all the while who "Ramchunder Doss" or "Colonel Jones," whose name he heard called, was when he was "Baboo Shastryia" or "Major Evans." It was as difficult to restrain the impatience of some as it was to accelerate the approach of others.

After a grand banquet at Government House the

Prince went to the entertainment prepared by a committee of Native gentlemen, at Belgatchia, a villa five miles away, from which the company did not get away till past midnight. What pleases Native gentlemen is not quite to European taste. There was a little too much smoke—too great a luxury of fireworks and illuminations to be agreeable to those who are so used to them by this time as to be very exacting and fastidious, but there were many pretty things. Above all, there was the intense wish to please. The dancing girls were so laden with clothes that only their faces and toes were visible, and dancing was lost in drapery.

December 25th.—Christmas Day. The Prince and the Viceroy attended Divine service in the Cathedral. It was a full choral service. Every seat was filled. The Communion-table was decorated with flowers, and the choir began the service by singing the Christmas Hymn, advancing in procession to the altar from the porch. The Prince sat with Lord Northbrook on his left, Miss Baring on the right. The Bishop and clergy were assisted by the Rev. Canon Duckworth. A charity sermon for distressed Europeans, remarkable for treatment and character, was preached by the Bishop. It contained no reference to the Prince's visit. It was an earnest and powerful appeal to Christians to set an example to the heathen. Every Englishman in India was a missionary; he became a minister of God or a minister of evil; he was charged with the burden of Christ. By his life was Christ's teaching judged. This principle of direct responsibility Bishop Milman insisted on most forcibly, concluding with an admirable appeal for aid to our distressed countrymen.*

* Bishop Milman died of a fever caught in an episcopal tour through the North-West Provinces in a few weeks afterwards.

The Prince, after his return from the Cathedral, drove to Prinsep's Ghaut, where thousands of natives and hundreds of Europeans, attracted by the *Serapis* dressed out with flags, had assembled. Two lines of sailors (Commander Bedford) and marines (Major Snow) were drawn up on the gangway, which was covered with scarlet cloth, and on pontoons extending from the shore to the ship. Outside, the officers of the *Serapis* and of the *Osborne.* Most of the blue-jackets had flowers in their breast. The deck was artfully transformed into a winter scene by means of shrubs and branches covered with cotton-wool to represent snow, which, with the aid of some glistening white powder, it did most successfully. Holly and ivy wreaths, fabricated on board, were suspended on the bunting-walls alongside inscriptions of "Welcome, merry Christmas!" "Happy new year!" "God bless the Prince of Wales!" "*Cead mille failthe,*" "Welcome." Old Father Christmas was duly represented. Across the forecastle was the inscription, "We wish you a prosperous journey and a safe return to us." A table prettily decorated, was prepared for lunch on the main-deck. "God save the Queen" having been played, the health of the Prince was drunk with Highland honours, the cheers being echoed by the crowd outside. The Prince proposed the health of Captain Glyn and the officers of the *Serapis*, to whom he paid some graceful compliments, adding the name of Commander Durrant of the *Osborne.* Captain Glyn, in returning thanks, expressed a hope that Major-General Browne would keep time in his 5000 miles' land journey with the Prince as well as the *Serapis* had kept her date. As the Prince bade the vessel good-bye, the crew rushed up into the rigging, cheering vociferously.

The Prince was accompanied by Lord Northbrook, Miss Baring, and the members of his personal staff, on a drive to the Viceregal Lodge at Barrackpoor in the afternoon. The name is better known to the English public as that of a Station at which the signs and tokens of a terrible trouble to come were first observed than as the pleasant retreat to which the Viceroy flies from the turmoil of Government House on Saturdays, returning on Monday, after a quiet day in the country, to his life of toil. There is a church near at hand, and a large population of officials who can afford to pay high rents for their bungalows are quartered on the banks of the river, at the other side of which is Serampoor. There is a noble park, in which the Bombax, not yet in flower, Casuarinas hung with creepers, Calabash trees, and many others, with the ordinary types of Bengal vegetation, are seen in great beauty. Times are changed since 1857. It has ceased to be a great Station. There was a quiet reception in the saloons of the Lodge in the evening.

December 26th.—After church the Prince made an excursion by water to Chandernagore. The visit delighted the residents in that pretty settlement. Some time ago it was supposed that France might be disposed to exchange it for an equal or larger slice of land in extension of Pondicherry. But times have changed, and any proposal of the kind now would be, it is said, embarrassing. The Governor was at Pondicherry attending a Council, but the Consul received the Prince. There was a smart guard of honour of Sepoys, tricolours, and British flags. A Royal salute was fired. The town band of Calcutta played "God save the Queen;" and although it was not till Saturday evening that the likelihood of the visit was known, the Colony turned out in black coats and white cravats. There was the inevitable address, of course, but it was short, and it was well read by an Irish girl named Wade, whose grace won complimentary remarks on the taste and elegance of Frenchwomen. "Soyez le bienvenu sur cette terre française, qui conservera longtemps le souvenir d'un si beau jour!" The President of the French Tribunal presented the French officials. The *vin d'honneur* and the usual toasts were drunk, after which the visitors passed in carriages through the neat little town. Chandernagore has been called an Eastern Arcadia. Certainly some of its people are simple enough. "Tiens!" exclaimed one to his neighbour when his Royal Highness proposed the health of the President. "Tiens! le Prince parle français donc!" By the time the Prince returned to the Ghaut all Chandernagore was there to cheer him, and cry, "Vive le Prince de Galles!"

December 27th.—There was a heavy dew at night, and at dawn there was a fog on the river which hid the opposite bank from view till 7 A.M. At 9 A.M. the Royal party embarked on board the *Rhotas* and her attendant floating house. The Prince, Lord Northbrook, &c., landed at Chandal, and drove to Government House, where there was to be another reception of Chiefs. All was ready by the time the Prince arrived. The Body Guard in their places; the Grand Staircase seamed with a broad red carpet; a guard of honour of H.M. 40th, with band and colours, and a glittering of gold lace under the portico and in the vestibule.

At five minutes to 12 A.M. a salute of fifteen guns; punctual to a moment, the Emissaries from the King of Burmah drove up in handsome carriages and four, with outriders, to the entrance. The Envoy-in-chief wore a circular casque of beaten gold, surmounted by a sort of steeple, with fantastic sprouts of the same metal. The members of the Mission had casques ornamented by flaps of velvet and gold, and wings of gold-embroidered velvet; their figures were enveloped in heavy folds of brocade.

But people who knew what to look at were principally concerned with their feet. They wore patent-leather shoes or bottines, and entered the presence without taking them off. When Sir Douglas Forsyth went to visit the King, he was required to take off his shoes. Henceforth the Court of Burmah can scarcely expect any British Envoy to forget the precedent set at Calcutta. No one could form an idea of the effect produced by the interview on the Burmese from their stolid features, closed mouths and sunken eyes.

At 12.15 P.M. the Maharaja of Punnah, only an eleven-gun Prince, but a very splendid person, attended by the Political Officer, was received. The Prince rules a small jungly State, with a population of 183,000, but is rich in the possession of a diamond-field close to his capital. He boasts a pedigree of 350 years of royalty; is a Bondeela, 28 years of age, and good looking; given to photography; very willing to improve his people. In his headdress sparkled numerous samples of the produce of his mines of great size and brilliancy, and his Sirdars were richly garnished with precious stones on their turbans, necks, arms, and fingers. Next an Embassy from the Nepalese Government was announced. It was led by Runoodeep Sing, Rana Bahadoor, and among its members was Bubbur Jung, son of Sir Jung Bahadoor, who is as fond of sport as his father; rides admirably, wins or loses steeple-chases and is quite of Young Nepal. He will be attached as aide-de-camp to the Prince's staff. The combination of the rakish headdress—a sort of skull-cap wreathed with pearls and emeralds, and decorated in front with an aigrette of diamonds, from which spirts up a stiff plume or brush of hair—with the scarlet coat and sash of a British General Officer, regulation overalls, strapped over boots, was effective. The

Sirdars wore uniforms like our artillery; several had the Indian medal and Lucknow clasp, and Colonel Tej Sing had the medal for the Thibet campaign, of the details of which we know very little indeed.

The Nepalese were eclipsed by Raghbeer Sing, the Raja of Jheend, and his followers, not so much by any great wealth of jewels, as by the noble bearing of the Chief and by the fine persons of some of his Sirdars. The Raja is only forty-two years of age, but his full beard is already grey, his features are very handsome, his figure tall, his manner full of dignity. A keen sportsman, a good soldier, a vigorous administrator, he has hereditary claims to the gratitude of the Imperial Government; for it was his father, Sarup Sing, who first marched against the Delhi mutineers and remained in camp till the city fell; his ancestors helped Lord Lake at a critical time, and held fast to the British Government in the Sutlej campaign. He is only an eleven-gun Raja, but his house has been rewarded by several grants of land. He was attended by Captain Lawrence. The dresses worn by the suite were distinctive; yellow turbans, pointed at the side, bound with fillets of gold cloth over the forehead, aigrettes of diamonds, flowing robes of brocade, and very tight pantaloons of white silk. Each man bore his sword by a belt from his side, instead of carrying it in his hand.

The Prince received a visit from the Maharaja of Benares at 1 P.M. His Highness was escorted to and from Government House by cavalry, and there was a guard of honour and band to receive him, and artillery detachment to fire his salute of thirteen guns. His carriage was drawn by four horses, the leaders ridden by postillions, the wheelers driven by a coachman on the box—the effect unusual, but not at all distressing to native ideas. Indeed, the amount of pain we cause them by our love of uniformity is very great. They like disparity. I was told of a Raja who was very much displeased because a new carriage sent from London made no noise on the highway, and was only satisfied when the local authority, by a happy thought, ordered the screws and bolts of the springs to be loosened, and so gave room for the needful clatter and jingle. The Maharaja is a Brahmin, with a 900 years' pedigree. He has a revenue of 80,000*l*. a year, of which more than a quarter (30,000*l*.) is paid to the British Government as revenue. He is learned, encourages education, and is gracious in manner. His position of Raja of the Sacred City, the holy monuments of which he has done a good deal to protect, gives him more consideration among the natives than he would be entitled to from his possessions. Of him more hereafter—*stat nominis umbra*—but he is much respected by his own people, and by Europeans, to whom he shows the greatest hospitality. He was most anxious that the Prince should visit his shooting grounds, where he promised good sport; but the programme would not admit of it, and the Prince expressed his regret that he could only pay him a short visit at his castle on the Ganges as he was on his way to Lucknow.

The Maharaja of Nahun was received at 1.15 P.M. Next came the Maharaja of Johore (seventeen guns; Political Officer, Captain Gordon; Secretary, Mr. Hole), Chief of a district of 20,000 square miles in the southern part of the Malayan Peninsula, above Singapore. His Chiefs, in dress and face, present a compromise between the Malay and the native of Hindostan. Lighter in colour, with round face and muscular frames, they seem as if they had fighting powers inside, and their vicinity to Perak made one study their appearance with comparative interest. The Raja affects no finery, has an open, frank manner, and has travelled much for an Indian Chief.

By this time the most indefatigable worshipper of State observances, and the greatest admirer of the picturesque, had probably grown a little weary of the uninterrupted succession of Chiefs and Sirdars, and diamonds, emeralds, rubies, and pearls had begun to look very much of the same size and brightness. But what must the officers, who were galloping up and down outside, meeting the Rajas at prescribed distances and seeing them off again, have thought of the length of the visits? The sun was very hot; and even in the Audience Chamber, where the punkah swung to and fro all day, the Prince no doubt felt grateful for the additional currents of air wafted from the yaks'-tails and the fans held by his attendants. To say the truth, there was, in the uniformity of pân and uttur and regulation courtesies, something which made one tire even of the sight of Major Henderson, as he conducted his friends to the presence, and feel glad when it was all over.

December 28th.—After receptions naturally come return visits;* the early part of to-day was devoted by the Prince to these acts of courtesy. The preparations of the Maharaja of Cashmere, who received the Prince at 11.30 A.M., were of extraordinary richness. There was a tent of Cashmere shawls outside the house. The walls were draped with shawls of immense value; the floors of the rooms were covered with the finest shawls. One felt as if he were walking over charming paintings, and destroying with Vandal foot works of great price. There was a dais shrouded in magnificent shawls at the end of the room; there was a shawl canopy for the throne or chairs of state. Rich as these were, the Maharaja and his Sirdars were richer still. They wore robes of stuff

---

* See Appendix.

which might be described as being thickened with a crust of exceeding fine jewels. From his Highness of Cashmere's residence the Prince went to that of the Maharaja of Johore, who made offerings of very characteristic work and fabrics from the Malay Peninsula. The Maharaja of Jeypoor was next in order, and very splendid in his presents and arrangements. After him, the Prince visited Holkar. The Prince next drove to the residence of the Maharaja of Jodhpoor, and with him closed the list of return visits for the day.

December 29th.—The Prince, at 11.30 A.M., drove to visit the Maharaja of Gwalior. Scindia has the good taste not to be too splendid in his ornaments. He did the honours royally; but when the Prince took his seat, he made a very low salaam with his hands clasped together before he sat down. The Begum of Bhopal, who had a very striking-looking *entourage*, next received a visit. After her Highness came the Chief of Rewah, whose armour-clad Sirdars were the grandest yet seen. Jheend, Punnah, and others followed, and then there was a welcome drive home to rest for a while.

After lunch the Prince attended the Calcutta races. It was arranged that an excursion should be made by special train at midnight to Goalundo, to have two days' boar-hunting and snipe-shooting; but the Prince thought it unadvisable to leave Government House, as he had caught a cold, which would not be improved in the jungle. He permitted those of his suite who desired it to go, and the famous Tent Club promised to give them excellent sport.

December 30th.—The Prince invited the Viceroy, Miss Baring, and a small party to lunch on board the *Serapis*. It was what is called a "change," and there was, somehow, an idea of a picnic connected with it. And odd it was to

CALCUTTA.—TENT-PEGGING.

think that not nine-and-ninety years ago all that was English within many miles of the scene of the little entertainment was represented by a handful of fugitives from the fort of Calcutta, ere it fell into the hands of Sooraj-ood-Dowlah, embarked in a few small vessels off Fulta, awaiting anxiously the arrival of Clive from Madras to avenge "the Black Hole," and, as it turned out, to win Plassey and to found an Empire. There were some not twenty-one years ago who would have followed the example of Governor Minchin and have escaped from Calcutta if they could. In the evening his Royal Highness honoured Sir A. and Lady Clarke with his company at dinner.

December 31st.—Tent-pegging—feats of horsemanship by troopers of the 10th Bengal Cavalry at 9 A.M. Tent-pegging means riding full tilt at a tent-peg driven into the ground and carrying it off on the point of the lance. If any one thinks it easy to do this, let him try, remembering that Indian tent-pegs are larger, longer, and stick deeper than those at home. Then rupees were put on the pegs to be knocked off by the Lancers. Handkerchiefs were laid on the ground, and one man managed to take three in succession in the same gallop. There were other exhibitions, somewhat of a circus character, but that the horses were ridden on the hard plain, and everything was done by hand, bit, and balance. The Prince was so much pleased that he gave a hunting-knife to the best man. A British trooper would have probably received the unexpected gift with much delight and *mauvaise honte.* The Towanna man was able to express a wish that he might be allowed to wear the knife when in uniform, and the wish was acceded to. The delusions prevalent about the covert sides of England, that no men can ride but Englishmen, and the fond faith of Irish foxhunters, that there is no race in the world like the natives of the Green Isle for hippodamic prowess, might be somewhat shaken if they had seen these swarthy gentlemen.

The Prince returned to Government House, and at noon drove out with the Duke of Sutherland, General Probyn, Dr. Fayrer, and the Rev. Canon Duckworth, to make a round of the principal Hospitals of Calcutta, from which he returned at 2 P.M. At the Medical Hospital and College, he was received by Dr. Clevege and the Professors and native teachers. He next went to the Campbell Hospital, Sealdale, where he was received by Dr. Woodford. He then visited the European Female Orphan Asylum, and was conducted over the establishment by Miss Clark, the lady superintendent, and ladies of the Committee. His Royal Highness expressed much pleasure at the healthy appearance of the children. At the Military Hospital he was received by Dr. Ray. Lord Napier also joined the party. His Royal Highness expressed himself pleased and satisfied with all he saw, and he certainly saw a good deal.

The day was wound up with a Garden Party at Belvedere, a Dinner at Government House, and the Grand Ball. The sporting party returned at 7 P.M. from Goalundo greatly pleased. There were no mishaps. Seven or eight boars were speared.

THE CHAPTER OF THE STAR OF INDIA.

January 1st, 1876.—The adjustment of the relative position of the Prince and of the Viceroy had caused considerable anxiety to good people at home before his Royal Highness set out on his journey. There were obvious objections to any person, however exalted, appearing to take precedence, in the eyes of the Chiefs and people of

India, of the representative of the Queen. The Viceroy would feel that he could not be the equal or the superior of the Prince. No ceremonial has such importance as a Durbar. It is a Court reception, in which each, according to his rank, is brought face to face with the representative of the Sovereign. But no one could hold a Durbar unless he were the representative of the Queen. Eventually it was suggested—I believe by Lord Northbrook—as a way of escape from these difficulties, that a Chapter of the Order of the Star of India, in which the Prince should act as High Commissioner, should be held at Calcutta, on New Year's Day.

All fashionable Calcutta was early awake, those who were to be in attendance being summoned for 7.45 A.M. At the distance of a mile from Government House, canvas walls had been erected in a long parallelogram. Along this were ranged tents for the Rajas and other personages who were to take part in the ceremony, so that each could pass into his tent, and remain there till it was time for him to take his place in the pageant. Opposite the entrance, in a Chapter-tent which was carpeted with cloth of gold, with the Royal Arms emblazoned in the centre, was an elevated dais. Above the dais a canopy covered with light-blue satin, and supported upon silver pillars. Beneath the canopy were two chairs, with silver arms, one with the Prince of Wales' "plumes," the other with a "crown," embossed on the back. On each side of and behind these chairs, were tiers of seats, those in front for members of the Order. Outside the tent were platforms for those fortunate enough to obtain tickets. Inside the enclosure were drawn up the marines and sailors of the *Serapis*, and a military band. On the left were infantry of the line; in front of the outer canopy was a tall flagstaff.

At 9.10 A.M. the artillery fired a Royal salute. A grand flourish of trumpets announced a very fine sight. First came Native servitors in liveries of scarlet and gold, two and two, bearing silver maces, spears, and wands of office. Next the Grand Marshal of the camp, Mr. Henvey, and Mr. Secretary Aitchison; then the Companions of the Order, two and two, one-half Natives, one-half Europeans. As the procession entered the Chapter-tent, the servitors ranged themselves right and left at the entrance.

Scarcely had the splendour of the stream of uniforms and costumes of the processions of the Companions toned down ere the procession of the Begum of Bhopal, the first Knight Grand Commander, entered, led by Colonel Osborne, the Political Officer, preceding eight Sirdars. Next came an officer bearing quaint devices on a silken banner. Her Highness, veiled, and swathed in brocaded stuff of many colours, over which was the ample light-blue satin robe, with white shoulder-knots, of the Order, was attended by two native pages in very handsome dresses and bare feet. Next came Mr. Trevor, the Political Agent, leading the procession of Sir Salar Jung. Eight Sirdars, dressed with that taste in the arrangement of colour and fashion of apparel, the joy of artists and horror of martinets, which the West has tried to destroy by "uniform," followed. Sir Salar Jung wore a small white turban, and a plain caftan of dark green cloth. His train was borne by two pretty pages, dressed in green and gold. In contrast to his studied simplicity, came next the Maharaja of Puttiala, who wore on his turban many fine diamonds, which were said to have once belonged to the Empress Eugénie, and the great Sancy diamond as a pendant. Lord Napier of Magdala came next. Well has the Colonel of Indian Engineers, who was summoned to

Lucknow eighteen years ago by Colin Campbell, won his honours. He took his seat next Sir Salar Jung, and courteously saluted him, the Begum of Bhopal and the Maharaja of Puttiala, who sat opposite to him.

The procession of the excellent Maharaja of Travancore, who is very like Mr. Buckstone, if one could fancy him in Oriental garb, came next. His Dewan and Sirdars were in the costume of their country, which is not so fine as that of Central India.

Next appeared Sir Bartle Frere, preceded by a banner with many an ancient quartering, his train held by two midshipmen. The Maharaja of Rewah followed. His procession, led by Major Bannerman, consisted of Sirdars, who would make a sensation in a London or Paris theatre. They were animated nuggets, ambulatory mines of jewels —one especially, who wore a suit of chain-armour, arabesqued breast and back-pieces, jewelled plume, casque of gold, and enamelled gauntlets. Rewah—reminding one of the great King of yore, on whose Palace wall the dread fingers wrote the pregnant sentence—wore a golden crown, exquisitely worked, blazing with gems. The Maharaja of Jeypoor's procession, headed by Colonel Benyon, included eight characteristic Thakoors and pages, whose doublets and trunk-hose of light-blue satin contrasted admirably with their dark faces. Next came Political Maitland, who headed the Maharaja Holkar's procession. That burly gentleman looked like an Indian Henry VIII. His pages were in Vandyck brown and gold. Next came the procession of the Maharaja of Cashmere, Major Jenkins in front. Eight most resplendent warriors and courtiers, finely shawled and jewelled, two and two, were eclipsed by the magnificent Maharaja, whose train was carried by pages in green velvet tunics and pink turbans, and who bore the ransom of a kingdom on his person. Last,

Colonel Hutchinson appeared at the head of Maharaja Scindia's procession. Brilliant as was the gorgeous Chief of Gwalior, the Europeans, at least, were not inclined to bestow on him much attention, for the Prince was now advancing. His household and officers in two lines preceded him. The Prince wore white helmet and plume, and Field-Marshal's uniform, almost concealed beneath the folds of his sky-blue satin mantle. His train was carried by naval cadets, Messrs. Grimston and Walshe, "blue boys," in cavalier hats and wigs, blue satin cloaks, tunics, trunk-hose, and rosetted shoes; pretty to look at, but decidedly anachronous, for the Order cannot claim any cavalier associations—but pages must be pages. The Prince took his seat on the dais, the Band playing "God save the Queen," all standing. The Viceroy ordered the Secretary to read the roll of the Order. Mr. Aitchison did so. Each member stood up as his name was called, bowed, and sat down. The Chapter was then declared open; the Secretary reported the business to be the investiture of the persons named in a warrant, directing the Prince to invest them, from the Queen, dated Balmoral, October 25th, 1875. The Viceroy and the members of the Order rose, bowed to the Prince, and sat down. The Prince then received from the Secretary the grants of the several dignities, which were handed to a page. He directed "the investiture to proceed."

First, the Maharaja of Jodhpoor was conducted from the tent in which he had been robed to the presence; the Under-Secretary bearing the insignia on a blue satin and velvet cushion. He was met at the entrance of the Chapter-tent by two junior Knights, and led up to the footstool of the Prince by Mr. Aitchison, who held him firmly by the hand, and indicated when he was to bow, kneel, walk backwards, and sit down. After the Queen's

INVESTITURE OF THE STAR OF INDIA.—CALCUTTA.

grant had been read, the Maharaja, having been decorated with a Knight's riband, badge, star, and robes, stood before the dais. He made two obeisances, and knelt. The Prince then placed the collar of the Order round his neck, and admonished him in prescribed form. Seventeen guns were fired. The Maharaja then rose, and, instructed by Mr. Aitchison, was led backwards, bowing with his face to the dais, towards the seat reserved for him. There his banner was unfurled to a flourish of trumpets, all standing. The Secretary proclaimed the titles of the newly-made Knight Grand Commander, and all resumed their seats. The account of one investiture must do for all. The Raja of Jheend was invested as G.C.S.I. The investiture of the Knights Commanders, Mr. Robinson, the Maharaja of Punna, Raja Mahun Kasee (Holkar's brother), Major-General Ramsay, General Runodeep Sing (Nepalese), Gunput Rao, and Faiz Ali Khan, followed. Mr. Robinson and Major-General Ramsay were also knighted. Mr. Chapman, Mr. Bullen Smith, and Baboo Degumber Mitter, received the badges of the Companionship, or third class of the Order. Then announcement was made by the Secretary that no more business remained. The Prince desired the Chapter to be closed. As the Prince emerged from the comparative darkness of the Durbar tent to the sound of a grand march, played by the military band, a Royal salute was fired, and the guard of honour presented arms. The spectacle of the processions leaving was by far the most picturesque part of the pageant. The Viceroy, the Grand Crosses, and the Grand Knights Commanders and Companions following in reverse order of their entry. The pomp of elephants, the noisy cavalcade of Eastern ceremonial were wanting, and there was no token of the public interest such a grand spectacle would arouse on the part of the inhabitants in any European capital.

As the Prince was going back to Government House, a native rushed towards the carriage. The Prince perceived that he held a paper in both hands, and was not at all perturbed. It was a petition. The natives have an idea that if one can give a petition into the Prince's hands, redress of grievances is certain.

In the afternoon the Prince, accompanied by the Viceroy, unveiled an equestrian statue of Lord Mayo on the Maidan, near Government House. The Prince expressed his melancholy satisfaction at unveiling the statue of one whom he had been proud to call his friend, and who would have left a great name among Indian Viceroys had he lived. On behalf of the widow, children, and friends of Lord Mayo, he thanked the Committee for what they had done in honour of his memory. After this ceremony, the Prince put on plain clothes, and drove to the Racecourse with the Viceroy, to witness a polo-match—an exciting contest between the Calcutta and Munipuri players; the former big men, on well-fed, well-groomed ponies; the latter light men, on ragged, poor-looking tats. The contest was rendered equal by the skill of the Munipuri men. The Prince next went to the display of fireworks on the Racecourse, which were not quite equal to expectation; but the spectacle of tens of thousands of faces lighted up by mortars, rockets, and coloured fires, was worth seeing. After the Royal party left the Race-stand an immense explosion occurred among the fireworks, but no one was hurt; and it greatly pleased the people, who thought it was part of the entertainment. At 7 P.M. the Prince drove off to see the fleet illuminated, and more fireworks were discharged from the ships; and after dinner he proceeded to the theatre, where there was a State night by Viceregal command. But not even the attractions of the Prince's presence and of Mr. Charles Mathews' acting could fill the house, and the Chiefs, who were expected to pay 100*l.* for a box, did not avail themselves as largely of the opportunity as the *beneficiaire* expected. Sir Salar Jung, the Maharaja of Rewah, and one or two more, however, did their best to appreciate "My Awful Dad." The veteran comedian was received with great applause by the English-speaking part of the audience, and at the end of the piece he was sent for and congratulated by the Prince. The play-bill will be found in the Appendix.

January 2nd.—The Prince, Viceroy, and party went to church at Fort William, and subsequently visited the Arsenal, where there is a collection of arms in good order. In the afternoon a steamer conveyed the Royal party to the Botanical Gardens. They drove back through Howrah, which was brilliantly illuminated, and halted at the Bishop's College, on the way. There was a concert of sacred music after dinner, by amateurs of great excellence, at Government House.

January 3rd.—Before 8 A.M. the Prince, attended by General Probyn and a few gentlemen, left Government House, on horseback, to see the 18th Bengal Cavalry exhibit their excellence in tent-pegging, feats of swordsmanship, and the like. There was not only tent-pegging, but a polo-match between five British champions and five Munipuri men. The latter scored five goals, to the astonishment of some of the spectators, who did not think it fair that an Englishman should be beaten at any sport by a native; but polo is the national sport of the Munipuris. These active little gentlemen would cut but a poor figure on their tats at a fox hunt. There was a regatta on the Hooghly at 2 o'clock. It must be an unkindly river for a regatta; the tide, up or down, races strongly, and although there is now no risk of fouling a dead Hindoo, the stream is not cleanly to look upon. The Prince created Mr. Stuart Hogg, the Chief Commissioner of Police, a Knight Bachelor; and, if it were any satisfaction to that gentleman to put "Sir" before his name, he had also the satisfaction of knowing that he had well earned the prefix by his work during the Royal visit. When "Sir Stuart" Hogg had been made and created, the Prince prepared for increment of his own honours, and was presented in due form at the University of Calcutta with the degree of Doctor, "honoris causâ," with immense acclamation. The paraphernalia of an English University seem out of place here; hoods, caps, stoles, gowns, are rather hot, but nevertheless they are appreciated; and the native graduates did not look at all amiss in cap and gown, surplice and robes. Left to themselves, the natives would very probably lie prone on their stomachs, *sub tegmine fagi*, or its substitute, listening to some ragged pundit or mollah, or sit on their hams around their teacher in tumbledown temple or mosque.

How it came about I do not exactly know, but it is probable that the Prince expressed a wish to see the zenana of some respectable native, and that the wish was made known to the worthy Hindoo of Bhawanipore, Mr. Mookerjee, who was only too happy to gratify it to-day. Miss Baring, Lady Temple, Miss Milman, Lady Stuart Hogg, and others, had, perhaps, some part in the *pourparlers*. There were hundreds of children assembled to see the Prince arrive; most of the little ladies held pretty bouquets, with which, out of loyal devotion, to pelt the Prince. These children may develop into Hindoo Bloomers, and establish Women's Rights' Associations, unless their wild shrieks of liberty be silenced in the leaden flood of caste and custom which has drowned so much thought and life in India century after century. Instead of salutes and flourishes, or bell-pulling, the Hindoos use conchs to announce the arrival of guests; the noise of these natural horns makes one rejoice that he is not among the Tritons. These were sounded often and long, for there were false alarms of the Prince's coming; but at last his carriage came in sight, and there was much conch blowing. His Royal Highness did not appear in the splendid attire which Mrs. Mookerjee and her fair friends, no doubt, thought a Prince should wear. Whether Baboo Jagadanund Mookerjee will ever get over the wrath of his co-religionists for the doings of this day time only can show. There is one fact revealed by the manner in which the occurrence was accepted by those concerned: Hindoo ladies, at all events, do not consider strict seclusion at all essential to their happiness. But it is dangerous to argue from a particular to the universal, and so it will be safer, perhaps, to say that some Hindoo ladies do not dislike being seen—at all events, by a Prince of Wales.

The delightful visit to Calcutta was over. In the noble reception-rooms of Government House there was one more gathering of notables to pay their respects to the Prince before his departure. Certainly no host could have done the honours of his house with greater taste and with more success than Lord Northbrook. The route from the Government House was lined with troops and people; and the Station, beautifully prepared for the departing guest, was like a scene in a Christmas pantomime. The cortege was half an hour late in arriving at Howrah, but the parting of the Prince from Lord Northbrook was not shorn of one pleasant word or kindly expression, and there were no doubt many there who bade each other farewell with sincere regret, albeit the cares of ceremony rather clip the wings of friendship. The strains of the military band were drowned in the cheers and voices wishing "God-speed!" as the train moved from the platform. The manner of utilising the Royal special train as a dormitory is now commended by much experience. The only loss the traveller suffers is that of such scenery as may be passed when he is comfortably asleep.

It may be necessary to state here, as I have not done so before, that at Bombay, Poonah, Ceylon, Madras, and Calcutta the Prince's bounty has been largely bestowed on the poor and needy, and on the charities which needed aid. The demands on the Royal purse—many from European institutions—have been very heavy and very various, and the donations made in the course of the journey already come to a large sum.

MUNIPURI POLO PLAYER.

PRINCE LOUIS HANSELS THE GAINEE-CART.

CHAPTER X.

Bankipoor—The Famine Officers—A great Satrap—Patna—Benares—A grand Camp—The last of the Tartars—Visit to the Raja of Vizianagram—Ramnagar—Fyzabad—The "Martinière"—Monument to the Faithful among the Faithless—Native Entertainment in the Kaiserbagh—Broken Collar-bones—Native Lucknow—Cawnpoor Well and Memorial.

JANUARY 4TH.—At the Bankipoor Station, which we reached early in the morning, there was a short halt for breakfast and change of dress. The Prince was received by Sir R. Temple, the officers, civil and military, of the district, and a vast concourse of people; salutes, guards of honour, "God save the Queen." But the feature of the reception was the well-equipped corps of mounted Volunteers (the Behar Riflemen) furnished by the planters and residents, whose appearance belied the evil reputation of the climate. Troops and police lined the road from the Station to the Camp, which was pitched on a plain, not very far from Patna, the ancient Palibothra, capital of the famous State —now a district (Behar) given up to opium and indigo—to which Megasthenes was sent as envoy by Seleucus, when little was known about Great Britain and Ireland by the most learned.

Sir Richard Temple had made preparations to show what a Lieutenant-Governor of Bengal could do. His Court, if not equal in splendour to that of the Viceroy, satisfied the spectator that he was a satrap of no ordinary magnitude and magnificence. Here was the crowning glory, not of his life—for he is young, ambitious, and able enough to look for greater honours—but of his career as a conqueror in the Famine Campaign. He had assembled the generals, officers, and privates of the vast army which had been engaged as his instruments, to be presented to the Prince of Wales.

Considering that there are, it is said, less than 100,000 Europeans in India, it was surprising to see what an assembly of ladies, in the most charming bonnets and most correct costumes, were waiting to welcome him. The avenue to the Durbar tent was lined by nearly four hundred elephants, caparisoned with great richness, the howdahs filled with people in gala dresses. The great multitude—Europeans on one side of the way and natives on the other—was loyal and picturesque; the loyalty of the Europeans expressed by cheers, waving of handkerchiefs, playing of bands, and discharges of cannon; the picturesqueness afforded by Rajas, Nawabs, and natives of inferior dignity. The Durbar marquee was a very spacious and stately but gaudy erection of canvas, hung with chandeliers. Patna is supposed to contain a good deal of disaffection and of religious fanaticism, which are encouraged by the presence of certain Mahomedan teachers; and it has been found necessary, I believe, to lock up a good many people whose pronounced opinions, or previous history, were of a nature to attract the attention of the authorities.

When the Prince had taken his place on the elevated dais under the canopy, whereon was placed a regal chair, the levee began, those distinguished by their exertions in the time of trouble being specially presented; but the anxiety of Sir Richard Temple to give information concerning the remarkable personages—and his personal knowledge seemed to be universal—had an effect which he did not anticipate; for the gracious bow was not always given to the owner of the name for which it was intended. That may seem but a small matter, but think of the anxiety of those who were looking forward to that recognition as their great reward, and of their chagrin when they found that their identity was not marked! There were Rajas and Zemindars of repute among the natives; and although now and then the "locals" might be heard muttering, "The old rascal ought to have been hanged in '58!" or, "One of the most seditious fellows in Behar!" generally they were well spoken of.

The levee was followed by a *déjeuner* in a very fine and lofty shamianah. The wives and families of the planters, and of the European residents generally were invited, and had full opportunity to see the Prince, as he sat at a slightly-elevated table at the end, with Sir R. Temple by his side. The health of "the Queen" was given, and then that of the Prince, which was received with great enthusiasm.

After this toast, the Prince proceeded to look at a panther offered by the sergeants of the 109th regiment. The three hundred and eighty elephants then passed in procession, and the Prince was amused at one very merry little fellow, who hopped about, danced, and waved his trunk in a comical manner. Amongst the gifts was a pair of very beautiful little oxen, not as large as Shetland ponies, which drew a light carriage like an artillery limber.

They were not easy to drive by those not to the manner born, as Prince Louis of Battenberg found when he made gallant essay to direct them. After an agreeable halt of three hours, the Prince returned to the Station.

From Bankipoor to Benares the country is flat but not quite uninteresting. It was disappointing to observe that in eighteen years no change had been made in the appearance of the people or of their dwellings. The weather is cold at night, and it was pitiable to see people here with their heads muffled up, at the expense of their brown legs, in a thin cotton cloth; a piece of calico was all their covering. They are no better off than the dwellers in the land of Egypt. In Egypt they are not harassed by cold at least; and a loin cloth and a skull cap are ample for the fellah's wants. The officials say these people are rich. There is always a story of wealth stored up in holes and corners—so they tell one in Egypt. But railway observations are not safe guides to knowledge, *pro* or *con.*, on any subject. It was nearly dark when the Royal train reached Rajghaut, the Station of Benares, but there was enough of light to give an ideal grandeur to those marvellous ghauts which have furnished so many subjects for the artist's pencil and the traveller's descriptive powers. And, truth to tell, these terraces descending from Temples, Palaces, and Choultries to the river's edge, look better through a medium of haze or moonlight than they do in the "garish light of day." The cortege drove over the bridge of boats from the right bank of the Ganges, and so through streets and roadways, the sides of which were crowded with people, out to the camp of the Lieutenant-Governor. The camp was enclosed by walls of canvas; the row of fourteen tents on the left was faced by another row of the same number. The main street, 1000 feet long and 230 feet broad, was bounded at the end by the

Durbar tents, on the left of which was a separate enclosure, 200 feet square. This contained drawing-room, bed-room, dressing-room, Equerry's room, a room for Lord Suffield, another for Mr. Knollys, two for personal attendants, and a tent for the guard—each room a large tent. They were all prettily furnished and decorated, the floors covered with rich carpets; a covered way led from the drawing-room to the tent of the Lieutenant-Governor, which was 70 feet long by 30 feet broad. Covered ways led from this saloon to a dinner tent. The Lieutenant-Governor, Sir John Strachey, Lady Strachey and family, lodged in tents to the right of the dinner-room. Each tent had a lamp in front, and the numbers and names were inscribed outside. Enter your own, and you find a charming carpeted quadrangle, divided into a bed-room and sitting-room, with a fireplace in which are blazing logs and glowing coals — not at all superfluous in this Indian winter—and, moreover, lights, tables, chairs, and every comfort a Rechabite of the most luxurious nature could desire—soft bed, and large bath, and ample space for life; smaller tents for servants within call, a complete establishment of attendants—plans of the camp—directions as to postal and telegraphic arrangements —rules to be observed in case of fire—clothes all ready laid out for dinner, of which the Camp bell and bugle give warning. The lamps and lights give one the idea of a busy street in high festivity; and when the company, are seated in the great tent, which is brilliant as a London ball-room, and one thinks that a few miles away there is a city of hundreds of thousands of people who would think it contamination to sit at the well-spread table, you understand how wide is the chasm which separates the life of the governing and the governed.

January 5th.—The Municipality of Benares presented

an address at 12.30 P.M. They welcomed the Prince to the most sacred city of the Hindoos, justly regarded and famous as the seat of their religion, philosophy, and learning, and associated from time immemorial in their minds with all that was pure and holy in their faith. Thousands of the devout annually assembled to worship there, maintaining under British rule the fullest freedom for their rites and ceremonies. They recognised in the Queen qualities as great as those of the Monarchs of Benares commemorated in the Hindoo epic, the 'Mahabharatam.' They thanked her Majesty for the personal assurance she had given of her interest in India, conveyed by the Prince's presence, and they watched his progress with unflagging interest. The Prince replied that it was a great pleasure to be thus received in the centre of all the nations and people of Hindoo origin, and to hear from those who knew them so well the feelings of their countrymen in all parts of India that under the British administration they enjoyed in the fullest freedom rites of worship according to the usages of their faith, and that privilege which was highly appreciated, perfect toleration. He would convey to the Queen their expressions of loyalty and gratitude. He was convinced it would give her sincere pleasure to learn that they appreciated the peace, contentment, and prosperity they enjoyed.

Before the Prince left Camp to-day there was an incident which deserves mention though it attracted little notice. "From an early hour" (as the chroniclers of the time have it), "six natives—venerable in aspect, not over splendid in attire, but bearing themselves like men conscious that they were not of common clay, might have been observed in the vicinity of the Royal quarters." The address by Mr. Carmichael on presenting them will explain better than any words of mine who they were, and the reason of their presence. He said :—

"The six gentlemen whom I present to your Royal Highness, Mirza Mahomed Sneed Bukht, alias Peary Sahib, Mozuffer Bukht, Nadir Bukht, Mouzoodeen Bukht, Rahemoodeen Bukht, Mahomed Mohsur Bukht, are lineal descendants of Mirza Jehan dar Shah, heir apparent to Shah Alum, the last independent King of Delhi and of the Timour dynasty!

"Shah Alum was desirous that his second son (called, when he reigned, Akbar Shah Saiee) should succeed to the throne. Hence a bitter feud arose between Jehandar Shah, the eldest son, and his father, and the former had to take refuge first at the Court of Lucknow, where a stipend was assigned to him for his maintenance by the Oudh Government, and later, in 1788, the British Government gave him and his family an asylum at Benares, making over to them for their residence the extensive range of buildings on the river face, called Shivala Ghat, and which had been sequestered for the rebellion of Cheyt Singh. The Prince Jehandar Shah died in May of the same year, and his descendants have since lived on the bounty of the British Government. As they have increased in numbers (the stipends which were many of them personal) have necessarily but ill sufficed for their maintenance. They are therefore in anything but comfortable circumstances, but still maintain their dignity, and are universally respected. They have ever been most loyal and grateful to the British Government for its protection and support.

I am told that the buildings in which they live are tumbling about their ears; and that poor as the owners are, they have dependents still poorer, who swarm around the place. Charity thrives in India. Hindoo and Mahomedan have vied with each other in past times in works which good political economists would assure them were of evil influence on society; and the foundations for keeping in idleness, if not competence, men, women, and children, which are so common, attest the greatness of their liberality and largeness of their sympathies.

After a levee for the district, European and Native, the Prince laid the foundation-stone of a new Subscription Hospital in Benares, halting on the way to hear the native pupils of the College, under the care of the Church Mission, sing, which they did very prettily.

The Prince then visited the Raja of Vizianagram, and inspected the Town-Hall, which has been built by the Raja in commemoration of the Duke of Edinburgh's visit. Thence the Prince proceeded to the famous Temples. It was necessary to walk to these edifices, as the streets are so narrow that it is with difficulty one can make room for the Sacred Bulls, which may be met at any moment taking a constitutional walk. To guard against the possibility of insult, and to prevent the crowding and "mobbing" which are not unusual where the visit of a Royal person is not quite so great a novelty, the buildings were cleared.

The Golden Temple and the Sacred Pool (which is a foul pool, covered with green scum, and emitting poisonous vapours of sulphuretted hydrogen), were duly inspected. These and the Great Temple of Ganesa, on ordinary occasions are thronged with priests, fakirs, pilgrims, devotees from all parts of India; but they were now carefully swept of "the perilous stuff," and there were only a few trusty Brahmins to exhibit the shrines, bulls, and holy places, under the guardianship of a strong body of police. The shops, where they sell the infinite varieties of brass idols, and flowers which are offered to the deities, were open. Among prints on the walls was recognised, not without merriment, the portrait of a celebrated French actress, who might be doing duty for the terrible helpmate of Shiva. Along the passages were stalls for the sale of the appropriate offerings to the god. It is strange that people under the influence of this faith should be mild and tolerant—that the female population should be remarkable for the exercise of every domestic virtue—chaste, faithful, devoted to their children. Of their tolerance the best proof is afforded by their indulgence of the missionaries who lift

ENTRY INTO RAMNAGAR.

their voices aloud against their idolatries under the shadows of the Temples.

The Prince drove thence to the Dourga Khound, in the suburbs. The monkeys cluster all over the pinnacles and ornaments of the Temple, which is painted with red ochre to imitate the colour of blood. They are very ugly impudent monkeys—red-haired, plump, and filthy. Too much familiarity has bred in them contempt for men, and they menaced the strangers with chattering and open mouths; but when they saw that their attendant priests were full of civility, and were preparing to feast them with parched grain and small parcels of sweetmeats, they came swarming down to the ground to the number of a hundred and fifty or two hundred, old and young, to partake of the offerings.

Shortly before sunset the Prince embarked in a handsome galley, with two sea-horses at the bow, which was towed by a steamer to the old fort of Ramnagar, four miles up the Ganges, where the Maharaja of Benares received the Prince on a canopied and garlanded landing-stage. It was the grandest and most characteristic reception possible. The river-bank was blazing with the twittering of *feux de joie;* the air lighted up by the discharges of artillery from the ancient parapets; the battlements of the fort were illuminated. Silver flambeaux and torches were held by people on parapets, walls and river-banks, which were as light as day. Preceded by mace-bearers, spearsmen, and banners, the Prince and the Maharaja were borne in gold and silver chairs, on men's shoulders, up the ascent from the river to the castle gate, between lines of matchlockmen and cavalry. Elephants, accompanied by wild music, marched on the left, shootee sowars rode on the right. Before the massive gateway, flanked by men in chain-armour, the Maharaja's infantry presented arms. There in the courtyard was a line of elephants, bearing gold and silver howdahs. In another courtyard were assembled the retainers and the officials of the household, who received the Royal visitor with profound salaams. The Maharaja led the Prince upstairs, where, after the usual presentations and a short conversation, a long file of servitors laid examples of gold brocade of the famed kinkob of Benares, Dacca muslin, and costly shawls at the Prince's feet, while the Maharaja sat, like a benevolent old magician in spectacles and white moustache, smiling, in his hall, with his hands joined in a deprecating way as each tray was laid on the ground, as though he would say, "Pardon that unworthy offering!" The Maharaja then conducted the Prince to a room where other beautiful presents were laid out on tables. In a third room a rich banquet was served, which was untouched.

The Prince mounted to the roof inside the parapet, whence a most marvellous scene presented itself. The surface of the Ganges was covered with tiny lamps, and, laden with these, the current flowed beneath the castle walls down towards Benares, and the little earthen vessels, bearing their cargoes of oil and wick, sparkled and glittered quite wonderfully. It seemed as though a starry sky were passing between banks of gold, for multitudinous Bengal lights were burning on the shores. The display of coloured fires from the walls of the castle and the extraordinary effect of the many-coloured flames on the mass of armoured men and on the upturned faces of the people evoked repeated exclamations of delight from the spectators. The river was flecked with fire. Imagine two miles of terraces rising from the water to temple and shrine, lit with oil-lamps, "packed" as close as they could stand or hang! Every line of masonry of minaret, mosque and temple, was marked out in light. The blackness of myriads of figures, set against vivid sheets of flame from the Bengal lights, gave a demoniacal aspect to the crowd. The Prince and party floated down the river from Ramnagar, pursued by flights of fire-balloons, to the landing-ghaut at Benares, where the carriages were waiting. Thence they drove to dinner to the camp, a distance of nearly six miles. The road was brilliantly illuminated.

January 6th.—The special train was ready at the temporary station, not far from the camp, at 8 A.M. The Maharaja of Benares, the Raja of Vizianagram, the Chief Justice and Judges, the Magistrates, the Major-General commanding the division, the aides-de-camp and staff were present. When the Prince was leaving, the Maharaja tendered him the last best proof of regard — his own walking-stick—a stout shillelagh, with a gold handle, and gold studs.

Travelling nearly all day to Lucknow. The scenery by the Oudh and Rohilcund Railway does not offer much variety. The country is a dead level, no great rivers, and not many streams, to bridge. Hitherto the Prince has visited regions blessed for many years by peace. Now he enters upon the scenes of great troubles, where traditions of the retribution inflicted on rebellion are recent, where confiscations and deposition have left many bitter memories, and where the fanaticism engendered in holy cities and by famous shrines keeps alive religious antagonism. At Fyzabad, the ancient Awadiah (Oudh), one of the most holy cities in India, which is much favoured by monkeys, where the train arrived at 1 P.M., Sir George Couper, the Chief Commissioner, staff, the magistrates, and officials, and Major-General Maude, commanding the district of Oudh, and his staff, received the Prince, who made a short halt at the station, and then continued his journey to Lucknow. There was little to note on the way; but

Oudh is less prosperous—to look at—than it was in 1858. Major-General Chamberlain and the Lucknow officials received the Prince at the Charbagh Station at 4.40 P.M. The cortege set out for the Royal headquarters, with an escort of the 13th Hussars, and made a fine show on its way; Fane's Punjaubees (now the 19th Bengal Cavalry), and the various regiments belonging to the Station, and strong force of Oudh police, lining the roads, the sideways of which were filled with crowds of natives. Lucknow has fairly been improved off the face of the earth. Hundreds of acres once occupied by houses have been turned into market-gardens. Swarded parks, vistas, rides and drives, far prettier than those of the Bois de Boulogne, spread out where once were streets, bazaars, palaces. They are like oceans beneath which thousands of wrecks lie buried. It was just possible to recognise Banks' Bungalow—now the residence of the Chief Commissioner—once Outram's headquarters; but the approaches to it baffled all attempts of memory.

January 7th.—A guard of the 65th Regiment, covered by a body of police, were on duty all night around the Bungalow. There was a native levee at 11 A.M. Next there came a European levee. The Prince then drove to the Dilkoosha. He was much interested in the building, which was the scene of interesting events at the two reliefs of Lucknow, and asked particularly about Peel's Battery, and the room in which the gallant sailor lay wounded; but the Dilkoosha is unsafe to enter. Thence the Prince drove to the Martinière. He descended to the vault where lie the remains of Claude Martin, a native of Lyons, "a simple soldier who died a general," and who bequeathed an enormous fortune to charitable purposes in the land where he gained it. Then he mounted to the roof, commanding a view of the country through which

VETERANS AT LUCKNOW.

Clyde advanced to the relief of the Residency. It is much changed, owing to the destruction of houses and villages. On his way back his Royal Highness drove round by the walls of Secunderabagh, and past the Kaiserbagh, through the Wingfield Park.

In the afternoon he laid the foundation-stone of the Memorial to the natives who fell in the defence of the Residency, which owes its origin to the happy idea, and its execution to the munificence, of Lord Northbrook. At 4 P.M. the 14th Regiment, the 65th Regiment, the 6th Bengal Native Infantry, the 41st Bengal Native Infantry, the G Battery, 19th Brigade, Royal Artillery, formed three sides of a square round the mound on which the Memorial is to be placed, just outside Aitken's Post, where the natives who fought in defence of the Residency were chiefly engaged. The survivors of the native defenders, who had been collected from Oudh and other parts of India, were near at hand in their old uniforms. Among those were old Ungud, the famous spy, and Canoujee Lall, the companion of Kavanagh in his daring venture, looking as young as he did in 1858. Sir George Couper, addressing the Prince, said they were assembled to honour the memory of the native officers and soldiers who fell in defence of the place, the ruins of which they saw around them. The behaviour of the Sepoys of Lucknow was simply without parallel in the history of the world. Under Clive at Arcot, Sepoys underwent great privations for their European comrades; but their fidelity was not tested like that of the men who resisted the adjurations of their brethren, comrades, and caste-men, not fifty yards off, calling them by name to desert the alien and infidel. Had they deserted, Lucknow must have fallen, and thousands of trained soldiers would have been free to march on Delhi. The loss of the Empire might not have been the result, but the difficulties of the handful who held the Ridge would have been enormously increased. Less distinguished services had been commemorated at the cost of the nation; but it was at his own expense that the illustrious nobleman who represented the Prince's Imperial mother in her Eastern dominions had directed the erection of the monument. That humble scene and scanty gathering would be historical, for this monument to Indian fidelity, bravery, and worth, would stand as a memento of the Prince's presence, and would be regarded with pride by Englishman and Asiatic alike when splendid pageants and stately ceremonials had been forgotten.

The Prince said that he had been requested by the Viceroy to lay the foundation-stone of the Memorial which he proposed to erect to the memory of the brave soldiers of the Native army who fell in defence of the Residency. He had great pleasure in giving effect to that request, and he was glad to have a share in doing honour to the memory of the gallant men who had set such a noble example of fidelity and of devotion to duty. It was not necessary for him to dwell on their deeds; history had celebrated them. Lord Northbrook, in erecting a monument to these soldiers, had done what would be gratifying to the whole army. As they passed it, on their way to or from their camps, European soldiers—officers and men—would feel they had in such men as those whose deeds were commemorated, comrades worthy to stand by their side in defence of the Empire, and Sepoys would feel proud of the honour done to the valiant soldiers whose courage and faithfulness reflected such lustre on their race and country.

The Prince then took the trowel, spread the mortar featly on the stone, which was lowered into its place, gave the magic three taps with the mallet, and declared it well and truly laid. The ceremony was over, but a happy unpremeditated thought of the Prince suggested that the veterans should be presented to him. The delight of the men when they were told of the honour in store for them was expressed in brightened eyes and trembling lips. They were led up by Major Cubitt, one of the gallant officers under whom they had served. There were some who had their grievances, and would have liked to take such a golden opportunity to say a word about their pensions. One murmured audibly, "Fourteen rupees a month, Shahzadah! It is not much, is it?" Another, led in by his sons, nearly blind from a wound, exclaimed, "Let me see him!" The Prince, understanding what he meant, told the officers to permit him to approach. The veteran, with his hand to his turban at the salute came quite close, peered into the Prince's face, drew a deep sigh, and said, "I thank Heaven I have lived to see this day and the Prince's face;" but when he felt that the Prince had taken his hand he burst into tears, and was led sobbing away. "One touch of nature makes the whole world akin." Taking all the circumstances and surroundings into consideration, the scene was most touching. When the Prince left, he had the satisfaction of knowing that he had rejoiced the hearts of the old soldiers by his kindliness. He would not allow them to be hurried by; he spoke to each one, ragged as he might be, squalid or unclean.

The generation which once thrilled with anguish or pride at the names of Lucknow, Cawnpoor, and Delhi, is growing old. The visitor may be inclined to dismiss the memories of those days as evil dreams when he hears the words of welcome and sees the rejoicings for the son of the Empress of Hindostan; but signs and tokens of that time of trial are around him, whether he will or not; they crop up in the language of the most guarded addresses; memorial churches and pillars bear witness to them; gardens and clearings, where once were multitudinous populations, tell what followed the outrages and crimes of that unhappy time.

After dinner at the Chief Commissioner's, the Prince, accompanied by Sir G. Couper, drove to the native entertainment given in the Kaiserbagh, once the Palace of the Kings of Oudh, and now the *chef lieu* of the offices of Government, a vast stretch of buildings covering more ground than the Louvre and Tuileries together. He was welcomed by the Talukdars in the Throne-room with "their modest tribute of allegiance and gratitude, which they fondly hoped he would accept as a fit emblem of the fealty of the Talukdars." This was a crown set with jewels.*

A great procession of these nobles made obeisance. Names were heard which brought back memories of troublous days—names of both friends and foes: the Raja of Bulrampoor, Bulwunt Sing, Prithee Poll Sing, and the like; now and then the title of some Sikh noble cropping up, and reminding us that land had been confiscated and that fidelity had been rewarded. After a time, Major Henderson stood forward, and expressed the pleasure of his Royal Highness at meeting so many native gentlemen, and his regret that time would not permit his making the acquaintance of each. The Prince then passed to the handsomely-canopied verandah outside the grand saloon to see the fireworks. These had quite a distinctive character; no spasmodic flights, or intermittent outbursts, of rockets, but continued activity—Catherine-wheels, fountains of fire, revolving-wheels, and balloons.

* The address is given in the Appendix.

The gateways, courts, and vast quadrangles were illuminated. A banquet was laid, to which the Prince paid a short visit to please his hosts. The natives crowded in to see the Europeans at table. Soon after 11 o'clock his Royal Highness left amid native salaams and European cheers.

January 8th.—An excursion was arranged for "pig-sticking" in a place where, although the country is rough, the sport could be enjoyed in perfection. The name of Onao will be remembered by those familiar with the history of 1857-8. The Prince rode hard; but the English horse has little chance with the boar, as the latter turns like a hare. There were many falls; some had two. The "pigs" showed great courage, fighting fiercely, charging savagely, and inflicting considerable injuries on the horses. In one run a boar, hard pressed, "kinked" (turned sharply round), and ran under the horse ridden by Lord Carington, which came down heavily. Lord Carington's left collar-bone was broken. Fortunately, Dr. Fayrer was close at hand—the bone was set—the patient carried to a shady grove, where he was put in a comfortable dooly, and thence borne to the hunting camp, where he was the object of the kindest care and attention. After luncheon "in the wild wood," the sport was continued, and many pigs were killed before the day was over.

The news that Lord Napier of Magdala had broken a collar-bone, in consequence of his horse falling with him, came to swell the list of casualties. The accident to the General-in-Chief caused great regret, and it was feared that he would not be able to take the field; but the telegrams represent him to be as ready to do so as if collar-bones were superfluous or needless articles in his human economy.

January 9th (Sunday).—The native press is very active

here, if not always very happy in its references to European ways, names, and manners; and there are several gentlemen in constant observation, note-book in hand, wherever the Prince goes. One of the native papers, at the end of a list of the suite, gave an account of "the attendants who take their meals in the mess-house of the first-class," to some of whom were attached amusing descriptions. "Bartlett Sahib, who discerns the qualities of Indian things" (Naturalist); "Jed Sahib" (Mr. Mudd), "who ascertains the qualities of vegetables" (Botanist), &c. They are hopelessly lost, however, about the Duke of Sutherland's pipers, who contribute so much to the effect of the state dinners on solemn occasions. Some of the old pensioners, Canoujee Lall, Ungud, and others, came to Camp and sat for their portraits to Mr. Hall, before the departure of the Royal party to Delhi. The Prince attended Divine service in the pretty church near Banks' Bungalow. At 4 P.M. he drove once more to the ruins of the Residency, descended at "Fayrer's House," and went over it with the former occupant and stout defender of the position, from whom the post takes its name. He visited the lines and sites of the batteries, and the cemetery, where rest, it is believed, the bones of Sir Henry Lawrence, and of the men and women and children who died during the investment. He thence proceeded by the river-side to the Iron Bridge by which Lawrence returned from Chinhut, and which Outram crossed to attack the city. After enjoying the view along the banks of the Goomtee, he went by the Victoria road to the Alumbagh, where he examined Havelock's monument. Most remarkable changes have been effected in the neighbourhood and in the city by wholesale demolition; but some things have been done which can scarcely be justified, unless it be maintained that it is our duty to keep alive bitterness of feeling, and to remind

Mahomedans that they are subject to a race which despises what they reverence, and desecrate what they consider holy. It may be quite right to convert the Kaiserbagh into Government offices and store-houses, and to appropriate the Chuttur Munzil (where, by the by, there was a very charming ball given by the club to the Prince, during his short sojourn in Lucknow), but the stolid indifference to native feeling manifested in the treatment of the Imambarra cannot be justified at all. Store away guns and ammunition there if you like; use the Mosque as church or chapel; but keep the place in decent order, root out the grass on the roofs, and remove the numbers and inscriptions in black and the hideous whitewash on the walls of the buildings. If we ever lose India, it will be from "want of sympathy."

The Prince did not visit the Native city. The Chandni Chowk, or main street, is too narrow to be traversed by carriages; elephants are too high. The Duke of Sutherland, Lord A. Paget, and several others of the suite walked through the bazaars and the principal thoroughfares. Kite-making and kite-flying flourish as of yore. The local authorities have had to prevent the ruinous results of betting on kites, skilled flyers being backed like horses in England. The people were inclined to be civil, but there is not a very cheerful air about them; and Lucknow, or what is left of it, has fallen from its high estate. There are still a few of the artificers who abounded here in the days of the Native Court—when Lucknow was like Paris under the Empire—workers in gold and silver, makers of curious jewellery, enamellers and pipe-stick embroiderers, workers of filigree ornaments, excelling in the inlaying of iron with silver, and these exhibited their wares every morning at the Commissioner's, and found many purchasers. They admitted that they liked the good old days, and that they did not admire being improved off the face of the earth. Altogether I doubt if Lucknow is quite friendly, whatever Oudh may be.

January 10th.—The Prince drove to Cantonments, to present colours to the 1st Battalion of the 8th Foot, a regiment with grand traditions, bearing a Royal Tiger as its badge, and among the names on its colours "Bhurtpore;" The ceremony, enlivened by music, and a hymn sung by the bandsmen, was watched with great interest by crowds of Europeans and Asiatics, and it was followed by a march-past. Two batteries of artillery went in an admirable manner. The 65th Regiment and the 14th Regiment did well, but they were eclipsed by the 6th Native Infantry—a splendid battalion, in handsome uniform, large turbans, Zouave trousers, and white gaiters—of which Colonel Holroyd might well be proud. The 41st (or Gwalior) Native Infantry, in blue and red turbans, gray facings with white lace, did not attract so much attention.

The Prince drove from the Chief Commissioner's house, attended by the authorities, after lunch, to continue his progress to Delhi, and was received at the Station with the usual honours. Having taken leave of Sir George and Lady Couper, to whom he expressed his sense of the pleasure his visit had afforded him, and having recognised the chief persons present, his Royal Highness proceeded on his journey. At 2.15 P.M. the special train left for Cawnpoor, and at 3.35 P.M. stopped near Onao to take up Lord Carington, who, a little pale, and with his arm in a sling, was certainly not in the least degree less cheerful. Pig-sticking has now led to three casualties, and has left its marks among the suite. Shortly before 4 P.M. we came to the hummocky grass-lands which border the Ganges. As the train swept over the stupendous bridge which spans

VISIT TO THE CAWNPOOR MEMORIAL.

the great flood, the spire of the church of Cawnpoor, and a few bungalows and trees came in sight. The Secretaries to the Government of the North-West Provinces, two of the Lieutenant-Governor's personal staff, the Major-General commanding the district, the Inspector-General of Police, the Judge, the Magistrate, Mr. Prinsep, ladies and gentlemen admitted by ticket, were on the platform of the Station, which is some distance from the city. The Prince drove first to the Memorial Church, which was still gay with Christmas emblems inside, and walked round the building, reading the inscriptions, without being "mobbed." The tombs outside the Church and the site of Wheeler's intrenchments were next examined. The clearances here have been on a vast scale also. The intrenchments have been levelled, the barracks pulled down. From Windham's *tête de pont* to the Memorial Church, nothing is left of the Station as it was in 1858, so one looks for ancient landmarks in vain. But in lieu of compound walls and bungalows there are fair parks, fine drives, and beautiful gardens, due, I believe, to Colonel Yule. The carriages were in request again, and after a drive from the site of the old Cantonments, stopped close to the gateway, which no unauthorised Native may enter. There the Prince got out, and the party walked to the building which marks the place of the fatal Well. There was deep silence as the Prince read in a low voice the touching words, "To the memory of a great company of Christian people, principally women and children, who were cruelly slaughtered here"—the name of the great criminal and the date of the massacre are cut round the base of the statue. No two persons agree as to the expression of Marochetti's Angel which stands over the Well. Is it pain?—pity?—resignation?—vengeance?—or triumph? The Prince then walked to the cemetery, hard by, examined the graves, and expressed pleasure at the neatness of the ground. He gathered some leaves from a shrub by the grave of Woodford, a gallant soldier who fell in Windham's engagement with the Gwalior Contingent, and left the scene of these sad events just ere nightfall for the residence of Mr. Prinsep, where his Royal Highness was entertained at dinner.

It was nearly 10 P.M. before the special train, with pilot engine in front, started for Delhi. The carriages were very comfortable; and if his Royal Highness has such accommodation as is due to his rank, the suite do not travel badly. With blankets and pillows, "the hardy traveller" can manage to make a night of it, and wake up in the morning refreshed by sleep.

"A HEALTH TO THE BROKEN COLLAR-BONE!"

THE REVIEW AT DELHI.

CHAPTER XI.

IMPERIAL DELHI.

The Royal Entry—The Camp—The Review—The March-past—Criticisms—Selimghur—The Kootab—Houmayoun's Tomb—The Manœuvres—Cavalry Field-day—Lahore—The Punjaub Chiefs—Return Visits—Reception at Jummoo—Games and Pastimes—The "Alexandra" Bridge at Wazirabad—Lahore—Sikhs *chez eux*—Umritsur—Agra—Procession to Camp—The Chiefs—The Taj—Excursions to Futtehpoor, Sikri and Sikundra—Visit to Gwalior—Scindia's Review—Rock of Gwalior—Return to Agra—Bhurtpoor to Jeypoor—The first Tiger—Amber City—Departure from Jeypoor.

JANUARY 11TH.—"Delhi! We shall be there in ten minutes!" It was true, indeed; we were close to the Imperial City! Delhi gained in one night's unconscious travel from Cawnpoor! There rose before us the fair frontage of Selimghur, the minarets of the Jumma Musjid. In a few minutes more the train was crossing the Jumna by the noble bridge, worthy of comparison with that over the Ganges at Cawnpoor.

The arrival at Delhi and entry of the Prince were attended with a pomp and circumstance well fitting the place and the occasion. The morning was all that could be desired; the breeze enough to dissipate the dust, and the temperature quite agreeable after the coldness of the night air. Inside the Station, Lord Napier of Magdala, the Staff of the Army, a glittering crowd of authorities, and officers of British and Native regiments of all arms, a guard of honour of 100 of the Rifle Brigade and 100 of Rattray's Sikhs. A Battery, 19th Brigade R.A., fired a salute. The escort consisted of A Battery of the A Brigade, a squadron of the 10th Hussars, and one troop of the 4th Bengal Cavalry. The procession was formed almost immediately; the Prince, in a Field-Marshal's uniform, with Sir H. Davies on the left, and Lord Napier of Magdala on the right. Major Bradford, Lord Suffield, the Duke of Sutherland, and Lord Alfred Paget, abreast; the Staff four abreast from left to right, three deep, in front; the suite in Royal carriages. Lines of soldiery, extending five miles, kept the route to the camp. From the Railway Station to Lothian road, the 11th Bengal Lancers, 7th Bengal Cavalry, 15th Hussars and 15th Bengal Cavalry. The esplanade was lined by C Battery, 19th Brigade; A Battery, 8th Brigade; B Battery, 8th Brigade; and 6th Bengal Cavalry; in front of the Jumma Musjid were the 5th Regiment and the 28th Punjaubees. As the Prince came in sight, the immense multitude, which had been sitting on the flight of steps leading to the grand gateway of the Temple, rose as by one accord. The Chandni Chowk was lined by the 31st Punjaubees, the 62nd Foot, the 5th Foot and the 26th Punjaubees, the 6th Foot, the 8th Foot and the 85th Foot, the 32nd Punjaubees, the 12th Foot, the 15th Sikhs and the 45th Sikhs (Rattray's). Then outside the city the 11th Hussars, 6th Bengal Cavalry, Central India Horse, 39th Foot and 51st Foot, 8th Native Infantry, and three batteries Royal Artillery. On the famous Ridge were six "green" regiments in line; the 1st Punjaubees, the 60th Rifles.

The Prince did not forget to notice either the stone monument, or the regiments which had actually fought upon the very ground they occupied before him—the living witnesses of the deeds by which the power of the Empire he represented was established. The 2nd Ghoorkas, on the right of the 60th Rifles, were opposite Hindoo Rao's house, which they held during the siege. The Prince stopped in front of the 2nd Ghoorkas and expressed his pleasure at seeing them in such an appropriate place. The procession next passed, the 3rd Ghoorkas and 4th Ghoorkas. Then the Sappers and Miners, a Mountain Battery, 33rd Native Infantry, 11th Native Infantry and the 73rd Foot. The road from the Ridge was lined by the 10th Bengal Lancers, the 4th Bengal Cavalry, two Batteries, and the 10th Hussars.

The Royal Camp was of grand proportions and beautifully ordered. The main street was formed by tents of great size, shrubs and flowering plants lining the edges of the avenue from end to end—the Royal marquees and enclosure at the extremity—in front, a parterre and a towering flagstaff; lamps before each tent; a sward as level, if not as green, as an English cricket-ground. The 10th Hussars and the Rifle Brigade, 4th Battalion, are the regiments nearest to the Royal Camp, which is a very proper arrangement, as the Prince is Colonel of both regiments.

After a time, the Municipality of Delhi, all Native gentlemen, were introduced to present their address. They said that they esteemed it a privilege to be permitted to give expression to their feelings of profound loyalty and devotion to the person and rule of their gracious Queen, and, on behalf of the whole community, of whatever race or creed, offered to his Royal Highness a hearty welcome to their ancient city. Since the Viceroy announced the intended visit, they had been anxiously looking forward to the auspicious event. Delhi, though small when compared with great capitals, such as Calcutta, Madras, and Bombay, could claim attention for its antiquities and historic interest. "For more than 1000 years it has been the seat of dynasties, which have risen, flourished, and passed away, leaving traces of splendour in the palace and the tomb, in mosque and temple, minaret and tower. Although no longer the seat of empire, it is flourishing. Three railways converge to it, developing trade and industry. It is still the home of the language of Hindostan and the seat of learning." It is their earnest wish that his Royal Highness may retain pleasing recollections of his visit, and that the remainder of his tour may be as full of interest as the commencement has been. The Prince thanked them for their welcome, and said he had looked forward with pleasure to his visit to their ancient capital, abounding in the earliest monuments of Indian magnificence and recollections of the greatest historical interest. The natural position of the city in the centre of Hindostan, where so many great lines of railway converge, must ever render Delhi one of the most important points in our Indian possessions. He was glad to meet them there, and much gratified in being able to convey to the Queen his assurance of the appearance of reviving prosperity in a city so famous and beautiful.

To the Englishman, Delhi represents merely the centre of a military system, which from time to time finds here its point of concentration. It is almost forgotten that it was but a short time ago the seat of power of an Empire, the capital of a dynasty retaining Imperial honours and privileges, and inflicting upon those who guarded both, such slights as now seem incredible. To us the city has no historical worth except that its name is hallowed by the exploits and by the extraordinary tenacity and efforts of the army "which held on to it," by the advice of Sir John

Lawrence, "like bulldogs," until the hour of hard-won triumph arrived, and the wretched descendant of the Great Mogul was carried off to a miserable captivity. But the Mahomedan and the Hindoo, whose memories are refreshed by ancient legends, and who love to dwell on the history of their past glory, having, in good sooth, no records of the present wherewith to be content, clothe the ruins of tombs and temples with an interest to which we are completely strangers. They have the heritage of the past divided between them in the enduring traditions of the great wrongs they wrought upon each other.

A Levee, which was attended by many hundreds of officers of all grades and of civilians, followed the presentation of the address, at the close of which the Native officers were presented.

Lord Napier of Magdala entertained the Prince at his own camp; but ample as was his mess-tent, there was not sufficient room for all the officers who might have expected to meet his Royal Highness. Some of the suite joined the staff at table in the magnificent Head-quarters' mess-tent. Others dined with friends in the ever-hospitable camp.

January 12th.—This was the day of the grand Review, to which so many soldiers, civilians, and fair ladies were looking with the greatest anxiety; and although the force, in comparison with that which one sees on any *Schauplatz* of the great military States in Europe was insignificant, it was for India a very respectable assemblage of all arms, the cavalry and artillery especially being excellent.*

The appearance of the force was very fine. The brigades of infantry, compact and glittering, were in the front line, the regiments in double companies quarter-

* For General Orders and list of Regiments see Appendix.

columns, in marching-past order, at thirty paces' interval. The cavalry regiments in quarter-distance column at thirty paces' interval in the second line; each brigade in rear of the centre of the division of infantry to which it was attached. The artillery at full intervals, with one line of waggons in rear, formed the third line. The sappers and miners, pontoon, and field telegraph train, formed the fourth line, with sappers on the right. The divisional generals were seventy-five paces in front of the centres of the divisions, and brigadiers fifty paces in front of brigades.

The Prince, who wore the uniform of a Field-Marshal, drove a couple of miles to the place where the horses were waiting under the charge of Mr. Prince. Cold as the night had been, and more than bracing as the morning air was, the sun waxed hot by noon, and the clouds of dust which arose from the plain were blinding. On getting out of the carriage, the Prince mounted and rode off, and there was a general "scurry" to follow. The horses were fresh, and those that were led became more frisky than ever at the sight of their companions going off full tilt. Before I was well in the saddle, my Arab reared, and then gave a buck-jump. He followed that up by another, which was unpleasant. "Give him his head, Sir!" cried Mr. Prince. I did so, but quite in a different way from that which my adviser meant, for in a moment I was on the ground, with an unpleasant consciousness of not being sure that I had not broken some bones. I was enabled to mount another horse; but I confess that, what with the effect of the shake, the heat of the sun and the weight of a helmet, I had but a very dim appreciation of the march-past.

As the Prince appeared on the ground, the Royal Standard was hoisted, and a Royal salute given along the line; the great crowd uttered a shout of welcome, and the fluttering of white kerchiefs from the dense line of carriages seemed like a ripple of surf against the background of the dark multitude. The Prince rode across to the right of the first line, and down the front, receiving the usual honours, bands playing, colours lowered, and so on, passing from right to left and left to right, till the inspection was complete. That was a pretty sight, scarcely marred by the dust that would rise to obscure for a moment the brightness of the cavalcade in which might be recognised the plumed pickel-haubes of Count Seckendorff and two or three Germans, the simple uniform of three American officers, the aigrettes of the Nepalese and the jewelled turbans of Native Chiefs, amid the uniforms of the officers of all branches of the two armies of the Crown in India. When his Royal Highness had taken up his place near the flagstaff in front of the Royal enclosure, the march-past commenced. His Royal Highness was in front, so that he could be seen by all; Lord Napier of Magdala, his arm in a sling, was on his left; Scindia was at a little distance on his right, somewhat in the rear with two or three chiefs. The Duke of Sutherland, Lord Keane (*en bourgeois*), Colonel Dillon, Mr. Knollys, &c., were on horseback in the Royal enclosure, but the military members and officers of yeomanry or militia of the suite were massed at the other side nearly opposite the saluting point. When the signal was given, the first line began to move, and for an hour and a half the stream of horse, foot, and guns flowed before us; and yet it would not have more than filled the muster-roll of a single foreign *corps d'armée*. As an officer said to me, "That army is able to march from the Himalayas to Comorin—from Madras to Bombay—but on one condition: the natives must feed it, and be ready to assist in the transport." There is no use attempting to discriminate and say what regiments appeared good and what bad; but it certainly did strike those accustomed to European armies, that the proportion of British officers to Native regiments was perilously small. Without at all detracting from the merit and proved excellence of Native troops under certain conditions, one could not help feeling that it was dangerous at the very moment when we are crying out against the inadequate number of officers available for duty in British regiments at home, to trust Native troops so very much to their own officers. However, Lord Napier is not only content, but he is powerfully supported on the point by the arguments and experience of General Norman. As to the Native army generally, without disrespect, and in fact with something like admiration, one may say to it, with the bully in the play, who, entering a tavern, put his sword upon the table: "Lie there, good blade! God grant that I may have no need of thee!" It was interesting to observe that the Queen's officers, as one may call them for the sake of distinction, did not speak of the appearance of the Native regiments at all, while the Indian officers had no eyes but for their own corps. The officers who belonged to the old irregular cavalry, notably the Punjaubees, are enthusiasts about the qualities of their men and the perfection of their organization, whilst the Queen's officers hold them in very poor estimation. Talking with a colonel of a crack English cavalry regiment, I was astonished to be told, in reply to a remark, "that the natives might surely be trusted on outpost duty," that they were the very worst men for that special duty he had ever seen; that they never knew how to post sentries, vedettes, pickets, and grand guards, and that in case of active service before an enemy he would never lie down to sleep if he thought the outpost service were confided to Native cavalry!

With some recollection of what happened down in the Valley of Baidar on a certain week in October, I could not help expressing a hope to myself that things were altered for the better in our own army since that time. The army of India costs as much as the British army, each in round numbers absorbing 15,000,000*l.* per annum, and certainly for 30,000,000*l.* sterling there ought to be, for a time of need, a force upon which the Empire can rely with the utmost confidence.

When the march-past was over, there was an advance of the whole force and a Royal salute, which had a very fine effect, and then the various arms marched off towards their camps. The great plain presented a most animated appearance. As to the camps spread out for miles, one thinks, when he sees them, and the towering elephants and hundreds of camels, the herds of sheep and goats, and multitudes of people, of a nation on the tramp—some great migration of a warrior horde. There is a method in all this apparent disarray; the tents are pitched with the precision which long practice in India gives. There are great civilian camps, native camps and bazaar camps; and the excellent plans issued by the Quartermaster-General's Department enable a stranger to find any corps he wants. These have their distinguishing colours and streamers, and the general effect as seen from an eminence like the Ridge is marvellously fine.

Lord Napier and many generals and officers dined with his Royal Highness; and the roll-call of the guests would have sounded well on the eve of any battle, albeit there were none who had fought at Solferino, Königgrätz, Gravelotte, or Sedan. Covers were laid for eighty. It was a right regal banquet; but one could not help thinking that there was something nomadic in the idea of a high festival of the kind in a tent—a tacit confession that "we've no abiding dwelling here"—that our mansion is like the house kept by the strong man armed. And then there came a ball in Selimghur. The manner in which this famous palace was arranged reflected credit upon the committee for the ball; but there were transformations not in the best taste, and adaptations which could scarcely have been grateful to those who had sympathy with ancient recollections. Selimghur has certainly not been improved by British occupancy. In the noble square stand red-brick barracks of amazing ugliness; but it has escaped the fate of the Imambarra at Lucknow, certainly one of the finest halls in the world, which was built as a canopy to the tomb of a King of Oudh, our friend and ally. All the world has heard of the Dewan Khass, wherein stood the "Peacock Throne." "If there is a Paradise on earth it is this! it is this! it is this!" But ideas of Paradise cannot be altogether realised in a pavilion filled with men in uniforms and evening dress, women in ball dresses, military bands playing Offenbach and Strauss, and, above all, a ceiling of a distressing colour. Nevertheless, when the dancing was at its height, and the dancers were seen whirling in the arched spaces, between rows of snowy columns, the scene presented by the marble "halls of dazzling light" was very brilliant. If the enjoyment of a succession of dances with charming partners, continued hour after hour, and a grand State supper could make men happy, there is no doubt the guests were in the most contented frame of mind when they were summoned to their camps and quarters to prepare, with the morning sun, for the manœuvres, for which the two leaders of the contending hosts had already set out.

January 13th.—Whilst the force was preparing for the grand operations before Delhi to-morrow and next day, an excursion of a very interesting character was made to-day to the Kootab Minar, on the way to which the Prince visited the beautiful tomb of Suftur Jung. The road lies through a country which presents the strangest aspect in the world. Delhi, in the words of Cunningham, is surrounded by ruins "which extend from the south end of the present city to Toogluckabad, ten miles; the breadth at the north is three miles, that at the south, four; Kootab to Toogluckabad, six miles; the whole area being not less than forty-five square miles, covered with ruins." And who founded the cities and built the palaces and made the strong places which are now but dust, rubbish and heaps of brick? The leaders of races who believed, each in his time, that his dominion would endure, just as we believe that ours must last for ever, or for as long as we wish. I was told that a recent English visitor, of some political eminence, was roused almost to fury by the sight of the magnificent monuments, because *he* did not know anything about the people to whose memories they were erected, and that he inveighed against the departed in that they were more honoured in their tombs than European worthies! The Mahomedan invasion, which established Shab-ood-Deen in power nearly 100 years after William had conquered England, found here a civilisation to which our ancestors had then no pretensions. An abstract of English history, intended for Native schools, came into my hands the other day, and I could not help thinking of the impression which must be produced on the reader by a summary of our wars civil and foreign, changes of dynasty, and violent deaths of kings. Kutb-ood-Deen, Nasir-ood-Deen, Toogluck, Feroze Shah, Baber, Shir Shah, Selim, Akhbar, Arungzebe—these are names not writ in water; to many millions they mean far more than Alfred, Richard Cœur de Lion, Edward the Black Prince, or Henry V. do to us, and yet our millions know nothing of them whatever.

At the Kootab there was a small camp pitched for the occasion. There was a military band, and lunch was laid in a large marquee. Many ladies were invited from Delhi. The Prince mounted to the summit of the Kootab, said to be the highest pillar in the world (it measures 238 feet in height), and viewed the wide-spread ruins of forts, tombs, mosques, and cities. He inspected the famous Iron Pillar, in which the natives still have a robust faith, in spite of practical demonstrations of the emptiness of it, and visited the well of Mehrowlie, where he was amused by the divers, who leaped into a pool eighty feet below them. Each man, before he jumped, threw a pebble to mark the spot, covered with green scum, which he intended to strike. The Prince, on his way back to the camp, stopped at Houmayoun's Tomb, where the Delhi princes surrendered to Hodson and met their death. This mausoleum struck me as one of the finest monumental buildings I had ever seen, when I visited it in 1858. Sombre, massive, vast, it is doubtless one of the grandest piles of the kind in the world; the effect of the red sandstone, relieved by the snow-white marble, the noble terraces, exquisite filigree windows, lofty walls, 290 yards long, is scarcely to be surpassed ; but it is falling somewhat into decay. In the great cemetery, around the magnificent mausoleum of Nizam-ood-Deen, which lies on the other side of the road to Delhi, a little nearer to the Kootab, are several fine tombs. Every traveller here has paid a tribute to the memory of the admirable Jehanara Begum, on whose tomb is inscribed the epitaph (translated):

> "Let no rich canopy cover my grave!"
> "This grass is the best covering for the poor in spirit!"
> "The humble, transitory, Jehanara—the disciple of the Holy Men of Cheest."
> "The daughter of the Emperor Shah Jehan."

However, for all her humble prayer, the lady reposes in a fine sarcophagus, which is surrounded by a screen of marble. General Sleeman mistook "Cheest" for a holier name, and claimed Jehanara as a Christian.

Delhi was illuminated, and the streets were crowded, as it was announced that his Royal Highness would drive through the principal thoroughfares to see the illuminations; but it was just as well that he did not pass through the city, for there are still budmashes whom all the arts of Major Bradford's agents could not inveigle out of their dens. On his return to Headquarters, the Prince, dressed in regimental uniform, dined with the officers of the Rifle Brigade, of which he is Colonel.

January 14th.—The force under Major-General the Hon. A. Hardinge—supposed to be advancing from the Punjaub to seize on the Ridge, and to hold it until an army, with which it was obliged to keep open its communications by Kurnaul, could come up—consisting of seven regiments of cavalry (Major-General Watson), divided into two brigades, under Colonels Hankin and Kennedy; thirteen battalions of infantry, under General Michell; Engineers, Pontoon train, and thirty-six guns, was in position about twenty-one miles north of Delhi, with its left on the Jumna and its right on Juteree, near the old Imperial road, to-day. A force of two brigades of cavalry, of three regiments each, under Miller and Annesley, and of eleven battalions of infantry, with four companies of Sappers and thirty-seven guns, including one mountain and one heavy battery, under Lieut.-General Sir Charles Reid, moved out to meet the attack.

Expecting to see a collision between Hardinge and Reid, the Prince drove in the afternoon to Alipoor, where horses were in waiting, mounted, and rode across the country. Operations commenced by Hardinge making a dash at a bridge on the Kurnaul road. Mounting eighty infantry on battery carriages and limbers, he opened fire on two guns, posted to defend the cross cut, which were covered by a regiment of cavalry. It may be doubted whether the cavalry could not have crossed the canal, taken the guns, and made short work of eighty isolated Riflemen. Hardinge seized the bridge, but there was no fighting. Reid did not intend to fight in the open. He scarcely made a show of defending the ground north of the canal. He was determined to stick to the Ridge whereon he had gained well-deserved honour in real warfare, so he intrenched himself, and left all the villages in front to Hardinge. It was no doubt a well-devised move, but it was not exciting; Reid might have obliged the world with a cavalry fight. However, he did not do so, and scarcely a shot was fired from the time of the arrival of the Prince till 3 P.M., when the operations, according to orders, terminated.

January 15th.—All were up and stirring to be on the ground in time, and soon after 10 A.M. the Prince and his suite were galloping over the plain towards the Jumna. Watson obtained leave from Hardinge to take his cavalry to his left and engage Miller's force. The affair, however, was not fortunate. There were forty-pounders on the flank of Watson's horse, which were also exposed to field batteries as they advanced in column. The umpires put several squadrons out of action. Cavalry, stopped by imperious umpires with positive assurance that certain puffs of smoke in the remote distance had put man and horse to rout, were by no means satisfied, for the results of actual practice near Delhi a short time previously tended to show that though where there was smoke there was fire, it by no means followed that where there was fire there was death. Meanwhile Hardinge reached the junction of the two roads with the canal. Stewart, to whom Hardinge gave over the command of the infantry, considered he might yet establish himself on the Ridge. Hardinge, however, saw the defenders were in impregnable positions in his front. He was checkmated, and acknowledged it.

Soon after 1 o'clock there was abrupt cessation of firing. Hardinge might have lost half his army by umpires'

THE SHAM FIGHT AT DELHI—PERILOUS POSITION OF SOME OF THE SUITE.

decisions without losing any credit with the general body of spectators, but he had demonstrated remarkably the daring of those who seized on the Ridge in 1857, and the impotence of those who lost such a position. There was but little knowledge of the value of the troops to be gained from what we saw, but to many the operations were of intense interest.

It is probable most of the spectators were glad that the fighting ended so soon—the troops engaged certainly were so, for the heat was not by any means agreeable. To the great *foule* the paramount attraction was the Prince's presence. Indeed, the position of his Royal Highness might be ascertained, not so much by the escort and staff around his person as by the crowd in eager chase, regardless of sun and dust, whose example was less impetuously followed by their cavaliers. Among one of the incidents on the way back to camp was the surprise of a party on an elephant, which suddenly became very restive and unruly. This was accounted for by the delivery of a brisk fire of musketry from a party of native infantry in dust-coloured (kharkee) uniforms, who, lying down close at hand, had not been seen till they actually began to fire.

January 16*th* (*Sunday*).—At night the cold was enough to cause the fires in the tents to be very welcome. Thermometer 34° at 6 A.M. Waking before daybreak, I walked out of the bedroom division, into the sitting-room, of my tent to light a candle. The fire was burning in the hearth, and I saw three figures, draped in white, seated motionless before it ; their backs were turned towards me. I paused to consider what they might be ; but ere the demand, in Hindostanee, "Who are you ?" ended, the three forms arose, towering as it seemed to a tremendous height, and vanished. They were three of the servants, who usually slept under the eaves and in the space between the outer and inner walls of the tent, and who, pinched by cold, thought they might creep in and sleep by the fire. One of these, Jewanjee, has attached himself in a most artful and surreptitious way to my establishment. I have seen him driven forth with vehemence, not to say violence, on several occasions ; but somehow or other he follows the camp from place to place, and will end, I am certain, by being placed on the fixed strength. There was rest in the camp all day. Divine service at headquarters.

Orders given for the departure of the party for Lahore, the baggage to be ready early to-morrow.

January 17th.—There is now an end of the Delhi pageant; in a day or two the busy city of canvas will have disappeared like a dream of the night, or a scene in a pantomime—the canvas houses will be packed up with their skeleton poles in commissariat stores; the grand tents of the Prince will be on their way to Calcutta; the regiments with their followers will be marching back to their stations; the civilians and their families and friends journeying to their scenes of labour; and all that will remain will be the eternal earth, the monumental Ridge, the wide-spread plains, the factor of *x* value, called the people, and many memories. This gathering has naturally enough given an impetus to the discussion on a subject of the most vital importance, the actual condition of the Indian army. I am sorry to perceive, however, that "there is too much heat to permit the truth to coagulate," as one of the American officers remarked. As the Prince desired to see the division under Major-General Watson work in the open, a field-day for cavalry was ordered this fore-noon. Three brigades, each three regiments strong, except the 4th, which had only two, were drawn up on the plain between the Kurnaul road and the Jumna. I cannot describe the movements, but it may be said the force was handled beautifully. When the brigades changed front to the left and formed in four lines for action, it was one of the prettiest sights imaginable. The flanks of the lines were carefully covered, in advance or retreat, and every disposition was made for mutual support. Successive charges of regiments in squadron were delivered, the front line retiring through the intervals, sustained by the next. A dash at the enemy's guns in extended order, made under cover of a dismounted force, was not so happy, as man and horse closed too much together, owing to inveterate habit, when the moment came to charge. As soon as the movements were over, his Royal Highness attended an amusing exhibition of soldiers' games and sports, tent-pegging, feats of arms, riding and polo playing.

The pleasant time here has not been without troubles. Captain Glyn is confined to his tent by an attack of dysentery. Bubbur Jung is so seriously ill as to give rise to anxiety among his people, who naturally consider him to be about the most important person in camp, and both must remain here after we have left.

The special train to Lahore left the Delhi Station before midnight. The Prince was escorted by a great body of officers, headed by Lord Napier of Magdala, with whom he had dined. The roadway was illuminated, and a pretty fashion in vogue at the military festivals here, of having soldiers, each with a torch in his hand, to mark the lines of camps, was followed all the way. The great *personnel*—suite, officers attached, servants and attendant natives—was safely stowed away, and the train moved off from the metropolis of the old Moguls out in to the night, amid tremendous cheers, on its way to the capital of the short-lived dynasty of the Sikh. The arrangements of Major-General Browne were complete. It was cold enough for all our rugs and wrappers, but when he comes, "Sleep is lord of all," and the clatter of the iron horse over many a famous battle-field did not disturb the weary travellers.

January 18th.—Lahore looked its best in the bright light of early morning as the special train slid up to the red cloth where the Governor of the Punjaub and the Military and Civil Staff of the Province, with a very large assemblage of Europeans, were waiting on the platform of the Railway Station which, ornamented with turrets and

A WAR-DANCE AT DELHI.

battlements, looks as though it aimed at being mistaken for a fortification. The Prince's cortege made a sweep round the town, passing the encampments of the Rajas of the Punjaub. Before each encampment floated the banner of the Raja to whom it belonged. In front stood in line, elephants, led horses in gold and silver saddle-cloths and jewelled caparisons; the Chief's armed retainers, regular and irregular, lining the roadway. The roll of drums, blare of trumpets, and clang and outburst of strange instruments saluted the Prince. Lance and sword, morion and cuirass, flashed, and all was light and beautiful. The very spirit of chivalry hovered over these martial faces and noble forms. Such might have been, but for that villainous saltpetre and those dastard firearms, a triumphant procession of Saladin or of Timour himself. The combination of colours forced the beholder to close his eyes for a moment and ask if it were a dream. Fenced in by this extraordinary pageantry, stood or squatted, silent, motionless, what some time hence will be designated by Native reformers "the majesty of the people." It was also on house-tops and on walls, and seemed much taken with the aspect of its Princely brother, whom it was able to recognise by reason of the gold umbrella carried over his head in the Governor's carriage. The flat roofs and carved lattices give the city a strong resemblance to Cairo before the improvements nearly demolished the Orientalism of the most Oriental of cities. There is, however, an Orientalism which is not altogether Indian in the aspect of the town and people—a mixture of the Punjaub and Krim Tartary, Jewish faces and Tartar dwellings.

There was so much to admire, that the way to Government House seemed very short—but it is four miles. Being an eminently practical people, we have made the tomb of a cousin of Akhbar into a residence for the Lieutenant-Governor, but it is said to have been occupied by a Sikh General before Sir J. Lawrence obtained possession. The living found it very comfortable. There was a guard of honour of the 92nd Highlanders, 100 strong, picked men, with pipers and colours, outside. As soon as the Prince had been introduced to the Lieutenant-Governor's family and Staff, and had changed his uniform, it was time to receive the address of the Municipality. They were ushered upstairs to the drawing-room, where the Prince stood in the midst of his Staff, and were presented by Sir H. Davies. The address was read by a Native gentleman.* It would have astonished members of an English Town Council to have seen their brethren of Lahore, in turbans of the finest gold-tissue, brocaded gowns and robes, coils of emeralds, rubies, and pearls, finer than any Lord Mayor's chain, round their necks.

A levee of European officers, officials, and private persons followed. When that stream ran out, another of a different character, far more sparkling and bright if somewhat more erratic, was turned on—a levee of the Native Chiefs.

The reception of these gentlemen was interesting, because they were a new type of men, and, moreover, exceedingly picturesque and brilliant. First came the Raja of Nabha, a Jat Sikh, escorted by cavalry, honoured with a salute of eleven guns, a guard of honour, and a band to play for him. He was met, on alighting from his carriage, by one of the Prince's aides-de-camp, and at the foot of the staircase by Major Sartorius, who conducted him up the stairs, all by "programme." He takes a great interest in his troops, on whose air the Prince complimented him,

* See Appendix.

to the Raja's evident pleasure. Next came the Raja of Kupurthulla, whom many remember at Lord Clyde's camp in Oudh towards the close of the great rebellion, full of vigour, fond of sporting, and never better pleased than when he was entertaining officers at a grand shikar, but now so broken that he is scarcely able to take part in conversation, although he speaks English with fluency. At 1.30 P.M. the Raja of Mundee appeared, an eleven-gun Chief from the Hills, where he rules a State, at one time much disturbed by questions of succession, till one John Lawrence turned his eye upon them. The result was that there wandered in indigent dignity about Simla an excellent gentleman, Meean Ruttun Sing, who must be recollected by visitors there in 1858, and above all by Lord William Hay, to whom he rendered efficient service in suppressing incipient trouble. Poor man! Some 300*l.* a year represented the whole of his allowance. He wrote a letter from Benares, years ago, the last I heard of him, with an address, which, translated, read—"From the street of the Beggarman living over the gutter." The present Chief is a Sanscrit scholar, and encourages the students and professors of that language.

The Raja of Faridkot, eleven guns, received at 1.30 P.M. The Raja of Chamba (eleven-gun man) put down for 1.28 P.M. The first is a Sikh, with a very nice little troop of soldiers. The second, a lad who takes great interest in affairs, came down to Delhi last year to assist at the Durbar. At 1.35 P.M. the Raja of Sukkut (eleven guns), a Rajpoot of the purest descent, Chief of a small State near Simla. At 1.50 P.M. the Sirdar of Kalsia; at 1.52 P.M. the Nawab of Pataudi; at 1.54 P.M. the Nawab of Loharu; at 1.56 P.M. the Nawab of Dujana; at 1.58 P.M. the Raja Shamshar Sing of Golar, a Hill Rajpoot, one of the best sportsmen in the Punjaub; none of these latter entitled to guns, the first only being served to uttur and pân by the Prince, the rest receiving it from one of the officers of his suite, and being conducted no further on their way than the foot of the staircase.

Later in the day the Prince went to see the Gaol, a model establishment abounding in ruffians. Among the latter must be reckoned a brace of Thugs, one of whom, aged 70, made the pleasant statement that he had murdered more than 250 people; the other, who looked as if he might have equalled his great master if time had permitted it, said that he could only account for 35. The older gentleman, by way of *experimentum in corpore nobili*, gave, by order, Dr. Fayrer's wrist a twist, the effect of which the latter felt next day.

The Prince next drove to the Citadel, and saw the sun setting over the broad plains and placid river from the tower from which the Lion of Lahore was wont to watch its rise. In the Armoury the Prince's attention was attracted by tiny cannon mounted on a revolving frame, which he was told belonged to Dhuleep Sing when he was a little boy, unconscious of the coming of the calm joys of Kelvedon and of the glory of the grandest bags of the season. At the Prince's request the toy was sent down to Bombay to be conveyed to England.

January 19th.—Although the Sikh and Hill Chiefs were in their persons, tents, equipages, and followings, perhaps the most picturesque persons of the various ruling classes summoned to pay their respects to the Prince, I daresay that an account of potentates of such limited political influence would not be read with much interest; in fact, I fear there have been too many details of the sort. But what can one do? There the Chiefs are, and for each there is a programme as strict as if he were King or Kaiser. Kalsīa, Sukkut, Chumba, Faridkot, Mundee,

Kuppurtulla, Nabha, Bahawalpur—names,—mere names! yet the rulers of these little States exercise more moral control over the people than all our magistrates, except in so far as it is our Government which is paramount to their rulers. Their tents; their henchmen; their arrays of horse and foot; their elephants, camels, musicians, these were of different degrees of magnificence; but the ensemble was always striking, and their presents offered in diversity, if not value, a contrast to the uniformity of medals, arms, whips, books, &c., bestowed on them. In their Durbar tents there were fine chairs beneath canopies of cloth of gold, upheld by silver poles, and lamps and chandeliers, and gaudy-coloured prints; the carpets were magnificent specimens of Cashmere and Persian work. When one thought of the money it must have cost to have got ready all that splendour, and to have carried it so far—from Mundee, for instance—and of the outlay on that mass of elephants, camels, and horsemen, and heard that the Chief was "hard up" before he came, it became subject for consideration whether the attendance would not be a cause of embarrassment hereafter. The absence of a Chief, however, would have been an affront, as with each "noblesse oblige." As their encampments formed two sides of a triangle, at the base of which was the Mausoleum of Runjeet Sing, they might, if philosophically minded, have set off their perfect security, and their immunity from the chance of being devoured by some Lion of Lahore, against the expenditure on this peaceful display. The return visits to Chiefs, and the opening of the Soldiers' Industrial Exhibition at Meean Meer, occupied the forenoon. By order of Sir G. Pollock, an immense quantity of Turcoman, Affghan, and Persian carpets, furs, pushmeena, puttoo, and various fabrics, was brought down for inspection to headquarters. The Prince bought many articles, others following his example, till none were left, and the merchants went away the second day rejoicing. There were also Hill men, with the finest falcons I ever saw, hunting-eagles, short-winged hawks, shaggy Thibetan mastiffs, rugged deer-hounds, to tempt purchasers, who had, however, to contemplate the possibility of their conveying the bargains on board ship without buying the natives in attendance. Among the novelties of Lahore must not be forgotten a *char-à-banc*, drawn by six dromedaries. How they were driven it is beyond me to say, but I know the leaders had a knack of turning round now and then to see what those who were behind were about.

Lahore has not increased in magnitude or in prosperity since it came under our rule; but it was decaying before Runjeet Sing gave it importance as the seat of his newly-established empire. Certainly if Lalla Rookh were to visit it now she could see nothing at all like what met her eye in the poet's dream, where "mausoleum and shrines, magnificent and numberless, affected her heart and imagination, and where death appeared to share equal honours with heaven." The engines which scattered showers of confectionery among the people in the public squares are replaced by the locomotive scattering hot ashes and pouring out steam at the station; the chariot of the artisan, adorned with tinsel and flying streamers to exhibit the badges of his trade, is now represented by a bullock-hackery. As to the great antiquity claimed for the city, some doubts are entertained by the writer of the capital little guide-book prepared for the Prince's visit. But the city, in his opinion, must have been founded between the first and seventh centuries of the Christian era. It was not till the reign of Akhbar that it attained its highest position as the centre of municipal activity. Jehangeer was fond of it as a residence, and fixed his Court here in 1622. He was, however, at Ajmere when he received Sir Thomas Rowe, an emissary from King James I.

In the evening there was a fete in the Shalimar Gardens: it was very cold; but the illuminations of the gardens were exquisite—long, broad ribands of lamps illuminating lakes, cascades, and islands, whereon stood white marble kiosks and temples—and the entertainment gave great satisfaction. I wish there had been more time to dwell on the buildings and doings here, for they were of great interest.

January 20th.—Last night it was bitterly cold. Dr. Fayrer says that it was 29° in his tent. My glass went down below freezing-point. There was a "scuffle" to get off, orders were given to start at 8 A.M., and the servants, European and Native, were torpid A guard of honour of the 92nd, drawn up with their band and colours in front of the Lieutenant-Governor's house, looked very cold indeed, with blue noses and knees; and the officers went up and down stamping their feet. I can quite understand, under the circumstances, the anxiety which has been expressed that the Prince might have some experience of the hot weather before he leaves. Indeed, if many of our friends had their way, they would use gentle violence to keep the Royal traveller in the Mofussil till "the rains" set in. Lord Aylesford, Lord Suffield, and Lord Carington remain at Lahore, owing to indisposition in the case of the two former, and in that of the latter to the accident from which he is fast recovering. There is a narrow-gauge line from Lahore to Wazirabad (twenty-six miles), of which the most that can be said is that it is better than no rail at all. The special train managed to reach Wazirabad in little more than two hours. Thence there is an excellent road, along which the party drove at a rapid pace. The country is a dead level, with few trees and a scanty population, and the steeple of Sealkote Church is seen far off, rising like a light-house out of the sea. It is scarcely possible to believe that Sealkote is one of the very hottest stations in India, for there is a delusive appearance of coolness given to it by the Himalayan ranges, crowned with snow, in the distance, and by the broad roads, shaded with overarching trees, which lead to the Cantonments. The Prince lunched with the 9th Lancers, and then continued the journey to Jummoo, twenty-seven miles from Wazirabad. On the way there is little to notice except the increasing dignity of the mountain chain in front. A splendid species of *Euphorbia* was common, and small forests of acacia and of the *Butea frondosa* dotted the plains along the roadside. It was 4 P.M. when the Prince, whose carriage was escorted by a troop of the 9th Lancers, entered the state of the Maharaja of Cashmere. An arch was thrown across the road; at the other side a deputation of Chiefs was waiting to receive the Prince. Seven miles from Jummoo, then quite visible on a low-lying spur of the Snowy Range—it is something like Aosta or Stirling as seen from the south—the Maharaja himself appeared with his principal Sirdars and a magnificent sowaree, and welcomed the Prince to his dominions. The cortege went at a rapid rate, but it was dusk before we reached the Towee. On the near bank there was a vast number of elephants. The carriages, halted at the top of a ridge, and we could look down on the broad river, covered with boats pulled by rowers in scarlet and yellow liveries, and dotted with men floating on skins, below us. On the other side, up the steep ascent to the ancient walls and the city gate, were lines of cavalry in armour, and of infantry. The old hill fort on the opposite side of the gorge was thundering out a salute, and astonishing

Himalayan wolves and jackals. When the Prince, mounted on an elephant with the Maharaja, led the procession across the river, joyous cries, ringing of bells, firing of guns and the clang of music, made an indescribable tumult. The road from the river-side up to the city, winding for two miles through roads and streets lighted up brightly, lined with the Maharaja's army, and filled with Hill people, Cashmerees, Lamas or priests from Leh and Ladak, Afghans, Sikhs, &c., presented the most original types and spectacle. On the summit of the ridge above Jummoo was a huge building—carpeted, and hung with shawls, pictures, and mirrors—built expressly for the reception at an enormous cost; it was only roofed a few hours ago. This pile was so frail withal, that the walls shook when the salutes were fired; and it was so damp, that his Royal Highness preferred the tents erected on the elevated plateau, as a *pis-aller* close at hand, between the Palace and the city.

It was dark by the time the Prince arrived at the Palace. I am not quite sure whether the presence of the detachment and band of the 9th Lancers was properly appreciated by the natives. Just as the dreadful noises produced by the instruments in which the Cashmerees rejoice cause Europeans great agony of ear, so did the former affect or really feel pain at the martial airs which the excellent band of the Lancers was performing. As the Prince's elephant was approaching the piazza in front of the Palace, the band, which had been in front, wheeled round and commenced to play "God save the Queen;" but the sight of the great beast was too much for the horses, which dispersed, capering and plunging, in spite of their riders, and sending the air to the winds. After the usual Durbar and ceremonies, the Prince was conducted to a verandah outside the Palace, and witnessed a fine display of fireworks, representing a general action. Afterwards there was a monster banquet, to which all the Europeans in the enormous encampment were invited.

January 21st.—Rain fell in the morning. A sporting party was arranged for the Prince, but it was not very

THE GUEST OF CASHMERE.

successful. Although his Royal Highness killed some deer and pig, the display of native sporting was a failure. A cheetah let loose at a deer ran after a dog. The dog turned, and the cheetah fled. A lynx was slipped at a fox; Renard showed fight, and lynx and fox made up and were friends. Nor would the lynxes follow hares which were loosed for them ; but Puss received scant mercy from the falcons, which invariably succeeded in killing them. Afterwards there was polo-playing by the Baltee Hill people, who have an evil reputation on this side of the Himalayan slope. The players, mounted upon ragged ponies and attired in bright-coloured silk, dividing into two parties, commenced the game; the multitude yelled with delight; but certainly there was no ground for approbation according to our notions. Pulwans, sinewy, active wrestlers, covered with oil, and very difficult to grasp, followed. Then spring-boards and two camels were brought out. The athletes, taking a short run, threw somersaults clean over the camels, one fellow leaping finally into the howdah of an elephant, which declined to have a repetition of the feat. The drawing of nets in the river revealed the fact that the fishers of Cashmere inherit the arts of Cleopatra, for fish were found all ready fastened to their meshes by the gills.

Procession was formed in the evening through the illuminated city to the old Palace, where the Maharaja gave a dinner to the Prince and a small party of Europeans. Then there was a weird performance of a sacred dancing drama by the Lamas from Thibet, which rivalled the best shows of the Royal tour. More fireworks ended the entertainment, which presented many novel and curious features.

January 22nd.—"Baggage at 7 A.M. The Prince and suite to leave at 8." And thereupon, long before dawn, great clamour in camp; for on all questions of transport, camels, elephants, and, above all, "natives," as they are called, express their feelings in very audible fashion—and frequently. Looked out at 6 A.M. It was very cold—an eager nipping air. Sentries, dressed in long fur coats, above which peered bayonet and plumes, and beneath which slipper-like shoes beat tattoo on the ground, were inviting the earliest rays of the sun to thaw them into life. Yellow-trousered, blue-coated policemen came on the scene; for it was feared that the shawls on the tables, and the satin *resais*, or coverlets of the beds in the tents, might be "conveyed" when we had left; and a hint was given by the officers in charge to the Cashmeree authorities. Wild Hill-men from Iskardo and Thibet; falconers, carrying eagles, falcons, noble peregrines and hawks; mountaineers, with dogs covered with hair as thick and coarse as the coat of a bear, cheetahs and Persian greyhounds; live deer, heads and horns of yak-deer and antelopes, brought from all parts of Cashmere for the Prince, were arrayed in front of the Palace.

Soon after 8 A.M. the Prince left Jummoo, in all the splendour of a state procession of elephants with magnificent trappings, and a grand "sowaree." His escort was furnished by the Maharaja's Cuirassier Lancer regiment, before which was borne a green and gold standard. There were bands of music with kettledrums and trumpets six or seven feet long. All the people turned out to look at the show, which certainly deserved the compliment. At the appointed seven miles' distance from the town the Maharaja took leave of the Prince, and expressed his deep sense of the obligation under which he was laid by the visit of the eldest son of the Queen. The Ministers and nobles came on to the British frontier, where there was a triumphal arch inscribed, "This road is for our illustrious Prince." The return was pleasant, if dusty, there being a short halt at Sealkote on the way. The Prince was called upon to perform an agreeable duty on his arrival at Wazirabad. He opened the grand bridge over the Chenab, which he named "Alexandra," after the Princess of Wales, crossed it *pro formâ*, and returned to a lunch

THE DEPARTURE FROM JUMMOO.

at the Station, where a banquet was set forth in a fine hall, handsomely decorated.

The journey from Wazirabad was continued at 3.40 P.M. by special train. It was quite dark (6 P.M.) when we arrived at the Lahore Station. The citadel, public buildings and streets were illuminated. The Prince drove to Government House, and was glad to find that the invalids who had remained behind were quite restored to health. His Royal Highness dined with the Lieutenant-Governor and Lady Davies, and went to the native entertainment, which was given at the College, in the Hall of which—a very fine room—a dais, covered with a scarlet carpet loaded with gold embroidery, was erected at the end. On the right an excellent full-length portrait of the Princess of Wales, and on the left a portrait of the Prince, painted, as the inscription stated, by order of the Maharaja of Puttiala, to commemorate the restoration of the Prince to health; along the walls were coats of arms, banners, and the emblazoned shields of the Punjaub Chiefs, the inventive work of Mr. Kipling's pupils. Underneath each shield was a Punjaubee, representing the district from which he came, armed to the teeth, standing on a pedestal. When the Prince was seated, the givers of the banquet were introduced — Rajpoots, Pathans, Beloochees. Among the 120 Chiefs were descendants of the Great Mogul, members of the Royal family of Delhi, of the Royal family of Afghanistan (one of whom, Shahzadah Shahpoor, actually sat on the throne), descendants of Nanuk, the founder of the Sikh faith, and of Govind, who made the Sikhs a distinguished nation. Then a number of Natives received one by one from the Prince's hands commemorative medals, ribands and rewards.

When the ceremony was over, the Prince ascended to the roof to witness the fireworks. It was worth miles of travel. The fort, parapets, and battlements illuminated, towered above a tumultuous sea of heads, which seemed to roll against the fiery barriers. The fireworks were heralded by fire balloons, which followed in a continuous stream, till the sky was loaded with novel constellations. People with naked swords, putting one in mind of Highland practices of a similar description, danced round great bonfires; but they were too far off to be as effective as they were meant to be. The wind somewhat marred the 1500*l.* worth of rockets, bombs, Catherine wheels, and fixed pieces, hissing, bursting, and blazing together, and out in twenty minutes. Eight Punjaubee girls in robes plated with precious metals and jewels were introduced, and, standing at some distance from the Prince on the roof, sang an ode composed in his honour in very doleful monotonous fashion. The Prince and the European ladies and gentlemen were led to the supper-room, which was laid out with six tables, at each of which covers for ten were laid. The Chiefs retired as soon as the Prince was seated. The Prince was escorted by the Native gentlemen to his carriage, and drove through immense crowds along the illuminated roads back to his head-quarters.

January 23rd.—Canon Duckworth celebrated Divine service at Government House, and the difficulty as to the choice between Lahore and Meean Meer in the matter of churches was thus happily solved. Later, the Prince, attended by the Lieutenant-Governor, by Mr. Thornton, and members of his suite, visited the Museum and other places of interest.

January 24th.—The Prince left the hospitable mansion of Sir Henry Davies for Agra at noon. The garrison of Meean Meer and the Lahore Volunteers furnished guards of honour and troops to line the streets. "The Chiefs present in Lahore and the officers in charge," as the official programme calls them, were present in places pointed out to them by Dr. Thornton, who has been indefatigable in all kinds of official and unofficial ways to make things go smoothly, and has rendered many services to the strangers, which cause them to feel great gratification at the news of his promotion. At the railway station Sir Charles Reid showed his plan of loading an ordinary train with artillery. In twenty minutes Captain Hawkins's battery (86 men and 94 horses) were placed in 17 ordinary waggons and 6 trucks attached to the Prince's train. When the Prince reached Umritsur, the horses and guns were run out, and opened as if for action, to the great astonishment of the crowd of Natives, in five minutes after the arrival of the train.

The Prince alighted under a salute from the fort, Govindghur, and drove through the streets to the building prepared for his reception. The route was lined and arched with artificial cypress-trees, gilded branches, and garlands, with the inscription, "God bless our future Shah in Shah!" and before every doorway were trays of rose-leaves. The Municipality—Sikh, Mussulman, and Hindoo—presented an address expressive of most fervent loyalty. The Prince afterwards visited the Church and the Mission School, where he was received by Mr. Baring, chief of the Mission. Several Native clergymen were presented—one a brother of the Raja of Kuppartulla; another, a well-known mathematical teacher; Emamadeen, a controversial writer. The great "sight" of Umritsur is the Golden Temple, wherein is the Holy Book or Grunt of Nanuk. Close by is the Temple, where all true Sikhs are or should be initiated. Multitudes assembled to see the Prince pass to the sacred place. Slippers were prepared for him, as the priests declared that he could not enter the Shrine without taking off his shoes. Several members of the suite visited the

Shrine before the Prince's arrival. But it was considered inexpedient for the Prince to visit the interior, and he surveyed the Golden Temple from the terrace, in sight of the crowd, who salaamed respectfully. Presents were given to the guardians of the Mausoleum at Lahore, from whom a curious epistle will be found in the Appendix,* and I think

A CLOSE SHAVE WHILE THE TRAIN WAITS.

there was also a donation made to those of the Shrine at Umritsur. The journey to Agra was continued at dusk.

It was close upon midnight when the train pulled up at the station of Rajpoorah, where the Maharaja of Puttiala was waiting to receive his guest. It may be assumed that

---

* See Appendix.

some, at least, of the passengers in the Royal train were rather sorry when they were awakened by a braying of bands, the firing of cannon, and the glare of a great illumination. The Maharaja, whose diamonds one can well get tired of hearing about, but which are always pleasant to see, was surrounded by his Ministers and officers. Carriages, guards of honour, and the Raja's troops were drawn up at the railway station. It is a very small place, an ordinary roadside platform, but it was made very fine with garlands, lamps, transparencies, and scarlet cloth. A grand palace of canvas, hung with silk shawls and carpets, with mirrors, chandeliers, and engravings and pictures, room within room, had been prepared. The banquet was brought from Calcutta. After the health of the Queen, the Maharaja proposed the health of the Prince of Wales. Amid discharges of cannon and pyrotechnic outbursts, the Prince bade good-bye to the delighted Maharaja, and continued his journey.

January 25th.—The red walls and towers of the Fort of Agra came in sight a little before 4 P.M. The train thundered over the grand bridge which spans the broad Jumna, now meandering through beds of sand. Presently up rose the clamour, to which all are so accustomed, that, as the miller wakes up when the clack of the wheel stops, so gentlemen who have been travelling so long to such accompaniments of music, voices, and cannon, consider something has gone wrong if they do not hear the familiar sounds at their arrival or departure, conscious though they be that not one note of sound or voice, nor one grain of gunpowder is expended in their honour. The Commissioner, the Major-General commanding the Division, the Brigadier, the Magistrate, the Station officers, &c., were on the platform. The A Battery, 15th Brigade Royal Artillery, headquarters and one squadron of the 10th

Hussars, two squadrons 16th Bengal Cavalry, and all the troops that could be collected in the Division were on duty. Along the road were stands and platforms belonging to Chiefs, communities, towns or districts in the Lieutenant-Governor's jurisdiction — Hindoo and Mahomedan, covered with tinsel, decked with streamers, and painted in the brightest hues in native fashion. In these, bands of musicians and spectators were seated. The names

PAINTING THE PRINCE'S ELEPHANT.

(*A Sketch at Gwalior.*)

of those who erected the stands, and inscriptions bidding the Prince welcome and invoking the blessings of God upon his head and upon his visit, were lettered upon them in Ordoo, Persian, or English. The procession was of truly Oriental pomp. The elephants, caparisoned with extraordinary richness, and painted in the patterns most in approval among the professors of elephantine decoration, were told off to their places, according to a printed list, so that no mistake could occur. They put me in mind of the great ships which I saw long, long ago, when the Queen made her first naval inspection at Spithead. It was a proud beast which salaamed, and sank down to the ground to receive the Prince. The howdah was of the richest fashion, and by reason of the umbrella and fans, and other apparatus of dignity borne by the attendants, the identity of him whom all had assembled to honour was plainly marked. Probably the mahout felt little satisfaction in knowing that he, one of the despised ones of the East, was the master of the wise and strong beast which was to bear so precious a burden. As some Admiral, leading the van of his fleet, amid great fluttering of streamers, discharge of cannon, and the cries of exulting multitudes, puts to sea, the Prince set out at the head of the magnificent procession, which was soon winding beneath the walls of the grand old fort. The members of the Government, the Chiefs and others, then fell in, so that there was a mighty train going up from the Jumna towards the camp. But the wind blew high, and the dust was of the most aggravating density and profusion, obscuring much of the brilliancy of the spectacle, and giving no small discomfort to the spectators as well as to those who took part in it. In front escorts of the 15th Bengal Cavalry and of the 10th Hussars. But why did not the bands play? Nothing could have been more inspiriting or have given greater finish to the procession than the performance of martial flourishes and music of a triumphal and joyous character. The camp, pitched on the old ground whereon the cavalry action was fought on the morning of Greathed's arrival with the relieving force from Delhi, was spacious and splendid, like that we have seen at Benares, and almost as grand as that we had just left at Delhi. When the Prince's elephant arrived in front of the Durbar tent, it faced round, and the elephants of the suite, following, wore, tacked, and ranged themselves in a curved line on the right; the European authorities, civil and military, Nawabs, Rajahs, and Sirdars passed in review, saluting the Prince—a *coup de théâtre* well conceived and admirably executed.

January 26th.—From "an early hour," which means any time last night, tomtom-ing, growling of camels, neighing of horses, trumpetings of elephants, and the infinite variety of tumult which vexes the dweller in tents, raged round the Headquarters' Camp; and as morning dawned, trumpet flourishes, bugle calls, and drumming attested the presence of British horse and foot. By 10 o'clock the *maidan* (or plain) outside the camp, access to which was strictly guarded by sentries, was crowded; and Agra poured out its thousands. The levee was well managed, people were told what to do before admission to the presence; but some leaving their shoes at the door by which they entered, had difficulty in finding them on their exit, an inconvenience as great to natives as if Europeans were left without their hats. Comfortable and capacious as the tents are, the interior must appear poor to eyes accustomed to coloured-glass chandeliers, huge mirrors, golden canopies, brocades, and gaudy-coloured engravings; but as one said, the presence of the Prince "makes them glow with light." After the levee fourteen Chiefs were received. At 11.30 A.M. seventeen rounds for the Maharao Raja of Boondee, whose cortege whirled up the main street amid blinding clouds of dust, with an escort of cavalry, three aides-de-camp, irregular horse, and retainers on foot in singular costumes. The Maharao, in his day a noted hunter, is a Tory Chief, a Rajpoot of the bluest blood, intensely Conservative, and a fine specimen of a native gentleman. The Prince won his heart by remarking that he heard the Maharao had attended a Durbar held by Lord William Bentinck, and had witched him by noble deeds of horsemanship. After him came the Raja of Bikaneer—a Lord of the Desert, whose capital is separated from the nearest road by 200 miles of rolling sand, which he and his retinue had crossed in the only ships which can navigate such seas—the famed camels of Bikaneer. The Raja has been to Benares, Lucknow, and Delhi; and has seen railways and steamers. Next was the Maharaja of Kishengurh, whose capital is exposed to novel influences, for the Rajpootana Railway now runs past it; the Chief has devoted himself to irrigation, and has executed tanks and other public works of great utility. It would surprise Lord Lake if he heard that a Maharaja of Bhurtpoor should visit a Prince of Wales at Agra! His army is well drilled; his State well administered; he breeds fine horses and keeps up a good stud. When the Maharaja took leave his face was radiant, for the Prince promised to have a few hours' duck shooting in his preserves, and this was honour indeed. After Bhurtpoor the Chief of Ulwar paid his respects—a good-looking lad, who sits his horse as if he meant to stick to it, and who plays "Badminton." He is a minor, but he has the learned pundit Munphool for his tutor; at the head of the State is an approved good administrator, Major Cadell, V.C., assisted by a Council Regency. The Ulwar stables are good, the stud very well selected, and English sires have been purchased to strengthen the stock. The Nawab of Tonk is Chief of a State which few persons in the Midland Counties, or even in Lancashire, ever heard of, and yet the Nawab's family rendered great services in the time of trial eighteen years ago. The Chief is remarkable for his hospitality to English travellers. He has a library and a good collection of arms. The Rana of Dholepoor followed, a bright-looking lad, who is being educated by Major Dennehy, to whom he seems much attached. The Maharaja of Oorcha, a hunter and sportsman, followed; after him came the Nawab of Rampoor—a poet and an invalid, whom the Prince invested with the insignia of the G.C.S.I., which he would have received had he been able to have attended the Calcutta Chapter. The Rao Maharaja of Duttia, who resides in a fine old fort, was next presented; then the Maharaja of Chickaree, son of the Chief whom Lord Canning in Durbar styled "Faithful among the Faithless." Last came the Raja of Tehri, the Maharaja of Shalpoora, and the Jagirdar of Alipoora.

In the afternoon the troops of the Nawabs and Rajas passed before the Prince—a strange *mélange* of elephants, camels, horses, bullocks, men such as Alexander might have led into captivity, knights in armour, artillery drawn by oxen, for an hour and a half. In the evening the Prince, after a banquet at headquarters, went to an evening party given by the Lieutenant-Governor in the Fort, which has been restored to a decent condition, and after a pleasant dance and supper returned to camp.

January 27th.—The Prince paid return visits to the fourteen Chiefs. When these visits were over, his Royal Highness drove through the suburbs, and after dinner he went to see the Taj illuminated.

Most writers who have tried their hands at a description of the Taj set out with the admission that it is indescribable, and then "proceed to give some idea" of it. I do not know how many of the fair ladies present agreed with Colonel Seeman's wife, who said to him, "I cannot criticise, but I can tell you what I feel. I would die to-morrow to have such a tomb!" Holy and profane men, poets, prosers, and practical people all write of the Taj in the same strain. "Too pure, too holy to be the

THE TAJ MAHAL BY MOONLIGHT.

work of human hands!"—"a poem in marble!"—"the sigh of a broken heart!"—"poetic marble arrayed in eternal glory!"—"the inspiration is from heaven—the execution worthy of it!" But the Taj, with 7000 spectators—7000 people who came to look at the Prince of Wales looking at the Taj! Well, it played its part to perfection.

Ascending the terrace, the Prince walked over to the shelter of the dark gateway of the mosque. Gradually there grew out, in all its fair proportions and beauty, framed in the purple of the starry heavens, the marble "Queen of Sorrow," which has power to dim every eye. Then trooping into the illuminated square came a band, and forthwith the soft tender notes of "Vedrai carino" floated through the night air. It may be doubted if Moomtaz-i-Mahul, or "the Exalted One of the Palace," would have quite approved of the music. However, Mozart was better than the *maestro* whose compositions next challenged the ears of the company. But the eye mastered every sense, and the loveliness of the Taj stole over the soul. In spite of blue lights, and lime lights, of lively dance music, of clank of spurs and sabres on the complaining marble, there was not a point which the peerless mausoleum could make which was for an instant marred or lost. Entering the tomb itself—the culminating glory—the party stood and gazed, almost trembling with admiration. Presently a clear, sustained note rose up into the vaulted roof of the tomb, and there found its counterpart, and the two commingled, swept upwards, and soared away, "till naught remained 'twixt them and silence." Again and again the notes soared, and the auditors stood breathless. Then came a few chords in sweet unison from four or five singers, but to my ear the effect was not so impressive as that of an old Moulvie's voice reading prayers when last I was there. That grand, grumbling chant awoke echoes which sounded like the responses of some vast congregation. The interior has been swept, garnished, cleaned, and, as far as can be, restored. If Shah Jehan could come back to earth, it is not too much to suppose that he would thank Sir John Strachey for the labour of love which has stayed the hand of the spoiler.

Moomtaz-i-Mahul died in childbirth of her eighth child. People have taken lately to abusing her husband and his times; but it may be recollected that about that very period of the world's history England was not quite a paradise; that we had a Star Chamber and other comforts for the conscience; were busy persecuting people we did not like; were preparing for a civil war and for the execution of our King, and were by no means in a condition to justify us in throwing stones at the builder of the Taj. We have done better since; and if there be no Taj or Sikundra to be put to our account, we hope we can say that our rule has, in the words of De Quincey, conferred on India "gifts higher by far than Mogul gifts of palace or serai, roads or tanks—the gifts of security, order, law, and peace."

After such a sensation, the Holy Jumna, with its placid bosom gemmed with star-like lamps, could offer little attraction. It was nevertheless pleasant to look down from the terrace and watch the tiny boats of earthenware, large as a coffee cup, bearing their cargoes of oil or cotton-wick, on the placid stream which multiplied their fires in the mirror of its waters; to look across at the wide expanse of gardens and kiosks, minarets, cupolas, and domes, writing their occult characters on the blackness of the night, and then to let the eye turn slowly on the Taj. There were, thank goodness! "for this occasion only," no fireworks. It was near midnight before the Prince was minded to quit the place.

January 28th.—The Prince rose early, but there was a good deal of what is called "rousing out" before the sportsmen were ready to start. The Maharaja of Bhurtpoor keeps a "sanctuary" of jungle, and had made arrangements to give his Royal Highness good sport. He met the Prince near a beautifully-arranged hunting camp. The "bag" consisted of eighty head. Another party went out pig-sticking. There were plenty of boars seen, but the country was bad, and there were no "spears."

In the evening there was a grand ball in the Fort. One may question the fitness of the Dewan Khass and the Dewan I-Aum for balls and suppers, but the scene was beautiful, and, though associations are rudely dislocated, these balls are as agreeable to the Prince, who is able to gratify so many Europeans, as it is agreeable to them to have an opportunity of seeing the Prince.

January 29th.—An excursion to Futtehpoor Sikri, a wilderness of stone, "attesting the vigour of Imperial selfishness and the futility of human aspirations." The road was guarded by escorts of 15th Bengal Lancers and the 10th Hussars. Fifty years did not elapse from the building of the city till its abandonment to owls and jackals. The Prince was shown round the temples by the eleventh descendant of the very fakir whose tomb constitutes the principal attraction to the natives.

January 30th.—The Prince attended Divine service at 11 o'clock. Sir J. and Lady Strachey, and the ladies and members of his household, and the various officers on duty and visiting the camp, formed a sufficiently numerous congregation under a large canopy in front of the Lieutenant-Governor's tents. Canon Duckworth officiated. On the right stood a squadron of the 10th Hussars, mounted; on the left a detachment of the Rifle Brigade. The native servants gathered in the rear, attracted by the ceremony; but, as the preacher spoke of the approach of the time when Christianity shall have taught all men to love each other, the business of the camp went on as usual; sentries paced up and down, orderlies galloped to and fro. Our little ship was leaving no track on the waters. The Prince, after lunching with Lord Mark Kerr and officers of the 10th Hussars, drove to a convent distinguished for good works, and visited the Christian schools and various other educational institutions. Sir Dinkur Rao had a long interview with the Prince.

The afternoon was devoted to an excursion to what is perhaps the grandest, as the Taj is certainly the most beautiful, tomb in the world—Sikundra, six miles from camp, where lie the remains of Akber (or Akhbar, or however else his name may be spelt), to whom India—Hindoo and Mussulman—accords the title of "Great," apparently with every reason. The road still shows the coshminars (round stone pillars), every two miles, which were erected along the Imperial Mogul routes, extending to Lahore, more than 700 miles from Agra. Near each was a watch-tower, and there were halting-places, and serais, and wells for travellers along the road. A grand gateway gives access to a garden, in which is the Mausoleum of red sandstone, 300 feet square, built in five stories, each diminishing from the base to the marble story at the height of 100 feet. Every terrace is ornamented with an arched gallery and cupolas, said to bear relation to the division of the Empire, over which he who rests below once ruled in dignity and power. Without going so far as Mr. Bayard Taylor, who considers Sikundra nobler in conception and more successful as an embodiment of Saracenic art than the Alcazar or Alhambra, it may be admitted that it stands among the grandest monuments of any kind ever reared by man.

Not more than 250 years have elapsed since it was finished. The son of the Queen of that England which was then represented in this land by a few adventurous merchants and mariners, and one or two wandering travellers, whose greatest wonder was that they were there at all, now stood before the sarcophagus within which lie the bones of the fourth descendant of Tamerlane, grandson of Baber, grandfather of Shah Jehan—stood there acknowledged heir to the sceptre, which had been wielded with such grandeur and might—future successor, if God wills it, to Akhbar the Great, whose titles one might read in the exquisitely carved inscriptions, ascribing to him "majesty and glory for ever." It was a fitting scene for a sermon on the rise and fall of Empires and on the vanity of human wishes.

January 31st.—The visit to the Maharaja of Gwalior was fixed for to-day, and as there is no railway it was necessary to prepare for a long journey by road, but the arrangements for posting the Royal party are, if possible, better than those for special trains. The carriages were ready in the main street at 9 A.M. There were relays and change of escort every six miles. At Dholepoor, the capital of the native State, some thirty-five miles from Agra, the Prince was received by the youthful Maharaja in a palace not yet completed, built expressly for the occasion. All the resources of the host were displayed. Music and dancers, elephants, armed retainers, chiefs and horses. The Maharaja, a charming boy, who speaks English well and delights in manly sports, became at once the friend of the Prince, who took to him greatly. There was a grand sowaree, and a *déjeuner* for the Europeans, &c. The Royal party at the border of the State crossed the Chumbul into Scindia's dominions by a bridge of boats.

A cavalry escort was drawn up seven miles from

Gwalior, the fortress of which had been in sight for a long time. Here Scindia received the Prince. Thence the cortege passed between lines of Mahratta cavalry to the entrance to the Lushkar (or "camp"), where infantry regiments were in line. The streets were thronged all the way through the city to the new Palace, where Scindia installed his Royal visitor in much state.

The Palace covers an area of 124,771 square feet, exclusive of the inner square, which is 321 by 321½ feet. The building is double-storied, and the wings and turrets are three- and five-storied. Its total length is 106 feet. The first story is Tuscan, second Italian Doric, and the third Corinthian order of architecture. The interior of the Reception-room is 97 feet 8 inches long by 50 feet broad, and it is 41 feet in height. The roof is arched with stone slabs 21 feet long, which enabled the architect to make the ribs prominent. They rest at each end on double Corinthian columns, which form a colonnade round the interior. The interior and exterior of the Palace form a combination of arcades and colonnades. Upwards of 300,000 leaves of gold were used to decorate the Reception-hall. The Grand Staircase-room is roofed with stone slabs 30 feet long; the room opposite to it is roofed in the same way. This room was used for dancing. The length of each of these rooms is 50 feet. The Grand Drawing-room, one of the finest saloons in the world, is hung with wonderful chandeliers, and decorated with enormous mirrors. The Prince's bedstead, washing service, and bath were of solid silver. The cost of the Palace was a little above 1,100,000 rupees. But the garden-walls, iron railings, gardens, furniture, glass, grand staircase, chandeliers, &c., cost about 500,000 rupees more. The area of the garden is about one square mile; there are several waterfalls and a number of fountains in it.

In the Palace and inner square there are 106 fountains and a waterfall.

There was a British dinner at the Palace, followed by a grand ball. The appearance of the saloons was very bright and gay, and the representative of the Governor-General for Central India, Sir H. Daly, did the honours with great kindness and success.

February 1st.—There was a review of "the army of Gwalior." At 7 A.M. a salute announced the arrival of the Prince of Wales. The Prince and Scindia then rode down the line side by side, bands playing and colours lowered. Scindia rode at the head of a truly "brilliant staff." He wore a scarlet tunic, with gold facings, diamonds, and gems, and the riband of the Star of India, his cap blazing with jewels, and ornamented with an egret plume rising from a diamond socket. On the Prince's return to the saluting post, the march-past commenced. The band played up the Gwalior version of "Garryowen." First came the general staff of the Gwalior army; next Scindia, alone. As he passed the Prince he saluted with his sword. It is said to have been the first time he has ever made such an acknowledgment. He was followed by ten Staff Officers riding abreast. Next, a troop of horse artillery, six-pounder smooth-bores, went by admirably in line. Another horse artillery battery followed almost equally well. Then came two nine-pounder field batteries, each gun drawn by six bullocks drilled to perfection, "with their humps dressed to a nicety," as some one said. Appia Sahib, Brigadier of Cavalry, and his staff followed. The first Regiment in the uniform of Close's old corps of the Gwalior Contingent, red tunics, buckskin breeches, long boots, and Afghan turbans. The second Regiment (regulars) blue tunics and red turbans; then a squadron of the 3rd Regiment of Hussars; the 4th Regiment of Lancers, in ultramarine blue uniforms, lance-pennons black and red, completed the cavalry. Each regiment was 400 strong. The five battalions of infantry which followed were armed with old smooth-bore percussion muskets. The men were well set-up and steady. Scindia took three regiments of infantry and two of cavalry to the right, to entertain the company with a display of tactics.

When Scindia galloped off to his sham fight, the Chiefs who were not attached to the corps rode up to the ground, and formed a very brilliant and interesting group close to the Prince. Their dresses were exceedingly beautiful; and wonderful as they were in colour—yellow, sky-blue, mauve, scarlet and pink—were matched with excellent taste. Some wore Damascened chain-armour armlets and thigh-pieces inlaid with gold. One Chief was in black satin surcoat, with bright red petticoat, chain-armour covered with gold plaques inlaid with pearls; another wore necklaces of pearls and emeralds over an enamelled breast-plate of fine steel, his satin cloak and coat trimmed with diamonds, earrings of emeralds and diamonds, and a waist-belt of precious stones gathering in his mauve pantaloons, and he sat in a saddle which appeared to be altogether of gold, with a cloth and housing set with pearls, emeralds, and diamonds. Several of the horses had anklets of precious stones set in silver on the fore-legs—in fact, as a predatory young gentleman observed, "the plundering of any one of these Sirdars would set up a man for life."

Meanwhile Appia, with the remaining infantry and cavalry, marched to the left, and took up a position, sending out a detachment of cavalry and guns to watch Scindia. Appia's guns were attacked by Scindia's cavalry; whose infantry moved up to sustain the attack. Aided by the fire of the artillery, they checked Appia's horse which engaged Scindia's right and threatened to outflank him. After several pretty movements, Scindia was declared to have won the day. The Prince expressed his satisfaction, and Scindia, overjoyed, declared that he would publish the Prince's eulogium in general orders to his army. It was, in truth, a very creditable display—*mais à quoi bon?*

In the afternoon the Prince visited the famous Fortress, and looked down on the city and the plain where Sir Hugh Rose defeated Tantia Topee, and where the heroic, if cruel, Ranee of Jhansee met her fate—a soldier's death. The fortress, which contains some much venerated and dilapidated temples and shrines, some used as places of confinement for political prisoners, overhangs Scindia's Palace and city very much as Edinburgh Castle imposes the town below; but as long as the British hold the great military Station less than three miles away and the open country, the Rock of Gwalior possesses no military importance; indeed, it is quite commanded by a ridge of similar formation at the other side of the road to Agra. However, Sir H. Daly and others maintain that it is very useful to Scindia to have a British garrison there, as he is thus protected against his own army and his subjects. Then there was a state visit to Scindia, who held a Durbar in the old Palace. The most notable feature in the reception was the great number of Mahratta Chiefs and Sirdars of importance who were present, and curious observances, such as the utterance in unison of a loud cry by the courtiers and the attendants (equivalent, *on dit*, to "God save the Queen"), when Scindia rose or sat down. Towards the close of the interview, Scindia, addressing the Prince, said:—

"I can command no language to express my gratitude for the honour the Prince of Wales has conferred upon me in thus visiting Gwalior—What can I say? On the

Scindias who have preceded me many honours have fallen—but on none has there been honour like this. This day will never be forgotten in Gwalior. I have nothing to show worthy of his Royal Highness. My palace, my troops, what are they to him? His attendance at my parade this morning in the heat and dust, the interest the Prince took in it, were out of his consideration for me. I am an ignorant man, almost without education. I know nothing of the English language. What I did this morning with the troops is an instance of what can be done by observation and labour—nothing more. Again and again I desire to express gratefully my appreciation of the favour the Prince has shown me; and when he sees the Queen, let him tell her from me, that I am, with hands clasped, her faithful servant for ever."

Scindia spoke these words with strong emotion and glistening eyes. After a moment's pause, turning to Sir H. Daly, he said: "One thing I would add. When the time comes for the Prince to ascend the throne, I hope he will remember Scindia."

There was a grand banquet in the evening at the new Palace. At the commencement of dessert, Scindia, with ten of his nobles, entered, and was handed by Sir H. Daly to a seat on the right hand of the Prince. Shortly afterwards the Maharaja proposed the health of the Queen, and then the health of the Prince of Wales. His own silver cup was brought to him, and he drank the toasts in champagne. The Prince's replies, which were translated by Sir H. Daly, appeared to give Scindia very great pleasure.

February 2nd.—Scindia came to the Palace at 9 A.M. to sit for his portrait to Mr. S. Hall, by desire of the Prince. At 10.30 A.M. all was ready for the return to Agra, and the Maharaja taking his Royal Highness by the hand, conducted him to the door of the carriage. On taking leave,

Scindia said: "It has been much to see your face, it is a grief to me that your visit is so short, and that you go away. I can hardly hope to see you again; but be this as it may, sometimes in England turn a kind thought to me. My state and everything I have is yours." The Prince replied, "that he should never forget Gwalior and the magnificence of his reception, and that he knew he had a friend in Scindia."

If Scindia could have uttered his heart's desire he would have probably said to the Prince: "Tell them to give me back my fortress." There can be no doubt that Lord Canning promised, in 1859, to restore it to him, but the plea of to-day for the non-fulfilment of the pledge is that Lord Canning did not promise to restore it at once, but made a proviso that the act should be performed at some convenient season. This is dangerous ground to take, especially if there is to be only one judge of the conveniency. The Prince, halting at Dholepoor to lunch on his way back to Agra, made an announcement, which was as agreeable to those who rejoiced in the good fortune of their companions as it was to the recipients, that the Queen would bestow the G.C.S.I. on Major-General Probyn, Major-General Browne and Dr. Fayrer, and the S.C.M.I. on Colonel Ellis, Captain Glyn and others. The party arrived at Sir John Strachey's camp as it was becoming dark. There were charming evening amateur performances in the Lieut.-Governor's tent after dinner on several occasions during the Prince's stay at Agra.

February 3rd.—A day of repose for all but a small party of sportsmen who went twenty-five miles from Agra to ground where wild boar were numerous. In the evening news was brought to the Prince, who was dining with the officers of the 10th Hussars, that Prince Louis of Battenberg had been thrown while in full career after a pig, and had been found senseless and with a collar-bone broken. Every one regretted this, for Prince Louis is a great favourite. Dr. Fayrer set off at once, and after a long and cold drive in an open carriage, found the patient, who was tended carefully by Lord Charles Beresford. Pig-sticking assumes a high position on the roll of casualty-causing sports. Lord Carington, a broken collar-bone; Lord Charles Beresford, teeth broken; Lord Suffield injured by his own spear; not to speak of falls, &c.; but the pig-stickers are veritable Gallios, and pursue the sport whenever they can. Colonel Owen Williams has got his hand in, so have Colonel Ellis and Mr. FitzGeorge, and Lord Aylesford is intact. There are some who do not tempt the fortunes of the field at all. On the whole, there are not so many people killed in the pursuit of pigs as in hunting the fox.

February 4th.—A special train of the Rajpootana State Railway was ordered for 8.45 A.M. for Jeypoor. At Bhurtpoor, where the Maharaja and his Court had been waiting for an hour, there was a great deal to see and but little time to see it. The guns of the famous old fortress thundered out salutes. The road to the moat, above which tower the crumbling walls that saw our troops twice fail to reach the summit, was lined with troops, clad in Sepoy uniforms, some with the old light infantry "wing" on the shoulders. The repulses of the British are celebrated in many paintings in the town. Crossing the broad ditch and passing the outer wall we came on a very thick brick gateway and wall, inside which lies the city. The streets are broad, and were well swept and clean. There were many triumphal arches, and every inch of footpath, window, and roof, was filled. The shops were shut. There was perfect silence till the carriage passed; then came a buzz of conversation and commentary. The route to the Palace was lined with a framework of bamboos, seven feet high, covered with pink calico. The staircase, corridors and floors of the Palace were covered with the finest kinkob and gold brocades, the walls being hung with the same. Pictures of the Duke of Wellington, Napoleon, the Prince Consort, and Queen Victoria were hung in the room where the Prince and party were entertained at lunch. The Maharaja conducted the Prince to the Station, and returned thanks for the high honour done to Bhurtpoor by the visit, which was very interesting to the strangers.

From Bhurtpoor the railroad traverses a plain, apparently level as a bowling-green, but in the vicinity of rivers the rains have cut deep and numerous ravines. At each half-mile of road there were pickets of armed horsemen. At every village were gathered Rajpoots, armed with sword and shield. Close to the city of Jeypoor, conical hills form continuous chains, on which are battlemented walls, fortresses of feudal Chiefs. From unexpected places came puffs of smoke and reports of cannon. The sun was getting low when the train stopped at the Station. As the Prince stepped out of the carriage, the Maharaja of Jeypoor advanced to welcome him at the head of his Court, and there was also the usual attendance of the official and unofficial Europeans on the platform. A procession was formed from the station through a great multitude—a double line, natives and Europeans, two elephants abreast. We passed through a gateway, and Jeypoor lay before us, a surprise and wonder for ever.

The world knows very little of its great men; and the number of people who are acquainted with the deeds of the Maharaja Jey Sing, who founded "the City of Victory" in 1728, is probably very small indeed, although astronomers must be acquainted with the name, at least, of the man who reformed the Calendar, and constructed the remarkable observatories at Benares, Jeypoor, and elsewhere. He laid down his capital, we are told, according to the rules of the 'Silpi Shastras,' and if so, it is to be regretted that these Shastras were not followed more generally, not only in India, but in England. In fact, Baron Haussmann might have been inspired by the genius which ordered this city :—" Between the gates of the Sun and Moon" (east and west) runs the main street, 2 miles long, and 111 feet wide; between the north and south gates is another street 1¼ mile long, and of the same breadth as the other. These streets are cut at right angles by others, 55 feet broad, and the rectangular blocks so formed are divided by streets 27½ feet broad! The town is surrounded by a crenellated wall of masonry, 20 feet high, and 9 feet thick, covered with rose-coloured plaster, pierced by seven gateways, each with two kiosks, and machicolations and screen walls; and there are bastions and towers with embrasures for guns at intervals. The streets have clean, broad pavements, and stone causeways for carriages. The shop-fronts, each shaded by a sloping calico or cloth pent of white, with broad, red stripes, giving a light and agreeable effect to the thoroughfares, open on the street. Projecting over the shops there is a broad ledge or terrace, putting one in mind of the old streets of Chester.

If I were to say that the houses look as if they were built of solid strawberry creams streaked in white arabesque, no adequate impression would be produced, simply because one cannot imagine houses of such material. And yet, out of confectionery, I have never beheld any street architecture of this kind. The houses vary from three to five or six stories in height, and are painted rose-colour picked out with white, with narrow windows and perforated stucco screens. The walls sometimes are mere pretences, blind frontages raised above the flat roofs. Nothing more light and pretty can be imagined than these streets with Venetian masts and flags, garlands, streamers, illuminated by an army of torch-bearers. There were some who tried to find out that it was a painted sepulchre, and dived into back streets, but it was only to discover that Brahminee bulls had an easy time of it, that fakirs were in much esteem, and that the shop-keepers were quite well aware of the value of the exquisite work in enamel, &c., for which Jeypoor is famous. The Prince was lodged in the Residency, where there were the usual festivities and ceremonies.

February 5th.—The environs are by no means destitute of tigers, and it is said that some of the Rajpoot Chiefs have a tenderness for the creatures—perhaps founded on a superstitious fear—and keep tiger reserves. Naturally enough, the animal which may at any moment eat the father or mother of a family, or the *spem gregis*, exercises a great influence over the popular imagination, and tigers rampant, couchant and passant, figure largely on the walls of the houses and temples. There is a short and safe method with the beasts when the Chiefs desire to kill them. Certain houses are erected in the valleys which the animals affect, and when one of them has been marked down by a "kill,"—that is, the slaughter of a calf or some edible of the kind—the sportsman takes up his post in one of the shooting-boxes, and beaters are sent to drive the valley; the tiger, who is of retiring habits when he has his own way, generally breaks away and gives a chance to the rifle as he passes. There was news of a "kill" this morning not far from the Residency, and the Prince set out to try his fortune, the Maharaja having made all the needful arrangements. The Royal party started in high spirits, some to hunt pig, others to shoot deer; the Prince to the rocky ravine in which the tiger was lurking. It had been the Maharaja's intention to station the Prince in the ravine; but the tiger having moved, he was placed in the upper story of a shooting-box, from which there was a clear view all round. Nearly two hours passed before the beaters came on the lair. Then the tiger was seen creeping, cat-like, towards the house. It came within thirty yards. The Prince fired. The tiger started off down the ravine at a trot. Again the Prince fired; the tiger rolled over, but recovered, and staggered into a hollow, amid thick brush. The Prince, who wished to follow the trail on foot, was dissuaded. He mounted Dr. Fayrer's elephant, and descended. The beaters threw stones into the ravine; the tiger emerged and walked slowly up the bank. The Prince fired twice; still the beast went on, badly hit though it was, and stumbling, rolled out of sight over a boulder. A beater, standing above, said, "It lies there." The party closed around, and there lay—tremendous still in death—a full-grown female, 8½ feet long. When it was laid out in the garden of the Residency, it was an object of much attention; the photographer was set to work, then came the naturalist to skin the carcass. The smell was abominable—a fetid odour, as though it were in a state of decomposition—but the tigress was very fat, and had she been allowed to live a few weeks longer there would have been three little items added to the population of Tigerdom. The carcass was placed on an elephant and borne in triumph to a little kiosk in the valley. There lunch was spread. The Maharaja, who lunched in the same room, but apart, congratulated the Prince on his success in a bumper, and requested his acceptance of a very large-bored tiger-rifle. There were grand illuminations all over

THE PRINCE'S FIRST TIGER.

the city, not because of the killing of the tiger, but on account of the Prince's visit. The Palace, which constitutes one-sixth of the metropolis, shone with myriads of lights; the gardens and tanks were lighted, the trees bore fiery fruit, fire rained from the citadel and the great range of fort-crowned precipices overhanging the city, and all devices known to Indian illuminators were lavished to the great delight of the people, who had come from every part of the State to witness the sight.

February 6th.—Divine service in the Residency at 10.30 A.M. There was afterwards an excursion to Amber, of which Mr. Julian Robinson wrote, "Compared to Jeypoor, it is Westminster Abbey to Covent Garden Theatre, or a mild, grave *sœur de charité* to a *pimpante*, frisky grisette." This is as true as another remark by the same writer, that Jeypoor "is the very millinery of masonry; the streets, compared to those of Agra or Calcutta, are a series of laces, ribands, frills and flounces." Amber is a fine solid sacque of brocade laid by for future generations to wonder at. The approach, by a road winding below a grand range of cliffs, and skirting a lake bordered with ruined castles, is a fit preparation for the sight of the great gorge, on one side of which tower the battlements of the series of temples which begin in the waters at their base, where sacred crocodiles swim in and out among the ruins of half-submerged colonnades and porticos. Amber is a city of the dead. There are more monkeys than men about Amber, and they are much respected by their relatives in the more developed stages who walk on two legs. The Dewan Khass, the Jess-mundur, the Sowaree Gate, in fact, all the magnificent buildings in the vast enclosure of battlemented walls, which climb up to the summits of the peaks dominated by forts, are of extraordinary beauty of design and elaborateness of execution; the walls of some of the Palace rooms are inlaid as if they were pieces of jewelry. No one should set foot on Indian soil without visiting Amber if he can. Lunch was spread on one of the terraces of the palace, and the cortege attracted a very great multitude of people as picturesque as the country they live in.

February 7th.—Early this morning the Maharaja appeared in the inner court of the Residency, walking up and down in front of the verandah, waiting till he could pay his respects to the Prince. He was followed by a train of courtiers, who moved just as he did, following him very much as though they had been so many joints in the tail of an animal. The little camp was astir. Servants busy packing up; crowds of box-wallahs hovering around with articles for sale. The Prince accepted a sword in an enamelled sheath gloriously jewelled ; a bag of gold mohurs struck at Jeypoor, and some photographs on a large scale, Many of the Princes of India take to photography, but the Maharaja is a master in the art. Almost every State in India, which aspires to gain the favour of the "Paramount Power," has set itself to copy British institutions. The Education Report of the Maharaja's College, the Rajpoot School, the Sanscrit College, and different branch schools in the city and in the State of Jeypoor, written in English, is now before me; and the great progress which has been made in ten years does honour to Mr. Kantee Chunder Mookerjee, the Principal of the College. There is also in my hands a report of the Jeypoor School of Arts, which was opened by the Maharaja in 1866, with a staff of teachers from the Madras School of Arts. Since 1869 it has been under the charge of Dr. De Fabeck, with the assistance of Mr. James Scorgee. The pupils are instructed in drawing, carpentering, modelling, bookbinding, electro-plating, watch-making, wood-carving, sculpture, embroidery, blacksmith's work, &c.; but, ah me! those "poor ignorant natives," who lived before us, and knew nothing of "principles of art," and had no art-instruction, conceived and executed works their more fortunate or better-taught descendants and their teachers can only faintly imitate. Take, for example, Jeypoor "enamel." Why, all the best workmen in London, Paris, Vienna, Rome, admit they cannot match this wonderful work! Our teaching will no doubt turn out a great mass of Brummagem craftsmen, but it is to be feared that with greater mechanical excellence it will "spoil the work." The articles made in the school meet with a ready sale, and the workshops are liberally patronised by Europeans and natives. The Principal has received high commendation from all the visitors, including Lord Mayo and Lord Northbrook, the latter of whom took the trouble of correcting an essay on art by a pupil of the College, which is printed for the "use of schools."

When the train was ready, the Prince walked with the Maharaja to the Station, which was a few hundred yards distant. One thing much affected the Maharaja—Would he ever see the Prince again? If not, might he venture to write to him—directly—now and then—to make inquiries after his health? The run to Agra was rapid and smooth. At six o'clock the party arrived in camp.

Here the ever-varying panorama of strange sights and scenes, processions, receptions, banquets, journeys, and hurrying to and fro day after day, cease for a while. Still the recollection of these, recent as they are, is not very distinct. There is scarcely any one among us—except, perhaps, the Prince himself, whose memory holds every fact in a vice—who can distinguish between one set of fireworks and another; remember what occurred at any one banquet which distinguished it from its fellows; identify a particular camp or quarter; or pretend to give a narrative of what he saw at any one place especially, without running the risk of confounding dates and events. When the Prince turned his face towards the Himalayas, there was a sensation of relief, a longing anticipation of such repose as the hunter's life would afford, and the taste of blood of tiger slain at Jeypoor had whetted the appetite for more. With what delight were uniforms, cocked hats, and laced coats carefully stowed away, and sent down country to be ready when the party emerged from the Terai!

The Duke of Sutherland and Mr. Grey are homeward bound, and Sir B. Frere and Canon Duckworth are going on a tour in the far North-West, whilst the Prince is away on his sporting excursion. Captain Glyn and Commander Durrant proceeded to Calcutta to take the *Scrapis* and *Osborne* round to Bombay for the Prince's homeward journey. Before his Royal Highness left he paid one more visit to the Taj, which was favoured by a lovely moonlight—not too direct and strong, but glinting at an angle which gave effect to the contour, and obviated the "blankness" of effect produced by its full glare. The Prince bade his kind hosts farewell, and at midnight the special train started for Moradabad, the farthest point towards the Terai to which the rail extends.

IN THE TERAI—BEATING FOR TIGER.

CHAPTER XII.

THE KUMAOUN—TERAI—NEPAL.

The Royal Shooting Camp—Sir H. Ramsay—Nynee Tal—An unlucky Dose—Pleasing Incongruities—Terai Scenery—Camp Personnel—A Day of Rest—The "King of Beasts"—Tigers and Tigerlets—"De Profundis"—The last Day with Ramsay—Enter Nepal—Sir Jung Bahadoor—Nepalese Civilities—An Elephantine Procession—Fighting-elephants—A good Beginning—An abstruse Joke—Taking to Roost—The terrible Proboscis—"Jung Pershaud is coming!"—Bigli Pershaud enters—"Cui Lumen ademptum"—Ballet-drill—The Reign of Terror—Departure from Nepal.

FEBRUARY 8TH.—Dreaming possibly of the Taj, or of the pleasant camp and the hospitalities of Sir John and Lady Strachey at Agra, stretched at length on the comfortable cushions of our railway carriages, and snugly wrapped in *resais*, we were borne through the night, taking no note of time, away to Rohilcund. An hour or so after daybreak the report of guns and a crash of music! What! Is there still a Durbar? Or is it only an address? Or is it a reception? Effectively, we were at Moradabad. Brigadier Payn, and the military and civilian staff of the district, a guard of honour, band and colours of the 18th Royal Irish, were waiting on the platform. Outside, detachments of the 28th Native Infantry and of the 3rd Ghoorkas, and a squadron of the 16th Bengal Cavalry to act as escort. Here there was breakfast, but, owing to the confusion and excitement of the native attendants, it was rather a feast of the Barmecide. The C Battery, 19th Brigade, had laid six-mile relays for the twenty-six miles to the shooting camp at Bahrinie, and the horses were ridden by the artillerymen at a tremendous pace over an excellent pucka road. The morning was fresh and the air delightful. Before us lay the great level plains of Rohilcund, green with the new crops and island-like clumps or topes of trees, which form a distinct feature of the landscape, the work of the old rulers, who planted them in the vicinity of the highways, and generally close to tanks and watercourses. The Ramgunga, meandering through the plains close at hand, recalled a time when its banks were lined by hostile Rohillas, and the country through which we were passing was in the hands of a mortal enemy. Now all looks peaceful and prosperous. Far as the eye can reach, hedgeless fields, vast herds of cattle, villages (which a man would give much to see in Ireland, or in parts of Scotland), in the far distance certain white streaks in the air—our first glimpse of the snow-peaks of the Himalayas. The first six-mile stage was done at the rate of sixteen miles an hour. We halted at the roadside, where there was a little camp, with commissariat, grass-cutters, and tents complete. It was a pleasure to see the smart non-commissioned officers and drivers — coats, boots, breeches, bits and buckles, with the genuine Woolwich glisten upon them—forming a nucleus for crowds of the apathetic and rather sulky-looking natives on the roadway. Buckles were undone in a trice, panting horses walked out, a new set of horses harnessed, and the carriages were off again. Stage after stage the same scene; the outline of the mountains northward growing more pronounced as the carriages rattled with the light-hearted company on towards the camp. The broad and well-laid road was lined by peepul and acacia, which rather hid the view; but towards noon certain white pyramids, like squat sugar-loaves, could be seen above the level, backed by a great forest of cornfields. "There are the tents!" It was the shooting camp at Bahrinie.

As soon as the Prince's cortege was visible, the 3rd Ghoorka guard of honour, and the detachment of the 15th Bengal Cavalry, turned out; about two hundred elephants were ranged on the side of the road, that his Royal Highness might see what preparations had been made by "the King of Kumaoun," as General Ramsay is called, to give him sport. Up fluttered the Royal Standard to the summit of the lofty flagstaff; the band played "God save the Queen." Here we are on the outskirts of the Terai. As a "forest" in Scotland means a mountain on which there are no trees, so the word "Terai," often applied to the wooded belt at the base of the Himalayas, is really the prairie which lies outside it for hundreds of miles. At this time of year it is as healthy as any part of Europe, but at other periods a deadly fever attacks Europeans and natives, except the peculiar people who live and thrive in the dreaded region. Farewell to carpeted tents and the luxuries of Agra or Delhi! But welcome, very welcome, the snug, blue-lined tent, very little better than a "pall," which afforded its grateful shelter! A large mess-tent, and the European servants, in black coats and white cravats, of Mr. Kellner, the German contractor, showed that even in the Terai it could not be forgotten that the Prince was present. Our camp was pitched by the roadside, close to a dense jungle; an undulating prairie, covered with high reeds and grass, stretched away to the foot of the mountains, where the Snowy Range was hidden by the outjutting shoots of the lower hills. It was arranged that only a certain number of his Royal Highness's suite should accompany him to Nynee Tal to see "the Snows," the great expanse of ice and snow in which Switzerland and all its mountains would be lost. Fortunately he reached the hill in time to behold the range of the Himalayas, lighted up by the setting sun, under their most favourable aspect, when the rose hue steals up from the darkening base over the pure white summits. As the day was yet young, those who were left behind thought they would make the most of it. There were great hunters amongst them — General Sam Browne, Colonel Dickens, Major Bradford, Major Prinsep, and others. It was suggested that we should beat the jungle, avoiding the district marked out for the Prince to-morrow, and in half-an-hour more we were crashing through a thick wood, in a way which, to a new comer, seemed to involve the danger of being swept off the elephant's back by branches, or torn by contending boughs. But a good mahout will guide these docile creatures much more easily than a steersman directs a boat. So the great procession went on, tearing through briar and brake, alarming cheetul, hog-deer, wild boar, peacock, and jungle-fowl. Now and then a fusillade, and a triumphant hurrah told that some victim had fallen; but there was more excitement than sport, till we came to a withered tree, on the branches of which were forty or fifty gorged vultures. "I am sure there is a kill," said Colonel Dickens, and—sure enough —there was the half-devoured carcass of a buffalo, left by a tiger so recently, that the stream was still discoloured where it had crossed. The word was instantly passed,

VIEW OF THE HIMALAYAS.—SUNRISE.

"No tigers, gentlemen!" just as one hears in an English covert, "No hens, if you please, gentlemen!" The elephants began to trumpet. I was on the left, close to a belt of wood, in grass that came quite up to the top of the howdah. "Look out!" exclaimed Major Prinsep, "there is something before you!" The grass was cleft asunder by some dark body, which showed for an instant like a porpoise in a tideway, and I fired. "Luggee!" exclaimed the shikarry behind me, "Luggee! He is hit!" "What was it?" asked I. The answer was terrible! Concurrent testimony declared that it was a splendid tiger. But I at least knew that if the tiger were hit he certainly was not killed. I had two guns in my howdah, one a rifle and the other a smooth-bore, and I had delivered a dose of buck-shot to the king of the jungle, which, at the worst, could only have caused him a disagreeable titillation. "Grief is for little wrongs—despair for mine." I had not the courage to reveal the fact, but somehow it leaked out, although I am not aware it was known to those most concerned till some time afterwards. "I am glad you got a shot at your tiger!" said one. "Wonder if he'll die!" exclaimed another. "Do you think you hit him?" asked a third. "No one expected a tiger there!" and so on. We returned to camp just as it was dark. The sun had not well gone down ere the chorus of jackals, wolves, owls, night-jars, and strange birds, filled the air. The wind came down keenly from the mountain ranges, and the comfort of fireplaces to which we had been accustomed in our grand tents was missed, so that some of the party resorted to the old Crimean practice of dressing to go to bed.

February 9th.—A concert of coughing, sneezing, chattering and shivering from the camp-followers around the tents awoke me this morning. The poor creatures from the south, with nothing but thin cotton robes to cover them, must have been miserable indeed. I believe we should all be more charitable if we lived in tents. As soon as the shooting-elephants had started to meet the Prince on his return from Nynee Tal, Lord Aylesford, Lord Carington, Colonel Williams, Colonel Ellis, Major Prinsep, &c., set out on horseback, under the guidance of General Browne, to a village six miles away. There we found Major Sartorius coming from Moradabad, who joined the party. The fleet of shooting-elephants having received its passengers on board, weighed, and stood in line across the ocean of pulse, grain, and barley, outside which we could see herds of black-buck; but long before we got within shot they vanished into the long grass. The ground literally swarmed with game—cheetul, buck, marsh-deer, and wild boars. My shikarry, Lall Sing, a trooper of the Central India Horse, must have been able to see through a stone wall. "Deko!" here—"Deko!" there—said he every moment, pointing as if he saw what was bounding away through the grass, while I might as well have tried to make out the clock of St. Paul's in a London fog. Occasionally the elephant whisked round, or started so violently as to cause one to hold on with might and main in the howdah, as "something" ran close to his legs. At last various game began to suffer, and deer, wild boar, partridge, black and red, para, &c., accumulated on the backs of the pad elephant. The courage of the boar is worthy of commendation. One, transfixed by a spear, turned upon the huntsman, and drove him to seek safety on the back of an elephant. Another, with a splendid "hog" mane and great tusks, charged the line, striking such dismay into the elephants, who preferred being rent behind to having a proboscis and tusk encounter in front, that the noble savage escaped. We reached camp at 7 o'clock. Here we found his Royal Highness, who had returned much pleased with his visit to Nynee Tal, although his first day was a blank.

After dinner, great logs were heaped up in front of the mess-tent; chairs were brought, and before the huge camp-fire, burning brightly, the Prince and the company sat listening to the delightful anecdotes of Sir Henry Ramsay, who invests the land and the people and the chase with fresh interest. He told us of a certain village in his territory where the people were terribly troubled by a tiger; so they sent for the wise man—the barabhar, I think he said—to charm the beast away with his drum and songs. The tiger, however, came out and ate the wise man—whereupon the villagers arose and migrated. "For," said they, "now that the tiger has eaten our sage, he will know all our secrets, and we shall have no chance of evading him."

The band of the 3rd Ghoorka Regiment has moved up with us. The strains of Verdi, Offenbach, Donizetti, and Mozart mingle with the howls of wolves and jackals. It is clear moonlight; the stars are shining brightly; above us tower the Himalayas. Who knows what lies beyond these snows? Who can tell what the crowd who sit afar, with their cloaks thrown around their heads, are thinking of, as they gaze at the white-faced strangers laughing and chatting so merrily in front of the camp-fire?

February 10th.—Three parties were formed, but no tiger was killed. After several blanks, the Prince and his party were posted by General Ramsay round a patch of deep grass and reeds, with water near it, in which a tiger was reported to be hiding. The elephants were sent in to beat. Unfortunately, the Prince was shifted to another place, and immediately after he had moved, a splendid tiger rushed out within twenty paces of where the Prince had been stationed. The Prince fired, but the grass was high, and the tiger, which received the fire of others, got off untouched. Subsequently a leopard started from the jungle, which the Prince wounded, and which was killed. However, the general shooting, deer and small game, was very successful.

February 11*th.*—Our objective point was Peepul Perao, thirteen miles to the eastward of our present camp. Each of the party has by this time got on pretty good terms with his mahout, his shikarry, and his elephant; but the wonderful way in which some of the former persist in never learning how to secure the howdah provokes great acrimony. As the unwieldy but not stupid brute which sustains the howdah plods along, the occupant sometimes feels that he is going steadily over on one side. The mahout, forcibly admonished of the fact, entreats the shikarry to step out on the back of the animal, to drag at the howdah to set it straight, or conjures two or three friends on pad elephants to come to his assistance. But it generally happens that at some crisis in the hunt you have to halt while the elephant lies down, and the howdah, with all its difficult apparatus of chains, ropes, and straps, is readjusted. At this time of year tigers are in the deepest swamps, where the grass rises many feet above your head; and the only chance of finding them is in diligently thrashing through the morass. Deep as these swamps and jheels are, they generally end in narrow guts, or taper away to comparatively bare spaces. What swarming life of birds! Duck, teal, kingfishers, reed warblers, painted and common snipe, rails, dappers, butcherbirds, partridge and quail; parrots, many sorts of thrush or grackles, woodpeckers, fly-catchers, owls; jungle-cock in the thick stuff, black partridge on the outskirts, and porcupines rustling over the dry watercourses; hares near the cultivated patches; by the edges of the woods, little burrowing creatures like marmosets! Above all, career eagles, falcons, hawks, buzzards, and kites. Orders strict—"No firing!" No matter what heads or tusks may be seen, not a shot is to catch the ear of some distant tiger and send him slinking away. Hour after hour the hunters sweep through great marshes and forests, where dâk, sal, teak, and peepul excite ever-recurring wonder. The absence of population in these regions is not remarkable when one thinks how people would be harassed by wild beasts and by fever; but still, to travel mile after mile through beautifully-wooded regions, where Nature seemed to give the most astonishing proofs of vigour and fertility, and find no trace of man, was startling! It is too much to say no trace, because we came upon wigwams belonging to people who had come down from the hills to feed their herds in the winter time—poverty-stricken, subdued, timid-looking creatures, of mild inoffensive aspect, clad in coarse cotton. Those who think that it is not an unpleasant half-hour when the cart advances with its Norwegian stove, and the cloth is spread on the grass in some pleasant dingle at home, would not disapprove of the arrangements made by General Browne for shooting-tiffin in the jungle. Not merely German waiters and the work of French cooks transported on the backs of elephants, but blocks of ice to cool the wine and water, and many other luxuries not at all to be despised by those who can get them when heated with the chase. When all hope of tiger was abandoned, the word was passed for "general shooting" homewards.

Peepul Perao, which we reached ere sunset, is a name only. Even the map-makers do not venture to give a local habitation to it. The once quiet glades now presented long lines of tents, blazing camp-fires and bustle of camp-life; the trumpetings of elephants, the neighing of horses, broke through the silence of the forest.

The camp contains 2500 persons. Without counting General Ramsay's separate camp establishment, there are 119 elephants, 550 camels, 100 horses, 60 carts drawn by oxen, many goats and milch-cows, sheep, and perambulating materials for food. There are nearly 600 coolies, 60 tent-pitchers, 20 men to supply water, 20 men to clean, 20 messengers, 75 non-commissioned officers and men of 3rd Goorkhas and their band, 20 troopers 11th Bengal Cavalry, 16 of the 28th Native Infantry, a detachment of native camp police (it will be observed the Prince's person is guarded by natives exclusively), and there are odds and ends which add to the total, without counting mahouts and their families and camel-men, assembled round the Prince and his thirty or forty Europeans. Certainly I should feel rather proud of myself if I were a wild beast and knew all this.

February 12th.—It is almost a certainty that the first sight that catches one's eye in the morning is the light, spare figure of General Ramsay smoking the inevitable cheroot, which, if unaccompanied by spirits or wine, must be one of the most wholesome articles of diet in the world, should we judge from the King of Kumaoun. The shooting camp was shifted to-day from Peepul Perao to Nuglah, about twelve miles away.

The first party had about eighty elephants. The second division had fifty. Covert after covert was beaten, but the landlords were not at home. General Ramsay did his best; but it is too early in the year, and it was labour in vain. When the flies are not out the tigers are in. The ground was so deep in places that the beasts floundered about as if drowning, and mine sunk so that the mud reached its lower jaw! The ground between the jheels, thickly wooded with *Butea frondosa*, euphorbias, elephant creepers, *Derris scandens*, dwarf-palms, and the dak-tree, leafless, but decked with profuse bunches of the brightest scarlet flowers. It was a relief to hear the word down the line—"You may fire at anything." And when the pad elephants were drawn up in camp at night there was a fair show of sambur, cheetul, nilghie, marsh-deer and pig. Eighteen Bhoteas, a Hill people, a cross between Monguls and Thibetans, of whom six were women, were brought down; but though they may be curious, they are not interesting. They were sketched by Mr. Hall, and they were photographed. They bore the ordeals with perfect composure. The women wore silver amulets, ornaments of turquoise and rude gems round their necks; some had silver nose, finger, and toe-rings, and anklets of uncouth workmanship. One man had a praying-wheel; others, who were professional beggars, produced the little drums by which they incite a desperate charity.

February 13*th*.—A day of rest. I walked over to General Ramsay's camp, where the Rev. Julian Robinson read service. The lock of one of my guns was broken by the shikarry. I was told that Ghole Mahomed, a blacksmith and general workman with General Browne, could repair it, so the gun was given to him, and he brought it over neatly mended—a new spring in. "You should not have worked on a Sunday," said I, "Mahomed." "It was a necessary work, Sahib," said he, "and your Book says it is lawful to do what is necessary on your holy day. How could you shoot to-morrow if I didn't mend your gun?" On my way from one camp to the other I saw a crowd of Natives hopping about in a very lively manner in a sort of circle, and at the same time striking with their sticks at something on the ground. It was at a small snake which was, they said, very venomous.

There are plenty of them here, but no cobras; pythons are numerous in the woods. It is remarkable that we have seen few snakes in India, where deaths from snake-bites amount to many thousands every year.

February 14th.—St. Valentine's Day. Dr. Kellett keeps a record of the game, and it is curious reading. Take "an off-day," for example:—"H. R. H., 2 para (deer), 1 pig, 3 black partridge, 1 kingfisher; Lord Aylesford, 2 mongoose, 1 para, 1 hare, 1 partridge, 3 plover; Lord Carington, 2 partridge, 1 cheetul; Lord A. Paget, 1 porcupine, 1 florican, 1 partridge, 1 hare; Fayrer, 2 para, 1 cheetul; Prinsep, 1 hare, 2 para, 3 partridge; Dr. Smith, 1 pig, 1 partridge," &c. The camp moved from Nuglah to Tandah; the shooters divided into four parties. The Prince's party, led by General Ramsay, moved across the open country in line, killing boar, deer, and partridge, till we reached the jungle. Presently sight was caught of two dark objects in the grass. They were bears. One was fired at and killed by Lord Aylesford. Mr. Macdonald called out, "Tiger gone back!" The elephants began to beat the jungle once more. The Prince was placed in the middle. In two or three minutes the elephants near him gave way, and looking across a small rivulet, I saw a bear, crouched as if listening, between the Prince and me. The Prince fired. The bear dropped, but got up and rushed out of the jungle, charging an elephant in its way. Several shots were fired, and it rolled over into the rivulet, struck by a fatal ball, but it had been hit by the Prince's first barrel. It was a sloth bear, of extraordinary size and weight. These creatures are exceedingly fierce and mischievous, and Mr. Macdonald has official knowledge of eight persons having been killed in two consecutive nights by one of them. The other parties were not successful.

The weather is cold at night, with variations of 40°

between 2 A.M. and 2 P.M. Quinine is taken according to prescription, but the country is considered quite healthy at this time of year. The people, who are called Taroos, a small-boned, quiet race, suffer much. They have taken to drink whisky as a national beverage.

The lion is called "the King of Beasts" by Æsop, but Æsop was an African. In the Indian jungle the tiger is king, and there is no royal road to shooting him; every other creature must be allowed to pass unscathed when he is sought; for to kill a tiger, hours of beating and watching and halting must be endured day after day without repining. There is indeed the excitement of knowing that at any moment the quiet patch of grass before your eyes may be rent asunder, and its yielding rushes and waving reeds may glow with the fire of that terrible eye and warm with the rich colour of that royal presence. One is told it is much nobler to descend into the jungle on foot and to seek the tiger in his lair, but gentlemen who pursue that sport are generally destroyed; certainly, whether safe or not, it would not be possible to pursue the sport here, for no living man could walk a hundred yards through the astonishing growth of reeds and tangled vegetation. It might be possible to get a tiger by sitting night after night watching on a roost up in a tree over a pool of water, or the carcass of a dead buffalo; but, in truth, the beasts are not abroad. "These confounded tigers are beating me," poor General Ramsay was wont to say, quite ruefully, night after night. They are like a needle, not in a bundle but in a stack of hay, and thousands of elephants in the jungle could not force them out.

February 15*th*.—From Tandah to Ooncha Gong, only a march of five miles, the beat extended over fifteen. For a long time there was tramp, tramp, tramp, through wood and swamp, and nothing worth shooting to see.

At last fortune began to smile. A great sloth bear was discovered sunning herself in the jungle, which started off with a scrambling run in the high grass. A quick shot from Mr. Colvin killed it. When the hunters went up they found two cubs, about the size of full-grown pug dogs, gambolling about their dam, as unconscious as herself of the cause of her sudden quiet. As soon as they found the strange beings were about to separate them from their mother, they fiercely snapped their little milk tusks at their captors. At last they were secured, uttering piteous cries, and fastened on a pad elephant. As soon as the carcass of the dam was hoisted up alongside the poor little fellows, they stilled their lamentation. At camp they were put into a box, and ate a dish of bread-and-milk without much pressing.

Towards four o'clock the hunters entered a covert in which the reeds and grass rose high above the howdahs; at times the elephants were restive. A para (deer) bounded past Lord Suffield. An instant afterwards there was a sharp cry. The line pressed on, and a tigress made a rush through the thick stuff. It is not easy to determine what happens on such an occasion. Every one who sees has a shot. Lord Carington was credited with the hardest hit; but Sir D. Probyn, who certainly made his mark, refused to claim any share in the skin. The tigress, hit through shoulder, head, and back, rolled over with a growl, which died into a moan, and with a few heaves of her striped sides lay stark, but not stiff. The milk still flowed from her paps. The natives ascribe many virtues to the natural food of young tigers, but no one was bold enough to test the truth of their assertions. They believe that the whiskers are a sovereign remedy for maladies incident to advancing years, and that tiger's fat is a specific for wounds and for sores which nothing else

CROSSING A NULLAH.

can cure. So here was a whole pharmacopœia stretched before us. The tremor of the elephants was explained when it was found that there had been three little tigers, some six weeks old, running about in the covert, playing with their mother. What became of these bereaved tigerlets? General Ramsay thinks their father will have nothing to do with them—that he will be very angry, in fact, if they come near him. If they were old enough they might pick up the fragments of his feast, and dispute the *disjecta membra* with jackals, wolves, and vultures, but he will not teach their young ideas how to hunt. The deer the tigress intended for their dinner was discovered, its neck broken and flanks rent by one stroke of those claws which now any one could feel with impunity.

February 16th.—The camp moved from Ooncha Gong to Sassoona. While enjoying very good sport in general shooting, two villagers brought positive news of tigers in a swamp of extraordinary depth. Lord C. Beresford and I were sent on to guard the farther end. We heard much shouting, and went to ascertain the cause. General Browne's elephant had sunk in a deep hole, from which it was extricated, after much hard work. Another met with a similar misfortune. This was unlucky, because the tiger was just before them. Lord C. Beresford had a shot at a crocodile, and a large bear was seen by the beaters. Search was made for the bear, but in vain. The Prince came to camp with a tigress (8 feet 6 inches long), and a fine sloth bear weighing over 250 lbs. and measuring 6 feet 8 inches, which he had killed after a long day's work; every one is pleased when there is a kill to reward General Ramsay's efforts. There were deer and pig, some florican, black partridge, and sundries to boot. A mailed ant-eater, or manis, was brought in alive. It could only be uncoiled by pouring water on it.* Colonel Owen Williams, to our great regret, was obliged to leave for England to-day.

February 17th.—There was a pleasant patter of rain on the canvas, and a sound of the kelassies trenching and digging round the tents, as if the force were sapping up to an enemy, last night. It was only making drains. The shower caused General Ramsay uneasiness, as the fords become impassable on small provocation. Had the rain lasted, the Prince would have been unable to shift his quarters, for the ship of the desert hates water, unless for drinking, and founders irretrievably in a few inches of mud.

It was 10.45 A.M. before the tents were struck, and the shooting party stood in single file westward, to beat the covert in which the tigress was killed yesterday. Unambitious shooters viewed with regret gorgeous peacocks, fly, sambur, cheetul, and wild boar bound across the path. When the scene of the kill was reached, the Prince and one body made a sweep round the swamp. The other guns were disposed in a semicircle at the extremity and on the flanks. At 12.50 P.M. the word was given to advance, and there arose the noise, like the hissing of a long rolling surf on the shingles of a beach after a storm, made by elephants moving through the grass and rushes. The elephant, resolved not to get into a hole if he can help it, thrusts his proboscis down in front, and sways it from right to left and left to right with the regularity of a pendulum, laying low the green wall with the "fleisen" sw-i-i-sh which the Germans say Homer meant when he wrote of "the much-resounding sea." The elephant, perhaps, would decide the question if we could only find

* It died on board the *Serapis.*

a mahout intelligent enough to understand it, and put it to him properly in elephant language. Suddenly there was a roar, which those who visit the Zoological Gardens on Sundays at feeding-times would ascribe to one of the largest carnivora. "It is a guddee* elephant that has gone down in a hole; that's all!" A good deal for the poor guddee, however, who had scarcely more than his head and proboscis over the mud, and who made a tremendous outcry over his situation. Elephants, unlike men, will always help a friend out of a hole—aye, more, they will help an elephant with whom they have not even a bowing acquaintance. At 1.45 P.M. passed through a forest filled with birds in infinite variety; trees, not one of which was known to the most learned of us, except as "a kind of" something or other, intersected by gullies and streams, with steep banks. It was very hard, but the tigers would not show. To add to the aggravation of a blank, there was scarcely one of the party who could not have killed a magnificent girow, or sambur or two.

The sun was getting low when the elephants made a sweep towards the smoke, rising high in the calm air, which indicated the site of the new camp at Nanuk Mutla. A few deer, hares, and black partridge, of the last of which Lord A. Paget made the largest bag, were added to the score.

The camp was pitched in a fine tope of mango and *Ficus vinosa*, near a favourite place of pilgrimage of the Sikhs, revered for the miracles of Nanuk Goroo. The Prince and his party came in at 8 P.M. with two young tigers. The third party saw a tiger swimming a river, and Ali Ashkar Khan got a long shot at it. We are, indeed, in Tigerdom, but the kings of the country will

* An elephant for the transport of game, &c., which carries only a pad.

not show us civility, though one ate a man to-day near us.

February 18th.—Several of the suite visited the shrine of Nanuk Goroo, and found many ascetics and pilgrims established round it, who never came to look at the Royal party. Mr. Girdlestone rode over this morning to make arrangements for the visit to Nepal. All our native followers must have passes. By the Governor-General's permission, Nepalese troops cross the Sarda to escort Jung Bahadoor. The whole party left camp together. The elephants formed a line of more than 600 yards long. At 12.30 P.M. the elephants crossed a quicksand in the bed of the Deva, which yielded but did not break. We soon came on marshy places swarming with duck, teal, and snipe. Ground so extensive required careful beating, and General Ramsay's lieutenants, Macdonald and others, aided by Major-General Probyn, directed the operations. It was near 2 o'clock when the elephants gave notice of something unusual in front. The line had contracted, forming a loop, with the Prince in the centre. Suddenly the grass moved, and a tiger bounded across in the direction of the Prince. Those who saw it called out, "Do not fire;" but at the moment some one fired from the other side of the loop, and the tiger turned before the Prince could get a shot at it. The beast charged the elephants, receiving fire from the howdahs and rolling over dead, close to the end of the line—a splendid male, 10 feet long, beautifully marked—shot through back, neck and head. Some of the party thought they saw a tigress going away at the same time, but Mr. Macdonald, who knows every inch of the jungle, thinks they were mistaken. It was dark when the Prince arrived at Kalteema, one short march from Bunbussa, on the Sarda. Here we were nearly at the frontier of Rohilcund, and the shooting excursion in

British territory terminated. The result did not answer expections. It is poor consolation to be told that a month later many tigers will be shot where now deer wander unmolested. There has, however, been a considerable amount of game killed, from bears and deer of various kinds down to florican, partridge, and snipe, and two large and two small tigers have been scored to the Prince and his friends. The life for those who enjoy perpetual change, especially on elephant-back, is interesting and healthy.

February 19th.—The tents were sent on to Bunbussa. One of the most curious sensations in the world is that of the dweller in tents when he finds his tent is gone, and that he is left out on the open, blinking his eyes in the sun, like an owl driven from his ivy-bush. I set off in my howdah, as, notwithstanding the jolting, I could read as I travelled. At 11.45 A.M. I noticed a milestone which informed the world that it was 27 miles to Phillibeet, and 13 miles to Bermudeo—I do not care if I never see that milestone again. At 12.15 P.M. there came to view another milestone, which stated that it was 29 miles to Phillibeet, and 11 miles to Bermudeo, so that my old elephant was gallivanting along at the rate of four miles an hour. But in that time what strange things my elephant and I had passed by and duly observed! There were strings of camels with their noses and tails connected by ropes—so a camel which would be high-minded because he knew his tail was compelling the head of the next to follow was humbled by finding his own nose obliged to obey the tail of his predecessor, and the pride of the first of the string had to undergo abatement when he became aware that a small boy was leading him by the nostril. There were men carrying all the quaintnesses of an Indian camp, boxes, labelled "Agra Ice Company,' dependent from the ends of bamboos; men with hooded falcons; men with greyhounds; old women on ponies; young women wearing breeches; men with no clothes on their legs and voluminous folds of calico on their heads; Sepoys guarding camels or elephants, or nothing but themselves; wallahs, with boarspears; soda-water bottles; curious and familiar articles, which put one in mind of the excellent story in Jacquemont's letters; cases with wine bottles, glistening in the sun, bearing the honoured names "Lafitte," "Château Margaux," and the like on their mendacious sides. Then a flock of goats and sheep, our milk and mutton. Thereafter, on an elephant, a red iron pillar, labelled "Post Office," and animated creatures of the same department on his back. Then a cheetah, hooded, in its ox-cart with two attendants, *Felis jubata*—purring like a gigantic tabby as its keeper stroked its head, and so on, mile after mile. Presently came in view a clump of trees and a few chairs by the roadside; a cloud of dust announced Sir Jung, who came up at a canter with a few officers. He dismounted and sat down, talking and smoking, while Mr. Simpson took a sketch of him.

The Prince of Wales came in sight about 1 o'clock. Sir Jung Bahadoor advanced on foot to meet him. Sir Jung then mounted and rode beside the Prince to the camp, where a guard of honour of the 3rd Ghoorkas and a cavalry escort were drawn up; and, after the usual formal visits, the rest of the day was passed in peace.

February 20th.—The Rev. Julian Robinson read service before his Royal Highness and the Europeans, with the exception of those who were obliged to go to the new camping-ground. Tents were struck after breakfast, that the luggage might be got across the river to Nepalese territory in time for dinner. By midday the tent of the

Prince, the mess-tent and shamianah, were the only traces of the encampment. The Prince remained at Bunbussa, on the British side of the Sarda, till 3 o'clock. He is about to enter a mountain jungle, where roads are unknown and camels travel with difficulty. The elephant must do all the work.

There were at least half-a-dozen bridges to be crossed before we reached the new camp at Jamoa, on the left bank of the river, for the Sarda, beautifully clear and impetuous, is now rather low. It forms an infinity of islands and is fordable at most places by elephants, but too deep for horses, and impassable for camels. The bridges are ingeniously made by filling osier-baskets with stones, and placing them together till they form a continuous chain of posts; on these branches are laid, and then earth, till a road is made for horses and hackeries, but not for elephants. The Prince was escorted by Sir Jung and his Sirdars. The British Ghoorkas remained on the other side. A Royal salute was fired by the Nepalese artillery. The Prince's camp was close to the tents of the Prime Minister, which were enclosed in a wall of canvas. Sir Jung took leave, and returned with his suite in full dress, blazing with diamonds. A Durbar was held. Sir Jung delivered a Kureeta from the Maharaja, expressing his great satisfaction at the honour of the Royal visit to Nepal, and conveying assurances of his attachment. In doing so, Sir Jung declared for himself he never could sufficiently acknowledge the kindness he had received from the Queen, the Prince Consort, and all classes of society when he visited England. He had been prevented by an accident from carrying out his intention to pay another visit to England, but he still cherished the hope. The Prince thanked Sir Jung for his expressions of good-will. Her Majesty was well aware of the services rendered by Nepal, and felt grateful for them, and she appreciated highly the assistance given by the troops under Sir Jung Bahadoor on an important occasion. Sir Jung Bahadoor said it had been his pride and happiness to have been able to afford the help which had been so highly esteemed. The government of Nepal had done what it could. Let the Prince assure the Queen that, if ever there was occasion, all the assistance Nepal could render would be cheerfully given. The Prince paid a return visit to Sir Jung. At each visit or Durbar there were presentations, so that each member of each suite was twice introduced. Two caged tigers and a splendid collection of birds were offered to the Prince. Many Impeyan pheasants (which the Nepalese call "duffa"), and argus (which they call "monal," the name by which the former are known by us), kaleege, coqplass, chickore, jungle-fowl, and a delightful little elephant, which salaams and performs many tricks, were also presented.

An enormous boa constrictor was dug out of a hole in a lethargic state, and roused by buckets of water poured down its throat. It was 18 feet long, as thick as a nine-pounder, and seemed an amiable reptile; but close at hand, coiled round a branch of a tree, was another of evil disposition, for when Sir Jung Bahadoor sent a man to cut the branch, so that the serpent fell with a heavy thud, it raised its head and moved menacingly, as if to attack us, but it eventually coiled itself round, and, like a true philosopher, went to sleep. Some Nepalese soldiers showed strength and skill in cutting trees, and there could be no doubt of their power to lop off heads and arms with their kookeries.

Sir Jung visited the Prince towards the close of dinner, and proposed the health of the Queen. After the toast, Sir Jung proposed the health of the Prince, and said that "it was felt he had done them the greatest honour in coming to Nepal."

We know very little of Nepal. There is no good map of the country; nor will there be any till a few engineers throw some light on the darkness. The present maps are specimens of what Colonel Thuillier would style conjectural geography. The kingdom extends for 500 miles S.E. and N.W.; it varies from 70 to 100 miles in breadth, which will give a superficies of 54,000 square miles. The population is estimated at 2,000,000, the revenue at 1,000,000*l*. The army consists of 14,000 infantry, 420 guns, of which six batteries are horsed, the others carried by coolies. There is a handful of cavalry, but the country is unsuitable for horses.

February 21*st*.—12.30 P.M.—The Prince has just returned, having killed his first tiger in Nepal. It is now lying stretched within a few yards of my tent, and a lamb might play with it, for there are in his body three wounds, any one of which would have been mortal; his eye, which I saw glaring with fire some minutes ago, is dull, his claws, once tremendous, retracted in harmless sheaths. What number of elephants and men were engaged in compassing his death I am not prepared to state; but I know that any one of them, brute or man, would have been sorry to have had a private interview with that mass of striped skin and inert muscle about 12 o'clock to-day. This tiger had been marked down close to camp, and it was resolved "by the authorities" that the Prince's first day in Nepal should not be a blank. Elephants were moored to blockade him, and men were stationed to keep up fires at night, so that he could not break through, according to tiger nature. The yells of the jemadars—"Roko!" (Halt), "Chelo!" (Go on), "Bāine-ko!" (To the left), "Dahine-ko!" (To the right)—the blows of the hircus—the shouts of mahouts—the crashing of branches above and saplings below—made the forest ring. As the great coil, each link of which was an elephant, moved on, a herd of deer, a confused mass of antlers and dappled skins, halted, like cavalry brought up midway in a furious charge. Then, taking council of despair, headed by a timid dame, they charged the elephants, which actually screamed with terror, and turned tail as the cheetul leaped over them. In another minute a tiger appeared, moving in an easy canter across our front, at a distance of some fifteen or twenty yards. He was growling as he ran. He seemed minded to go at the elephants, but he changed his intention of a sudden, and thought it best to consider the situation in the seclusion of a small natural shrubbery. Into this he dropped, and was lost to view. The elephants closed in round the spot. The Prince and Sir Jung appeared. The tiger, after two or three growls—the bellow of an angry bull and the snarl of a dog commingled —leaped through the brushwood. The Prince fired. One! two! The last shot turned him. He rushed into the covert. His side was exposed to the Prince. The next report of the rifle was followed by a yell of pain; the tiger raised itself, rolled half over, and fell as the second barrel sent a bullet through its body. The apparition of open jaws and glaring eyes sank down into the grass, which waved fitfully to and fro for a second or two; then all was quiet. There was the usual cautious advance of the shikarries; and, looking down from their howdahs, all saw the creature stretched out dead. He was a full-grown male, 9 ft. 6 in. long. Had he not been stopped just at the right moment he would certainly have been "on" to a man or an elephant.

The afternoon's sport was inaugurated by a display rarely given to any one to witness—a procession, in single file, of 700 elephants. The Prince sat for three-quarters of an hour watching the column cross the Sarda. To each elephant there were at least two persons—the mahout and a man on the pad; several carried three or four people. Unless you see what mountains of sugar-cane and green food an elephant can stuff down his throat, you can form no idea of the vastness of the commissariat arrangements. When the elephants were all in position, they wore ship from line stem and stern to line ahead, and began to move over the prairie.

Tiger-talk may be monotonous, but I regret very much that I did not see the making of the wonderful "bag" which the Prince brought into camp. No less than seven tigers fell; of these six, including that in the forenoon, were shot by the Prince. Five were killed in a single beat, which did not last more than an hour. The Prince killed two with single shots; he disposed of three tigers in two or more shots each, and one was accounted for by "outsiders." The scene of slaughter was an island, with sparse forest and thick jungle, on the Sarda, such as tigers love. It was not easy for eyes unaccustomed to the work to make out tigers in the grass. The Prince steadily refused to listen to advice. "Fire just before you, Sir! There he is in front!" He would not fire at an object he did not see. Once, the elephants being close alongside, his Royal Highness crossed over and shot the beast from Sir Jung's howdah. When three or four tigers were to be seen like so many cats in a London square, it was natural that sportsmen should feel excited; but, on the whole, the general feeling was that the creatures were not as "game" as they might have been. An old hand observed, "When they have seen as much of the gentlemen in stripes as I have done, they will think them far more interesting in the long grass than when they are on the howdahs, or clawing the mahouts off." The Prince's shooting drew forth the encomiums of the great Nepalese shikarry, who has killed to his own rifle more than 550 tigers, and who hopes to score at least 600 before he quits the field.

One of the beasts which perished to-day—a tigress, fetid, lean, and hideous—was not content with deer; she was a man-eater. The clothes and bones were found near the spot where the murderess met her doom. It is generally an old or sickly tiger which takes to man-eating. Too slow or too weak to run down deer, he pounces on some poor wayfarer; and once he has found out how easy a prey man is, never tries for any other food. Another had killed nine bullocks and buffaloes belonging to one village. Is it not a comfort to feel that justice is overtaking the creatures, though, as they are cats with teeth, claws, and stomachs, they must have "their rats and mice and other small deer"? It will be many a long year before Nepal ceases to keep up a breed of tigers; and as we sit at dinner news comes that there are some not very far off.

February 22nd.—Close to the river, apart from his fellows and tended by a few chosen followers, lives a monster of force and, if one is to believe his eye, of cruelty. He is happily restrained from mischief by great ropes secured round his legs and fastened to the trunks of large teak-trees, but for all that he is fenced in and guarded sedulously. His head is painted blood-colour, so is his neck and the upper part of his body. Two small furrows over his cheeks marked by unholy ichor trickling from his head, show that he is "must." This is Jung Pershaud, the champion elephant of the Nepalese woods. There are Bijli and other famous chiefs in camp, but none equal to him. They are kept to engage the males of the wild herds. The first day we entered Nepal it was rumoured that there was a herd not far distant, and last night Sir Jung told the Prince that he had sent out his fighting-elephants, and hoped to let him see the sport. Orders were given for every one to be ready next morning at 7 A.M.

CAMP-FIRE IN A BANYAN TOPE. NEPALESE BAND PLAYING.

The party, led by Sir Jung, started accordingly, and went full speed through woods and swamps, across ravines and rivers, up and down nullah-sides, over old moraines, crashing through brake and copse with the tumult of a hurricane. The trained pads are urged by the mahout, and by a man who hangs on by a strap behind and belabours them with a wooden mallet, and go shuffling along at the rate of eight miles an hour. The wild, unencumbered with mahouts and mallet-men, are faster than the domesticated animals. Excited spies came galloping down the hillside to report that the fighting-elephants could not come up with the fugitive. After two hours' full cry—and no one can imagine what music the yells of drivers, the shouts of the leaders, the trumpeting, the snapping of reeds and saplings, and the rushing noise through swamp and grass make—some of the elephants showed signs of distress, and many were far behind. Sir Jung suggested that they should give up—"he did not know whether the Prince would think it worth while to go on." The Prince decided on going on, and away they went once more, the fatigued beasts now and then cooling their sides and expressing their indignation by spouting jets of water from their proboscis over their backs, careless of who was on the pad, even though it were the Prince, who came in for the full benefit of a douche, till at last a second halt was called. It was noon. In a few minutes a scout came up with news that the wild champion was engaged with Jung and Bijli. Sir Jung, in trepidation, came up. "You must mount at once; the herd may break this way, and no one's life is safe." The Prince was now twenty-five miles from camp, and it was impossible to witness the engagement. However, on the way they came on the conquered beast between its captors, his legs tied together—with downcast ears, drooping head and dejected proboscis. Before the morning the greater part of the herd were taken.

February 23rd (*dies carbone notanda*).—The Prince had a long day, and killed a tigress; its cub was taken alive. A word anent my own misfortune. I was posted outside a jungle, with Mr. Kellett on one side, Mr. Smith on

THE PLEASURES OF THE CHASE.—PAD ELEPHANT.

the other, and the other guns moving up towards us. The day was hot, the flies were troublesome, and I took out a newspaper and began to read. Suddenly, Lall Sing cried, "Deko! Deko!" and put a gun into my hand just as the elephant made a quick swerve, and there cantered out of the reeds, within fifteen yards of me, the very finest tiger (of course) I ever saw. He was in a hurry and in a rage too. I pulled on him. Alas! the stop was on. By the time I was on him again the tiger was off in the covert; but I cherished the idea I had hit him. There was a general search, but he was seen no more. Every one said, "You ought to have killed that tiger." However, I have seen a good many missed, and so fortify my spirits.

February 24th.—The district having been swept clear of tigers, the camp was struck at 10 A.M., and was transferred to a "lodge in a vast wilderness," eight miles off, called Mahullea. The Prince started with Sir Jung for a wood within a few hundred yards of the camp. The usual tumult began. Presently from the right came a few clear notes from a bugle. It was answered from the left. "Halt!" The line halted, for these trained corps are regulated like an army, form on centre or flanks, wheel and turn at command. There was a movement in the thick grass, and the Prince looking down could see something. He fired. The grass was agitated. He fired again, and all was still. The elephants closed up. There lay a very beautiful, full-grown leopard, dead, killed by the first shot; the second was supererogatory. The elephants re-formed and closed, until a shout announced that a tiger had been seen in a piece of grass. His Royal Highness fired. A growl from the grass — no movement; another shot—another growl. In a second afterwards out leaped the tigress, to the great discomfiture of the elephants, which flourished their trumpets, and behaved as sagacious creatures might be expected to do. The tigress was in her hiding-place again in an instant; two shots fired into the grass failed to displace her. She relapsed into an attitude of expectancy, and would not stir. In vain was she addressed in bad language and hooted at. An elephant was ordered to go in and stamp her out; he declined. To show that he acted on principle, he took a sapling and snapped it right across the animal's back. She only growled. Projectiles were hurled into the grass—oranges, Taunus, soda, and Apollinaris water bottles. Sir Jung seized the hunting-hat of the Raja behind him, and threw it at the tigress. That would not do, so he flung his own pith cap on the animal's head. Out she came, clawed her way through the convulsed and agitated throng of elephants, and made off. The Prince was close behind, got a good view, fired, and, struggling convulsively, the tigress expired. Thus in less than an hour a leopard and tigress were killed close to our camp of Mahullea.

February 25th.—To-day there was such a hunt as it comes rarely in any man's lifetime to see or enjoy. A herd of wild elephants, led by a tusker of enormous size, strength, and courage, who had engaged and beaten Sir Jung's best, was discovered in the forest some seven miles from camp. Sir Jung vowed they should be his. I started an hour or two before the Prince left camp, for I wished to ride quietly and have a look about me. There is no fear of losing one's way in the forest. There are always parties of soldiery sent in advance. There is also the track of the "pads;" but it can be followed to a certain extent only by a horseman, as the elephant can go where the horses would be smothered, swept away, or pounded hopelessly. I overtook Mr. Simpson, of the 'Illustrated

London News,' and Mr. Johnson, of the 'Graphic,' on the same elephant, proceeding in friendly rivalry, and entered a forest of sal and dak, leafless, but glorious with scarlet flowers. After an hour and a half, I halted beyond the dry bed of a stream filled with boulders. In a few minutes afterwards Sir Jung galloped up with the Prince. He wore a quaint jockey cap with gold-laced peak, a suit of hemp of English make, and a pair of antigropelos, which are much in favour among the Nepalese. The Prince wore a shooting-coat of the colour which tradition says was the favourite wear of the hero of Killiecrankie, boots, and breeches. At 11 o'clock Sir Jung pulled up and said he would wait for news of the wild herd, which could not be very far off. The halt afforded time to read the newspapers. In one was a *jeu d'esprit*, which caused some amusement. Sir Jung desired to have the joke explained; and his secretary, paper in hand, with an assiduity which was scarcely attended by the success it deserved, for a quarter of an hour or more sought to thrash out the fun of the four lines of English into choice Hindee. Sir Jung's face became graver and graver; at last he gave it up.

Up came a Ghoorka hunter with full particulars. The indomitable tusker was covering the retreat of the ladies of his family to a pass a few miles ahead. Jung called to horse at once, leading at a hand-gallop through the "glades," like the wild huntsman of the German song; but it was by no means "over the downs so free"—for there were too many "ups"—river-beds, boulder-beset, steep-banked, and besnagged by giant stumps. The horses seemed to know what was required of them. All that was needed was to look out sharp for the "checks," which, to horsemen riding hard in file, with excited horses, were much to be deprecated. It was a relief to come to a stream, so rocky-bedded, deep, and "ugly," that some dismounted, and all had to pull up. When all were on the other side, Sir Jung turned up the left bank for a few hundred yards. The horses were given over to the syces. The party proceeded up the river-bed till they reached a very steep bank, up which Sir Jung climbed, followed by the Prince. The river flowed out of a deep valley close at hand. It was down this gorge the tusker was expected to come. A screen was made by the Ghoorkas with their kookeries. Down in the gorge below us the wild tusker ought to encounter the redoubtable warriors who were hastening up. Every eye was turned towards the glen. The stalls and boxes were filled, the theatre was ready, but the actors did not appear. Sir Jung became impatient, jumped on the back of one of the Nepalese, and with two men at the side of his "mount," to steady him, was borne down the rocks, over the river-bed, and up the hill on the opposite side by his roadster, at a wonderful pace—certainly six miles an hour. He was lost to sight ere one could finish a comfortable laugh. In a quarter of an hour he appeared, urging his bounding biped on his mad career. The wild tusker was making for the pass in which we had halted when the joke was *not* explained. All that remained for it was to ride with all speed to the place we had left. The harder Sir Jung rode the better spirits every one was in and the better the horses went. How it was no one came to grief is not to be understood. The old halting-place—a moraine—was reached, and all dismounted. Scouts were sent out, and it was proposed that lunch should be eaten. But, lo! Sir Jung interrupted the hasty meal. "We are dead men if the elephants break down upon us. We must all get into trees." "But the horses?" "They must do the best they can. God will take care of them." He

SIR JUNG IN THE JUNGLE.

was in earnest, and in evident alarm, and there was no time to inquire into the reasons he had for supposing that horses would be more favoured by Providence than their riders. The Prince, who laughed at the idea of a tree at first, was persuaded to yield. Close at hand was a fine banyan, with spreading branches; and on these, some thirty feet above, the Nepalese constructed a perch with their kookeries. The Prince clambered up to this stage; Lord A. Paget, *magnâ adjuvante catervâ*, followed. Prince Louis of Battenberg, whose arm was still in a sling, shared a fork lower down with me. It was wonderful to witness the agility and *accrochant* powers of the suite. But this display of latent talent and physical force went for nothing. The elephants did not come. The tusker had gone clear away through the forest between our roosting-place and the camp.

Sir Jung's face was a picture to see, and if looks could kill, the fugitive was a dead elephant. "Call up the pads. Let the Prince mount at once," he exclaimed. But his Royal Highness expressed a wish to ride, and thereby secured the success of the day; for there can be no doubt it was only the speed of the horses which enabled the party to come up with the runaway and bring him to bay; and, finally—but I anticipate. If Sir Jung rode before, he flew now. It is wonderful how we got through that gallop; for, to the difficulties of the nature already mentioned to be negotiated, there was added the violent shying of the horses at the trumpeting pads. In ten minutes there was an awful clamour on our flank. Hundreds of pads, with mahouts and mallet-men, yelling like maniacs, passed at full speed in a succession of brown waves through the glade. The trackers had hit off the spot where the tusker had passed. They were in full pursuit. Sir Jung turned towards the plain. When the horsemen reached the verge of the forest, they saw before them, in a plain of high grass, a huge brown back, borne along on invisible legs, reminding one very much of a half-submerged whale cleaving its way in a placid sea. The cheer that burst forth—a joyous English hunting "Tally-ho!" "Hark-forward!"—was such as was never heard before, and will probably never be heard again, in Nepalese jungle. The cry took the hunted elephant aback. He paused, raised his proboscis inquiringly, looked round with an air as of one who would say, "What manner of men be these?" then, after a brief survey, he resumed his course for the swamp. The instant the elephant stopped, Sir Jung shouted, "Shahzadah! Take care! Look out, all of you! You must not go near him! In that long grass you have no chance of getting away!" But when he saw the elephant was moving away, he clapped spurs to his horse and, keeping outside the thick grass, galloped in a line parallel to the course of the beast. Away went the Prince, away went every one, *ventre à terre*, with a "Hark-forward!" that made the woods echo. Very soon the horsemen were careering in front of the monster, on a piece of burnt prairie, where the reeds were so thick and stiff as almost to force one's foot out of the stirrup. It could be seen that he was sore distressed. He had been on the move incessantly from dawn; had travelled over mountain and valley; had no time to rest or to eat; his sides were heaving, his gait was heavy, he tossed his head wearily from side to side, showing one, and but one, very large tusk and the stump of another. But he was tremendous in bulk and stature. He came on, bigger and bigger as he loomed above the cleared space. Then, his proboscis extended, his tail straight out, he stood and looked around; suddenly uttering a shrill cry, he made a run at the horsemen who were circling

THE HUNTERS HUNTED.

before him. There was something so ludicrous in the gait and attitude of the charging elephant that every one, as he bent down on his saddle and rode literally for his life, burst out laughing—all except Sir Jung, who, with one eye over his shoulder, kept calling out, "Look out, Prince! Take care, Prince!" ("Shahzadah! Kuberdar!") But though the speed at which his strange, shambling shuffle carried him along was extraordinary, the beast was much too fatigued to continue it very long. He halted, blew a note of rage, swaying his head to and fro, and flapping his ears. It was of the utmost consequence to keep him in the open, and take as much out of him as possible, till the fighting-elephants could come up. In a moment the horsemen wheeled and swept round him, Sir Jung shaking his fist and using the most opprobrious terms to the indignant animal. Down went his head, up went proboscis and tail once more. This time he turned straight on the Prince, who was shaking with laughter as he put his horse—a splendid Arab—to his top speed. Fast as he went, the terrible proboscis was not many yards behind for a second or two; but the pace was too great to last. The horses evidently had the pull in this ground; and there was nothing to fear but a fall or stumble, and then—well—"nothing can save you!" Over and over again the bold attack and precipitate flight were repeated. It was now Mr. Rose, now Lord Suffield, now Lord Carington, who was singled out, as one happened to be nearest. All the party had the honour of a run in turn. Lord Alfred Paget* and Lord C. Beresford, who had remained on pad elephants, not expecting such a finish to the day, were out of the hunt; and Prince Louis of

* I am told Lord A. Paget, mounted on a pad elephant, had an excellent view of the whole scene.

Battenberg had given a jar to his broken collar-bone, and was returning to camp.

All this time we were expecting the champions; we were but the *velites* engaging the enemy till the solid infantry could come up. Repeated messengers were despatched to hasten the fighting-elephants; but the redoubtable Jung Pershaud was rather done about the legs, as is the manner of giants, and could not travel fast, and Bijli Pershaud was far in the rear. The hunted elephant, either too much fatigued to charge his persecutors any more, or having duly reflected on the best course to pursue, now set off at a quick walk in the direction of the marsh from which it was above all things desirable to keep him. In vain the horsemen capered in front of him, rode up to his flanks, and passed within switch of his tail. On he went, like a porpoise through a shoal of herrings, sweeping his proboscis right and left. It was exciting to be able to get so close to him; it was irritating to be so powerless to control his course or divert him from his purpose. Nearer and nearer loomed the tall rushes, the waving reeds, the long feathery grass of the swamp. "He will escape, by Jove! Can nothing be done? Where are those wretched elephants?" The Prince, Sir Jung, all make a final and close attack; but he is not to be led away. He enters the swamp, the rushes and tall reeds close behind him; he is lost to sight. There is an exclamation of something more than disappointment; but Sir Jung says calmly, "We are sure of him when Jung Pershaud comes up. That fellow will not go far; he cannot leave the marsh." There was a belt of trees close at hand. All sat down in the shade. A Nepalese was sent up a tall tree. "He sees the elephant," said Sir Jung. "The haramzadah is in a pool, splashing and cooling himself. It is as I expected." As the champions who are coming down have names, and "haramzadah" is not a nice one, I shall call the runagate Miserrimus.

Half-an-hour and more passed. All this time the army of pad elephants had been rounding the edge of the swamp, and we could see them draw up in a dense living barrier. Sir Jung sent off an aide-de-camp every five minutes. "He will quite recover," said Sir Jung, "if this goes on, and be able to fight his way out, perhaps!" At last a bell, like that of a town-crier, was heard ringing from afar. There was a joyous cry, "Jung Pershaud is coming!" The head of the great brute, painted a bright red, came in sight above the reeds. He was plodding heavily along, but with an evident air of business about him; and, as if he had to keep an appointment with his antagonist in that precise spot, he went straight into the swamp. When Miserrimus heard the strange clang of the bell swinging from Jung Pershaud's neck coming down on him, he slowly turned and swept away the reeds with his proboscis, so as to get a clearer view. Miserrimus had only one tusk and the stump of another; but his perfect tusk was a beauty, and it ended in a very fine point. This he lowered, as if to receive cavalry. Jung did not give Miserrimus much time for reflection. He was a trained bruiser, and he was larger than the other, big as he was. Jung, moreover, had two very strong tusks, cut short, indeed, but still 4 ft. or 5 ft. long, and bound round with brass rings to prevent fracture. Jung, raising his proboscis with a flourish, ran in, and when within a foot of his enemy's weapon swerved a little, and gave him what I can only term "a clout" on the side of the head. Miserrimus turned a little to get his sole tusk to bear. Jung, passing on towards his quarter, gave him a ram right on the beam, which fairly "reeled" him half over. The thud was like a stroke on the big drum in a silent theatre. It was followed by a fearful, battering, ram in the quarter gallery. That was enough for Miserrimus. "There's more," quoth he to himself, "where that came from;" and as Jung drew back to administer ram No. 3, his antagonist fairly bolted, and, with unexpected nimbleness, set out for the open country, leaving Jung to beat the empty air. Miserrimus had evidently mastered the situation. "This trained assassin is bigger and stronger than I am, but I am more fleet of foot. I am refreshed by my bath, and I'll make for the forest, where horses cannot follow me. As for these pads —disgraceful females—I'll sweep them away like flies." Thus meditating, he received a dig in the stern from Jung Pershaud, which nearly sent him on his wise head, and quickened the resolve. There was a tremendous squelching in the grass, and in a minute more Miserrimus came out, heading for the wooded ridge. As he calculated, the pads and smaller fighting-elephants turned in the most abject terror. Jung made one more strenuous attempt to engage him, but Miserrimus was at least two knots faster; he slipped into the very wood in which we were, long before the other could reach it.

Horsemen in a forest have no chance of escaping an elephant. Sir Jung's anxiety was intense. "Don't go near him! Keep him in view, that is all!" It was marvellous to see how the elephant, resistless as fate, crashed along, only turning for the larger trees. Miserrimus continued his career till he reached a small stream, and saw he would have to cross some open ground before he could reach the great forest. All our hope now was in Bijli Pershaud—the "Lightning" conqueror. The Prince had ridden out of the belt, expecting to see the fight renewed outside, and I was following, when I saw Sir Jung riding among the trees as fast as he could manage it, with Mr. Girdlestone's Arab horse-breaker "Bill" and Captain Grant after him.

On the skirts of the wood was a deep, ditch-like stream. Sir Jung went at it and cleared the brook, but the horse very near lost his balance and slipped in. "Bill" sailed across like a bird. Captain Grant was over at the same moment; I was obliged to go a little higher up. The horse breasted the bank, and sent me skimming gracefully along the ground on the other side; but as my Arab did not attempt to run away, I was enabled to mount, thanks to Captain Grant, and follow my leader. I was surprised to see Sir Jung suddenly pull up outside the forest, shake his fist, and hear him pour out a volley of invective on some one inside. "He is abusing the elephant," said Captain Grant. "He is insulting his female relations, and calling him every name in the world!" And there, sure enough, standing against a tree, was Miserrimus listening intently to Sir Jung, as if he were taking notes for an action of defamation. There were only the four of us. Whether he thought he could finish the little lot off-hand, or that his feelings were roused to madness by a remark affecting the reputation of his deceased mother, I cannot say; but without sound or note of warning, like a house undermined by a flood, he plunged into the stream, and was at us in a moment. At this supreme moment Bijli Pershaud emerged from the covert a few yards away. Not so large as Jung Pershaud, but comparatively fresh, and of great courage. Miserrimus saw his new antagonist. He halted. "Fly from him! never!" So he set his fore legs a little apart, lowered his head and prepared for battle. Rash and ridiculous Miserrimus! You are doomed. Bijli came on at full speed, and the two met with what ought to have been concussion of brains and smashes of frontal bones. It was a terrific encounter. Bijli was the quickest. Whether he was aided by the craft of man on his back or not, he delivered a tremendous blow on the port bow of Miserrimus which shook him from stem to stern, and seemed to spring a leak. Still Miserrimus tried to find sea-room for a run, but Bijli had fairly "got him" now on his flank and kept to it. When Miserrimus ran, Bijli ran too, and, being faster, was always able to resume his station on the beam, and ram him before he could tack or wear. The Prince came in time to see the final defeat of Miserrimus, who, after several rallies, had just been caught *en flagrant délit* close to a tree. Bijli gave him a ram against it, which made the branches quiver. This was repeated. Miserrimus seemed quite stupified. The attendants of the small fighting-beasts, who had now come up, passed a turn of rope round his hind leg, while Bijli sought to engage his attention by giving him resonant whacks over the head and eyes with his trunk. But Miserrimus felt the rope and broke away before it could be secured. He ran once more, followed by the relentless Bijli, pursued by the small fighting-beasts, and encircled by a cloud of horsemen. It was almost his last effort. Bijli gave him a stupendous and crashing ram in the quarter, which nearly sent him over. Then, and then only, poor Miserrimus said, as plainly as elephant could say it, "I give in!" There must be some elephant language as plain as any spoken words. He dropped his proboscis, as a vanquished knight lowers his sword-point, blew a feeble tootle of a trumpet, full of despondency—a cry for mercy—and stood screening his shame with his huge ears. Bijli accepted the surrender on the instant. He approached in a fondling sort of way, wound his proboscis round the captive's neck, and, I daresay, complimented him on his very handsome resistance. "But, after all, Miserrimus, the odds were against you. There was old Jung Pershaud, and you beat him, and did very well; but I am 'Bijli,' you know!" As Miserrimus was thinking what answer to make to these compliments, the knaves with the ropes were at work again, and this time they made good their knot. He, however, gave a tottering run, which put the horsemen to flight, but there was no chance—a great rope trailing behind him, Bijli and four fighting-elephants beating him over the head, and battering his poor sides! Miserrimus stood still. Bijli stood before him, two elephants patted him with their trunks, and jammed him between them on each side till a rope was made fast to the other hind leg, and both were secured. He was now regularly taken into custody. The deed was done, and the brave and chivalrous old warrior was beaten to his knee. And lo! it was then discovered that Miserrimus was blind of an eye. He had, no doubt, lost it in the same fight in which his tusk had been broken off. Bijli had got at the blind side of Miserrimus. When this discovery was made, there was pity for Belisarius, and Sir Jung said, "I will let him go if the Prince expresses a wish that he should be set at liberty, but I hope to be allowed to offer his Royal Highness the tusk." The Prince at once demanded grace for the captive, and he was led away to a great tree, where he was moored by a veritable cable; but he made one great effort to get away, and strained the tree to its summit ere he submitted. The cruel ropes, not as they always do for the good ship at sea, held fast. Then he uttered one very bitter cry. It is said that his wives answered him from afar, but for this I cannot vouch. There he stood, sullen and silent, rejecting with scorn the sugar-cane held out at arm's-length of his proboscis. Next morning Miserrimus was set free, and went off in search of his family, who treated him, I hope, with the respect due to the brave and unfortunate. When Sir Jung came over to the Prince's camp-fire that night, he was accompanied by men bearing the beautiful tusk, which had been sawn off soon after we left. So ended the elephant hunt, which was perhaps the "best day" in India.

February 26th.—There were two beats marked out, but the Prince returned without having had any sport, though led by Sir Jung himself. The camp elephants and camels had got on the ground and spoilt the shooting. The second party which went out for general shooting, in charge of Mr. Moore, Magistrate of Bareilly, beating across a grassy plain, came upon a fine tiger, which Mr. Moore fired at and hit. The tiger sprang on the elephant of Mr. Robinson, placing one claw on the rifle, so that he could not fire, and tearing the mahout's leg. The elephant swung around, the tiger fell off, but sprang at the elephant again and clawed it cruelly. It then leaped on the mahout of the elephant carrying Colonel Ellis, and was tearing him down when Colonel Ellis, leaning down over the howdah, fired his rifle, and the tiger dropped, but not till it had lacerated the elephant's ear and the man's knee and leg. Surgeon Kellett dressed the men's wounds, and the injured mahouts and elephants were sent back to camp. Half an hour afterwards another fine tiger was started, and killed in the open by a general volley, so that this was a great day for the outsiders, who had never expected such good fortune.

February 27th.—Mr. Robinson, none the worse for his tiger scare yesterday, read service. In the afternoon Sir Jung obtained the Prince's assent to display his army. The advance guard was composed of some dozen Lancers, well mounted, and dressed like our own native cavalry, Nepalese cap and crescent instead of turbans. Then a battery of six four-pounder brass guns. Each gun was slung on two bamboos, carried by ten men—four and six—muzzle and breach. Each limber was carried by twelve men, two men carried the ammunition in leathern cases on their backs. There were five artillerymen to each gun. In less than a minute the battery was in action; in a minute it was out of action, in retreat. Then the battery was halted, counter-marched, advanced. "Halt! action! front!" These lascars could get a battery over ground which would beat mules. The Rifle battalion, tall men in red tunics, like those of the British infantry, dark-blue facings and white braid, dark-blue trousers with red cloth stripe, dark-green Ghoorka cap with white circular roll round it, the badge (inverted crescent and sun) in front, and a chain of German silver on the upper part of the arm to the shoulder-strap. They were armed with muzzle-loading rifles, like our old Tower Miniés, made in Nepal; and in addition to the bayonet, carried the national kookery. The battalion went through the ordinary exercise to English words of command. When all appeared to be over, the band struck up a polka, and the whole battalion, moving at every bar from left to right and right to left, began the manual and platoon exercise, words of command being supposed to be given by bars at regular intervals, the oscillating movement being all the while maintained. The pains—in more senses than one—that battalion endured to learn this exercise can scarcely be comprehended. Only a ballet-master could give due credit to the performers. The battalion, in open order, next went through the bayonet exercise to the same polka, swaying as at the beginning, in accord with the music.

There was then a grand march-past, the Prince taking the salute. The band played "God save the Queen" and "God bless the Prince of Wales." It was altogether curious—the Heir-Apparent, in shooting-dress, in the midst of the Nepalese Terai, facing a regiment in which, if I am not misinformed, there was more than one real Pandy who burnt powder against us in 1857-58.

February 28th.—The camp was raised to-day, and the party shot across country to the site of the encampment called Mooza Panee. The sport was excellent. No less than four tigers fell. The Prince got one tiger, one boar, &c.; Lord Suffield got one tiger (a very aged and worn-looking fellow, whose appearance gave rise to suspicions); Lord A. Paget got one tiger (7 feet 4 in.), and Mr. Rose one tiger. In the general battue one of the beasts sprang on the Prince's elephant, and tore the cloth on which the howdah rested, coming very close to Peter Robertson. Another tiger escaped owing to a diversion made by a swarm of bees, which made a most savage attack on the party at a very critical moment, and stung the Prince very severely. The general destruction of cheetul, pig, &c., was very great, and Mooza Panee proved to be an excellent shooting station.

February 29th.—*Shrove Tuesday.* We are moving to the sanctum sanctorum, Bahminie Tal, the private and peculiar preserve of Sir Jung. The forests were set blazing, and in all directions, to keep the game in; the air was filled with volumes of black smoke. This succeeded very well, and the sport was admirable as soon as the hunters got to their beat. The angle of the Nepalese Terai formed by the bend of the Sarda is covered with forest, swamps, and prairies, and is specially reserved for tigers, one reason being that men and women cannot, or, at least, believe they cannot, live there as soon as the unhealthy season begins. In Kumaoun and in Rohilcund Terai there is too much progress to favour the increase of tigers, and the Prince, when thanking General Ramsay, comforted him by observing that he knew the country was improving, and that it was not to be expected tigers could thrive there

THE TIGER'S ALLIES.

as well as men. Among other spoils, the Prince killed a curious maned tiger, said to be peculiar to Nepal. There was a heavy bag brought to the new camp.

March 1st.—Sir Jung was unable to accompany the Prince on account of illness, but the sport was good and the ground abounded in game. "Flies!" There never was anything like them in the jungle hereabouts, not in Egypt at its worst! I begin to pity the tigers, which are driven out of their haunts by these pests; but I have no feeling of anything but wonder for the men who voluntarily go forth to be tortured by flies in order that they may kill tigers. These are smaller than the British flies, but to the eye they are otherwise alike. They seem quite content with the nutriment they extract from pith hats, leather, gun-barrels, howdah seats, dry leaves, old newspapers, or anything on which they settle, and I am quite prepared to believe that in April they are so numerous that it would not be possible to put a pin's point to the back of a man's coat without disturbing a fly. In seven days will begin the unhealthy weather. On the 8th of March commences the reign of fever over all who are not Taroos, which will drive the Nepalese out of the woods as if they were fly-tortured tigers. It is, however, rather unfair of the fever to have made some reconnaissances before its time. The Prince killed a fine tigress with six cubs (unborn). Lord Suffield shot a tiger which assumed a very menacing attitude, and obliged him to fire in self-defence; and an odd lot of porcupines, deer, wild boar, pea-fowl, black-buck, duck, snipe, partridge, and plover were laid out before the tents when the shooting parties returned in the evening.

March 2nd.—A telegram, which left no doubt that the illness of Canon Duckworth, of which news came a couple of days ago, had assumed the form of typhoid fever, caused general regret in camp. The Prince requested Sir Joseph Fayrer to start for Lahore, which is more than 500 miles away. At 10 A.M., although not quite recovered from the effects of his fall at the elephant hunt, he set out by elephant to the nearest railway station, where a special train was ordered. The country is by no means exhausted, notwithstanding the quantity of game killed. There was another good bag. The Prince shot a tiger upwards of 10 feet long, and the outside party enjoyed good shooting. In the evening the Prince and his suite were presented to the ladies of Sir Jung Bahadoor's family, his wife and his daughter-in-law, and two other relatives, who received the visits in a large tent. They were all very interesting in appearance and costume, and one was very pretty.

Sir Jung still suffers from fever, and several of the Nepalese officers are indisposed; but the Europeans are generally in good case, though the sun be exceedingly powerful.

March 3rd.—We moved to Duknabagh on the Sarda, opposite Moondia Ghat. Hearing a hue and cry at the back of my tent this morning, I went out just in time to see a fine para fairly hunted down. Another deer was taken in camp yesterday evening in a similar fashion. The Nepalese also exhibited their skill in taking fish, driving them with elephants up to a line of stake nets. There are boats or pontoons moored at the other side, and the fish, when they seek to leap over the nets, find they have got from Scylla to Charybdis. The jeels teem with snipe and coarse carp, but no one cares for birds or fishes when there is such abundance of grand game. The Prince got two fine tigers; Prince Louis killed one; and there was a good score of pig, para, cheetul, &c.

March 4th.—Before the camp broke up there was an attempt made by the photographer to "take" the Prince and his shooting-party in their howdahs. These dear old elephants will do anything but keep ears, proboscis, and tails quiet; their ears are very large—no one can deny that the proboscis is a great feature—so that it is not easy to get a good negative of the "hathi," no matter how steady the outside passengers may be. This morning Sir Jung and his brethren came over to be subjected to the operation, and two groups were taken of the united parties. The shooting excursion to-day yielded a very fine tiger, 10 feet long and 19 inches round the forearm, to the Prince's rifle. There was also a deer hunt and a wild boar chase organised, but the results were not very important, and it is our last day in Nepal—the end of the visit to these happy hunting grounds. To-morrow we move to the British side of the river. Guns and ammunition must be stowed away to-night, and the Prince's days in India may now be easily numbered, though his arrival in England is not to occur before May.

March 5th.—In the forenoon the Rev. Julian Robinson read Divine service. At noon Sir Jung and his brethren were seen coming from their camp, his Excellency bestriding a man, as is usual when he is in small health and does not mount his horse. The Prince met him at the entrance to the tent, and led him to a seat of honour. It was a farewell Durbar. The presents for Sir Jung included several very fine rifles, a silver statuette of his Royal Highness in the uniform of the 10th Hussars, and many other valuable souvenirs. His brothers and relatives were presented with rifles and other arms, &c. Sir Jung begged Mr. Girdlestone to express his sense of the great obligations under which the Prince had placed Nepal, and those who had received marks of munificence far beyond anything that they deserved at his hands, and the Durbar was broken up.

The less agile members of the suite were disconcerted when they were told that they would have to cross the river on pad elephants. The procession moved down to the river Sarda, bright, clear, and blue as the Rhone at Geneva, but twice as broad. The elephants could just ford it, causing the occupants of the pads on their island-like backs to squirm with the apprehension that the beasts would take to swimming. The Prince was delighted at the idea of having a swim across on an elephant; but the idea did not please Sir Jung, and the elephants gained British soil in safety by the ford. The camp was beautifully situated under a magnificent mangoe tope close to the river, which looked so tempting that some of the party mounted elephants, and went down to the most likely pools, where they tried fly and spinning for marseer, but in vain. Only one of these fish was caught by the anglers, who were not numerous—Lord Aylesford, Major Prinsep, and myself—in the several attempts we made on different occasions.

March 6th.—The end of our pleasant holiday in the Terai to-day! Eager to come and eager to go. The mahouts appeared to take leave. Even the hathies were brought up to make salaam. The artful Jewanjee, the venerable bheestie, the kelassie, &c., duly paraded before my tent, but they were readily disposed of. Chitties and baksheesh, and away they went contentedly. After breakfast, Sir Jung, Bubbur Jung, Runodeep Sing, and other Nepalese officers came to camp to bid the Prince farewell. When Sir Jung was told that what he said yesterday in Nepal had appeared already in London he did not evince the smallest astonishment. Indeed, it would be very hard to excite that feeling, or, at least, to induce him to permit any expression of it to be detected in his face; I doubt if he would have allowed any trace of emotion to have been visible had he been told that his speech had been duly printed in the moon. The leave-taking between the Prince and his officers, and the Nepalese Prime Minister, his relatives and followers, was of a very kindly and friendly nature.

"TU POTES TIGRES RABIDOS, MACALLISTER, DUCERE."

"MARTYRS TO THUGGEE."

CHAPTER XIII.

Bareilly—Allahabad—Chapter of Investiture of the Order of the Star of India —The Prince and the Viceroy—Jubalpoor—More Thugs—Visit to Holkar— The Residency at Indore—Arrival in Bombay—Farewell to India.

MARCH 6TH (*continued*).—At 11.30 A.M. the Prince's equipages set out for Bareilly. A new road had been made for many miles through the forest, and the cortege bowled along at a famous rate through "Topey," Rohilcund. At Phillibeet the Rampoor Chief had made a small but pretty encampment, in which there was a room of gauze, supported on silver poles, under a great tree. Here one could enjoy the air without being pestered by the flies. Of Bareilly we saw nothing but illuminated roads; but there were some of the party who had good reason to remember one hot day in May, in 1858, when, outside its mud walls, the Ghazees broke through Colin Campbell's stout Highlanders, and the Rohilla horse charged our siege-train.

Major-General Sam Browne—to be formally "Sir Samuel" to-morrow—left an arm not far from the side of our route. The Prince repaired from the Nawab's house to the mess of the 18th Royal Irish, where the evening passed so pleasantly that I am not quite sure if the special train to Allahabad was not a little later in starting than the programme had it. From Bareilly, which the Prince left at 10.20 P.M., there was a continuous run, by special train, of nigh twelve hours by Shahjehanpore (where Hale made such a stout defence when the Moulvie came down on the 82nd regiment, in 1858), to Lucknow, Cawnpoor, and Allahabad, which was reached at about 10 A.M.

March 7th.—There was much to be done, short as the Prince's stay was here. Lord Northbrook had arrived to see the last of his much wandering guest. Sir Bartle Frere and Dr. Fayrer arrived from Lahore, where they left Canon Duckworth making fair progress towards recovery. There was a grand reception at the Station, and a State procession to the Lieutenant-Governor's house. An address was presented by the Municipality, to which the Prince made an appropriate reply.

A Chapter of Investiture of the Order of the Star of India was held at 1 P.M. Major-General S. Browne, V.C., Major-General Probyn, and Surgeon-General Fayrer were invested as Knights; and Colonels Ellis, Michael, and Earle, Majors Bradford and Henderson, and Captain Baring as Companions. In the afternoon, the Prince drove to the Fort and Canning Town. There was a large dinner at the Lieutenant-Governor's residence. The Prince and Lord Northbrook had a long conversation before his Royal Highness went to the station, to which he was attended in the same state as when he entered Allahabad in the morning. The train went off before midnight, amid loud cheers from a great crowd on the platform.

March 8th.—Travelling all night on the East India Railway to Jubalpoor, and all day on the Great Indian Peninsula Railway to Candwah (or Khandwa) on the way to Indore. At Jubalpoor there was one of the prettiest receptions possible, and a halt for breakfast at the hospitable mansion of Mr. Grant.

Afterwards the Prince was invited to see seven miserables who had been for thirty-five years in gaol, having committed an incredible number of murders in pursuit of their profession as Thugs. Their lives had been spared because they had turned approvers. What lives! Five-and-thirty years within the prison walls! The Prince questioned them as to their trade and their feats in pursuit of it. I cannot say that, had we not known they were Thugs, we should have thought them remarkably villainous-looking—except one man, the most "venerable" of all, who had a hideous leer and ferocious mouth, and who could scarcely refrain from chuckling when he said, in reply to a question as to how many people he had disposed of, with his hands together in a deprecating way, "Sixty-seven!" I was experimented upon by this old gentleman, who, slipping the noose over one of my wrists, instantly gave it a turn outwards, and produced a disagreeable sensation of numbness, and a tingling sensation in the fingers and up the arm. When the Prince was about to retire, there was subdued talk among the Thugs. Mr. Morris, who had been speaking to them, said they had a petition to offer to his Royal Highness. "What is it?" "They beg, sir, that you will be pleased to order that instead of three rupees a month, their present allowance, each of them shall receive four. It will make them quite comfortable." The Prince smiled, and said that, "If it could be done he hoped the increase might be granted; very few of them would live long to enjoy it." They appeared as delighted when the Royal words were communicated to them as if they had just secured a fresh victim, and had found a purse of gold on its body.

At Sohajpoor, 122½ miles from Jubalpoor, lunch was laid out in the station, which was charmingly prepared for the Prince. Then the journey continued for five long hours. At Candwah, where the Prince dined, there was a long halt. Here the Holkar State Railway, narrow-gauge, commences, and we had to shift to much less comfortable carriages. At one o'clock in the morning the special train left the station, and the party travelled slowly all night.

March 9th.—It was 6.30 A.M. when the train drew up at Chowral on the Nerbudda, 57 miles from Candwah, the present terminus of Holkar's line to Indore. Refreshments, tents and a large pavilion were prepared for the party. Sir H. Daly, Major-General Montgomery, Colonel Watson, Majors Bannerman, Cadell, Forbes, &c.; the Malwa Bheel Corps, the Bhopal Battalion, the C troop Royal Horse Artillery, the 3rd Hussars (detachment), the band, colours, and guard of honour of the 108th Regiment, detachment of the 23rd Regiment, were waiting. Open carriages and relays of artillery horses at intervals of six miles all the way to Indore—an exceedingly interesting ascent of the Vindhya Range. On the high lands in the famous opium district of Malwa, fields of poppies were spread out like carpets of Turkestan, far as the eye could reach. Five miles from Indore the glistening of arms attracted attention, and presently we made out a great triumphal arch, spanning the road. As the Prince approached, Holkar came forth with his chiefs to welcome him. He wore a Mahratta turban, the riband and badge of the Star of India; a fine collar of diamonds was his only ornament save a brilliant-ring—a single stone of great size.

All the men that Holkar could turn out were under arms, and formed a picturesque if irregular line for more than four miles to the town. The Bhopal Battalion and Malwa Bheel Corps lined the road. I think it was observed by most of us that the air of the people in the quasi-Independent or Treaty States is bolder than it is in parts of India immediately under British rule. It was also remarked that several of the houses in the city had shutters up and jalousies closed. The people seemed prosperous, and we heard of great wealth in the place. The Prince was escorted by the Maharaja and his Sirdars to the house prepared for him by Sir H. Daly, but there was no incident worth noting. The Residency has undergone some changes for the better since the days when it was held so bravely; but there is still the staircase remaining by which Durand made his escape with the survivors of that dreadful 1st of July, nineteen years ago. There was a levee after the departure of the Maharaja, and the Chiefs of the district attended it in order to pay their respects.

At 5 P.M. the Prince visited the Rajas of Thar, Rutlam, Jourah, and Dewas, in acknowledgment of their attendance at the Residency; after which he paid a visit to the Lallbagh, where his Royal Highness was received in Durbar. Holkar led him to a room where his presents were laid out, first taking off a brilliant-ring and putting it on the Prince's finger.

A State dinner followed in a pavilion erected for the occasion at the Residency, to which eighty European ladies and gentlemen received invitations. Holkar gave the health of the Queen, whose rule, he said, was founded on the principle of doing justice to Princes and poor alike. After his health had been proposed by the Prince, he expressed the honour he felt at being visited by the son of the Queen at his poor capital, and begged to assure her of his loyal attachment. General Daly translated the speech, to which the Prince made an excellent reply. The Prince remained in conversation with the Maharaja's Minister for some time, and then went to the ballroom, where the European ladies and gentlemen from the Stations round about had assembled.

March 10th.—The third volume of Sir J. Kaye's 'History of the Sepoy War' has reached India, and the account of the Indore Mutiny has provoked keen criticism. As I look out of my tent I find it difficult to picture the scene on that terrible day when the guns were pouring shot into the house above which now floats the Royal Standard of England, and when Travers gathered up his handful of horsemen for that desperate charge. There are gardeners watering beds, from which come the perfume of roses; the only noise audible, and it is quite loud enough, is from the camels and the hackery-wallahs waiting for our baggage.

The Prince received the Chiefs of smaller note, and the officers of the Bhopal and Malwha Bheel Corps. Five men of the Central India Horse who charged the guns on the 1st of July, 1857, seemed more than rewarded by the Prince's notice and the few words acknowledging their services. A group of Bheels performed graceful dances; the men with bows and arrows, and garlands in their hair, dancing together; the women, with heads and faces covered, and arms and legs ornamented with gold bands, also dancing in separate sets, to the sound of rather harmonious native instruments. The Prince, before his departure, thanked Sir H. Daly for his exertions in Central India, and for what he had done at Gwalior and Indore, and the Royal thanks were well and worthily bestowed. The departure of the Prince from Indore, his last excursion in India, was made in the same form as his entry; and if I have said nothing more about these, it is because no matter how the occasion and locality may differ, there is necessarily a monotony which I, at least, cannot dispel. Holkar took his leave at the pandal at which he had received the Prince, and there was a pleasant drive over the plateau and down the Alpine road which descends the ghaut, to the special train at Chowral.

"We shall be in Bombay to-morrow morning! Just think of that! And then in two days more we are off towards home! Hurra, my boy! Hurra!" The train started at 6 P.M., and reached Candwah, 57 miles, at 8.40 P.M. Here there was a banquet; that is, there was a remarkable bill of fare: but the dishes set forth thereon were by no means to be found on the table. Lord Suffield, in honour of the day, proposed the health of the Princess of Wales, for which the Prince returned thanks, and, in doing so, paid a tribute in most gracious terms to the officers in his personal suite and to those who joined him in India, and attributed much of the success which had attended his trip to their efforts.

March 11th.—It was 11 A.M., and the sun was already unpleasantly powerful as the ever-vigilant artillerymen announced the Prince's arrival outside the Churchgate Station, Bombay. The station was carpeted, and the pillars wreathed with flowers. On the platform there were the Governor, the Commander-in-Chief, and all the authorities, for there was to be a procession to the Dockyard. A guard of honour was furnished by the Marine Battalion; the Governor's Body Guard and a squadron of the Poonah Lancers were told off as escort. The Staff preceded the carriages, and his Royal Highness sat in the last carriage of all with the Governor. Parsee ladies in the brightest colours that dye can make formed groups of enthusiastic admirers, even though they were compelled now and then to content themselves with the sight of umbrellas only, for the sun was very hot. It is said, indeed, that many people went away because they were tired of waiting in the heat. One of the Bombay papers, excusing the city apparently for a lack of decorations, said that there was no time to allow of any extravagant display. But perhaps it would be more polite to say that the departure of the Prince was not an event which could be welcome to the city or to India. There was a continuous line of people for about two-thirds of the route, at various points there were isolated groups of Parsees, knots of Hindoos and Mussulmen; and the European store-houses, shops, hotels, and the like, presented an array of pleasant faces from window, balcony, and roof, the owners of which cheered and waved handkerchiefs, and expressed their delight at seeing the Prince again. The first battalion of the 2nd Queen's, the 4th Bengal Native Infantry, the 20th Queen's, and the 21st Bengal Native Infantry were drawn up along the route. The platform and stands inside the dockyard-gate which had been prepared for the Prince's reception on his arrival from the railway station were occupied, but the Chiefs were there no longer. Instead of the welcoming inscriptions there was inscribed in golden letters over the portal the words "God speed you!" A group of naval officers from the fleet was posted at the entrance; a guard of honour of the G.I.P. volunteers, and guard, band, and colours of the 2nd Queen's. There were many there, no doubt, who bade good-bye to friends and acquaintances among the suite with but little likelihood of meeting again in this world; but there were doubtless fast friendships formed, which will be renewed, let us hope, on this side of the grave in a less sunny climate.

The Prince stepped on board the steam-launch. Thirteen ships of war saluted. The *Serapis*, freshly decked with white paint and re-gilt, was nobler to look at than any bucentaur. It was so pleasant to think that instead of going to wed the Adriatic, the Prince was bound for home! There was something more than official warmth in the cheers with which he was greeted, something more than the multiplied echo of Captain Bedford's regulation "Hip! hip! hurray!" as, cocked hat in hand, that gallant mariner directed the enthusiasm of the men in the answering cheers aloft when he came alongside. The day was spent on board, but the Governor invited the notabilities of Bombay to have the honour of meeting the Prince at Malabar Point at a farewell dinner. The entertainment was in all respects very agreeable.

March 12th.—At 11 A.M. the Prince attended Divine service on the quarter-deck. Mr. York read the service and preached a good sermon, but did not attempt "to improve the occasion." The land-breeze tried in vain to temper the muggy heat which wrapped us all round like a blanket, and at the best that same breeze is but a sorry and deceitful ally. It is difficult to agree with people in their praises of the climate of Bombay. Sir Joseph Fayrer certainly will not admit that it deserves commendation. Reports of sickness have led to the issue of orders that if any natives go off they are not to be allowed to come on board again. Hence great despair. The melancholy Madrassee is a sad sight, but for profundity of grief, the Bombay boy seems far to surpass him. Admiral Macdonald gave a farewell dinner to the Prince on board the *Undaunted*, to which the senior officers of the fleet were invited.

March 13th.—Just this day, seventeen weeks ago, the *Serapis* cast anchor in Bombay Harbour. The Prince has travelled nearly 7600 miles by land and 2300 miles by sea, knows more Chiefs than all the Viceroys and Governors together, and seen more of the country in the time than any living man. Soon after dawn all were alive and stirring between decks—not so much stirring, indeed, as trying to stir, for it was with difficulty one could move until the Chinese and a detachment of sailors had cleared the boxes, bales, baggage, bundles, parcels of all kinds. About these mounds of private property the native servants wandered disconsolate. No doubt in many hours of hard work their souls had been cheered by the thought that when we had gone they would appear all glorious in their scarlet coats, slashed with gold-lace, adorned with the silver plume of the Prince, and perambulate the bazaars, the admiration of all their fellows! But Major Sartorius had issued a ukase. The clothing must be given up. Finally it was settled that the gold-lace should be taken off, and that the clothes should be dyed another colour, and given back to the servants. The whole matter quite unimportant, but for the proof of microscopic vision and of thoughtfulness on the part of the authorities.

Sir Philip Wodehouse, attended by Captain Jervoise and Mr. Lee Warner, came on board at 1 P.M.; next, Rear-Admiral Macdonald and Sir Charles Staveley arrived soon afterwards. Then came the deputation—Parsee and Hindoo merchants for the most part, and three or four Europeans—Dr. Hewlett, Mr. Maclean, Mr. Peddar, &c., with the farewell address of the Bombay Corporation. The Prince requested Mr. Káráka's (the chairman) acceptance of a souvenir—one of the medals presented to Rajas.

Sir Jamsetjee Jeejeebhoy and his family had a farewell audience. Major-General Sir Samuel Browne, V.C., Major Bradford (special service), Major Henderson (political service), Major Ben Williams (in charge of the transport and stud, &c.), Major Sartorius, V.C. (in charge of the *personnel* of the camps), whose services the Prince so fully appreciated, came to take leave. There was certainly no exaggeration in the compliment paid by the Prince, when he associated these officers with the success of his Indian tour. Sir Samuel Browne—his friends take away the last two syllables of his Christian name—had to arrange trains, carriages, from the beginning to the end. Any one who saw how quietly all was done would admit that "General Sam's one hand and arm are worth two of most people's." Major Bradford had charge of the Prince's personal safety. His quiet vigilance never relaxed; nothing escaped him; his surveillance extended from Ceylon to the Himalayas, and even into Nepal; no one would ever think he had any more onerous work than playing a hand at lawn tennis. Most amiable, gentle, and kind of men, he was obliged to create small Siberias on occasion, and the number of people who "got locked up" all of a sudden will never be known, not even if a return be moved for in the House. Major Henderson's experience rendered his assistance in ceremonies of state of the highest value. If any came to grief on the horses which Major Williams provided, it was not the fault of that excellent officer; and Major Sartorius's name and services are too well known to render any eulogy of mine necessary.

Admiral Macdonald was the last to leave; with full eyes he bid the Prince "Good-bye!" It was 3.45 P.M. Then came the strokes of the bell, which set the engines in motion. The Prince stood on the bridge as the *Serapis* slowly forged ahead. The farewell salute was fired. As soon as the smoke cleared away, the signal "God speed you!" was seen flying from the *Undaunted*. The *Serapis* made reply, "Thanks! We look forward to next meeting!'

Through the drifting vapour of gunpowder, the shore, growing dimmer and dimmer, as it reflected the fading rays of the declining sun, was watched, until the outlines of the hills faded into cloudland, and darkness fell on the face of the waters. The Colaba Light long threw its sheen on the foam which marked our wake, but was lost at last amid the stars. Farewell to India!

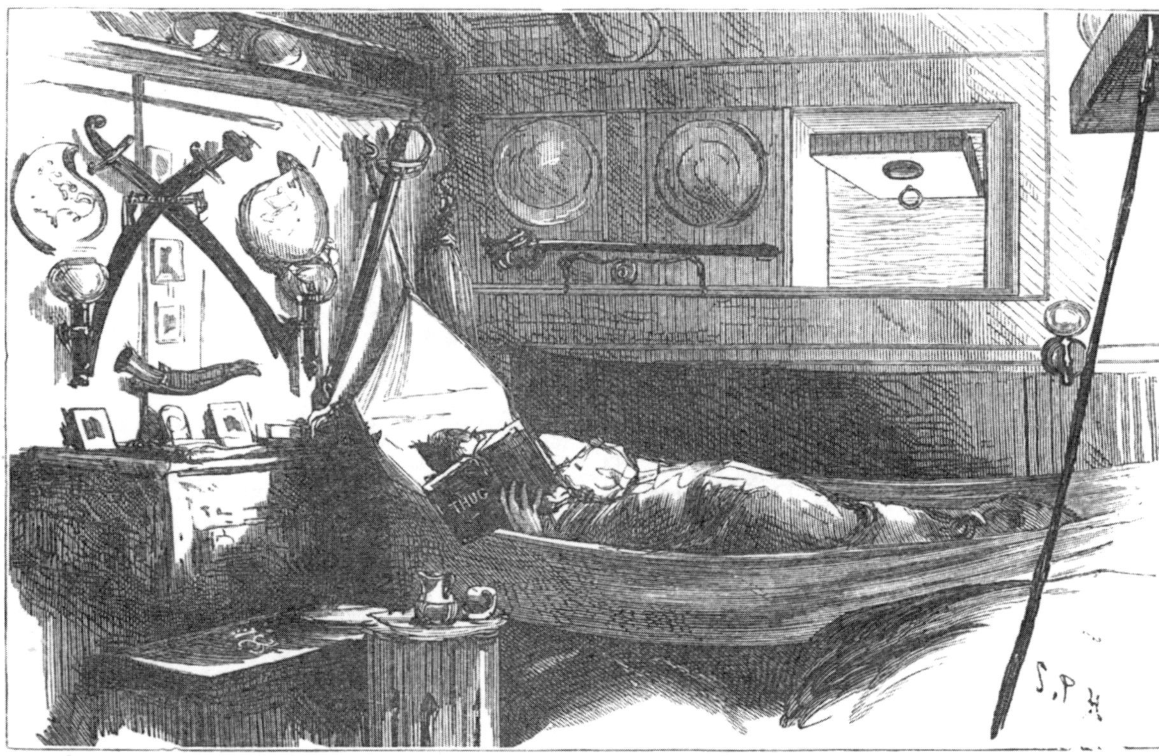

ON THE WAY HOME.

UNDER ONE FLAG.

CHAPTER XIV.

Homeward Bound—St. Patrick's Day—A Stern Chase—Aden once more—Perils by Night—Visits on Board—Suez—Lord Lytton—Cairo—The Khedive—The Grand Duke Alexis—The 'Svetlana'—Alexandria—A Rat-Trap—Malta—Gibraltar.

MARCH 14TH.—Those who were on the shady side of the ship on the voyage out have now the full advantage of the rising sun, and as he is rather strong in these parts, the benefit is not as much appreciated as it probably would be in England about this time of year. At noon, latitude 18° 4′ N.; longitude, 69 °2′ E.; distance run, 218 miles. Aden Light House distant 1419 miles. Some curiosity was felt to see how the elephants would behave. Nothing could be better or more composed than their conduct. The cheetul presented at Ceylon has complete freedom of the ship, the Prince's state cabins and bedroom included, but particularly affects the smoking saloon. She appears to live on anything, eats fresh vegetables or cotton-wool, and has been known to accommodate her appetite to putty and tobacco. At 10.15 P.M. passed the *Peshawur*, bound with mails for Bombay. Signal was made to the *Osborne* to follow and get papers.

March 15th.—At 8 A.M. a slight breeze sprung up, but it soon died away, and there was little to do but to read; the papers proved a great solace. The intelligence that the Queen would assume the title of Empress of India had reached before the *Serapis* left in the ordinary way and had been much discussed, and the reports of the debates in Parliament, which were received by the last mails, were read with profound interest. No incidents.

March 16th.—Thermometer 80°. At noon, Aden 893 miles distant; latitude, 15° 59′ N.; longitude, 60° 4′; distance run, 273 miles.

March 17th.—"Incidents" scarce, as usual. The *Osborne* came alongside, in order to exhibit her two elephants salaaming. One of the playful little tigers made a sudden clutch at Mr. Hall as he was passing him, and tore his pantaloons from knee to ankle. The four-horned deer took it into its foolish head to jump into the sea and was lost. A distribution of a very small piece of shamrock, sent last mail by a thoughtful compatriot, gave little sprigs to Lord Charles Beresford, Dr. Watson, Captain Gough, Lieut. Lambert, Lieut. Lowry, and Lieut. Burrowes. The band at and after dinner played a selection of Irish airs in honour of the day by desire of the Prince.

March 18th.—Signal made to the *Raleigh* to put on all speed and chase, as if to ram the *Serapis*, then running over twelve knots an hour. A stern chase is a long chase, but the *Raleigh* vindicated her reputation, coming up in a masterful style as if to send us to the bottom, when, with a light touch of the helm, she shot past as close as her yard-arms would permit on our starboard quarter. The Prince was on deck. The way in which the *Raleigh* was handled gave him great satisfaction. It was curious enough to see the figure-head and read the name of the hapless courtier breasting the Arabian seas as she passed us.

Sunday, March 19th.—A breeze right astern; very grateful. It was dark as the *Serapis* approached Aden. We had great difficulty in our moorings, as the wind was strong. A good deal of nervousness and electricity about. It was exciting, for there were only four inches of water under the ship's bottom. The Resident, Brigadier Schneider, came off with Colonel Penn and the staff of the Station. They were disappointed that the Prince had not arrived in time to go ashore, where everything had been prepared to do him honour.

The purchase of Socotra has given satisfaction, and it is accepted as a sign of active interest for which people living at Aden are very grateful, because they are very much like the signal-men at the Clapham Junction, who witness a continual succession of trains going and coming. There is uneasiness about the comparatively defenceless condition of Aden. There is a want of 11-inch guns, and in due time let us hope this want will be remedied.

March 20th.—The coaling finished at 2.15 A.M., and the *Serapis* and *Osborne* were steaming out of Aden Roads before 3 A.M. Perim was in sight at 11.30 A.M. Some languid excitement was created in the afternoon by the appearance of the P. and O. steamer, which we had left behind at Aden, coming up fast astern, the *Raleigh*, with all sails set, overhauling both.

March 21st.—At 1.15 A.M. the look-out saw something dark in the water, with a white streak at its base.

"Breakers ahead!" We were running right on Lebaju Island, but it was a considerable distance off. Our course was altered at once, and, in doing so, the ship came broadside towards the sea, which at once availed itself of the opportunity to have a run inside, rousing up the sleepers, who, with many cries of distress, had to make shift for dry quarters. I was amongst the sufferers, and, kicking off my wet sheet, crept up into the saloon and slept on a sofa. At 5.45 A.M. the P. and O. steamer *Assam*, going eastwards, signalled that she had service-letters; slowed, and took them on board. The P. and O. *Hydaspes*, which had dropped behind, came up hand over hand at dusk, and before nightfall was out of sight. We had 30 additional stokers, and 16 Arabs, making 96 hands in all; but 40 of the crew and marines were sent down to the stoke-holes, for which they receive double pay.

March 22nd.—At 8 A.M. our speed was little over 10 knots, but the wind from the north came through the ship and reduced the heat to 78°—a very agreeable change. Deck tennis. No incidents.

March 23rd.—A visit was paid by the port tiger to the larboard tiger. One got loose and had a little play, very much by itself, on deck before it was minded to turn into its cage. Speed down to 9·4 knots. At noon observations gave lat. 23° 33′ N., long. 36° 59′ E., distance run 235 miles. Dædalus Light, 111 miles; Suez, 465 miles. The mountain ranges over Berenice came in sight just before dinner.

March 24th.—At 6 A.M. the *Osborne* was despatched to Suez to telegraph to Lord Lytton at Cairo that the *Serapis* would not arrive in time to receive him to dinner, but that she would probably reach Suez at 2 A.M. The new Governor-General is a personal friend of the Prince.

It seems very appropriate that the Prince returning

from India full of fresh impressions, should meet in Egypt the representative of the Crown, now Imperial, who is going to Hindostan to carry out a policy which will doubtless bear marks of the agencies developed during the Royal tour, and the sympathies and objects indicated in the addition of the title of Empress to those by which the Queen has hitherto been known to her subjects. At noon the Suez Light-vessel was still 210 miles distant, Shadwan S. point 37 miles; lat. 25° 56′, long. 34° 29′ E. Siesta, deck tennis, reading, music, enable us to get over the day, and there was the excitement of the usual "lottery" concerning the hour of arrival, which was won by Major-General Hardinge.

March 25th.—There was a very picturesque reception at Suez at 8 o'clock this morning. The weather delicious; men-of-war and merchantmen decked in their best; the quays of the noble docks decorated with flags and lined with troops. Lord Lytton, who was accompanied by Lady Lytton and Colonel Burne, came on board at 9 A.M., and the Prince had a long conversation with him after breakfast. The interview was all too short; for the train was timed to reach the Egyptian capital at 6.45 P.M., and the Governor-General was very desirous to take away as much daylight with him as he could down the Straits of Jubal; but no doubt it was of mutual advantage. At Cairo the Prince found the Khedive, his sons, and the Grand Duke Alexis waiting to receive him, and his welcome was cordial and stately. We were installed in our old quarters in the Gezireh Palace, the rooms very much as if we had left them yesterday. The Grand Duke Alexis, a tall, stalwart sailor, with massive brow, keen blue eyes, and a pleasant smile, came to dinner. He has a frank manner, which tends perhaps in the direction of abruptness, as if the sea air had a little corroded the Imperial varnish, but he is a very good officer, and he certainly was very gracious and agreeable to the suite. We found the Court in a state of great depression. Nubar Pasha's familiar face and kindly presence are missed—he is once more out of office—this time it is said never to be restored, and Chereef Pasha is master of the situation, as far as the Khedive permits any minister to be so, for he is "*maître chez lui.*" The statement that the Khedive had requested that Mr. Cave's report should not be published had produced the utmost astonishment and anger, and at the present moment "the English interest" is very much down indeed. But who, to see the Khedive doing the honours to-night at the Opera (where we had *Flick und Flock* and *La Pruova di un Opera Seria*, admirably given, Signor Fioravanti reviving the recollections of Lablache in Campanone), could have supposed that his Highness had to pay 4,000,000*l*., and to be ready with 600,000*l*. in a fortnight, and that the Finance Minister had no money, and said he did not know where to get any? He was as light and *debonnair* as ever, and two princes were lodged in his palaces, and entertained sumptuously every day. The Prince remained at Cairo from the 25th of March till the 1st of April. It was desirable to avoid the inclement weather which generally prevails in England at this time of year, and it was also necessary to adhere to the time fixed for the visits to the Courts of Spain and of Portugal before the Prince arrived home. Telegraphic communication was easy, and there were daily bulletins which diminished anxiety. The time passed pleasantly, as it always does for those who are guests of the Khedive till the Khamseen wind set in, and that is an infliction that even his resources cannot evade or alleviate.

I do not propose to continue the daily record of events. There were operas and the theatre, concerts and banquets at the Palace, dinners, great and small, excursions, and, I may add, alarms; for in the midst of all this gaiety, there was Turkey near at hand struggling with wide-spread revolt and menaced with ruin, in which Egypt must be in some measure involved; there was imminent trouble at home, immense financial pressure; war with Abyssinia only just suspended by overtures of doubtful submission from the enemy. But the Khedive never exhibited any symptoms of *malaise*, irritation, or despondency. Like the Lord Mayor of London who expressed his belief that the metropolis would get on very well as long as the Thames was not taken away, the Viceroy seems to think that Egypt has nothing to fear as long as the Nile pours down its beneficent flood. His fertile brain is for ever busy with plans for the development of the influence and resources of the country, from the embellishment of Cairo to the extension of his power to the confines of Zanzibar. As under Papal rescripts the Kings of Spain and Portugal claimed all the Indies, East and West, the Khedive holds that he is entitled as successor of the Caliphs of Egypt to push his empire till arrested by some stable, well-established power. He desires to have a neutral territory guaranteed by some European Power between Egypt and Abyssinia, but will not consent to give a foot of sea-coast. The Coptic Abouna, whom he regards as the great mischief-maker, is said by Mr. Flad, who is now in Cairo, to be largely engaged in the Slave-trade. The same authority declares King Johannes to be a monster of cruelty, and holds that there will be no peace in Abyssinia till it is ruled by Egypt or by some strong power—the best solution of the difficulties of the situation, he thinks, would be the selection of Theodore's son, now in England, to be King, under Egyptian protection. There were excursions to the Pyramids and to Sakkarah, and quail shooting;

but the Khamseen was quite well developed on the 31st of March, the last day of the Prince's residence. During the week we lost Sir Bartle Frere's society—the *mitis sapientia Læli*—and Lord Alfred Paget's co-operation in doing whatever was to be done in the way of "life," for by the Prince's permission they proceeded direct to Europe. On the 1st of April the Prince bade farewell to the Khedive at the Cairo Station. The special train left at 2.45 P.M., and arrived in Alexandria at 7 P.M. There was a large and rather tumultuous crowd, and the streets were filled with people all the way to the dockyard. There boats were waiting, and once more the *Serapis* received the Royal traveller and gave his followers welcome shelter. There was a large dinner on board, at which the Grand Duke Alexis and the senior officers of his suite and of the Russian corvette *Svetlana* were present. The Prince, after the health of the Queen, proposed that of the Czar; and the Grand Duke, in returning thanks, gave the health of the Prince, which was received with the heartiness inspired by the satisfaction that he was on board safe and well after the accomplishment of a most interesting and valuable enterprise.

April 2nd.—At 8 A.M. the *Raleigh*, *Research*, *Invincible*, *Svetlana*, and the Egyptian ships and batteries saluted the Prince's flag. It blew hard; there was a chopping sea in harbour. Divine service at 11.30 A.M. The Grand Duke Alexis gave a dinner on board the *Svetlana*, to which the members of the suite were invited. The evening passed very agreeably; and after an interchange of toasts, in one of which the Grand Duke observed it was not the least agreeable incident to him that it was a Russian frigate which was the first foreign vessel to receive the Prince on his return from visiting the Indian possessions of England—at which there was much cheering—the party mounted to the upper-deck, where there was a very characteristic and interesting entertainment given by the crew—one of the *equipages* of the Imperial Guard—very fine, soldierly-looking sailors. They sang admirably those sweet and rather melancholy melodies which one hears chanted by Russian regiments on the march, as well as some livelier airs, and these were interspersed with dances, but the *chef-d'œuvre* was a musical drama or operetta, in which the deeds of the pirates of the Volga were recounted by a tall, picturesque sailor, whose solos were sustained by spirited choruses. As he sang, he walked round and round in the semicircle of sailors, now and then advancing to the company with a great air of bravado, and delivering his words with immense animation in a rich, round voice. After cordial farewells, the party returned to the *Serapis*, where all was in readiness to sail next morning, if the weather permitted.

April 3rd.—At 5.15 A.M. the *Serapis*, followed by the *Invincible*, *Raleigh*, and *Research*, weighed and stood out of Alexandria Harbour. The frigates, and the batteries, from Ras El Teen to the windmills, roused up the sleeping city with a salute, which drowned the cheers of the sailors. There was a heavy roll on the bar; but the harbour has been so much improved that there was none of the anxiety about touching, which certainly would have been not unfounded some years ago in such a sea. At 8.45 A.M. the fog-horn sounded, and a gun was fired from the senior officer as a warning to the squadron before entering a bank of haze. A few minutes afterwards a flash of lightning came straight down from a small, round, black cloud, and struck the sea a couple of miles from the *Serapis*. It was followed by a short roll of thunder, abrupt as the report of a great gun. The haze lifted in an hour and a half. The *Invincible* and the *Raleigh* were in sight; but the *Research* had dropped away astern.

THE PRINCE OF WALES ON BOARD THE 'SVETLANA,' CAPTAIN H.I.H. THE GRAND DUKE ALEXIS.

The thermometer marked 65°, and men complained of cold. The manis,* the curious mailed ant-eater, died to-day, and it is a positive fact that three several persons when told of it, in order to try them, fell into the trap, and gravely said, "Peace to his manes!" There is no punishment for such offences except recording them.

April 4th.—Now here is a fact to note. From the time the Prince landed in India till this morning there has not been a shower of rain. I except Ceylon, where it rained torrentially. There was a dreeping shower at Jummoo, and a patter for five minutes on the tents in the Terai. Now, in this sunny Mediterranean, we are favoured with a downpour. But it is quite calm. Somehow or other the sun was "brought down" in a lucid interval at noon, and our run from Alexandria was put at 268 miles, distance from Malta 489 miles (lat. 33° 7′ N., long. 23° 52′ E.).

April 5th.—The sea is in a rascally humour. It is too cold to have the ports open, but there are strong plate-glass slides adjusted to the port-holes, which seem to fit very nicely and to be quite reliable, as the Americans say—it is a good word after all—for keeping out the waves. Trusting to the appearance, I went to sleep, and in the middle of the night was suddenly awakened to the certainty that the sea had surged in through the port, and that my blankets and cabin were saturated. The rats have become very active. My boots suffered especially; so my ingenious and kindly neighbour, Lord Charles Beresford, prepared a trap, in which several of the miscreants were caught, but not being quite so confident of the results of his mechanical ability as I should have been, I removed the undevoured boots, and was duly objurgated for my

* A Pengolin. *Manis tetradactyla.*

unfeeling conduct in "spoiling sport and taking away the bait." The rigging full of pretty fly-catchers and *motacillæ* all day; but there are scoundrel kestrels about, which, having probably chased them out to sea, pursue their prey on board. They boldly strike their victims and pick them to pieces on the yard-arms.

April 6th.—At dawn Malta was in sight just like a cloud in the west, and at 7 A.M. the little *Helicon* came in view, dancing over a rolling sea, with the Admiral Sir James Drummond's flag aboard, and bags of letters for the squadron. As soon as the *Serapis* was within a mile of St. Elmo the saluting began; when she opened the entrance to the great harbour, the thunder of guns from forts and ships, and cheers from parapet, and ringing and tinkle of bells made such a clangour as was quite wonderful.

No less than eight addresses were proposed for presentation to the Prince on landing. These were condensed into one, or, more properly speaking, one address was made to do duty for the island, which desired to express its loyalty through eight different channels — masonic, clerical, ecclesiastical, legal, medical, educational, aristocratic, and commercial.

There were some pretty touches of Oriental, or, at least, of Southern sentiment and taste in the details of the preparations. When the Prince landed, he saw before him the statues of eight Grand Masters of the Knights of St. John —L'Isle Adam, who led the Order to Malta and established it there after the conquest of Rhodes by Solyman; La Valette, the gallant defender of the island against Moustafa, and the hero of the famous siege, on which the eyes of Europe were fixed so long, whose name is perpetuated in that of the city; De la Sangle, the legislator; La Cassière, the founder of St. John's Church; Vignacourt, the builder of the great Aqueduct; Cottoner, the creator of "the lines"; Manoel, the constructor of the great fort; and Emmanuel de Rohan, who gave a code of laws to the island, and died just in time to escape the melancholy distinction of being the last Grand Master. It was a good idea to line the noble staircase of the Palace, up which the Grand Master was wont to ride on the day of his election, with non-commissioned officers of the corps in garrison. There were numerous presentations at the Palace, but there was no levee.

The enthusiasm of the multitude was a very agreeable testimony to the popularity of the Prince; it can scarcely be maintained that British protection can be unpopular if the Heir to the Crown can be received so warmly. The people, who are not rich, subscribed largely to decorate the streets, prepare transparencies and fireworks. The dinner given by Sir W. and Lady Van Straubenzee was one of the grandest which the old Palace had ever seen since the great banquet on the occasion of the surrender of the island to the French.

April 7th.—There is an old gentleman named "Paolo,"—what his other name is I know not—holding office high among the servitors, in the Palace, who is among the institutions of Malta. He first came into office with General Ponsonby, and since that time he has seen nine Governors come and go; and, like the major-domo at the White House, Washington, he regards himself as the only stable part of the administrative machine. He knows every inch of the building, and is especially conversant with the gallery of armour, where there are many interesting things, for which see the Guide-books. Paolo says, "No people rule this place very long, but it will always be strangers who will do so. The Maltese belong to no one, and must be taken care of." However, there is a nationality, but it certainly has no claims to be Italian, and the most intelligent of that intelligent Maltese race, feeling the pressure of increasing population, are given to projects of founding colonies in Africa, where their people certainly thrive and flourish. There is, at any rate, plenty of room for them between Algiers and Egypt.

The 98th Regiment, Sir Colin Campbell's favourite corps, received new colours from the Prince on the Floriana Parade-grounds to-day. Although it did good service in China and the Punjaub, it had now no distinctive appellation. It was first raised as "the Prince of Wales's Tipperary Regiment"; how it lost that title I am unable to say. After the ceremony, which is one of the most tedious that ever was invented, at least for those who have to look at it, the garrison, which consisted of the 42nd Highlanders, the 71st Highland Light Infantry, the 74th Regiment, the 101st Regiment, and the British and Maltese Artillery, about 4000 strong in all, marched past the Prince.

There was a State dinner at the Palace. It is Lent time, and there is only one day during the Prince's stay considered eligible for rejoicing. The old Catholic families of Malta did not think it right to attend the ball at the Union Club in the evening. Certainly their absence was scarcely noticed, for the rooms were well filled, and the committee had done everything to render the entertainment worthy of the Prince; but it would have been more agreeable to one's notions of the becoming had the native nobility and gentry been present.

April 8th.—There was a pretty exhibition of artillery practice from the batteries to-day, but the results must have satisfied non-professional people that "sound and fury" *may* "signify nothing." Shortly before noon the Prince drove to St. Elmo, and took up a position on the concrete roof of the magazine below the Light House.

It had been intended to have experiments with torpedoes in conjunction with practices from the batteries, to show the Prince the range of the new armament, and the powers of resistance; but the Telegraph Company called attention to the danger to the submarine cables, and, as scientific officers would not give an assurance that these apprehensions were not well-founded, the torpedo experiments were postponed.

The practice was at floating octagon targets 16 feet long, at 1200, 1500, and 2000 yards, from 11-inch guns, 110-lb. breechloading Armstrongs, 80-lb. and 64-lb. Palliser's converted guns, and began from the batteries soon after noon. The general fault of the firing was that the shots were "short." Certainly the result seemed to justify the impression that an ironclad moving seven or eight knots an hour at 1500 yards could subject guns *en barbette* and in casemates to destructive fire without much danger of being injured. The *Devastation*, flying the Danish flag, which had been saluted at noon as it was the King of Denmark's birthday, steamed out of harbour for Gibraltar. Naval men said she could have laid Ricasoli, St. Elmo, and Tigné in ruins. The clamour was tremendous, and as far as picturesque effect went the scene was beautiful. None enjoyed it more than the native aides-de-camp, Anoop Sing and Afzil Khan, who have been our quiet and observant companions from Bombay. The Prince then left St. Elmo and drove to the Lascaris platform, overlooking the great harbour, to witness a general fire from all the works to resist an enemy, represented by two gunboats, one from east and the other from west. The parapets were lined with infantry. Every sea-face battery opened, at ridiculous distances, on the gunboats, and continued till their ammunition was exhausted. It was very pretty, but useless. Everything was soon hid in smoke. The noise was tremendous. The gunboats were miles away. When all was over they steamed in, and claimed the capture of the place.

The Prince lunched at Sir Victor and Lady Houlton's, and after dinner at the Palace went to the Opera, where there was a creditable performance of *La Muette de Portici*.

Palm Sunday.—April 9th. — The Prince attended Divine service at the Protestant church, which was crowded. Bishop Sandford preached. At the conclusion of the service the Prince drove with the Governor and party to Vedella, to lunch, and returned about 4 P.M. As the steam-launch was going across with the Prince and his party, who were to dine with Colonel Macdonnel and the officers of the 71st Regiment, she encountered a nasty chopping sea from the Custom House Stairs to Ricasoli, caused by the wind blowing straight up the harbour. A little uneasiness, not to say anything about the wetting, was felt for a few moments as to our prospects of landing. Fortunately the officers had prepared a floating platform, which rendered access to the causeway not so difficult as it would have been without such assistance. The wharf was illuminated by torches held by soldiers of the 71st. They lined the way to the entrance to the barracks. The ascent was steep, and the good-humoured remark that no one who lived in such a place ought to ask people to dinner, was at one time generally assented to. A very agreeable evening, however, caused small initial impediments to be forgotten.

April 10th.—Torpedo "experiments," were made in presence of the Prince, who was posted not very far from the site of one of old Draguts' batteries during the famous siege. Well! Given the increase of power on the part of the attack derived from steam ironclads and rifled ordnance since Draguts' time, and the corresponding development of the power of resistance by these same agencies, plus torpedoes, it might be inferred from what we saw to-day that things were very much as they were. When the torpedo exploded under an object which was so good as to allow itself to be taken expressly to be blown up, the torpedo blew the object up and killed many fishes as well—a new source of supply to a beleaguered garrison. I do not think his Royal Highness was quite satisfied with what he saw, or considered that torpedoes, so far, could defend Massamuschett Landing or the Lazaretto. Let us hope "non tali auxilio, nec defensoribus istis, Malta eget." This was our last day in Malta. There were many things to be done, visits to be paid, and small ceremonies and duties attended to. The people were busy taking down faded garlands, triumphal arches and Venetian masts, before the Prince went off to the *Serapis* in the evening. There a banquet was given on board to the Governor, and to the chief people of Malta, British and Maltese, which was of a very agreeable character, although not destitute of the formal attributes of a State dinner.

April 11th.—One more stage on the journey home. At 8 A.M. the *Serapis* left her moorings, off Custom House Stairs, and steamed out to sea on her way to Gibraltar. The Prince's flag was duly honoured by a general salute from ships and forts. The thermometer, 60°, warned us that we were running westwards, and away from the sun. As the ship ran along shore, one of the Scotch servants was much excited on being shown "St. Paul's Bay." "Hech!" he exclaimed, "I'd sooner ha' seen yon than a' the Peeramids in Egypt and a' the Rajaws in Ingey!" And why not?

April 12th.—Latitude 37° 44′ N., longitude 8° 34′ E. Run 264 miles. Cape de Gatt 526 miles, Gibraltar 684 miles at noon. In the midst of a conversation on a most interesting subject, the Prince's attention was caught by the appearance of one of the natives attending the elephants, who was holding his hand to his mouth, from which there was a trickle of blood. He went to the man, followed by Sir D. Probyn, and was told that the mahout had been struck by a sailor because he desired him not to tease the elephant. The Prince at once ordered an inquiry to be made. The culprit was an A.B. of good standing. Captain Glyn, who well knew the risk of "setting up Jack's back" against the natives and the animals on board, did not, nevertheless, hesitate to order condign punishment. I think it was a pretty "bed of justice," and that had it been seen in India it might have been worth a battalion to us at least.

April 13th.—A strong East wind—squally; all square canvas set, the *Osborne* spreading all her wings, and the *Raleigh* very fine to look at under her great tiers of sail. There was so much play about the ship that fiddles were put on the dinner-table, perhaps their third appearance since the Prince left Brindisi. It is cold at night, and the gentlemen who swing on board at ease feel very glad of an extra blanket in their cots.

April 14th.—The wind is said to be changeable always; but to-day it really seemed to blow in different directions at the same time. There were dozens of vessels, of all sizes and nationalities, bowling along on their respective courses, as if each had a witch to fill her sails. At noon we were in latitude 36° 37′ N., longitude 2° 20′ W. "I beg your pardon, Sir," said an old salt to me, "but its somewhere just about here we seed the sea serpent in 1870." "Who were 'we'?" "Well, Sir, asking your pardon, it was aboard the *Palace* we was. But the captain wished us to say nothing about it, for, says he, if it gets out that we say we seed the sea serpent, there's not a man will ever be employed again! But we seed it sure enough! The whole watch, about a cable's length off, and just as big as our funnel." And so I believe he did.

April 15th.—"The Rock" was in sight at dawn. It is a subject of much mirth to our young gentlemen—and, indeed, to some of the old ones—that the Spanish Governor of Algesiras, opposite, designates himself "Commandant" (or Governor) "of Gibraltar, in temporary occupation of the English;" but it is only of late years that there disappeared from the superscription of English coins a title not less ludicrous. The sense of possession, however it may be vilipended by philosophers and advanced thinkers, is unquestionably agreeable. A man is proud of belonging to an Empire of great extent, and assumes that he is *pro tanto* and *per tantum* better than the native of a country which has not made acquisitions. I once heard a great statesman make what he thought to be a complete answer to a politician, who was denouncing a certain course of action as tending to reduce England to the position of Holland, by exclaiming, "And I have yet to learn that a Dutchman is less happy or prosperous to-day than his forefather was when the Seven Provinces were dominant at sea, and when they were distracted by efforts to maintain their colonial possessions!" The great statesman never felt the throb—foolish, it may be, but capable of driving a good deal of heroic blood through one's veins—which the heart gives when the sight of the flag awakens the sentiment of the proud King.

"Ich heisse
Der reichste Mann in der getauften Welt:
Die Sonne geht in meinem Staat nicht unter."

And that was what one felt in travelling back from the East, so that the irruption of the red flag with the white crescent on it at Suez seemed almost anomalous and improper. But what do the Spaniards think of our Union Jack fluttering above Calpé? Probably very much as the Moor over yonder, who has not only to sigh over the fair land he has lost, but to submit to the flag of his despoiler on his own shore. Strong wind, sea high. The Moorish coast, rocky, bold, and barren, visible through the port, and the white houses over Tetuan very distinct. At 7.45 A.M. heard the ships and batteries saluting.

The *Serapis* moored alongside the coal-quay in less than half an hour afterwards. Scarcely had she made fast before the Duke of Connaught was seen coming down the quay. The Duke was delighted to find the Prince in such excellent health, and said he had never seen him looking so well. There could be no doubt of the good dispositions of the inhabitants of the Rock, and of their desire to do all they could to render the visit of the Prince agreeable. The procession to the Convent was made in state, and there was certainly no reason to find fault with the reception; streets crowded, windows and houses filled, flowers, garlands, triumphal arches, banners and flags all along the route; the cheers of the great multitude exceedingly hearty. After a levee at the Convent the Prince accompanied the Duke of Connaught to his quarters, where he partook of luncheon. There was a disagreeable pull from the Watergate Quay to the *Serapis*, in order to dress for a banquet at the Convent at 8 o'clock.

The news of the death of the Maharaja of Puttiala (which came to-day) was heard with sincere regret by the Prince, to whom the young Maharaja had exhibited great friendship and regard.

April 16th.—When Bishop Sandford had ended service, Sir J. D. Hay appeared on board with a deputation from the Emperor of Morocco, Cid Aly Mesfeewy, Envoy

Extraordinary, Said Abdallah Benabdil, &c.; and though there was not a diamond or emerald among them that I could see, and their attire was simple indeed—white turban and bournous, and yellow slippers—I am not sure that they were not as noble of presence as any Raja or Nawab of them all.

Easter Monday, April 17th.—Gibraltar still *en fête*. Crowds in the streets. Nothing to be seen but flowers and garlands, flags, lanterns. The foundation-stone of the New Market-place was laid by the Prince with Masonic ceremonies, the proceedings being opened by a long and somewhat lugubrious address, of a religious character, by a Dissenting minister. The Masonic manifestations which had been suppressed at Malta found large expansion here. The engineers complain that the defences of Gibraltar suffer exceedingly from constant changes at home. Plates and guns are subjected to continual alterations. As the size of the cannon is increased, the emplacements become obsolete. Casemates intended for 18-ton guns are quite useless for 35-ton guns. The emplacement for the new 35-ton gun to be mounted at the Alexandra battery, on the end of the New Mole, was laid by the Prince in the afternoon. The garrison, consisting of five regiments, paraded at 3.30 P.M. on the ground outside the Watergate. The Spanish Governor of Algesiras came over to the Review to pay his respects to the Prince, and to have a look at the outside of his temporally abstracted fortress, accompanied by a staff of Spanish officers and by a small escort of serviceable, if not neat-looking Lancers. The Prince entertained the Duke of Connaught and a large party on board. Covers were laid for fifty-five. The company went on shore to witness the fireworks, and the lighting up of the streets and of the Rock. The illuminations on shore, to our practised eyes, were not quite overpowering, but the marine works of that sort, and the pyrotechnic effects of the fleet were admirable.

April 18th.—Excursion to the cork-wood of Rondo; a very agreeable day, in spite of showers. I was told that there were two hundred police and soldiery posted in various spots round the scene of the picnic, out of sight. The Prince dined in the evening with the Rifle Brigade, and went off to the theatre afterwards. It blew great guns. The guests of the Rifle Brigade, and those who attended the theatre, had to contend with great difficulty respecting transport—the rain fell in torrents—the supply of vehicles in Gibraltar is not unlimited. Combine these conditions and imagine the result.

April 19th.—The storm passed away. The 4th (King's Own) had the honour of receiving his Royal Highness at lunch. There were soldiers' games at the North Front afterwards, and the struggle between the Royal Artillery team and the sailors (of the *Raleigh* principally, I think) in the "Tug of War" evoked the finest feelings of the services; and when the sturdy gunners, who had been at work mounting ordnance, parbuckling, heaving and hauling carriages and shot for months, pulled the tars over, it was too much for one ancient mariner; he blew his nose suspiciously, and would not speak to any one for ten minutes. From the games the Prince returned to change his uniform, and the 23rd Royal Welsh Fusiliers entertained him at dinner in their mess-room. The festive proceedings which were arranged to celebrate the Royal visit were wound up by a grand ball. As they were to start for Cadiz early next morning, the Prince and the Duke of Connaught went on board the *Osborne* from the ball-room.

THE ONLY BULL-FIGHT THE PRINCE SAW IN SPAIN.

CHAPTER XV.

Departure from Gibraltar—Arrival at Cadiz—Seville—Cordova—Madrid—Toledo—The Escurial—The Palace Tapestry—The Armoury—The Review—Festivities—Arrival at Lisbon—Public Entry—Belem Castle—Royal Entertainments—Excursion to Cintra—Palace of Ajuda—Departure from Lisbon—*Serapis* Dinner to the Prince—Land in Sight—"The *Enchantress* is coming"—Home at Last!

APRIL 20TH.—At 7 A.M. the *Osborne* was running along the coast on her way towards Cadiz. It was understood there should be no saluting, but the *Devastation*, *Swiftsure*, *Raleigh*, and *Research* manned yards and fired, the batteries joined, and in a few seconds Gibraltar was completely hidden in a cloud of thick, white smoke. The weather was cloudy, and rain fell at intervals. Passing near the Pearl Rock we could not but wonder at the neglect of measures to mark a spot made so unpleasantly familiar by our naval misfortunes. At 12.30 the *Osborne* was running into Cadiz. The Prince landed incognito at 3.45 P.M. Special trains, however, are not easily "smuggled through," and there were crowds at all the stations up to

Seville, where their Royal Highnesses arrived at 6.45 P.M. in time for dinner. The Count of Mirasol and two high officers of the Court were waiting on the part of the King to receive them.

Although there were no public functions at Seville, no part of the tour was more thoroughly enjoyed than the entertainments provided for the Royal travellers. The Princes attended the races, which had been postponed till their arrival; went to the theatres; visited the famous Tobacco Manufactory; picnicked in the gardens of the Monpensier Palace; saw the "fun" of the Fair, which was then at its height; inspected at their ease Cathedral, churches, museum, Alcazar, la Caridad, picture-galleries. Their presence gave eclat to many assemblages, and the splendour of the equipages placed at their disposal necessarily attracted attention. However, the Sevillanos, on the whole, were not demonstrative. It was delightful to be in a city where there were neither reviews, receptions, state banquets, illuminations, nor fireworks, and where without any "wild shrieks" there was the full enjoyment of liberty. Perhaps it was just as well that there was a rigid resolve to resist the blandishments of the quaint posters on the walls, giving the names of the performers who were to operate on "*los toros*" in the ring, and representing tremendous bulls on the rampage.

The Royal party left Seville on the 25th of April, and at 5.15 P.M. the special train reached Cordova. The Princes drove in carriages provided for them by the courtesy of gentlemen of the city, to the Cathedral. The people assembled at the station and at the entrance to the building were scarcely remarkable for courtesy or good manners. The canons and higher dignitaries received the Princes, and led the illustrious visitors through every part of the vast edifice. The choir, the mosque, the treasury, the richly embroidered robes and plate were inspected, and finally their Royal Highnesses ascended the tower, from which there is a fine view of the city. At 9 P.M. the Royal party continued their journey, travelling all night in the Royal carriages. The train arrived at 8 A.M. (the 26th of April) at Aranjuez, where Mr. Layard, the members of the British Legation, and a deputation of Spanish officers were waiting to welcome them. In two hours more they reached Madrid. A guard of honour, with the band of an Engineer regiment, was drawn up at the station. The young King exchanged most cordial greetings with the Prince of Wales and the Duke of Connaught.

The crowd of English and strangers inside the station cheered loudly. The state carriage left the station, the Prince sitting on the right of King Alfonso, the Duke of Connaught and Prince Louis of Battenberg opposite. The Prince of Wales was dressed in the uniform of Field-Marshal, and the Duke of Connaught in that of the 7th Hussars. Other carriages followed with the suite. The full-dress liveries were very handsome, and the equipages well appointed. The Royal party drove to the Palace through a mile and a half of crowded streets. The cortege was preceded by a body of the Royal Guard on horseback. The people in the streets were very respectful, and took off their hats, but there generally was no cheering except from foreigners. It is not the habit in Spain to utter loud cries, unless under excitement of a political character or of warlike demonstration.

The reception at the Palace was very stately; the approaches and staircases lined by halberdiers in effective uniforms, cocked-hats, broad lapelled coatees of blue with white facings, white knee-breeches, and long black gaiters. Upon reaching the grand apartments, King Alfonso presented the Royal Princes to the Princess of the Asturias, ladies of the Court, the grandees, and officials. The English Princes then presented the members of their suites to his Majesty, who gave them a most gracious reception. In the afternoon the King and the Princes visited the Museum, rich in masterpieces of Murillo, Velasquez, Titian, and in noble specimens of the Flemish and Dutch schools. There are some French paintings, but no examples of English masters in the galleries. Here the Royal party spent a considerable time.

There were great crowds along the Prado and Buen Retiro in the afternoon to see the Prince. Madrid wears an animated aspect. The list of festivities is full, and promises to tax the energies of those who will have to take part in them. The Prince of Wales declined an invitation to a bull-fight, which it was proposed to give on a large scale in his honour. There was a banquet at the Palace, remarkable for the display of plate and for great splendour of appointments, after which the King and Princes went to the Theatre. The opera was *Il Trovatore.*

April 26th.—The King accompanied the Prince of Wales and Duke of Connaught to Toledo. The Royal party left Madrid by special train at 9 o'clock, breakfasted *en route*, and reached Toledo in two hours. At the station a guard of honour was drawn up, and breaks drawn by magnificent mules were waiting to convey them through the quaint old city. The visitors first examined the Hospital built in 1504, which has been justly called "one of the architectural gems of the world."

Thence they proceeded to the great manufactory where Toledo blades, as well as arms of all kinds—the machinery moved by the waters of the Tagus—are still made to perfection.

The Churches, surrounded by the mass of the mediæval city—the Bridge, the Market-place, and the Cathedral, rival of Seville's glory, next challenged attention. The clergy of the Cathedral displayed the wondrous silver, some of which dates from the tenth century, miracles of art, when art was at its best, and opened shrines and reliquaries, seldom seen or heard of, which have escaped heathen and Christian pillage, for the Prince's inspection.

After an interesting drive through the old and tortuous streets they went to the Alcazar, converted by King Alfonso into a military college, where 400 students are educated on the Woolwich system.

The special train arrived at Madrid soon after 5 P.M. The Princes dined with the King, and afterwards went to the Opera, where *Aïda* was performed to a house crowded from floor to ceiling with all Madrid could show of rank and beauty—and both still are left to her.

After the Opera, the King and the Princes went to the ball given by the "Dukes" Fernan Nunez (*i.e.* the Duke and the Duchess) in honour of the occasion. The ball was in all respects a great display of the luxury, refinement, splendour, and wealth, of the *noblesse* of Spain, and remarkable for the grace and beauty of many of the ladies, whose presence adorned the magnificent salons.

April 27th.—In the forenoon the Prince paid another visit to the Picture Gallery, where he remained until it was time to return to the Palace to prepare for the grand review. The Duke of Connaught visited the Armoury and the interesting and beautifully kept Museum of Artillery. The latter is especially rich in armour of the time and of the person of Philip II. and of Charles V., trophies from the battle of Lepanto, a suit of mail of Columbus, swords of Cortes, of El Gran Capitan, and many beautiful and curious arms. Three stands of English colours were among the trophies on the walls. The sword which Francis I. surrendered at Pavia was carried off by the French in 1808, and is represented by a facsimile.

At 2 o'clock all Madrid was in the streets or in the windows of the houses. It was a fête day. Shops were shut and all business suspended. In the capital of a nation which has just escaped from the horrors of civil war after hard-fought battles, in which for weary months Spaniards stood face to face with Spaniards, where wounded soldiers hobbling about the streets, war medals and ribands on many breasts, attest the fact, it was strange to observe the general gaiety and abandon of the crowd. The people were packed as closely as they could stand long before the time fixed, quiet and orderly, waiting patiently for the march-past. The troops were drawn up on the Prado under a pure blue sky and warm sun worthy of India.

At 2 o'clock King Alfonso, in the uniform of a Spanish General, the Prince in Field-Marshal's uniform, the Duke of Connaught in the uniform of the 7th Hussars, preceded by cavalry, attended by the Generals Caballos, Prima del Rivera, Echagues, San Roman, Cotoner, Makenna, Zapatero, Rinzdana, Azcarraga, Beaumont, Ping, Salavera, and followed by a brilliant *Etat-Major*, rode down the Prado, which was lined by the cavalry, infantry, and artillery assembled for the Royal inspection.

The review was the most remarkable military display which the young King has seen since the day he entered Madrid. The force consisted of four regiments of cavalry, four battalions of engineers, one battalion of civil guard, fourteen battalions of the line, one of artillery, and eighty guns. The first division (Vargos) extended from the Obelisk de la Castalana to the Cibeles Fountains. The second (Terreros) from the Botanic Gardens to the Gate Atocha. The cavalry, under the Count de Combres Altas, from the

Gate of Atocha to the Canal; the artillery (General Prat) from the Alcala Gate to the Prado. The second division was formed of the 3rd regiment of Grenadiers, the regiment of Grenada, and the battalion of the Caçadores of Manilla. The cavalry consisted of the regiments "Del Rey, Reina," "Pavia," and "Alfonso the Twelfth." The wheeled artillery was formed in column from the Porte of Alcala, with mountain artillery between the "Obelisk of the 2nd May" and the Museum. The defile was a very striking spectacle. No one who has derived his impressions of Spain from the Stock Exchange, Cuban insurrections, Carlist wars, or recent European history, can realise the grandeur that clings to the old Catholic Monarchy, and the strength of the military spirit which so often placed Spain at the mercy of a *pronunciamiento*. In all that refers to the ordering of a military show the review was perfect. First came the Palafreneros of the Palace and the Royal Guard, the escort of the generals, the Regiments of Manila, Ciudad Rodrigo, and Catalano, of the first division. The Chasseur battalions were well received. After the infantry next came Engineers and Telegraph Companies; then the mountain batteries (pieces of four), one mule carrying the wheels, one the limber, one the carriage, and one the caisson or tumbril, 36 pieces in all; then the Chasseurs; after which the *Guardia Civil*, 1400 strong, in picturesque uniform—cocked hats with white borders, blue coats with red breasts, white pantaloons, black gaiters, whose appearance could not be easily surpassed. Next came the light and heavy artillery, Krupp guns, drawn by very fine mules, a total force of 80 pieces. After these regiments of cavalry. The Princess of the Asturias sat in the balcony of a house near the Ministry of War.

It was near 5 o'clock before the review was over, and the King and the Princes returned to the Palace at 8.

After the review the Prince visited the Countess of Montijo. There was another State banquet at the Palace at night.

April 28th.—At 11.20 the King with his Royal guests, set out in travelling dress for the Escurial. Special train, of course. It was very cold; the snow-covered ranges of the Guadamarara gave an Alpine aspect to the plains, beyond which rose a line of hills, whereon the great bulk of the Escurial, resembling a truncated pyramid, could be presently discerned. Patrols of civil guard were placed at intervals along the line. There was no crowd at the stations, nor, for the matter of that, did there seem any considerable population, Villa Alba, which we passed at 12.20, being the most extensive hamlet within sight. The country put one in mind of the least cultivated parts of Kerry. Fields, surrounded by stone walls, broke the monotony of rocky expanses, sometimes covered with scrub-wood, occasionally quite destitute even of so much verdure. The aspect of the country so black as to give the impression of a peat-moor, over which the roads ran like white ribands, caused us to wonder that any one could have selected such a site for a palace, until we thought of the character of the man who had reared the Escurial. Certainly he could have offered the excuse that there was plenty of stone close at hand for the building. Within half a mile of the Palace there are some poplars, white houses, red tiled roofs, and a red church, with two steeples. At 12.35 the train stopped at the end of the journey. A crowd of 600 or 700 people and the authorities were waiting; outside the station were Royal carriages, remarkable for the splendour of the ancient trappings. The harness of the mules was made of silk, and the housings and mountings very remarkable and curious. Outside the Palace a guard of honour was mounted by cadets and pupils of the Military School founded on the principle of the Theresianum at Vienna. King Alfonso acted as guide through the immense pile—a palace, a cemetery, a library, and a museum—where the sombre soul of Philip II. seems to brood in monumental granite. Little more than 300 years old, the Escurial appears to be as far removed from our times as the Parthenon or the Serapeum, yet the massive blocks of stone are so fresh that they are not incongruous with the marble slabs which stonemasons are fitting to-day to the sides of a new cemetery destined for the Princes and Princesses of Spain who have not reigned.

It was so cold in the gloomy halls and vast corridors that the King requested all to keep on their hats. Although La Houssaye destroyed or carried away enormous quantities of relics, plate, and objects of art, the Escurial is still a wonderful mine of most valuable and interesting books, manuscripts, and tapestry. The Royal party inspected the chapel in which, as all the world is erroneously told, Philip heard the news of the battle of Lepanto without emotion; the place in which he was told of his great reverse; the crypt in which he lingered and died; the dread mausoleum in which are ranged sarcophagi of the Kings of Spain, beginning with that of Charles V., Emperor and King, and ending with that of Ferdinand VII. There is one prepared wherein may repose the remains of the crownless Queen now in exile. Beneath it is a marble tomb, which the young King pointed out to the Prince of Wales, saying, "There is where I shall lie one day."

With the exception of a short interval for refreshment in one of the rooms of the Palace, the day was spent wandering over the Escurial. At lunch the King spoke with much feeling of his English comrades, of his instructors, and of his friends at Sandhurst. "I might be tried as a deserter if they could catch me," said he, "for I went away on leave of absence, but I came on to Madrid, and I never returned to duty." At 4.30 P.M. the special train started amid loud cheers from the young cadets and students, and in an hour reached Madrid. Here the train to the north was waiting, and the King and Prince bade good-bye to the Duke of Connaught, who, accompanied by Lord Gordon Lennox and Mr. FitzGerald, started for Paris *en route* for England.

When the Prince returned to the Palace, he found the grand corridor which surrounds the inner court hung with the most magnificent tapestries—Italian, Flemish, French, and Spanish—which had been taken out of their lurking-places by order of the King, and suspended over the doors on one side, and over the windows on the other, that the Prince might see them. This corridor is rectangular, and runs over the corridors on the ground-floor; and each side is probably sixty yards long. On one side are the entrances to the staircases and suites of apartments. The other sides "give" on the court; and as the winters are cold, and the springs not always genial there, it has been found desirable to place glass doors and windows on the outer side, so as to form a protected walk. These marble alleys are guarded by halberdiers in picturesque uniform, with an air of intense respectability. They have something to guard. From end to end each of these four sides was lined with pieces of tapestry, some of vast size—30 or 40 feet long by 20 high—tacked side by side as close as they can hang. There are at least eighty pieces up at present. Some of these are said by competent judges to be worth thousands of pounds sterling. When these pieces were put up it was naturally supposed that they were all the Palace could boast of, except such as were fixed in the Royal apartments. But there are, it seems, many more. "How many? Twice?" "Yes; many more than twice." "Ten times as many?" "Oh dear, yes!" "What! more than 800 pieces of tapestry?" "Oh, yes! There are 2500 pieces, many finer than these!" Cosas de España, indeed. But very magnificent. There are four large pieces, for example, before my room, each of which is a large page from the history of Alexander; but there were once six. The two missing pieces have been discovered in Vienna, but no one knows how they found their way there. When the figure of St. Anthony was cut out of the glorious Murillo in the Cathedral at Seville, and was traced to New York, one might guess at the nature of the motive-power which led to the robbery; but it is not so easy to imagine how two great pieces of tapestry could have been taken out of the Royal Palace at Madrid and conveyed to Vienna, at a time long subsequent to any connection between Austria and Spain, except that which was thus so strangely established.

In the evening the King and the Prince honoured Mr. Layard with their presence at dinner, and at a ball afterwards at the British Legation. Next day all Madrid talked with wonder of the presence of a King of Spain at the house of a foreign Minister.

April 29th.—This Palace contains an exquisite chapel, to which the members of the Royal Family and Household repair every morning for mass. There is also a library of vast extent and value, but in considerable disorder as yet, for the librarian, a most obliging and learned gentleman, recently appointed, has only commenced his work of arrangement and classification. A glance at the old catalogue, however, reveals the existence of many treasures, and some "Hours" belonging to Charles V., Philip I. and II., &c., are most exquisite specimens of missal illumination and binding. I suspect there are great discoveries to be made in the sea of shelves piled up room after room in the lower story of the huge edifice. Then the Armoury is another joy for ever such as Sir Samuel Meyrick or good Mr. Planché would have exceedingly rejoiced to see. Ford scarcely does justice to the rare and charming things which are enshrined in the Armeria and other national establishments, but in matters of art he is quite excellent. The Prince permitted nothing to escape, and in the young King he has an indefatigable and enthusiastic cicerone. An old courtier of Philip II. would have died, or fainted at the least, could he have met the King of Spain walking about the stables in a shooting-jacket and "pot-hat," with a gentleman in similar costume, who was heir to the Crown of England. The Royal coach-houses are filled with vehicles, which excel those of Vienna in cumbrous magnificence; and there may be among them the carriage in which "Jack and Tom" set out from the Earl of Bristol's to the first interview with the Infanta in that romantic expedition of "Baby Charles." The jewels which the thrifty James did not scruple to send to Madrid, valued then at 150,000*l.*, seem to have "left not a rack behind." Poor Infanta! Hapless Charles! There is something very touching in the simple remark of the Princess, "Had he loved me he would not have quitted me!" The results of a happier ending to that wooing may well exercise the fancy. After a day of comparative quiet, and some hours spent in examining objects of interest, the Prince of Wales drove out and paid visits to Marshal Serrano, the Duke and Duchess of Sesto (rejoicing rather in the title and name of Marquess and Marchioness of Alcaniçes), Señor Canovas del Castillo, and the Duchess of Montijo. He also attended a sitting of the Chamber of Deputies (Cortes), where a solemn debate on some

Railway Bill was proceeding with great dignity, and had an opportunity of seeing the most eminent orators and members, for the house happened to be very full. After dinner at the Palace, the King and Prince went to the Theatre, where they saw the only "bull fight" which it was permitted his Royal Highness to witness in Spain. "Pepe Hillo" was but a mockery and a mimicry. The bull was a sham, and the horses were not real; but, what was best of all to see, there was a seguidilla charmingly danced by a beautiful and graceful girl, who received well-deserved compliments. Then came a ball of a very stately kind, given by los duques de Bailen (the Duke and Duchess of Bailen), at their fine Palace of Portugaleté, where the King and his Royal visitor were received by all that was distinguished in Madrid, the last festivity in honour of the Prince, which brought his pleasant sojourn to a fitting conclusion.

April 30th.—A forenoon of adieux, and reception of friendly visits.

At 3 P.M. the Prince left the Palace for the Railway Station, where a special train was in readiness, for Lisbon. King Alfonso drove the Prince to the station in an open carriage, with postillions in uniforms of blue and crimson. The suite followed in three four-horsed Royal carriages. The King and Prince were met at the station by Mr. and Mrs. Layard, Señor Elduayen, and others. All the travellers were in plain clothes. There was no crowd at the station. The Civil Governor of Madrid, the Duke of Sesto, and other Spanish nobles accompanied the Royal party. The Prince shook hands warmly with the King, the Duke of Sesto, Mrs. Layard, General Velasco, Señor Elduayen, Sir John Walsham, and others, bowing repeatedly to those on the platform as the train moved off. "The Prince carries away a most pleasant remembrance of his visit." Among the many of the King's suite who did so much to make the English strangers comfortable, the Marquis of Alcaniçes and the Count Morphy must not be forgotten. Mr. Layard came on to Aranjuez, where he took leave of his Royal Highness. The train arrived at Manzanares La Mancha at 7.15 P.M., and, after a short halt, went very smoothly all night.

May 1st.— Passing Badajos station at 6.30 A.M. some were aware of band playing, of a crowd, and of a detachment of the omnipresent Civil Guard drawn up on the platform. Nothing was to be seen of the famous fortification until the train had passed out of the station, when, looking back, one could make out part of the fort, with a flagstaff above it, the houses of the town below, and a church steeple, beyond which lay a hill, which appeared as if it were powdered with snow. This resolved itself subsequently into the town of Elvas, where we saw a crowd of burly, apathetic-looking country people, their heads bound round with red kerchiefs, as if they had just got out of bed, and apparently waiting on business, not curiosity; differing very much in appearance from the smaller, more excitable-looking Spaniards, and, indeed, not very well-favoured or intelligent looking. At 11.10 A.M. crossed the Tagus, and entered upon scenery of much softer and more interesting character than that of the country outside Madrid. The British Minister and the Portuguese Minister, the Viscount de Sagres, and officers, sent to welcome the Prince, were waiting an Entroncamento, where there was lunch, and a halt for half an hour. At 3.30 P.M. the train arrived at Lisbon. King Louis, who wore the uniform of a Portuguese Admiral, with the Grand Cross of the Tower and Sword, and the Titular King Don Fernando in the uniform of a Portuguese Field-Marshal General, with the Grand Cross of the three Portuguese Orders, were waiting to receive his Royal Highness, and gave him a very warm greeting. The ministers, the principal authorities, the British admirals, Seymour and Phillimore, and the officers of the fleet in the Tagus, the diplomatic and consular officers, and a large assemblage of ladies and gentlemen, who were admitted on the platform, also welcomed the Prince. In the Railway Station some 500 ladies were seated on rows of chairs, and rose to wave their handkerchiefs. The windows were crowded. The Band of the 5th Caçadores played "God save the Queen." The Portuguese aides-de-camp and officers were presented to the Prince—Senhor Fontes, President of the Council, the Minister of Finance, Senhor Andrade Corso, Minister of Foreign Affairs, Senhor Serpa Pimentel, Senhor Cardoso Avelino, Minister of Public Works, &c. &c. The King and Prince drove slowly through the streets, which were lined with all the available troops.

There was no display of flags in the city. There was no triumphal arch. There was not a "welcome," or a single banner. There was not, as far as I heard, what would pass muster in the smallest English village for a cheer. Nevertheless, the reception was most gratifying. Standing closely packed for at least two miles in the streets, which they crowded so as just to leave room for the carriages to pass, the good people of Lisbon, and of the country round, waited in the hot sun till the Prince arrived, and, as he passed along almost within a hand's breadth of the front ranks of men and women, the former uncovered their heads, and the latter waved their handkerchiefs, or showed, by their best smiles, how glad they were to see the Heir of the Throne of Great Britain and Ireland. The ships of the squadron in the Tagus saluted with excellent effect as soon as the cortege came in sight. Arrived at the Palace of Ajuda, the King presented his ministers and officers to the Prince, who in turn presented his suite to their Majesties. His Majesty looks younger than he is (thirty-eight), and, like many other members of the illustrious House of Coburg, has light hair and blue eyes. He takes an active part in the work of Government, has seen much of the world, is a good naturalist (versed especially in ornithology), a friend of the arts, favourable to the emancipation of commerce from all imposts which are not absolutely needed for revenue, and anxious to abolish as far as possible all traces of the protective policy which was so much in vogue in Portugal—as in other places—a short time ago. The Prince Royal and the Infante Dom Affonso are nice-looking lads, with a strong resemblance to their Royal mother, who is as like to King Victor Emmanuel as a comely lady with a profusion of blonde *crêpé* hair and of refined presence can be to El Re Galantuomo. Prince Ferdinand of Saxe-Coburg, a man of taste and letters, quite gained the hearts of all the visitors by his extraordinary pleasantness, kindness and *bonhomie;* and they all agree that a more gracious, agreeable, and witty Prince was not met with on their travels than the very tall gentleman who reminds one a little of Napoleon III., and a little of Don Quixote—as drawn by Doré—and who is able to talk in nearly if not all the languages of Europe. The party proceeded to the Palace of Belem, where the Prince and his suite were quartered comfortably, and spent the evening quietly.

May 2nd.—There came, this forenoon, a deputation of British subjects to Belem with an address, which the Prince received. The King arrived after lunch, and had a long conversation with members of the suite.

The concert at the San Carlos in honour of the Prince gave a good opportunity to the Portuguese ladies of showing their toilettes, diamonds, fine hair and eyes to advantage, of which they availed themselves very generally. The aspect of the theatre was bright and beautiful; and when the Kings, *de facto* and Titular, the Queen, the Princes, the Prince of Wales, the ministers and officers of the Court, and noblemen and gentlemen were seated in the Royal box, which occupies the centre of the grand tier, the spectacle presented by the audience flashing with brilliants and blazing in State uniforms, lace and orders, was as fair a gala theatre as could well be witnessed.

May 3rd.—The Prince paid a visit to the Convent of Bon Secours (Bom Soccorso), near at hand, this forenoon, and was much gratified by the arrangements. He was conducted over the rooms and gardens by Father Smyth, and was entertained by the performance of one of the nuns, who sang "Kathleen Mavourneen" to a harp accompaniment very tenderly. The ladies are principally from Ireland. In the afternoon the Prince gave lunch on board the *Serapis* to Dom Ferdinand and a small party, and then he led them on a visit to the iron-clads. After dinner at Belem the Prince and the party attended a grand Ball given by the King and Queen at the Palace of Ajuda.

May 4th.—An interesting excursion to Cintra—the Prince taking one party to the Chateau of King Ferdinand—Lord Suffield, General Probyn, Sir J. Fayrer, Mr. Knollys, Mr. Hall and I, being directed to visit the Viscount of Montserrat, an English gentleman, who has a pretty country house on the side of a hill some distance below the peak on which the Royal castle is perched. The villa commands a charming prospect, and is surrounded by well laid-out grounds; but the combination of modern furniture in the halls and rooms of Saracenic architecture is scarcely pleasing. The Prince drove off at 10.30 A.M. The second party at 11.15 A.M.—the carriages drawn by mules. It is a pleasant well-known drive of 28 kilometres; but at some distance, three or four miles from the Viscount's gate, the road was broken, and our party had to leave the carriages and walk. The visitors were delighted, and after spending a very agreeable day, returned to Belem to dinner at 7 P.M. The city and the heights on both sides of the Tagus were illuminated at night, and there was a grand display of fireworks from the fleets, in which the heavens joined with thunder and lightning.

May 5th.—The day was observed as a complete holiday. At 3 P.M. the King came down the Tagus and visited the Prince at Belem Palace. The Royal galley was rowed by eight oarsmen, and there were two State galleys for the suite. The fleet manned yards and saluted as the Royal flags passed.

The King and the Prince then went on board the galleys off the stairs, and landed at the Arsenal, whence they proceeded, mounted on horseback, through crowded streets to the Dom Pedro Square, to inspect the greatest assemblage of troops ever seen in Portugal. The march-past began at 5 P.M., and occupied over an hour and a quarter. The artillery was very good, comprising upwards of one hundred guns, mostly Krupp, and mountain artillery drawn by fine mules. The cavalry consisted of a regiment of Lancers, two regiments of Hussars (one regiment very good), a brigade of Rifles, and two brigades of infantry. The Rifles were smart-looking and soldierly; but the ground was most unfavourable for a march-past, being only one side of a small square, on which the immense crowd closed in, notwithstanding the efforts of the police and soldiery.

At 8.30 P.M. the King, Prince of Wales and a distinguished party dined with Admiral Seymour on board the *Minotaur*. The King, in a well-turned speech, proposed the health of Queen Victoria. As the toast was being drunk the *Black Prince* fired a salute of twenty-one guns. Then the Prince of Wales proposed the health of the King of Portugal, on which the *Resistance* fired a salute of twenty-one guns. When the health of the Prince was proposed by the King, the *Black Prince* saluted. On the Royal party leaving the *Minotaur*, the ships lighted up, and rockets were discharged from the fleet with beautiful effect.

May 6th.—The Portuguese bands are very "brassy," and the smart regiment on duty at Belem has one of the most effective; so that what with the playing of the national air of Portugal, the fanfares, various other musical exercitations, when important visitors come and go, the court-yard and corridors are resonant from an early hour in the morning. The Marquis of Souza-Holstein was kind enough to take me to see many most interesting institutions. I was particularly entertained and instructed by the treasures in the Torre de Tombo, in the vast pile of the old convent of St. Bento, which now accommodates the two Houses of Parliament and contains the national archives. The collection of early charts, especially of Africa and the East Indies, is admirable. One of these, of the fifteenth century, gives what looks like an exact representation of Lake Nyanza. The records of the Inquisition, the banners with the motto, "Exurge Deus," &c., the former filling immense rooms, are to be seen in perfect order. I read the process of the last act of the Holy Office at Coimbra, in which a nun was accused of having given way to Jewish practices, of keeping Friday holy, refusing certain food, &c., for which it would seem she suffered death; but it was explained to me very particularly that the officers of the Inquisition did not inflict the punishments. The civil power was called on to punish a crime, and those condemned of heresy were merely handed over by the ecclesiastical tribunal to meet the legal consequences of their guilt! The National Printing Office and the Academy are admirably conducted.

There was an extraordinary gathering of vehicles and people at the Races. All Lisbon was out on the Belem course; many glad of a holiday to see the Royal personages, some interested in a new sport—a very great concourse, who remained all day under a hot sun and in a cold wind, quite happy and contented. The King conferred decorations on the Prince's suite.

The banquet at the Palace of Ajuda was very brilliant. Covers were laid for one hundred guests on tables glittering with the plate of the House of Braganza. It was nearly half-past nine when the Prince led the Queen to the Banqueting-hall, followed by the King, King Ferdinand, the Infante, Ministers of State, Admirals, Foreign Ministers, and *Corps Diplomatique.* One of the most powerful bands ever heard was stationed in the gallery at one end of the hall, and effectually obviated any necessity on the part of the company to engage in conversation. The King, after a felicitous allusion to the Prince's presence, said there were three healths he could not separate—"*Dieu garde la Reine, votre gracieuse et auguste mère, qu'il protége le Prince de Galles, et veille sur la nation anglaise.*" * The Prince of Wales proposed the health of the King, and expressed the pleasure he felt at his visit to Portugal.

May 7th.—The scene on the departure of the Prince from the Tagus to-day was a fitting prelude to his welcome home. Nothing could be more bright and gay than the appearance of Lisbon—the sun lighted up the terraced hills which, springing from the water's edge, are lost among

* See Appendix.

the serrated heights of Cintra. The population, ever fond of holidays, swarmed along the quays, and crowded the pierheads. The Portuguese Squadron, and the Fleet under Rear-Admiral Seymour, were dressed. The vessels moored in the river displayed their national flags.

Having been the guest of the King and lodged so pleasantly in his Palace at Belem, it was natural that the Prince should desire to receive the members of the Royal family on board his own ship under the British flag. There is something of the old maritime grandeur of the Portuguese nation to be seen in the maintenance of antique-looking galleys of many oars, with the rowers dressed in antique liveries, somewhat like those worn by our Thames watermen in the early part of the last century, which are still used for Royal occasions. A steam-launch—except when it is tearing through the upper waters of the Thames, to the disturbance of the placid angler and of swaggering swans and to the great discomfiture of punters and rowers—is no doubt a practical, useful creation; but it yields in all requisites of state and dignity to great galleys moved by oars, such as are still extant on the Bosphorus and on the Tagus. The Prince drove to the chapel of the British Legation, where Divine service was performed by the chaplain, Mr. Pope. When service was over, the Prince proceeded in a steam-launch to the *Serapis*, and was received with the usual honours at 12.30 P.M. The ship looked as if she had just come out of dock, sides snowy white, gilding fresh, rigging all taut. It was a very gala day on board. There were guards of honour, bands, buglers on the decks, and officers in full dress at the sides; and as the Royal guests and Admirals mounted the ladder there were salutes, flourishes, and all due forms and observances of respect. The Prince of Wales received the Titular King, his Majesty

Dom Ferdinand, at the top of the companion, and was engaged in conversation with him and the Infante Don Augusto for some time before King Luiz I. and Queen Doña Maria Pia came alongside. Yards were manned, the crews cheered, and salutes were fired in both fleets when the Royal party embarked, and when the Portuguese flag was run up to the main of the *Serapis*. A guard of honour of the Royal Marine Light Infantry under

JACKO V. JACK.

Major Snowe and Lieutenant Burrowes, the Marine Artillery detachment under Lieutenant Lambert—the *Serapis* band, were drawn up to welcome their Majesties. Soon after 2 o'clock lunch was served, and when it was over the party ascended to the upper-deck saloon, and wandered over the decks, where tigers, cheetahs, cheetuls, elephants, dogs, the bear, horses, asses, birds, monkeys, displayed teeth, claws, tusks, feathers, tails, and other attractions. Everything on board was an object of interest to the

Royal visitors. The two little elephants, not more than six feet high, were brought out by the mahouts with great gravity, and the Kings and Princes proceeded to mount and to take a little ride round the deck in turn. Officers and crew were delighted that their pets afforded so much gratification. At last the time for parting came. The Titular King, the Infante his son, and their suite, departed. The Queen, her sons and ladies of honour, went next; but the King still lingered as if loath to part with his cousin. At 5.20 P.M. the Prince appeared at the top of the port ladder with King Luiz. Once more the Portuguese national anthem was played, the marines presented arms, the crew on the yards, led by Commander Bedford, gave three good cheers, and the King, after one more cordial farewell, stepped into a galley and went off to his corvette to escort the Royal squadron out of the Tagus. The word was given, "Undress ship! Prepare to slip." The wind was strong on the port bow. There was a strong current and a tremendous tide running; it was full fifteen minutes before the *Serapis* could turn. The landscape was beautiful. It was a very charming bit of colour—such as Claude could have painted and would have loved. A large, somewhat washed-out-looking sun descending towards the sea-horizon through lemon-tinted clouds, the hue of which came broadening up the Tagus, and throwing in its career a mellower tinge on the tiers of white houses from the water's edge to the hill-tops; Belem—a castle made expressly for Claude to paint—standing out clearly on the sea face; close at hand old-fashioned boats and curious crazy-looking craft, galleys, caravels and feluccas, side by side with men-of-war in their pride of impenetrable sides and tremendous armaments—these would have suited the painter well: nor would he have found it amiss, as flashes of fire and curling clouds of smoke leaped and spirted from the sides of the iron-clads. The *Minotaur*, *Black Prince*, *Triumph*, *Resistance*, *Monarch*, flying together Portuguese and British ensigns from the main-tops, dressed in flags, yards manned, marines on quarter-decks, moored in a double line; and the crews on board the Portuguese ships, which were in excellent order, burst into a great clang of music and cheers as the *Serapis* steamed down the lordly avenue, and the hills of the Tagus re-echoed the familiar, and let us hope always welcome, sounds of a British salute. The Prince, on the bridge, acknowledged the salutes by touching his cap repeatedly as he passed each ship, and gave a friendly wave of the hand to Admiral Seymour and his officers on the deck of the *Minotaur*. At 6 P.M. the *Serapis*, rapidly leaving the rolling cloud of smoke and the cheering sailors astern, was close to Belem. The Portuguese corvette, with the King on board, had been in collision with the *Raleigh*, which telegraphed, "Portuguese corvette has run into us, and has I fear suffered some damage." The *Raleigh* was none the worse otherwise for an accident, the blame of which may be shared, if not divided. At 6.15 P.M. the guns of Belem Castle saluted, Fort St. Julian followed, just as it was getting dusk, and the Prince was at last homeward bound without any halting-place on his journey.

May 8th.—At noon, lat. 41° 23′ N., long. 9° 45′ W.; distance run 170 miles; distance to Finisterre 95 miles. About four hours before Finisterre was sighted there came on a strong blow from the north-east, which mounted to "6" at times, and up rose the sea, and down went ports. It was so far unfortunate that the change occurred, as the evening had been selected for the dinner given by Captain Glyn and the officers of the *Serapis* to the Prince. Mr. Morier, the British Minister, Colonel Annesley, 11th

Hussars, Colonel Macdonell, 71st H.L.I., Lieutenant Gough, 10th Hussars—to whom his Royal Highness gave passages on board the *Serapis*—were invited. The dinner-table was laid on the main-deck, in a space between the port side and the masts, which was screened off by flags, and the band was stationed forward near the ward-room. Captain Glyn, in proposing the health of the Prince, took occasion to allude "to the interest which he had shown in the officers and men of the ship, and to the qualities which had endeared him to all on board. In the name of the officers he requested the Prince of Wales to accept an album with photographs of the ship's officers and detachments of the marines and crew, as a souvenir; and as the state of the sea would not allow them to indulge in Highland honours, he could only ask them to drink the Prince's health with three hearty cheers." This was done most enthusiastically; the book was handed to the Prince. He said "he did not require any photographs to keep him in mind of those among whom he had passed so many pleasant hours and days, but it was agreeable to him to accept such a proof of their kindly feelings. They had one and all done everything in their power to promote the success of the voyage and to contribute to his comfort, and there was not one of them, from the Captain who commanded down to the stokers who worked at the furnaces, to whom he was not personally indebted." The Prince, gave "the health of Captain Glyn, the officers and men of the *Serapis*," and added to that toast "the health of Commander Durrant, and of the officers and men of the Royal yacht *Osborne*, and the health of Captain Tryon and of the officers and men of H.M.S. *Raleigh*," and expressed his high sense of their services. Captain Glyn, in returning thanks, remarked, that among other advantages of the Prince's tour was the opportunity of becoming personally acquainted with so many officers of the Navy; although the Prince was a soldier by profession he had endeared himself to the Navy by the interest he took in all that concerned its welfare. The Prince had seen no less than four different squadrons of her Majesty's Navy, comprising more than one-half of the whole fleet, and his acquaintance with them could not but be a source of great satisfaction to the service. Lord C. Beresford returned thanks for the *Raleigh* and *Osborne*, and signal was made that "the Prince drinks to the health of the ships," which was duly acknowledged in the early morning. Then there were more toasts and speeches, music, a little quadrille, and the company broke up and went to bed, all in the highest spirits, despite an abominable adverse wind, and the premonitory symptoms of what was to be expected in England—violent colds, which attacked several of the party.

May 9th.—Strong north-east wind. The sea high, but the *Serapis* has little to fear from the waves even of the Bay of Biscay as long as they come at her right in front. Her speed, however, was reduced to a knot. Lat. 44° 50′ N., long. 8° 43′ W.; Ushant 263 miles N.E.

May 10th.—The calm of the voyage home, after so many months of excitement and tumult, was very agreeable, although it was "enjoyed" in a wild, cold sea. There was, however, a sense of solitude just now, for, strange to say, there were no ships in sight. At noon difficult observations gave lat. 48° 15′ N., long. 5° 30′ W.; Yarmouth 220 miles; Ushant 20 miles S.W. At 1.15 P.M., the squadron being abreast of Ushant, the *Raleigh* was sent in to signal, that the latest news of the Royal squadron might be transmitted to London, and then our course was shaped across Channel for the shores of Old England.

May 11*th*.—An hour after midnight the welcome light of the Start was made out, and at 2.15 A.M. it was seen well on the beam. The first sight which greeted the eyes of the early risers through their ports this morning was the appearance of a few white perpendicular streaks far away above the surface of the crisping waters, which through the glass resolved themselves into the chalk cliffs near Portland. Shanklin Light was visible at 7.35 A.M.; and as the familiar scene unfolded itself and grew nearer and nearer, like some well-known panorama, every eye was strained up the narrow stretch of water between the Isle of Wight and the mainland. At 10 A.M. the *Alberta*, with the Royal Standard flying, and a steam tender, probably the *Pigmy*, in attendance, were reported to be in sight.* It was not the *Alberta*, however, all the same, but the *Enchantress*. She was wisely lying at anchor in comparatively smooth water; for the sea off the Needles was rough and tumbling. At 10.15 A.M. the *Serapis* passed the Needles, and a little yellow yawl, with two men on board, flying a red burgee, came bowling down to meet her. One of these, an elderly gentleman, stood up, and cheered so vigorously that he attracted the Prince's attention, and may rest satisfied with the honour of being the first Englishman who was seen to welcome his Royal Highness in British waters. A large yacht ran down next to meet us; but whilst the squadron was passing by the Shingles the channel was comparatively clear, till it was near Yarmouth, when steamers, laden with people, who swarmed like bees on the decks, stood out to greet the Prince, and almost rubbed their sides against the *Serapis*.

---

* It was the *Sprightly*, which the Admiralty had placed at the disposal of Dr. Birdwood, C.S.I., who had been directed by order of the Prince to board the *Serapis* as soon as possible to take charge of the presents. Not one package belonging to the Prince or his suite went astray.

The *Enchantress*, in obedience to signal, weighed and steamed towards Yarmouth, in advance of the *Serapis*, in quest of smoother water. At 10.45 A.M. Fort Victoria saluted; but somehow the saluting from ships and forts was, it seemed to those on board, rather late. Soon the great ship approached the object on which all were gazing intently, which was quietly steaming ahead. The Prince was on the bridge, glass in hand, with his eyes fixed on the *Enchantress*, which (happily named) had the Princess's standard flying, and was laden with a precious burthen. By degrees the Princess of Wales and her children were distinguished amid the crowd on her deck. When she was close to Yarmouth the *Serapis* "slowed," and the *Enchantress*, altering her course, came down towards her, and in a few minutes was passing close on her port side, so that men could make out the faces of those on board quite plainly. Then the crew from the rigging, the officers on the decks, and all on board the *Serapis*, gave three cheers and a few cheers more, which must have proved that their throats, at all events, were not affected by the climate of India; and as the yacht rounded the stern of the *Serapis*, and came up on her starboard quarter, so that every one could see the Princess and her children looking up towards our deck, men confessed that they felt a little inclination to gulp down something in their throats. The band played "Home, Sweet Home," the marines presented arms as she passed. The *Serapis* anchored at 11 A.M., the barge was lowered at once, and the Prince immediately went on board the *Enchantress*. It may be imagined with what joy he was welcomed! In a quarter of an hour the Princess of Wales and the Royal children left the yacht and came on board the *Serapis*. The officers of the ship, the guard of honour of the marines and the band were drawn up on the main-deck facing the com-

"A LEVÉE OF PETS."

panion, the gentlemen of the Prince's suite extending in a line along the deck up to the entrance to the saloon. The Princess had a gracious smile or a pleasant word for those who were known to her as she passed to the saloon. To the Royal children the great ship seemed a treasure-house of wonder and delight, for there were tigers and tailless dogs, elephants, deer, horses, ostriches, leopards, birds, diminutive ponies and cattle, monkeys, to be exhibited, visited, petted or dreaded. At 12 P.M. the *Serapis* weighed, and steamed towards Portsmouth. On her way the Duke of Edinburgh came on board to welcome his Royal brother.

The scene at the landing at Portsmouth was a becoming prelude to the greeting which the whole country gave the Prince of Wales on his return from the visit to India, which will be for ever a great landmark in the history of the Empire.

HAVEN AND HOME.

APPENDIX.

APPENDIX.

I.

SUITE OF THE PRINCE OF WALES.

1. His Grace the DUKE of SUTHERLAND, K.G.
2. The Right Honourable SIR BARTLE FRERE, G.C.S.I., K.C.B.
3. The LORD SUFFIELD (Lord-in-Waiting and Head of the Household of H.R.H. the Prince of Wales).
4. MAJOR-GENERAL the LORD ALFRED PAGET (Clerk Marshal to H.M. the Queen).
5. The EARL of AYLESFORD.
6. MAJOR-GENERAL PROBYN, C.B., V.C. (Equerry in Waiting to H.R.H. the Prince of Wales).
7. LIEUT.-COLONEL ARTHUR ELLIS (Grenadier Guards, Equerry in Waiting to H.R.H. the Prince of Wales).
8. Mr. FRANCIS KNOLLYS (Private Secretary to H.R.H. the Prince of Wales).
9. SURGEON-GENERAL FAYRER, C.S.I. (Physician to H.R.H. the Prince of Wales).
10. CAPTAIN the Honourable H. CARR GLYN, C.B., Royal Navy (Aide-de-Camp to H.M. the Queen, Commanding H.M.S. *Serapis*).
11. COLONEL OWEN WILLIAMS (Commanding Royal Regiment of Horse Guards).
12. LIEUTENANT the LORD CHARLES BERESFORD, M.P., Royal Navy (Aide-de-Camp to H.R.H. the Prince of Wales).
13. CAPTAIN the LORD CARINGTON, Royal Horse Guards (Aide-de-Camp to H.R.H. the Prince of Wales).
14. The REVEREND CANON DUCKWORTH (Chaplain to H.M. the Queen and to H.R.H. the Prince of Wales).
15. LIEUTENANT AUGUSTUS FITZGEORGE, Rifle Brigade (Extra Aide-de-Camp to H.R.H. the Prince of Wales).
16. COMMANDER DURRANT, Royal Navy (Commanding Royal Yacht *Osborne*).
17. Mr. W. H. RUSSELL (Honorary Private Secretary to H.R.H. the Prince of Wales).
18. Mr. ALBERT GREY (Private Secretary to the Right Honourable Sir Bartle Frere).
19. Mr. SYDNEY HALL (Artist in the Suite of H.R.H. the Prince of Wales).

First Mess.

Mr. DOWNIE (Page).
„ GRIMM (Valet).
„ MACDONALD (Jäger).
„ BONNEMAIN (Chief Cook).
„ SCURTI (Assist. Cook).
„ PRINCE (Stud Groom).
Mr. MACALISTER (Duke of Sutherland).
„ FEELAN (Lord Suffield).
„ ISAACSON (India Office).
„ BARTLETT (Naturalist).
„ MUDD (Botanist).
„ ABRAHAM (Assist. to Mr. Isaacson).

Second Mess.

BLACKBURN (Sergeant Footman).
GURR (Footman).
PALMER (Footman).
CHANDLER (Wardrobe-man).
ROBERTSON (Assistant Jäger).
MITCHELL (Cook's Apprentice).
COOLIDGE (Groom).
WRIGHT (Lord Carington).
POTTER (Lord Alfred Paget).
MYSON (Lord Aylesford).
TREADWELL (Sir Bartle Frere).
EVANS (Colonel Ellis).
GILLARD (Major-General Probyn).
TOM FAT (Lord C. Beresford).
JAMES (Dr. Fayrer).
MALT (Mr. FitzGeorge).
PHIPPS (Colonel Williams).
MCLACHLAN (Duke of Sutherland).

II.

THE LANDING IN BOMBAY.

The following notification, issued by the Political Department, gives the details of the entry and procession :

"HIS ROYAL HIGHNESS THE PRINCE OF WALES arrived at Bombay at 9 A.M. on the 8th instant in Her Majesty's Steam Ship *Serapis*.

"On the *Serapis* entering the harbour a Royal salute was fired by the ships of war under the command of his Excellency the Naval Commander-in-Chief and by the saluting battery.

"At 10 A.M. his Excellency the Commander-in-Chief of her Majesty's Naval Forces in India and Rear-Admiral Lambert, C.B., proceeded on board Her Majesty's Steam Ship *Serapis*.

"At 3 P.M. his Excellency the Viceroy and Governor-General, attended by his Suite, arrived at the Dockyard and proceeded on board Her Majesty's Ship *Serapis*. His Excellency was received at the Dockyard by a Guard of Honour; and on his embarkation Royal salutes were fired from the saluting battery and by Her Majesty's Ships of War. While on board the *Serapis* his Excellency the Viceroy presented the Foreign Secretary to the Government of India and the Members of his own Personal Staff to his Royal Highness the Prince of Wales.

"At 3.25 P.M. his Excellency the Governor of Bombay, attended by his

Staff, and conducted by the Superintendent of the Bombay Marine, proceeded on board Her Majesty's Steam Ship *Serapis* under the usual salute from the saluting battery, and was presented to his Royal Highness by his Excellency the Viceroy. His Excellency was accompanied on board by the Chief Justice, his Excellency the Commander-in-Chief, the Members of Council, and the officer commanding the troops in Bombay, who were presented to his Royal Highness by his Excellency the Governor of Bombay.

"At 3.45 P.M. the Governor of Bombay, and Staff and the Officers who accompanied his Excellency, returned to the Dockyard.

"At 4 P.M. his Royal Highness the Prince of Wales, accompanied by his Excellency the Viceroy, and attended by his Suite, quitted Her Majesty's Ship *Serapis* in the Royal Barge under a Royal salute from Her Majesty's Ships of War.

"His Royal Highness landed under a salute of 21 guns from the saluting battery, and a Guard of Honour of European Infantry was drawn up opposite the landing-place.

"His Royal Highness was received on landing by his Excellency the Governor of Bombay, the Chief Justice, his Excellency the Commander-in-Chief, the Roman Catholic Bishop, the Members of Council, the Judges of the High Court of Judicature at Bombay, the Additional Members of Council, the Commissioner in Sind, the Commissioner of Customs and Opium, the Revenue Commissioners, the Secretaries and Under-Secretaries to Government, the Chairman of the Corporation of Bombay, the Chairman of the Bench of Justices, the Municipal Commissioner, and the Sheriff of Bombay.

"The Native Princes, Chiefs, and Sirdars assembled in Bombay in honour of his Royal Highness, attended on the occasion."

PROCESSION.

On Horseback.

The Assistant Quartermaster General, Bombay District.
The Deputy Assistant Quartermaster General, Bombay District.
A Squadron of the 3rd Hussars in column of Fours headed by the Band of the Regiment.
A Battery of Royal Horse Artillery in column of route.
A Squadron of Poona Horse in column of fours.

The Officer Commanding Poona Horse.	The Officer Commanding 1st Bombay Lancers.
The Brigade-Major.	A Staff Officer.
Brigadier-General Phayre, C.B., Aide-de-Camp to the Queen.	Brigadier-General Gell, Commanding Bombay District.

A Detachment of His Excellency the Governor's Body Guard.

Carriages of His Excellency the Governor of Bombay.

1. Captain Spencer, Aide-de-Camp to His Excellency the Governor of Bombay.
   Captain Anderson, Aide-de-Camp to His Excellency the Governor of Bombay.
   Captain Grey, Aide-de-Camp to His Excellency the Governor of Bombay.
   Jemadar Shaik Cassim, Aide-de-Camp to His Excellency the Governor of Bombay.
2. C. S. Close, Esq., Surgeon to His Excellency the Governor of Bombay.
   Lieut. MacIlwaine, R.N., Aide-de-Camp to His Excellency the Governor of Bombay.
   Captain Daniel, Aide-de-Camp to His Excellency the Governor of Bombay.
   Captain Makellar, Aide-de-Camp to His Excellency the Governor of Bombay.
3. E. R. Wodehouse, Esq., Private Secretary to His Excellency the Governor of Bombay.
   Captain Jervoise, Military Secretary to the Governor of Bombay.
   Captain Wodehouse, Aide-de-Camp to His Excellency the Governor of Bombay.
   Lord Hastings.
4. His Excellency the Governor of Bombay.
   Sir Bartle Frere, G.C.S.I., K.C.B.
   Captain Fawkes, Aide-de-Camp to His Excellency the Governor of Bombay.
   A Detachment of His Excellency the Governor's Body Guard.

Carriages of His Royal Highness the Prince of Wales.

1. Captain FitzGeorge, Aide-de-Camp to His Royal Highness the Prince of Wales.
   Albert Grey, Esq., Private Secretary to Sir Bartle Frere.
   W. H. Russell, Esq., LL.D., Honorary Private Secretary to His Royal Highness the Prince of Wales.
   S. P. Hall, Esq.
2. Lord Carington, Aide-de-Camp to His Royal Highness the Prince of Wales.
   Francis Knollys, Esq., Private Secretary to His Royal Highness the Prince of Wales.
   Surgeon-General Fayrer, C.S.I., Special Duty with His Royal Highness the Prince of Wales.
3. Major Bradford, Special Duty with His Royal Highness the Prince of Wales.
   Reverend Canon Duckworth, Chaplain to His Royal Highness the Prince of Wales.
   Lord Charles Beresford, Aide-de-Camp to His Royal Highness the Prince of Wales.
4. Major Williams, Special Duty with His Royal Highness the Prince of Wales.
   Lord Aylesford, Equerry to His Royal Highness the Prince of Wales.
   Colonel Owen Williams, Equerry to His Royal Highness the Prince of Wales.

5. Lord Suffield, Lord-in-Waiting to his Royal Highness the Prince of Wales.
 Lieut.-Colonel Ellis, Equerry to his Royal Highness the Prince of Wales.
 Major Henderson, Political Officer with his Royal Highness the Prince of Wales.
 Major Sartorius, V.C., C.M.G., Special Duty with his Royal Highness the Prince of Wales.
6. Duke of Sutherland, K.G.
 Lord Alfred Paget.
 Major-General Browne, C.B., V.C., Special Duty with His Royal Highness the Prince of Wales.
 A Detachment of His Excellency the Viceroy's Body Guard.

Carriages of His Excellency the Viceroy and Governor-General.

1. Lieutenant Cavendish, R.N., Flag Lieutenant of His Excellency the Commander-in-Chief of Her Majesty's Naval Forces in India.
 Lieutenant Foley, R.N., Flag Lieutenant of the Rear-Admiral Second in Command.
 Captain Farmer, Aide-de-Camp to his Excellency the Viceroy.
2. The Rear-Admiral Second in Command.
 Captain Evelyn Baring, Private Secretary to His Excellency the Viceroy.
 Captain Jackson, Aide-de-Camp to His Excellency the Viceroy.
 The Honourable F. Baring, Aide-de-Camp to His Excellency the Viceroy.
3. His Excellency the Commander-in-Chief of Her Majesty's Naval Forces in India.
 C. U. Aitchison, Esq., C.S.I., Secretary to the Government of India.
 Colonel Earle, Military Secretary to His Excellency the Viceroy.
 Captain Biddulph, Aide-de-Camp to His Excellency the Viceroy.
 A Detachment of His Excellency the Viceroy's Body Guard.

<table>
<tr><td rowspan="2">The Adjutant of the Viceroy's Body Guard (on horseback).</td><td>HIS EXCELLENCY THE VICEROY AND GOVERNOR-GENERAL.</td><td>HIS ROYAL HIGHNESS THE PRINCE OF WALES.</td><td rowspan="2">The Commandant of the Viceroy's Body Guard (on horseback).</td></tr>
<tr><td colspan="2">The Equerry in attendance on his Royal Highness.</td></tr>
</table>

The Commissioner of Police (on horseback).
A Detachment of His Excellency the Viceroy's Body Guard.

Carriages of Native Princes invited to take part in the Procession.

The Deputation from His Highness the Nizam.
His Highness Syajee Rao, Gaekwar of Baroda.
His Highness the Maharaja of Mysore.
His Highness the Maharana of Meywar (Oodeypur).
His Highness Siwajee Chutraputtee Maharaj, Raja of Kolhapur.
His Highness Maharao Shree Mirza Rajay Pragmuljee, G.C.S.I., Rao of Cutch.
His Highness Kesrusingjee Jewunsingjee, Maharaja of Edar.
His Highness Meer Ali Morad of Khairpur.
His Highness Mohubut Khanjee, K.C.S.I., Nawab of Junagarh.

His Highness Jam Shree Vibbajee, Jam of Nawanagar.
His Highness Rawul Shree Tukhutsingjee, Thakur Saheb of Bhaunagar.
His Highness Rah Shree Mansingjee, Raj Saheb of Dhrangadra.
Gumbheersingjee, Raja of Rajpipla.
His Excellency Zorawur Khan, Dewan of Pahlanpur.
Bismilla Khan, Nawab of Radhanpur.

Carriages of other Officers and Gentlemen taking part in the Procession.

1. The Chief Justice of Bombay.
   His Excellency the Commander-in-Chief.
2. The Honourable A. Rogers, } Members of Council.
   The Honourable J. Gibbs, }
3. The Honourable Sir Charles Sargent.
   The Honourable Mr. Justice Bayley.
4. The Honourable Mr. Justice Kemball.
   The Honourable Mr. Justice Green.
5. The Honourable Mr. Justice West.
   The Honourable Mr. Justice Nanabhai Haridas.
6. The Honourable A. R. Scoble.
   The Honourable Major-General Kennedy.
7. The Honourable Colonel W. C. Anderson.
   The Honourable E. W. Ravenscroft.
8. The Honourable Rao Saheb W. N. Mundlick.
   The Honourable Rao Saheb Becherdass Ambaidass.
9. The Honourable Nacoda Mahomed Ali Rogay.
   The Honourable Khan Bahadoor Padamjee Pestonjee.
10. The Honourable Donald Graham.
11. The Chairman of the Municipal Corporation.
    The Municipal Commissioner.
    The Sheriff of Bombay.
    A Squadron of the 1st Bombay Lancers in column of Fours.

POONAH.

PARADE STATE.—15*th November*, 1875.—(Page 179.)

	Corps.	British Officers.	Medical Officers.	Native Officers.	Non-Commissioned Officers.	Drummers and Musicians.	Rank and File.	Total.	Horses.	Guns.
	Head Quarters, 4th Brigade, R. A.	1	..	..	..	..	..	..	1	..
	Head Quarters, 9th Brigade, R. A.	1	1	..	1	1	..	2	4	..
	A–4 Royal Artillery	3	..	..	12	2	75	89	92	6
	E–4 Royal Artillery	2	1	..	11	1	75	87	94	6
	E–9 Royal Artillery	1	..	..	4	1	44	49	56	3
	Sappers and Miners	7	1	6	18	4	204	226	8	..
1st Inf. Brigade.	2–7th Fusiliers	14	1	..	24	52	536	612	3	..
	1st Grenadier Regiment N. I.	7	1	14	31	48	374	453	5	..
	8th Regiment N. I.	4	1	12	33	36	472	541	4	..
	15th Regiment N. I.	4	..	7	24	28	328	380	4	..
2nd Inf. Brigade.	2–15th Foot..	11	1	..	24	43	490	557	3	..
	13th Regiment N. I.	4	1	9	23	30	312	365	4	..
	17th Regiment N. I.	5	1	12	30	13	433	476	5	..
	19th Regiment N. I.	6	1	9	20	29	259	308	6	..
	Grand Total ..	70	10	69	255	288	3602	4145	289	15

BOMBAY. —(Page 182.)

After the presentation of colours to the Bombay Marine Battalion on 16th November, there was a review before the Prince. The following was the Parade State :

Corps.	Field Officers.	Captains.	Subalterns.	Native Officers.	Sergeants, Duffedars, and Havildars.	Trumpeters and Drummers.	Rank and File.	Total.
D–C. Royal Horse Artillery	1	1	1	..	7	2	78	87
3rd Hussars	..	2	2	..	5	27	112	144
1st Light Cavalry (Lancers)	2	3	1	9	19	4	173	196
Poona Horse	2	1	2	12	23	4	185	212
6th Brigade R. A.	2	1	2	..	6	5	121	132
1–2nd Queen's	1	2	5	..	12	3	300	315
20th Regiment N. I.	4	3	1	12	39	44	411	494
21st Regiment N. I.	3	1	1	15	25	29	413	467
26th Regiment N. I.	1	2	1	10	21	39	278	338
Grand Total	16	16	16	58	157	157	2071	2385

After the march-past Sir C. Staveley issued the following G. O. C.:

The Commander-in-Chief has the gratification to announce that the Field-Marshal His Royal Highness the Prince of Wales, having reviewed the troops, both European and Native, at Poona and Bombay, the first he has seen in India, has been graciously pleased to express his approval of their appearance on parade, and of the steadiness and precision of their movements.

RETURN VISITS.

There were printed programmes for each visit made to, and each return visit made by the Prince, and one will serve, *mutatis mutandis*, for all. The directions were undeviatingly observed, and the programmes were useful guides, as notes of what to observe in the case of each Chief were pencilled on the back. There were also *libelli* issued by the Government, giving accounts of the State and family of each Chief, generally adorned by photograph:

FOREIGN DEPARTMENT.

FORT WILLIAM, December 27, 1875.

Return Visit of His Royal Highness the Prince of Wales to Maharajah Scindia, G.C.S.I.

His Royal Highness the Prince of Wales will return the visit of his Highness the Maharaja Scindia on Wednesday the 29th day of December, at 11.30 A.M. A deputation, consisting of the four principal members of his Highness's suite present in Calcutta, will wait on his Royal Highness the Prince of Wales at Government House, at 10.45 A.M. precisely, to conduct his Royal Highness to the private residence (No. 5, Alipoor) of the Maharaja. His Royal Highness will be attended by Major P. D. Henderson, Major R. W. Sartorius, and by such members of the personal Staff as his Royal Highness may appoint. The Maharaja, accompanied by the Political Officer on duty with his Highness, will receive his Royal Highness the Prince of Wales under the portico of his house as his Royal Highness alights from his carriage, and will conduct his Royal Highness to a seat, which will be immediately on the Maharaja's right hand. On the right of the Prince will sit Major P. D. Henderson, Major R. W. Sartorius, and the personal Staff. On the left of the Maharaja will sit the Political Officer on duty with his Highness, and beyond him the Maharaja's relatives and attendants, according to their rank. After a short conversation, the Maharaja's relatives and attendants will be presented to his Royal Highness by the Political Officer on duty with the Maharaja, and will offer the usual nuzzurs, which will be touched and remitted. At the close of the interview the Maharaja will present uttur and pân to his Royal Highness the Prince of Wales, and one of his

Highness's principal attendants to the other officers present. The Maharaja will take leave of the Prince under the portico of his Highness's house. The four members of his Highness's suite who met his Royal Highness will return with his Royal Highness until it shall be the pleasure of his Royal Highness to dispense with their attendance. A Guard of Honour will be drawn up at the Maharaja's house, and will salute on the arrival and departure of his Royal Highness. His Royal Highness will be escorted by the Body-Guard. Full dress will be worn by all officers on this occasion.

P. D. Henderson, Major, Political Officer on duty with his Royal Highness the Prince of Wales.

NEW YEAR'S NIGHT.—(Page 377.)

The bill of the play on the occasion of the Prince's visit on New Year's night to the Theatre, Calcutta, was as follows:

ENGLISH'S THEATRE, 7, LINDSAY STREET.

Directress—Mrs. E. English.

TO-NIGHT, SATURDAY, 1st JANUARY, 1876,

His Royal Highness

THE PRINCE OF WALES'S

STATE NIGHT BY VICE-REGAL COMMAND,

AND

Benefit of Mrs. English.

Tenth appearance in India of the Celebrated and World-Renowned

CHARLES MATHEWS,

The greatest Comedian of the age, and acknowledged as such by the World.

The Performance will commence (by Command) at 9.30 P.M. precisely, with Charles Mathew's latest London success and own Comedy, entitled,

MY AWFUL DAD!!

Mr. Adonis Evergreen—Mr. Charles Mathews (his Original Character).

Richard Evergreen (his son, aged 27) .	Mr. G. Barrett.
Prince Kotchacoff	Mr. H. Walton.
Humphrey Lovekin (aged 40)	Mr. H. Jordan.
Fibs, Clerks to Richard Evergreen . .	Mr. C. Vere.
Nibs, Clerks to Richard Evergreen . .	Mr. Cooke.
Dibs, Clerks to Richard Evergreen . .	Mr. F. Stuart.
Cruets (a Waiter)	Mr. F. Stuart.
Matilda Weddagain	Miss Annie Baldwin.
Emma Marigold	Miss Edith Wilson.
Mrs. Biggs	Miss Sallie Turner.
Charlotte Fitzplantagenet (*née* Griskin)	Miss Nellie Vincent.
Evangeline Clara Vere-de-Vere (*née* Tadpole)	Miss Marie Kean.

To conclude with (by special request),

LITTLE AMY ROBSART!!!

OR, YE QUEEN, YE EARLE, AND YE MAYDENNE.

QUEEN ELIZABETH	Mr. G. Barrett.
EARL OF LEICESTER	Miss Edith Wilson.
EARL OF SUSSEX	Miss Marie Kean.
EARL OF ESSEX	Miss Ellen Kemp.
EARL OF SURREY	Miss Mabel Howard.
SIR WALTER RALEIGH	Miss Nellie Vincent.
TRESSILIAN	Miss Annie Howard.
VARNEY	Mr. H. Walton.
WAYLAND SMITH (a Vagabond). . . .	Mr. F. Mervin.
TONY FOSTER	Mr. F. Stuart.
MIKE LAMBOURNE	Mr. H. Jordan.
AMY ROBSART	Miss Topsey Venne.
JANET	Miss Stella Balham.

SCENERY by HERR M. FREYBERGER.

MUSIC ARRANGED BY MR. ALFRED PLUMPTON.

On this occasion the interior of the House will be festively decorated, and the exterior brilliantly illuminated by Messrs. FREYBERGER and ANDERSON.

The FLORAL DECORATIONS of the exterior and interior of the House have been entrusted to Mr. M. BAKER, the Florist.

The Royal Box will be fitted up by Messrs. Lazarus & Co.

PRICES OF ADMISSION.

Upper Tier Boxes with Six Seats	Rs.	1,000	each	= £100
Lower Tier Boxes with Five Seats	„	500	„	= 50
Stalls	„	30	„	= 3

Maharajahs, Rajahs, Nawabs, Chiefs, and the *élite* of Calcutta who may wish to reserve Boxes on this interesting occasion are solicited to communicate through their Agents, or by letter with Mrs. English, or with Herr M. Freyberger, 14 Chowringhee Road.

THE DELHI REVIEW.—(Page 407.)

The following is an account of the force which was present at Delhi on the 12th January, 1876:

ARTILLERY.

Royal Horse Artillery.

A. Battery, A. Brigade	Major F. G. Ravenhill.
C. Battery, A. Brigade	Major F. A. Whinyates.
D. Battery, A. Brigade	Major P. E. Hill.
A. Battery, C. Brigade	Major M. M. FitzGerald.

Field Artillery.

A. Battery, 8th Brigade	Major W. J. Finch.
B. Battery, 8th Brigade	Major A. Dixon.

F. Battery, 8th Brigade	Major D. S. Pemberton.	
A. Battery, 19th Brigade	Major A. H. Davidson.	
C. Battery, 19th Brigade	Major E. H. Dyke.	
F. Battery, 19th Brigade	Major W. Manderson.	

Mountain Battery.

6th Battery, 13th Brigade	Major H. A. Tracey.	

Heavy Battery.

No. 1 Battery, 23rd Brigade	Major P. H. Harcourt	Three 40-pr. Armstrong B.L.; two 8-inch mortars; two 5½-in. cohorns.

CAVALRY.

10th Hussars	Major Lord Ralph Kerr.	
4th Bengal Cavalry .. (Hindustanees—general mixture of various classes.)	Col. G. C. Hankin	6th of the Old Army. Did not mutiny.
10th Bengal Lancers .. (Sikhs, Pathans, &c.—class troop system.)	Major O. Barnes ..	2nd Regiment, "Hodson's Horse."
2nd Punjab Cavalry .. Punjab Frontier Force —class troop system.)	Captain F. Lance ..	Raised by Major-General Sam Browne before Mutiny. Commanded by him throughout Mutiny.
11th Hussars	Lieut.-Col. A. L. Annesley.	
5th Bengal Cavalry .. (General mixture of various classes.)	Major H. R. Osborne.	
1st Regiment, Central India Horse.	Captain H. M. Buller.	
13th Hussars	Lieut.-Col. H. C. Russell, C.B.	
6th Bengal Cavalry .. (Hindustanees, Sikhs, Jats, &c.—class troop system.)	Major G. A. A. Baker.	Old 8th Irregular Cavalry. Commanded by Colonel Richardson before the Mutiny; still commanded by him.
15th Bengal Cavalry.—"Mooltanee Horse." (Men from the banks of the Indus and the Deyra Jat, under their own hereditary Chiefs.)	Major G. A. Prendergast.	Raised during the Mutiny by Major-General Cureton in the Derajab. All Pathans, calling themselves Ben d'Israeli. Their last migration, 250 years ago, was from Candahar. They are not Affghans.
15th Hussars	Lieut.-Col. J. E. Swindley.	

7th Bengal Cavalry .. (General mixture of various classes.)	Captain H. C. Creak	The old 17th; "Liphott's Regiment."
11th Bengal Lancers.—"Probyn's Horse." (Sikhs and Afghans—class troop system.)	Major R. E. Boyle	Raised by Wale, who was killed at the head of the Regiment at Lucknow. Succeeded by Probyn.

ENGINEERS.

Bengal Sappers and Miners.	Col. F. R. Maunsell, C.B.	

INFANTRY.

73rd Regiment	Major J. W. Barnes.	
11th Native Infantry .. (General mixture of various classes.)	Major P. H. F. Harris.	Formerly 70th.
33rd Native Infantry .. (General mixture of various classes.)	Lieut.-Col. J. T. Harris.	Raised during the Mutiny at Allahabad. Composed of various classes, of which the shepherds and agriculturists prevail. Presumed to be a low-caste Regiment, because not composed of Brahmins, Rajpoots, &c.
4th Battalion, Rifle Brigade.	Lieut.-Col. H. R. L. Newdigate.	
3rd Goorkhas .. .. .. (Class Regiment.)	Col. A. Paterson.	
4th Goorkhas .. .. .. (Class Regiment.)	Lieut.-Col. J. P. Turton.	
2nd Battalion, 60th Rifles	Lieut.-Col. H. P. Montgomery.	
2nd Ghoorkas, Sirmoor Battalion. (Class Regiment.)	Lieut.-Col. D. Macintyre, V. C.	Taken into the British service as a Regiment. Had fought against us. Fought on our side against the Sikhs in the Sutlej, with the 60th and Cooke's Rifles. Held Hindoo Rao's house throughout the siege of Delhi.
1st Punjab Infantry .. (Punjab Frontier Force.)	Major F. J. Kean ..	Coke's Rifles. Raised by Coke for Frontier service in 1850. Largely composed of Affreedis. Held the Ridge with the 60th and the 2nd Ghoorkas during the siege. Casualties since formation have amounted to about 680.
39th Regiment	Col. R. H. Currie.	
51st Regiment	Lieut.-Col. C. Acton.	
8th Native Infantry .. (Rajpoots, Hindustanees, Pathans, Sikhs, &c. — class company system.)	Col. T. A. Carey ..	Old 59th. When stationed in the Punjab, enlisted a large number of Sikhs and Pathans.

Regiment	Commanding Officer	Remarks
1st Battalion, 8th Regiment.	Lieut.-Col. G. H. Cochrane.	
85th Regiment	Major W. Hallowes	
32nd Native Infantry.—"Pioneers." (Muzbee Sikhs—class regiment.)	Lieut.-Col. G. A. Williams.	Raised for service at Delhi. Altogether composed of Muzbi Sikhs. Served during the Mutiny in Bhootan and in the Umbeylah Pass.
2nd Battalion, 12th Regiment.	Lieut.-Col. J. M'Kay.	
15th Native Infantry .. (The Loodianah Regiment, Sikhs, &c.—general mixture.)	Col. G. H. Thompson	All Sikhs. Called the Loodianah Regiment. Existed before the Mutiny as an Irregular Regiment. Was raised in what were called the Protected States.
45th Native Infantry .. (Rattray's Sikhs—class regiment.)	Major F. M. Armstrong.	All Sikhs, excepting one Company of Dogras (Hill men). Sikhs drawn from the neighbourhood of Umritam. Originally a Police Battalion, and brought into the line in recognition of its distinguished services under Colonel Rattray.
62nd Regiment	Lieut.-Col. S. G. Carter.	
28th Native Infantry .. (Punjabees—class company system.)	Lieut.-Col. W. C. Hamilton.	The old 16th. Largely composed of Sikhs, Punjabees, and Pathans.
31st Native Infantry .. (Punjabees—class company system.)	Major H. L. C. Bernard.	Raised in the Mutiny. Four Companies of Sikhs; remaining four Companies of various castes—Punjabees, Musalmans, &c.
1st Battalion, 6th Regiment.	Lieut.-Col. T. L. Bell.	
26th Native Infantry .. (Punjabees—class company system.)	Lieut.-Col. C. M. Longmore.	Raised when the Mutiny broke out, and numbered 18th. Sir Herbert Edwardes was said to have collected all the budmashes about Peshawur and neighbouring hills, and regimented them under Lieut.-Colonel (then Lieutenant) Williamson—a good Frontier officer, well acquainted with the Frontier tribes.
5th Punjab Infantry .. (Punjab Frontier Force—class company system.)	Major J. W. McQueen.	One of the old Frontier Regiments. Served throughout the Oudh Campaign under the then Major Vaughan.

A Class Regiment—for instance, Ghoorkas, Cureton's Mooltanee Cavalry, the 1st, 2nd, and 3rd Native Infantry—all Hindoostanis.

A Class Company Regiment would have, for instance, two or three

Companies of Sikhs, a Company of Hindoostanis, a couple of Companies of Musalmans, a Company of Goojurs, a Company of Akeers, occasionally a Company of Ghoorkas, a Company of Affreedis, &c. &c.

The Bengal army consists of about 43,000 men, 19 regiments of cavalry (cavalry regiment about 480 men), and 49 regiments of infantry (infantry regiment about 700 men). The Punjab Frontier force of about 12,000 men.

In the Bengal army there are about 8000 Sikhs, 13,000 Mahomedans. The remainder are Hindoos of various castes.

The regiments raised for service in the Mutiny had four British officers only. After that war the complement was increased to six; a seventh was added as a reserve for civil employ. It is to be remembered that each regiment has, besides its full complement of native officers, two per Troop or Company, who should be, and are in the good regiments, what the Captains and Subalterns are in British regiments.

RETURN of the CAVALRY DIVISION, the 17th January, 1876.

DIVISIONAL STAFF.

Brigadier J. Watson, C.B., V.C. .. .. .. Commanding Division.
Lieut.-Colonel Hugh Gough, C.B., V.C. .. Assistant Adjutant-General.
Major S. de A. C. Clarke, 4th Hussars .. Assistant Adjutant-General.
Lieutenant F. C. Burton, 1st B. C. .. .. Assistant Quartermaster-General.
Major W. H. Macnaghten, 13th B. C. .. Orderly Officer.

1st CAVALRY BRIGADE.

Colonel C. Gough, C.B., V.C. .. .. .. Commanding.
Captain W. Clayton, 9th Lancers .. .. Brigade-Major.

TROOPS.

10th Royal Hussars—Major Lord Ralph Kerr commanding—265 sabres.
2nd Punjab Cavalry—Captain F. Lance commanding—226 sabres.
10th Bengal Lancers, "Hodson's Horse"—Major O. Barnes commanding—225 sabres.

2nd CAVALRY BRIGADE.

Colonel J. Miller, 13th Hussars .. .. .. Commanding.
Captain A. P. Palmer, S.C. .. .. .. Brigade Major.

TROOPS.

11th Prince Albert's Own Hussars—Lieut.-Colonel Lyttelton Annesley commanding—220 sabres.
5th Bengal Cavalry—Major H. Osborn commanding—279 sabres.
1st Regiment Central India Horse—Captain H. Buller commanding—279 sabres.

3rd CAVALRY BRIGADE.

Colonel G. C. Hankin, S.C. .. .. Commanding.
Captain G. Luck, 15th Hussars .. .. .. Brigade-Major.

TROOPS.

13th Hussars—Lieut.-Colonel B. Russell, C.B., commanding—260 sabres.
4th Bengal Cavalry—Major M. Prendergast commanding—255 sabres.
6th Bengal Cavalry—Major G. A. A. Baker commanding—266 sabres.

4th CAVALRY BRIGADE.

Colonel T. Kennedy, S.C. .. .. Commanding.
Captain H. R. Abadie, 9th Lancers .. .. Brigade-Major.

TROOPS.

15th Hussars—Lieut.-Colonel J. E. Swindley commanding—279 sabres.
11th Bengal Lancers, "Probyn's Horse"—Major R. E. Boyle commanding—291 sabres.

Total of all ranks, 2857.

HUGH GOUGH, Lieut.-Colonel,
Assistant Adjutant-General.

Camp of Exercise, 18th February, 1876.

FORCE ORDER.

(*Issued by Scindia at Gwalior, on 3rd February*, 1876.)

The march-past on the 1st instant gave satisfaction to the Field Marshal His Royal Highness the Prince of Wales, who greatly praised the Commanding Officers. It is therefore notified on the part of His Highness the Maharaja to the Commanding Officers that they are to impress this on their hearts with gladness of spirit, and to continue to perform their respective duties in a creditable and exemplary manner, in order that the fame of the force and of themselves may be lasting.

THE PRINCE'S FAREWELL TO INDIA.

"FORT WILLIAM, *March 17th*, 1876.

"His Excellency the Viceroy and Governor-General has the satisfaction of publishing, for general information, the following letter, which he has had the honour of receiving from his Royal Highness the Prince of Wales :—

"'*H.M.'s Ship "Serapis,"* BOMBAY, *March 13th.*

"'MY DEAR LORD NORTHBROOK,

"'I cannot leave India without expressing to you, as the Queen's Representative of this vast Empire, the sincere pleasure and the deep interest with which I have visited this great and wonderful country. As you are aware, it has been my hope and intention for some years past to see India, with a view to become more intimately acquainted with the Queen's subjects in this distant part of her Empire, and to examine for myself those objects of interest which have always had so great an attraction for travellers. I may candidly say that my expectations have been more than realised by what I have witnessed, so that I return to my native country most deeply impressed with all I have seen and heard. The information I have gained will, I am confident, be of the greatest value to me, and will form a useful foundation for much that I hope hereafter to acquire. The reception I have met with from the Princes and Chiefs, and from the Native population at large, is most gratifying to me, as the evidence of loyalty thus manifested shows an attachment to the Queen and to the Throne, which, I trust, will be made every year more lasting. It is my earnest hope that the many millions of the Queen's Indian subjects may daily become more convinced of the advantages of British rule, and that they may realise more fully that the Sovereign and the Government of England have the interests and well-being of India very sincerely at heart. I have had frequent opportunities of seeing Native troops of all branches of the Service, and I cannot withhold my opinion that they constitute an army of which we may feel justly proud. The "march-past" at Delhi of so many distinguished officers and of such highly disciplined troops was a most impressive sight, and one which I shall not easily forget. I wish also to state my high appreciation of the Civil Service, and I feel assured that the manner in which their arduous duties are performed tends greatly to the prosperity and the contentment of all classes of the community. I cannot conclude without thanking you, and all those in authority, for the facilities which have enabled me to traverse so rapidly so large an extent of country, and rest assured I shall ever retain a grateful memory of the hospitality tendered by yourself and by others who have so kindly received me.

"'Believe me, my dear Lord Northbrook,

"'Yours very sincerely,

"'ALBERT EDWARD.'"

ADDRESSES.

THE following are Addresses, which present characteristic points :—

POONAH.

"We beg to approach your Royal Highness with every feeling of loyalty and respect, to offer our congratulations on the occasion of your Royal Highness's visit to this city.

"The blessings of peace and good government which we enjoy have endeared the rule of Her Most Gracious Majesty the Queen to all her Indian subjects, and we hail the advent of your Royal Highness among us as a new proof of the great interest Her Majesty and your Royal Highness take in all that affects the well-being of the countless inhabitants of this land.

"The city of Poonah, though comparatively poor in point of wealth, is rich in historical renown. It is the capital of the Deccan and the chief city of the great Mahratta nation. Your Royal Highness will see many larger, handsomer, and wealthier cities in other parts of India, but will find nowhere a more loyal, intelligent, or closely united community than the one which now welcomes your Royal Highness through us their representatives.

"May the God of all nations bless and preserve your Royal Highness and Her Royal Highness the Princess of Wales, your noble consort, long to adorn the proud positions your Royal Highnesses at present occupy, and in future years may your Royal Highness look back on your visit to Poonah with feelings of kindly remembrance.

"With the deepest respect we beg to subscribe ourselves your Royal Highness's most faithful and loyal servants."

AHMEDABAD.

(*Presented at Baroda.*)

"We, the Naggarsheth of Ahmedabad and others, on behalf of ourselves and our fellow-citizens, desire to express our feelings of loyalty and devotion to her Majesty the Empress of India, and the great pleasure which we feel in approaching your Royal Highness as her Representative.

"Your Royal Highness's short sojourn in Guzerat may have impressed on your Royal Highness the fact that this Province is more than any other distinguished by a spirit of industry and commercial enterprise; and that the people in general are, in consequence, lovers of peace and liberty, which we happily enjoy under the benign sway of her Gracious Majesty the Queen. The people of this Province are to be found engaged in trade in distant parts of this great country and even beyond it. Hence the language of Guzerath is, properly speaking, the commercial language of India. This language is being very fast improved and enriched with useful literature, under the auspices of the Educational Department and by individual efforts. We are trying to establish a College in our city, that the blessings of higher education, derived from English literature and European science, may be placed within the reach of the people; and we hope to succeed in our undertaking by the support of Government, which is so essential to success. The railway has given an impetus to its trade, and it has still better prospects before it when the line on the North shall connect Guzerath with Rájputáná and Upper India. The fevers of Guzerath, which were once a terror to the population, have been much mitigated by the wise sanitary and medical arrangements made by Government.

"Our city, which historically is the chief city of Guzerath, as shown by numerous ancient architectural relics, is peopled by traders, workmen, and artificers, who depend for their support on their own industry and labour, for which the cotton, silk, and gold-thread manufactures afford a great scope.

"It has unfortunately suffered greatly by the recent flood; but the whole country has shown its sympathy by prompt and generous assistance, and we hope it will ere long recover its former prosperity.

"We pray that God may bring your Royal Highness's travel through India to a happy close, and that it may afford your Royal Highness opportunities of knowing the real state and wants of your future subjects. We are, therefore, earnest in the hope that it may be productive of much good to this country, and be the means of strengthening between Great Britain and India those feelings of cordiality and reciprocal confidence which mutual acquaintance and knowledge are sure to engender."

SURAT.

(*Presented at Baroda.*)

"It is our high privilege to approach Your Royal Highness with feelings of loyalty and devotion, and to offer on behalf of the general community of the ancient City of Surat our congratulations on the occasion of Your Royal Highness's visit to the Province of Gujerat.

"Whilst we lay no claim to prominence in geographical position, in wealth, or in magnificence, we look back with pride to historical traditions which begin with the landing at Surat of the first British Ambassador in Hindostan, more than two and a half centuries ago, and we can challenge any city in India to show a longer or more intimate connection with the British Government.

"It would not have been in accord with such historical associations, if we had allowed this august occasion of a visit to Gujerat of the Heir Apparent of Her Most Gracious Majesty Queen Victoria, under whose benign rule we have so long enjoyed peace, prosperity, and the benefits of improved institutions, to pass without offering to you personally an assurance of our loyalty and devotion to the Throne, and our continual prayers for the welfare of Your Royal Highness.

THE MAHOMEDAN LITERARY SOCIETY.

The following remarkable address was presented to Sir Bartle Frere, with a view to its being laid before the Prince:

"The undersigned Members of the Committee of Management of the Mahomedan Literary Society of Calcutta, on behalf of the Society comprising Members of the Mahomedan Community from various parts of India, venture to approach your Royal Highness with a most cordial and most loyal welcome.

"Of all the many vicissitudes and chances through which, within living memory, it has been the lot of our country to pass, the most auspicious occurred on the day on which, under Divinely appointed Wisdom, your Royal Highness's August Mother, who rules over a hundred kingdoms and hundreds of millions of hearts, undertook the charge of a troubled empire, to give peace and hope to the people for ever, and imbue them with the consciousness of Royal protection and regard. But however mighty and signal the change, now barely quarter of a century since, which was made on the occasion, the external form and machinery of Government remained the same, and only the learned amongst us and those busy in public affairs could understand the nature as well as extent of the revolution that had taken place. The vast bulk of the population, unable to realise an abstract idea of Supreme Power diffusing itself through and sustaining all things, hungered for a visible presence and embodiment of Royalty; and the advent of your Royal Highness fulfils their anxious desire, while it proves that the great Lady, our Beloved Queen, whose goodness and graciousness are over all Her dominions, is ever mindful of our welfare, and will never neglect the prayer of loyalty and affection.

"That the enthusiasm evoked by your Royal Highness's visit is not the mere outburst of a holiday sentiment, the reception which your Royal Highness has experienced in other parts of India has no doubt testified. To the people of Bengal, and particularly the Mahomedan portion of them, it is fraught with memories which will live in their history to come. The overthrow of our Indian Mahomedan Dynasties by the conduct and valour of the British Nation is recent enough to have left behind some memories of the glories of some of our Moslem rulers. But the justice, humanity, and universal toleration of the British Nation have obliterated the past for us; and, in accordance with the instincts of our human nature, we longed for the moment when we could, as now, regarding your Royal Highness as representing our Gracious Sovereign, look upon the object of our most precious love and reverence.

"It is not permitted to us, who have signed the Address, to speak in our collective capacity as politically representing the Mahomedan Community of all India or all Bengal; but each can individually bear witness to the fact that in his own immediate will, from the highest to the lowest, the inmost recesses of Mahomedan feeling have been stirred in a manner in which their depths have never been moved before; that a reanimated sense of personal fealty to your Royal Highness's family has dawned over them; and that your Royal Highness, as our future King and Emperor, is the centre of a world of devotion and allegiance becoming intensified day by day.

"The special function assumed to itself by the Mahomedan Literary Society is to promote among our co-religionists a knowledge, and also an inclination for the study of the physical sciences of the West. As a means to this end, opportunities are seized upon for bringing about occasions of intercourse between European gentlemen of scientific and learned repute and members of the Mahomedan Community, and thus fostering the germs of mutual good-will between the race of rulers and of the ruled. In the furtherance of such a cause we respectfully solicit your Royal Highness's countenance and encouragement.

"However poor and inadequate the expression, we beg your Royal Highness's acceptance of this humble tribute of sincere and lasting homage; we implore the Almighty Ruler of the world to shower down untold blessings upon your Royal Highness, and your Royal Highness's illustrious family."

AGRA.

"The Municipal Commissioners of Agra desire to express fervent loyalty and devotion to Her Most Gracious Majesty Queen Victoria, our Sovereign, and our great joy on the occasion of this visit with which your Royal Highness has been pleased to honour this city. Within sight of the walls of that ancient fortress which bears witness to the magnificence of former Emperors we welcome your Royal Highness, the representative of a Sovereign whose Empire extends far beyond the limits of the sway of the mightiest monarch ever enthroned at Agra. We gratefully recognise in the justice and tolerant impartiality of our Empress Sovereign's rule, imperial qualities which especially distinguished the wisest of the House of Timour—the founder of this city which welcomes you to-day—Emperor Akbar. The joy and pride which we now feel would have been completed had it been possible for her Royal Highness, the Princess of Wales, to honour us with her gracious presence on this auspicious occasion. We believe and trust that the tour of your Royal Highness through India will tend to draw closer the ties which bind her to England, and will be a source of benefit to this country as well as of pleasure and interest to ourself."

The Native Christians of the Punjaub.

"We, your Royal Highness's humble servants, approach your august presence. We do not represent any great State or city, but we are a little flock gathered, by the grace of God, in the course of about thirty years 'out of every kindred, and tongue, and people, and nation' of this Province; a flock which by the power of God is increasing day by day.

"We rejoice exceedingly that your Royal Highness has honoured this country with your presence; for, as subjects of Her Most Gracious Majesty the Queen, in addition to that prosperity which all the people of this country derive from Her Majesty's Government, we have received even greater blessings under British rule, namely, those spiritual blessings which are imperishable and far better than this world's treasures.

"God has now given us a most welcome opportunity of offering to the Heir Apparent to the Throne of this country a tribute of our devotion and respect, and of assuring your Royal Highness how deeply we feel indebted to those Christian people, of whose labours and self-denial we are the fruit. We have been called to God by foreign missionaries, who, in giving us spiritual instruction and support, have displayed an energy and endurance which the Christians of India in generations to come will not forget. For although this Government does not in any way interfere with religious belief, still Christian people have found under British rule an opportunity of proclaiming in this country the Word of God, which has been the means of great blessing to other lands, and by which the darkness of this land is being gradually removed, and light and purity are being diffused.

"With great pleasure and thankfulness, we beg that your Royal Highness will be graciously pleased to accept copies of the Sacred Scriptures in Urdu, Persian, Punjabi, and Afghani, which have been translated by foreign missionaries for our benefit, and we pray that the rule of Her Most Gracious Majesty the Queen, whose piety and holy life are an example to her subjects, may be established and prolonged, and also that the Divine protection may ever be vouchsafed to your Royal Highness, that you may be enriched with heavenly blessings, and in all things glorify God through our Lord Jesus Christ."

Lahore.

"We beg humbly to express our thanks that it has pleased the Heir Apparent of the Throne to honour with his presence this distant portion of Her Majesty's dominions; for we see in this auspicious visit, following that of his Royal Highness the Duke of Edinburgh, another proof of the warm interest taken in our welfare by our Gracious Sovereign and the members of the Royal Family.

"Though distant from the Capital of England, and among the youngest sons of her Great Empire, we claim, in common with our countrymen, a foremost rank among the loyal subjects of the Crown; for, placed at the north-western door of India, on the borders of regions untraversed by Europeans, and mindful of our own past history, we are in a position to appreciate even more than others the benefits of British Rule.

"For those great benefits we hope ever to evince in acts, as we now express in words, the gratitude of a faithful people."

The Managers of Runjeet Sing's Mausoleum.

"We the Managers of the Mausoleum beg to approach your Royal Highness with feeling of the deepest loyalty and offer our cordial welcome for the visit paid to this edifice, consecrated to the relics of the departed Royalty of this country. We never expected such an unusual honor, ever since, the memorable visit of his Grace, the Duke of Edinburgh. It is however realized. We rejoice in it, and once more pay our homage to your Royal Highness for the honor once done.

"It is very perperous for the Commons, and we are really immaculated to have a personal appearance of a Royal Prince. We have nothing to adore our Lord स्पमाट the Emperor, according to Hindoo Sastras Bhugbutgellah 11 Section 27 verse नरानाचंनरा घिपा "Nurranuncho Nuradheephann," also Adage देवीस्वरवा जगदीस्वर *Delhisuro bah Jugodisoro* and in Mahomedan's ظل الٰلی *Zoolilah*, i.e. the Emperor is a shadow of Almighty. This Mausoleum was erected by the Raja Khurk Sing, son of Maharaja Runjeet Sing, in the year 1839, nearly thirty-six years ago.

"Though Lahore is far inferior to other Presendencies in almost in every respect which your Royal Highness visited, the fidelity and loyalty which we feel warm in our bosom will for ever remain unchanged for your Royal Highness and Her Majesty the Queen of Britain. We sincerely pray for health, happiness, and safe journey of your Royal Highness through this country, and remain,

"With the greatest respect your Royal Highness's

"Most obedient and devoted subjects and humble servants,

"Nursing Prosand Roy (*for the* Grinthians).

"*25th January*, 1876."

The Municipal Council of Kandy.

"The prosperous condition of the Kandyan country, the peace and security which every Native homestead, scattered throughout this important Province, is now privileged to enjoy—the material and social advancement of the people—the contentment which is apparent among the different sections of the community—are, it is our pleasing duty to acknowledge, but a few of the beneficial results which have marked the British rule in this Island.

"The introduction of wise and beneficent laws, and the continued efforts which have been made to promote the interests of all classes, have tended to foster feelings of loyalty and attachment to the Government, which we feel confident will be strengthened by this visit of your Royal Highness."

The Talukdars of Oudh.

"We, the Talukdars of Oudh, as faithful subjects of the Empress of India, most humbly and dutifully offer to your Royal Highness, the illustrious representative of the Royal Family, a cordial welcome to this remote corner of her Majesty's realm. That your Royal Highness, after long travels by land and sea, should have deigned to honour us this evening with your Royal Highness's presence, makes our hearts proud as well as thankful; and the present occasion, when our eyes have been gladdened by the sight of our future Emperor, will ever remain with us a fond and honoured tradition.

"Although we have owed allegiance to the British Crown for the comparatively brief period of a score of years, we can assure your Royal Highness that our fealty is as firmly established as if it had been handed down to us through a long succession of dynasties; and we humbly trust your Royal Highness will convey to our august Empress the assurance that the Talukdars of Oudh, though the last to become her Majesty's subjects in India, are second to none in the sincerity of their loyalty.

"Nay more, your Royal Highness, we know that our loyalty to the British Government is both reasonable and right; for it is to the benign rule of your Royal Mother that we owe the security of our rights and vested interests, as well as the permanence of our position, dignity, and rank, as the landed aristocracy of Oudh.

"At the same time, we assure your Royal Highness that we are grateful to the British Government for its efforts to improve the general condition of the people of the Province. We are thankful that reforms are from time to time introduced into every branch of the Administration,—not abruptly but gradually; and with that due regard to ancient rights and time-honoured customs which alone can produce a useful and lasting reform.

"We would further entreat your Royal Highness to convey to your

Royal Consort our humble assurance that, though the boundless ocean prevents us from laying the tribute of our devotion at her Highness's feet, it is none the less certain that the majesty of her presence reigns supreme in our hearts.

"In conclusion, we humbly approach your Royal Highness with this modest tribute of our allegiance and gratitude, which we fondly hope your Royal Highness will deign to accept as a fit emblem of the fealty of the Talukdars of Oudh to the British Crown."

POETICAL ADDRESSES.

THE hyperbole of Oriental poetry appears very ludicrous when translated by those who give not the inner meaning, but only the bald dictionary correlatives of the words of the poet. It is not for the purpose of ridiculing what may be a very creditable production that I quote a few lines of a Sanscrit poem, by Raghunath Rao Vithal Vinchoorkar, described as "First-class Sirdar; Companion of the most exalted Order of the Star of India; Raja Oomdut Oolmulk, Bahadoor," entitled 'The Indian Journey of the Prince of Wales,' printed at a native press in Bombay, and dedicated to the Prince. The translator was assisted by the Professor of Sanscrit at the Elphinstone College. The poem commences with a eulogium on England as a "famous country on the terrestrial globe which, endowed with prosperity, shines verily in the north-western quarter with a heavenly glory. Whose brave things, like the autumnal suns, delighted their Padma-like friends (Padma being a species of lotus, blooming in sunlight), and brought on a pallor to the host of their Kumuda-like enemies (Kumuda being a species of lotus blowing open in moonlight) by their ray-like hands. Whose forces, consisting of numberless ships, moving on the bottomless sea, cause her enemies to sink by their very sight in the ocean of the world, in half a moment." We are told that the sea, "inaccessible in consequence of frightful animals with cave-like mouths, swimming within its bowels, and dreadful to look at, because of waves as high as mountains," is the fort within which this country dwells. London is compared to a beautiful woman, shining with ornaments, on the banks of the Thames, "where shine very lofty palaces, various factories, libraries containing books stored by renowned scholars, charity houses, and an observatory built of marble; lovely mountains and pleasant rivers, trees and creepers full of fruits and flowers, and very delightful forests, abounding in beasts of every variety." The genealogy of the Prince is next given, beginning with "a King named George, who was of good deportment, like a shining pearl," and who, by his "white and fair conduct, made his subjects red and devoted." A footnote tells us that in the original there is very pretty play upon words, which I presume cannot be turned into English. India is described as having been "enjoyed with violence by intoxicated, wicked, and oppressive kings," and as having taken shelter under the great Queen, "seeing whose astonishing beauty, people formerly desirous to see Rati have slackened their wish, and are content with Her Majesty, who, seated on the throne, with the lamps of the diadem gems of tributary Princes whirling round her lotus-like feet, is worthy of being looked at by all people, like Royal splendour incarnate on earth." After an outburst of praise for all she has done in the spread of science, and of all the arts that promote the good of men, the poet says: "She levies taxes for our prosperity, dispels all our fears, and cherishes us with affection: Victoria is therefore our mother-like Queen." The cause of the Prince's journey is tersely put. "Disputes often take place in Parliament respecting the real state of the Queen's subjects. Some say, 'her Hindoo subiects are poor; their miseries are great;' others say, 'it is false.' Was it, then, to decide the matter that the Queen sent her own son?" The question is not answered by the poet; but he evidently infers that some such object was at the bottom of the journey. He asks, "Did the Queen send out her eldest son at once, because conscious that it is of advantage to inquire whether officers appointed by herself act in conformity with the rules laid down for the protection of her subjects? India is well worth such a visit. The best of countries; the fertile land where gold and gems are found; the inhabitants of which were in olden time versed in arts, and rich in learning, and which became an object of desire to Western kings in consequence of its wealth." The arrival at Bombay is next set forth: "When the Queen's son set his foot on land from the barge, the terrestrial globe seemed to be shaken by the thundering of guns." The Princes received him from "his palace-like ship," and bowed low when they saw "the person of the son of the paramount Sovereign." "The Queen's representative appointed to protect India" supported the Prince, and the people, "with their lotus-like eyes dilated through delight," saw him step into the middle of the carriage. "Then, as the sun sank down, the moon, in the shape of the Prince by his charming lustre, rising, blew open the Kumuda-lotuses of the eyes of people in Bombay." An enumeration of all the blessings which the Queen has bestowed on India—"the telegraph, which carries intelligence swiftly," ships, "carriages moved by fire," "hospitals for the poor," machines for printing newspapers, libraries, "the pursuit of female education," trade, "unrestrained acquisition of freedom," "travelling unattended with trouble," and "roads free from the fear of bandits." "Of Her through whose grace" all this is obtained "this Prince is a son, and certain to be our King. He is learned; the appreciator of merits; benevolent; bountiful; the very ocean of kindness; the hater of the crowd of wicked people; modest, just, and the lover of truth. Long live this Prince, our Lord! adorned with so many excellent qualities." He is described as "the water-basin for the growing creeper of Politics; the ocean of the rising moon of genteelness; the mountain on which grow the shining gems of virtues;

the arani of the fire of valour; the pleasure hall for the lovely maiden of knowledge; the wearer of the true ornaments—the ruby of honesty and the abode of real joy." He is "the young paramount Sovereign" giving "the honour due to each of the subordinate Princes" at Bombay, Madras, Calcutta, and in the "city of Delhi, of world-wide fame, once the seat of great Mohomadan rulers." Viewing at Delhi "the large array of troops displayed by the Commander-in-Chief, he, with all his suite, sank instantly in the ocean of wonder. Having thus seen what is worthy, and pleased himself, and pleased the people, he set off for England. All chiefs, whether pure Kshatrias, Brahmins, Vaisias, Sûdras, Mohomedans, Buddhas, or Jains, differing in caste as they do, unite in praying for ever to the Almighty for the good of the Prince in forms proper to their several faiths."

The Superintendent of State Education in Indore, Raojee Wasudeva Tullu, M.A., wrote "a Welcome Address":—

"All hail! Victoria's son, thrice welcome hail!
With hearts full joyous, we thy presence greet.
Hail! youthful prince! we now ourselves avail
To speak our hearts, with love and joy replete.

"As when the Lord of Stars, in days of yore,
First from the deep to azure sky arose,
Thus, from a land ten thousand miles and more,
Thy visit charms all eyes, that joy disclose."

Remembering how, that when the Prince has left, the Maharaja remains behind, the Superintendent of State Education pays a delicate compliment or two to his immediate master:—

"In blessed Mâlwà rich, the first is Indore land,
Which now is graced by England's future king;
Here rules TUKOJI wise. Let friendship's band
In close alliance these two powers bring.

"Sprung from her lineage is TUKOJI wise,
Who sees his subjects pleased, himself is pleased;
So too, thou, Prince, are pleased in thy allies,
When they from cares and troubles are truly eased."

The poet in the verse alludes to the descent of Holkar from Ahalyá "a Queen divine, a unique Hindoo Princess, Nonpareil."

SPEECH of the MAHARAJA OF PUTTIALA.—(Page 437.)

"January 24th.

"This occasion on which your Royal Highness, our future Emperor, and the most beloved son of our gracious, glorious, and illustrious Sovereign, the Queen, has been pleased to condescend to accept this my humble entertainment, and thus to bestow a very high honour on this State, is a source of great pleasure and pride to the Puttiala family.

"The family of Puttiala is very proud of this, that seventy-three years ago, since friendly relations have been made with the British Government, it has by the series of its continued, long, and uninterrupted services, attained an especial predominance, distinction, and conspicuousness over all the other Native States of Hindoostan, and has, owing to this, always gained the favours and kindness of the British Government, which, it is hoped, will always be continued on this faithful family.

"This place, known by the name of Rajpoorat, although it has lately been reckoned as one of the gates of the capital of Puttiala, is not a very large city, and is very insignificant in itself. It does not pretend to have any very large ancient buildings or anything of historical importance, so as to attract the attention and curiosity of your Royal Highness, whose condescension therefore, in making time, in order to grant me the honour of entertaining your Royal Highness at such an insignificant place as this, is a vivid proof of that special favour of Government with which this State has always been treated. I therefore avail myself of this opportunity to offer my sincerest and most heartfelt thanks to your Royal Highness for the same.

"These few tents in which this poor entertainment is offered to your Royal Highness are not fit for the Royal entertainment of a Royal guest, but there is an adage in this country which is very appropriate here—

"'Sudar hir ja ke nushinud sudar ast.'

That is, 'That wherever the Chief is, it is the chief place.'

"This night will be a memorable event in the history of the Puttiala family, and the thought of my being the first of the family in having the honour of receiving our future Emperor in my territory is very pleasing.

"I am well convinced that your Royal Highness and her Majesty the Queen are fully aware of the services, loyalty, and devotion of my family, and if they are ever required in any dark emergency, which God forbid, I am ready to come forward with all I have, sacrificing even my life. I earnestly hope that the feelings of loyalty and faithfulness which I have received as a heritage from my forefathers will go down to my successors, and that they will always take pride in them.

"Before concluding this my humble address with the fervent prayer for the long life and sound health of her Gracious Majesty the Queen, your Royal Highness, and all the members of the Royal family, and for the uninterrupted continuance of the British rule in India, which has been full of great and many blessings to us, I propose to you gentlemen present in this assembly, this toast, the good health of his Royal Highness."

THE KING OF PORTUGAL'S SPEECH.—(Page 564.)

" Ce n'est pas là première fois qu'un prince anglais vient en Portugal, mais c'est pourtant la première qu'une visite officielle a lieu et je la considère comme la preuve évidente des bons rapports entre l'Angleterre et le Portugal. Je m'en félicite de ce que pendant mon règne cette visite ait lieu. Je m'en félicite parce que c'est une visite de l'Angleterre au Portugal. Je m'en félicite parce que c'est la preuve que c'est ce prince, qui, un jour, portera la couronne d'Angleterre qui vient au nom de la Reine et de son pays donner l'assurance aux traités qui nous lient comme alliés depuis plusieurs siècles. Je m'en félicite, parce que deux peuples qui ont les mêmes principes politiques, jaloux tous les deux de leur indépendance et pour qui le mot patrie est une vérité et non un mensonge, se donnent l'accolade fraternelle de deux peuples libres dans leurs institutions et également identifiés avec leurs dynasties constitutionnelles. En saluant Votre Altesse, il y a trois santés que je ne veux pas séparer : Dieu garde la Reine, votre gracieuse et auguste mère. Qu'il protége le Prince de Galles, et veille sur la nation anglaise."

THE NATIVE PRESS.

THERE is in each Presidency an officer with functions corresponding, in some degree, to those of the Chief of the Press Bureaux in foreign countries, whose business it is to furnish the Government with a weekly *précis* of the articles in the Native newspapers relating to foreign and domestic policy, administration, internal affairs, &c., and to direct attention to complaints and misstatements, but he has no power of control or censure. These reports are "confidential," and are only sent to the Governor and the higher officials of each Presidency. The tone of some Native papers is so very hostile to the Government, and to the magistracy generally, as to excite uneasiness, and to invite the consideration of measures of repression. The younger and less experienced members of the Civil Service are much in favour of a vigorous censorship and of stringent press laws, whilst they assert, at the same time, that the Native press has small influence, and that no one should pay attention to it. Those who advocate repression lose sight of, or undervalue, the immense benefit to Government of learning what the people are saying of their rulers. I here give some translations of articles in Native papers published in Bombay, Madras, &c :—

'*Vedanta Nirnaya Pathricai*' (Tamil newspaper), dated 15*th November*, 1875.

"His Royal Highness the Prince of Wales set out from England on the 11th October, 1875, to visit India. This was ordered by her Majesty Queen Victoria, and by the most Honourable the Parliament of England. It will ever be memorable, by honours and amusements, in all the places where he will stay during his voyage or journey. He went over to France, where in the capital, the Government and the inhabitants paid him respect, and honoured him as the great Prince of Great Britain. When the steamer *Serapis* touched at Aden, the chief members of the Government of the place, and other officials and people, congregated near the sea-shore, where the 25th Regiment of Infantry was placed as Guard of Honour, and escorted him with Royal honours, chanting 'the God Save the Queen.' An Address was then read to him by Kavoojee Dui Shaw, a nobleman of the place, which was answered by the Prince. And then, on the 8th of

November, the *Serapis* arrived at Bombay, where also a great deal of honour and special respect was paid to the Prince. If convenient, we shall advert to this subject in our next issue.

'Vedanta Nirnaya.'

"The steamer *Serapis* was in sight at the Port of Bombay on the 8th ultimo. Three guns were fired to denote the arrival of the Prince. All the people of the city, who were expecting since a month, rejoiced exceedingly. A salute of twenty-one guns was fired solemnly from the men-of-war. The rays of the morning sun appeared on the waters of the sea, and shone like golden beams. In all the ships in the Roads colours and flags were hoisted. At which time males and females came in dense crowds to the sea-shore, and were quite taken up by the scene, where there was a great clamour of ships borne by the hands of the sea maidens. Then, about half-past 4 o'clock in the afternoon, Lord Northbrook, the Governor-General of India, and Sir Philip Wodehouse, the Governor of Bombay, together with the chief officials, went up to the *Serapis*, and visited the Prince with respect; after which the Prince, attended by the above nobles, landed from the *Serapis*, and, walking gently, got up in the middle of an embellished building near the Beach. There were high seats prepared on each side, so as to contain nearly five hundred persons. In the main road were spread superior carpets. Near that building stood the Regiment of European Fusiliers in parade, and paid the due honours. The band played 'God save the Queen.' Immediately her Royal son, standing in the midst of the assembly, advanced two feet forward, when an Address, prepared by the Committee of the City Decoration, was read by Dada Bahee Baheramjee, which was then put into a fine covered case, and was presented into the hands of our Queen's son. To which the Prince replied properly. Again the Shahzadah had interviews with every native King with much pleasure, and, when he was going in his Royal carriage towards the Government House, Parsee maids, well dressed, met him in the road, and poured showers of flowers at his feet, and sprinkled odorous scents. Being struck with astonishment, the Prince halted awhile, stooped his head, and paid them his respects. And then, going along in procession through the decorated streets, he was dropped at the Government House. He went, after a few days, to Poonah and Baroda, in the Bombay Presidency, where also the respective inhabitants welcomed him, and he had the pleasure of witnessing many sights of wrestling and wild-beast fighting. He was much pleased with one Pilanteen, who played upon a rope, or very cleverly walked upon it, suspended by the power of steam-machine. We are now obliged to stop, as it will take too much space if we want to relate all."

From the 'Andhra Bhasha Sanjavani' (Telugu), Madras, 13th November, 1875.

" We are glad to hear that his Royal Highness the Prince of Wales has resolved upon subscribing for and seeing the English newspapers of India, during his stay here. We are of opinion that this is beneficial, but we regret to observe that the vernacular papers have not been fortunate enough to be blessed with the Royal glance.* Perhaps his Royal Highness might have been under the impression that the opinions and sentiments of the teeming millions of India could be understood through Anglo-Indian papers. We consider this as quite erroneous; most of the Anglo-Indian papers are conducted by Englishmen. No doubt there are some English papers under the direction and editorship of the natives; but they generally follow the purely English papers. Thus, those papers give expression rather more to what Englishmen think of the natives than to what the natives think themselves. Is it possible to grasp native opinion from such papers? Whatever may be the firm footing of the British in India, still this country will go by the name of Hindoostan rather than by the name Anglostan. Differences of opinion are as inevitable as differences of colour and caste. Is it not on account of this that our Government are subscribing for and paying attention to the sentiments expressed in the vernacular papers of this Presidency. Consequently, it is desirable for our Prince to acquaint himself with the opinions of the Natives as the Government are doing. Although it may be asserted that the aim of our Prince, in subscribing for those papers, is to patronise his people, and not to know their opinions; still are not Indian vernaculars, languages like his own? Are not the Hindoos, equally with the English, acceptable to our Prince? Can the ruled be looked upon by the rulers as foreigners? Have not British rulers been ever justly famed for treating all these various subjects equally and impartially? Under these circumstances we most humbly solicit the great generosity of his Royal Highness the Prince of Wales, who is an ocean of intelligence, to subscribe for and favour with a glance the vernacular as well as the Anglo-Indian papers."

'*Jerida-i-Rezgan*' (a newspaper started in Madras by the Mahomedan community, expressly for the Tour of the Prince), 16*th December*.

" His Royal Highness the Prince arrived at Madras, and the people, long expecting, now have the means of representing the pleasure attending his Royal Highness's joyful arrival. We are unable to write in his praise; he possesses a thousand merits, and we are unable to explain one-tenth of them. The people of this place were in dark, and by the arrival of the Most Noble the Prince, the light has spread out, and his lustre is shone on them as a rising star throws his light on the earth. Praise be to (Alla) God, who has given us such a joyful day!"

* It is not given to every one to understand Telugu.

The same, 22nd December.

"For a few days Madras had the pleasure in greeting the joyful arrival in the happy town: but now our Most Noble Prince has left our shores, we see nothing but dulness and quietness. For this separation we feel very sorry. If it had been in our power, we would not have allowed him to depart."

From '*Veltikodegone*' (Tamil newspaper), 18*th December*.

"The precious son of her Majesty, the Queen, his Royal Highness the Prince of Wales, born by the blessing of the Happy One, the transcendant Holy Height, whose beginning, middle, and end are incomprehensible, approached the Perambore Railway Station at 7 A.M. on Monday last, when the officers of the Railway Company, who awaited to receive him there, poured over the Prince a shower of various sorts of odorous flowers, such as lilies, rose, jessamine, lotus, and the like, sprinkled on him rose-water, atter, and other essences of odour, which were kept filled up in different trays of gold set with precious stones, paid him all possible respect, and taking hold of him by his hand (vivid as the crimson colour of lotus), delightfully inducted him into a well-decorated apartment where the floor was covered with carpets of various colours interwoven with gold. Within about half-an-hour, after having visited the workshop and other places and having put on a Royal robe, he got into the train and approached the Roypooram Station at about a quarter-past eight. The ornamental decoration and workmanship at the Railway Station were such as to ravish the spectators' sight. His Grace (the Governor) the Duke of Buckingham, the Chief Justice of the High Court, the Protestant Bishop, the Right Rev. Dr. Fennelly, Bishop of the Roman Catholics, the Government Secretaries, and others, as well as the Native Princes and Rajahs of the five different soils, and others, having wished him a long reign, cheerfully welcomed the Prince, who in return paid them respect by raising up his hand of crimson colour. By this time the military officers fired the guns. All those and every one of the spectators, who waited with inexpressible anxiety the whole previous night, with their eyes wide awake, exposing themselves to the fulgent and frigid rays of the moon, as well as the darting rays of the morning sun, fearless of the dangerous consequences of the deed, no sooner heard the report of the guns, than they got up and stood with their hands folded and their mouths closed, in the fashion of Oriental loyalty usually shown to Sovereigns.

"However diffident we may feel as to our powers to express the excellent manner in which the Thumboo Chetty Street, commencing at the terminus up to the Madras Government House, was decorated, yet we shall try our best endeavours to remove that, as well as the feebleness of our pen, and describe the same as far as practicable.

"The diffidence is entirely owing to the extreme degree of our inability to the task, since the Alldishasha himself (the Seven-Hooded Dragon subterranean supporter and the Divine Commentator of all the Gravimaties) has gone down feeling rather too shy; as this grandeur is far above his powers of expression, he is not adequate to the task. In streets on both sides, coloured flags were hoisted; artificial groves of trees, such as coca, palmyra, date, and plaintains, were exhibited, so thickly that they appeared to touch the ethereal regions.

"Heroic military officers and vehicles of Hindu Kings moved on in Royal procession. To feast their eyes with the colours (flags) on the Railway building the people, conscious of their unworthy vision or sight, attempted to perform penance for better eyes than theirs. There was a green canopy set up within the boundary limit of the Railway Terminus, and it presented a superhuman workmanship. On the front of each of the pandals there was an inscription of the British national anthem, 'God Save the Queen.' In the pandal there was hung an angelic relique which showered on his Royal Highness a profusion of flowers. The Prince, whose face was attactive as the moon, being pleased at this, smiled. Immediately Ramasaumy Chettiar offered his loyal respects to the Prince, who returned his thanks. From the Fort Esplanade up to the Government House the green pandals were all so excellently beautified, like her Majesty's Windsor Castle, near that water fountain, in England, presenting a view of recreation. Orchards from Wallajah Bridge up to Munro's statue, there were on both sides raised-up benches prepared for the students of all the schools of Madras, whose numbers defied calculation. A portion of them chanted songs of congratulations to the Prince and praises of the Deity. Then the Prince stopped his Royal vehicle a little, and with pleasure listened to melodious numbers.

"His Royal Highness observed the carefulness and watchfulness of the respective schoolmasters by the side of their students, and was indescribably satisfied with their devotional attention to their duty. The side benches prepared for the officials and other officials were not enough for their number, crores and crores of them standing under the powerful sun, unmindful of the beams of the day-maker, like the blind praying for eyes who have realised their wish; when it was quarter after nine the Prince entered into the Government House. The multitudes, expressing doubt if there was ever such a scene beheld, returned home. On that evening his Royal Highness went to the Guindy Park Government House; the following day, being the day of his late father's anniversary, the Prince kept at home at Guindy."

'*Oomdatool Akbar*' (Oordoo Paper), *20th December.*

"By the blessing of Almighty, His Royal Highness the Prince of Wales arrived at Madras, and the people of this place consider it a very fortunate day in their life. In place of showers of rain, they are pleased with showers of pleasure; the beauties of flowers of the garden and trees are in no way to be compared with the pleasures derived by the arrival of our Noble Prince. We offer our prayer to Almighty God, that the Prince may arrive safely at his destination.

"After his Royal Highness had witnessed the last General Military Review near the Government House, sitting under the gold, shining, triple-crowned umbrella, supported by the pillar set with carbuncle, diamond, crystal, cat's eye, emerald, lapis lazuli, and blue-gem, he was much transported with joy. He was again overwhelmed in the ocean of delight by the exhibition of fireworks, which laughed to scorn our Indian fireworks. The skilful European workmen, who came from England for the purpose of preparing these powder combinations, were able in the secrets and mysteries of nature to change from minute to minute, for more than three hours, the aspect of the blue sky into crimson-red, emerald-green, saffron. Crores of people were thunderstruck, and imagined that the sidereal heaven itself has been translated into the earth, and crores again uttered cries that the stars were melted and poured down. Crores put forth the opinion that the bushy rockets dashed upwards to measure the distance between the celestial and terrestrial orbs. In like manner the fireworks exhibited on *Scrapis*, and on the Body-Guard ships, were vieing with each other. As these were observed to dive into and emerge from the sea—sight quite novel to people like ourselves—we stood with our eyes wide awake, so as not to wink even."

From the '*Andhra Bhasha Sanjavani*' (Telugu), Madras, 11th January, 1876.

"From the commencement of the British rule in India, to the time of the arrival of his Royal Highness the Duke of Edinburgh and his Royal Highness the Prince of Wales to this land, Viceroys and Governors of the different Presidencies acted as if they were British Sovereigns. Even the Collectors and Judges of the several districts and the British Residents and Political Agents, behaved themselves (towards the natives of India and Native Princes and Chiefs) in a similar manner. This was owing to the neglect which the Royal Family of Great Britain, who are the sole masters of India, showed towards this country by not visiting it. Not only did those gentlemen look upon themselves as British Kings, but even the people at large were under the same impression. Such being the case, how could loyalty find a place in the breasts of our people? His Royal Highness the Duke of Edinburgh visited the Indian shores. It was through this that such a thing as loyalty sprouted up on the Indian soil. By the present visit of his Royal Highness the Prince of Wales, the plant of Loyalty has struck deep root here. The people at large are now in transports of joy, at being able to see with their *own* eyes the son of their Queen, nay, their future Emperor. Also, they are full of hopes of being favoured with similar visits at frequent intervals hereafter. Just as tortoises, in the fable, boast themselves of having the moon as their King, similarly the people at large, hitherto had to speak of some *great Queen* in an unknown and distant land, as their Protectress. They had to share the sorrow of being ruled by representatives and servants of their Sovereign, as in the Mahometan times. They had the dissatisfaction and grief of never being able to feast their eyes with a glance at their Sovereign. But all these disappointments and griefs have now become things of the past. The Native Rajas and Chiefs, without being any longer the poor victims of Government servants, are full of ever-progressing joy and well-merited loyalty, because they have now the honour and happiness of seeing with their own eyes and conversing freely with their British Prince. It is a matter productive of great benefit (both to the rulers and the ruled) that our Prince is becoming personally acquainted with native Princes, and is charming their hearts with deserved respect and honour.

"As another result of this visit, many of the chief servants of the Government will, casting aside their (usual) arrogance and superciliousness, behave themselves with humility, and act with the full knowledge of the fact that the Native Rajas and Maharajas, Chiefs, &c., are more respectable than they, and that, after all, they are but *servants*. They will henceforward conduct themselves in harmony with the respect and honour due to the Native Princes, and the native community at large. These Princes and the natives of India will act with gratitude and loyalty towards the British Government, which protects them voluntarily without being entreated (as the eyelid does the eye). We think that it will be by far the most beneficial thing both to India and the British rulers, if our Prince of Wales, the heir to the British Crown, is pleased to become a High Court of Appeal over the Governors-General and Governors of the various Presidencies, especially as his Royal Highness is now becoming personally acquainted with India and its wants.

"In the second place, we are very glad to find our Prince invested with full authority by our Great Queen, to confer titles on the deserving. We need hardly say that we rejoice in the fact of the Prince judiciously exercising that authority now. But we feel it incumbent upon us to say a few words on *one point*, with reference to the investiture of titles. We do not see any reason why we should keep our opinion in the background. We shall then candidly set it before our readers. It is that all those titles which have been conferred till now have been bestowed upon Maharajas, Rajas, high Government officials, Counsellors, wealthy folks, and, in fact, on principal paid servants of the Government, and on these only. But no titular dignity has become the lot of praiseworthy lovers of learning and pursuers of poetry. Considering deeply, are not great pundits and poets deserving of honour from Kings? Is it proper that such men should be thrown into utter oblivion? Will not the wealth of learning and blessing of poetry shine perpetually, conferring great happiness, pleasure, and honour, not only upon its lovers, but also upon all those who have a special knowledge of the language, without becoming the property of foreigners? Therefore, it will be a great boon both to the public and to these literate poets, if our wise British Prince is pleased to bestow upon these titles as they deserve. By thus honouring pundits and poets, our Prince will be loudly praised by all as a great connoisseur and patron of learning."

The following are translations by Natives of the accounts of visits and return visits in Madras:

"THE TANJORE QUEEN.

"This Royal Lady was not able to come in time to meet his Royal Highness the first day, but she came in a special train on the next day, in company with the Moplay Dorai (son-in-law), and the Princess's Consort, in the Sabha Mantapam (the Royal Court), the next Thursday, in the afternoon. The Prince received them with all joy and respect. As the Tanjore Lady should not be seen by male members of the assembly, they let down a curtain between her and the Prince. Behind the curtain with the Queen were standing three ladies. When the Queen had put out her golden hands, the Prince with pleasure shook hands with her. After a few seconds, the Queen put out her hands, holding a golden belt, on which his Highness's name was inscribed, which the Prince received, and thanked the Queen. Then the Moplay Dorai (Sakaram Saib) spoke with the Prince for a little while; after which the Maha Ranee put her hand out again, when the Prince, giving her a gem-set ring, on which his name was engraved—'*Albert Edward*'—shook hands with her. There is nobody competent to estimate the value of the workmanship of the ring. The Prince presented to the Tanjore Queen a picture or a portrait of his Royal Mother, Queen Victoria. After a few more words, the Royal guests took leave of each other. When the Maha Ranee came in, thirteen guns were fired, and when she left, another salute of thirteen guns was fired."

"RAJAH OF COCHIN.

"The Prince of Wales, with his retinue, Bartle Frere, &c., proceeded to the residence of the Rajah of Cochin, on the Thursday evening, at 4½ o'clock, to give him a return visit. The Rajah stood at his gate, and receiving the Prince with all respect, took him to the Royal Home, and, after a few words of etiquette, gave him the following presents:—A silver plate, made very exquisitely by six artisans, and ear-rings and neck ornaments and hand ornaments; and one pair of gold bangles, made by a goldsmith of Kusumba, light-red description. The latter mentioned jewellery was intended for the Princess of Denmark. Then two mats, of superior and curious workmanship, were also presented. The presents given by the Prince to the Rajah of Cochin were a gold breast-plate * for memory. On one side of it was the picture of the Prince, and on the other side the Prince of Wales's feather-sign; also a gold watch and a gold chain. The front plate of the watch was crystal. A thick, rich ring, on which the Prince's feathers were carved; a sword with ivory handle. The case was made of steel, on which was carved 'Given to the Maha Rajah of Cochin Rama Vurma by the English Prince.' A book also, on the 'Priests and Warriors of the Middle Ages,' was presented. After this interview the Prince went to the residence of the Prince of Arcot. The Dewan of Cochin, the Chief Justice, Soobraminya Pillay, and Teroo Venkatacherry, Judge of the Trichoor Division, went with him," &c.†

---

* A medallion.

† It will be seen that the Native chroniclers took small note of the retinue, but were particular about the names of their own people. The Anglo-Indian papers adopted the same principle.

NOTES.

INDIAN SNAKES.

WHEN the Prince visited the General Hospital, on the 31st December, as mentioned in page 370, he saw a very remarkable collection of snakes, which are kept there for the purpose of testing the efficacy of the various supposed antidotes of which the virtues are from time to time urged on the notice of the medical authorities by enthusiastic believers. These were specimens of the—

1. *Ophiophagus Elaps.*—A snake which grows to the length of twelve feet, and which has the agreeable *gourmandise* of eating any snake he can get. He is a congener of the Cobra, and is "very deadly."

2. *Naja tripudians* (Cobra di Capella).—Of which there are at least three varieties, all most venomous and deadly.

3. *Bungarus cæruleus*, or "Krait."—A fearful little wretch, of a blue steel colour, ringed with white, and with a snow-white belly; a deadly insidious reptile, frequenting the thatch of houses, and even the beds of the indwellers, or dropping from the rafters, &c., on their heads and shoulders. He is not more than three feet long, but "he will serve." "Can such things be, and overcome us like a summer cloud without our special wonder?"

4. *Bungarus fasciatus.*—This is larger than the Krait and not so common; very retiring in his habits, of rural tastes, living in the fields instead of houses. He is coloured black and yellow, and is fair to look upon.

5. *Daboia Russellii* (called by Gray *Daboia elegans*, and known as the Tic Polonga in Ceylon, Borah in Bengal).—The Chain Viper, one of the most powerful and deadly in the world. But it not so common as the Cobra or Krait; and chiefly frequenting fields and grass-patches, it kills cattle, &c., rather than human beings.

6. *Echis carinata.*—A very small, active, aggressive and deadly viper; common enough in the Punjaub, North-West Provinces and Madras, and not unknown in Bengal. It gives some notice of its dangerous presence by the rustling noise made by its scales as it moves ("Carinata").

There were several large and hideous-looking snakes in the boxes with these deadly species, but they were comparatively or quite innocuous. Some were crotaline, which are poisonous but do not kill. And note a strange fact!—

7. All fresh-water snakes are harmless: all salt-water snakes (*Hydrophidæ*) are most poisonous! Fortunately, few people come in contact with the latter. They may be seen in thousands on the banks in the Indian seas at certain times of the year. The gentlemen who exhibited

the snakes, and the natives in attendance upon them, seized the deadliest with the utmost *sang froid*, and showed us the fangs distilling crystalline "drops of death." There were some wretched dogs outside in various stages of dissolution and torture, the state of which would have moved the hearts of anti-vivisectionists. And yet who could object to such testing of antidotes, the success of any one of which would arm science with the means of saving many thousands of human lives every year? As yet no specific has been discovered for well-injected snake-poison.

ON THE CHOLERA OUTBREAK IN 1875.

There was acute disappointment caused to thousands by the change of programme, which not only deprived the Prince of the opportunity of visiting some of the most interesting scenes and districts in India, and of enjoying the sport which was to have been expected in the Annamally Hills, but rendered extensive preparations, native and European, to do him honour and give him appropriate welcome quite abortive. That the reasons which led Dr. Fayrer to oppose the visit of the Prince were well founded, the following figures, which are taken from the official return laid before the Army Sanitary Commission, will show.

The deaths from Cholera in the districts which the Prince would have visited were as follows :—

	1874.	1875.
Madras and Mysore	313	97,051
Hyderabad, Rajpootana, and Central India	4	14,649

It is quite true that there was also a great increase of deaths from Cholera in districts which the Prince traversed, but the danger to be especially avoided was the outbreak or increase of Cholera in large camps and congregations of people where the disease was known to exist. That 1875–6 was a Cholera year may be shown from the following table of deaths :—

	1874.	1875.
Oudh	68	23,381
Bombay	37	47,573
North-West Provinces	6396	41,106
Punjaub	14	14,643

Altogether, it is much to be thankful for that there was no outbreak in the Royal Camps.

Description of Instruments presented by the Maharaja of Benares. The originals of the first five are found in the Hindu Observatory, Benares.— Jan. 5, 1876.—(Referred to in Page 390.)

1. DIGANŚA-YANTRA.—An instrument for finding the degrees of Azimuth of a planet or star.

2. DHRUVA-PROTA CHAKRA-YANTRA.—An instrument for finding the degrees of declination of a planet or star.

3. YANTRA-SAMRÁT (Prince of Instruments). For finding the distance (in time) from the meridian and the declination of a planet and star, and of the sun; and the right ascension of a planet or star.

4. BHITTI-YANTRA (a mural quadrant). An instrument for finding the sun's greatest declination and the latitude of the place.

5. VISHUVAD-YANTRA (the Equinoctial circle). An instrument for ascertaining the distance (in time) of the sun, or of any star from the meridian.

N.B.—The method for finding all these is given in 'The Mánamandira Observatory,' by Pandit Bápú Deva Śástrí.

6. PHALAKA-YANTRA (invented by Bháskarácharya).—An instrument for finding the time after sunrise.

The detailed account of this instrument may be found in the translation of the Siddhánta-śiromani, by Lancelot Wilkinson, Esq. ('Bibliotheca Indica," p. 214.)

7. CHAKRA-YANTRA.—An instrument for finding the altitude and zenith distance of the sun, and also the longitude of planets. ('Bibliotheca Indica,' p. 212.)

8. CHÁPA-YANTRA (semi-circle).
9. TURÍYA-YANTRA (a quadrant).
} Instruments for finding the zenith distance and altitude of the sun.

10. ŚANKU (Gnomon). From its shadow are ascertained the points of the compass, the place of the observer, including latitude, &c., and time.

The Armillary Sphere represents the following circles:—namely, the Prime Vertical, Meridian, Horizon, Equinoctial, Ecliptic, &c., and by the threads that are fastened within the globe Hindu Astronomers determine the parts of any spherical triangle on the globe.

The detailed account of this sphere may be found in the translation of the Siddhánta-śiromani, by Lancelot Wilkinson, Esq. ('Bibliotheca Indica,' pp. 151–176.)

From the Maharaja were also offered satchels and caps worked by the ladies of his own household, velvet mats, fifteen pieces of kinkob, fifteen velvet mats embroidered in gold and silver, window-curtains embroidered on silk and muslin, jewelled and enamelled swords, spear with revolving pistol attached; models of the Fort of Ramnagar; an armillary globe illustrating the Hindoo system of astronomy; a gold-enamelled inkstand, a model of the Maurpankhi, or "peacock-boat;" boxes of photographs; a model of the great Observatory of Benares in silver and sissoo-wood, with an English description of the various instruments by the "Astronomer Royal" of the College, in other words, the astronomical pundit; a clock, made in the Maharaja's house by an artisan in his employ, showing the signs of the Zodiac, phases of the moon, dates of the month, days of the week, hours, and minutes; a model of a larger clock of the same kind in the inner Court of the Ramnagar Fort; a translation of the Queen's 'Life in the Highlands' into Hindee, each page illuminated, bound in marble and gold, with a diamond in each corner, the Royal Arms on one side and those of the Maharaja on the other, printed at Benares, and illuminated in the fort by an artist in the service of the Maharaja, the marble executed at Agra from designs by the Maharaja, the whole enclosed in a velvet case.

THE GOLD AND SILVER GUNS, BARODA.

(Page 208.)

These are four in number, two of gold and two of silver; but there are people who say or believe that the "gold" guns are of silver-gilt. They are 3-pounders. The carriages are drawn by white bullocks of remarkable beauty, caparisoned in *robes* of cloth of gold and gilt trappings; even their horns are gilt. The limbers are covered with plates of silver, and the tumbrils and caissons are plated with the same metal, gilt. The report is very peculiar, sharp and metallic, with "a melodious twang," like that with which Aubrey's ghost was heard to vanish. The golundauze (gunners) are dressed in rich and fantastic uniforms to match this strange artillery. Altogether the battery would be a very rich capture, and "a charge on the guns" of Baroda would be very tempting to unprincipled and needy cavaliers.